AMERICAN DEMOCRACY

AMERICAN DEMOCRACY

Tenth Edition

Michael N. Danielson

Princeton University

Walter F. Murphy

Princeton University

HM Holmes & Meier Publishers, Inc.

New York ▪ *London*

Published in the United States of America 1983 by

Holmes & Meier Publishers, Inc.
30 Irving Place
New York, N.Y. 10003

Great Britain:
Holmes & Meier Publishers, Ltd.
131 Trafalgar Road
Greenwich, London SE10 9TX

Library of Congress Cataloging in Publication Data

Danielson, Michael N.
  American democracy.

  Rev. ed. of: American democracy / Walter F. Murphy,
Michael N. Danielson. 9th ed. c1979.
  Includes bibliographies and index.
  1. United States—Politics and government.
I. Murphy, Walter F., 1929–   . II. Murphy, Walter F.,
1929–   . American democracy. III. Title.
JK274.D243 1983   320.973   83-4313
ISBN 0-8419-0839-7

For Duane Lockard

Our colleague, our friend, and our teacher

Preface

The typical pattern of life for Americans is to be born in institutions (hospitals), to be educated in institutions (schools), to work for institutions (corporations), to worship in institutions (churches or synagogues), to pay taxes and obey the laws of institutions (legislatures) in order to avoid other institutions (courts and prisons), and finally to die in institutions (hospitals again or homes for the aged). Indeed, sociologists hold the view that the most obvious escape from this network of controls, the family, is itself an institution, though of a less formal sort than most.

The message is clear: We cannot shape our destinies unless we learn to cope with, if not control, the institutions that it is our particular fortune, good or bad, to encounter. And the one institution that pervades our society is government. It taxes our income and our purchases; uses our money to provide goods and services for some members of society; regulates the size of the houses we can build, the speed at which we can drive our automobiles, the conditions under which we can use alcohol and other hallucinogens; monitors the purity of the air we breathe, the water we drink, and the food we eat; sets the amount of money we must pay our employees or be paid by our employers; claims authority to make us serve in the armed forces and to specify the rules under which we can pass on our worldly goods to our heirs.

We have revised this book in the hope of making more comprehensible to intelligent and interested students the way that governmental institutions in the United States operate—how they influence our lives and how we, in turn, may influence them. Our focal point is how public policy gets made under the Madisonian system of fragmented, fractured power that characterizes our politics. To understand that system, of course, one must also understand the competing theories of popular government and limited government on which the political structure rests as well as the larger social and economic cultures within which it operates. We have thus tried to go beyond an explanation of institutions and their interactions to an exploration of the relationships among these organizations and the larger social system.

At the outset we warn that this approach requires concentration; it demands close attention to linkages among ideas, institutions, processes, and a larger set of cultures. We try to cut through some of the complexities of the American political system, but we make no claim to simplify: For those relations are by no means simple and they are connected to each other in intricate and important ways. To the extent that one fails to grasp their complexity and their linkages one misunderstands American politics. In this area, to simplify is to oversimplify. Decades of teaching have convinced us that most students prefer complex truth to simple falsity and have the intellectual capacity to distinguish between the two.

As is our custom, we have compiled many debts in this revision. For reading portions of the manuscript we are indebted to Professor Barbara Jean Nelson, Peter Benda, and Gregory Keating; for research assistance to Bonnie Berry, Jeffrey Danielson, Shirley Gilbert, Rosemary Little, and Kathleen Neeff; for typing to Jessica Danielson, Patricia Danielson, Nancy Grandjean, and Holly Murphy; for encouraging us to undertake a new revision, Max Holmes; for editorial help (and discipline) to Jane Cullen; for careful copy editing to Nancy Guelich; for patience and even some understanding to our wives. We shall, of course, accept full responsibility for our errors, though we do not promise to do so gracefully.

Michael N. Danielson
Walter F. Murphy
Princeton, N.J.
December, 1982

Contents

★ PART II

The Constitutional Framework

★ PART III

The Process of Politics

PART IV

The Congress

10 The Legislative System and Lawmaking 292

PART V

The Presidency

11 Presidential Leadership 334

12 The President and the Executive Branch 374

☆ PART VIII

Conclusion

PART **I**

The Framework of American Politics

1 Politics and Government

Politics deals with who governs and how. In pungent language, politics involves three questions: "Who gets what, when, and how?"* More elegantly, we can say that *politics is concerned with the authoritative processes that determine the goals of a society, mobilize its resources to achieve these goals, and distribute rights, duties, costs, benefits, rewards, and punishments among members of that society.*

Authoritative processes are those processes whose decisions the vast majority of the people accept as binding. People may accept them for a variety of reasons, including habit, tradition, respect for certain procedures, or loyalty to particular persons or institutions. In Western democracies, citizens tend to accept most governmental decisions as authoritative. In other systems, people may or may not see public officials as legitimate rulers, and in some circumstances large segments of a population may look on another organization or individual as the legitimate leader, at least for some purposes. A bishop or guerrilla chief, for instance, may make decisions that a sizable minority or even a majority of citizens consider superior to those of presidents or parliaments. Considered this way, *politics encompasses all activities of individuals and groups, public and private, with respect to governing societies.*

This definition is broader than that in everyday use, because people commonly limit the meaning of the term *politics* to political parties, campaigns and elections, and activities of elected officials. Of course, those are central aspects of politics, and much of the remainder of this volume examines them in detail. But politics also includes many other kinds of behavior that we cannot ignore. Equally important, politics is not a dirty word, nor are all politicians venal. That some are corrupt is as obviously true as that some bankers embezzle, some union leaders take bribes, some doctors pad their bills, and some lawyers pay for perjured testimony. In this world, politicians can claim a monopoly neither on sin nor on virtue. But the game they play—making decisions that can bring war or peace, prosperity or poverty, slavery or freedom—is vital to society's survival.

Participants in politics usually seek the support of government for their goals. Thus, a group alarmed about the spread of pornography demands that the local police chief prevent showings of an X-rated film, while the theater operator goes to court to secure an injunction against

---

* This now classic question is Harold D. Lasswell's and first appeared in his *Politics: Who Gets What, When, and How?* (New York: McGraw-Hill, 1936).

Force can be used by government to ensure compliance with its policies on the part of those who feel no moral obligation to obey, as in the arrest by the U.S. Coast Guard of three drug smugglers off the Florida coast. (Official U.S. Coast Guard Photo)

picketing on his property by the antipornography group.* Advocates of the "right to life" demand that government protect the unborn by making abortion illegal. Slum dwellers pay their rent to the city rather than to their landlords in the hope that their money will be used to make desperately needed building repairs. Federal officials are urged to lower waste discharge standards by meat packers, whose complaints about the

---

* An injunction is a court order which prohibits or requires a specific action.

high costs of pollution control are echoed by local political leaders fearful of unemployment and loss of tax resources.

Government is the focus of political interaction because it makes and enforces many of the rules in modern society. Indeed, federal, state, and local governments regulate a wide range of individual, group, and corporate behavior; they levy taxes, set and enforce standards of behavior, confer licenses and franchises, and create rules regarding the distribution of all sorts of costs and benefits. Equally important as the scope of governmental rule making is the fact that governments usually can enforce their decisions more effectively than other social institutions. In a stable political system, citizens generally (although not always) feel a moral obligation to follow the law. It is this feeling of obligation that confers what is called *legitimacy* on governmental action. But should moral obligation fail, public officials have force—the police, the national guard, or even the army—to ensure by brute power that a policy will be carried out. Even though governmental use of force is subject to many important restraints in the United States, official use of raw power always remains a real possibility.

Furthermore, those with governmental authority usually command a preponderance of the instruments of coercion. This near-monopoly means that they can imprison people for real or alleged crimes, conscript young men and women for regular armies or guerrilla cadres, exterminate groups of people as Hitler did the Jews or Stalin his opponents, or allow the possession of slave laborers as Americans did until the Civil War. Alternately, political action can remove conditions of terror and slavery, end famine and pestilence, discourage drug abuse, fight organized crime, and restore civil rights.

 DEMOCRACY

Americans commonly speak of the process by which their political decisions are made as *democratic*. Unfortunately, that word is among the most vague and value-laden terms in any Western language. "Democracy" can refer to a town-meeting style of government in which all citizens are present and have equal voting power; it can mean government by an Athenian assembly whose members are selected by lot or serve in rotation; it can refer to a representative form of government in which delegates are chosen by any of a variety of electoral processes. "Democracy" says nothing about the extent of governmental power. A democracy may, as in the United States, limit the authority of government, or it may exercise total authority in the name of the people.

When we speak of *American democracy*, we are talking about a political hybrid, a government in which citizens can participate, operating in a particular cultural context, under certain legal rules, and through a certain set of institutions and informal processes. What is involved, as Chapter 3 explains in more detail, is a mix between popular government and limited government. In a pure democracy, the will of the people is supreme. In a limited government, the constitution imposes restraints on what the ruler—whether a single person, a small group, or a majority of the adult population—can do. Thus, to the extent that the people rule in the American political system, they do so subject to important legal restrictions, many of which are spelled out in the Bill of Rights, the first ten amendments to the Constitution. As a result, we should speak of the United States as having a *republican form of government*, or a *free government*—a term the Founding Fathers liked—or a *constitutional democracy*.

The American version of constitutional democracy is also a *representative form of government*. To the degree that the people "rule," they do so by having a right to speak their minds on public issues, to organize other citizens, and, at regular intervals, to vote for or against candidates who wish to become their representatives. The people also "rule" in the sense that the representatives, who are subject to periodic re-election, are typically anxious to anticipate the moods and preferences of the voters—although how they anticipate or even discover those moods and preferences involves processes that are often more mystic than scientific. "To speak with precision about public opinion is a task not unlike coming to grips with the Holy Ghost," as V. O. Key once remarked.[1] Yet at election time public opinion can become as real to governmental officials as the Holy Ghost is to traditional Christian theologians.

American government is also permeated with the concept of *equality*, a notion whose meaning is only slightly less varied than that of democracy itself.* At very least the Constitution's command of "equal protection of the laws," requires "one person, one vote" in the political sphere as well as even-handed justice from the courts. At the same time, the Constitution forbids governmentally imposed restrictions on social mobility or economic opportunity because of race, sex, religion, or ancestry. Living up to even these minimums has posed immense practical problems that the American system has yet to overcome.

Given the fact that people are not equal in talent and ambition and do not share the same interests and moral codes, political equality is difficult for the government to maintain. If left alone, some individuals will inevitably want, seek, and obtain a disproportionately large share of many goods and services, including political power.

It is also obvious tha all Americans are not equal in terms of political influence. Candidates who compete for public office are rarely just plain

---

* *Equality* is discussed in the context of political culture in the next chapter, in the context of voting rights in Chapter 8, and in the context of civil rights in Chapter 15.

FIGURE **1-1**

**Public Attitudes on Major Issues
during the 1976 Presidential Campaign**

(In percent)

Agree   Disagree   Don't know

The Federal Government should see to it that every person who wants to work has a job.

| 70 | 26 | 4 |

It is not in our interest to be so friendly with Russia because we are getting less
than we are giving them.

| 50 | 33 | 17 |

The right of a woman to have an abortion should be left entirely up to the woman
and her doctor.

| 67 | 26 | 7 |

Government spending for military defense should be reduced.

| 37 | 52 | 11 |

Laws against polluting the environment should be relaxed to help solve the energy crisis.

| 45 | 44 | 11 |

Racial integration of the schools should be achieved even if it requires busing.

| 22 | 71 | 7 |

The Federal Government now runs many programs for health, education and the
poor. It would be better if these were run instead by the states.

| 63 | 24 | 13 |

SOURCE: *New York Times*, February 13, 1976. The New York Times/CBS News Poll sur-
veyed 1,463 respondents by telephone as part of a continuous effort during the
presidential election year. © 1976 by The New York Times Company. Reprinted by
permission.

folks, although they frequently pretend to be. They are members of an elite, typically better educated, wealthier, and far more astute in the arts of manipulation than the average citizen. They are often surrounded by other elites—bankers, financiers, union officials, lawyers, interest-group leaders, or journalists—whose political resources also set them apart from the average citizen. Even professional politicians are not equal in political influence, and they must compete with each other for power. One of the arenas of competition is the marketplace for popular votes. It is principally because of competition in this particular market that we can speak of the United States as having a strong democratic element in its government. And because in that marketplace all votes are supposed to count the same, we can speak of some measure of political equality.

The problem of equality has other troublesome dimensions. In the United States, the notion of political equality has been coupled with an ideal of social equality, an ideal that goes far beyond equal treatment by government officials or "one person, one vote." It means an absence of informal social barriers as well. Because social practice, like political practice, has not always lived up to its ideals, governmental action is necessary to strike down religious, economic, ethnic, and, most important in the American context, racial barriers against social mobility. But the concepts of limited or constitutional government and representative democracy hamper this sort of governmental action. Ideals to the contrary, a majority of Americans have been quite willing to allow informal social barriers to exist. Indeed, they have invested a good deal of their ingenuity in constructing these barriers.

★ THE INEVITABILITY OF CONFLICT

Conflict arises from disagreements about both ends and means. Individuals, groups, and governmental agencies differ over what should be done and how to tackle problems on the public agenda. One major source of political conflict is fundamental: Should government intervene at all in a particular problem? Apartment dwellers battle with landlords over proposals for rent control. The American Medical Association and private insurance companies try to keep the federal government out of health insurance, while labor unions and consumer groups work for universal national coverage of medical expenses. Conflicts over governmental involvement are likely to be especially bitter when strongly held personal beliefs are challenged, such as the constitutionality of prayers in the public schools, use of public funds to provide abortions, or court orders requiring busing to desegregate schools.

Once government does become involved, the potential for conflict increases substantially. Some interests seek to enlarge government's

Almost everyone agrees that cleaner air is desirable. Conflicts arise, however, over specific ends—the question of how clean the air should be. Conflict also results from disputes over the means of reducing air pollution—what sorts of controls are needed at what cost. A major party to such conflicts has been the power industry, which has been forced to make substantial investments to reduce emissions at generating plants such as this one in New Mexico. (Public Service of New Mexico)

role, others to restrict public activity. Welfare programs, for example, constantly generate conflict over who should receive public assistance as well as how much. Further conflict usually arises over the effectiveness of particular policies, programs, and agencies. Consumer groups, for instance, charge that the Federal Aviation Administration is not sufficiently independent of airplane manufacturers when it assesses the safety of commercial jets. Airlines, on the other hand, argue that FAA has inadequate funds and personnel to monitor the nation's airways safely and efficiently.

Allocating responsibilities among public agencies and levels of government also causes political conflict. City officials and their supporters in Washington quarreled for years with transportation interests about having federal transit programs in the Department of Housing and Urban Development or in the Department of Transportation. Similar disputes arise over whether food stamps for the poor should be administered by the Department of Agriculture or the Department of Health and Human Services. Increasing the likelihood of conflict is the existence of 50 state governments and almost 80,000 local governments. State and local officials battle with the federal government, as well as with each other, for control over various programs and tax resources. For their part, nongovernmental participants in politics favor assigning responsibilities to the agency or level of government most likely to advance their interests. Thus, residents of middle-class suburbs want to maintain local control over land use and housing programs, while civil rights and fair·housing groups prefer state or federal agencies to be responsible for locating subsidized housing.

Competition among existing programs and their supporters for scarce public resources is another important source of conflict. Building an antiballistic missile system may mean ending a school lunch program. Expanding foreign aid to Egypt and Israel is likely to reduce funds available for the poorest nations of Africa and Asia. Hiring more police officers can leave less money for public health. Paying teachers higher salaries often forces school officials to cut back on books and other supplies, reduce special forms of instruction, or delay the construction of new facilities.

Conflict also results because public activities almost always involve costs and benefits that cannot be measured merely in dollars. A new network of highways may ease traffic but bring more air pollution; heavy dependence on foreign sources of petroleum has led to strong demands for public policies that will foster use of domestic energy sources such as soft coal, Alaskan oil, and offshore petroleum. At every turn, however, environmental interests have challenged proposals that threaten to increase sulphur and other pollutants from coal, or alter the ecology of northern Alaska, or imperil the fragile environment of coastal areas.

Political conflicts usually arise because of competing interests rather than lack of information or expertise. With growth of government has come an enormous increase in availability of technical information to many participants in politics. Experts often disagree among themselves, however, and these disagreements increase rather than decrease political conflict. Some top naval officers, for example, argue that giant aircraft carriers are essential to national defense. Other experts contend that supercarriers are too vulnerable to justify expenditure of $2.4 billion

One of the four Nimitz-class supercarriers in service in 1982. Over 6,000 sailors serve on one of these massive nuclear-powered vessels, which support almost a hundred warplanes. (United States Navy)

per ship. The point is that information and technical skills rarely are used neutrally in political conflicts. Instead, public agencies and other political participants tend to use expertise to advance their own interests and undermine the arguments of their opponents. Nuclear scientists within the atomic industry and the federal Nuclear Regulatory Commission produce analyses that conclude that atomic power plants are safe. Other scientists insist just as adamantly that nuclear generating facilities pose unacceptable risks of monumental disaster.

Despite the variety and intensity of political conflict in the United States, few of these disputes concern the fundamental arrangements of government. To be sure, large numbers of Americans are dissatisfied with the performance of public officials and agencies, with waste and corruption in government, and with rising tax burdens. But even so, most citizens do not seriously question the legitimacy of the basic features of the American political system. Groups seeking equal rights for women or higher social security benefits try to influence the government rather than overthrow it. Those not satisfied with Supreme Court rulings on school prayers are more likely to try to change the membership or jurisdiction of the Court than to have the Court abolished. Of course, these general rules have their exceptions, as groups on the extreme left and right have periodically sought radical change in the American system. And the Civil War stands as a bloody reminder of what happens when conflicts over difficult issues like slavery, tariffs, and territorial expansion come to involve basic governmental arrangements like the nature of the federal union.

 BIG GOVERNMENT

Government—the target of most political activity—has grown steadily in the United States. In 1982, the federal government, the states, and the more than 79,000 local governments spent $1,005 billion, which accounted for 33.2 percent of the gross national product.* Over $746 billion of this total was spent by the federal government. To collect and spend these funds, government employed 16 million civilians, over 13 million of whom worked for state and local governments.

Underlying the growth of government has been social, economic, technological, and political change. Urbanization and industrialization have made Americans less self-sufficient, and their increased interdependence has generated demands for more public services and

---

* The gross national product (GNP) refers to all the goods and services produced within the United States.

FIGURE **1-2**   **The Budget Dollar: Fiscal Year 1983 Estimate**

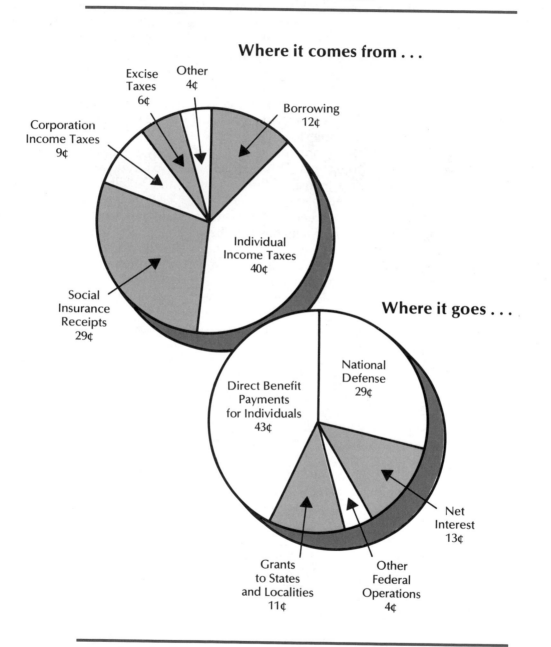

Where it comes from . . .

Excise Taxes 6¢

Other 4¢

Corporation Income Taxes 9¢

Borrowing 12¢

Individual Income Taxes 40¢

Social Insurance Receipts 29¢

Where it goes . . .

Direct Benefit Payments for Individuals 43¢

National Defense 29¢

Net Interest 13¢

Grants to States and Localities 11¢

Other Federal Operations 4¢

SOURCE: Executive Office of the President, Office of Management and the Budget, *The United States Budget in Brief, Fiscal Year 1983* (Washington, D.C.: Government Printing Office, 1982).

governmental regulation of private enterprise. In addition, these demands have brought about the organization of all sorts of interests pressing for increased governmental activity of one kind or another—or for less of it. Political leaders have responded and have also generated new demands of their own, in the form of such programs as Woodrow Wilson's New Freedom, Franklin Roosevelt's New Deal, and Lyndon Johnson's Great Society. Paralleling urbanization and industrialization in the twentieth century has been the expanding role of the United States in world affairs, which has greatly increased the military, diplomatic, and other international activities of the national government and so its size and complexity.

Particularly striking in recent years has been the growth of government's social programs. Between 1962 and 1982, federal spending for human resources increased thirteenfold, from $30 billion to over $390 billion. Underlying this rapid expansion of specific federal programs and assistance (and parallel developments at state and local levels) were many of the forces that account for the general growth of government.

Popular support for social security, for example, has produced a steady widening of eligibility for participation in the program. The lengthening of life spans also increases the number of recipients of benefits. As a result of these developments, one out of every six Americans was collecting social security benefits in 1982. Equally important, benefits rose rapidly in recent years because of both inflation and political pressures for more adequate levels of assistance for the elderly. In general, popular programs expand with population and political pressure, and government becomes bigger.

A spectacular example of the growth of government is provided by the food stamp program. Food stamps were first distributed in the 1960s as a means of improving the diet of very poor families and individuals. Later, a series of legislative changes and administrative actions broadened the program. As a result, well over 20 million people received food stamps in 1982, compared with fewer than a million in 1966. This enormous expansion combined with larger benefis to send federal outlays for food samps from under $100 million in 1966 to over $11 billion in 1982.

With the growth of government has come specialization. Specialized agencies, personnel, and programs—in short, bureaucracies and bureaucrats—have developed at all levels of government. The Department of the Interior, responsible for most of the 738 million acres of federal land, including the national parks, forests, wilderness areas, and wildlife refuges provide a striking example of this process. Interior regulates strip mining, leases offshore oil fields, controls mineral and grazing rights on public land, and builds dams to increase the supply of water in the parched west. At the top of this federal agency are the

secretary of Interior; an under secretary; solicitor; and assistant secretaries for congressional and legislative affairs; fish and wildlife and parks; land and water resources; energy and minerals; and policy, budget, and administration. Most of the Interior's work, however, goes on within its main divisions: the National Park Service; the Fish and Wildlife Service, the Bureau of Reclamation, the Bureau of Mines, the Bureau of Land Management, the Bureau of Indian Affairs, and other specialized agencies.

Governmental agencies like the Department of the Interior produce rules, regulations, services, facilities, assistance, and information. Almost every kind of economic activity is affected by such rules and regulations. The federal government regulates transportation, communications, petroleum and natural gas, generation of electric power, atomic energy, food, drugs, consumer products, job safety, wages and hours, labor relations, equal employment opportunity, automobile safety, environmental protection, banks, securities dealers, and scores of other transactions and enterprises. State governments regulate insurance companies and public utilities and license lawyers, doctors, dentists, barbers, undertakers, engineers, and a host of other professionals. Local governments set taxi and transit fares, enforce building codes, regulate land use, and prescribe minimum health and sanitary standards for all sorts of enterprises.

Among the major services provided by governments are those concerned with education, health, police, fire, public transportation, and mail delivery. Except for the postal service, the principal responsibility for actually providing these public services rests with local governments, although the state and federal roles in financing education, health, and transit steadily rose during the 1960s and 1970s. Largely through federal funds, government provides assistance to millions of citizens in all income groups. Social security is available for the elderly, unemployment compensation for those out of work, welfare and social services for the poor, public housing for low-income families, aid to the blind and disabled, and medical assistance for the aged. Assistance also goes to veterans, farmers who have suffered crop damage, victims of floods and other natural disasters, and a wide variety of business enterprises. Many of these activities involve governments' providing facilities—schools, police stations, firehouses, hospitals and clinics, community centers, welfare offices, housing units, and post offices. Other governmental responsibilities involve construction and operation of public facilities, such as highways, airports, transit systems, parks, military bases and equipment, research laboratories, and testing facilities.

In carrying out these responsibilities and in collecting the taxes to finance them, governments consume an enormous amount of paper—statutes, regulations, reports, instructions, forms, press releases, and judicial rulings. The federal government alone requires over 10,000 different forms and reports. These generate more than 500 million responses annually, and are estimated to require 1.3 billion hours to prepare. A major corporation like Standard Oil of Indiana files 250 reports each year with more than 40 governmental agencies. As programs evolve, new rules and regulations are constantly issued. Following enactment of the food stamp legislation by Congress, rules for the program were developed in 1965, rewritten in each of the next three years, and again in 1972. After 1972 the rules were revised twenty-seven times before being rewritten once more in 1974. And in 1975 alone almost 500 regulations affecting food stamps were issued.

More often than not, the results are torrents of rules and regulations in bureaucratic gobbledegook that is almost incomprehensible. Consider, for example, the design standard for swimming pools set forth by the Consumer Product Safety Commission: "The slide shall be designed so that any side forces on the user induced by prior lateral curvature will be reduced to zero upon exit from the slide runway."[2] Over 90,000 pages of federal regulations were in force in 1982, and the cost of complying with them was estimated at more than $120 billion. Even though the Reagan administration came to office pledged to reduce governmental regulation, its agencies issued over 5600 new federal rules in 1981.

Big government, with its red tape, alphabet soup of agencies, and expanding programs, troubles most Americans. Among those questioned by the Gallup Poll in 1967 and 1977, more saw big government as a greater threat to the nation than big business or big labor.* Rising taxes

---

* The 1977 Gallup survey indicated that 39 percent of the respondents feared big government the most, 26 percent big labor, 23 percent big business, and 12 percent had no opinion; see George Gallup, " 'Big Government' Seen as Nation's Top Threat," *Sunday Times Advertiser* (Trenton, N.J.), January 30, 1977.

Wayne Stayskal. Reprinted by permission of Tribune Company Syndicate, Inc.

are universally disliked, as are mounting fees for all sorts of public services. Taxpayers' revolts have swept like wildfire through the American political system in recent years, producing restrictions on taxing and spending in many states and bolstering support for politicians like Ronald Reagan who promise to cut taxes and slash spending. When increasing costs are combined with declining levels of service, as in the post office, concern is even greater. Widespread inefficiency, the ineffectiveness of many governmental programs, and the persistence of corruption further increase public dissatisfaction.

Big government also troubles some people because of the threat posed by its police and intelligence agencies to privacy, freedom of expression, and other basic rights. In recent years the Internal Revenue Service, the Federal Bureau of Investigation, and the Central Intelligence Agency have confessed to a series of felonies that would make a Mafia don blush. Other citizens are deeply distressed by the prospect that social programs, high taxes, and economic regulation will undermine individualism, property rights, and free enterprise.

During the past two presidential campaigns, big government—and particularly the burgeoning national government—was a prime target of the candidates of both major political parties. Gerald Ford, who inherited the presidency after the resignation of Richard Nixon in the wake of the Watergate scandals, warned that "Any government big enough to give you anything you want is big enough to take everything you have."[3] Jimmy Carter campaigned successfully against Ford, arguing that only an outsider like himself who was untainted by previous service in Washington could tame the federal monster. Four years later, Carter in turn was swamped by Ronald Reagan, the former governor of California, who had been crusading for years on the need for less government.

While most people share concerns about big government, they also tend to favor *more* public involvement in areas of particular concern to them. Almost everything the government does reflects long, hard work by some interest group pressing for governmental intervention. Elected political leaders typically are responsive to insistent demands that government do something about a problem. Thus, candidates who condemn big government, bureaucracy, and red tape rarely oppose all efforts to expand government after election to office.

Once a program is begun, groups that benefit from that particular activity usually provide strong support for its continuation and enlargement. Few programs survive without strong backing from these "clientele" interests. And many of the most influential supporters of particular programs are outspoken critics of big government in general. Farmers, for example, tend to favor less governmental spending, but not in areas that benefit them directly—agricultural research, food programs, irrigation projects, price supports, and the like. Business interests which heartily endorsed most of the Reagan administration's budget cuts protested loudly against reduced federal funds for the Census Bureau, Agriculture Department, Bureau of Labor Statistics, and other data-gathering agencies which produce detailed information on population, income, consumption, employment, investment, farm production, health, and scores of other activities.

The fact that government with all its inadequacies plays an indispensable role in the everyday life of almost every American also partially offsets concern about big government. Clean water to drink, sewage disposal, schools, public safety, highways, public transportation, and scores of other esential services are provided by government. Because of federal environmental regulations, the air everyone breathes contained 25 percent less sulphur dioxide in 1980 than in 1970. Cars produced in the 1980s under strict federal emission standards emitted less than one-fifth the carbon monoxide of those manufactured in 1970. Mandatory federal requirements for seat belts and other safety devices on auto-mobiles played a major role in reducing the highway death rate by one-third since 1965.

Also vital to life for millions of Americans are the social programs that are the cause of so much public concern and criticism. Almost 11 million people receive sustenance through the federal government's program of Aid for Dependent Children. In addition, there are 23 million individuals who have their diets and incomes supplemented through the food stamp program. And 36 million people receive monthly social security benefits. Although benefits and costs have risen steadily and so increase political conflict, payments under most social programs are grossly inadequate to provide a decent standard of living for recipients. Revised in 1972 to allow payments to rise with the cost of living, social security by itself still does not provide enough income for the aged to escape poverty. Payments under the Aid for Dependent Children program, which is administered by state and local govern-ments, have been kept at miserably low levels in many states, and nowhere have they kept pace with inflation. Further reducing the help provided by most social programs is their incomplete coverage of those who need and are eligible for assistance. And following the election of Ronald Reagan in 1980, federal expenditures for many social programs were sharply curtailed.

The ambivalence of most Americans toward big government and its social welfare activities was strikingly illustrated in a survey conducted in 1977 by the *New York Times* and CBS News. As indicated in Figure 1-3, a substantial majority of those polled opposed governmental welfare programs in general. But even larger majorities favored specific public efforts designed to provide financial assistance, health care, and lower food prices for the poor. Similar mixed attitudes exist in most areas of public policy, as indicated in the results of a poll on environmental policies conducted by *Newsweek* in 1981. Majorities agreed in general with the desirability of protecting the environment, but even larger ma-jorities favored specific policies likely to increase pollution.

☆ PUBLIC POLICY

Public policy is what government does about a particular problem. Typically, public policies involve a series of decisions by public officials rather than a single decision. The nation's policy toward Lebanon, or its public-land policy, or its policy on tax credits results from a variety of public actions. First, certain officials make a decision to act, usually in response to

FIGURE **1-3**   **Support of Welfare Depends on the Program**

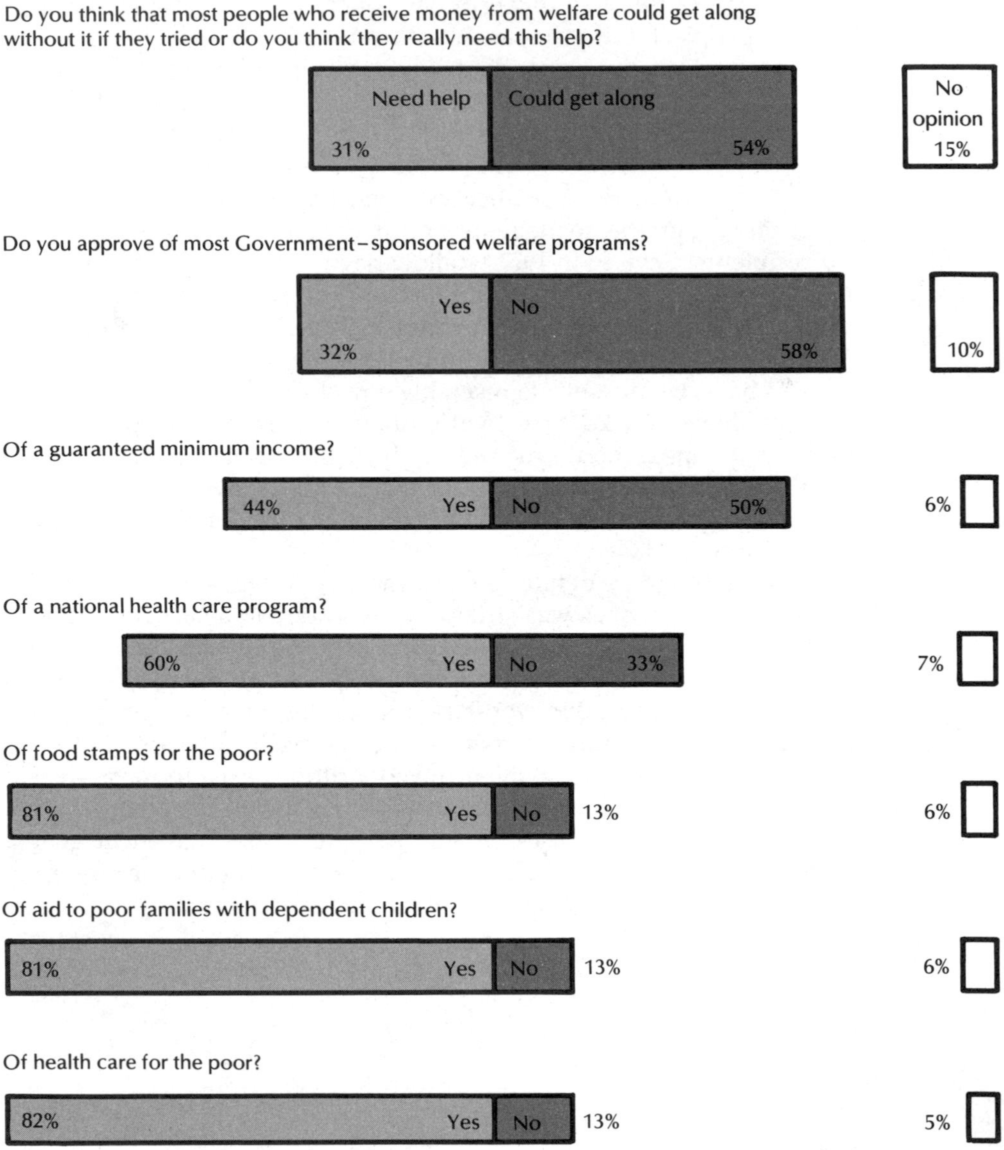

Do you think that most people who receive money from welfare could get along
without it if they tried or do you think they really need this help?

Need help	Could get along		No opinion
31%	54%		15%

Do you approve of most Government–sponsored welfare programs?

Yes	No		
32%	58%		10%

Of a guaranteed minimum income?

44% Yes	No 50%	6%

Of a national health care program?

60% Yes	No 33%	7%

Of food stamps for the poor?

81% Yes	No 13%	6%

Of aid to poor families with dependent children?

81% Yes	No 13%	6%

Of health care for the poor?

82% Yes	No 13%	5%

SOURCE: New York Times/CBS News Poll, *The New York Times*, August 3, 1977. © 1977 by
The New York Times Company. Reprinted by permission.

TABLE **1-1**   **Public Views on the Environment**

	Agree	Disagree
Government rules to protect the environment are worth the extra cost.	58%	36%
To help solve energy problems, the rate of environmental improvement should be slowed down.	36%	55%

	Favor	Oppose
Easing restrictions on strip-mining	48%	39%
Reducing auto-exhaust regulations that increase the cost of new cars	42%	53%
Increasing oil exploration and other commercial uses of federal lands other than national parks	76%	19%
Relaxing clean-air standards to allow industry to substitute coal for imported oil	55%	36%
Enlarging the area for offshore drilling of oil	70%	22%

SOURCE: Adapted from *Newsweek,* June 29, 1981. All rights reserved. Reprinted with permission. The poll was conducted by the Gallup Organization with a sample of 745 adults.

particular problems and situations, pressures from various interests, and special concerns of officials. Then they must select particular courses of action among alternatives. The importance of the problem, which will affect its claim to political, administrative, and budgetary resources, must be determined. Once an overall policy has been decided on, it needs to be implemented. Officials must assign responsibilities for carrying out the policy, settle administrative arrangements, and determine procedures. In the course of implementing the policy, all sorts of decisions have to be made about applying or not applying the general policy to specific instances.

Rarely, however, are public policies developed and implemented in a neat procession of decisions. Instead, new developments and considerations affect determinations at each stage. Experience with implementing a policy may lead to minor basic revisions. Group demands for certain policy goals that were not satisfied in the development of the general policy may be met in executing the policy. Benefits distributed

"HANG IN THERE, SONNY... SOMEBODY WILL COME ALONG TO REPLACE YOU!"

Gamble, © 1981 The Florida Times-Union

by a policy may strengthen a particular interest group's ability to secure still more funds or more sympathetic treatment in the implementation of the policy. Moreover, public policies constantly affect each other. Thus, policy toward Israel is influenced by foreign policies involving Egypt, the Soviet Union, and other nations, as well as by defense policies, foreign aid policies, and the government's need for support for other policies from domestic interests favorable, hostile, or indifferent toward Israel.

Public policy is expressed in a variety of ways, both formal and informal. Public policies dealing with the structure of government, the powers of its basic components, and the rights of the people and the states are set forth in the Constitution. State constitutions and municipal charters sketch similar public policies. Many state constitutions also contain a variety of other policy statements—for example, descriptions of the highway system or allocations of school aid, which in the case of the national government are the subject of legislation rather than constitutional provisions.

Law is an extremely important formal source of public policy. *Legislation* or *statutes* (also called *ordinances* in some local governments, and collectively called *statutory law*) are those public policies formally enacted by legislative bodies. *Treaties* and *executive agreements* are policy statements that grow out of international relations. Treaties are agreements with foreign nations that are signed by the president and ratified by the U.S. Senate, whereas executive agreements are similar documents that do not require formal actions by the Senate. *Executive orders* are policy determinations by the president, the governor of a state, or a mayor, and the authority to issue them is derived from constitutional or statutory law. *Administrative rules, regulations,* and *standards* are policy determinations by administrative agencies designed to implement constitutional provisions, laws, treaties, or executive orders. Another major source of formal policy statements is *judicial opinions* and the *rulings of quasi-judicial bodies* like the Federal Communications Commission or the Securities and Exchange Commission, whose decisions have much the same impact as court orders.

Despite the importance of such formal statements, many policies are expressed informally, particularly when they are being implemented. Every day hundreds of thousands of public officials decide informally which laws to enforce and how strictly to apply administrative standards. The policeman who permits cars to exceed the speed limit by five miles an hour is revising the formal policy stated in statutes. So is the building inspector who does not enforce a section of the building code whose standards cannot be met by most older buildings. Laws, administrative regulations, and other formal policy statements may be informally altered for all sorts of reasons—convenience, practicality, constraint of time, bribery, fear, deference to the power of certain groups and individuals, racial or ethnic prejudice, or the desire for electoral support.

Informal determinations of public policy occur throughout the whole social system as well as in governmental processes. Policy can be vitally affected by White House aides who pass the word that only deserving members of the president's party are to be considered for judgeships, by civil service officials who manage to find serious flaws in the credentials of homosexuals, by welfare investigators who turn their backs on chiseling, by executives of oil companies who secretly agree to keep their tankers at sea to create an oil shortage to drive prices up, or by union leaders who decide their members will not load ships bound for the Soviet Union.

A good example of the evolution of public policy is provided by the space program. Born in the late 1950s, the civilian space program grew rapidly under Presidents Kennedy and Johnson, reaching annual expenditures in excess of $5 billion in the mid-1960s and culminating in the landing of Apollo 11 on the moon in 1969. Growing political resistance to the costs of the space program led to a tapering off of expenditures during the following decade. But interest in manned flight revived in the late 1970s, with increased emphasis on the commercial and military aspects of space flight. (National Aeronautics and Space Administration)

 SUMMARY

We have said enough to make it clear that public policy results from an interplay among a complex mix of cultural, social, economic, constitutional, political, and institutional forces. The remainder of this volume examines many of those factors in detail. We shall concentrate on policy making at the national level, but the reader must keep in mind that formal and informal decentralization of power permeates the entire political system. Participants in state and local politics play a major role in making and implementing national policies.

The next two chapters describe the cultural, social, and economic setting in which political activity takes place. Chapters 4 and 5 look at basic constitutional arrangements that affect policy making, the system that James Madison and other Founding Fathers designed to distribute and so restrict power within the national government and between the nation and the states. We then turn to the processes of politics, examining such problems as the concept of power, the organization and functions of political parties, the electoral machinery for choosing public officials, and the diverse ways in which voters respond to appeals by parties and individual candidates. In Chapters 9 through 14 the emphasis shifts to the political institutions that bear responsibility for making policy, the operations and mutual restraints among Congress, the presidency, the bureaucracy, and the judiciary. Chapters 15 and 16 take up in detail certain problems of civil rights and criminal justice.

The final chapter tries to evaluate the performance of and the prospects for the American political system. A central concern in this concluding appraisal is the capacity of the system as a whole to make and carry out public policies that can coherently and effectively attack problems that gnaw at the country. What we hope emerges from the entire volume is a more sophisticated appreciation of the difficulties of reconciling competing, even conflicting, demands. These conflicts, and the power relationships that determine their outcome, are the essence of politics.

NOTES

1. *Public Opinion and American Democracy* (New York: Alfred A. Knopf, 1961), p. 8. Professor Key was one of the wisest analysts of American politics in the twentieth century. His work includes major contributions to the understanding of political parties, public opinion, voting behavior, and state and regional politics.
2. *Federal Register*, January 19, 1976, p. 2357.
3. Quoted in "Big Government," *Newsweek*, January 15, 1975, p. 34.

SELECTED BIBLIOGRAPHY

Anderson, James. E. *Public Policy Making* (New York: Holt, Rinehart and Winston, 1979). A succinct introduction to the policy-making process, which identifies the major aspects of policy formulation, implementation, impact, and change.

Dahl, Robert A., and Charles E. Lindenblom. *Politics, Economics, and Welfare* (New York: Harper, 1953). A classic examination of planning and policy making within complex political systems.

Davies, J. Clarence III. *The Politics of Pollution* (New York: Pegasus, 1970). An analysis of the many participants in environmental politics, and the conflicts among them.

Derthick, Martha. *Policymaking for Social Security* (Washington: Brookings Institution, 1979). A detailed examination of the various participants involved in the politics of social security.

Fritschler, A. Lee. *Smoking and Politics* (3d ed., Englewood Cliffs, N.J.: Prentice-Hall, 1983). A fascinating study of the forces at work inside and outside government which shape public policy: in this case, the health warning on cigarette packages.

Kaufman, Herbert. *Red Tape: Its Origins, Uses, and Abuses* (Washington: Brookings Institution, 1977). A deft appraisal which concludes that red tape is an integral aspect of political institutions.

Pechmann, Joseph A. *Setting National Priorities: The 1983 Budget* (Washington: Brookings Institution, 1982). The thirteenth in an annual series of volumes which analyze the consequences of the major determinations in the federal budget.

Reagan, Michael D. *The Administration of Public Policy* (Glenview, Ill.: Scott, Foresman, 1969). A description of the linkages between substance and process in the development and administration of public policy.

Wildavsky, Aaron. *Speaking Truth to Power: The Art and Craft of Policy Analysis* (Boston: Little, Brown, 1979). A comprehensive, provocative approach to the complex task of analyzing public policy.

2 American Political Cultures

Political behavior and governmental institutions are shaped by a nation's physical setting, patterns of development, social structure, belief systems, values, and goals. Most of these conditioning factors, in turn, are affected by the nature of a national political system and the public choices it makes and seeks to implement.

☆ THE CONTINENTAL SETTING

The political system of a nation is influenced by such physical factors as the country's location and natural resources. In these respects, the United States could hardly have been more blessed. When it was small, underpopulated, and weak, it was also remote, both in terms of interest to and distance from the great powers of the world. To the north, Canada was a sparsely settled outpost of the British Empire; to the south, Mexico, once it gained independence, wanted only peaceful coexistence. To the east was an ocean, and to the west an almost uninhabited subcontinent that invited exploitation.

Physical isolation was enhanced by natural wealth. On both sides of the Appalachian Mountains the climate was generally temperate and the soil fertile. A series of rivers provided a network of inland trade routes, and the seacoast was indented with sheltered harbors. Scattered about the country was an abundance of resources—wild animals for food, hides, and furs; grassy plains for cattle; timber for houses; gold and silver for adventure and quick wealth; and, for the industry that would come later, coal, oil, natural gas, iron, copper, lead, and bauxite.

In 1840, Alexis de Tocqueville, a Frenchman who traveled widely in the young nation, could speak of the "magnificent dwelling place" and the "immense booty" that fortune had left to Americans. That abundance has played a critical psychological as well as physical role in the American experience. Great prosperity, and an illusion of even greater prosperity, attracted wave after wave of immigrants and sent them as well as older inhabitants searching out and developing the natural wealth of the country. Often these people came as the downtrodden, but they came to better themselves, not to accept poverty. The myth of rags to riches may have seldom materialized, but social and economic advancement was possible and became the American dream, creating a surge of energy and hope.

Immigration and social mobility combined to help Americans maintain a myth of equality.[1] It was not that all people were equal—they certainly were not, in wealth, education, talent, or political power. But

29

the pull of an expanding economy and the push of the next sweep of immigrants did give most of the white poor more and more material benefits. It was not so much that their proportionate share of the good things of life increased, but that the number of good things available at a low price multiplied.

Industrialization

Until 1900, the frontier played a major role in American development. So did industrialization, but before 1860 its impact had been gradual. Some small-scale manufacturing had appeared during the colonial period. After independence, and shielded by a protective tariff, factories

"*Every twenty minutes, another small farmer disappears. You're next.*"

P. Steiner, © 1982 The New Yorker Magazine Inc.

grew slowly but steadily. The Civil War, however, created massive demands and started American industry off on a spiraling curve that has continued, despite frequent recessions and occasional depressions, for more than a century. Technological advances in production occurred at the same time that technological advances in transportation opened vast markets and made raw materials easily accessible.

European demands during World War I further bolstered American industry, so that by 1918 the United States had become not only the creditor of much of the world but also the biggest of the industrial nations. After the disastrous years of the Great Depression, World War II catapulted the American economy off once more with a momentum that sustained rapid economic growth for more than thirty years. During this period, industrial production increased nearly threefold, employment grew by 53 percent, and average incomes (adjusted for inflation) almost doubled.

Today, the manufacturing industries that spurred rapid growth—steel, farm machinery, automobiles, machine tools, appliances—are in decline. Thousands of jobs in steel mills, auto assembly lines, rubber plants, textile factories, and other industries have permanently disappeared, resulting in high unemployment and dashed hopes across the old industrial belt of the Northeast and Midwest. Computers and other high technology industries now are the most dynamic sectors of the economy. Also expanding rapidly are service jobs—retail sales, hotels, restaurants, repair, recreation, training, and other personal services. McDonald's, with an estimated work force of 350,000, employed two and one-half times as many people as U.S. Steel in 1982. But these new growth sectors of the economy create relatively few jobs for displaced industrial workers, because of geographic, educational, skill, and wage differentials.

Urbanization

Industrialization greatly altered the distribution of the American population. The new factories and their demands for labor stopped immigrants at the cities and also sparked a steady exodus from the farms to metropolitan areas. In 1800, only 6 percent of Americans were living in towns with populations over 2,500; by 1870 the proportion had risen to one-quarter. By 1900 it was up to 40 percent, and by 1980 more than three out of four people in the United States were living in urban places of more than 2,500. A better sense of the spread of urbanization is provided by data on metropolitan areas—cities and their surrounding suburbs, or in the case of some newer areas, suburbs surrrounded by newer suburbs. In 1980, 169 million Americans—almost three-quarters of the nation's citizens—were residing in metropolitan areas. The 323 *standard metropolitan statistical areas* covered 16 percent of the nation's land.*

But even these figures underestimate the physical reach of urbanization. The arms of the megalopolis have been spreading out like the tentacles of a hungry octopus, scooping up surrounding land for industrial parks, research laboratories, shopping centers, and suburban housing developments. "Strip Cities," like the one reaching from north of Boston to south of Richmond, Virginia, the one bordering all the southern arc of Lake Michigan, and the one stretching from the Mexican border along the coast of California north above Santa Barbara, are turning huge stretches of country into urbanized belts that make old geographical and political boundaries impractical for dealing with many social problems.

The growth of cities, metropolitan areas, and urban regions is a consequence of what have been called "two revolutions," one piled on top of the other.[2] The first of these revolutions is the rise of the urban way of life. The second is its diffusion and dispersal over the countryside. Underlying the "first revolution" has been migration to the city, primarily in response to industrialization.

The "second revolution," the rapid outward movement of urban populations, has resulted from acceleration of the natural tendency of cities to grow at their edges. Rapid outward expansion was made possible primarily by mass production of automobiles. Since 1920, suburban areas have been growing increasingly faster than central cities. By 1980, 102 million Americans lived in suburbs, 34 million more than resided in central cities, and 44 million more than lived outside metropolitan areas.

As people and jobs have moved outward, most older cities have stagnated. All of the major cities of the northeast and midwest had fewer residents in 1980 than in 1950. The biggest declines were in Boston, Cleveland, Detroit, Pittsburgh, and St. Louis, each of which lost at least 30 percent of its population.

In all of these cases, losses in population would have been far greater had the outward movement of white families not been offset by the growing migration to the city of blacks and Hispanics—most of them poor and uneducated. Between 1950 and 1980, millions of blacks moved to central cities, a migration which raised the cities' proportion of black residents from 12 percent to 23 percent. During the 1970s, Spanish-speaking migrants substantially outnumbered black newcomers; and in 1980, over seven million Latinos lived in central cities. As a consequence

---

* Standard metropolitan statistical areas, or SMSAs, are cities with 50,000 or more residents and the surrounding governmental jurisdictions, usually counties, which have economic and social links to the city. In addition, SMSAs can consist of contiguous suburban areas without a city of 50,000 or more at the core.

of these trends—and despite the fact that many blacks and Hispanics have also moved to the suburbs—most cities are separated from the surrounding suburbs by substantial racial, ethnic, income, housing, and educational differences.

Exceptions to these patterns are found primarily among the younger cities of the south and west. Growing up in the era of the automobile, these cities developed at much lower density than had the older cities of the northeast and midwest. As a result, many urban cores in Florida, Texas, Arizona, and California are more suburbs than cities in the traditional sense.

Unlike the typical older city, most of the newer cities have continued to experience rapid growth. Houston, the sixth largest city in the nation, more than doubled its population between 1950 and 1980, adding 1,000 new residents a week during the 1970s. During the same three decades even more spectacular growth rates occurred in Tampa, Jacksonville, El Paso, Phoenix, San Jose, Albuquerque, and Tucson.

By the 1970s, metropolitan growth began to slow as increasing numbers of Americans were attracted to life in smaller towns and rural areas. The dispersion of jobs was one factor in the rebirth of many small towns. Even more important was the growing desire for a simpler life in smaller communities, away from the congestion, crime, pollution, and impersonality of the metropolis. Housing also is typically cheaper outside metropolitan areas, and access to outdoor recreation easier. Adding to this outflux has been the aging of the population, increasing the number of people whose residence is not tied to work, and who seek less expensive, safer, warmer and more attractive places to live on pensions and social security checks.

A Changing Population

Industrialization and urbanization have stimulated enormous population growth. The small nation of 4 million in 1790 added 36 million residents by 1870. Then, as the impact of industrial change and urban growth began to transform American society, population expanded rapidly, both as a result of natural increase (the excess of births over deaths) and of immigration from abroad. In the past sixty years, the 1920 population of 105 million more than doubled, reaching 226 million in 1980.

By the 1980s, however, population growth had slowed in the United States. The annual growth rate during the 1970s was 1.1 percent, compared with 1.5 percent over the previous two decades and 2.0 percent between 1870 and 1920. Underlying this decline have been social and family changes which reduced the birth rate substantially. Lower birth rates have combined with longer life spans to produce an increasingly older population. In 1980, one in nine Americans was sixty-five or older, compared with one in twenty-two in 1929 and one in thirty-five in 1870.

In recent years, immigration has again become a major factor in demographic change. Over 800,000 immigrants entered the United States legally in 1980—including 140,000 refugees from Cuba and Haiti—almost as many as came annually during 1900–1910, the peak decade of earlier immigration. Another half million or more aliens enter the country illegally each year. Altogether, legal and illegal newcomers account for about one-third of the United States' annual population growth. The new immigrants are primarily from Asia and Latin America, rather than from Europe as in the past. California rather than New York is the principal destination for the latest waves of people seeking political freedom, economic opportunity, religious tolerance, and a better life in America.

Another important feature of the changing demography of the United States is accelerating movement of people from the older industrial and urban heartland of the northeast and midwest to the sunbelt areas of the south and west. The rapid growth of newer cities such as Houston, Phoenix, and Tampa reflects the westward and southward movement of Americans, a migration to warmer climes and economic opportunities created by industries based on petroleum, electronics, and other new technologies. During the 1970s, western and southern states accounted for 90 percent of all the nation's population growth, and in 1980 the geographical center of population moved across the Mississippi River for the first time.

TABLE 2-1   **Shifting Sources of Immigration to the United States, 1959–1979**

Region of Origin	Percentage of Immigrants	
	1959	*1979*
Europe	60.9	13.4
Latin America	19.8	38.6
Asia	8.9	41.4
Canada	8.9	3.0
Africa	1.1	2.6
Oceania	0.5	1.0

SOURCE: U.S. Immigration and Naturalization Service

A sign at a California shopping center underscores the rising tide of migration from Asia to the nation's most populous state. (David Strick, New York Times Pictures)

American Society

This collage of wealth, work, isolation, immigration, industrialization, and urbanization has forged a complex society full of contradictions. The contrasts of American life abound: romantic love and high divorce rates, Hollywood sex symbols and Disneyland, urban blight alongside magnificent monuments, marvelous medical research and a mania for cigarette smoking, anger at the young for dulling their minds with marijuana but approval of cocktails before lunch and dinner, eminent symphony orchestras and blaring rock bands, resounding testimonials to human dignity and equality together with insidious racial and sexual discrimination.

Americans created an economy which provides most citizens with comfortable housing, good food, and excellent medical and dental care. They spend millions of dollars annually for recreation—color television sets, boats, second homes, golf, fishing, bowling, whiskey, and long vacations. Yet even play means hard work for Americans; they tend to consume leisure rather than enjoy it. At times it has seemed that the Protestant ethic of hard work has gone mad in America and has created a mass rat race of people working compulsively harder and harder to win higher salaries, more responsibility, and less enjoyment. In recent years, however, there has been a notable reaction against this kind of existence. In all sorts of occupations, there has been a rejection, particularly by younger Americans, of the regimentation imposed by large organizations and a search for alternative lifestyles oriented toward individual fulfillment.

The frenzied labor of American adults has bought for future generations the advantage of the widest dispersion of educational opportunities in the world. The median number of years of schooling for adults in the United States now exceeds twelve. A college education has become the normal expectation of most middle-class teenagers and of large numbers of working-class children as well. In 1979, over 11.5 million students were attending colleges and universities. The high income earned by doctors, lawyers, and engineers evidences the rewards that a highly technological society bestows for advanced training.

Despite the great emphasis on education and despite the respect Americans accord academics, there is a noticeable current of anti-intellectualism in American thought. Perhaps the challenge of survival on the frontier and later of competition in the dog-eat-dog economy of the nineteenth century discouraged philosophical speculation and encouraged pragmatic approaches. Does it work? Does it make a profit? Does it allow me to get ahead? These are the typical questions Americans have asked, not: How does it fit into a broad interpretation of the cosmos? Indeed, if Americans can be said to have developed any national philosophy, it is a philosophy of pragmatism, which pushes aside abstract speculation and favors more practical questions about actual results.

American society is permissive as well as pragmatic. With Dr. Benjamin Spock's book on child-raising the bible of the last generation of parents, family life has become very democratic. In recent decades, many schoolteachers have urged children to express themselves, to give their own opinions rather than to regurgitate the rote recitations that used to characterize much of what we call education. The point is not that there is no discipline in the family or school, but that there is considerably less than in the American past or than in the present of most other nations.

The informality of American business life, where president or owner often insists on being addressed by first name or initials, may be partly a means of softening the savagery of competition. But the usual practice of the more successful corporations has been to encourage employees to exercise initiative, blue-collar workers as well as top officials. Even the military is becoming less authoritarian. The traditional model of the general as the "heroic soldier" who earned his reputation for blood and guts and demanded instant and unswerving obedience is being superseded by a managerial model, in which the general more often persuades and leads than commands.[3]

⭐ THE CONCEPT OF POLITICAL CULTURE

Like a nation's physical setting and resources, its social customs and ideals can influence the character and operation of its governmental system. To take account of this shaping force, political scientists have developed the concept of political culture. In its most general and useful sense, *political culture refers to politically relevant ideas and social practices.* It is a concept that calls attention to the fact that habits of action, norms of conduct, symbols of good and evil, and even basic notions about the nature of God and man can influence the ways people behave in political contexts and the ways in which they evaluate the political behavior of others.

To be sure, not all social arrangements and not all prevalent ideas are politically important, but many are. Even something as basic as language may play a significant role. One noted political philosopher has speculated that the existence of the word "leader" has increased the chances for the success of democratic government in English-speaking nations over such countries as Germany and Italy, where the closest words are more equivalent to "commander" or "director."[4] One would expect a society in which fathers usually exercise authoritarian control over family life to foster very different sorts of political relationships from a society in which there is considerable give-and-take in family decision making. One would also expect people who grow up under rigid class structure to have different patterns of political behavior from people reared in a classless society.

Although few societies provide neat contrasts, there is evidence to indicate that to a large extent the expected relations between society and politics do take place. People accustomed to participate in decision making in the family, at school, or at work tend to participate more in political life and to feel more competent to influence governmental decisions. The connections, however, between social background and political behavior are neither simple nor universal. Among other important factors is personality. For instance, people who feel least competent politically are usually not those who have been denied opportunities to participate in other social situations, but those who have had such opportunities but did not take advantage of them.[5]

Moreover, traffic between politics and other social relations is not along a limited-access highway. New governmental policies frequently interact with old social customs to precipitate fundamental changes. And these changes occur not only in the way people behave politically but also in relationships within supposedly more basic groups like the family or the church.

"Our government," Supreme Court Justice Louis D. Brandeis once noted, "is the potent, the omnipresent teacher. For good or ill, it teaches the whole people by its example."[6] American concepts of equality owe much to Jefferson and Lincoln. George Washington and Chief Justice John Marshall helped shape our views on nationalism. Certainly Presidents Franklin D. Roosevelt, John F. Kennedy, and Lyndon B. Johnson were primarily responsible for converting minority views about the desirability of the welfare state into an accepted part of American life. Chief Justice Earl Warren's pronouncement for the Supreme Court in the school segregation case in 1954 changed a great deal of thinking about human dignity in general and race relations in particular.[7]

More generally, it is a plausible hypothesis that much of the permissiveness of current American life is a by-product of political democracy. Extolling the virtues of debate and popular participation in governmental affairs has a perceptible spillover into the arenas of the family, classroom, office, and church.

SYSTEMS OF BELIEFS

Basic ideas about human nature, authority, religion, and the purposes of life have broad political relevance. The framers of the American Constitution, for instance, were deeply aware of the frailty of virtue. Products of Protestant culture, they were influenced by the doctrine of original sin—human nature is fundamentally weak; people want to do good but are inclined toward evil and selfishness. Thus the framers found attractive a governmental scheme for checking ambition against ambition. "But what is government itself," James Madison asked in *The Federalist*, "but the greatest of all reflections on human nature? If men were angels, no government would be necessary."[8]

Ideas about fundamental philosophic principles as well as beliefs directly linked to politics are more likely to be normative than descriptive. That is, they are more likely to consist of notions about what is right and proper than descriptions of what actually happens. These ideas thus form a kind of moral screen through which people filter information and perceive and judge political reality.

One can speak in two senses of a system of beliefs. First, there is evidence that an overwhelming proportion of Americans endorse democratic political principles. Most are convinced that democracy is the best form of government, that public officials should be elected by a majority vote, and that every citizen should have an equal opportunity to participate in politics. Americans also believe that members of the minority have the right to criticize the majority's choices and to try to win a majority over to their views.[9] The concept of the basic equality of human dignity would probably receive equally enthusiastic endorsement.

Second, in many important respects, the political outlooks of Americans differ from those of citizens of other countries. A study conducted by Almond and Verba showed that, compared to British, Germans, Italians, and Mexicans, Americans tended to be more trusting of their fellow man, to see more altruism in other people, to look more on political participation as a duty of the average citizen, to think of themselves as more influential in their national government, and, except for the British, to be more likely to expect fair and equal treatment from public officials.[10]

Almond and Verba also found that Americans were prouder of their governmental institutions, but more recent surveys show a marked drop in American trust in their political system. The Survey Research Center of the University of Michigan reported in 1964 that 62 percent of a national sample of adults had a high level of trust in the federal government. Over the next few years that figure fell steadily, and at the time of President Nixon's forced resignation in 1974 had plummeted to 25 per-

TABLE **2-2**   **A Decade Later—Attitudes Toward Watergate in 1982**

Watergate was a very serious matter	52%
Watergate was just politics	45%
Don't know	3%
To what degree has Watergate reduced your confidence in the Federal government?	
(a) a great deal	21%
(b) somewhat	45%
(c) not at all	30%
(d) don't know	4%
Abuses of presidential power could happen easily again	53%
Lessons of Watergate will probably prevent similar abuses of presidential power	42%
Don't know	5%

cent. Declining trust during this period was strongly influenced by the Watergate scandal, the Vietnam war, race relations, assassination of U.S. and foreign political leaders, and disregard of basic rights by intelligence agencies. Although there was some increase in trust in government in recent years, levels remained much lower than in the past. Americans also were pessimistic about the prospects of abuses of presidential power, as indicated in Table 2-2.

Another indication of changing public attitudes toward government is the rise in tax evasion and the growth of a vast underground economy based on unrecorded cash transactions. The United States historically has had a very high rate of tax compliance compared with most other political systems. By 1981, however, the Internal Revenue Service was reporting that almost $100 billion in taxes were not paid, an amount three times that of 1973. The underground economy was estimated at $500 billion in the early 1980s, and growing at twice the rate of the economy as a whole.

 **CULTURAL DIVERSITY**

We must talk of *many political cultures* when we analyze most modern nations. Patterns of child-raising, educational and religious training, and economic relations vary greatly from social group to social group in America. An immigrant child raised in a strict Irish Catholic family and educated by authoritarian nuns is apt to have been exposed to a set of influences very different from that of a black child who came to maturity in an urban ghetto or on a Mississippi cotton farm, or of a white Protestant youngster who grew up in an affluent suburb where discipline was light.

In similar fashion, we should not expect anything approaching unanimity on most political issues. What we know about public opinion indicates that consensus on general principles rarely includes agreement on specific policies. To a middle-class white, for example, equality for blacks may refer to their right to live in decent housing in the central city, not next door in a suburb, or to compete for a blue-collar job, not a managerial position. To many blacks, equality means preferential treatment to compensate for centuries of injustice. To a conservative, the right of a minority to try to persuade the majority of the error of its ways may not include the right of a communist to speak in a public hall or at a street meeting. To radicals, free speech may mean the right to shout down those who advocate "immoral" or "fascist" propositions.

Table 2-3 summarizes responses of a sample of adults in Ann Arbor, Michigan, and Tallahassee, Florida, who had averaged over 95 percent agreement on the democratic principles listed in the previous section and indicates just how quickly consensus disappears when it is confronted with practical problems of application. On only three of the seven statements listed—the rights of blacks to run for office and of socialists to speak and a desire to restrict voting on city tax measures to

TABLE 2-3   **Responses to Questions about Civil Rights**

Statement	Percent Agreeing
Antireligious speeches should be allowed	63
Socialist speeches should be allowed	79
Communist speeches should be allowed	44

Statement	Percent Disagreeing
Only informed people should have the right to vote on a city referendum	49
Only taxpayers should have the right to vote on city tax measures	21
Blacks should not be allowed to hold public office	81
Communists should not be allowed to hold public office	46

SOURCE: James W. Prothro and Charles M. Grigg, "Fundamental Principles of Democracy: Bases of Agreement and Disagreement," *Journal of Politics*, XXII (1960), 285.

taxpayers—were about eight out of ten respondents in agreement. In no instance did the answers approach the consensus reached in reply to questions about general principles of democracy.

The Silent Majority

The dominant political culture in America has been shaped largely by the values of the white middle class. Its general beliefs in popular participation and election, majority rule and minority rights, and equality before the law are widely shared. But these beliefs are usually abstract rather than particular. Often they have little to do with how people view concrete public issues. To many middle-class Americans, political participation may mean only voting regularly and perhaps writing to a senator or calling a local official about a problem. To most other Americans, political participation means even less. On the whole, to the average citizen politics is neither a very important nor an interesting part of life's circus. In 1980, more than two out of every five American adults denied that they cared very much in a personal way about the outcome of the presidential election. During the same year, less than a third of the people indicated they were very much interested in the presidential campaign.

As such responses suggest, the political knowledge of most citizens is slight. Even during national campaigns, Americans are likely to have little detailed information about issues that candidates, journalists, and political scientists consider important. The average citizen seldom engages in serious political discussion. When he or she does, it is likely to be with people who have the same opinions.

There is a cluster of private citizens, mostly from the upper and upper-middle class, who are highly informed and deeply concerned about politics. Among this group, an opinion about a specific problem tends to be a consistent piece of a more general and coherent political orientation. These people are typically well educated and sometimes have experience in practical politics. However, they form a small minority, accounting for less than 10 percent of the adult population.[11]

Apparently, despite lack of knowledge and lethargic participation, widely shared affection for the basic system continues even when levels of political trust are running low. A survey by Louis Harris and Associates in 1972 indicated that 90 percent of the respondents were convinced of the basic soundness of the American system of government, despite the fact that fewer than 30 percent had a great deal of confidence in Congress or the federal executive. Throughout American history, foreign observers have been struck by the reverence with which Americans view their Constitution. Politicians and political institutions rise and fall in public esteem, but the Constitution seems to persist as a symbol of virtue as much as a charter for government.

Running alongside respect for the Constitution is suspicion of governmental power. "I am not," Thomas Jefferson wrote in 1787, "a friend to a very energetic government."[12] Something akin to that attitude can be seen in the responses to questions put by the pollsters. Americans may say that they favor governmental action on problems that affect them directly—keeping railroads running or increasing social security benefits, for example. At the same time, however, those people are apt to respond negatively to broader questions about increasing governmental power. Although these reactions may seem to be logically contradictory, they reflect a recognition of the need for governmental action and at the same time a yearning for the independence and individualism that Jefferson treasured.

The Professional Politician

Even very interested and articulate private citizens often differ from professional politicians in the way they look at politics. The professional's world is shaped by the fact that he (or she) has far more political resources at his command. As a generalist—a nonspecialist—the professional may know less about some particular problems than do many highly educated private citizens, but politicians know where to find expertise if needed. More important, politicians devote their working time, not just their leisure, to politics. Acquiring and using political skills are the politician's life work; and success provides other resources. If an incumbent, the professional has the authority of office and the prestige it provides. If not in office, the professional politician may still have considerable influence with those who head governmental agencies.

Private citizens seldom have a sophisticated understanding of how to translate general principles of democratic government into workable political rules. For the professional, "the rules of the game" are likely to be tangible guidelines.[13]

The most basic of these professional rules is acceptance of elections as the proper means of determining who should govern. To look at the frequency of coups d'état around the world is to appreciate that respect for the ballot box is hardly an inborn trait. The political espionage and sabotage run by the White House in the infamous Watergate scandals of the 1972 presidential campaign indicate how brittle such respect can be even in the United States.

Other rules of the game include listening to constituent complaints, permitting groups likely to be affected a chance to be heard before government takes action, allowing opposing legislators a reasonable opportunity to speak, keeping one's word to officials from the opposing party as well as one's own, not looking closely into the campaign financing or tactics of colleagues unless serious abuses come to light, and respecting the constitutional prerogatives of other governmental agencies even while sharply disagreeing with their decisions. Professional politicians generally observe these rules because they know that they have to work year after year with other professionals, that they will have to run for re-election at frequent intervals, and that in their careers they may hold a variety of offices in several branches of government.

Even the amateur who gets deeply involved in politics is apt to see a different world than does a professional. The amateur typically enters the political arena with a single, immediate policy goal in mind. The professional, on the other hand, is accustomed to dealing with many issues so steadily and constantly "that few of them have the ultimate soul-saving importance for him as they do for amateurs . . . . Politics for [amateurs] is a means to an end, and what counts is to gain that end. To the professional, in contrast, what counts is to endure."[14]

The Poor

Patterns of behavior, belief, and expectation are greatly influenced by an individual's economic circumstances. Most striking are the differences between those who are more or less affluent and those who live in dire poverty. In 1981, 32 million Americans lived below the poverty level.* Some of the poor are people who are too lazy, too undisciplined, or too oriented toward immediate gratification to cope with life in a technological society. Some, like the hoboes of an older generation or the hippies of a more recent one, simply prefer a lifestyle that cannot be measured in economic terms. But the vast majority of the poor are impoverished neither by choice nor by sin. Instead, they are "largely those un-equipped by reason of some disability—age, sickness, or other physical incapacity, lack of education or training, discrimination because of race, or some other circumstance over which they had no control—to find gainful employment either in the private or public sectors of the economy."[15] Those who live in poverty are disproportionately black, members of other racial minorities, very old, or very young. If old, the poor tend to be sick, unemployed, and unemployable. If young, they often come from broken homes and have received education inadequate to equip them for competition in American society.

Michael Harrington, whose book *The Other America* played a major role in awakening national interest in the problems of the poor, sees

---

* The poverty-level line is defined by the federal government in terms of the amount of money it takes a family in a particular area to pay for minimally adequate food, shelter, and medical care. In 1981, the poverty line for a family of four was $8,287.

poverty as "a culture, an institution, a way of life."[16] The poor have family structures, sexual mores, and political outlooks different from those of middle-class citizens. "To be impoverished is to be an internal alien, to grow up in a culture that is radically different from the one that dominates society."[17] Those doomed to live in the empty shadows of poverty are vulnerable to hate—of themselves as well as of others—as they catch glimpses of the world of prosperity.

Poverty also has tremendous implications—although still largely potential implications—for the structure as well as the policies of the American political system. Until the late 1960s, the poor were politically mute and unimportant, despite their numbers. More recently, poor blacks, Chicanos, Puerto Ricans, Indians, and Appalachian whites have become "politically visible." Obviously, 32 million people represent an enormous political potential. The vast majority of the poor, however, remain ineffective in the political arena. Only about three out of five

Don Wright, The Miami News

TABLE **2-4**

Poverty in America, 1981

	Number	*Percent of Poor*
Age:		
Under 18	12,324,000	38.7
18–64	15,645,000	49.2
Over 64	3,853,000	12.1
Residence:		
In central cities	11,231,000	35.3
In suburbs	8,116,000	25.5
Outside metropolitan areas	12,475,000	39.2
Race:		
Whites	21,553,000	67.7
Blacks	9,173,000	28.8
Hispanics	3,713,000	11.7

SOURCE: U.S. Bureau of the Census.

adults within the lowest income brackets even claim to vote regularly, and the actual proportion is smaller. In comparison, about nine out of ten people with higher incomes go to the polls. Nor do the poor usually belong to unions, clubs, or other organizations that can dramatize their plight and represent their interests as poor people. In political life, the poor are fatally handicapped by their lack of resources. Most are too ignorant, too young and unsophisticated, too sick, too miserable, or too old to achieve anything like their political potential.

Blacks

The National Advisory Commission on Civil Disorders stated in 1968 that the United States was "moving toward two societies, one black, one white—separate and unequal."[18] The striking eloquence of this sentence obscured the fact that it was fundamentally wrong. The United States has comprised many societies, and race has drawn the most obvious and enduring line of division. Since the first slaves were taken ashore in Virginia in 1619, America has had a black society that has been distinctly separate from and decidedly unequal to the white societies. The black man, wrote W. E. B. Du Bois at the beginning of this century, "ever feels his twoness—an American, a Negro; two souls, two thoughts, two unreconciled strivings; two warring ideals in one dark body."[19]

No more accurately, of course, than one can speak of *a* Caucasian society can one speak of *a* black society. Many social, economic, educa-

Demonstrators on Capitol Hill protest slashes in social programs on May Day, 1982. (Shephard Sherbell, Picture Group Photo)

tional, and political differences exist among the 26.5 million blacks in the United States. There are some rich blacks, although not very many. More and more blacks have moved into the middle class and have incomes, education, attitudes, and values similar to those of white middle-class Americans. In 1980, the average black had completed 12 years of school, compared with 8.2 years in 1960 (and 12.5 years for the average white in 1980). And 37 percent of all black workers held white-collar jobs in 1980, about three times as many as in 1960. Despite these gains, there remain masses of black poor, from the small rural farms to the large city ghettos—more than one of every three blacks fell below the poverty line in 1981. The poor of both races bear the same burdens, but the colors of their skin have usually generated enough prejudice and distrust to keep them from acting as close allies. True assimilation of blacks into white American life at any social or economic level has been rare.

As a result of imposed separatism, a set of black subcultures has grown up, with some practices and speech patterns running back through the slave cabins to Africa. Not only do customs and habits of dress frequently differ, but rural and ghetto blacks often speak what is in many respects a different language from white-middle-class English.[20]

Like whites, blacks have moved from lonely farms to even lonelier urban centers. In 1940, about two-thirds of blacks lived in southern states; by 1980, the proportion had fallen to 45 percent. But even more than from south to north, the pattern of black migration has been from farm to city. Wherever blacks live, most have grown up in an environment more hostile than that of the typical white. If they are poor or near-poor, blacks witness violence almost daily. The black trusts fellow humans less than does the white, and with good reason. A black male is four times more likely to be robbed than a white, and a black woman is three times more likely to be raped than a white female. Blacks are also much more likely than whites to be stopped by police and subjected to humiliating searches or to be hauled off to a police station for questioning.

A black can expect to live seven fewer years than a white person of the same sex, to enjoy three-fifths the income, and to suffer more than twice the unemployment rate. Blacks also bear a disproportionate burden of the costs imposed by cutbacks in governmental spending because of their greater dependence than whites on welfare, public health and housing, job training, and other social programs. Thus most blacks neither have nor can reasonably expect to gain in the near future the material goods that the average white earns. Despite substantial gains, discrimination remains an integral part of every black American's life.

In these circumstances, it is hardly surprising that blacks have created their own political subculture. They, too, may endorse the basic principles of democracy, but to them majority rule may mean white domination and minority rights a black dream. When they express their political views, blacks, compared to whites, assert greater general trust in the federal government and are much more strongly in favor of specific federal programs to carry out school desegregation, to enforce fair employment practices, and to provide jobs and minimal standard of living for all citizens. On the other hand, blacks register far less satisfaction with local government. They are much more critical of such public services as garbage collection, recreational facilities, schools, and, most of all, police protection.[21]

One of the more important political differences between blacks and whites is not merely the way in which they judge events but also the way each group tends to see—or not see—the same event. For instance, almost eight out of ten whites interviewed during the 1968 presidential campaign said they thought that most black protests had been violent, while fewer than three out of ten blacks so perceived the same demon-

TABLE 2-5   **White / Black Opinions about the Federal Government**

Statement	Percent Agreeing	
	Blacks	*Whites*
The federal government has gotten too powerful	15	59
The federal government should make sure everyone has a job and a good standard of living	81	30
The federal government should make sure Negroes get fair job treatment	89	38
The federal government should make sure Negro and white children can go to the same schools	89	37

SOURCE: Center for Political Studies, University of Michigan, American National Election Study Series, 1968

strations. The race riots of the 1960s underline these differences in perception. Blacks tended to find the causes of the riots primarily in social deprivation and saw them as the result of a discriminatory system. Whites, on the other hand, were far more likely than blacks to blame looters or "agitators." Blacks were more likely than whites to look for cures in social reforms, while close to a majority of whites saw a solution in stiffer police measures. Whites also claimed awareness of far less discrimination against blacks than did the blacks. Although whites conceded that blacks were worse off than they themselves were, a majority felt the cause was in the blacks themselves rather than in social conditions brought about by discrimination. A decade after the riots, the proportion of whites who saw no evidence of economic discrimination toward blacks had risen as indicated in Figure 2-2. Blacks in 1978 were more pessimistic about race relations than in 1968, with more feeling that whites don't care about blacks, that there was little progress being made in reducing racial discrimination, and that there was little hope of eliminating racism in the foreseeable future.

Despite improving conditions for many blacks and the easing of discrimination, race remains one of the fundamental sources of conflict in American society. Martin Luther King, Jr.'s dream in the 1960s of people of all races living together in harmony remains a distant goal in the 1980s. King, and generations of blacks before him, had dreamed the American dream, the same dream that brought waves of immigrants from Europe, Asia, and Latin America to the United States. It was a dream of enjoying that equality of human dignity which the Declaration of Independence had proclaimed to be a self-evident truth, that equality before the law which the Fourteenth Amendment had enshrined as a fundamental constitutional principle, and that material prosperity which had been achieved by millions of other Americans.

FIGURE 2-1

Attitudes on Racial Discrimination in the Urban North, 1968 and 1978

BLACKS

On the whole, do you think most white people in your town want to see blacks get a better break, do they want to keep blacks down, or don't they care?

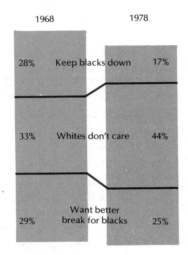

1968   1978

28%   Keep blacks down   17%

33%   Whites don't care   44%

29%   Want better break for blacks   25%

BLACKS

Would you say there has been a lot of progress in getting rid of racial discrimination over the last 10 or 15 years? Or would you say there hasn't been much change for black people?

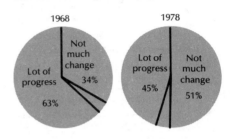

1968   1978

Lot of progress 63%   Not much change 34%

Lot of progress 45%   Not much change 51%

BLACKS

Do you think there will always be a lot of racial prejudice and discrimination in the United States, or is there a real hope of ending it in the long run?

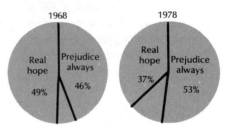

1968   1978

Real hope 49%   Prejudice always 46%

Real hope 37%   Prejudice always 53%

WHITES

Do you think that many, some or only a few blacks in your city miss out on jobs and promotions because of racial discrimination?

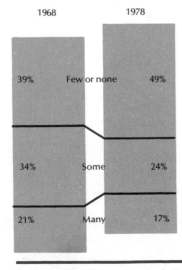

1968   1978

39%   Few or none   49%

34%   Some   24%

21%   Many   17%

SOURCE: 1968—Survey Research Center, University of Michigan; 1978—New York Times/ CBS News Poll, *The New York Times,* February 26 and 27, 1978. © 1978 by The New York Times Company. Reprinted by permission.

For many blacks, the dream of equality in a racially integrated society is a dangerous fantasy rather than a guiding hope. A century of second-class citizenship, of living in sharecropper shacks or rat-infested urban ghettos, has cut an inevitable swath of bitter disillusionment. One response has been black separatism. In the 1920s, Marcus Garvey advocated a return to Africa. More recently, Black Muslims have preached the need for the creation of a black nation carved out of the southern states. Calls for "black power" and "black liberation" reflect the rejection of white society by some contemporary black leaders.

Few blacks, however, actively support racial separation. The results of the survey conducted for the Commission on Civil Disorders indicated that barely 6 percent wanted their children to go to a black school or believed there should be a separate black nation or that whites and blacks could not have close friendships. At the same time, running through these and other survey data is strong support for black cultural identity and economic independence. Almost all blacks believe that they should take more pride in their history and that there should be more businesses operated by blacks. A substantial majority agrees that, where possible, blacks should buy from stores run by blacks. More recently, 79 percent of the black respondents in a *Newsweek* poll indicated that they would prefer to live in a racially mixed neighborhood rather than in an all-black area.[22] What emerges is a portrait showing that "a substantial number" of blacks want *both* integration and black identity."[23]

White Ethnics

Rising self-consciousness among blacks has been accompanied by an intensification of ethnic consciousness among many working-class whites. The movement for black pride and power has not only generated fears among whites whose forebears were immigrants from Ireland, Italy, and central eastern Europe. It has also increased the sense of separation from the culture of white, Protestant, and affluent America that these people have long felt.

Disdained by WASPs (White Anglo-Saxon Protestants) and typically by preceding waves of immigrants as well, the Irish, Italians, Poles, and other ethnic groups tended to settle initially in neighborhoods already populated by their own people. A common set of ties to family, friends, and customs in the old country, a common language, and a common religion (usually Catholic), plus a tightly knit family, held most of these people together against the strange and sometimes hostile behavior of the Anglos. "The point about the melting pot is that it did not happen."[24] Indeed, a smorgasbord would provide a more fitting analogy of American society: a rich variety of separate offerings, yet with a degree of similarity in flavor, much of it imparted in recent years by the leveling influence of television.

Ethnic influence on social behavior can be seen most clearly in the working-class neighborhoods of older cities as one goes from an Irish to an Italian or Polish community. Similar distinctions appear more subtly in the personal styles of life, most especially in family structure. The bonds of affection and, perhaps more significantly, of interdependence that still tie second- and third-generation Italians or Polish families into a unit have weakened among the Irish and seldom exist at all among white middle-class Protestants.

To a large extent, the Germans, Scandinavians, Irish, and Jews have left the working classes and are diffused through the middle and upper classes of America in the suburbs in which these classes largely live. Italians, Poles and other Slavs, Greeks, and Czechs are still disproportionately made up of manual and skilled laborers, and remain aware of their differences from each other and from the rest of Americans.

The working-class ethnics are also acutely—and proudly—conscious of having earned the right to be Americans. They shed a disproportionate share of blood in the first three wars of this century. They also feel that they, not the government, lifted themselves out of the stink of poverty. By their own hard labor, they sweated their way up from the slums. Thus white ethnics tend to be parochial in their outlook and wary of public welfare programs. Their own harsh struggle for survival has left scars of distrust of the world outside the family or neighborhood.

Hispanic Americans

Almost 15 million Spanish-speaking individuals were living in the United States in 1980. Growth of the Hispanic population has been rapid—the increase during the 1970s was 60 percent—and Latinos will outnumber blacks by the end of the century. Like blacks, most Hispanics have been victims of pervasive discrimination which has limited employment, housing, and educational opportunities. The price of discrimination has been particularly high for Chicanos, migrants from Mexico who for decades were blatantly exploited by the dominant Anglos of Texas, New Mexico, Arizona, and California. In other respects, the Latino experience has resembled that of European ethnics. Few Hispanics arrive able to speak English; they share a Roman Cathlic religious heritage; and they come from a variety of homelands—Mexico, Puerto Rico, Cuba, the Dominican Republic, and Colombia. Some, most notably the business and professional refugees from Castro's Cuba, have assimilated relatively easily; others have found no way out of the sprawling barrios of Los Angeles, San Antonio, Miami, and New York.

Like other newcomers, Latinos have paid heavily for their entry into

American society, in terms of hard work, poor public services, bloodshed, poverty, and dashed hopes in the land of opportunity. Low rates of political participation and exploitation by unscrupulous Anglo and Latino political leaders have reduced their impact on the political system. During the 1970s, however, Hispanics began to flex their political muscles, electing increasing numbers of their own to local councils, state legislatures, and Congress. Latinos and their political leaders have grown more aggressive in their quest for greater recognition of the Hispanic population, its numbers, language, and other special needs. They favor governmental efforts to help the disadvantaged, but feel that federal social programs have been aimed primarily at blacks, to the detriment of the Latino poor.

In recent years, more and more minority groups have sought to enhance their political power through organizations such as La Raza Unida, a Chicano group organized in southern Texas. (United Press International)

Women

In many respects, the political behavior of women resembles that of men. More education and income increase the likelihood that women will vote and otherwise participate in politics. Class, racial, and ethnic affiliations have much the same effect on voting and political attitudes of women as on those of men.

Women, however, also face special obstacles that derive from their historically subordinate role in American society. Sexual stereotyping related to prospective social roles reduces educational and economic opportunities for many women. Automatic assignment to females of responsibilities for child care and domestic life limits the horizons of large numbers of women. Male dominance of households, social groupings, and organizations restrict female participation and influence in all sorts of activities. Nor have women enjoyed the same legal rights as men, although recent changes have improved their legal position considerably. Women were not guaranteed the vote in federal elections until the Nineteenth Amendment in 1920. As a consequence of these barriers, women fill a disproportionately small share of the positions of influence in the American economic, political, and social life.

During the past decade, growing numbers of women in the United States have rebelled against their subordinate status. In a variety of ways, women's liberation has raised the consciousness of females and sensitized males about the position of women. Given the enormous diversity of attitudes in the female population, however, the women's movement has been cross-cut by other social, economic, and political forces. Catholic women are less likely to favor abortion than other women. Black women are more concerned about racial discrimination than their white sisters. Married women and single females have different interests on some issues; middle-class women differ from welfare mothers on others. An important factor in the defeat of the proposed Equal Rights Amendment to the Constitution, which was vigorously supported by groups such as the National Organization of Women, was the opposition of many women with conservative political, social, and religious perspectives.

Despite this diversity, large numbers of women have mobilized politically to support efforts to eliminate sex discrimination in employment, to secure more effective and less humiliating laws dealing with rape, and to demand more positions of leadership in all aspects of American life. More and more women are running for—and winning—public office. And in 1981 a woman was appointed to the U.S. Supreme Court, leaving the presidency and vice-presidency as the only remaining male bastions in American politics. Even more important, fewer women automatically accept the subordinate roles which the dominant male society traditionally assigned them. One evidence of this change is the

TABLE **2-6**   **Number of Women Holding Elective Office, 1975–1981**

	1975	1980–1981	1983
Congress	21	21	23
Statewide offices	30	34	37
State legislatures	610	908	ca. 992
County governments	456	1,144	1,128
Municipal governments	4,650	14,176	14,464

SOURCE: Eagleton Institute of Politics, Rutgers University, National Information Bank on Women in Public Office.

growing divergence of women's positions on a number of important issues from those of men—with women more skeptical of defense expenditures, more supportive of social programs, and more concerned about the quality of life than men.

★ VIOLENCE AS A CULTURAL TRAIT

All social groups in the United States have been exposed to the glorification of *the rule of law* that runs through American culture.* Alongside the hallowed stream of traditional law and order, however, has run a clearly discernible trickle of thought justifying, and at times glorifying, violence. It may be a remnant from a frontier society that depended heavily on self-help for survival, for there is a strong theme of violence in the legends of Daniel Boone, Davy Crockett, James Bowie, Wild Bill Hickok, and Buffalo Bill Cody. Moreover, much of what passes for literature today is often an assorted mixture of sex and sadism. In the popular novels about Lew Archer and Travis McGee and on the television screen or comics page are peace officers such as T. J. Hooker or Dick Tracy, who automatically settle their disputes with guns, knives, lasers, knees, or, in moments of relative reason, fists. As one of television hero Matt Dillon's victims observed from the perspective of a barroom floor, "That marshal is awful sudden."

The Robin Hood theme of a generous criminal crusading against injustice has also been popular in the movies and on television. The

---

* The rule of law means that all governmental actions must be based on previously announced general rules, thus the idea of a "government by law" rather than a "government by men."

Hollywood productions of the lives of Frank and Jesse James made them out to be misunderstood lads whose murders and robberies were just boyish forms of social protest against overly acquisitive railroad officials. More recently, films like *Bonnie and Clyde* and *Butch Cassidy and the Sundance Kid* made light of the murder of dozens of people.

Even serious American writers like James Fenimore Cooper, Edgar Allan Poe, Stephen Crane, Ernest Hemingway, and Norman Mailer have been fascinated by violence. At one level, they deplored its use, but again and again they returned to it, exploring in fine detail death struggles on the frontier, on the battlefield, or in the bullring.

Underlying this preoccupation have been frequent resorts to illegal or "extralegal" violence all through American history. Indeed the country was conceived in a revolution against tax collectors and came to its maturity in a gruesome civil war. The gory chronicle of two centuries includes the Boston Tea Party; farmer rebellions; riots against the draft in New York during the Civil War, against Catholics in Philadelphia, against blacks in the midwest, and against Orientals in the far west; bounty hunters; Indian fighters; feuds like that of the Hatfields and the McCoys; Pinkertons and union men beating and bombing each other; the gang warfare of Prohibition; wars among rival families of Mafiosi; the kidnappings and robberies by the Symbionese Liberation movement; and the assassinations of four presidents.

Violence has been a recurring theme in the unhappy history of race relations in America. Before 1861, there were at least 250 abortive slave revolts, including Nat Turner's rebellion in 1831 and John Brown's raid in 1859. It took a civil war to end slavery, but even that bloody conflict did not eliminate violence from racial relations. The Ku Klux Klan and less-organized white mobs lynched more than 3,000 blacks from 1882 to 1959. The north experienced savage race riots, in Springfield in 1908, East St. Louis in 1917, Chicago in 1919, and Detroit in 1943. Churches were bombed and civil rights workers in the south frequently beaten and sometimes murdered while white police actively or passively cooperated. In the 1960s, race riots in northern ghettos became such a common happening as to merit no headlines outside the affected city; and in the 1960s and 1970s, a few black gangs aped the Klan's racial terror by assassinating policemen and randomly robbing and sometimes murdering white private citizens. Police retaliated in some cities with brutal attacks on Black Panthers and other militant groups.

When H. Rap Brown, a black militant leader, said that violence was as American as apple pie, he was offering a reasonably accurate description of a part, although only one part, of American culture. The thread of legal, peaceful change may be a stronger one; but the recurrence of violence indicates a persistent failure of the political system to achieve its avowed goals of ensuring both justice and domestic tranquillity. This

Armed workers and Pinkerton agents clash during the Homestead Strike in 1892.
(The Bettmann Archive, Inc.)

failure is hardly unique to America. A generalization about European history that applies to Asia, Africa, and Latin America as well as to the United States holds that "collective violence has flowered regularly out of the central political processes. . . . The oppressed have struck in the name of justice, the privileged in the name of order, the in-between in the name of fear."[25]

In defense of the American system, one can note that a nation carved out of a wilderness has absorbed millions of immigrants from almost every race, religion, and region of the world.[26] The significant points may be that there has been so little rather than so much violence and that such a small proportion of it has been directed against the system itself. Furthermore, there is a difficult moral dilemma here that has confounded political philosophers over the centuries: In many circumstances, violence may be the only alternative to submission to tyranny. On the other hand, resort to violence to correct major injustices when peaceful means are available can threaten the existence of society. No one has yet constructed a scale to weigh such matters objectively.

 POLITICAL SOCIALIZATION

If a society is to survive for any substantial period of years, it has to pass on from generation to generation its morally approved beliefs and customs. Sociologists refer to this process as *socialization*. *Political socialization is the means by which a political system indoctrinates a new generation, as well as a means by which members of the new generation learn to become mature political participants following an old or a new set of values.*

Experiences in early childhood, even though not directly political, begin the educational process. In relations with parents, brothers, sisters, and other playmates, the child discovers something about authority, obedience, punishment, and the opportunities, benefits, and costs of freedom. Indoctrination with moral values by the family or church helps the child construct ideas about justice, fair play, and permissible limits of behavior.

Later, children transfer these more universal notions to the political world. In the United States, they begin to do so very early in life. Even before they go to school, American children are very much aware—and proud—of their national identity. By the second grade, if not before, many of them think of themselves as Democrats or Republicans, although this partisan identification is almost totally emotional. Children usually have favorable attitudes toward those in positions of authority. Perhaps as a carry-over from a permissive family environment, most young American children look on the police, the mayor, and the president as "good men" who do "good things" for people. By their early teens, childen are reasonably well informed—compared to their parents—about politics. By their mid-teens their views are usually sufficiently firm so that they can fit their specific policy preferences into a more general political orientation.

It is probable that this learning process continues through much of life. As a young person builds up experience with party workers and governmental officials, initially uncritical attitudes toward authority moderate and become more sophisticated. But psychologists still believe that early experiences make the most lasting impact on a person's outlook on life. It may well be that the strong emotional attachments of children to country and government are what keep people loyal in later years to their political systems, despite the frequent failures of all such systems to fulfill their promises.

Political socialization operates in a number of formal and informal ways. The patterns of trust, obedience, and freedom of preschool years have important political spillovers. In addition, children may hear discussions of political affairs, and parents or other family members may "explain" some current event. These "explanations" are likely to be very simplistic and highly moralistic, couched in terms of the good guys (us) against the bad guys (them). In school, the authority of the teacher and the principal is added to that of the family. Children are taught, though they do not necessarily believe, such principles as "Good boys and girls obey their teachers" or "Good boys and girls settle their differences without hitting each other."

More formally, saluting the flag, reciting the pledge of allegiance, and singing the national anthem reinforce national identity. So does repeating legends of heroes like George Washington and Abraham Lincoln, whose truthfulness and honesty are often stressed more than their political accomplishments. Reading and teaching in history, geography, and civics provide a pool of specific, although simplistic, information about national ideals and traditions.

Even religious instruction may play a role. In inculcating ideas about the Deity, churchmen indirectly teach something about the nature of authority and the necessity of obedience. Furthermore, many religious groups, especially the Catholic Church, frequently go out of their way to praise the political system and to stress the smooth compatibility between fidelity to their theology and loyalty to America.

Not all groups in society experience the same processes of socialization, either formal or informal. Nor, of course, do all persons react to the same influences in the same way. Uniformity of socialization is impossible in a culturally diverse country, especially one where wealth is so unequally divided. Even among young children, differences in social class, religion, and race are accompanied by differences in political orientation. Black children, for instance, tend to display less feeling of

A moment of pride. Some of 1,205 individuals from 67 countries taking the oath of United States citizenship in New York City in 1978. (Neal Boenzi/The New York Times)

political effectiveness than do whites. Blacks also develop earlier than whites a less idealized outlook on governmental officials.[27]

Adult immigrants go through a much different form of political learning. First of all, they have the difficult task of uprooting old national identifications and loyalties, building new ones, and perhaps accepting new standards of civic conduct.

Historically, socialization of waves of immigrants often reversed the usual generational process. It was the children who passed American culture on to their parents. They learned the new ways in the neighborhood and, more important, in school—more often than not, for Catholic immigrants, a parochial rather than a public school—and brought the new customs and beliefs home to their parents both in words and in behavior that would not have been tolerated in the old country.

The foreign immigrant's socialization is usually more formal and direct than that of the natural-born citizen. Because he or she often goes through the process as an adult, the immigrant is likely to receive more political education from reading, from lectures, and from direct contact with public officials than from the slow process of gradually being exposed to more and more complex relations. The federal government suggests that all aliens interested in becoming citizens read several volumes intended to provide quick socialization by providing lists of ideals of American government.

Government plays a direct role in the process of socialization, both for the immigrant and the native-born. As we have seen, the example of public officials can stir respect or contempt for prevailing customs, processes, and values. The speeches, opinions, and writings of presidents, governors, legislators, and judges can help shape political beliefs. The way professional politicians campaign, run their offices, and train other professionals makes them carriers both of the general political culture and of the more particular rules that allow the system to operate.

Socialization, of course, does not mean merely preserving the cultural status quo, although it often has that effect. It can also be an instrument for change. The Russians, the Chinese, the Japanese after World War II, and the Germans both under Hitler and since World War II have deliberately tried to educate children away from old political standards and patterns of conduct. No educational system can ever be politically neutral. By its practices as much as its teaching, it inevitably encourages some kinds of political conduct and discourages others, just as the political system inevitably influences the content of beliefs transmitted.

Moreover, socializing processes may be so effective that they promote unintended change. They fill some people with such high political ideals that when they reach adulthood they cannot accommodate those ideals to a world inhabited by fallible humans. In those circumstances people may react against the system and become either bitter revolutionaries or cynical apoliticals. In neither case are they likely to see much use in working within an existing political system.

★ PATTERNS OF POLITICAL CULTURES

One can speak of *an* American political culture only in the most general sense. It is much more accurate to talk of *political cultures*. Yet there are forces undermining diversity. Mass communications are a particularly important leveling force. Movies, radio, and most of all television are providing common patterns of speech. More significant, they generate, especially among young children, common standards for individual, social, and political behavior. This power to shape the collective psyche of the nation is awesome, apparently too awesome for most television producers to appreciate, or, if they do, to bring them to agreement on what the content of this socialization should be.

Whatever the long-range effects of television and other means of communication in unifying American culture, at the moment the United States is still pluralistic. These cultural divisions affect the way people look at, and behave in, politics.

Without a deep and widespread belief that the governmental system, for all its faults, is basically fair and reasonably efficient, *political stability* cannot last, especially not in a nation whose people are so different from one another. Without a wariness of governmental power, *political freedom* may not last long. If stability and freedom are to have a substantial chance of coexisting, trust in and wariness of government have to coexist. Perhaps the greatest danger to freedom occurs when a low level of trust in a democratic regime is accompanied by a lack of fear of political power itself.

 SUMMARY

The American political system developed in a unique physical and social setting. A broad continent with abundant resources permitted the growth of a large, rich, and powerful industrial nation. Within its boundaries, diverse peoples came together to produce a highly urbanized and interdependent society. Despite the diversity of its citizens, agreement on basic democratic principles is substantial in the United States. On more specific issues, however, Americans tend to disagree, with political attitudes often reflecting class, racial, and ethnic cleavages. Political values are transmitted from generation to generation by the process of political socialization. This process in turn is influenced by the various political cultures that coexist in the United States. In some respects, these political cultures have been losing some of their distinctiveness because of the growth of national instruments of communication and other unifying influences on American life. In other ways, however, differences among political cultures continue to have a powerful influence on voting, attitudes toward authority, positions on many public issues, and feelings toward members of other races, classes, and groups.

NOTES

1. David M. Potter, *People of Plenty: Economic Abundance and the American Character* (Chicago: University of Chicago Press, 1954), especially Chapter 4.
2. York Willbern, *The Withering Away of the City* (University, Ala.: University of Alabama Press, 1964), pp. 9–10.
3. Morris Janowitz, *The Professional Soldier: A Social and Political Portrait* (New York: The Free Press of Glencoe, 1960).
4. Giovanni Sartori, *Democratic Theory* (New York: Frederic A. Praeger, 1965), p. 97.
5. Gabriel A. Almond and Sidney Verba, *The Civic Culture* (Princeton, N.J.: Princeton University Press, 1963), chap. 12. For a useful overview—and an annotated bibliography—on the role of personality and politics, see Fred I. Greenstein, *Personality and Politics: Problems of Evidence, Inference, and Conceptualization* (Chicago: Markham Publishing Co., 1969).
6. *Olmstead v. United States*, 277 U.S. 438, dissenting opinion (1928).
7. *Brown v. Board of Education*, 347 U.S. 483 (1954).
8. *The Federalist*, No. 51 (New York: Random House, 1937), Modern Library Edition, p. 337.
9. James W. Prothro and Charles M. Grigg, "Fundamental Principles of Democracy: Bases of Agreement and Disagreement," *Journal of Politics*, XXII (1960), p. 276.
10. Almond and Verba, *The Civic Culture*, Parts II and III.
11. For a discussion of the scarcity of political knowledge and sophisticated citizens, see Philip E. Converse, "The Nature of Belief Systems in Mass Publics," in David E. Apter, ed., *Ideology and Discontent* (New York: The Free Press of Glencoe, 1964), p. 206.
12. Jefferson to James Madison, December 20, 1787; quoted in Alpheus T. Mason, ed., *Free Government in the Making*, 3rd ed. (New York: Oxford University Press, 1965), p. 320.
13. An excellent discussion of the concept of the "rules of the game" can be found in David B. Truman, *The Governmental Process* (New York: Alfred A. Knopf, 1955), Chapters 12, 14, and 16.
14. Charles Frankel, *High on Foggy Bottom: An Outsider's Inside View of Government* (New York: Harper & Row, 1968), pp. 9–10.
15. Committee for Economic Development, *Improving the Public Welfare System* (New York, April 1970), pp. 9–10.
16. Michael Harrington, *The Other America: Poverty in the United States* (Baltimore, Md.: Penguin Books, 1962), p. 22.
17. Ibid., pp. 23–24.
18. *Report of the National Advisory Commission on Civil Disorders* (Washington: Government Printing Office, 1968), p. 1.
19. W. E. B. Du Bois, *The Souls of Black Folk* (Chicago: A. C. McClung & Co., 1903), p. 3.
20. See William W. Ellis, *White Ethics and Black Power: The Emergence of the West Side Organization* (Chicago: Aldine Publishing Co., 1969).
21. See the data collected in Angus Campbell and Howard Schuman, "Racial Attitudes in Fifteen American Cities," in *Supplemental Studies for the National Advisory Commission on Civil Disorders* (Washington: Government Printing Office, 1968), especially in Chapter 4.
22. See *Newsweek*, March 9, 1981, p. 31.
23. Angus Campbell and Howard Schuman, "Racial Attitudes in Fifteen American Cities," p. 6.
24. Nathan Glazer and Daniel P. Moynihan, *Beyond the Melting Pot: The Negroes, Puerto Ricans, Jews, Italians, and Irish of New York City* (Cambridge, Mass.: Massachusetts Institute of Technology Press, 1963), p. 290.
25. Charles Tilly, "Collective Violence in European Perspective," in Hugh Davis Graham and Ted Robert Gurr, eds., *Violence in America: Historical and Comparative Perspectives*, A Staff Report to the National Commission on the Causes and Prevention of Violence (Washington: Government Printing Office, 1969), I, 5.
26. Henry Fairlie, "The Distemper of America," *Interplay*, IV (1969), p. 6.
27. See the articles collected in Charles S. Bullock, III, and Harrell R. Rodgers, Jr., eds., *Black Political Attitudes: Implications for Political Support* (Chicago: Markham Publishing Co., 1972), Part I.

SELECTED BIBLIOGRAPHY

Almond, Gabriel A., and Sidney Verba. *The Civic Culture: Political Attitudes and Democracy in Five Nations* (Princeton, N.J.: Princeton University Press, 1963). A path-breaking study of political culture in five democracies.

Dahl, Robert A. *A Preface to Democratic Theory* (Chicago: University of Chicago Press, 1956). An analysis of the underpinnings of American democracy that rejects much accepted lore.

Dawson, Richard E., and Kenneth Prewitt. *Political Socialization* (Boston: Little, Brown, 1969). An excellent introduction to the study of political socialization.

Glazer, Nathan, and Daniel P. Moynihan. *Beyond the Melting Pot: The Negroes, Puerto Ricans, Jews, Italians, and Irish of New York City*, 2nd ed. (Cambridge, Mass.: Massachusetts Institute of Technology Press, 1970). A study of the sociology and politics of ethnic groups that has far broader importance than for New York City alone.

Handlin, Oscar. *The Uprooted* (New York: Grosset & Dunlap, 1951). A dramatic account of immigration to the United States and its impact on the immigrants.

Harrington, Michael. *The Other America: Poverty in the United States* (Baltimore, Md.: Penguin Books, 1962). A social reformer's angry account of the condition of the American poor, which helped turn national attention to the problem of poverty in the 1960s.

Hochschild, Jennifer L. *What's Fair? American Beliefs About Distributive Justice* (Cambridge, Mass.: Harvard University Press, 1981). An examination of what people think about the distribution of wealth in the United States, and the implications of these beliefs for the political system.

Jencks, Christopher, et al. *Inequality: A Reassessment of the Effect of Family and Schooling in America* (New York: Basic Books, 1972). An important—and much discussed—effort to gauge the effects of children's IQs, educations, and social backgrounds on their ultimate economic achievement.

Jennings, M. Kent, and Richard G. Niemi. *Generations and Politics: A Panel Study of Young Adults and Their Parents* (Princeton, N.J.: Princeton University Press, 1980). An intensive examination of intergenerational political socialization which provides insight into recent changes in political beliefs of individuals in the United States.

Lipset, Seymour Martin. *Political Man* (New York: Doubleday, 1960). A series of essays by a political sociologist, evaluating the conditions that make for democratic stability.

Mason, Alpheus T., ed. *Free Government in the Making*, 3rd ed. (New York: Oxford University Press, 1965). An extraordinarily useful collection of essays and documents illustrating the development of American thinking about politics.

Myrdal, Gunnar. *An American Dilemma* (New York: Harper, 1944). This book has become a classic in the study of race relations and has a great impact on American political and social thought.

Novak, Michael. *The Rise of the Unmeltable Ethnics: Politics and Culture in the Seventies* (New York: Macmillan, 1971). A well-written, hard-hitting yet sympathetic study of the working-class white ethnic.

Potter, David M. *People of Plenty: Economic Abundance and the American Character* (Chicago: University of Chicago Press, 1954). A leading historian's view of the linkages between physical richness and the development of American life and "national character."

Simon, Carl P., and Ann D. Witte. *Beating the System: The Underground Economy* (Boston: Auburn House Publishing Co., 1981). An examination of the many elements of the underground economy and its costs to government.

Tocqueville, Alexis de. *Democracy in America,* Phillips Bradley, ed. (New York: Kropf, 1945). After a century and a third, still one of the most perceptive analyses of American democracy, a classic in the study of American politics.

Wattenberg, Ben. *The Real America* (New York: Doubleday, 1974). A celebration of the accomplishments of the American system, based on a mass of social and economic data.

Wilson, William Julius. *The Declining Significance of Race* (Chicago: University of Chicago Press, 1978). An analysis of the black lower class which concludes that class has become more important than race for American blacks.

PART **II**

The Constitutional Framework

3 The Constitutional System

A nation's cultural and social systems, its physical setting, the state of its technology, and its relations with other nations all interact with that fundamental set of political rules which we call a *constitution*. Indeed, a constitution that did not fit a society's cultural patterns and physical needs would soon either change those patterns and needs or, more likely, itself shrivel up and die. An effective constitution not only allows government to meet immediate problems but also helps shape society's ideals and practices. "A living constitution" refers to a basic legal order that is truly part of a nation's life, one capable of being adapted by public officials to fit changing problems and also of shaping official and private judgments about what is proper and improper in public affairs.

★ THE NATURE OF A CONSTITUTION

A Constitution as an Instrument of Government

Recognizing these reciprocal relations, some scholars have viewed a constitution not as a document or even as a particular arrangement of political institutions, but as a way of life. Insofar as they are right, a nation's constitution is only one manifestation of its political culture, a statement of the objectives and ideals of that society and an explanation of the means that can be lawfully used to achieve those ends.

Logically, then, we can define *a constitution as an instrument of government expressing a set of general political principles about society's ideals, objectives, and legitimate processes.* To be effective, a constitution must not only fit existing cultural standards and be capable of meeting current problems but must also be capable of being "adapted," as Chief Justice John Marshall said in 1819, "to the various *crises* of human affairs."[1]

As an instrument of government, a constitution distributes power among governmental institutions. It specifies—often in broad, sometimes in vague, and occasionally even in confusing terms—who can perform what kinds of publicly binding actions. As an instrument of government, however, a constitution usually does much more. Typically it also restricts governmental power in order to protect certain rights of the individual.

The idea of a constitution as a limitation on government is largely the product of long struggles in medieval and early-modern Europe against various forms of political tyranny. Intellectual justifications for those struggles have been rooted in such notions as *natural law* and *natural rights*—beliefs that human beings have certain obligations and rights that existed before organized society and that continue to exist within society, retaining superiority over any laws that society enacts. Although the doctrine of natural rights flourished during a more religious age, today its groundings are likely to be purely secular. Occasionally, however, its theological foundation becomes clear. "Men," Justice William O. Douglas once wrote, "do not acquire rights from government; one man does not give another certain rights. Man gets his rights from the creator. They came to him because of the divine spark in every human being."[2]

As an instrument of government, a constitution may also serve as a symbol of the nation and its ideals. As such, it helps indoctrinate new generations to accept both the political system itself and particular aspects of the nation's dominant political culture or cultures. In performing this function, a constitution may allow government to cope with crises by applying old rules in new ways while at the same time retaining cherished links with traditional values and processes. Thus a constitution may help unify a people who are angrily divided over particular issues of public policy, reminding them that they are all citizens of the same country, believers in the same goals, and heirs to the same heritage.

Constitutionalism and Democracy

The heart of the notion of *constitutionalism* is that government and society are subject to a body of law that is superior to the immediate will of any governmental official, or to the majority of the community, or, as long as the constitution remains in force, even to the immediate will of the entire community. Most simply, the content of constitutionalism is summed up in the phrase "the rule of law." Its heart is a moral principle that government, even government of, by, and for the people, can act legitimately *only* insofar as it follows certain procedures that the constitution specifies. For instance, if a constitution said that no one could be punished without a fair trial, a government would violate the essence of constitutionalism if it punished without a fair trial a single person for treason, even if every private citizen (other than the accused) in the country and every public official were absolutely convinced that the accused was guilty.

American constitutionalism also includes a belief that certain kinds of governmental action are prohibited, regardless of the procedures followed. For instance, the First Amendment forbids Congress to establish a religion. Thus it would be illegitimate for Congress to require, even by means of a properly adopted statute, all citizens to become Episcopalians, even if all persons in the country were already Episcopalians.

Amending a constitution is almost always a possibility (see below, pp. 71–74). But in the absence of such an amendment, any official or private citizen who took his or her duty seriously (and in the United States every public official takes an oath to support the Constitution) would be obligated to vote against any policies that contradicted constitutional commands. If those policies won, even by an overwhelming vote, the conscientious individual would—in the absence of a constitutional amendment—still be obliged to refuse to carry them out. In short, one of a constitution's functions is to play a role similar to that performed by natural law in more religious times; that is, to serve as a body of principles superior to all other political obligations.

Constitutional Permanence and Change

If analysis could stop at this point, the art of politics would be simple. Unhappily, neither the world of action nor the world of ideas is quite so neat. Among the many complications are two problems: What is "the Constitution"? and how flexible are its terms?

Does "the Constitution" refer only to the document of 1787 as amended, or does it refer as well to certain norms that can be deduced from that document as well as to historical practices? If the answer is only the document, then the American Constitution would not include judicial review—the authority of judges to declare unconstitutional acts of executive or legislative officials—or executive privilege—the authority of the president to keep certain matters relating to his powers under Article II secret from Congress or the courts. Neither, in that limited sense, would "the Constitution" include a right of an individual accused of crime to a presumption of innocence, a right to have one's guilt proved beyond a reasonable doubt, a general right to privacy and bodily integrity, or a right to equal treatment from the federal government.

The broad wording of many clauses of the written Constitution has allowed interpreters to deduce such rights and authority from the document itself. But these efforts at textual explanation have often been strained. Rather, the overarching theory of constitutionalism as well as historic practices have provided the real bases for such "deductions." What remains unclear—and of crucial political significance—is how constitutional interpreters deduce specific rules from a general political theory and how they determine which historic practices become engrafted onto "the Constitution."

Closely related is the problem of permanence and change. Earlier we noted that an effective constitution must be supple, capable of changing to meet society's changing needs. Amending the document is

Jack Ohman. Reprinted by permission of Tribune Company Syndicate, Inc.

one answer, but in the American system that process is cumbersome at best. The amending process has two steps: proposal, then ratification.

Congress may itself propose an amendment, providing two-thirds of those voting in both houses approve, or it may call a national convention at the request of two-thirds of the states. (Congress has never used the latter procedure, partly out of concern for what such a convention might do, once in session. It is difficult to forget that the Philadelphia Convention of 1787 also met only to amend the Articles of Confederation.) Having proposed an amendment, Congress may require ratification either by state legislatures or by special conventions meeting in the states. In either case, three-quarters of the states must approve for the amendment to become part of the Constitution.

Since 1788, more than a thousand constitutional amendments have been introduced in Congress; but, through December 1982, Congress has approved only thirty-one by the necessary two-thirds vote, and the states have ratified only twenty-six. Ten of these, the Bill of Rights, were proposed in 1789 and ratified in 1791, and two of the others—the Eighteenth and the Twenty-first, dealing with Prohibition—cancel each other out. Those statistics—only fourteen effective amendments since 1791—illustrate the difficulties of the process and hint at the availability of other modes of adaption.

The latest proposed amendment to meet defeat was one that would have guaranteed equal rights to women. It failed to secure ratification despite a congressional extension of the time allowed for states to approve until 1982. Later in that same year, the Senate passed a proposal to amend the Constitution to require, in peacetime, a balanced federal budget, unless three-fifths of each house of Congress specifically voted otherwise. The measure failed to secure the necessary two-thirds majority in the House, but proponents promised to renew the battle in the new Congress. If adopted, the budgetary amendment would change the nature of the political system more sweepingly than any amendment since the Thirteenth, Fourteenth, and Fifteenth, adopted after the Civil War to end slavery and require the states to respect the equal rights of blacks. Indeed, no amendment has ever curbed federal power in the social and economic sphere.

Another answer to the problem of constitutional development, and one the American system has tended to rely on, is to change the Constitution by interpretation. This practice means that clauses of the constitutional document might not retain the exact same meaning for each generation and that practices valid at one time may lose their legitimacy.

Some officials justify shifts in interpretation by claiming that the fundamental principles of the Constitution do not vary, but their applications must change. That assertion may be comforting; it even contains some truth. The Constitution's essential purpose of protecting maximum feasible liberty may remain constant, but what is "maximum," what is "feasible," or what is "liberty" may change over time. Yet, however easily one may dismiss the first two kinds of changes as being of degree rather than kind, the last sort of change can be fundamental in nature. When such alterations occur, the very symbolism of the Constitution may be vital for society, confirming continuity with the past even as it permits change.

As in deciding what is legitimately deducible from the constitutional document or an integral part of a larger constitutional practice, interpreters face problems of extraordinary complexity and importance. Understandably, their work—and more often that not the "interpreters" are the justices of the Supreme Court—is likely to foment political controversy. Many efforts to amend the Constitution—recently, for example, to allow prayers in public schools, permit closer governmental regulation of abortion, outlaw busing to achieve racial balance in schools, or authorize states to create electoral districts unequal in population—have been angry reactions to decisions of the Supreme Court. Over the span of American history, several such proposals have been adopted: the Eleventh Amendment, to limit federal judicial authority to hear suits against states;[3] the Fourteenth, in part, to reverse the Court's ruling that a black man could not be an American citizen;[4] the Sixteenth, to validate a federal income tax;[5] and the Twenty-sixth, to overcome a ruling that Congress could not authorize eighteen-year-olds to vote in state elections.[6]

★ FRAMING THE AMERICAN CONSTITUTION

The Framers' Objectives

The men who met in Philadelphia in 1787 to amend the Articles of Confederation were familiar with the ideas and problems we have been discussing. Nevertheless, they were confident that they could create political arrangements that would "bestow the blessings of liberty" on themselves and their "posterity" by combining both constitutionalism and popular participation. Had they not succeeded, they would have been hooted through history as arrogant fools.

An astute combination of *constitutional liberty* and *popular participation* were not the only objectives of the framers. They also tried to ensure a high degree of *political stability*. And they also knew that, if their work was to endure beyond their own time, they would have to look beyond immediate problems and fashion a political structure that could cope with crises whose specific shapes they could not even dimly foresee. Thus they had to formulate general principles rather than a detailed code.

On the other hand, if their constitution was to have any future at all, it would first have to meet existing difficulties; and those people at the convention who wanted their ideas to develop into reality would have to persuade other delegates to join with them in proposing the plan as well as to convince political leaders in the states to agree to such a scheme. "We must," Gunning Bedford of Delaware said, "like Solon make such a government as the people will approve."[7] His plea was echoed by colleagues who said they would accept the best constitution possible and not hold out for unrealizable ideals.

Government under the Articles of Confederation

At the time, the nation was seriously handicapped by shortcomings of government under the Articles of Confederation. Those Articles had not

"Remember, gentlemen, we aren't here just to draft a constitution. We're here to draft the best damned constitution in the world."

created a national political system, but only "a firm league of friendship" among sovereign states. Each state had retained "its sovereignty, freedom and independence, and every power, jurisdiction and right, which is not by this confederation expressly delegated to the United States, in Congress assembled." Congress consisted of a single house to which each state could send two to seven representatives, who were more like ambassadors to the United Nations than like today's congressmen. Regardless of the number of its representatives or its population, each state had one vote, and it took an affirmative vote of nine states to exercise any of the very few national legislative powers. Indeed, one could make a strong case that Congress could not legislate at all. Its enactments were essentially proposals to state governments; and, lacking any effective executive department, Congress had no means of enforcing those suggestions. The central government, under the Articles, could "resolve and recommend but could not command and enforce."[8]

In foreign affairs, the Articles ostensibly gave Congress authority to speak for the United States. Again, however, absence of an effective executive and inability to command individual citizens meant that Congress could only request the states to carry out whatever agreements its diplomats might negotiate. In this context of political impotence, other nations tended to treat the Confederation with indifference or contempt.

Historians disagree about whether one should label as a crisis the events leading up to Congress's call to the states to send delegates to Philadelphia for the purpose of proposing amendments to the Articles. Certainly, however, inability to negotiate commercial treaties vital to the prosperity of a small agricultural nation contributed to dissatisfaction. And, in domestic affairs, widespread debt, a revolt of poor farmers in Massachusetts under the leadership of Captain Daniel Shays, and a threat of tariff wars among the states alarmed governmental officials and politically aware private citizens. Thus one obvious and immediate objective of the framers had to be creation of a stronger national government that could further "prosperity" and "domestic tranquility."

On the other hand, having just rebelled against an oppressive government, that generation was in no mood to obtain law and order by substituting American for British tyrants. The greatest need in constructing a government, James Madison wrote shortly before the Philadelphia convention, is to "render it sufficiently neutral between the different interests and factions, to controul one part of the society from invading the rights of another, and at the same time sufficiently controuled itself, from setting up an interest adverse to that of the whole Society."[9]

The Framers

Like the old moral precept "Do good and avoid evil," Madison's constitutional prescription was not easy to fill. Fortunately, most of the fifty-five men who met at Philadelphia were able and practical as well as ambitious and self-confident. Although their average age was only forty-three, collectively they had already had considerable experience in the real world of politics. Forty-two had served in the Continental Congress; several were in fact serving while participating in the convention. Seven had been governors and twenty had been members of state constitutional conventions. As a group, they were also extraordinarily well trained for the times. Twenty-six had a college education, more than thirty were lawyers, three were college professors, and two were college presidents.

These delegates were not representative of Americans. Most obviously, all were white males. Only the most radical democrats of the time considered women and blacks among "the people" entitled to political participation. Few delegates could speak for small yeomen farmers, and virtually none either had been an urban worker or could claim to be a spokesman for these "mechanics and artisans." Rather, the framers were almost all men of financial means, social stature, and professional reputation: creditors not debtors; gentlemen farmers, merchants, bankers, lawyers, and governmental officials. They had large, tangible financial stakes in creating a political system that would provide both stability and freedom. Thus they were motivated by self-interest as well as by patriotism.

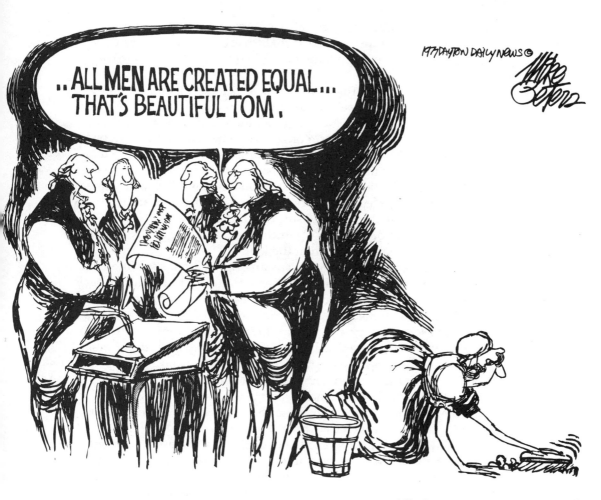

Mike Peters, Dayton, Ohio, Daily News

A few of the more famous leaders of the Revolution were at Philadelphia—George Washington, Benjamin Franklin, Alexander Hamilton, James Madison, James Wilson, George Mason, Oliver Ellsworth, and Edmund Randolph, for example. But other revolutionary leaders were absent. John Adams and Thomas Jefferson were serving abroad as diplomats; Tom Paine was living in Europe; Sam Adams was too old to come; John Hancock was Governor of Massachusetts; and Patrick Henry, although chosen as a delegate, refused to attend, saying, "I smelt a rat!" In all, only eight of the fifty-six who signed the Declaration of Independence were present.

The Framers' Political Philosophy

Despite marked similarities in social class, the framers vehemently disagreed among themselves on many vital issues, such as how to divide power within the national government or between the national government and the states.

For John Dickinson of Delaware and Alexander Hamilton, monarchy had not yet lost all appeal, whereas Ben Franklin, James Wilson, and sometimes even the wealthy New England merchant Nathaniel Gorham spoke for a more democratic form of government than finally emerged. Luther Martin of Maryland was among the principal advocates of retaining strong state governments, while Wilson and Madison were the leaders of the faction wanting a powerful national regime. Many delegates were also deeply troubled by slavery (Madison, for instance, argued that it was "wrong to admit in the Constitution the idea that there could be property in men"),[10] but no one could think of a way of abolishing the institution and keeping the south in the Union.

There were also areas of consensus among the framers. Moreover, what notes we have of their deliberations indicate that, like bright participants in a seminar, they learned from each other.[11] Most of them probably agreed with Madison's prescription for constitutional government—one strong enough to control any part of society but not so strong as to be able to set itself up against society. For these men, government was a dangerous but necessary institution; and, if they had been faced with a clear-cut choice between constitutionalism and democracy, they would have quickly opted for constitutionalism. Five years earlier, Jefferson had summed up their views: "An elective despotism was not the government we fought for."[12]

Given the heavy democratic element in most state governments, however, the framers never had any real option of excluding popular participation. Furthermore, most of the delegates actually wanted popular government both in the sense of widespread approval of the new constitutional system and also in the sense of the people's having a limited but real part in choosing public officials. Madison argued on several occasions that popular election of at least one house of the legislature was "essential to every plan of free government."[13] Like many of his colleagues, he would have limited suffrage to those who owned property, but proponents of this restriction claimed that 90 percent of the population would still have been able to vote.

Nevertheless, as a group, the men at Philadelphia feared tyranny by a majority as much as tyranny by a monarch. When they used the term "democratic," it was typically as a criticism. The label that they preferred for their bold plan to wed constitutionalism with democracy was "free government," an imaginative but delicate marriage of liberty and restraint, of popular participation and constitutional limitations.

Many of the framers' notions about government derived from their view of human nature. On the one hand, they were aware of man's capacity for evil. They were influenced in part by the writings of the seventeenth-century English philosopher Thomas Hobbes, who claimed that "life is a restless seeking of power after power." Even more so, they were influenced by a Calvinist concept of original sin and the corruptibility if not the corruption of mankind. Having grown up in a relatively poor society but one rife with political struggles, they understood that power could be as alluring a temptation as money. According to Bedford of Delaware, "Give the opportunity [to use power], and ambition will not fail to abuse it."[14] Then, turning inward to the convention itself, he reminded delegates:

> Look at the votes which have been given on the floor of this house, and it will be found that their [delegates' states'] numbers, wealth, and local views, have actuated their determinations. . . . Pretences to support ambition are never wanting. . . . *I do not, gentlemen, trust you.* If you possess the power, the abuse of it could not be checked; and what then would prevent you from exercising it to our destruction?[15]

Madison spoke in more general terms: "In truth, all men with power ought to be distrusted to a certain degree."[16]

On the other hand, this bleak outlook was tempered by other ideas that were in the wind. As children of the "Age of Reason," many framers also had faith in the power of the human intellect; and many people of their generation, most notably Jefferson, hoped that by learning from experience and using his mind man could improve morally as well as intellectually. Writing in *The Federalist* No. 55, Madison summed up the framers' mixed view of human nature: "As there is a degree of depravity in mankind which requires a certain degree of circumspection and distrust, so there are other qualities in human nature which justify a certain portion of esteem and confidence."

The framers' pessimism made them see government as necessary to protect people from one another, and also as dangerous because humans were no more apt to be moral in public than in private affairs. But their faith in reason gave them courage to believe that they could devise institutional arrangements that would channel behavior toward civilized conduct.

Besides holding a belief in the necessity of government and in constitutional limitations and a somewhat pessimistic view of human nature, the framers were hardheaded men of practical experience. They had faith in reason, but wanted reason anchored to hard facts rather than wafting around abstract theories. "I believe," William Paterson of New Jersey told the delegates, "that a little practical virtue is to be preferred to the finest theoretical principles, which cannot be carried into effect."[17] As men of affairs, they knew American politics firsthand, but many of them had also read widely about ancient Greek and Roman history as well as more recent political developments in England and on the Continent.

Compromises

The framers' differences on many specific issues created a series of sharp disputes. But their agreement on certain fundamentals—coupled with their pragmatic outlook—allowed them to compromise most of these. For the long run, the most important negotiations turned on slavery. On that question, John Rutledge of South Carolina told the convention, hinged "whether the southern states shall or shall not be parties to the Union."[18] Faced with a choice between a single nation with slavery or two nations, one with and one without slavery, the framers gave in to southern demands, even though most of the delegates, including the southerners, personally thought that slavery was morally wrong.

Probably to salve their consciences, the framers adroitly avoided using the term "slave" or "slavery" in the Constitution. In fact, the document made few indirect references to this "peculiar institution," thus leaving it almost entirely to state control. Article I provided that, for purposes of apportioning representatives in Congress, a state's population would be computed "by adding to the whole number of free persons . . . excluding Indians not taxed, three fifths of all other persons." Furthermore, Article IV, Section 2 placed on free states an obligation to return runaway slaves to their masters. The language of this section was a masterpiece of disingenuity:

> No person held to service or labour in one State, under the laws thereof, escaping into another, shall, in consequences of any law or regulation therein, be discharged from such service or labour, but shall be delivered up on claim of the party to whom such service or labour may be due.

As a sop to antislavery sentiment, Article I empowered Congress after 1808 to forbid "the migration or importation of such persons as any of the states now existing think proper to admit"—a long-winded way of saying that Congress could prohibit importation of slaves. And in 1808 Congress promptly used this authority, although that action did little to abate the slave trade *within* the United States.

At the time, the framers thought of the "great compromise" as that involving state representation in Congress. With larger states adamantly insisting on representation by population and smaller states just as firmly insisting on equality, the convention almost blew apart. Oliver Ellsworth of Connecticut and John Rutledge finally worked out the obvious solution of equal representation of states in the Senate and representation by population in the House.

Another of several important compromises involved admission of new states into the Union. Some delegates feared the possible political orientation of western settlers and proposed a clause specifically providing for preferred status for the thirteen original states. Delegates who wanted free and rapid development of the west to enlarge and strengthen the Union urged a guarantee that new states would be ad-

Advertisement for a slave sale, 1784. Congress used its constitutional authority to prohibit the importation of slaves in 1808, but legal buying and selling of slaves within the United States continued until the Civil War. (Courtesy of the Library of Congress)

Negroes for Sale.

A Cargo of very fine stout Men and Women, in good order and fit for immediate service, just imported from the Windward Coast of Africa, in the Ship Two Brothers.—
Conditions are one half Cash or Produce, the other half payable the first of January next, giving Bond and Security if required.
The Sale to be opened at 10 o'Clock each Day, in Mr. Bourdeaux's Yard, at No. 48, on the Bay.
May 19, 1784. JOHN MITCHELL.

mitted on the same basis as the original thirteen. The only compromise the framers could agree on was silence. Article IV, Section 3 says: "New states shall be admitted by the Congress into this Union. . . ." Later, Congress by statute and the Supreme Court through constitutional interpretation opted for equality between old and new states.

⭐ THE CONSTITUTIONAL STRUCTURE

"Happily for America," Madison modestly noted after the convention adjourned, he and his colleagues at Philadelphia had pursued a "noble course." They had "paid a decent respect to the opinions of former times and other nations" without allowing "blind veneration for antiquity, custom, or for names to overrule the suggestions of their own good sense" and "the lessons of their own experience." Combining history and reason, he claimed, the men at Philadelphia had accomplished "a revolution which has no parallel in the annals of human society. They reared the fabrics of governments which have no model on the face of the globe."[19]

The new national government of which Madison spoke had far more power than the old. Congress could act directly on private citizens. It could tax and spend; "regulate commerce with foreign nations, and among the several states, and with the Indian tribes"; coin and borrow money; create a national system of courts; establish an army and a navy; and "make all laws which shall be necessary and proper" to carry out any of the powers granted to any branch of the national government. To enforce federal laws and treaties, the Constitution also established an executive department, chosen independently of Congress and headed by a president. By its own terms, the Constitution also provided that federal laws and treaties as well as the Constitution itself took precedence over state regulations.

The states, of course, retained much of their traditional political power, but were not the equals of the new federal government. At that, some delegates, including Madison, believed that the national government was not as powerful vis-à-vis the states as it should have been. But, as on most issues, they were willing to compromise to obtain an agreement that could become operative.

Limiting Power by Prohibitions and Elections

As one would expect, the framers did more than grant and distribute power. In express terms they forbade Congress and/or the states to perform certain actions, for example, passing bills of attainder* or ex post facto laws.** But the framers were not naive, simple-minded men who thought that writing "thou shalt not" into a constitution would prevent abuse of power. They were, after all, aware of the history of the Ten Commandments. Popular elections, Madison said, formed "the primary control on the government."[20] Officials who periodically were obliged to go, hat in hand, to the people to ask to be allowed to retain their jobs would find it difficult to behave arrogantly between elections.

Limiting Power by Sharing Power

But these checks by prohibition and election would not be sufficient, Madison admitted; "experience has taught the necessity of auxilliary precautions." Responding to Bedford's argument about abuse of power, Madison said that for those holding public office, "ambition must be made to counteract ambition. The interest of the man must be connected with the constitutional rights of the place."[21] To stir up a jealous clash among ambitions and to cement an identification of interest and rights, the framers divided—"fractured" is more accurate—governmental power. First, they made a virtue out of the necessity of the states' continuing to operate as important units of government. By increasing the power of the national government, leaving the states with a generous residue of power, and refusing to draw clear boundaries between the two, the Constitution made it inevitable that state officials would fear federal encroachment and federal officials fear state trespasses.

At the national level, the framers further splintered power among three branches, the legislature, executive, and judiciary. They did not, as Madison conceded, provide for a "separation of powers." Rather they created a system in which separate institutions share power.[22] Congress—itself split into two houses that often compete with each other—must exercise its legislative power in conjunction with the president, who can call the two houses into special session, adjourn them if they cannot agree on a time for adjournment, recommend legislation to them, and veto bills that they pass. Moreover, in enforcing the law he, no less than judges, must interpret statutes. And, because the language of legislation is often vague and Congress has on occasion passed a new statute without fully explaining its effect on existing law, the president's

---

* A legislative act that, without judicial trial, convicts a specific person of a crime and orders him or her punished.

** A law that makes an act, innocent when committed, a crime, or that retroactively lowers the amount of proof needed to convict for a particular crime, or that retroactively increases the punishment for a specific crime.

discretion here can be quite broad. Moreover, a president's first obligation is to obey the Constitution, not Congress; and more than one chief executive has refused to carry out an act of Congress because he has believed it to be unconstitutional. Less dramatically, presidents have typically not been zealous in executing laws they believe unwise.

The whole matter of responsibility for the legislative process is muddled for several reasons: Executive agencies often draft the bills that congressmen debate, modify, and finally pass; the president and his staff often actively lobby in Congress and stir up public opinion for or against important proposals; and, most important, bills that become law confer a great deal of discretion on the president. In sum, as we shall see in Chapters 10–12, probably the most significant function of the president in domestic affairs is to act as chief legislator. With congressional power shared among 535 people, usually only the president can provide effective leadership.

Judges also share in legislative processes in that they must interpret the same statutes as does the president. Moreover, because the Constitution proclaims itself to be law, judges have asserted that they have authority to interpret that document. "It is emphatically," Chief Justice John Marshall said in 1803, "the province and duty of the judicial department, to say what the law is."[23] As a result, judges can define the legitimate scope of Congress's power to enact laws, to conduct investigations, and even, in some circumstances, to seat its members.

In interpreting statutes and the Constitution, judges are often accused of "judicial legislation." Frequently those charges are correct. By enacting vague statutes, Congress invites judges and administrators to indulge in creative interpretation. One cannot, for instance, mechanically apply a law that sets as a standard "the public interest." And the great clauses of the Constitution are often equally imprecise. For instance, Article I's listing of congressional power does not mention "interstate commerce." Rather, it confers on Congress authority to regulate "commerce among the several states," without defining "regulate," "commerce," or "among"—and the last omission may be the most serious of all, since the word "among" in the late eighteenth century was as likely to mean "within" as "between more than two." Similarly, the Fourth Amendment prohibits only "unreasonable searches and seizures," not all searches, not even all searches without a warrant. And the Fifth and Fourteenth Amendments do not flatly forbid federal and state governments to take life, liberty, or property, but only "without due process of law"; and no judge or lawyer or scholar has yet been able to offer a precise definition of "due process" that many other judges, lawyers, or scholars would accept. Faced with the task of interpreting such language, judges must act creatively, obtaining their values, as Justice Benjamin N. Cardozo said, not from law, but "from life itself."[24]

The president shares in judicial authority in that he directs, through the attorney general, all civil and criminal suits begun in the name of the United States and may, except in cases of impeachment, pardon any person convicted of, charged with, or suspected of violating federal law. The pardoning power even extends to those convicted of criminal contempt of court for disobeying an order from a federal judge. In addition, the president nominates all federal judges and often selects people who he believes will decide cases in ways that he thinks correct. Furthermore, final responsibility for enforcement of judicial decisions falls on the executive, and presidents have on occasion treated this responsibility as requiring careful discretion rather than automatic action.

Congress also shares in judicial power, the Senate in confirming or rejecting judicial nominees and both houses in regulating the size, organization, and jurisdiction* of the federal courts. Like the president, senators and representatives have often used their authority to try to shape the development of law.

Moreover, in their investigations of activities that might merit federal regulation, congressional committees frequently "punish" witnesses by forcing them to face television cameras while responding to questions about their pasts that can ruin reputations and wreck careers as well as merely embarrass. As an accusing body in impeachment cases, the House of Representatives exercises a quasi-judicial function; and if the House impeaches, the Senate sits as a trial court to determine the guilt or innocence of the accused federal official.

Nor does executive power exist in an airtight compartment. Judges can interpret executive orders, just as they can statutes. And, in interpreting the Constitution, courts have on numerous occasions set limits to executive authority. Congress has even wider avenues of influence into administration. The Senate can confirm or reject the president's nominees for his own cabinet and several thousand other executive posts. Perhaps more important, Congress also determines the organization of all departments within the executive branch and by its control over appropriations can affect the minutest detail within federal agencies as well as the general direction of administrative policy. Indeed, many chiefs of federal offices are likely to pay more attention to senators and congressmen on appropriations committees than to presidents.

Networks of Jealousy

The general picture that emerges from this description is that of several networks of overlapping grants of authority to separate institutions,

---

* "Jurisdiction" refers to the basic authority of a court to hear and decide certain kinds of controversies. Article III of the Constitution allows Congress very broad authority to give jurisdiction to or take it away from federal courts.

each staffed by people chosen in different ways and at different times, who have access to different sorts of information, are responsible to different constituencies, and are moved by different kinds of institutional loyalties as well as by competing personal and institutional ambitions. Each of the three branches has its own primary core of power, but each of the other branches to some extent shares in the exercise of that power. It is highly unlikely that either Congress, the president, or the Supreme Court can take any important action either without the cooperation of another branch or else without seeming to trespass on the domain of one or the other branch.

Thus wariness and jealousy form the normal state of affairs within the national government no less than between state and federal levels. It is only a slight exaggeration to say that Madison and his colleagues tried to build a constitutional structure that would, on the one hand, stir up recurrent disputes among envious governmental officials and, on the other hand, supply each of them with a sufficient number of checks on the others to keep those disputes within tolerable limits.

Restricting the Power of the People

Because they distrusted all men and not merely public officials, the framers also wanted to restrain the power of a majority of the people. "In all cases," Madison told the convention, "where a majority are united by a common interest or passion, the rights of the minority are in danger."[25] The remedy, he said, was for government to encourage development of a wide range of interests within society. In short, he wanted "to enlarge the sphere, and thereby divide the community into so great a number of interests and parties, that in the first place a majority will not be likely at the same moment to have a common interest separate from that of the whole or the minority; and in the second place, that in case they should have such an interest, they may not be apt to unite in the pursuit of it."[26] One specific way to encourage growth of what we would call "pluralism"* was to make sure, because it "was politic as well as just," that "the interests and rights of every class should be duly represented and understood in the public Councils."[27]

On the negative side, the framers were aware that federalism, vast distances, and poor means of communication would make it difficult for

---

* In a general sense, "pluralism" refers to the existence within a particular community of people of different social classes, occupations, religions, ethnic backgrounds, educations, values, and races. That is the sense in which the word is used here. In a somewhat more specific sense, "pluralism" refers to particular arrangements for sharing political power among the different groups that make up a society. Chapter 5 discusses pluralism in detail.

a majority to identify and unite around a common interest separate from the rest of the community. If such a majority did develop, they also hoped that it would be hobbled by the system of restraints on public officials. The framers reinforced these barriers by staggering terms of office for national officials and by providing that they be responsible to different constituencies. Originally, only members of the House of Representatives were elected directly by the people. Having only one-third of the senators chosen at the same time (and selected by state legislators who may have been elected a year or two earlier) would hamper any group from gaining control of Congress at a single election. The Electoral College, as it initially functioned and still can function, put additional brakes on the ability of a national majority to choose a president. And, of course, federal judges, because they would be nominated by the president and confirmed by the Senate, would be even more insulated from popular pressures.

The Bill of Rights

As proposed and ratified, the Constitution did not have a separate bill of rights to protect individual liberties from government. The body of the document contained a few prohibitions against state and federal action; but as we have seen, the framers had little faith in "parchment barriers'" preventing abuses of power. Moreover, as Madison expressed it:

> Wherever the real power in a Government lies, there is the danger of oppression. In our Government, the real power lies in the majority of the Community, and the invasion of private rights is *chiefly* to be apprehended . . . from acts in which the Government is the mere instrument of the major number of Constituents.[28]

Thus the framers thought that they had effectively protected individual rights by retaining but restricting state governments, impeding the ability of a majority to control the federal government, establishing a government under law, limiting the authority of the new government to powers expressly delegated or reasonably implied, and, most important, by creating a network of overlapping and interlocking grants of authority so that each branch of government would have a vested interest in preventing the others from abusing power.

Despite such weighty arguments, many delegates to the state ratifying conventions had opposed the new Constitution because it did not include a bill of rights; and two states, North Carolina and Rhode Island, had not yet ratified the document when the First Congress assembled in 1789. Although no explicit bargain had been struck to amend the Constitution in exchange for ratification, Congress was, nevertheless, under heavy pressure to add a listing of fundamental rights.

Earlier, Madison had thought a bill of rights unnecessary. He admitted to Jefferson, who was still in Paris, that such an enumeration of rights might become part of the political culture and so serve as an internalized check both on what private citizens demanded and on what officials tried to do. But, he concluded, given the sort of system that the framers had constructed and the inherent difficulties in formulating language that would protect rights and permit action needed in emergencies, omission was not a serious defect.

In reply, Jefferson took up the objections to a bill of rights and attempted to rebut each of them. The thrust of his reasoning, however, was brief:

> In the arguments in favor of a declaration of rights, you omit one which has great weight with me, the legal check which it puts into the hands of the judiciary. This is a body, which if rendered independent, and kept strictly to their own department, merits great confidence for their learning and integrity.[29]

These men, Jefferson claimed, would be able to resist popular impulses to restrict liberty.

Wanting to calm fears about the new government, desirous of persuading North Carolina and Rhode Island to join the Union, and intellectually convinced by Jefferson, Madison took the lead in guiding through Congress the Bill of Rights, the first ten amendments to the Constitution. In justifying such action, he adapted Jefferson's reasoning and incorporated it into his own general theory of checking power against power:

> If they [the Bill of Rights] are incorporated into the constitution, independent tribunals of justice will consider themselves in a peculiar manner the guardians of those rights; they will be an impenetrable bulwark against every assumption of power in the legislative or executive; they will be naturally led to resist every encroachment upon rights expressly stipulated for in the constitution by the declaration of rights.[30]

★ THE CONSTITUTIONAL SYSTEM AND THE NEED FOR ENERGETIC GOVERNMENT

With its grants of power to the national government, the new Constitution inspired enough confidence both within the country and abroad that the United States could survive as a politically stable nation. Over the decades since 1787, the flexible and general nature of those constitutional clauses has allowed public officials to adapt grants of power in ways that enabled them to cope with most crises. During those years, the democratic element in the American system has grown in size and strength, as popular participation has expanded from white, male property owners, to white males, to whites, and finally to all citizens having a right not only to cast a vote for members of the House of Representatives but also for senators and, although still not directly, for the president as well.

If American government now includes more democracy than the framers would have included under "free government," the general wording of constitutional clauses has also allowed judges to protect, often in imaginative ways, constitutional rights against equally imaginative efforts at subversion. Perhaps most significant, the Thirteenth, Fourteenth, and Fifteenth Amendments extended both the democratic notion of equality and the constitutional objective of individual liberty across racial lines. The Nineteenth Amendment and judicial interpretations of the Fourteenth have come close to acknowledging women to be full-fledged members of the political community.

Successes and Failures of the System

The framers did not believe they were constructing a utopia, nor did they succeed in doing so. As we have already indicated and will continue to point out, the warts on the American political system—for example, long tolerance of slavery—are large; moreover, as some old warts have fallen off new ones have grown. Yet, on the whole, the framers built well. The greatest success of the Madisonian system of federalism, popular elections, and interlocking power shared by separate institutions has been that the United States has generally had both *popular participation* and *limited government*. While instances of serious oppression by federal officials have occurred, those instances, when compared with cases in similar spans of history in other nations, have been relatively few. To the extent that the framers tried to construct an enduring constitutional system that would increase the chances of prosperity, they also succeeded quite well. As Chapter 2 pointed out, Americans have historically been a "people of plenty," in large part because of natural resources, but also in part because of relative political stability.

On the other hand, the great weakness of the Madisonian system is that it makes *positive* action by the federal government always difficult and often impossible. And frequently, positive federal action has been necessary to remove the tyranny of one citizen over others or of state officials over their own citizens. Freeing the slaves, protecting civil rights of minorities, guarding the public against the greed of giant monopolies in industry and labor, providing adequate medical care for the poor and aged, reversing the course of large-scale economic recessions or depressions—all these have required positive federal action. And that action has come slowly, in piecemeal fashion, and sometimes not at all.

In short, the Madisonian system of sharing and checking power tends to foster the interests of people who are content with the status quo. And that system is hard on political newcomers: in past generations, Indians, slaves, women of all races, and immigrants from Europe and Asia; more recently, blacks, Chicanos, and Puerto Ricans, the poor generally.

Generally speaking, the Madisonian system can accommodate positive federal action in only three or four situations. First, where matters are not controversial, Congress, the president, and the Supreme Court routinely agree. Little dispute, for instance, arises about paying salaries to civil servants or interest on the national debt, although there may be great controversy about the proper size of either. Second, in the opening stages of great national emergencies, especially those involving foreign affairs, Congress and the president tend to work closely together, with Congress usually deferring to presidential wisdom. As wars or other crises stretch out, however, presidential wisdom typically tarnishes, and legislators begin to reassert independent judgment.

Third, and more normal, are situations in which opposing leaders—and usually the president and his agents come off slightly the better in this game—can arrange a compromise that allows limited positive action in exchange for benefits to those who oppose such action. A fourth situation—perhaps really a variant of the second or third—may occur when an energetic and skillful president is able to mobilize patronage, patriotism, and public opinion to persuade congressmen to accept sweeping new policies. Among the most striking examples is Lyndon B. Johnson's astute manipulation of the public mood of sorrow and guilt after the assassination of John F. Kennedy to push Congress to adopt several meaningful civil rights statutes and to begin a bold "war on poverty." Almost as dramatic was Ronald Reagan's pushing through Congress in 1981 fiscal policies reducing taxes and federal spending, to a large extent abandoning the economic theories on which national social and economic policy had been based since at least 1936.

Despite such striking usages of power, in its political orientation the Madisonian constitutional system tends to be more negative than positive. "The purpose of the Constitution and the Bill of Rights," Justice William O. Douglas wrote for the Supreme Court, "unlike more recent models promoting a welfare state was to take government off the backs of people."[31] The American Constitution created a long and successful union of democracy and constitutionalism. But, whether the Madisonian Constitution can cope with current crises—or whether current political leaders possess sufficient skills to adapt that Constitution—remains an open question, one that each generation of Americans has, from its own special perspective, faced.

 **SUMMARY**

This chapter has explored the concepts of constitutionalism and democracy and the way in which the framers of the American Constitution tried to blend the two into a living political system. We have also taken a quick overview of how the national government functions under that system, leaving to the following chapter the task of examining federal–state relations, and to the rest of the book the work of filling in the skeleton of constitutional structure with the flesh and muscle of political processes.

NOTES

1. *McCulloch v. Maryland*, 4 Wheaton 316 (1819).
2. *The Anatomy of Liberty* (New York: Trident Press, 1963), p. 7.
3. The case was *Chisholm v. Georgia*, 2 Dallas 419 (1793).
4. The case was *Dred Scott v. Sandford*, 19 Howard 393 (1857).
5. The case was *Pollock v. Farmers Loan & Trust*, 157 U.S. 429 (1895).
6. The case was *Oregon v. Mitchell*, 400 U.S. 112 (1970).
7. Charles C. Tansill, ed., *Documents Illustrative of the Formation of the Union of the American States* (Washington: Government Printing Office, 1927), p. 315. (Unless otherwise indicated, references to Tansill refer to his reprinting of James Madison's notes on debates during the convention.)
8. Clinton Rossiter, *1787: The Great Convention* (New York: Macmillan, 1966), p. 52.
9. James Madison, *Vices of the Political System in the United States* (1787); reprinted in Alpheus T. Mason, ed., *Free Government in the Making*, 3rd ed. (New York: Oxford University Press, 1965), p. 172.
10. Tansill, p. 618.
11. See John P. Roche, "The Founding Fathers: A Reform Caucus in Action," *American Political Science Review*, LV (1961), 799–816.
12. "Notes on Virginia," reprinted in Mason, *Free Government in the Making*, p. 165.
13. Tansill, p. 126.
14. Ibid., p. 165.
15. Ibid., pp. 834–835.
16. Ibid., p. 358.
17. Ibid., p. 771. (Here the reference is to the notes taken by Robert Yates at the convention rather than by Madison.)
18. Ibid., p. 588.
19. *The Federalist*, No. 14.
20. Ibid., No. 51.
21. Ibid.
22. Richard Neustadt makes this point most emphatically; see his "Presidential Government," *International Encyclopedia of the Social Sciences*, XII, 451, 453.
23. *Marbury v. Madison*, 1 Cranch 137, 177 (1803).
24. *The Nature of the Judicial Process* (New Haven, Conn.: Yale University Press, 1921), p. 113.
25. Tansill, p. 162.
26. Ibid., p. 163.
27. Ibid., p. 461.
28. G. Hunt, ed., *The Writings of James Madison* (New York: G. P. Putnam's Sons, 1904), V, 272.
29. Reprinted in Mason, *Free Government in the Making*, p. 325.
30. Reprinted in Hunt, *The Writings of James Madison*, V, 385.
31. *Schneider v. Smith*, 390 U.S. 17, 25 (1968).

**SELECTED
BIBLIOGRAPHY**

Beard, Charles A. *An Economic Interpretation of the Constitution* (New York: Macmillan, 1913). This famous book argues that in drafting the Constitution the
Founding Fathers were strongly motivated by their own peculiar kinds of
financial interests.

Beitzinger, A. J. *History of American Political Thought* (New York: Dodd, Mead,
1972). An excellent analysis of the origins and development of American
political ideas.

Bessette, Joseph M., and Jeffrey Tulis, eds. *The Presidency in the Constitutional
Order* (Baton Rouge, La.: Louisiana State University Press, 1981). An interesting collection of essays that fulfill the title's promise and speak of "the constitutional order" as much as of the executive as a peculiar institution.

Bowen, Catherine Drinker. *Miracle at Philadelphia* (Boston: Little, Brown, 1966).
An account of the Philadelphia convention for the general reader.

Brown, Robert E. *Charles Beard and the Constitution: A Critical Analysis of " An
Economic Interpretation of the Constitution"* (Princeton, N.J.: Princeton University Press, 1956). With Forrest McDonald and Staughton Lynd, Brown has
been one of the leading critics of Charles Beard's views of the Philadelphia
convention.

Elliot, Jonathan. *The Debates in the Several State Conventions on the Adoption of the
Federal Constitution* (Philadelphia: J. B. Lippincott, 1888). A useful but very
incomplete selection of documents relating to the states' ratification of the
Constitution. Merrill Jensen is editing a much more comprehensive collection, which may run to twenty volumes: *The Documentary History of the
Ratification of the Constitution* (Madison: State Historical Society of Wisconsin,
1976—).

Farrand, Max. *The Framing of the Constitution* (New Haven, Conn.: Yale University Press, 1913). One of the first popular accounts of the Philadelphia convention.

————, ed. *The Records of the Federal Convention of 1787* (4 vols.; New Haven,
Conn.: Yale University Press, 1911, rev. ed., 1937). Although the title is
misleading—most of the materials are not records but informal notes—these
volumes are valuable compilations of sources bearing on the work of the
Philadelphia convention.

The Federalist. The title given to the collection of newspaper articles written by
Alexander Hamilton, John Jay, and James Madison in support of the proposed constitution during the debates on ratification. Available in many
editions; among the most useful is that by Benjamin F. Wright (Cambridge,
Mass.: The Belknap Press of Harvard University Press, 1961).

Fisher, Louis. *The Constitution Between Friends: Congress, the President, and the Law*
(New York: St. Martin's Press, 1978). A thoughtful, well-written introduction
to the actual workings of the constitutional system.

Friedrich, Carl J. *Constitutional Government and Democracy*, 4th ed. (Waltham,
Mass.: Blaisdell Publishing Co., 1968). What has become a classic examination of constitutionalism and constitutional systems.

Harmon, M. Judd, ed. *Essays on the American Constitution* (Port Washington,
N.Y.: Kennikat Press, 1978). A series of lectures by leading scholars on the
Supreme Court and constitutional interpretation.

Jensen, Merrill, *The Articles of Confederation* (Madison: University of Wisconsin Press, 1940). An analysis of the drafting of the Articles and the system thereby established.

Jillson, Calvin C. "Constitution-Making: Alignment and Realignment in the Federal Convention of 1787," *American Political Science Review,* LXXV (1981), 581. An excellent analysis of the shifting coalitions of states at the Philadelphia convention. For another important article, see the citation, above to John P. Roche's work in note 11.

Kelley, Alfred H., and Winfred A. Harbison. *The American Constitution: Its Origins and Development,* 6th ed. (New York: W. W. Norton, 1982). One of a number of excellent histories of constitutional development from colonial beginnings to the present.

Loss, Richard, ed. *Corwin on the Constitution* (Ithaca, N.Y.: Cornell University Press, 1981). A collection of articles by Edward S. Corwin, the greatest of American constitutional commentators.

Lynd, Staughton. *Class Conflict, Slavery, and the United States Constitution* (Indianapolis: Bobbs-Merrill, 1968). A provocative "radical" view of social and economic factors that shaped decisions during the revolutionary and founding periods.

Mason, Alpheus Thomas, ed. *Free Government in the Making,* 3rd ed. (New York: Oxford University Press, 1972). A superb collection of materials chronicling the development of American constitutional and political thought.

————. *The States Rights Debate: Antifederalism and the Constitution,* 2nd ed. (Englewood Cliffs, N.J.: Prentice-Hall, 1976). A stimulating series of brief essays examining the "ambiguous interplay" of arguments over the formation of the Constitution.

McDonald, Forrest. *We the People: The Economic Origins of the Constitution* (Chicago: University of Chicago Press, 1958). One of the more important critiques of Beard's thesis concerning the economic motivations of the framers of the Constitution.

Rossiter, Clinton L. *Seedtime of the Republic* (New York: Harcourt Brace, 1953). An excellent analysis of the intellectual ferment during the colonial and Revolutionary periods.

Storing, Herbert J. *What the Anti-Federalists Were For* (Chicago: University of Chicago Press, 1982). An analysis of the political thought of those who opposed the Constitution in 1787–88.

Wills, Garry. *Explaining America: The Federalist* (New York: Doubleday, 1981). A controversial reinterpretation of the partnership of Hamilton and Madison in writing *The Federalist*.

Wood, Gordon S. *The Creation of the American Republic, 1776–1787* (New York: W. W. Norton, 1972). A thoughtful and perceptive study of the development of American political ideas from the Declaration of Independence to the framing of the Constitution.

4 The Nation and the States

The framers of the Constitution sought to limit government by creating a national government that would coexist with the states. At the same time that they wanted a set of strong national political institutions, they feared highly centralized power. These fears and the strong commitment of most Americans in the late eighteenth century to local self-government produced political arrangements in which the states retained significant responsibilities. By forging an uneasy partnership between the federal government and the states, the Constitution provided the framework for the evolution of a complex set of relationships among the national government, the several states, and the thousands of political subdivisions of the states—relationships characterized by conflict, cooperation, and, most important, constant change.

⭐ FEDERALISM AND THE CONSTITUTION

Federalism refers to a political system that divides power on the basis of area—a national government and a series of local, state, or regional governments. Under a federal system, constituent units are guaranteed certain powers, and their consent is usually required for alterations in the basic arrangement. Federalism may be contrasted with a *unitary* or *centralized government*, such as that of Great Britain, in which local units are created by and subject to the control of the central government.

Every federal system reflects a compromise between concentration of power at the center and preservation of autonomy within the constituent units. To endure in the modern world, such a system must be able to adjust to change because no nation's social, economic, and political conditions—and thus problems—remain constant. In the United States, the bargain between nation and state was struck in an isolated, thinly populated, agrarian society. It has survived civil war, territorial expansion across a continent and beyond, a fiftyfold increase in population, development of an industrial economy and an urban society, global wars, and consequent multiplication of demands on all governmental institutions. In the process, American federalism has been transformed from a relatively simple set of constitutionally prescribed relationships between nation and state into a complex mosaic of interactions among public agencies and private associations at the national, state, regional, metropolitan, county, municipal, and neighborhood levels.

A Strong National Government

As we saw in Chapter 3, the Constitution created a central government that was much stronger than what had existed under the Articles of Confederation. Since 1788 the national government has had authority to rule the people directly, not merely by recommendations to the states as was the case under the Articles. Moreover, the Preamble of the Constitution explicitly says that the national government draws its authority from "the people of the United States," not from the several states as separate political entities. The Constitution also denies the states a role in formulating foreign policy and forbids them to issue paper money, tax imported or exported goods except to the extent necessary to pay the cost of inspecting them, impair contracts, grant titles of nobility, enact bills of attainder, or pass ex post facto laws.

In addition, Article VI of the Constitution clearly announced a doctrine of national supremacy:

> This Constitution, and the laws of the United States which shall be made in pursuance thereof; and all treaties made under the authority of the United States, shall be the supreme law of the land; and the judges in every State shall be bound thereby, any thing in the Constitution or laws of any State to the contrary notwithstanding.

This clause renders invalid any effort by a state to infringe on the Constitution or any federal statute or treaty that lies within the authority of the national government to enact. Furthermore, it provides that in any area of public policy where both the national and state governments may legitimately be active—control of commerce, for example—the national law shall supersede inconsistent state law or even, the courts have ruled, a compatible state statute that may impose problems of different administrative interpretations.[1] In addition, state authority may have to give way completely before national authority in certain vital areas like national security, where Congress may claim a "dominant interest" and has woven a pervasive scheme of public policy for the nation.

To balance these provisions of the Constitution, the Tenth Amendment declared that all powers not delegated to the federal government were reserved to the states or the people. A hasty reading of this amendment might lead to the view that there were two watertight compartments of authority: the powers of the federal government as enumerated in the Constitution and a vast residue of state power. Unhappily for those who like simple political structures, no such clear-cut division of power exists. While the Tenth Amendment serves as a constitutional reassurance of the viability of the states, it does not restrict national authority to those functions specifically listed in the Constitution. Several times during the debate in Congress on this amendment, proponents of states' rights tried to insert the word "expressly," so that those powers not specifically delegated to the federal government would be reserved to the states, but each time they were voted down.

These matters are closely related to the provision of Article I, Section 8, the "necessary and proper" clause, with its sweeping implied power to the national government:

> The Congress shall have power . . . to make all laws which shall be necessary and proper for carrying into execution the foregoing powers, and all other powers vested by this Constitution in the government of the United States, or in any department or office thereof.

In 1819, in *McCulloch v. Maryland*, the Supreme Court spelled out the implications of the doctrine of implied powers.[2] In question was the constitutionality of Congress's establishment of the Bank of the United States. No clause of the Constitution mentioned congressional authority to charter banks or other corporations. But speaking for a unanimous Court, Chief Justice John Marshall held that, when coupled with the "necessary and proper" clause, the expressly delegated powers of Congress to borrow and coin money, to collect taxes, to regulate commerce, to raise armies, and to wage war implied Congress also had authority to create institutions that would enable it to carry out its work. Marshall rejected limiting the power of Congress to choose whatever means its members thought most convenient:

> We think the sound construction of the constitution must allow to the national legislature that discretion, with respect to the means by which the powers it confers are to be carried into execution, which will enable that body to perform the high duties assigned to it, in the manner most beneficial to the people. Let the end be legitimate, let it be within the scope of the constitution, and all means which are appropriate, which are plainly adapted to that end, which are not prohibited, but consist[ent] with the letter and spirit of the constitution, are constitutional.

The concept of *implied powers in the federal government* is not easy to reconcile with a doctrine of *reserved state powers*. Once it is conceded that the national government has implied as well as expressed powers, the exact limits of national authority become difficult to fix. As a result, the question of implied powers has been a constant source of controversy, conflict, and compromise among the parties to the American federal partnership.

Guarantees to the States

The Constitution protects the physical integrity of the states by forbidding the federal government to change a state's boundary without that state's consent. The Constitution also imposes some positive obligations on the federal government: it must guarantee to states "a republican form of government," guard them against invasion, and, at request of a state's legislature or governor, protect against domestic violence.

The guarantee of a republican form of government has had little impact on federal-state relations. The Supreme Court has said that enforcement of this clause belongs to Congress and the president.[3] But neither branch of government has been willing to define what constitutes a "republican form of government," much less guarantee such institutions to the states.

More controversial has been the obligation to protect a state against domestic violence. In general, the president has waited for a request from state authorities before acting. On occasion, however, he has gone ahead without any such request and has defended his action by asserting that enforcement of federal laws required intervention by federal troops. For example, against the wishes of the governor of Illinois, President Grover Cleveland sent an army regiment to Chicago in 1894 during a railroad strike, claiming that this action was necessary to protect interstate commerce and to keep the mails moving.[4]

The practical effect of the federal guarantee of territorial integrity has been to freeze state boundaries. Without the consent of state government, there is no way to satisfy those who would separate northern and southern California or have New York City secede from New York State. Not since 1820, when Maine was detached from Massachusetts, has a state legislature actually consented to a revision of its boundaries. At the opening of the Civil War, when Virginia seceded from the Union, a group of western counties refused to join the Confederacy and formed the state of West Virginia. After the war, with Union troops in command, Virginia had no alternative to "consenting."

Admitting New States

Awareness of the country's vast potential for further growth led the framers of the Constitution to grant virtually unrestricted power to admit new states to the Union. Vermont and Kentucky came in as the fourteenth and fifteenth states in 1791 and 1792. Alaska and Hawaii became the forty-ninth and fiftieth states in 1958 and 1959.

Congress is under no legal obligation to admit a new state in any given situation. Generally, Congress has required local experience with self-government, support for statehood from a majority of the electorate of the proposed state, and sufficient population and resources to support state government and pay a share of federal taxes.

Few territories, however, acquired statehood merely by meeting these conditions. Long after Alaska and Hawaii had met the traditional requirements, their admission was blocked in Congress. Because both territories were noncontiguous to the existing states, many congressmen

Hawaii becomes the fiftieth state in 1959. (The Bettmann Archive, Inc.)

felt a dangerous precedent would be established by breaking the geographical solidarity of the country. Opposition also came from southerners who believed that members of Congress from Alaska and Hawaii would support civil rights legislation. Partisan considerations also played a role, since Republicans feared that Alaska would send Democrats to Congress, and Democrats objected to Hawaii for the opposite reason. Not until 1958 did the supporters of Alaskan statehood prevail in Congress. With Alaska's admission, it proved easy to admit Hawaii a year later.

For three-quarters of a century following adoption of the Constitution there was much argument as to whether states might withdraw from the Union. This issue was settled on the battlefields of the Civil War. In 1869 the Supreme Court gave legal approval to what had already been determined by force of arms when it declared that the "Constitution, in all of its provisions, looks to an indestructible union, composed of indestructible states."[5]

Interstate Obligations

In their relations with each other, the states are directed by the Constitution: (1) to give full faith and credit to each other's official acts; (2) to extend the same privileges and immunities to citizens from other states that they extend to their own citizens; and (3) to deliver up fugitives from justice at the demand of the executive authority of the states in which the crimes occurred.

The *full faith and credit* provision has been subjected to a great deal of intricate judicial interpretation. For example, the Supreme Court has held that the clause requires each state to recognize private contracts made under the laws of other states. Thus, a contract made in Ohio for the sale of land can be enforced in the courts of Texas. Similarly, marriages performed or granted under the laws of one state are valid in all other states. Divorce, however, raises more complicated problems, and judges have ruled that a state may refuse to recognize a divorce granted by another state.

The *privileges and immunities* guarantee means generally that a state must extend to citizens from other states the rights to acquire and hold property, make contracts, engage in business, sue and be sued, on the same basis as these rights are granted to its own citizens. But a state need not follow the literal meaning of the guarantee in all respects. It may, for example, deny to citizens of other states the "privilege" granted its own citizens to attend its university. On the other hand, a state cannot deny out-of-staters a privilege like use of its highways. Custom and common sense have had a good deal to do with drawing the line between privileges that must be granted and those that can be restricted. The same is true of the surrender of criminals. Although the obligation is prescribed in the Constitution in binding language, in practice, state officials have occasionally refused to surrender fugitives at the request of other states. Federal judges have consistently refused to order state authorities to meet this obligation imposed by the Constitution.

TABLE **4-1**

Local Governments, 1977	
Counties	3,042
Municipalities	18,862
Townships	16,822
Special Districts	25,962
School Districts	15,174
Total	79,862

The Place of Local Government

As far as the Constitution is concerned, there are only two levels of government—the national government and the states. The Constitution makes no specific reference to local units of government—counties, cities, school districts, townships, and the like. From the constitutional point of view, these 79,862 units are all state subdivisions, created by the states and responsible to them. As such, local governments are subject to all restrictions and prohibitions that the Constitution places on states. Their purposes, powers, and status, however, are determined by the states, except that a state cannot grant to a subdivision authority or functions that it does not itself possess.

★ NATIONAL POWER AND STATES' RIGHTS

Perhaps the most important feature of the Constitution with respect to federalism has been its flexibility concerning boundaries of power between the national government and state and local governments. This flexibility has permitted national power to expand to respond to social, economic, technological, territorial, and political changes. It also has facilitated innovation and adjustment in intergovernmental relations. Because of the fundamental issues involved, the evolution of the federal partnership has generated persistent conflict throughout American history between those favoring a stronger national government and those dedicated to preserving states' rights.

Growth of National Power

Underlying the national government's enormous expansion of activities has been the development of a modern industrial society with a national economy, nationwide networks of transportation and communications, and an increasingly interdependent and urbanized population. With these developments, more and more problems have become national in scope and impact and have generated demands for national action. State and local governments can deal with most national economic and social problems only in a piecemeal fashion. No state could control giant multinational corporations like Standard Oil or Du Pont or a national union like the AFL–CIO. The federal government has the authority—though not always the capacity—to treat problems comprehensively. In a period of widespread unemployment, the federal government can analyze the causes of unemployment without regard to states' political boundaries. It can attempt to eliminate gross differences among the states with regard to levels of health, welfare, income, and economic development. Washington can insist that there are certain essential standards of individual freedom, civil rights, and racial equality that must be accepted and maintained throughout the nation.

Development of national power has also produced national organizations—business, labor, farm, civil rights, and other groups—that focus their political energies on the federal government. Concentrating on Washington means considerable economy of effort for organized interests, since there is only one Congress or Department of Labor, compared with fifty state legislatures or state labor agencies. The fact that members of Congress and federal administration often have been more responsive to group demands than states and localities has reinforced the desire of many organized interests to achieve influence in Washington.

One major reason for the national government's greater responsiveness is the superiority of its financial resources. Throughout much of the nineteenth century, the expansion of federal activities was paid for by proceeds from tariffs and sale of public lands. During the past fifty years, the growth of national government has rested on its formidable powers to raise money through income taxes and borrowing. Federal taxes also have the political advantage of nationwide application, which means they do not place the taxing unit at a competitive disadvantage, as state and local taxes frequently do.

Federal involvement also has been spurred by the inability or unwillingness of states and localities to respond effectively to widespread demands for governmental action. Failure of most states to regulate effectively the industrial combines of the late nineteenth century led to the expansion of national controls over business during the progressive era (1885–1915). The devastating impact of the Great Depression of the 1930s on state and local fiscal capabilities created a governmental vacuum that was filled by the far-reaching innovations of the New Deal. Many of the newer federal programs have resulted from pressures from urban areas, which, before the Supreme Court's reapportionment decision of the 1960s, were systematically shortchanged by state legislatures dominated by rural interests.[6] A final stimulus to national action has been the ineffectiveness of many state and local governments in dealing with complex problems. Given these financial, political, and administrative weaknesses, those who want government to "do something" often turn to Washington for action.

Last but hardly least important, national power has grown because occupants of the White House and Congress have used the most readily available instrument—the authority of the federal government—to advance their policies, value preferences, and favored interests. Instructive in this respect is the case of Ronald Reagan, who came to Washington in 1981 pledged to get the federal government "off the backs" of the American people by reducing federal regulation and transferring federal responsibilities to the states and localities. While Reagan worked to keep these promises, his administration at the same time was seeking to expand power when necessary to promote its interests. Reagan advocated giving federal officials more authority to scrutinize tax returns, to reduce welfare fraud. The Reagan administration also sought to discourage sexual relations among teenagers by requiring that parents be notified when birth control devices were provided to those under eighteen by family planning clinics receiving federal funds.

States' Rights and Decentralization

"Government close to the people" has long been the rallying cry of those opposed to enlarging the role of the federal government. Defenders of states' rights see state and local officials as nearer and more responsive to the electorate than federal officials and thus better able to adapt governmental action to diverse local needs.

One may ask, however, whether state and local governments are all that much closer to the people than the federal government. A larger proportion of voters participates in national than in state or in local elections. News broadcasts, magazines, and newspapers typically devote more attention to national affairs than to state or local politics. Survey research indicates that the average citizen tends to be better informed on national issues than on issues contested at the state capitol or in city hall. Moreover, the decentralized administration of many national responsibilities means that citizens often have more frequent contact with federal officials in such agencies as the post office, Social Security Administration, Internal Revenue Service, or Department of Agriculture than with state and local agencies.

Equally questionable is the assumption that small size automatically promotes responsiveness. States and cities that are small have not been noticeably more responsive to citizens' demands than larger ones or than the federal government.

Moreover, those whose interests have been enhanced by decentralization frequently have used their influence to frustrate rather than advance democracy and the general welfare. As one study of federalism emphasized: "The main beneficiary [of federalism] throughout American history has been Southern whites, who have been given the freedom to oppress Negroes, first as slaves and later as a depressed caste."[7] In general, the cause of states' rights has usually enlisted the staunchest defenders of the status quo. These interests have sought to minimize governmental activity by lodging responsibilities in state capitals, where prospects of inaction were usually higher than in Washington.

To be sure, the federal system does provide opportunities for those units which can muster the resources and the political support to innovate and expand. Wisconsin pioneered in developing unemployment compensation. California led the nation in evolving a superb and costly system of higher education, in which some form of advanced training is available to every high school graduate. New York City extended effective protection to a wide range of civil rights far in advance of most jurisdictions. More generally, states have bolstered executive leadership, enhanced administrative capabilities, developed more diversified and responsible legislatures, and strengthened their finances. But less enterprising or poorer states and localities have lagged far behind their more dynamic neighbors. For all its wealth and growth, Texas devotes relatively little of its resources to social programs and urban needs.

Competition between states also limits experimentation. Policy makers in a state may hesitate to embark on experiments that might raise taxes because they fear that business will move to a state with lower taxes. Federal leadership, for example, was necessary to develop an adequate social security system. Furthermore, some experiments are beyond the fiscal resources of most state governments, or they involve problems too far-flung to be resolved by individual states or even adjoining, cooperating states.

Decentralization, then, involves costs as well as benefits. Despite substantial improvements in many jurisdictions in recent years, government in the state capitals and at the grass roots all too often is ineffective, unresponsive, and corrupt. Perhaps the most serious weaknesses are the differences that result from the dependence of state and local services on taxable resources located within their boundaries. The cost and quality of education, availability of public health care, level of welfare and employment assistance, and burden of taxes for every American are determined to a considerable degree by where he or she happens to live. These differences in services and taxes, particularly at the local level, are heightened by forces of urban growth and change that have created sharp disparities between metropolitan and rural areas, between city and suburb, and among suburbs.

A favorite image of the champions of states' rights pictures states and localities as shriveling appendages of an all-powerful national government manned by bureaucrats who seek to dominate every phase of public life. To support this contention, critics point to the enormous growth in the activities and domestic expenditures of the federal government. Then they conclude that Washington's gains have been at the expense of states and their subdivisions. This approach conceives of federalism as a "zero-sum" game, in which increased national power automatically means reduced state and local authority. The zero-sum approach, however, ignores the fact that governmental activity has been expanding at all levels.

Today, state and local governments are spending more money, employing more people, and engaging in more functions than ever before. In fact, state and local government is one of the fastest-growing sectors of the American economy. Between 1950 and 1980, state and local expenditures increased 709 percent. During the same period, the gross national product rose only 518 percent. In 1980, states and localities spent $432 billion, compared with $377 billion spent by the national government for domestic purposes. More than 13 million people work for state and local government, more than four times the number of federal civilian employees.

Equally important, state and local governments play a primary role in most of the areas of governmental activity that have the greatest bearing on the quality of individual and community life. Their activities have a direct, substantial, and often intimate impact on individuals. As parents, citizens are concerned about how the state and the community foster the health, welfare, and education of children; they are affected by municipal zoning and planning, by housing or slum-clearance programs, by fire and police protection, by collection of garbage, by recreational opportunities.

 FEDERAL AID

Federal assistance provides an important source of funds for state and local governments, making the superior resources of the national government available for financing locally administered services. A *grant-in-aid* is a sum of money derived from a tax levied and collected by a higher level of government.

Through grants, the federal government has often been able to advance national priorities without assuming full responsibility for functions within the traditional sphere of state and local jurisdictions. In the process, Washington has provided the states and their subdivisions with a substantial portion of the resources needed to tackle some of their most pressing problems. Federal aid has stimulated new state and local activity in a wide range of programs. Because recipients must meet federal standards, grant programs have raised the level of competence and professional skill of state and local employees. Federal grants have also redistributed wealth from prosperous to less prosperous areas, thus permitting higher standards of governmental service and performance to be set and implemented for the nation as a whole. Finally, development of the grant mechanism has moderated demands for more drastic forms of centralization that would clearly diminish the state and local role in the federal partnership.

FIGURE **4-1**   **Federal Grants to State and Local Governments, 1972–1981**

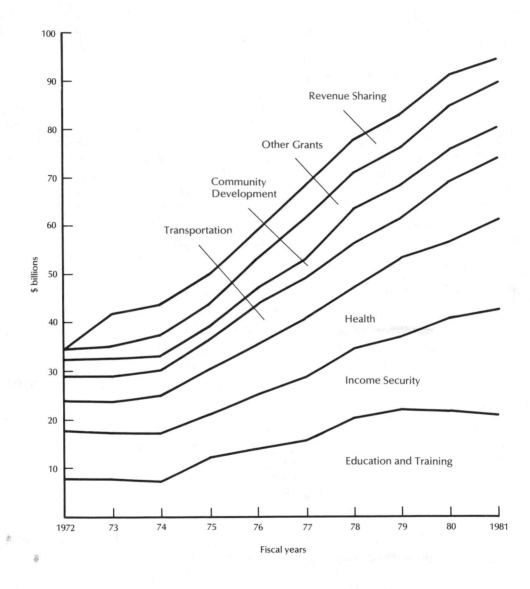

SOURCE: Office of Management and the Budget.

Between 1955 and 1981, federal grants to state and local governments increased from $3 billion to over $94 billion. Equally dramatic was the increase in the number of federal aid programs. During the heyday of Lyndon Johnson's Great Society, Congress enacted sixty-seven new programs, twenty-one dealing with health, seventeen with education, and others concerning economic development, urban problems, and manpower. In the 1970s, federal assistance was available to states and localities for more than 500 programs, administered by over 150 bureaus and offices in a score of federal departments and agencies.

Paralleling the expansion of federal programs has been a vast increase in the number of state and local recipients of assistance. In response to federal requirements, states created scores of regional comprehensive health planning agencies under the Partnership for Health Act and hundreds of regional law enforcement districts under the Safe Streets Act. Over four hundred metropolitan and regional agencies were established to comply with federal planning and coordinating requirements in programs affecting urban, community, and regional development. Federal aid has also been extended to nongovernmental groups, professional associations, and private businesses. In Johnson's war on poverty, federal funds supported programs administered by community action agencies, often established outside regular governmental channels and administered by private boards of directors. Under Medicare, the federal government has in effect contracted with private insurance companies to handle claims of persons over sixty-five and with professional associations to determine the eligibility of hospitals and nursing homes for participation in the program.

Categorical Grants

Until recently, almost all federal assistance was provided in the form of *categorical grants*, that is, grants made for specific purposes, such as constructing hospitals, providing school lunches, or financing public housing. Typically, categorical grants involve federal requirements or conditions. In addition to using the funds for the specific purposes of the particular program, the state or locality receiving federal aid must comply with a variety of program, performance, materials, administrative, and personnel standards. Most categorical grants also require that a proportion of the federal money be matched by the recipient, with the exact matching provisions varying from program to program. For interstate highways, the state share is 10 percent, for example, and for acquisition of open space the matching requirement is 50 percent.

The rapid growth of federal aid brought mounting criticism of categorical grant programs. A major charge was that the conditions—or "strings"—attached to federal grants undermine the independence of

Federal aid at work—an addition to a police station in California under construction, with help from a public works grant from the Economic Development Administration. (U.S. Department of Commerce, Economic Development Administration)

state and local governments. Federal grants, critics argue, inevitably shift control to Washington. At the same time, requirements for matching funds cause state and local budgets to reflect federal objectives rather than state or local priorities.

Complexity and proliferation of categorical programs have also caused serious problems in administration. At the state and local level, many agencies lack the political skills and organizational capabilities needed to master the esoteric art of "grantmanship," in order to secure grants which are loaded with complicated procedures and requirements. Fraud is also an increasingly serious problem, particularly for local agencies that administer grants for welfare, health, housing, and job training. At the federal level, programs frequently overlap. Coordination among agencies and programs is often weak, and interagency conflict common.

Another major concern has been the focus of most categorical grants on rather narrow objectives, such as a particular kind of housing or training program. Federal conditions and restrictions often prevent development of programs adapted to particular state or local circumstances. Even more important as pressures mount on state and local budgets, federal aid fails to provide funds for many public needs not covered by particular categorical programs.

Unhappiness with the complex array of specialized federal aid programs has led in recent years to efforts to develop new approaches to intergovernmental financial relationships. One of these efforts resulted in the enactment of *revenue sharing* in 1973. Another has focused on distributing aid in broadly defined *block grants*. The election of Ronald Reagan in 1980 set the stage for serious consideration of proposals for far-reaching changes in the structure of federal-state-local fiscal relations, changes designed to reduce substantially the role of the national government in domestic affairs.

Revenue Sharing

Proposals for *sharing national revenues* are almost as old as the republic. In 1805, President Thomas Jefferson called for a "just repartition" among the states for "canals, roads, arts, manufactures, education and other great objects." Three decades later, President Andrew Jackson distributed a $50 million federal surplus to the state governments. Revenue sharing surfaced again in the 1960s in a plan that would have distributed 1 percent of federal income tax collections to the states for their unconditional use. President Lyndon Johnson dropped the proposal when it stirred a hornet's nest of opposition from liberal, labor, and urban interests who argued that state governments would misuse unconditional grants. Similar protests came from federal agencies administering grants and from groups that were benefiting from specific federal programs.

Despite these objections, support for revenue sharing mounted steadily, spurred by fiscal problems of state and local governments and criticisms of categorical programs. Among the staunchest advocates were governors, who wanted shared revenues funneled through the state capitals. Mayors, on the other hand, demanded that a sizable portion of the funds be reserved for local governments. Local officials also wanted assurances that revenue sharing would supplement rather than supplant categorical assistance.

After extensive negotiations had produced consensus among state and local leaders, President Nixon proposed in 1971 to distribute $5 billion a year among the states and localities with no strings attached. The debate that followed underscored the diversity of views and interests encompassed by the complex federal partnership. Critics opposed distribution of national tax revenues without detailed federal controls, and the spending of federal funds by state and local officials who did not bear the political burden of imposing taxes. Questions of fairness were raised, both by those who felt that states and localities that taxed themselves lightly would be rewarded, and by those who wanted state and local needs, not population, to be the prime criteria for distribution of federal revenues.

Revenue sharing survived these attacks largely because the alliance of state and local officials remained cohesive and reached into every congressional district. The legislation that emerged from Congress in 1972 provided for distributing $6 billion annually. Concern over the plight of the older cities led Congress to reserve two-thirds of the revenue-sharing pool for localities, as well as to revise the formula for distributing funds to local governments so that it favored poorer jurisdictions.

Funds received under federal revenue sharing have been used for a wide variety of purposes. A substantial portion has financed programs that were already in existence, like police and recreation. Allocations for specific purposes have reflected state and local priorities, major public concerns, and the power of various interests. As a result, far more revenue-sharing funds have been expended for police and fire protection than for welfare programs and other activities that are not valued by local voters.

Despite strong support from state and local officials, revenue sharing became a tempting target for those seeking to trim the federal budget in recent years. Mounting federal deficits, argued some, meant there were no revenues to share. Budget cutters also were attracted by the simplicity of revenue sharing—a large amount of federal outlays could be saved with one slice, compared to the many parings of categorical programs that would be required to save the same amount. Revenue

'Have you noticed the terrific crosswind?'

Etta Hulme, Fort Worth Star-Telegram. Reprinted by permission of
Newspaper Enterprise Association

sharing to the states proved particularly vulnerable because of the apparent financial health of many sunbelt states, and the state portion was eliminated by Congress during the Carter administration.

Campaigning against Carter in 1980, Ronald Reagan supported continued revenue sharing. Once in office, however, he too found the remaining $4.6 billion in unrestricted aid to local governments an attractive target for reducing federal spending. But Reagan's proposal to cut revenue sharing provoked cries of outrage in city halls and county courthouses across the nation, and a Congress responsive to this influential constituency kept revenue sharing intact, at least through Reagan's first two years in office.

Block Grants

The same concerns that stimulated development of revenue sharing have spurred efforts to consolidate categorical programs into *block grants.* As the name implies, block grants provide assistance for broad rather than narrow functions. A housing block grant, for example, can be used for any form of housing assistance. Categorical grants, on the other hand, are restricted to particular kinds of housing efforts, such as construction of low-rent public housing, or rent supplements, or urban renewal, or neighborhood preservation. Block grants typically involve fewer federal conditions, permitting the state or locality to determine how to spend the funds within the general program area. Block grants thus combine the program focus of categorical assistance with the fewer restrictions and greater flexibility of revenue sharing.

Block grants raise many of the same concerns as revenue sharing. Mayors resist block-grant proposals that would channel federal funds to the states rather than the local governments. Civil rights groups argue that the interests of minorities would be more difficult to advance under block grants than in more narrowly focused and more closely monitored categorical programs. Localities that have been particularly successful in securing categorical grants resist changes that threaten to reduce their share of federal aid. In Congress, committee and subcommittee chairmen do not welcome dilution of their control over individual programs. Nor are members of Congress eager to forgo their personal identification with successful applications for special grants and lose the gratitude of local officials who have been helped on their way through the federal aid maze.

Relatively few block-grant proposals successfully ran this gantlet before the election of Ronald Reagan. In 1981, President Reagan seized on block grants as a means of accomplishing a number of his major objectives—reducing federal spending for social services, transferring power to the states, and lessening federal involvement in domestic affairs. He persuaded Congress to consolidate over fifty categorical programs into nine block grants to be administered by the states. The largest consolidation was in education, where thirty-three programs for such activities as school libraries, gifted students, and science teacher training were merged. At the same time, federal funding for these activities was cut 25 percent, a move that further jeopardized the future of many of the specialized programs which lost their separate identities and funds.

Restructuring Federal Aid

During the 1970s, the increasing complexity of intergovernmental relations spurred growing concern from many participants in the federal partnership. In the forefront of the critics was the Advisory Commission on Intergovernmental Relations—composed primarily of federal, state, and local elected officials—which repeatedly denounced the proliferation of federal programs, the blurring of distinctions between national, state, and local roles, and the resultant costs in effective and responsible government. To reform what it saw as an overloaded federal system, the commission recommended sorting out responsibilities between national and state governments. Washington would assume full responsibility for functions such as welfare, unemployment insurance, and housing, while the states would handle education, public safety, and health care. Strong support for a fundamental realignment came from elected state officials, with the National Governors Association and the National Conference of State Legislatures calling for action in Washington.

Ronald Reagan was more than receptive to these ideas, since he had been campaigning for years against the federal government and its aid programs. Reagan complained that "federal bureaucrats now dictate where a community will build a bridge or lay a sewer system. We have lost the sense of which problems require national solutions and which are best handled at the local level." As president, he was "determined to restore power and authority to states and localities—returning as much decision-making as possible to the level of government where services are delivered."[8]

In 1982, Reagan proposed a complicated swap with the states: the federal government would assume responsibility for medical aid for the poor, while the states would take on the full burden of food stamps, welfare, and more than forty other programs. To help the states finance these new responsibilities, Reagan called for creation of a "federalism trust fund," financed primarily by federal excise taxes on alcohol, gasoline, and tobacco, which would provide $28 billion in additional revenues to the states. Almost immediately the plan was ensnarled in controversy. Particularly unhappy were the governors, who liked neither the financing arrangements nor the proposed division of burdens. Welfare, the governors argued, should be a national responsibility because poverty results from national economic conditions. City officials bitterly protested that they would get less help from the states than they had from Washington, and would be at the mercy of state legislatures controlled by unsympathetic representatives from suburbs and small towns. Beneficiaries of the targeted federal programs saw little hope of influencing most states to continue funding such activities as foster care, child abuse, health clinics for migrant workers, urban mass transit operating subsidies, or low-income energy assistance.

That realigning the responsibilities of the various levels of government raises all sorts of conflicts should surprise no one. The stakes are high, and the road between lofty principles and political realities full of potholes, detours, and other perils. At root, arguments about the division of powers among the federal partners deal with what kind of a nation we are. Are problems like poverty, unemployment, urban blight, and inadequate medical care national problems, or problems best handled in various ways by the several states? Should the federal government establish minimal levels of assistance, or can the states be relied on to take care of the needs of their citizens? There are no easy answers to these questions, which have embroiled Americans since the formation of the federal union, itself an effort to realign the responsibilities of the nation and the states.

What does emerge clearly is that federal aid makes a substantial difference in determining what kind of policies are pursued in the American system. After many federal programs were consolidated into block grants in 1981, few states moved to maintain the various specialized activities at their former levels. Instead, as a Florida law maker explained, states have their own priorities and respond to different constituencies than Congress:

> The Legislature is going to have to take a hard look at the programs turned over to us and determine which of these the state really needs. First of all we can't afford to maintain all of these programs even if we wanted to. Then there are three practical things you have to remember: One is that the poor do not represent an active constituency; second, politically it is easier to cut social services; and third, people are embarrassed by Florida's reputation for crime and they want something done about it.[9]

★ DECENTRALIZED POLITICS IN THE FEDERAL SYSTEM

A key factor in debates over the distribution of power and money among the federal partners is the decentralized nature of the American political system. Despite the development of a national economy and growth of a strong central government, the political power of senators and representatives still derives from the voters in particular states and localities. As a result, Congress—and through Congress the federal executive—is highly responsive to the needs and demands of the states and localities. Because of this responsiveness on the part of federal officials, governors, mayors, and other subnational officials play important roles in the various dramas over revenue sharing, block grants, and realigning fiscal responsibilities.

This responsiveness assures state and local governments of a major role in federal programs. Despite conditions attached to categorical grants, primary responsibility for implementing federally aided activities belongs to state and local officials. In almost all grant programs, the federal role normally remains financial and supervisory. State highway engineers locate and build roads, local school superintendents hire the teachers and establish the curriculum, state welfare officials set the

"IT'S FROM THE WHITE HOUSE...THEY'VE RUN OUT OF ROOM!."

Dana Summers, Dayton Journal Herald

levels of payment and criteria of eligibility for most public assistance, and city aides negotiate complex arrangements for urban renewal. Other state and local officials make thousands of policy choices that largely determine who benefits from federal aid, under what conditions, and at what costs to the various components of a particular constituency. Revenue sharing and block grants further increase the scope of state and local influence over use of federal funds.

At the heart of this decentralized system are political parties that disperse rather than centralize power. It is difficult to find more decentralized national institutions in any modern society than the Democratic and Republican parties. The basic rules of the party system are largely determined by state law. Except during presidential elections, most party funds are collected and distributed by state and local party organizations. Both national party organizations are federations of fifty state parties. These committees exercise no significant control over party personnel in the states. Normally the national party leadership plays no role in selecting candidates for Congress, governorships, state legislatures, or local offices.

Underlying the absence of centralized political parties is the decentralization of the rewards of political activity. For most participants in politics, the opportunities for elective office, government contracts, and other benefits are greater at the state and local than at the national level. Of more than 500,000 elected offices in the United States, only 537 are federal positions; and only the president and the vice-president among these 537 are elected nationally rather than from state or local districts. Opportunities for jobs and contracts are also more numerous at the state and local levels because three out of every four civilian government employees are hired by states or localities. Moreover, many patronage jobs in the federal government are distributed to the party faithful through state and local party leaders. Party decentralization is further enhanced by the broad scope of state and local activities. As a result, these governments control a significant proportion of the rewards essential to the sustenance of political parties. The fact that state and local officials play a major role in determining how more than $94 billion in federal aid will be spent also helps nourish the parties at the grass roots.

Of all these elements of the decentralized party system, none is more important than the fact that congressional constituencies are rooted in one state at most, and more commonly in one small area. Members of Congress usually make sure that officials from their constituencies share in spending federal money. The sensitivity of the average congressman to the needs of his district also assures that state and local interests are protected in the federal administrative process. A state's objections to regulations proposed by the federal welfare administration, a city's failure to secure a manpower training grant, or a suburb's efforts to persuade the Bureau of Public Roads to reject a state highway department's proposed alignment for an interstate route all draw congressmen into the administrative aspects of intergovernmental relations.

☆ A GOVERNMENT OF SHARED POWER

The net effect of decentralized politics is to produce a widespread sharing of power. All of the money that comes from Washington is spent at the state and local level. Federal controls are tempered by political realities, as well as by bonds of professionalism and sharing of goals among federal, state, and local officials who work together in a program area. As a result, there is no neat division of functions between the nation and the states and their subdivisions. Instead, the various components of the federal partnership interact in a multitude of ways to provide the wide range of public services that are the shared responsibility of federal, state, and local government.

Decentralized Federal Activity

Both sharing of responsibilities and dispersion of power are promoted by the fact that most federal activities are administered in local communities by local people working for the national government. The great majority of employees of the largest federal agencies, including the Department of Defense, the Veterans Administration, the Postal Service, and the Departments of Agriculture, the Treasury, and the Interior, are scattered throughout the country. By custom, U.S. attorneys and marshals, federal district judges, and, where possible, heads of FBI offices are residents of the areas in which they serve. Locally based federal employees staff veterans' hospitals, maintain national dams and flood control projects, and keep the voluminous records of the old-age insurance program. By the nature of their work—and of congressional appropriations—most have to cooperate closely with their state and local counterparts. And almost all bring to their jobs the same range of values and attitudes that characterize the people in the community in which they work.

Federal-State-Local Interaction

Intergovernmental cooperation extends far beyond activities financed by federal grants. Informal cooperation is the most pervasive form of sharing. Federal, state, and local agencies with common concerns find it mutually advantageous to keep each other informed about their activities and problems and profit by one another's experience. All the levels of government cooperate in collecting and distributing information on everything from prices and incomes to births and deaths. Federal and state officials jointly inspect banks, utilities, and food processors; they investigate many crimes and accidents together; and they work side by side in preserving order and providing relief during disasters and riots. The federal partners share the services of many public servants such as health inspectors and agricultural specialists. They also lend personnel and equipment to one another, train personnel across intergovernmental lines, and provide each other with various goods and services.

Law enforcement, an area of paramount state and local responsibility, illustrates the variety and adaptability of the modes of federal-state-local cooperation. For years, the Federal Bureau of Investigation has helped train state and local police officials. Its fingerprint files were developed with the aid of local police, and those files as well as other information and technical resources are readily available to police departments throughout the nation.

Given the scope of intergovernmental activities, conflicts inevitably arise among federal, state, and local officials. Among the causes of friction are differences in perspective, professional outlook, legal responsibilities, budgetary capabilities, constituency needs, and partisan affiliations of political superiors. Conflict also results from normal human desires to seek credit for things that go well and to avoid blame for those that go awry. Thus, the local police chief complains that the FBI receives all the praise when a joint federal-local operation foils an airline hijacking, while state and federal civil emergency officials blame each other for the inadequacies of relief measures in the wake of a disastrous flood. In a system as complex as the American federal partnership, the temptation to pass the buck is great, especially when pressures are intense, issues controversial, or partisan interests endangered.

Different perspectives are a frequent source of conflict in a decentralized political system. Take the case of airports, which are operated by local agencies, financed in part by federal grants, and linked together by the national government's air traffic control system. Officials of the Federal Aviation Administration approach questions such as flight schedules and noise from the perspective of a nationwide system, while airport agencies are preoccupied with a particular setting. Responding to local concerns, airports have restricted takeoff and approach patterns and night flights, moves which federal officials criticize as detrimental to the efficient operation of a national system of commercial aviation. Federal criticisms are shared by the airlines, which would prefer a single system of federal control to the current necessity of dealing with scores of local airport agencies.

Finally, conflicts arise because of policy differences. In 1982, for example, the Reagan administration developed a plan for civil defense, whose centerpiece was evacuation of 145 million Americans in urban areas and near military installations to less vulnerable regions. Like all civil defense plans, the new scheme required federal-state-local cooperation, but many localities refused to participate, including two of the nation's largest cities, New York and Philadelphia. Critics scored the federal evacuation plans as wildly optimistic. "How are we supposed to feed 19,000 people?" asked the mayor of a town of 1,000 in West Virginia. "We have only two food stores. It's difficult to feed ourselves."[10] Washington's efforts also were attacked by anti-war groups, who argued that evacuation planning increased the likelihood of thermonuclear war because it deceived people into thinking that such a war could be survived. The Federal Emergency Management Agency responded to its reluctant federal partners by indicating that all federal emergency assistance could be withheld from communities that refused to participate in the relocation program.

Interstate Cooperation and Competition

Relations within the federal system do not always involve the national government. By their cooperative efforts, states have always met some of their needs for coordinated governmental activities. One example is the demand for *uniform state laws* that arises from the need for identical treatment of certain issues by individual states. Among the statutes recommended by the National Conference of Commissioners on Uniform State Laws, the most widely adopted are a criminal extradition* act, a gift-to-minors act, a partnership act, a narcotics act, and a simultaneous death act. But, because state courts are under no obligation to interpret identical laws in the same way, there is no guarantee that uniformity of administration will result from these enactments.

Another means of securing cooperation among states is the *interstate compact*, an agreement between two or more states. Since 1921, over a hundred compacts have been concluded, many of which established continuing interstate agencies to operate bridges, ports, parks, and mass transportation, as well as to develop metropolitan and regional plans, coordinate state policies, and exchange information. The earliest and perhaps best known of such agencies is the Port Authority of New York and New Jersey, established in 1921 by joint action of New York and New Jersey to build and operate interstate transport and terminal facilities in the New York metropolitan area.

Destructive economic competition among the states under the Articles of Confederation was a major factor in the creation of a federal union with a strong national center at Philadelphia in 1787. But the "united states" have hardly been harmonious over the past two centuries. Competition and conflict have been fueled by substantial differences among the states in terms of population, size, wealth, resources, economic base, and amount of land owned by the federal government. These variations are reinforced by political decentralization, which enables states to have different kinds and levels of taxes, services, facilities, and regulations. States use their powers to seek competitive advantages over other states—such as by lowering taxes or easing environmental regulations to attract particular industries. Competition has been enhanced by the expansion of the national government, as states and localities vie for federal aid, contracts, and facilities.

---

* *Extradition* is the process by which one government transfers a person within its jurisdiction to another government that wishes to try that person for a crime committed within its own jurisdiction.

 **SUMMARY**

Federalism involves a division of power between a central government and territorially based constituent units that have an independent base of authority. The Constitution established a strong national government with important specific powers and broad implied powers. The Constitution, as well as national laws and treaties, is the supreme law of the land and thus prevails in any conflict with actions taken by the states. Within this basic framework, national powers have steadily expanded in response to economic, social, and political changes. Dedication to local self-government and the pervasive decentralization of the American political system, however, have continually nourished states and localities. Much of the national government's growth in domestic affairs has come from the use of federal assistance to state and local governments in the forms of categorical grants, block grants, and revenue sharing. As a result, state and local officials bear primary responsibility for implementing national programs. Despite constant conflict and controversy, the American federal system demonstrates remarkable durability because of its capacity for sharing of power and adjusting to change.

NOTES

1. See especially *Pennsylvania v. Nelson,* 350 U.S. 497 (1956).
2. 4 Wheaton 316, 421 (1819).
3. See *Luther v. Borden,* 7 Howard (1849); and *Pacific Telephone Co. v. Oregon,* 223 U.S. 118 (1912).
4. See the decision of the Supreme Court in *In re Debs,* 158 U.S. 564 (1895), a case that grew out of this episode.
5. *Texas v. White,* 7 Wallace 700 (1869).
6. See *Baker v. Carr,* 369 U.S. 186 (1962) and *Reynolds v. Sims,* 377 U.S. 533 (1964).
7. William H. Riker, *Federalism: Origin, Operation, Significance* (Boston: Little, Brown, 1964), p. 152.
8. Speech to the National Association of Counties, July 13, 1982, see *New York Times,* July 14, 1982.
9. Ralph Haden, speaker of the Florida House of Representatives, quoted in John Herbers, "Legislatures and Governors Battle for Control of U.S. Block Grants," *New York Times,* January 18, 1982.
10. Mayor A. J. Jorishie, Webster Springs, W. Va., quoted in Reginald Stuart, "Some Local Officials Refuse to Plan Mass Relocation in an Atom Threat," *New York Times,* May 15, 1982.

SELECTED BIBLIOGRAPHY

Anderson, William. *The Nation and the States: Rivals or Partners?* (Minneapolis: University of Minnesota Press, 1955). One of the best general treatments of the American federal system.

Elazar, Daniel J. *American Federalism: A View from the States* (New York: Thomas Y. Crowell, 1966). A useful analysis of federal-state-local relations from the perspective of the state capitol.

Goldwin, Robert A., ed. *A Nation of States: Essays on the American Federal System* (Chicago: Rand McNally, 1963). A series of provocative essays on federalism by a group of leading scholars.

Grodzins, Morton. *The American System: A New View of Government in the United States.* Daniel J. Elazar, ed. (Chicago: Rand McNally, 1966). The major writings of one of the most influential students of American federalism.

Hale, George E., and Marian Lief Palley. *The Politics of Federal Grants* (Washington: Congressional Quarterly Press, 1981). A thorough introduction to the grant-in-aid system as it operated during the 1970s.

Macmahon, Arthur W., ed. *Federalism: Mature and Emergent* (New York: Doubleday, 1955). A large collection of essays on various aspects of federalism in American politics.

Mason, Alpheus T. *The States Rights Debate: Antifederalism and the Constitution* (2nd ed., Englewood Cliffs, N.J.: Prentice-Hall, 1972). An analysis of the historical origins of the current and recurrent debate about national power and states.

Nathan, Richard P., and Charles F. Adams, Jr. *Revenue Sharing: the Second Round* (Washington: Brookings Institution, 1977). A report on the use of revenue sharing funds based on the experience of selected state and local governments.

Reagan, Michael D. *The New Federalism* (New York: Oxford University Press, 1972). A timely appraisal of revenue sharing and the implications of the Nixon administration's efforts to reshape the federal system.

Riker, William H. *Federalism: Origin, Operation, Significance* (Boston: Little, Brown, 1964). A systematic, original, and critical analysis of federalism.

The Process of Politics

5 Politics and Power

As the first chapter pointed out, politics is concerned primarily with power. *Political power involves having others feel, think, or act as one wants with respect to governmental and other authoritative decision making.* Political power can be exercised in one of two ways. First, an individual or a group can shape decisions by government that affect other individuals or groups. Second, an individual or a group can create an intellectual or emotional climate in which others are unable to raise issues detrimental to the interests of the powerful individual or group.[1] This second aspect of power has been called the "mobilization of bias," since it involves the ability of powerful interests to shape values, attitudes, myths, and rules within a political system.[2] Thus, political power is exercised both in making governmental decisions and in excluding issues from the political arena.

⭐ SOURCES OF POLITICAL POWER

Political power comes from many sources. Among the more important are the right to vote, the right to speak out, wealth, official position, organization, popularity, knowledge, and force. Except for the right to vote, all these sources of influence are distributed unequally among citizens. And even the vote is used with varying skill and frequency by different individuals and groups. Moreover, the sources of political influence are not mutually exclusive. Knowledge, for example, can be purchased with wealth. Money certainly makes it easier to communicate with others or to organize for political action. Almost always, in the United States, the legitimate use of force is reserved to those with official governmental positions.

Wealth

Money, it has been said, is the mother's milk of politics. Wealth provides the resources for campaign contributions and other means of access to government officials. It affords control over jobs and credit, which can easily be transformed into political influence. Corporate wealth creates sizable organizational resources—specialists, publicists, lobbyists, and lawyers ready and able to serve the political interests of the corporation's managers, directors, and larger stockholders. The airlines, for example, spent $2.8 million in one recent year to hire lawyers to defend their interests before the Civil Aeronautics Board, compared with a $20,000 expenditure on the part of public interest organizations appearing before the CAB.

With wealth, particularly inherited wealth, come deference and social standing, both of which are important sources of political influence. Wealth can buy an excellent education, highly skilled assistance in dealings with government, and control over information through ownership

Copyright 1979 by Herblock in The Washington Post

of mass media. Money can also supply the talents of pollsters, advertising experts, and campaign specialists—as well as television time, billboards, newspaper ads, and mass mailings—to advance a cause or personal ambitions.

Durability is another important aspect of money as a source of political power. The wealthy tend to keep their economic resources over a long period of time, and usually pass their fortunes on to their family. As a result, wealth is "doubly powerful, not only for what it can purchase now but for what it can buy in the future. . . . Men of wealth can afford to wait, to bide their time while maintaining continual pressure on behalf of their interests."[3]

Money's usefulness and durability as a source of political influence have led many observers of the American scene to conclude that political power is concentrated largely in the hands of the wealthy. This "power elite," as C. Wright Mills called it, is composed of top corporate, military, and governmental leaders, most of whose members come from wealthy families.[4] According to Mills, this tightly knit group rules in the interests of the rich and big business.

A similar picture emerges from many studies of local influence which have found that political influence is derived almost exclusively from economic and social power. Control over the local political system, some analysts believe, is exercised by a cohesive and stable business elite that rules in its own interests.[5] From the perspective of these studies of national and community power, the rich form a "governing class," which "owns a disproportionate amount of the country's wealth, receives a disproportionate share of its national income, contributes a disproportionate number of its members to governmental bodies and decision-making groups, and dominates the policy-forming process through a variety of means."[6]

There can be no doubt that the rich have more than their proportionate share of many of the resources on which political power is based. But is wealth the single most important source of political power? Does the political influence derived from economic resources overshadow other sources, permitting the wealthy to dominate politics? The supporters of the power-elite approach are right in saying that a cohesive economic elite dominates political life in some places and prevails more generally on some issues. But the power elitists have failed to demonstrate conclusively that the sources of political influence available to the economic elite enable them to prevail all the time.

The utility of political resources available to the economic elite depends on a number of other factors besides money: the sources of influence available to other participants in a particular political system, the nature of the issue at stake, and the characteristics of the political arena in which that issue is being contested. Also limiting the influence of the wealthy is a lack of agreement on all political issues among economic notables. The common fact of being multimillionaires produced little agreement on most political questions between liberal Democrat John F. Kennedy and conservative Texas oilman John Paul Getty. Disagreement is common among major corporate interests on most issues. Automobile manufacturers and insurance companies, for example, cross swords on what kinds of safety devices should be required on vehicles. Trade legislation commonly divides big business along the lines of the benefits seen in freer or more restricted foreign commerce.

Opposing the power elitists are scholars who have been labeled "pluralists." They assign must less significance to wealth as a source of political power. Instead, they emphasize the variety of sources of influence and the dispersal of these sources across a wide range of individuals and groups. Pluralists, however, do not believe that sources of power are evenly distributed among Americans; they identify many kinds of elites, most of them not based on money alone. In their view, the wealthy share power with elected and appointed public officials, political parties, and all kinds of nongovernmental groups:

> businessmen, trade unions, politicians, consumers, farmers, voters, and many other aggregates all have an impact on policy outcomes; . . . none of the aggregates is homogeneous for all purposes; . . . each of them is highly influential over some scopes but weak over many others; and . . . the power to reject undesired alternatives is more common than the power to dominate over outcomes directly.[7]

Official Position

Formal roles within government—that is, being a member of Congress, agency head, school board member, or the like—provide a key source of political power. Unlike other participants in politics, who must persuade governmental officials to act, officials themselves have authority to act.

Legislators vote on bills, approve budgets, and confirm or reject executive nominations. They can also investigate other governmental officials as well as private citizens, including directors of huge corporations, presidents of labor unions, officials of presidential election campaigns, and kingpins of organized crime.

Presidents, governors, and mayors make thousands of decisions personally, and they delegate large amounts of their authority to political appointees and bureaucrats. Under the law, the president and other federal officials are empowered to enter into agreements with foreign nations, draft individuals into the armed services, and contract with private suppliers for everything from intercontinental ballistic missiles to toilet paper. Other officials determine eligibility for public assistance, inspect motor vehicles for compliance with safety regulations, and acquire private property for a wide variety of purposes. Members of boards of education set local school policies and often school tax rates as well. Regulatory agencies determine rates for gas and electricity, insurance premiums, and practices regarding sale of stocks and bonds. Judges have authority to levy fines, settle estates, and send people to jail. Judges can also set aside actions of other officials if they conclude that those actions conflict with laws or the Constitution.

By their nature, however, formal governmental roles are restricted sources of political power. In general, the influence derived from public office can be used only for specific functions within a particular governmental jurisdiction. A school superintendent may secure substantial political influence from the authority to manage a local school system. But this official position is not likely to provide much influence in such matters as the location of a new highway or the closing of a military base. Like that of most other officials, the school superintendent's official power is limited to a specific function and governmental jurisdiction.

To be sure, holding an official position may provide an individual with other sources of influence. Knowledge and experience, popularity or deference, an important role in a political party, or a substantial increase in personal wealth can result from holding public office. By the same token, access to other sources of influence can bolster the utility of an official position. In addition to his formal powers, the president typically derives political influence from his popularity and his role as a national party leader. A wealthy governor or member of Congress may use personal funds in order to increase the expert assistance available in exercising official responsibilities. A federal administrator with a strong professional reputation may attract more support for his or her program than another official who is not well known. J. Edgar Hoover amassed great influence during his long service as director of the Federal Bureau of Investigation, because of the sensitivity of much of the information that passed across his desk and because of his skill in using this information in dealings with presidents, members of Congress, and others inside and out of government.

The influence of most officials is also limited by their tenure in office. Official sources of power typically cannot be transferred from one office to another, or from public to private life. The city buildings commissioner who resigns to accept a judicial appointment has the same formal powers as other judges, who may or may not have held previous governmental positions. The state legislator who is elected governor derives formal authority solely from those provisions of the state's constitution and statutes dealing with the chief executive. In office, the president of the United States is one of the most powerful individuals in the world. But this source of influence terminates abruptly with the inauguration of his successor, or, in Lyndon Johnson's apt phrase, when the plug is pulled.

To be sure, popularity, experience, or wealth gained in one public position may increase influence in another governmental office or in private life. The former state legislator now serving as governor is likely to benefit from earlier experience in dealing with the legislature. A tax lawyer who worked for the Internal Revenue Service and a retired Air Force general employed by a defense contractor will certainly draw on the knowledge and associations acquired in official roles to enhance their influence. An ex-president may derive influence from the prestige that follows him out of office from his role as an elder statesman. These sources of influence, however, are a far cry from the enormous institutional power of the presidency itself.

Pluralists view official positions as critical sources of power. In a classic pluralist study made in New Haven, Robert A. Dahl concluded that public officials play most of the central roles in political life. Officials were more likely than others to be full-time, knowledgeable, professional participants in politics. Dahl found the mayor to be the most influential individual in New Haven. His official sources of power enabled him to bridge a variety of issues and political arenas. As a result, the mayor's influence was broad in comparison with the more specialized political resources of nongovernmental participants, even wealthy citizens.[8]

Members of the power-elite school, on the other hand, downgrade the role of official position as a source of independent political influence. They see politicians and bureaucrats as dominated by the economic elite, whose members are statistically overrepresented in the highest positions of public leadership. Certainly public officials do not always exercise their authority without outside influences. Officials are often strongly influenced by wealthy individuals and corporations. But the notion that public officials are always subordinate to an economic elite is an oversimplification. Officials are also influenced by labor unions, environmentalists, religious and radical groups, veterans' organizations, organized crime, and many other interests. Equally important, public officials, because of the substantial sources of political power inherent in their official positions, frequently are *the* decisive participants in politics.

Organization

For large numbers of Americans, *collective action* is a significant source of political influence. Business, labor, agriculture, professions, regional and neighborhood groups, religious faiths, racial and national groups, teachers, veterans, conservationists, consumers, pensioners, women, motorists, consumers, women's liberationists, sportsmen, homosexuals, public officials—most interests in the United States are organized to some extent.

A rally of homosexuals in New York, part of the growing political activism of gay Americans, which has become an important factor in cities like New York, Houston, Atlanta, and San Francisco. (© 1980 Martin A. Levick, from Black Star)

All organizations facilitate collective activity by people who share common objectives and who try to influence government to promote their aims; but organizations differ widely in effectiveness as well as goals. Some have considerable financial resources, large staffs, and skilled leadership. Others are "letterhead" organizations with little behind them but stationery and a single individual's zeal. A few organizations have a broad range of political interests. Most, however, are specialized and become politically involved only when their particular interests are at stake. Some organizations are concerned primarily with politics, most notably political parties. A far larger number of groups that become involved in politics are organized for other purposes, like winning economic benefits from employers, facilitating exchanges of information within a profession, promoting a religious faith, or sharing a common recreational interest. The political effectiveness of an organization also depends on the unity of its members, their commitment to the organization's goals, and their willingness to support the organization.

Political parties are particularly important groupings, and we discuss them in detail in the next chapter. The Democratic and Republican parties are large organizations that seek to win the active support of millions of voters. Consequently their appeals are broad and their programs typically deal with a wide range of problems. By contrast, because its appeal typically is narrow and its program limited, an interest group is usually supported by only a small minority of the population. In general, a party is primarily interested in winning control of the government, while an interest group is mainly concerned with influencing particular governmental decisions. But these distinctions are blurred in practice. Having won control of the government, a party cannot avoid responsibility for shaping many public policies. On the other hand, an interest group may seek to elect its supporters to public office to secure its policy goals.

Historically, the most effective interest groups have been those based on economic interests. Business, labor, and agricultural groups have been the most successful in employing organizational resources to influence government. Nevertheless, these broad groupings are not very cohesive. Labor often is torn between rival aims of various unions and of skilled and unskilled workers. Small farmers have little in common with the huge agribusinesses that farm thousands of acres. Manufacturers, banks, insurance companies, retail merchants, and other businesses have remarkably diverse interests. Moreover, on some political issues, business and labor groups in the same industry may be more closely identified with each other than either is with other business and labor organizations.

Most professions also have strong organizations that from time to time become politically active. Through the American Medical Association, doctors have sought to block or curtail federal programs to finance medical care for the elderly and the poor. The American Bar Association has an obvious interest in the structure, procedure, and personnel of the courts, as well as in many specific issues of public policy that affect lawyers. In general, professional interest groups take very conservative positions. While claiming to be anxious about maintaining high professional standards or serving the public good, these groups often are principally concerned with protecting the vested interests of their members, especially by limiting competition.

Organizations representing war veterans find a powerful incentive for political activity in such issues as pensions for former GIs and medical care for disabled veterans. But their political activity also has encompassed such issues as national defense and foreign policy. The largest veterans' organization is the American Legion, which is controlled and administered by a group of conservative leaders. This organization illustrates the enormous power wielded in all kinds of interest groups by their professional staffs. It is doubtful whether the average member of many groups shares—or even knows about—the views of the paid workers who run the organization. For example, the typical member of the Automobile Association of America probably is not aware of the strong pro-highway views of AAA's Washington staff. One reason that public officials often ignore organizations is their knowledge that the group's professional staff does not necessarily represent the views of rank-and-file members.

As the role of government has broadened to encompass more and more activities, politically oriented organizations have proliferated. Economic interests have become ever more specialized, with almost every conceivable industrial, service, financial, and commercial activity now represented in the nation's capital. The consumer movement, concern over the environment, and the upsurge in interest in governmental reform that followed the Watergate scandals have also spurred the creation of new groups such as Common Cause, Friends of the Earth, and Ralph Nader's Public Citizen organization. Specific issues and concerns continually spur the formation of new organizations, such as the Women Against Military Madness and the National Right to Life Committee. Of particular significance in recent years has been the proliferation of conservative organizations such as the Moral Majority, seeking political action on religious and family issues such as abortion and school prayer.

Pluralists point to the broad range of group and organizational activity as further evidence of the dispersal of sources of political power in the United States. "Few if any groups of citizens who are organized, active, and persistent," argues one pluralist, "lack the capacity and opportunity to influence some officials somewhere in the political system in order to obtain at least some of their goals."[9] But corporations, the wealthy, middle-class citizens, and industrial workers are far more organized, active, and persistent than the poor, the aged, members of minority groups, and others most in need of organizational resources. One study of political participation concluded that

> organizations increase the political gap [between more advantaged and less advantaged groups], for the simple reason that those who come from advantaged groups are more likely to be organizationally active. Upper-status groups are, to begin with, more politically active. They are also more active in organizations. And, because the latter type of activity has an independent effect in increasing political activity—over and above the effects of socioeconomic status—their advantage in political activity over the lower groups is increased.[10]

Knowledge and Information

Knowledge may not be power, but it is a source of political influence whose importance steadily grows. In an increasingly complex society, knowledge and information are indispensable to effective participation in politics. The substance of political life as well as its procedures requires more and more technical competence. For example, settling disputes over hazards to health posed by nuclear generating plants necessitates evaluating advice from nuclear physicists. Determining permissible contents of automobile emissions requires help from chemical and mechanical engineers as well as from specialists in respiratory diseases. The process of electing public officials enlists the talents of campaign specialists, fund raisers, publicists, and pollsters. Operating the government requires personnel specialists, budget officers, efficiency experts, computer programmers, and hundreds of other kinds of technicians.

The wealthy, large corporations, governmental officials, and major organizations enjoy tremendous advantages in acquiring knowledge and experts. And the ability to control the content and dissemination of information is as important as access to knowledge. This source of political influence is also concentrated in the hands of a few hundred individuals and corporations. They control the broadcast networks, own radio and television stations, and operate wire services, newspapers, and magazines. In sum, they and their employees determine what the public sees, hears, and reads.

Control of information provides the press with influence over other participants in politics. Most public officials, groups, and individuals cannot communicate with the public unless the press and television pay attention to their activities and opinions. Moreover, public attitudes are shaped by the way in which reporters and editors present objectives and actions of various participants in politics. The press is also the principal

"Boys, you know I can't answer a question of such a sensitive nature with only one camera and microphone!"

Grin and Bear It, by Lichty and Wagner, © 1980 Field Enterprises, Inc. Courtesy of Field Newspaper Syndicate

means by which officials and political activists communicate with each other. "Most congressmen," notes a former presidential aide and cabinet member, "never read even a partial text of any presidential message. They read about it in the *Washington Post*."[11]

Political activists are intensely aware of the importance of the communications media. They hire press agents, hold news conferences, prepare publicity releases, arrange "photo opportunities," and organize their activities around reporters' deadlines and broadcasters' schedules. Governmental officials and other political participants leak stories to the press, withhold information, demand equal time, and curry favor with publishers, editors, columnists, commentators, and reporters. Organizations sometimes bring economic pressure to bear by contracting for or canceling advertising. Nor are public officials reluctant to criticize "biased" coverage of their activities or even, in the case of radio and television, to threaten greater federal regulation to ensure "impartiality."

All participants in politics employ propaganda in order to influence public opinion. Propaganda may be true, false, partly both, biased, or distorted. It may be narrowly aimed, or it may seek the broadest national good. But its fundamental purpose is to influence public opinion on a particular issue. To accomplish this objective, public relations experts generally rely on the same techniques used to advertise consumer products.

Consider, for example, a pair of television commercials prepared by Republicans and Democrats during the 1982 congressional campaign, which claimed credit for increases in social security and blamed the other side for threatening benefits. The Republicans' TV spot showed a kindly old letter carrier on the steps of a vintage house, telling the viewer:

> I'm probably one of the most popular people in town. I'm delivering Social Security checks with the 7.4 percent cost-of-living raise that President Reagan promised. He promised that raise, and he kept his promise. In spite of the sticks-in-the-mud who tried to keep him from doing what we elected him to do.

The Democrats countered with a commercial showing a social security card being cut away by a Republican scissors, accompanied by the following message:

> The Republicans all say they believe in Social Security, a sacred contract with the American people. That's what they say. Look at what they do. In 1981 they tried to cut cost-of-living increases by $60 billion over 10 years. In 1982 they said either increase Social Security taxes or cut $40 billion to help balance the budget. When are they going to stop? Not until it hurts. It isn't fair. . . . It's Republican.[12]

The realities of the politics of social security are complex, but the task of the political propagandist typically is to reduce issues to simple and emotional terms.

A classic instance of political propaganda is afforded by the American Medical Association's long campaign against national health insurance.[13] Direct pressure on Congress by lobbying with individual legislators was only a small part of an enormous "educational" campaign conducted for the AMA by public relations experts. Thousands of billboards, newspaper advertisements, and radio commercials and millions of leaflets decried "socialized medicine." Almost ten thousand other organizations were persuaded to endorse the AMA's position. "Canned" editorials denouncing the evils of federal health assistance were distributed to newspapers. As a final touch, paintings of a physician at the bed of a sick child were sent to individual doctors to be displayed in their waiting rooms; the caption read:

KEEP POLITICS OUT OF THIS PICTURE

When the life—or health—of a loved one is at stake hope lies in the devoted service of your Doctor. Would you change this picture?

Compulsory health insurance is political medicine . . . .

Popularity

Political influence is often derived from personal qualities which enable some individuals to lead effectively, or to be respected by others, or to win votes in elections. Political popularity also can be rooted in an individual's attributes, such as social standing, family background, birthplace, race, religion, or ethnicity. Personal followings forged from these links built the political bases of generations of American politicians in rural county seats and big-city wards. Popularity also results from personal accomplishments in business, the arts, sports, journalism, as well as public office. In an age of celebrities, it is hardly surprising that the President of the United States is a former movie actor, and that two of the rising young stars of national politics initially won public renown as athletes: Representative Jack Kemp of New York, a former quarterback for the Buffalo Bills; and Senator Bill Bradley of New Jersey, an all-American basketball player at Princeton, who played professionally with the New York Knicks.

In modern society, popularity is strongly affected by publicity, by the amount of attention that an individual is given by the mass media. Office holders and office seekers are preoccupied with their "image," with how they appear to the public. Public relations specialists constantly seek to present the most favorable aspects of their clients, often manufacturing public personalities for politicians that bear little resemblance to the real person. Other experts assiduously measure the "popularity" of office holders and candidates through opinion surveys, whose results often are treated as revealed truth by both the beholders and the beholdee. Increasingly, popularity has become a commodity, rooted less in personal attributes and more in the institutions which have the means to make and break images. These include the press, the campaign technicians, corporate and other major campaign contributors, and government itself, which provides the grandest settings of all to create images—the Oval Office, the steps of the Capitol, the crowded committee hearing, the frenzied reporters at a press conference.

American Indians protest in front of the White House in an effort to dramatize their grievances against the federal government. (© 1978 Frank Johnson, from Black Star)

Protest

Groups that lack other sources of political power are most likely to use protest as a means of bolstering their influence. The main purpose of protest is to dramatize grievances or causes. By drawing attention to their problems, protesters hope to arouse the feelings of others, who will then put pressure on the target of the protest. When a group of black students in Greensboro, North Carolina, staged the first sit-in at a chain store in 1960, they did not pose a serious financial threat to the local store. But chain store executives could not ignore sympathetic reactions from around the country. A demonstration in Greensboro was only a trivial incident, but picketing in major cities in the north and midwest, all presented on evening television news programs, was a different matter.

Typically, the condition that leads people to protest in the first place—lack of other political resources—hampers effectiveness. Successful protests usually require excellent organization as well as leaders who can attract the attention of reporters. Protest activities must be planned and led, rather than just merely "happen." Funds have to be raised from sympathetic individuals and groups. Information needs to be distributed to protesters and the press. Technical skills often are required—such as those of lawyers if legal action is taken to halt the protest.

In the past two decades, protests have been employed by a widening range of interests, including many who possess other political resources. Anti-abortion groups, organizations seeking a freeze on nuclear weapons, landlords, police officers, and numerous other participants in politics have organized demonstrations to dramatize their demands, often by providing photogenic events for television's news cameras. For all groups, the utility of protest depends on the availability of other political resources. No group can protest endlessly, thus the demands of those who lack other sources of power are most easily ignored or discredited.

Force

"Political power," in the words of Mao Zedong, "grows out of the barrel of a gun."[14] Because physical force is an extremely potent source of political influence, government in the United States exercises a virtual legal monopoly over its use. The military services and law enforcement agencies are authorized to employ deadly force in limited circumstances. Other officials, such as those who operate prisons and jails, may use physical force to detain individuals who have been convicted of violating the law or are suspected of crimes.

Governmental agencies often misuse their authority to employ force. One example is the brutal behavior of guards in many prisons. Another is the forcible detention by the federal government of more than a hundred thousand American citizens of Japanese descent during World War II. Local police power has often been employed to defend the status quo. Cities under the sway of political machines like that operated by Frank Hague in Jersey City used the police to intimidate voters, political opponents, and hostile newspapers. Not so long ago, city officials often repaid corporate executives for campaign contributions by using police to break strikes and disrupt the organizing activities of labor unions.

The power of the police has been used in recent years to put down demonstrations by blacks, striking farm workers, opponents of the Vietnam war, and foes of nuclear power plants. On the national level, federal troops have been used to quell domestic disturbances ranging from the Whiskey Rebellion of 1794 to the ghetto riots of the 1960s. The Civil War represents the resort to force by government to settle a dispute that could not be resolved through more conventional sources of political influence.

Government's "legal" monopoly over force is not quite the same as a real monopoly. Other participants in politics have derived political influence from raw force. As Chapter 2 pointed out, there is a strong strain of violence in American culture. Political parties, organized crime, and agents of business and labor have threatened voters and political opponents and occasionally attempted to resolve political disputes through beatings or even shoot-outs. At times, law enforcement agencies have let groups violently settle disagreements among themselves or have—as the FBI did a few years ago with radical black organizations—even egged on groups to fight each other. And the assassinations of Presidents Lincoln, Garfield, McKinley, and Kennedy, as well as the political murders of Martin Luther King, Jr., and Robert F. Kennedy, and the attempted assassinations of Presidents Franklin Roosevelt, Harry Truman, Gerald Ford, and Ronald Reagan, all illustrate that violence can be an extremely important, if very fleeting, source of power.

★ USING POLITICAL RESOURCES

Political resources such as wealth, official position, organization, popularity, knowledge, and force are sources of power; they are not power itself. Availability of such means does not guarantee influence in a particular situation. Instead, the sources of power provide potential in political relationships. The usefulness of a particular source of power depends on the nature of an issue, participants' goals, and resources available to other parties. Moreover, some participants are more willing

A stark reminder of the role of violence in American political life is provided by the funeral procession of President John F. Kennedy, who was killed by an assassin's bullets during a visit to Dallas, Texas, on November 22, 1963. (United Press International)

than others to use their resources for political purposes; and some are more expert in employing them. They may have more time available for political activity, as is the case with public officials in contrast with most businessmen. Elected officials and other political professionals may also have acquired more skill in converting potential influence into actual power.

A Multitude of Political Arenas

Relatively few participants in politics have resources that are usable in a wide range of political arenas. Instead, the utility of sources of influence tends to be specialized. Like government itself, political activists specialize in defense, international trade, banking, taxation, education, housing, health, social security, welfare, public lands, or environmental protection. Equally important is the territorial distribution of responsibility within the federal system among nation, state, and local governments.

Because of the specialization of influence, a lawyer experienced in immigration matters cannot use his resources as effectively in a dispute over the location of high-tension power lines in a residential area. An admiral responsible for procurement of antisubmarine weapons derives considerable influence over this activity from his official position, organizational resources, and expert knowledge. None of these specialized resources, however, is likely to make the admiral particularly effective as a participant in political arenas dealing with baby-food additives or the location of waste disposal facilities.

This multiplicity of political arenas contributes to dispersion of power in the United States. Different levels and agencies of government have different responsibilities. This power tends to be exercised in particular political arenas by different participants. A study of political influence in the nation's largest city concluded:

> Decisions of the municipal government emanate from no single source, but from many centers; conflicts and clashes are referred to no single authority, but are settled at many levels and at many points in the system: no single group can guarantee the success of the proposal it supports, the defeat of every idea it objects to. . . . Each separate decision center consists of a cluster of interested contestants, with a "core group" in the middle, invested by the rules with formal authority to legitimize decisions . . . and a constellation of related "satellite groups" seeking to influence the authoritative issuances of the core group.[15]

As the chapters that follow indicate, similar statements can be made about political parties, Congress, the federal executive, and most of the other political arenas that comprise the American governmental system.

Participation

Participation in politics involves attempts to turn political resources into political influence. Most individuals and groups participate only in those political arenas in which they think they have interest. Stakes are broader in some arenas than in others. Race relations and highway building, for example, attract more participants than does regulation of barber shops.

Those who participate most in politics tend to have roles that require substantial involvement, either as governmental officials or as holders of politically oriented positions in business, unions, and other organizations. Most governmental and organization roles, however, dictate a narrow range of political involvement. Bureaucrats typically participate only in those political arenas in which their authority is exercised. Private organizations usually do not become involved until they perceive a specialized interest of their own.

Only a small proportion of participants have sufficient resources or interests to participate in a wide range of political activities. Among the most active participants in politics are elected executives and their staffs, members of Congress and other legislative bodies, and judges. Private parties who participate in a broad scope of activities include the press, civic groups such as Common Cause and the League of Women Voters, and general-purpose business and labor groups like the Chamber of Commerce, the Committee for Economic Development, and the AFL–CIO.

Aside from voting, most Americans participate in politics infrequently, and their scope of involvement typically is narrow. Less than 10 percent are members of groups that are primarily political in nature, and only one in five citizens has been in contact with a governmental official. Typically, involvement results from a local problem—a zoning change, a traffic accident, a proposal to integrate schools, or the like—and that involvement usually ends when the issue is resolved or the conflict eases.

Participation is closely related to social and economic standing. Those who participate the most tend to have higher incomes, more education, and higher-status occupations. Conversely, those who are least involved tend to have low incomes, little education, and low-status jobs. For most Americans, "politics is a remote, alien, and unrewarding activity."[16]

Some who fail to participate are totally inert politically. Others are satisfied with things as they are, or perhaps more frequently are not sufficiently dissatisfied to divert time and energy from their other pursuits. Many do not participate because their resources are limited. Such people often see involvement as futile, given the massive resources of public officials and established groups.

Senior citizens have become increasingly vocal in their political demands, and no issue arouses more fervor among the elderly than social security. (Bob North, Picture Group Photo)

Voting, the only political resource employed by most people, has little direct effect on most political outcomes or the workings of governmental institutions. Elections rarely alter the behavior of bureaucracies with which citizens must deal. Moreover, connections between candidates and policies are often obscure. For example, the victors in the 1964 and 1968 presidential elections promised peace in Vietnam, but both President Johnson and President Nixon proceeded to wage war for the next four years.

Even in the case of voting, however, increased participation can enhance the influence of a group or an interest. A good example is provided by the growing political power of the 23 million Americans who have reached their sixty-fifth birthday. Rapid expansion of the ranks of the elderly has increased their political significance. Older people tend to vote more than younger individuals; many also have more time and experience to devote to political activities. Another factor stimulating the political involvement of senior citizens is their heavy dependence on government for social security, Medicare, and subsidized housing. The combined membership of groups such as the American Association of Retired Persons, the National Council of Senior Citizens, and the Gray Panthers exceeded 15 million in 1982. Increased political mobilization and participation have made elected officials and government agencies more and more responsive to "gray power." The result has been new tax breaks for senior citizens, more public facilities and programs for older people, sharp hikes in social security and other benefits for the elderly, restrictions on mandatory retirement, and widespread opposition by elderly voters to school budgets and other spending programs that threaten them with higher taxes.

⭐ A SYSTEM OF MANY ELITES

We have said enough to make it clear that, on the whole, we disagree with the belief of power elitists that political power in the United States is concentrated in the hands of a small group of wealthy people. The American political system, however, is hardly the participatory utopia pictured by some pluralists. Large numbers of Americans lack resources to participate effectively in any political arena. As a result, significant influence is distributed among a relatively small proportion of the population. People with power tend to be white males, among whom American-born Protestants are overrepresented. The influential usually have college educations and incomes well above average. They almost always hold positions of leadership in government, business, and other organizations.

Those with substantial political resources secure many benefits from the political system. A supposedly progressive federal tax system actually places heavier relative burdens on lower- and middle-income families than on the very rich. Most federal housing subsidies—in the form of mortgage assistance and income tax deductions—benefit homeowners rather than the poor. Large farmers and agribusinesses have been the principal beneficiaries of massive agricultural programs. Public officials and businessmen defend huge subsidies for aircraft companies, the merchant marine, and the petroleum industry as essential to a healthy economy. Many of these same people, however, attack subsidies for unemployed mothers with dependent children as undermining self-reliance and thrift.

"*I'm terribly sorry, sir, but in the process of cutting out programs for the poor we inadvertently cut out a program for the rich.*"

Dana Fradon, © 1979 The New Yorker Magazine, Inc.

Alliances of public and private power tend to dominate many political arenas. Coal companies, the United Mine Workers, the Federal Bureau of Mines, and state regulatory agencies have cooperated on such issues as mine safety and strip mining. Many government agencies with regulatory responsibilities—for example, the Federal Trade Commission, state utility commissions, and local zoning boards—are often dominated by the very groups they were created to control. Public power also is frequently delegated to influential private organizations. For example, county agents in the Department of Agriculture's extension program are appointed by a powerful private group, the American Farm Bureau Federation. Many state medical, bar, engineering, and other private associations exercise public power over licensing, certification, and other prerequisites to the practice of a profession. In the process, these private interests use their public authority to reduce competition.

Few such advantages are possible for those who lack political resources. The groups that are most dependent on government—the poor, blacks, Chicanos, Puerto Ricans, Indians, migrant farmhands, unskilled workers, and some of the elderly—have the least influence. On the whole, they vote less frequently and have fewer organizational resources than their fellow citizens. Because of their lack of power, governmental officials can afford to ignore or heavily discount the interests of these people.

Consequences of Powerlessness

The lives of the poor, and racial minorities are in large part shaped by their lack of political power. The federal minimum wage system does not include many of the lowest-paid jobs, such as farm labor. When workers in low-paying jobs reach retirement, they have to survive on inadequate social security benefits, supplemented by charity, private or institutional. While surplus agricultural commodities overflow government warehouses under programs designed to keep up food prices, hundreds of thousands of American poor go hungry and old people eat dog food. Under a national housing policy that proclaims the goal of decent shelter for all, federal programs have replaced the slums of low-income families with new housing, but at rents that former residents rarely can afford.

Typically lacking education, legal assistance, and organizational resources, the poor are placed at a tremendous disadvantage by laws governing relations between landlord and tenant or between lender and borrower. Again because of their lack of politically useful skills and resources, powerless groups tend to receive the harshest treatment from police, judges, prison guards, and probation officers. Public health facilities for the poor are usually overloaded and understaffed, although poorer Americans have a much higher incidence of health problems than middle-class people. Welfare recipients contend with a complex system that provides insufficient assistance at great cost in terms of human dignity. Moreover, because the children of the poor tend to attend the worst schools, and drop out early, the outlook for the next generation remains bleak.

Political resources are difficult to create among impoverished groups. Few members of a powerless group have the time, energy, or personal resources to devote to political activity. Even protest, the most readily available means, is not a very effective substitute for more durable sources of political influence. Talented leaders like Cesar Chavez of the United Farm Workers Organizing Committee can help overcome some of these disadvantages. The efforts of skilled and dedicated professionals, such as those found in civil rights organizations, can provide the poor and minority groups with desperately needed political resources. So can the availability of organizational resources for the poor through

A small part of the 637 million pounds of surplus cheese accumulated by the U.S. Department of Agriculture as a result of dairy price supports that cost the federal government $2 billion in 1982. To prevent spoilage, 30 million pounds of the cheese were distributed to needy families in 1982. (Brad Bower, Picture Group Photo)

such governmental programs as the ill-fated war on poverty. Welfare clients, public housing tenants, parents of black schoolchildren, and residents of poor neighborhoods have also organized in recent years for political action. In so doing, some of these groups have gained influence in political arenas that most affect the poor.

Despite these successes, creating and maintaining political resources for the poor is an arduous task. Organizations serving the poor and minorities frequently depend heavily on government agencies, foundations, or other institutions controlled by outsiders. These groups must compete with other participants who hold official positions, have more reliable sources of political influence, and have more political experience. Without significant redistribution of wealth and access to other political resources, the poorer segment of the population is likely to remain relatively powerless. At the same time, poorer Americans' lack of political resources greatly reduces the likelihood of such a redistribution.

The meager political resources of poor people were underscored during the first years of the Reagan administration. The 1980 election result was in part a repudiation of past policies aimed at reducing poverty. Reagan promised Americans less government, more free enterprise, and more freedom for individuals to succeed or fail—a formula that quickly proved disastrous for the poor. When the chips were down in Washington, poor people counted for little as Congress approved sweeping budget cuts which devastated those least able to defend their interests—welfare and food stamp recipients, public housing tenants, and Medicaid patients. Cuts in federal aid also weakened legal services, community, tenant, and other organizations which battle unequal odds in defense of the poor. "We are all so powerless and dependent," said one despairing welfare recipient, "now they are saying to us, 'You can't be dependent on the state any more,' before we have the means to be independent."[17]

Black Power

Black Americans have faced particularly severe problems in acquiring political resources. First slavery then segregation cut blacks off from most sources of political influence; thus they received few educational opportunities. And, even in an absence of prejudice, a poor education severely limits economic opportunities. Blacks—like Indians and Hispanic Americans—have lower average incomes than whites, are more likely to be poor, and have fewer organizational resources. Until recently, blacks were formally excluded from politics by the denial of the vote in many states. And when blacks have been able to participate in politics, their influence was often limited by racist attitudes among white Americans.

Inevitably, political involvement of blacks has been shaped by their unique position in American society. They have had to struggle for even the right to participate in politics. Almost all their meager political resources have been devoted to the fight for equality—for the right to be treated like other citizens in jobs, housing, schooling, and other public services. Lacking access to most sources of political influence, blacks in the past relied heavily on legal action. Throughout the first half of the twentieth century, the courts were the key political arena for the National Association for the Advancement of Colored People and other groups representing black interests.

During the 1950s, frustration with the slow pace of change that courts could manage turned blacks to other means of registering dissatisfaction. Large-scale protests against racial separation began in Montgomery, Alabama, where a young minister named Martin Luther King, Jr., directed a successful boycott against the city's segregated bus lines. King and his organization, the Southern Christian Leadership Conference, stressed direct action in the form of demonstrations, protests, and boycotts, rather than lawsuits and lobbying, favored by traditional groups like the NAACP. The dramatic and direct aspects of protest appealed to frustrated blacks who lacked other sources of political influence. In the wake of the boycott in Montgomery, sit-ins, freedom marches, rent strikes, school boycotts, and other forms of mass protest were employed by increasingly militant blacks across the nation.

Out of these racial confrontations, and from the new leaders and organizations spawned by protest, came the demand for *black power*. In one sense, black power resembles the "Irish power" on which urban political machines were built during the nineteenth century. It involves using racial solidarity as a source of political influence by having black voters, black organizations, and black officials work for black interests. From this perspective, black power means capitalizing on the concentration of black voters in an area to elect black officials, or defeat hostile white candidates, or press for particular policies and programs.

For many blacks, however, black power involves more than following the traditional political strategy of ethnic solidarity. They see black power as essential to black self-determination. Their goal is freedom from the social, economic, and political domination of whites. Some black leaders stress use of black power to secure economic independence, urging blacks to build up and patronize their own business establishments. Even more important for many black spokesmen is freedom from white cultural dominance. For these people, black power must be expressed in terms of black pride. They urge blacks to develop values and institutions based on their own history, lifestyles, and aspirations.

Advocates of black power have differed widely on the best means to secure political power. Martin Luther King, Jr., was a passionate advocate of nonviolence and peaceful protest. Demonstrations were also the principal weapon of the Congress of Racial Equality. The Student Nonviolent Coordinating Committee emphasized working within the existing political system by concentrating on registering potential black voters in the south. More militant black groups, however, have embraced force, violent rebellion, and terrorism. Some leaders of the Black Panthers have said armed force is the only effective instrument of black power. More recently, the Panthers have de-emphasized violence in an effort to broaden their political base. Slogans like "All Power to the Sniper" frightened away much black support. Indicative of the changing perspective of the Panthers on political means was the candidacy in 1973 of one of the organization's leaders, Bobby Seale, for mayor of Oakland. Seale attracted sufficient support to force a run-off election with the victorious candidate. Four years later the Panthers helped elect Oakland's first black mayor with a vigorous voter registration drive and efforts to get blacks to the polls.

Black leaders disagree about ends as well as means. Despite emphasizing mass action and radical rhetoric, Martin Luther King's dream of an integrated society linked him to the traditional objectives of the NAACP, middle-class blacks, and white liberals. Toward the other end of the spectrum have been outspoken separatists like the Black Muslims. For the Muslims—who also have mellowed in recent years—black power has been a means to create a separate black nation of Islam, which would be forged from a part of the United States. In between are those who see integration as unattainable and political separation as unrealistic. For them, black power is a means of providing blacks with the political resources to control those institutions that affect their lives—local schools, police departments, welfare bureaucracies, and public hospitals.

From these diverse views of black power, a few common themes emerged in the 1970s. First was agreement on a need to bolster self-respect among blacks. Second were efforts to create greater unity among blacks. Some black leaders have been attracted to the possibility of a black political party, which would capitalize directly on the potential support of the 16.5 million blacks of voting age. As the next chapter points out, the attractions of organizing a new party are always tempting to leaders of a minority group. But blacks constitute only about 11 percent of the electorate, hardly enough to win control of any governmental structure above the local level. If, however, leaders can persuade more blacks to register and can offer a realistic threat of shifting their support to one party or the other or of forming a third party at critical points, blacks could exert more political influence at the national level than they have in the past. But there are substantial risks in solidarity. In 1980, nine of ten blacks supported Jimmy Carter, leaving them almost no leverage with President Reagan.

At the local level, electoral politics can pay higher dividends than in Washington. Although blacks could never control Congress or even a state legislature simply by virtue of their numbers, they can, if they mass their power, dominate many older cities. Blacks already form a clear

Mayor Kenneth Gibson of Newark is one of the steadily growing corps of black elected officials who emerged in the 1970s as the principal spokesmen for blacks. Gibson is shown addressing the United States Conference of Mayors, the major lobby for the big cities, during his tenure as the organization's president. (Wide World Photos)

majority of the population in Washington, Atlanta, Detroit, Newark, New Orleans, and Baltimore. By 1981, there were more than 5,000 black elected officials at the state and local level.

Compared to whites, blacks now vote in about the same proportions, but they engage less often and less actively in political campaigns and contact public officials less frequently about personal or community problems than do whites. These differences are closely associated with differences in socioeconomic status.[18] Actually blacks in the higher socioeconomic ranks participate even more frequently and actively than do whites of similar backgrounds. The rub comes in the fact that a majority of blacks fall in the lowest one-sixth of the country on the usual measures of socioeconomic status.

Thus, black leaders face the same circular problem as others who seek to bolster the political influence of disadvantaged groups. They need positive governmental action to improve the socioeconomic status of their people. Yet low socioeconomic status is typically accompanied by unawareness of political opportunities and an inability to exploit those that are perceived. At the same time, the economic advance of large numbers of blacks in the 1970s eroded black solidarity. Like other Americans, upwardly mobile blacks seek to separate themselves from the poor and their problems, and in the process they develop political interests based more on class than on race.

Neither calls to use the ballot more wisely and more often nor exhortations to utilize other forms of participation offer an easy solution to the problem of political resources for blacks. The volatility of race in America imposes severe restrictions on both the speed and the quantity of gains that blacks can achieve by the political processes. Efforts to heighten the awareness of the black community may make whites more aware of their own identity and perhaps even frighten them into greater political activity. To avoid the dangers of a backlash while still mustering the black support needed to build political power requires skills of a rare sort.

☆ AN INHOSPITABLE TRADITION

One of the problems faced by those who lack political influence is the attitude of most Americans toward power and its role in public life. Demands for black power or brown power or student power disturb those who believe that conflict is undesirable. Most people feel that issues ought to be settled on their merits rather than by exercise of political influence. The fact that most individuals or groups accept the resolution of an issue on its "merits" only when the merits or existing rules favor them does not diminish the widespread dislike for conflict, politics, and power.

Most Americans want statesmen rather than politicians or power brokers for leaders. Thus, those who exercise significant power usually mask its use. Typically, they claim that they are acting in the public interest, or following established procedures, or seeking economy, efficiency, justice, or some other admirable goal. Those who use power blatantly find themselves criticized for being selfish or undemocratic.

Politicians have always sought to capitalize on these negative attitudes about politics. Anti-politics became particularly attractive to candidates for office in the aftermath of the Watergate scandal. Jimmy Carter based his successful campaign for the presidency in 1976 on his status as an "outsider" with no connections to the political world of Washington. In office, Carter repeatedly sought to place himself above politics by refusing to compromise with Congress and by appealing directly to the people for support of his programs.

Public distrust of power has also contributed to the maintenance and elaboration of a complex governmental system that disperses authority widely. As Chapter 3 showed, desire to limit official power was a principal concern of the authors of the Constitution. The result was a sharing of powers, checks and balances, overlapping terms of office, and a federal system. State constitutions in the nineteenth century scattered governmental authority even further, providing for election of a host of executive officials, detailed restrictions on state and local governments, and created independent agencies to carry out governmental functions.

Pluralists see the fragmentation of governmental authority as essential to prevent concentration of power, to protect minority rights, and to ensure peaceful settlement of disputes. The importance of these goals should not be belittled. Equally important, however, is the fact that dispersal of governmental authority has not prevented concentration of great political power in the hands of certain public officials, most notably the president, governmental agencies like the Department of Defense, and large corporations, trade associations, major labor unions, and such organizations as the American Medical Association. By and large, decentralization of governmental responsibilities play into the hands of influential and experienced participants who understand the complexities of the system.

The result is a political system which offers many advantages to the powerful in their quest to protect their interests. As one detailed study of political influence concludes: "Every proposal for change must run a gauntlet that is often fatal. The system is more favorable to defenders of the *status quo* than to innovators. It is inherently conservative. . . . If plans are radical, they seldom survive; if they survive, they seldom work major changes in the going system."[19]

SUMMARY

Political power involves getting others to feel, think, or act as one wishes. It comes from a variety of sources—wealth, official position, organization, popularity, knowledge, force, and the right to vote. These resources are not evenly distributed in society, any more than are the skills in using such resources. Most sources of political power are specialized. Individuals and groups typically exert their influence in particular arenas rather than in politics generally.

In the United States, power tends to be dispersed rather than highly concentrated in a power elite. Substantial influence, however, is distributed among a relatively small proportion of the population, composed primarily of white males with above-average incomes and educations who occupy positions of leadership in government, business, and other large organizations. The poor and members of disadvantaged minority groups have the least political influence, a circumstance that gravely handicaps efforts to improve their economic and social conditions. Because of the bitter heritages of segregation and discrimination, blacks, Indians, and Hispanic Americans have faced particularly severe problems in acquiring and using political resources.

For all individuals and groups, the exercise of political influence is conditioned by the hostility of most Americans to open use of power. Public distrust of power has shaped American politics from the colonial period to the present, in the process contributing significantly to the fragmentation of authority at all levels of government.

NOTES

1. These two aspects of political power are emphasized in Peter Bachrach and Morton Baratz, "Two Faces of Power," *American Political Science Review*, LVIII (1962), pp. 947–952.
2. See E. E. Schattschneider, *The Semi-Sovereign People* (New York: Holt, Rinehart and Winston, 1966), p. 71.
3. David Ricci, *Community Power and Democratic Theory* (New York: Random House, 1971), pp. 168–169.
4. See C. Wright Mills, *The Power Elite* (New York: Oxford University Press, 1956).
5. The classic studies of community power were undertaken by Helen and Robert Lynd in Muncie, Indiana: see *Middletown* (New York: Harcourt Brace, 1929) and *Middletown in Transition* (New York: Harcourt Brace, 1939). Also significant is Floyd Hunter's analysis of influence in Atlanta, Georgia, in *Community Power Structure* (Chapel Hill, N.C.: University of North Carolina Press, 1953).
6. G. William Domhoff, *The Higher Circles* (New York: Random House, 1970), p. 109.
7. Robert A. Dahl, "Business and Politics: A Critical Appraisal of Political Science," in Mason Haire and Paul F. Lazarsfeld, eds., *Social Science Research on Business* (New York: Columbia University Press, 1959), p. 36.
8. See Robert A. Dahl, *Who Governs?* (New Haven, Conn.: Yale University Press, 1961).
9. Robert A. Dahl, *Pluralist Democracy in the United States* (Chicago: Rand McNally, 1967), p. 386.
10. Sidney Verba and Norman H. Nie, *Political Participation in America: Political Democracy and Social Equality* (New York: Harper & Row, 1972), p. 208.
11. Joseph A. Califano, Jr., quoted in "Washington's Press Corps," *Newsweek*, May 25, 1981, p. 88.
12. Quoted in Martin Tolchin, "The Battle of the Social Security Ads," *New York Times*, July 19, 1982.
13. For an excellent analysis of the early stages of this campaign, see Stanley Kelley, Jr., *Professional Public Relations and Political Power* (Baltimore, Md.: Johns Hopkins University Press, 1956), Chapter 3.

14. Stuart R. Schram, *The Political Thought of Mao Tse-tung* (New York: Frederick A. Praeger, 1963), p. 209.
15. Wallace S. Sayre and Herbert Kaufman, *Governing New York City* (New York: Russell Sage Foundation, 1960), p. 710.
16. Dahl, *Who Governs?*, p. 279.
17. See "Welfare Officials Surprised at Silence of Poor over Cuts," *New York Times*, February 10, 1982.
18. See Verba and Nie, *Political Participation in America*, Chapter 10.
19. Sayre and Kaufman, *Governing New York City*, pp. 716, 719.

SELECTED BIBLIOGRAPHY

Bachrach, Peter. *The Theory of Democratic Elitism* (Boston: Little Brown, 1967). A succinct critical evaluation of the concept of the political elite.

Carmichael, Stokeley, and Charles V. Hamilton. *Black Power: The Politics of Liberation in America* (New York: Random House, 1967). An angry analysis of political power and the role of black Americans in the political process.

Dahl, Robert A. *Pluralist Democracy in the United States* (Chicago: Rand McNally, 1967). The pluralist perspective on the American political system.

———. *Who Governs?* (New Haven, Conn.: Yale University Press, 1961). A classic study of democracy and power in an American city.

Domhoff, G. William. *The Higher Circles* (New York: Random House, 1970). An elitist analysis of the role of the "governing class" in American political life.

Graber, Doris A. *Mass Media and American Politics* (Washington: Congressional Quarterly Press, 1980). An introduction to the impact of the mass media on political behavior in the United States.

Hess, Stephen. *The Washington Reporters* (Washington: Brookings Institution, 1981). A fascinating exploration of the role of the press in the nation's capital.

Key, V. O., Jr. *Public Opinion and American Democracy* (New York: Alfred A. Knopf, 1961). A thoughtful attempt to place sociological knowledge about public opinion into a meaningful context.

Lindblom, Charles E. *Politics and Markets: The World's Political-Economic System* (New York: Basic Books, 1977). An appraisal of the power of large corporations which concludes that they dominate American politics.

Lowi, Theodore J. *The End of Liberalism* (New York: W. W. Norton, 1966). An examination of the fusion of public and private power in American politics.

McConnell, Grant. *Private Power and American Democracy* (New York: Alfred A. Knopf, 1966). An analysis of the influential role of private groups in the making of public policy.

Mills, C. Wright. *The Power Elite* (New York: Oxford University Press, 1956). A classic and iconoclastic statement of the elitist perspective on American politics.

Polsby, Nelson. *Community Power and Political Theory: A Further Look at Problems of Evidence and Inference* (New Haven, Conn.: Yale University Press, 1980). A spirited critique of elitist approaches to the study of political power by one of the most outspoken pluralists.

Ricci, David. *Community Power and Democratic Theory* (New York: Random House, 1971). A critical review of elitist and pluralist approaches to power and democracy.

Skolnick, Jerome H. *The Politics of Protest* (New York: Simon and Schuster, 1969). Originally a task force report to the National Commission on the Causes and Prevention of Violence; a broad survey of protest movements with an excellent chapter on black politics.

Tolchin, Martin, and Susan Tolchin. *To the Victor: Political Patronage from the Clubhouse to the White House* (New York: Random House, 1971). An entertaining examination of a key political resource and its use throughout the American political system.

Truman, David. *The Governmental Process* (New York: Alfred A. Knopf, 1951). A comprehensive analysis of the operation of the American political system as seen through interest group activities.

6 The Party System

Ideally, political parties perform a number of important functions in a democracy. For candidates seeking public office, a party mobilizes voters, organizes the government for those who are successful at the polls, and helps recruit new personnel for both these tasks. For citizens, parties supply information about political issues, clarify and simplify alternatives, and offer a choice among solutions. In addition, because political parties are continuing bodies, the citizenry can hold them responsible for achievements and failures, primarily by rewarding or punishing candidates at the next election.

Over the years, the American party system has developed three principal characteristics. First, at the national level, it is a two-party system. Since the 1790s, there have almost always been two, and only two, serious contestants for control of the national government. Second, the parties usually agree on many fundamentals of political philosophy and do not offer radically different programs to the voters. Third, each of the two national parties is decentralized. Party policy is more likely to be the result of bargaining among leaders at many levels of the party structure than of decisions made at the top.

⭐ PARTIES AND INTEREST GROUPS

Before examining these characteristics of American political parties, we need to distinguish between political parties and interest groups. As we saw in the last chapter, an interest group is typically concerned with a single public policy or a set of related policies. In contrast, political parties involve themselves with a wide range of public policies. Specifically and more fundamentally, parties try to win control of the machinery of government in order to make those policies effective.

To attain its more limited goals, an interest group normally uses one or more of three basic techniques: electioneering, lobbying, and propagandizing. In electioneering, the group helps a party or individual candidates who appear favorably disposed to the group's objectives. Lobbying is an effort to persuade public officials, whatever their initial feeling about a group, to adopt and enforce its policies. Propagandizing is a longer-range version of the other two techniques. Essentially, it consists of "educating" the public to believe in the group's objectives and so to elect officials sympathetic to the group's goals.

Political parties also use these three techniques—including lobbying among their own members holding public office, because party leaders cannot always count on their support. For a party, however, the main techniques are, in the short run, electioneering and, over the longer haul, propagandizing. Interest groups may use these techniques to help a few candidates win office or to gain support on a small cluster of issues; party leaders are aiming for control of the government itself. The policy is *the* objective for interest group leaders. For most party leaders, on the other hand, policies are usually intermediate steps toward the primary goal of winning the next election.

Occasionally, an interest group that commands a large following is tempted to enter more directly into electoral affairs by becoming a political party. The Prohibition party, a one-issue organization that sought a ban on sale of alcoholic beverages in the years before adoption of the Eighteenth Amendment, provides a good example. So do the foes of abortion who run candidates under the banner of the Right to Life party. For most groups, however, direct electoral involvement as a political party has few attractions. The variety of interests in the United States means that any group with limited aims will appeal to no more than a small segment of voters. Moreover, given the way in which the electoral system is organized, narrow appeals are not likely to win any elections at the federal level and few at the state or even local level. On the other hand, if a well-organized interest group shrewdly bargains for the support of a party or candidate in exchange for help at the polls, the benefits can be both immediate and relatively inexpensive.

Unions, representing a large and frequently well-organized minority, have been most often tempted to form parties. Labor parties have been organized in England, Ireland, Australia, and other countries, as well as in a few American states. Their efforts have met with some success, for labor in a highly industrialized area is a sufficiently numerous group to have a chance of winning an election. But labor's electoral prospects are not good unless a labor party is able to broaden its appeal to include farmers, professionals, tradespeople, or other groups.

Interest groups function more easily as political parties in countries that use an electoral system based on proportional representation. To win seats under proportional representation, parties need secure only a small proportion of the popular vote. Once in parliament, a narrowly based party may be able to negotiate its way into a governmental coalition and so exercise considerable direct influence on public policy. In the United States, however, a successful candidate usually must obtain a majority of the vote. Thus, most groups are discouraged from creating political parties to advance their particular interests.

THE TWO-PARTY SYSTEM

The Constitution is silent about political parties and about such important party matters as presidential nominating conventions and direct primary elections, and legislative caucuses. Because political parties were known in 1787 (though not in the modern sense), the Founding Fathers' omission was probably deliberate. At the end of his presidency, George Washington expressed the attitude of many of the Founding Fathers when he warned against the "baneful effects of the spirit of party." It is also probable that some members of the Philadelphia convention realized the inevitability of political parties in American government. James Madison seemed to sense this in *The Federalist*, Number 10, published in November 1787:

> A landed interest, a manufacturing interest, a mercantile interest, a monied interest, with many lesser interests, grow up of necessity in civilized nations, and divide them into different classes, actuated by different sentiments and views. The regulation of these various and interfering interests forms the principal task of modern legislation, and involves the spirit of party and faction in the necessary and ordinary operations of government.

Development of the Two-Party System

Whatever the thoughts and wishes of the men at the Philadelphia, by the beginning of Washington's second administration, two political parties were already operating. Washington himself had come under the influence of Alexander Hamilton and consistently sided with him against Thomas Jefferson in controversies over public policy. This factional dispute within the cabinet became a party battle when Jefferson and James Madison created a coalition of small property owners and farmers to oppose Hamilton's policies. In 1793, Jefferson resigned from the cabinet, and in a few years the *Republicans* (as the Jeffersonians called themselves) were a full-fledged political party, challenging the administration's pro-British foreign policy and conservative economic policies.

During this period, the followers of Washington and Hamilton preempted for themselves the name of *Federalists*, although the Jeffersonian ranks included many of those who had led the original Federalist cause in the fight for adoption of the Constitution. The new Federalists, like the old, were pre-dominantly an elite group composed of men of wealth and substance. In contrast to the imaginative and energetic Federalist campaign of 1787–1788 in support of the Constitution, the new Federalists were curiously negligent about forming local party organizations to compete with Jefferson's Republicans for support among the growing electorate. Out of touch with new voters and lacking the machinery to

The familiar party symbols—the Democratic donkey and the Republican elephant—were well established by the end of the nineteenth century. (The Bettmann Archive, Inc.)

mobilize conservative voters, the Federalists were routed in the election of 1800. By 1816 they had ceased to exist as a party. The lesson of their disaster was not lost, however. Leaders of all succeeding parties have realized that to win office one must win votes; and to win votes one must have organizations working at every electoral level.

After the disappearance of the Federalists, the nation experienced a short period of one-party rule. Although the surviving party—Jefferson's Republicans—tried to encompass all political viewpoints, it could not satisfy every political, economic, and social interest. In the 1820s two warring factions developed within the party, the Democratic Republicans and the National Republicans. The split grew until by 1840 each of the two factions, now called *Democrats* and *Whigs*, had taken on the character of a national party.

Through the mid-1850s the two parties fought on almost even terms. But with the death of Whig leaders like Henry Clay and Daniel Webster and the worsening crisis over slavery, the Whig coalition between eastern capital and southern planters disintegrated. Of the various third parties competing for national status, the new *Republican* party was most attractive to Whigs as well as to many northern Democrats. In 1856, the Republicans rallied behind General John C. Fremont and made a respectable showing in the presidential campaign. In 1860, their candidate, Abraham Lincoln, carried only a minority of the popular vote but won a solid majority in the Electoral College. The Democrats and Republicans had become the main contestants in the American two-party system.

They were to remain so. No third party has come even close to capturing the White House in the years since 1860. Only in 1912, when the progressive wing of the Republican party broke from the regulars to nominate Theodore Roosevelt as the Bull Moose candidate, has a third party polled as many votes as the losing candidate of the major parties. Yet third parties have continued to have a voice in American politics. Former Vice-President Henry Wallace and Senator Strom Thurmond ran serious third-party campaigns for the presidency in 1948, as did Governor George Wallace in 1968 and Representative John Anderson in 1980.

Why Two Parties?

One of the questions that has most puzzled foreign observers of American politics is why the United States has a two-party rather than a multiparty system. Most modern democracies have multiparty systems, including England and Canada. There is no satisfactory single answer; instead, a number of forces have encouraged a two-party system.

First, there are historical factors. The colonists brought with them a two-party tradition. It is easy to exaggerate its influence, however, be-

"People are forgetting their old patriotisms. . . . like 'our party, right or wrong!' "

Grin and Bear It, by Lichty and Wagner, © 1975 Field Enterprises, Inc. Courtesy of Field Newspaper Syndicate

cause England in the eighteenth century did not have a party system in the modern sense. Yet the factional divisions between British Whigs and Tories had some effect on colonial ideas of politics. After independence, Federalists and Antifederalists divided over the adoption of the Constitution. A few years later came the split between the Federalists in power and the Jeffersonians out of power. The basic appeal to two social groups—by the Federalists to men of means and substance, and by the Jeffersonians first to small farmers and later also to the growing working classes in the cities—set the pattern that exists today.

Certain American institutions have also played a role in creating and preserving a two-party system. First, the framers of the Constitution chose a presidential rather than parliamentary form of government. Masses of voters owing allegiance to three or more parties will have more difficulty selecting a president than a majority of multiparty representatives in a legislature will have in compromising their differences and picking a prime minister. The constitutional requirement of majority agreement, whether the president is chosen by the Electoral College or by the House of Representatives, has further limited the number of presidential candidates and thus the number of political parties. The election of a single chief executive in each state and at local levels has also encouraged would-be factions to unite behind a single candidate and aim for that golden target, a majority vote.

Another institutional arrangement that has operated to foster a two-party system is the election of members of Congress from individual districts. In a single-member district only one party can win an election.* In such circumstances third parties are discouraged unless they can achieve voting strength sufficient to compete with the established major parties. The Constitution does not demand election of members of the House of Representatives from single-member districts, but Congress has by law required single-member districts throughout most of American history. Furthermore, the election of senators from a particular state in different years makes each state a single-member district for senatorial elections.

As a result of these structural features, third-party candidacies must surmount the fear that votes cast for the third party will not only be wasted but may help elect the candidate that a voter prefers least. In 1980, supporters of President Carter hammered away at the theme that votes by dissident Democrats for the third-party candidacy of Representative John Anderson would help put Ronald Reagan in the White House. At the same time, Republicans who were attracted to Anderson were urged to return to the fold in order to prevent Carter's re-election. By election day, defections from Anderson dropped his final share of the popular vote to 7 percent, less than half the support that polls had indicated at the start of the campaign.

Social factors have been more important than electoral arrangements in maintaining the American two-party system. Where a society is beset by political cleavages based on geographic, socioeconomic, ethnic, or religious lines, conditions are ripe for a multiparty system. Where there is relatively little class consciousness and where political divisions cut across religious, ethnic, geographic, and socioeconomic lines, a two-party system has a far better chance of taking firm root. In such a situation, "the stakes of politics are smaller, and the kinds of tolerance, compromise, and concession necessary for a two party system's majoritarian parties can prevail."[1]

There is class consciousness in the United States, as we saw in Chapter 2, as well as significant societal divisions along economic,

---

* A single-member district elects one representative to a legislative body. Districts that elect two or more legislative representatives are known as multimember districts.

Steve Greenberg, Daily News, Los Angeles

ethnic, religious, geographic, and, most important, racial lines. Each of the two major parties does tend to direct its appeal to certain groups, and, as Chapter 8 will indicate, these groups often respond positively. Compared to countries such as France and Italy, however, class and other social divisions are relatively indistinct among whites in the United States. As long as blacks and other racial minorities were politically passive, racial differences imposed only limited stresses on the governmental system.

Appreciating the relative political, if not psychological, homogeneity of the white electorate, leaders of both parties have always tried to appeal to a wide spectrum of interests. Each party may gather its basic strength from particular economic and social groups, but each has usually tried to gain support from all segments of society. It has been a rare platform that has not offered something to all parts of society. But the growing significance of racial cleavages has complicated the task of building biracial coalitions. In 1968 and 1972 the Republican party developed a "southern strategy," which gave up any hope of winning the black vote of the northeast. The Republicans successfully concentrated on capturing the white vote in the south and picking up enough support from traditional Republicans and worried white Democrats in the border states, the midwest, and California, as well as working-class whites in urban areas, to obtain a majority in the Electoral College. In 1976 and 1980 the Republicans shifted their appeal more toward the rapidly growing states of the sunbelt, in the process continuing to ignore black voters, an overwhelming majority of whom supported the Democratic ticket in these presidential elections.

Consequences of the Two-Party System

Because there are only two major parties, it is probable that in a presidential election year one or the other will win both the presidency and a majority of both houses of Congress. The peculiarities of the American electoral system make it possible, of course, for one party to gain the

TABLE **6-1**   **Party Control of Presidency and Congress, 1945–1982**

Years	President	House	Senate
1945–46	Democratic	Democratic	Democratic
1947–48	Democratic	Republican	Republican
1949–50	Democratic	Democratic	Republican
1951–52	Democratic	Democratic	Democratic
1953–54	Republican	Republican	Republican
1955–56	Republican	Democratic	Democratic
1957–58	Republican	Democratic	Democratic
1959–60	Republican	Democratic	Democratic
1961–62	Democratic	Democratic	Democratic
1963–64	Democratic	Democratic	Democratic
1965–66	Democratic	Democratic	Democratic
1967–68	Democratic	Democratic	Democratic
1969–70	Republican	Democratic	Democratic
1971–72	Republican	Democratic	Democratic
1973–74	Republican	Democratic	Democratic
1975–76	Republican	Democratic	Democratic
1977–78	Democratic	Democratic	Democratic
1979–80	Democratic	Democratic	Democratic
1981–82	Republican	Democratic	Republican
1983–84	Republican	Democratic	Republican

Candidate Ronald Reagan seeking blue-collar votes in Youngstown, Ohio, as part of his successful effort to win support from elements of the traditional Democratic coalition. *(Newsweek,* John Ficara)

White House while the other wins a majority of seats in the House and Senate. Such divided victories have happened only three times since 1848, however—in 1956, 1968, and again in 1972, and in each case, a Republican president faced a Democratic Congress. In 1980, Ronald Reagan's decisive victory over Jimmy Carter helped the Republicans capture the Senate, but the Democrats were able to retain their majority in the House of Representatives. It is in off-year elections that the party not in control of the White House is more likely to obtain control of both houses of Congress. Such a division has occurred in six of the twenty-one off-year elections in this century.

By making it possible for one party to control the government, the two-party system puts great pressure on party leaders. To achieve the goal of party control they must win a majority, or close to a majority, of the popular vote. This requirement means that a party cannot concentrate on one interest (for example, big business or organized labor) to the exclusion of all others. Nor can it depend solely on one region of the country (for example, the northeast or the south) for victory. Thus, the two-party system fosters the formation of electoral coalitions. Typically, the Republican party has brought together the financial and corporate interests of the northeast, farmers and small-town residents of the midwest, and white-collar workers, professionals, and other suburbanites throughout the nation. More recently, Republicans have focused attention on the prosperous states in the southwestern, Rocky Mountain, and Pacific Coast regions. The Democrats, on the other hand, have historically united—at least for purposes of electing a president—the south, blue-collar workers in urban areas across the country, a portion of white-collar workers, small farmers, liberals, and blacks.

Exceptions to the Two-Party System

Although basically the United States has a two-party system, certain reservations must be made. First, for long intervals many states have had one-party systems. The south for almost a century after the Civil War offered the most obvious example of a regional one-party system. Furthermore, from 1914 to 1954, in only twenty-six of the then forty-eight states did the minority party win 25 percent or more of presidential, senatorial, and gubernatorial campaigns.[2] Examining elections from 1956 through 1973, Austin Ranney could classify only twenty-three of the fifty states as having truly competitive two-party systems.[3] In most election years, less than half the 435 congressional districts involve serious two-party contests.

In recent years, these one-party monopolies seem to be giving way, both in national elections and, though less markedly, in state campaigns as well. During the 1960s, Republican presidential candidates won Alabama, Georgia, Louisiana, Mississippi, and North Carolina once, and Florida, South Carolina, Tennessee, and Virginia twice. In 1972 Richard Nixon took every state in the old Confederacy from the Democrats. Although the Republicans lost ten of the eleven southern states in 1976, Gerald Ford ran almost as well in the south as he did elsewhere in the nation, winning 45 percent of the popular vote there compared to 49 percent nationally. And in 1980, even an incumbent southern Democrat, Jimmy Carter, lost every southern state but his native Georgia to Ronald Reagan. The results of senatorial and congressional races have been less dramatic, but they tell a similar story of Republican gains. When the Ninety-eighth Congress convened in January 1983, half of the 22 senators from southern states were Republicans, as were 34 of the 116 southern members of the House.

The second reservation that must be made about the two-party system is that third parties have been a constant part of the American political scene. Free Soilers, Greenbackers, Populists, Farmer-Laborites,

Prohibitionists, Bull Moosers, Socialists, Dixiecrats, Progressives, American Independents, and even Communists have won state and national office.

Despite short lifespans and influence restricted to single states or small geographic areas, third parties have often made important contributions to public policy. Many of them have won enough support to threaten the balance of power, and that threat has sometimes forced leaders of major parties to respond to pressures they would have preferred to ignore. Often the third party has taken a more decisive stand on issues than has either of the major parties. But whenever it has appeared that any large number of voters were being attracted to such a party, one (or both) of the major parties has been sufficiently impressed to take over at least a part of the third party's program, thus cutting the ground from under it. For example, the small vote polled by Henry A. Wallace's Progressive party in 1948 resulted in part from the Democratic party's move to the left on civil rights and labor-management relations, a move stimulated by the Progressives' appeal to liberal Democratic voters. So too in 1968 Richard Nixon undercut some of George Wallace's support by implying that a Republican administration would slow down the push for civil rights for blacks. Once in the White House President Nixon continued to erode Wallace's constituency by means of lax enforcement of civil rights laws.

★ PARTIES AND IDEOLOGY

A second key characteristic of the American party system is a lack of fundamental differences between the major parties. Each usually presents to the voters an image that differs from the other's more in matters of rhetoric and style and policy detail than on fundamental issues of political philosophy. Both parties are likely to make appeals to citizens of all social classes and geographical areas. Both accept the basic, though vague, principles of constitutional democracy. Both reject socialism and endorse a free-enterprise system modified by a degree of governmental regulation.

Why Few Basic Differences?

Part of the explanation for the absence of fundamental differences can be traced to the lack of class consciousness of the bitter sort that has divided many nations. Most immigrants knew what a class-riven society was; they bore on their backs and in their souls many of its scars. As each new wave of immigrants came, it was overwhelmed as much as absorbed by America, and for most the old hatreds softened into fears and suspicions. And the newcomers followed the twin American dreams of prosperity and equality. Without a high degree of class antagonism, development of parties with strong commitments to particular programs or ideas becomes very difficult.

In this country an appeal pitched only to blue-collar workers may well fall on uncomprehending, if not deaf, ears, as members of the Students for a Democratic Society discovered in the late 1960s when they moved off the campuses and tried to "radicalize" factory workers. America's relative lack of class consciousness can also be traced to the absence of a feudal tradition, the comparative prosperity of the economy, the existence of a frontier to absorb dissident elements, the ideals of egalitarianism, and the political castration of blacks and radical movements. As a result, the dominant political standards of American society have been those of the middle class. No national party can wander very far from its standards without risking disastrous defeat.

Furthermore, the two-party system encourages formation of coalitions. As we have seen, to control the national government party leaders must make a broad appeal. Given the diversity of American backgrounds, outlooks, aspirations, and loyalties, it has been difficult, even in times of severe crisis, to organize a majority coalition behind a specific and all-encompassing party program. An easier alternative for national party leaders is the vaguely worded statement of ultimate goals— glowing allusions to "The Great Society," for example, or to "binding up the nation's wounds"—with little systematic development of general ideas and few specific proposals for achieving these broad purposes. Even the New Deal was a combination of uncoordinated and at times conflicting individual policies, geared as much to satisfying each of the diverse groups in Roosevelt's grand coalition as to overcoming the Great Depression through a coherent, coordinated governmental system.

An additional factor militating against clearly defined party positions is the indifference of many Americans to politics. Even when people are troubled, public opinion is not likely to be neatly divided into two camps. Just before the 1968 election, after seven years of intense public debate on American policy in Vietnam, the Survey Research Center of the University of Michigan found the following distribution of opinion about what the United States should do:

Pull out of Vietnam entirely	19.5%
Keep our soldiers in Vietnam but try to end the fighting	36.7%
Take a stronger stand even if means invading North Vietnam	33.5%
Other	3.3%
Don't know, no answer	7.0%

Public opinion may also be internally contradictory. The same people who disapprove of big government in Washington and want to cut federal spending may favor building new atomic-powered aircraft carriers, increasing aid to veterans, or expanding highway networks.

Significance of Party Differences

Despite the absence of a deep ideological gap between the major parties, Democrats and Republicans do differ in their general orientations toward public policies. The popular impression of the Democrats as the more liberal and the Republicans as the more conservative party is essentially accurate, although there are liberals and conservatives in each party. Delegates to the two national conventions—a group that includes members of Congress, governors, state and county party leaders, and other party activists—differ markedly along party lines in their attitudes toward a whole series of political issues. Democrats have favored more governmental activity to protect the civil rights of minority groups, more governmental regulation of business, less regulation of labor, more public ownership of natural resources, higher taxes on busi-

TABLE 6-2

Party Unity* Votes in Congress, 1974–1980

		Total roll calls	Party unity roll calls	Percent of total
1980	Both Chambers	1,135	470	41
	Senate	531	243	46
	House	604	227	38
1978	Both Chambers	1,350	510	38
	Senate	516	233	45
	House	834	277	33
1976	Both Chambers	1,349	493	37
	Senate	688	256	37
	House	661	158	36
1974	Both Chambers	1,081	399	37
	Senate	544	241	44
	House	537	158	29

*Party unity roll calls are those on which a majority of voting Democrats oppose a majority of voting Republicans.

SOURCE: *Congressional Quarterly Weekly Report,* January 25, 1975, p. 199; November 13, 1976, pp. 3173–3174; December 16, 1978, p. 3447; and January 19, 1981, p. 79.

ness and upper-income groups, and more of an internationalist orientation toward foreign policy than have Republican leaders.[4]

The different approaches of the two parties can also be seen in a comparison of the concepts of the presidency held by Democratic Presidents Wilson, Franklin Roosevelt, Truman, Kennedy, and Johnson with those of nearly all the Republican incumbents of this century. The most notable Republican exception, Theodore Roosevelt, took a grand view of his office, as did each of the Democrats. For these men, the presidency was a position of dynamic power, a post from which to control the executive bureaucracy, to push social and economic legislation through Congress, to exercise leadership in international affairs, and to shape public opinion in favor of strong governmental action. Republican presidents typically have been less activist, and some, like Taft, Harding, and Coolidge, were very nearly inert. Since World War II, America's expanded role in the world has made Republican presidents as energetic in foreign relations as their Democratic counterparts. In domestic policy, however, Eisenhower, Nixon, Ford, and Reagan generally sought to restrict rather than expand the national government, by stopping Congress from acting, by reducing spending, and by cutting back or eliminating social welfare programs.

Voting records in Congress provide another indication that there is a meaningful difference between the two parties. Party affiliation is the most significant factor associated with congressional voting behavior. While party unanimity is rare in Congress, party cohesion is not. Although party unity has been declining on Capitol Hill, especially in the House, party still exerts a strong pull on most representatives and senators, as Table 6-2 shows.

★ DECENTRALIZATION OF AMERICAN POLITICAL PARTIES

The third important characteristic of the American party system is decentralized organization. Power within each party is diffused. Rather than a chain of command running down from the top of the party hierarchy, there are only many avenues of persuasion, requests, demands, threats, and bargaining. Each of these is a two-way street, and sometimes the traffic in demands and threats is heavier going up than down.

Neither party enlists or organizes members on a national or centralized basis. In fact, membership in either party is difficult if not impossible to define. It does not involve paying dues or subscribing to any particular set of doctrines. Frequently, party membership is nothing more than a state of mind, many people who call themselves Democrats or Republicans never bother to vote. Among those who participate in elections, a vote cast in the party primary is the usual indication of party membership. In most states, a citizen who votes in the primary of one party is barred from voting in the primary of another for a period of several months or years. In a few states, however, primaries are "open," and voters are legally free to change party allegiance and vote in either primary, or both. Nothing, of course, prevents any individual from voting for the other party's candidates at the general election.

Politicians also can switch parties with ease, constrained only by credulity of voters. John Connally was elected Governor of Texas as a Democrat, then switched parties to seek unsuccessfully the Republican presidential nomination in 1980. John Lindsay rose to political prominence as a liberal Republican member of Congress and Mayor of New York City. While Mayor, he became a Democrat and an unsuccessful contender for the presidential nomination of his new party in 1972. And Ronald Reagan, the champion of the Republican right for a decade, is an ex-Democrat.

Decentralization is also apparent in the complexity and disorder of party organizations. Overlap and conflict in organizational structure are common. In addition, formal organization is frequently supplemented by informal organizations that wield actual power. For example, presidential candidates typically put together personal staffs that usurp many of the campaigning functions of their respective national committees. As we have already seen in Chapter 4, federalism also plays an important role in decentralizing American parties because it provides independent bases of political power.

Party Machinery for Winning Elections

Generally speaking, party machinery, whether formal or informal, has one of two functions: winning elections or running the government. Of these two types of party organization, the first is more decentralized.

The basic unit of the party machinery for winning elections corresponds to the basic unit of electoral administration, the *precinct*, or election district. Here, the party organization may consist of only one person, the precinct captain. Particularly in large cities, he or she may have a small staff of assistants, usually part-time volunteers. Historically, it was at the precinct level that most of the personal contact between party officials and party constituencies occurred. Today these grass-roots party organizations have atrophied in much of the nation, particularly in the suburbs and the rapidly growing metropolitan areas of the sunbelt. Above the precinct in urban areas is the *ward organization*, again perhaps consisting of only a few people. The next unit in the party hierarchy is the *county committee,* composed typically of precinct captains. Most of the 3,000-odd county chairmen in each party are influential figures who play a role in nominations, party finance, patronage, and other party matters.

One step above the county committee, at least on paper, is the *state committee.* Depending on local laws and customs, its members may be elected or may hold their offices by virtue of their position in county organizations. The functions that state committees are supposed to perform vary widely from state to state, but they frequently include coordinating the campaign work of county committees, calling state party conventions to nominate candidates for office, and arranging the administrative details for primaries.

Although much of the organization and operation of party machinery at the local and state level is prescribed by state law, party machinery is strictly a matter of custom at the national level. The two parties, however, have established very similar patterns of organization. There are four main agencies, or agents, heading the national parties: the *national convention,* the *national committee,* the *national chairman,* and the *national committee secretariat.* In addition, the parties have *congressional campaign committees* organized and controlled by the party groups in each house of Congress.

The *national convention* is the formal assembly of some 1,200 to 3,200 delegates* from the fifty states and the federal territories, who meet every four years amid television cameras, bunting, bands, and extravagant oratory. The national convention's task is to select the party's candidates for president and vice-president and to determine party policy by writing and approving a document called the *party platform,* in which a stand, forthright or evasive, is taken on the issues of the day. Apart from these functions, the national convention has little authority. It has nothing to do with the nomination of the party's candidates for Congress, nor can it compel congressional candidates to pledge support to the party's platform.

During the four-year period between conventions a party is supposedly run by the *national committee* and the national chairman. The national committees are composed of members from each state, territory, and the District of Columbia. Ordinarily, a national committee meets only on call by the chairman, and such calls are infrequent. Its main task is to determine the date and place of the national convention, often a difficult job, as the competing claims of different cities must be sorted out. The national committee also makes the rules under which delegates to the national convention are chosen. The committee, how-

---

* There is a difference between *delegates* and *votes* in a national convention. Some delegates may have only a half-vote.

Demonstration after the nomination of Ronald Reagan at the National Convention of the Republican party in Detroit, 1980. (© Gilles Peress, Magnum Photos, Inc.)

ever, never actually runs the party, nor does it determine party policy, although it may ratify proposals laid before it by the chairman or party members holding public office. Individual national committee members, however, frequently wield considerable power in their own states and within the federal government.

The *national chairman* is chosen by the national committee every four years after the nomination of the presidential and vice-presidential candidates. In practice the chairman is the personal choice of the presidential nominee, and the committee merely ratifies the name suggested. The first and most important task confronting the new chairman is the party's campaign for the presidency. The national chairman is also ac-

Delegates at the National Convention of the Democratic party, 1980. (© Philip Jones Griffiths, Magnum Photos, Inc.)

tive in congressional campaigns, but here power and responsibility are shared with the Senate and House campaign committees. Between elections, the national chairman's day-to-day duties are varied. He keeps in close touch with state and local party organizations, makes many speeches, and works constantly to raise party funds. Never has a national chairman become a "boss" in the sense that state and local chairmen sometimes have. Rarely does the national chairman have anything to do with the actual operation of the government itself, unless he also holds a governmental post.

The party *secretariat* attracts little attention, but this salaried staff attached to the national committee and its chairman is extremely impor-

RONALD REAGAN

April 30, 1982

Mr. Michael N. Danielson
283 Hartley Avenue
Princeton, New Jersey 08540

Dear Mr. Danielson:

We are in the midst of the biggest political battle waged in our
country in the last forty years. I know the outcome will affect
you directly.

The battle I am talking about is between those who want to
continue the welfare state built on high taxes, massive deficits
and federal subsidies and those who are forced to pay for it: you
the taxpayer.

On numerous occasions I have appeared on national television to
address the American people on the critical issues that we face.
I have repeatedly warned that our nation is in the worst economic
crisis since the Depression.

In response, Congress recently passed major elements of my economic recovery plan. This plan is designed to avert an economic
calamity in the future that could hurt every family in America.

. . .

Over the last few months, the liberal Democrats and their powerful
allies, in and out of the government, have attacked and distorted
every part of our legislative program. And that is just the
beginning.

They will intensify their full-scale attacks in the weeks and
months to come as I submit new legislation to limit the growth of
government and restore our defenses.

It is clear to me the liberal Democrats and the special interest
groups will do everything in their power to reverse the results of
the 1980 election by trying to win a major victory in the 1982
election.

Your contribution will enable our Party to challenge and refute
these political attacks and elect candidates who will vote to
carry out the mandate entrusted to me by the American people in
1980.

Your help will mean a great deal to me personally, and more
importantly, I believe it will help our country.

I will be meeting shortly with Chairman Richards to review these
projects. I will be anxious to know if enough funds have been
raised to expand this nationwide debate and help our candidates
win elective office in 1982.

Sincerely,

Ronald Reagan

Ronald Reagan

RR/klr

In his role as party leader, the president lends his name to a variety of fund-raising
efforts. This letter was sent to potential contributors by the Republican National
Committee as part of the effort to raise funds for Republican congressional
candidates in 1982.

tant to the vitality and the effectiveness of the party. Its organization varies from time to time and from party to party. Its functions are to write speeches for important party members, supply research assistance, help raise money, keep track of political trends, prepare publicity releases, handle correspondence with state and local party agencies, and engage in a great many housekeeping tasks whose successful performance, although not publicized, does much to build party unity and strength for the next campaign. With the growing sophistication of modern fund-raising and campaign methods, technical assistance has become an increasingly important task for the staffs of the national committees. Particularly important are direct mail solicitation, use of radio and television, and computer applications. After the 1980 census, the Republican National Committee undertook an ambitious effort to provide staff and computer assistance to state parties in order to redraw congressional and state legislative district lines to the advantage of Republican candidates.

The national conventions, committees, chairmen, and staff are focused on the presidency; their primary concerns are presidential—nominating the party's candidate, winning the White House, and, for the party in power, serving the political interests of the president. Party members in Congress have created their own national organizations to provide assistance in congressional campaigns. Over the past decade, the role of these groups has expanded, particularly in the House of Representatives. Most active have been the House Republicans, who raised $50 million for the 1982 election, which the Republican Campaign Committee spent on research, television commercials, fund raising, candidate recruitment, and field representatives who provide advice on everything from direct mail techniques to achieving tonsorial splendor with a blow dryer. The other congressional party committees have lagged behind the House Republicans, but all have been increasingly active in raising campaign war chests and providing candidates with help. In the process, these efforts have made congressional elections less localistic, since much of the assistance from Washington emphasizes national issues and campaign themes.[5]

Party Machinery for Running the Government

Party machinery for winning elections has relatively little to do with running the national government. Indeed, any attempt by the national chairman or national committee to exert pressure members of Congress is apt to meet vigorous resistance. To be sure, county chairmen and other party officials offer advice on the distribution of patronage and convey to officeholders requests for favors that may affect the formation or administration of important public policies. More important in Washington, however, are the party organizations that parallel governmental machinery. Each party has units inside Congress, including a caucus, a steering or policy committee, and a floor leader to try to shape policy making. (These we shall examine in Chapter 10.) National party officials are supposed to be in close touch with the executive branch if the party controls the presidency. In reality, the White House staff, other presidential advisers, and the cabinet are more often the instruments through which party control of the administrative aspects of government is exercised.

The president, of course, is the chief of his party. In staffing an administration, presidents seek not only to run the government efficiently but also to keep the party organization together by rewarding friends and punishing enemies. The president's control over party machinery is far from absolute. But his immediate access to the press and the television networks, the enormous prestige of his office, and his power over patronage provides sustained opportunities for him with party leadership. Like it or not, other party leaders have to live with the fact that the public at large usually identifies the president with his party, and the fate of many of the party's candidates at the next election is strongly influenced by the public image of the president.

The opposition party, on the other hand, has no powerful national leader around whom to rally. Supposedly, the leader of the minority party is the defeated presidential nominee, but his actual position is ambiguous. His rejection by the voters to some extent counterbalances his nomination by the party for the nation's highest office, and commonly he is leader in name only. As Adlai Stevenson, twice titular head of the Democratic Party, commented:

> The titular leader has no clear and defined authority within his party. He has no party office, no staff, no funds, nor is there any system of consultation whereby he may be advised of party policy and through which he may help to shape that policy. There are no devices such as the British have developed through which he can communicate directly and responsibly with the leaders of the party in power.[6]

Adding to the difficulties of the titular leader are rivals within the party. Leaders who opposed his nomination are rarely persuaded of the error of their ways by having the electorate confirm their views. Other presidential hopefuls, looking to the next nomination, are rarely eager to increase the power of a prominent rival.

If there were no more to the story, the titular leader's position would be unambiguously impotent. But, as Stevenson himself admitted, the press and public often look on the titular leader as the spokesman of his party. Whether or not he deserves that role, there is rarely any other person who has a legitimate claim to speak for the party. Senators, congressmen, and governors represent interests that are too parochial, and aspiring presidential candidates have not yet won the approval of the national convention. "Despite its ambiguity, perhaps even because of it," three close students of the American party system conclude, "the titular leadership has become a post that offers many opportunities for initiative, at least for a first time incumbent."[7]

Federalism and Party Decentralization

As Chapter 4 pointed out, federalism in the formal governmental structure increases the decentralization of power within the party system. There are more than 79,000 units of government in the United States and more than a half million elective political offices. An independent source of revenue or an elective office means a potentially independent base of power for state and local party leaders and elected officials. Governors or mayors who refuse to support an energy program on which the president's prestige depends cannot be fired by the president, even though they are of the same party. Nor can the president dismiss a senator or representative who consistently attacks the administration's foreign policy or votes against administration bills. Each of these officials is elected by a local or state constituency and is legally responsible only to that constituency. If the locally based official is sure of electoral support, he can thumb his nose at the president, at party colleagues, or at any other official.

Congress has been wary of centralizing power in Washington and usually stipulates that state and local officials share in administering national programs. State and local officials actually spend federal grants, and so power moves away from national party leaders. In addition, almost every member of Congress spends considerable congressional time—and his staff spends even more—talking to administrators about problems constituents at home are experiencing, once again diffusing national party influence. Representatives and senators can apply more formal pressure in questioning agency heads or bureau chiefs during annual appropriations hearings or at special investigations. A president's ability to control his bureaucracy is typically proportional to his ability to control Congress; and seldom can even the most astute president exercise control over senators and House members from his own party.

Decentralization does not always affect parties at the state or local level, and in some areas discipline is strict and real power centered in the hands of one individual or a small group of people. The literature and folklore on colorful, and not always honest, city and county bosses is as enormous as it is fascinating. The fragmented power structure of the national parties has helped bosses run their machines. Decentraliza-

President Carter confers with Democratic governors at Camp David. Party ties provide the president with political supporters among elected officials throughout the nation, but the independent political base of these officials means that support must be cultivated rather than commanded. (White House/United Press International)

tion of government and party power means local control and "plays into the hands of the boss . . . he has contact with all the elements of the party system, but he usually is beyond the authority of any higher echelon of the party. He has and uses the weapons of discipline to keep control over his organization, but he is usually free of effective control or discipline from above."[8]

Increased prosperity, the spread of civil service, wider assumption by governmental agencies of social welfare functions once exercised by party officials to keep poor immigrants loyal, and the declining economies of the industrial cities have cut into the number and efficiency of bosses. Yet disciplined local political organizations survive, particularly in ethnic neighborhoods in northeastern and midwestern cities.

Although these organizations have much less power than in the past, they continue to play an important party role, largely because of their ability to control disciplined blocs of voters in primary elections. Political bosses also survive because some people need, or believe they need, a political broker who listens sympathetically to problems and has enough organizational strength to intervene with a particular government agency. A father, for example, who has denounced politicians and bossism all his life may turn to a state or local political leader when his son or daughter has trouble getting into the medical school of the state university. A contractor who wants a bigger share of paving jobs complains not to a purchasing agent of the county but to its political taskmaster. Citizens like these represent sources of power as much as did the impoverished and disoriented immigrants of the gaslight era. The individual who can help them soon becomes a repository of good will—the substance of which bosses are made.

If Americans widely believe that politicians are engaged in a dirty business, it is partly because many private citizens persist in using party organizations for personal gain, from fixing a traffic ticket to legitimizing by ordinance and statute otherwise illegal business practices worth thousands or even millions of dollars. In locales where machines survive, the party boss and his aides are accessible to citizens who want some governmental act of commission or omission for which they are willing to make some suitable payment. In other areas, a party functionary may merely be an intermediary who "introduces" a citizen to appropriate governmental officials and tries to secure a sympathetic hearing for the individual. Often, particular party leaders are known for their close relationship with governmental officials—one with the police department, another with the prosecutor's office, another with the tax assessor, and so on.

⭐ REFORM OF THE PARTY SYSTEM

At the turn of the century the American party system was the principal target of political reformers. Their specific goal was to curb the power of the boss. To this end they fought for nonpartisan elections, in which candidates' party affiliations would not appear on the ballot. In other areas, they fought for primary elections, which would take the power to nominate candidates away from party leaders. The party system is still the target of political reformers, but ironically the goal of many is now to strengthen party leadership, to centralize power within the parties, to shore up party discipline, and to broaden the representation of women, blacks, younger people, and others within the party structure. The overall objective of the newer critics is to make the parties more responsive to the popular will and more responsible for the behavior of their elected candidates.

The decentralized, compromising character of the national parties has been severely criticized on the ground that such parties fail to fulfill two essential functions. First, they do not present the voters with a clear choice on the really important public issues. Indeed, they frequently fail even to discuss the really important issues. There is, critics charge, "a vast boredom" in American with party politics. "Because it has failed to engage itself with the problems that dog us during our working days and haunt our dreams at night, politics has not engaged the best in us."[9]

The second criticism of the American party system is that its diffusion of power causes a diffusion of responsibility. Because no one individual or one committee or one convention can set party policy, no individual or committee or convention can be held responsible. Some critics argue that the United States usually has a four-party rather than a two-party system, with the Democrats and Republicans each having a congressional party and a presidential party. These fractured parties are not able to effect consistent governmental policies, and the voters are unable to hold either party, as a party, responsible for the action or inaction of its members while in office.

Some political scientists see many virtues in the existing party system. Pendleton Herring argued that a democratic society can survive only where there is a constant reconciliation of conflicting economic and social interests. He claimed that a party politician performs an essential social role by acting as mediator. Herring also defended political parties because they appealed to a wide variety of groups and won their support by offering something to each. "The accomplishment of party government lies in its demonstrated ability for reducing warring interests and conflicting classes to cooperative terms."[10] Herring and others have asserted that the vague ideologies of the two parties make it possible for people who have clashing interests to live together in peace. If the lines of conflict were ever drawn too clearly and the stakes in politics set too high, the danger of the defeated faction's refusing to accept the result of an election would increase. Its members might conclude that, having lost so much, they would be better off opposing the result with violence than permitting the government to pursue unacceptable policies.

★ THE PATTERN OF THE PARTY SYSTEM

We deliberately chose the term "party system" for this chapter, because "to speak of a party *system* is to imply a patterned relationship among elements of a larger whole."[11] What we have described and analyzed is a pattern of relationships. The three main characteristics of the American party system—two parties, with few fundamental differences, and with decentralized organizations—are so interrelated that it is difficult to say which are causes and which are effects of the others, or how the consequences of each shape the consequences of the others.

Because a two-party system encourages efforts to form majorities, it encourages the formation of broad-based electoral coalitions. The relative absence of deep and antagonistic class cleavages also discourages ideological stands, as does a respected written Constitution. These factors also encourage electoral coalitions, which in turn facilitate a two-party rather than a multiparty system. A presidential form of government and a winner-take-all electoral arrangement for congressional seats also encourage two parties and move parties to stress social unity rather than divisiveness. At the same time, such political arrangements are feasible only where class consciousness is low.

A pluralistic society spread over half a continent makes federalism an attractive political arrangement. Federalism, in turn, creates independent bases of power for local politicians and works against disciplined national parties. Undisciplined national parties are not likely to be able to unite on ideology and comprehensive programs. The dangling bait of a majority vote and the apparent middle-of-the-road and rather indifferent political attitude of large portions of the electorate move the parties to make similar appeals to similar groups of voters. At the same time, the similarity of these appeals may tend to make large blocs of voters somewhat lukewarm in their attention to politics and, since they have been educated in an environment of political moderation, to adhere to the middle of the political road.

This reasoning does not lead to a conclusion that the party system is unchanging. In many respects, it has changed over the years and will continue to change in the future. Most important of these changes is the declining importance of political parties to most participants in American politics. As the next chapters indicate, voters are less attached to parties than in the past, candidates rely less on party labels, campaigns are based on television and modern marketing techniques rather than party organizations, and a variety of organizations compete with parties for campaign funds and electoral influence. As indicated in Figure 6-1, the proportion of the population that identifies most strongly with either

FIGURE **6-1**   **Party Identification, 1952–1960**

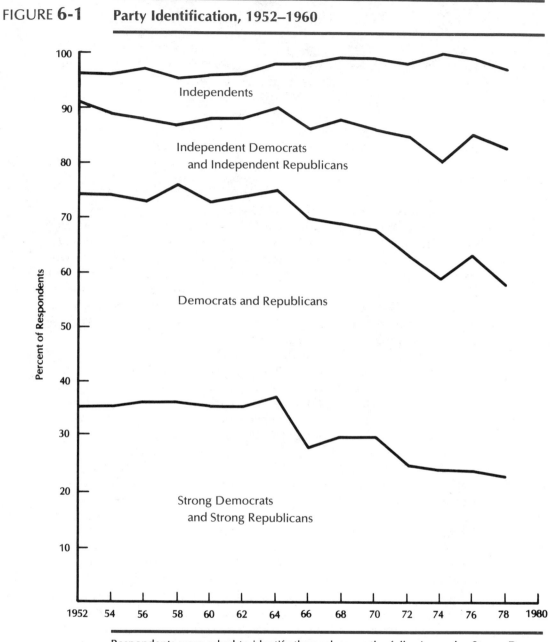

Respondents were asked to identify themselves on the following scale: Strong Democrat, Democrat, Independent Democrat, Independent, Independent Republican, Republican, Strong Republican.

SOURCE: Center for Political Studies, University of Michigan.

party has been declining, while the number of independents and those whose party loyalties are weak has been on the increase. The impact of television has been particularly potent, as emphasized by a recent report on the future of political parties in the United States:

> By giving candidates and officeholders direct access to voters, television has replaced the political party as the principal network of political communication. Moreover, by giving that access to anyone who can afford to buy television time, or is shrewd enough to gain notoriety without buying it, television can also create instant candidates out of theretofore unknown persons, persons who, without television, would have had to invest years of party activity and survive the judgment of peers and party officials before having the opportunity to go before the voters.[12]

Pressures for change also come from within the parties, particularly from partisan activists who would like to transform their party into a more coherent and ideological organization. In 1964, conservatives sought to swing the Republican party sharply to the right, a move that if successful would have brought about sweeping changes in the nature of the party system. The stinging defeat of Senator Barry Goldwater in the 1964 presidential election convinced Republican leaders to halt the voters' abandonment of their party by uniting behind Richard Nixon, who was more moderate on most issues than Goldwater and his supporters. In 1972, many of Senator George McGovern's backers and at times the candidate himself saw his campaign as an effort to restructure the party system by moving the Democratic party decisively to the left. The disastrous results of that election convinced most Democratic leaders that a feasible reshaping of the party system cannot stray too far from the middle of the political road.

Despite the apparent lessons of these elections, a substantial faction of the Republican party under the banner of Ronald Reagan sought in the 1970s to transform the GOP into an avowedly conservative party. For Reagan, "a political party is not a fraternal order. A party is something where people are bound together by a shared philosophy."[13] Reagan's victory in the 1980 presidential election brought into office the most conservative national administration in half a century. But the Republican party under Reagan continued to encompass a broad sweep of the political spectrum, and within its scope there was considerable disagreement on the tenets of a shared philosophy. And, predictably, the loudest complaints came from the ideologues on the Republican right, who criticized Reagan for appointing too many moderates, for softening his stance on China and the Soviet Union, for embracing huge federal deficits, and for failing to press aggressively for constitutional amendments on abortion and school prayer.

Richard Wright, The Providence Journal-Bulletin. Reprinted by permission of United Feature Syndicate, Inc.

Thinking in terms of interrelated components of a party system does not imply that positive steps should not be taken to reform that system. What the concept of a party system does indicate is that reform is a much more difficult process than merely tinkering with the mechanics of party organization. The concept of a party system suggests that successful reform of the party system is likely to have widespread effects throughout the entire governmental and social system in the United States. If power within the parties were to be effectively centralized and if they were thus converted into disciplined, programmatic bodies, headed by leaders who had real power, changes in the basic structure of American politics would follow. Not only would relations between the president and Congress be affected, relations between the nation and the fifty states would also change. Furthermore, fusion of the scattered fragments of power into the hands of leaders of disciplined parties might very well materially affect the relationship of the individual to government. Far-reaching changes also would result from the reorientation of the parties along sharply defined ideological lines.

The existing splintering of power makes governmental action difficult and thus often frustrates demands for new and needed policies. But by making governmental action difficult, that splintering also sometimes helps protect individuals and minorities against oppressive governmental action.

⭐ SUMMARY

Political parties perform extremely important functions in a modern democracy. They mobilize electoral support at the polls, simplify alternatives for voters, dramatize issues and candidates, and provide a means of organizing government after elections. Unlike interest groups, which usually concentrate on a particular policy goal, political parties seek to win control of the machinery of government. In the United States, a party system has evolved characterized by the existence of two major parties that are highly decentralized and not separated by fundamental social, economic, or ideological differences. The result is a party system that encourages the formation of governing majorities, but does not provide sufficient party cohesion or discipline to permit parties to dominate the government.

NOTES

1. Frank Sorauf, *Political Parties in the American System* (Boston: Little, Brown, 1964), p. 30.
2. Austin Ranney and Wilmore Kendall, *Democracy and the American Party System* (New York: Harcourt Brace, 1956), pp. 161–164.
3. Austin Ranney, "Parties in State Politics," in Herbert Jacob and Kenneth N. Vines, eds., *Politics in the American States: A Comparative Analysis*, 2d ed. (Boston: Little, Brown, 1971), p. 87. See also Duane Lockard, *The Politics of State and Local Government*, 2d ed. (New York: Macmillan, 1969), pp. 176–177.
4. Herbert McClosky, Paul Hoffman, and Rosemary O'Hara, "Issue Conflict and Consensus among Party Leaders and Followers," *American Political Science Review* LIV (1960), 406–427.
5. See Steven V. Roberts, "Parties' Outlook: Distinctly National," *New York Times*, May 4, 1982.
6. Adlai Stevenson, *What I Think* (New York: Harper, 1956), pp. ix–x.
7. Paul T. David, Ralph Goldman, and Richard Bain, *The Politics of National Party Conventions* (Washington: Brookings Institution, 1960), p. 84.

8. Lockard, *The Politics of State and Local Government*, p. 211.
9. James M. Burns, *The Deadlock of Democracy*, rev. ed. (Englewood Cliffs, N.J.: Prentice-Hall, 1963), p. 1.
10. Pendleton Herring, *The Politics of Democracy* (New York: Henry Holt, 1940), p. 132.
11. V. O. Key, Jr., *Politics, Parties, and Pressure Groups* (New York: Thomas Y. Crowell, 1964), p. 206.
12. *The Future of American Political Parties*. The Sixty-Second American Assembly, April 15–18, 1981, Arden House, Harriman, N.Y.
13. Quoted in Jon Nordheimer, "Reagan Urges His Party to Save Itself by Declaring Its Conservative Beliefs," *New York Times*, December 16, 1976.

SELECTED BIBLIOGRAPHY

Agar, Herbert. *The Price of Union* (Boston: Houghton Mifflin, 1945). Stresses the role that political parties have played in American history in furthering compromise and building consensus.

Bass, Jack, and Walter DeVries. *The Transformation of Southern Politics* (New York: Basic Books, 1976). An informed effort to update the analysis in Key's *Southern Politics* listed below.

Binkley, Wilfred E. *American Political Parties*, 4th ed. (New York: Alfred A. Knopf, 1963). Provides historical background for the present-day party system.

Burnham, Walter Dean. *Critical Elections and the Mainsprings of American Policies* (New York: W. W. Norton, 1970). A "revisionist" interpretation of American politics that argues that the party system will undergo drastic realignment.

Converse, Phillip E. *The Dynamics of Party Support* (Beverly Hills, Calif.: Sage Publications, 1976). An analysis of the factors influencing party identification.

Crotty, William J., and Gary Jacobson, *American Parties in Decline* (Boston: Little, Brown, 1980). An inquiry into the nature and causes of the declining role of political parties in the United States.

Fairlie, Henry. *Republicans and Democrats in This Century* (New York: St. Martin's Press, 1978). An English journalist's iconoclastic view of party politics in the United States.

Greenstein, Fred I. *The American Party System and the American People*, 2d ed. (Englewood Cliffs, N.J.: Prentice-Hall, 1970). A short but insightful introduction to American parties.

Hofstadter, Richard. *The Idea of a Party System: The Rise of Legitimate Opposition in the United States, 1780–1840* (Berkeley: University of California Press, 1969). An analysis by a distinguished historian of the gradual establishment of what we have come to call political parties.

Key, V. O., Jr. *Politics, Parties, and Pressure Groups*, 5th ed. (New York: Thomas Y. Crowell, 1964). The last edition of the standard—and, in many ways, the classic—textbook on American political parties.

———. *Southern Politics in State and Nation* (New York: Alfred A. Knopf, 1949). A brilliant analysis of the politics of one section of the United States.

Lipset, Seymour Martin, ed. *Party Coalitions in the 1980s* (New Brunswick, N.J.: Transaction Books, 1981). A collection of essays explores the implications of the 1980 election for the Democrats and Republicans.

Schattschneider, E. E. *The Struggle for Party Government* (College Park, Md.: University of Maryland Press, 1948). In contrast to volumes by Agar, Herring, and others, this pamphlet presents a plea for stronger and more highly disciplined parties.

Sundquist, James L. *Dynamics of the Party System* (Washington: Brookings Institution, 1973). An analysis of party realignments, which seeks to explain changes in the American party system.

7 Elections and Campaigns

In discussing the American party system, Chapter 6 spoke of winning public office—gaining control of government—as the primary goal of political parties and the chief characteristic setting them apart from interest groups. This chapter looks at the electoral process, the means by which the national political system as a functioning constitutional democracy chooses all of its legislators and two of its executive officials.

⭐ SUFFRAGE AND DEMOCRACY

A minimum requirement of democratic government is that *principal officers who make public policy should be elected by the people for limited terms.* Although hardly controversial, this prescription leaves open such vital questions as who are the "principal officers," from what constituencies shall different sets of officers be chosen, what constitutes a "limited term," and, of course, just who are "the people."

"Principal Officers"

There is no objective test to distinguish "principal officers" from minor political officials. Certainly heads of executive offices such as the attorney general and the secretary of defense make important policy decisions, but to some extent so do almost all governmental officials. At the national level, only those principal officers who serve as president, vice-president, and members of Congress are elected. Far more offices are elective at the state and local level. Indeed, some states overwhelm voters with a "jungle ballot," a long list of candidates for offices ranging from governor, lieutenant governor, state cabinet members such as the attorney general, three levels of judges, state legislators, county officials, local council members, mayor, and coroner. There are more than half a million elected officials serving in state and local governments, compared to the 537 elected federal officials—a president and vice-president, 100 senators, and 435 representatives. Voters seldom even know the names of the candidates for most state and local offices, and where candidates' party identification is unclear, choice has a large element of randomness.

Constituencies

American colonial history made it inevitable that national legislators would be chosen from within the states. Once the Constitutional Convention had decided that there was to be a single executive who would not be selected by or from Congress, a national constituency became necessary for the election of the president.

"Limited Terms"

"Limited terms" posed additional problems for the framers; and in their typical fashion, they adopted a pragmatic compromise: two years for members of the House of Representatives, six for senators, and four for the president, all being eligible for re-election. Like many compromises, this solution has not ended debate. Proposals have frequently been

D. Reilly, © 1981 The New Yorker Magazine, Inc.

ELECT CHALMERS

HE DOESN'T KNOW MUCH MORE THAN YOU DO.

made to lengthen representatives' terms to four years and to restrict the number of terms a national legislator may serve. In the latter vein, the Twenty-second Amendment limits a president to two four-year terms or, if the president initially takes office on the death or disability of the incumbent, to a maximum of ten years.

"The People"

The framers spoke eloquently of "We, the people," but they skillfully avoided offering any definition of who those people were. Alexander Hamilton's alleged reference to the people as a "great beast" probably did not accurately reflect the delegates' sentiments. Nevertheless, many of them deeply feared democracy. As we saw in Chapter 3, the framers wanted popular *approval* of the political system but not necessarily much active popular *participation*. As part of their artful dodging, they left the question of suffrage—the right to vote—pretty much to the states. Senators were to be elected by state legislatures, representatives by voters who possessed "the qualifications requisite for electors to the most numerous branch of the state legislature," and members of the Electoral College, who formally choose the president, were to be selected in each state "in such manner as the legislature thereof may direct." Again, this compromise marked the beginning, not the end, of debate and development.

★ THE MARCH TOWARD "ONE PERSON, ONE VOTE"

As the idea of equality gained strength and its logic extended to politics, the concept of "one person, one vote" gradually became an ideal of American political culture.

Constitutional Changes

Formal constitutional amendments have played a part in broadening the suffrage and in shifting control over decisions about who can vote from the states to the federal government. The Supreme Court has ruled that, in forbidding states to deny persons equal protection of the laws, the Fourteenth Amendment generally prohibits discriminatory regulations of the right to vote. The Fifteenth Amendment, specifically bars state or federal abridgment of the right to vote "on account of race, color, or previous condition of servitude." The Nineteenth Amendment, which became part of the Constitution in 1920, forbids discrimination in voting because of sex. The Seventeenth Amendment, adopted in 1913, provides for direct, popular election of U.S. senators by those persons qualified to vote for members of Congress. The Twenty-third Amendment, which went into force in 1961, gives the District of Columbia three votes in the Electoral College, but makes no provision for elected representation of Washington's residents in Congress. The Twenty-fourth Amendment, operable since 1964, forbids denial of the right to vote because of failure to pay poll taxes* or other levies, and the Twenty-sixth Amendment, adopted in 1971, lowers the minimum voting age to eighteen.

Formal constitutional amendments tell only a small part of the story of the expansion of voting rights. White, male suffrage had become almost universal before the Civil War, and these advances had come through political processes at the state level. Furthermore, when constitutional amendments have been successful, they have reflected earlier changes in political attitudes. For example, before the Seventeenth Amendment was proposed, most states already had provided for popular choice of senators. Similarly, adoption of the Twenty-fourth amendment occurred after the poll tax was no longer a significant factor in the exclusion of blacks and other poor southerners from the polls. The story was much the same with the Nineteenth Amendment's extension of suffrage to women. Adoption in 1920 climaxed nearly a century of agitation, marked toward the close by mass demonstrations, violence, and jailings. But the amendment came after fifteen states had granted full female suffrage and many others had conferred limited voting rights. The Twenty-sixth Amendment also came after years of debate over the unfairness of drafting eighteen-year-olds into the armed forces while refusing to allow them to participate in choosing officials who decided on war and peace.

The history of the Fourteenth and Fifteenth Amendments was radically different. They were not anchored in established customs, nor were they products of long debates on black suffrage; even many abolitionists had argued before and during the Civil War against allowing freed slaves to vote. Moreover, in southern states, where almost all blacks then lived, the amendments lacked legitimacy among the white majority. Not only did they violate the wishes of most whites, but the Radical Republicans—those in control in Washington—had also made ratification of these two amendments a prerequisite for southern states to regain their prewar status. Worsening the situation was a general lack

---

* A *poll tax* is a general tax of a fixed amount, levied on all persons, regardless of income or property. The tax was used to establish a citizen's eligibility to vote, and payment was a prerequisite to receiving a ballot. Those who did not wish to vote usually did not have to pay the tax. To increase its effect on the poor, the poll tax typically was cumulative. Failure to pay the tax for the two previous elections meant that a citizen had to pay for all three years before being permitted to vote in the next election.

of even elementary political knowledge among newly freed slaves and consequent scarcity of black leadership. These amendments thus represented the hopes of a group of northern whites and blacks only temporarily dominant in the federal government. But without a strong base of power in either the north or the south, the amendments signaled merely a small beginning to full political participation by blacks.

Black Ballots

Historically, southern whites used three different means of keeping blacks from the polls. The first, simply physical violence, or threats of violence, was patently illegal, although no less effective for this fact. The second means, economic reprisal—for example, firing a black who tried to vote or denying the individual credit at local stores—was also sometimes illegal but more subtly so. Third, there was a continuous search for a "legal" means of keeping blacks from voting: "literacy" tests administered in such a way as to allow discrimination against blacks and poor whites; "grandfather clauses" that permitted a citizen to vote without taking a literacy test if his or her grandfather had voted; "white primaries" that barred blacks from participation in primary elections, which until recently were the real elections in the one-party south; and poll taxes that discriminated against lower-income whites as well as blacks.

The Supreme Court declared many of these legal charades unconstitutional, but southern officials could pass new laws as fast as judges could invalidate them. Blacks trying to register for the first time were often confronted with a battery of evasive maneuvers. Some registrars held office hours at irregular times and were simply not available when blacks showed up. Other registrars arbitrarily refused to accept such standard identification as a driver's license, or required that a prospective black voter bring in two already registered voters (that is, whites) to identify him. There were also cases in which registrars rejected black applicants for such minor errors as underlining rather than circling "Mr." on an application form.

Not until after the Supreme Court's ruling in 1954 on school segregation did public and official moods become receptive to national legislative and administrative action to end discriminatory voting practices.[1] After passing a pair of ineffective statutes in 1957 and 1960, Congress, prodded anew by federal judges, by the U.S. Commission on Civil Rights, and by the growing political power of northern blacks, zeroed in on the principal evils of literacy tests and other discriminatory procedures for registering voters. The Civil Rights Act of 1964 made a sixth-grade education a presumption of literacy and required that all literacy tests be administered in writing, unless the attorney general gave special

Blacks flock to the polls in rural Peacetree, Alabama, in 1966, part of the dramatic increase in voting by southern blacks which resulted from enactment of the Voting Rights Act of 1965. (United Press International)

permission. The statute also forbade unequal administration of registration requirements and made it illegal for state officials to refuse to allow a prospective voter the franchise because of immaterial errors on registration forms.

Although more effective than its predecessors, this statute proved to be defective in many respects, leading Congress to pass a new law in 1965, the Voting Rights Act. The heart of the 1965 statute—which applies to all elections, state or national, primary or general—is a series of specific, practical remedies. This act allowed the attorney general to suspend operation of any state or local voting test of literacy, education, or character that he believed had been used to discriminate. It also provided that any new local or state regulations affecting voting rights had to be approved by the attorney general. In 1975 Congress simplified the statute by outlawing all literacy tests. The Voting Rights Act also allows the attorney general to declare that federal supervision is necessary to ensure fair voting in a particular locality.

This federal show of force encouraged black organizations to intensify their registration drives in the south and in the north as well. The number of enrolled black voters climbed dramatically. As a result, blacks became an important voting force even in the deep south, and increasing numbers of blacks were elected in constituencies with substantial black populations. The growing power of blacks at the polls also was a significant factor in producing lopsided majorities in Congress in 1982 for an extension and strengthening of the Voting Rights Act. Particularly important was the new provision which instructed the federal courts to consider the "totality of circumstances" in cases of alleged discrimination in voting. The new language was prompted by decisions of the Supreme Court which had held that blacks must prove that discrimination had been intentional, which is far more difficult to demonstrate than a discriminatory effect in the light of the "totality of circumstances."

Current Voting Requirements

Today voters are required to meet four general conditions. These pertain to citizenship, age, residence, and registration. There is nothing in the Constitution that limits voting to citizens, and in the past states allowed aliens to vote. Now, however, citizenship is an absolute requirement in every state. Historically, states have also required citizens to be residents for rather lengthy periods before they could vote, often twelve months or occasionally even several years. In an amendment to the Voting Rights Act in 1970, Congress effectively eliminated residence requirements for voting in presidential elections. Two years later, the Supreme Court declared a Tennessee law requiring a year's residence to vote in a state election to be a violation of equal protection of the law. Thirty days, the justices said, provided ample time for the state to prevent fraud, but in 1973 the Court sustained a state requirement of fifty days' residence.[2]

Each state administers these requirements by means of a system of registration. Typically, a prospective voter must go to a local governmental office during specified times of the year, offer proof of age, residence, citizenship, and have his or her name entered on the electoral rolls. Most states now provide for permanent registration; that is, once a voter is enrolled he or she may continue to vote at each election. To prevent fraudulent voting through use of names of those who have died or moved away, some states require registration every few years.

While useful in keeping elections honest, registration is a deterrent to voting, particularly when offices are not open year round or periodic registration is necessary. Seldom are even two-thirds of people otherwise eligible to vote actually registered. Those who do not register are disproportionately black, Latino, poor, and under thirty, and are also more likely to be Democrats than Republicans.

Voting and Legislative Apportionment

Apportionment involves distribution of seats in a legislature among electoral districts. Unfair apportionment of legislative seats may dilute the value of a vote. That dilution can be accomplished by *gerrymandering*—drawing lines of electoral districts to give one party, area, or set of interest groups advantages over others either by making districts unequal in population or by placing boundaries in such a fashion that certain interests are likely always to lose. Malapportionment may also result from inaction in the face of major shifts of population. As late as 1964 it was common to find urban and suburban congressional districts with populations three to four times those of rural districts in the same state, and imbalances were even more dramatic in most state legislatures.

In 1962, the Supreme Court made a landmark decision, ruling in *Baker v. Carr* that it was a violation of the Constitution for a state to allow the lower house of its legislature to become malapportioned.[3] Two years later, the Court extended *Baker* and held that states had a constitutional obligation to ensure that the districts from which members of the U.S. House of Representatives are chosen are approximately equal in population.[4]

Then in 1964, *Reynolds v. Sims* held that both houses of a state legislature had to be apportioned on the basis of population.[5] The Court said that the democratic ideal of "one person, one vote" was a constitutional command subject only to the specific exceptions of the U.S. Senate and the Electoral College. "Legislators," Chief Justice Earl Warren wrote for the Court, "represent people, not trees or acres. Legislators are elected by voters, not farms or cities or economic interests." During the 1970s, the Supreme Court moved away from the near-mathematical uniformity among districts that had been demanded by the Warren Court. While retaining the general principle of "one person, one vote," the Court under Chief Justice Warren Burger has permitted states rather wide leeway in applying that maxim, allowing, for instance, Virginia's electoral districts to vary in population by as much as 16.4 percent.[6]

Advocates of reapportionment had hoped that reform would produce better-qualified legislators, more effective law-making institutions, and greater concern for urban problems. More equitable apportionment certainly has helped produce more diversified legislative bodies, as more women, blacks, Latinos, and younger Americans have been elected in the two decades following *Baker v. Carr*. Metropolitan areas also are far better represented in Congress and state legislatures than in the past. But most of these seats have gone to suburban areas and the newer cities of the south and west rather than the older industrial cities, whose declining population has led to losses rather than gains in legislative representation in recent years.

New district lines often have been drawn to protect incumbents. This kind of bipartisan logrolling reflects interests that professional politicians share with each other, regardless of party. "It is hardly surprising," one scholar has commented, "that legislators, like businessmen, have collaborated with their normal adversaries to eliminate dangerous competition."[7]

Moreover, it is practically impossible to draw electoral districts without conferring some partisan advantages; and, where one party has

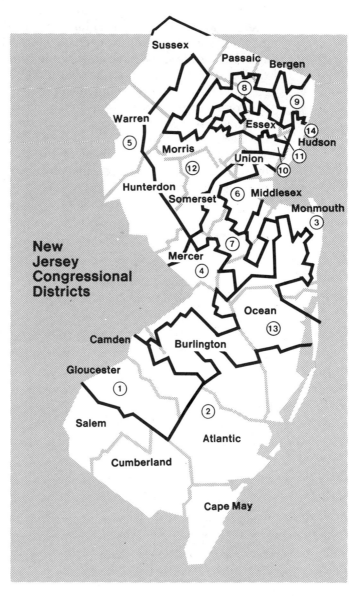

New Jersey's congressional districts after reapportionment following the 1980 census were of equal population, but hardly compact. Among these weird shapes, note in particular the seventh district, quickly dubbed the "fishhook." This district was designed to enable the Democrats—who controlled the State House—to elect another member of the House. (© 1982 by The New York Times Company. Reprinted by permission)

been able to do so, it has usually taken full advantage of every opportunity to cling to power. Judges are well aware of the possibility of gerrymandering districts of equal population, and on one occasion the Supreme Court struck down a crude effort to district blacks out of city government.[8] But it remains to be seen whether judges can—or will try to—cope with more subtle efforts where there are no racial overtones.

Even if most House districts were approximately equal in population, there would still be wide variations in representation in Congress. First, the Constitution's guarantee to each state of two senators—a provision that it requires unanimous consent of the states to change—means that in 1982 California had one senator per 11.8 million people and Alaska one senator for every 200,000. The House also poses problems. Each state must have at least one congressman, and in 1982 three states had total populations below the 520,000 of the average district.

There is another way in which the democratic nature of the House of Representatives is skewed, the so-called "swing ratio"; that is, electoral results do not always correspond completely to patterns of voting. In a perfectly representative system, a party receiving 51 percent of the votes would obtain 51 percent of the states, but no country can be divided into electoral districts that always produce such mathematically pure results.

TABLE 7-1   **Seats and Votes in the House of Representatives**

| | Percent Democratic* | |
Year	Votes	Seats
1964	57.5	67.8
1966	51.3	56.9
1968	50.9	55.4
1970	53.4	58.6
1972	51.7	55.9
1974	57.6	66.9
1976	56.2	67.1
1978	54.4	63.4
1980	51.2	55.7

*A two-party vote

SOURCE: Adapted from Edward R. Tufte, "The Relationship between Seats and Votes in Two Parties," *American Political Science Review*, LXVII (1973), 540. The authors have added 1976–1980 data.

⭐ ELECTING MEMBERS OF CONGRESS

Every other November, voters choose the entire membership of the House of Representatives and one-third of the Senate. The Constitution allows Congress to determine the number of seats in the House, and currently that number is 435. Every ten years, following the census, Congress redistributes those seats among the states according to population—with the proviso, of course, that each state has at least one representative. The Constitution itself fixes terms and minimum qualifications for Congress. Senators must be thirty years old and have been citizens for nine years. Representatives must be at least twenty-five and have been citizens for seven years. All are required to be residents of their states at the time of election, but "resident" has sometimes been liberally construed. Representatives are not legally obliged to be inhabitants of the districts they serve, but almost invariably they are.

Article I of the Constitution and the various voting amendments discussed earlier in this chapter give Congress broad authority to regulate elections, both primary elections and general elections, at which national officials are nominated and chosen. Although Congress has passed important legislation against racial discrimination, various forms of fraud, and large financial contributions, it has by and large left other kinds of regulation to the states.

Nomination of Congressional Candidates

Elections in the United States typically consist of a two-step process. First comes formal nomination, then a general election.

As with most public officials other than president and vice-president, the *party primary* is the normal means of nominating both senators and representatives; but the form of these elections differs widely from state to state. Most use *closed primaries*, in which participation is limited to voters who have declared their party allegiance either at registration or at the primary itself. There are, of course, provisions for changing loyalty, but having voted in the primary of one party usually bars a citizen from voting in the primary of another for a period of a year or longer. A few states use a system of "open" primaries, allowing voters at each primary to decide in whose election they will participate. In practice, the distinction between the two types is not always sharp; a closed primary can be so loosely administered as to be almost indistinguishable from an open system.

Timing provides another variation in primaries. There is no national primary day; dates for House and senatorial contests range from March through October. This staggering makes it virtually impossible to focus

TABLE 7-2   **Party Changes in the House of Representatives, 1972–1982**

| | Number of Seats | | Seats Changed | |
| | Democrats won from Republicans | Republicans won from Democrats | | |
Year			Total	Percent
1972	14	8	22	5.1
1974	49	6	55	12.6
1976	12	10	22	5.1
1978	10	22	32	7.3
1980	3	27	30	6.9
1982	27	4	31	7.1

the attention of voters in different states on the same issues of public policy, and it reinforces the power of local politicos at the expense of national party leaders.

In many states, especially in the south, the primary often serves as the real election. Between 1950 and 1978 more than 60 percent of congressional candidates won the general election by at least a margin of 60–40, indicating the outcome was never seriously in doubt. Although "safe" districts in one election can become bitterly contested battlefields a few years later, the fact remains that only a rather small number of seats changes party hands at any one election. Table 7-2 presents some figures from recent years to demonstrate this point. Even in recent landslides, turnover in seats has not exceeded 13 percent of the House.

Off-Year Campaigning

In *midterm* or *off-year elections* for Congress, the national parties are relatively inactive. There is no party platform and, more important, no presidential contest to focus attention nationally. As a result, the process seems more like several hundred individual campaigns than a single election.

But, as in other phases of life, appearances are sometimes deceiving in politics. Off-year congressional campaigning is most certainly a highly decentralized process, with each candidate having great leeway in choosing strategies. Still, national affairs do exert a powerful influence that brings more coherence to the result that individual candidates may intend or prefer. Practicing politicians and students of politics have long been aware that the president's party almost invariably loses congressional seats in off-year elections.

Explaining this phenomenon and predicting its magnitude in any election are obviously politically important. And it was an effort to wrestle with these problems that led Edward R. Tufte to a relatively simple formula that accurately predicts the national distribution of votes in off-year congressional elections.[9] Two elements are involved: the president's popularity just before the midterm election as measured by the Gallup Poll; and general economic conditions as measured by the real, disposable income per person. (The actual distribution of seats, as we saw earlier, is affected by the so-called swing ratio.) Statistical techniques aside, the significant point is that midterm elections function as a sort of national referendum on the president's general performance and more particularly on his management of economic affairs.

FIGURE 7-1   **Changes in House Seats by President's Party,* 1948–1982**

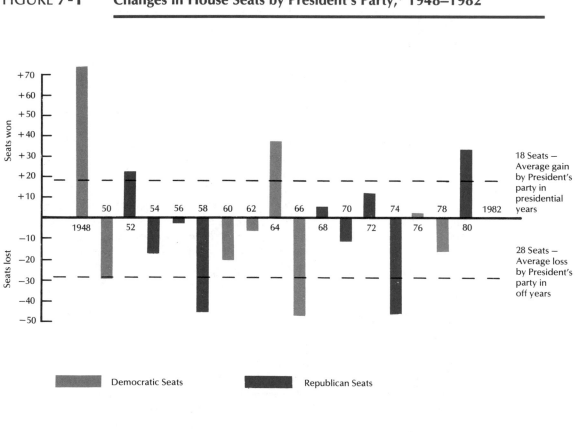

*Party of winning candidate in presidential election year.

ELECTING THE PRESIDENT

After much debate, the framers compromised on an Electoral College to select a president and vice-president. Each state legislature can choose its members of the College—equal to the number of the state's representatives and senators—as it sees fit, although all now use popular elections. Technically it is for a slate of such electors and not for a president or vice-president that voters cast their ballots. The winning electors meet in their respective states at a time designated by Congress and vote for a presidential and vice-presidential candidate. The ballots are forwarded to Congress and counted in the presence of both houses. Originally, the electors voted for two persons without designating either office. The person receiving the largest number of votes, providing it was a majority, would be president, and the person with the second-highest number vice-president. If no person had a majority, the House of Representatives was to select one of the five highest on the list to serve as president; each state was to have one vote in this process, and a majority of all the states was required for election.

The election of 1800, when party lines were first clearly drawn, revealed a serious flaw in this plan. All the electors from the Jeffersonian party cast their first two votes for Thomas Jefferson and Aaron Burr, intending the first to be president and the latter vice-president. But, since both men had the same number of electoral votes, the only way of breaking the tie was for the House of Representatives to choose. Because it was clear that the same result would prevail in subsequent elections if political parties continued to be active, the Twelfth Amendment was added to the Constitution, directing electors to cast one vote specifically for president and one for vice-president. If no person obtains a majority, the House—with each state having one vote—chooses the president from the three candidates with the largest number of electoral votes, and the Senate chooses the vice-president from the two leading candidates.

Presidential Primaries

For almost a century and a half, the major parties as well as many minor organizations have nominated presidential candidates by national convention. Historically, state party organizations used their own conventions or caucuses to choose delegates to the national convention. In this century, however, more and more states have required that delegates be chosen through primary elections. In 1980, thirty-six states held presidential primaries, twice the number scheduled in 1968.

Increased reliance on primary elections to select the delegates who choose presidential candidates has changed the nominating process in fundamental ways. Primaries broaden opportunities for presidential candidates to attract attention and support, and as a result tend to increase the number of candidates for each party's nomination. More important, primaries open the nominating process to mavericks, outsiders, and politicians from small states. Primary victories gave the 1972 Democratic nomination to George McGovern of South Dakota, a senator from a thinly populated state who was well to the left of his party's center of gravity. Four years later, an obscure former governor of Georgia won national attention in the primaries and was able to capture the Democratic nomination from a host of better-known adversaries. Increases in the number and importance of primaries have lengthened presidential campaigns. Candidates now launch their formal campaigns as much as two years before their party's convention. By contrast, campaigns lasted less than six months as recently as the 1960s.

Emergence of primaries as the key battleground for the presidential nomination is closely related to other developments in American politics. The decline of party organizations and bosses who played pivotal roles in the brokered conventions of the past created a vacuum in which primaries have flourished. No longer can a candidate afford to rely on party leaders and funds as Hubert Humphrey did as late as 1968—during a campaign in which he entered no primaries. Today, candidates must build their own organizations and sources of support. Moreover, the process is interactive, since the spread of primaries has further reduced the role of party leaders in selecting and controlling delegates, and their influence over candidates.

Another factor in the equation has been the growing reliance of candidates on television and media-based campaigning techniques. Advertising on television provides candidates with a means of waging campaigns in a variety of states with primary elections scheduled at different times. And media attention—the network news shows as well as the national news magazines and newspapers—is essential to attract supporters and contributors. Where once judgments about winning and losing candidates were made by party professionals, now they are made by the *CBS Nightly Report, Time,* and the *Washington Post.*

Despite these developments, the importance of primaries varies from year to year and state to state. A strong incumbent president eligible for re-election does not have to pay much attention to primaries. At the other extreme, primary contests are likely to be decisive for the party out of power when the competition is among several candidates whose ability to attract votes outside of their own state or region is untested. How "important" primaries are likely to be in any year largely depends on: (1) the number of active candidates (the greater the number, the more likely primaries are to sift out candidates who cannot generate substantial public support); (2) timing; and (3) technical rules under which primaries are conducted.

The last two points require elaboration. Because these contests are scattered from February to June, timing of victories and defeats can be crucial in creating the illusion of momentum. An early victory may thrust a candidate into prominence and attract further support and money. In 1976, Jimmy Carter's early victories persuaded *Time* and *Newsweek* to put his picture on their covers and to structure feature stories around him, transforming Carter from a little-known former governor into a household word across the country. Similarly, a victory in one of the last major primaries—California or Ohio, for example—may propel a candidate into the convention with a considerable psychological advantage.

Conversely, an early defeat may crush a candidate almost before the campaign gets started, and a late defeat may give the impression of ebbing strength and frighten supporters away. It is always desirable, of course, for an aspirant to do well in any primary—and thus it is prudent to stay out of any contest in which the candidate is doomed to be drubbed. But if time and other resources are scarce, it is generally wiser to concentrate on winning early and late. One important and obvious qualification is that the candidate must also gain a share of large delegations like those of California and New York, regardless of when the primaries occur.

The technical rules under which primaries are run also affect both strategy and results. In some states, what are called primaries are really little more than public opinion polls, and the results do not bind delegates. Winning these contests is less useful than winning in states that require delegates to support candidates on one or more ballots at the convention.

A second critical issue concerning the rules pertains to who gains what from a primary. One rule may give the state's entire delegation to the candidate who wins the most votes; a different rule may provide that candidates will receive shares of delegates proportional to their shares of the popular vote. A third rule may divide delegates by electoral districts and provide either that the winner in each district will take all the votes or that the front runners will share those votes proportionately. These rules can make a decisive difference. In 1972, "proportionate shares" would have sent George Wallace into the Democratic convention with by far the largest number of committed delegates. Under a winner-take-all system, Hubert Humphrey would have had the most delegates, although not a majority. Only under the districting rule, which the Democrats used most frequently in 1972, could the eventual nominee, George McGovern, have been the front runner.

For 1976, the Democrats adopted a rule forbidding winner-take-all primaries and encouraging proportionate shares. In the context of thirty-two primaries and at least a dozen candidates for the nomination, one result was the elimination by mid-spring of most candidates. A second outcome was that more than 80 percent of the delegates to the convention arrived with at least their first-round votes already pledged; and Jimmy Carter had a clear majority. Thus the change in the Democrats' rules did not accomplish its principal purpose of re-establishing the convention as the arena in which the real as well as the formal choice would be made. Party leaders were thereby denied their cherished role as brokers, pasting together a winning coalition from among various factions.

An unresolved problem is that presidential primaries usually draw only a small portion of eligible voters to the polls. In fact, as few as 2 percent of a state's population of voting age may actually participate, and rarely does the figure exceed one-half. On the average, less than 40 percent of those legally able to vote turn out for presidential primaries; the percentage slipped to 28 percent for 1976 and 24 percent in 1980.[10] The matter is further muddled by the fact that, while most of those who vote in primaries are party loyalists, participants may also include a substantial share of dissidents who are voting *against* a set of policies or people rather than *for* a candidate. Thus a candidate's ability to win a primary is frequently a very poor measure of real popular support.

Presidential Nominating Conventions

Democratic and Republican national conventions may have from 1,200 to 3,200 delegates, many with only a half vote. The size of a state's delegation is determined by complex formulas that weigh both the state's population and its support for the party. Nevertheless, the more populous states tend to be underrepresented, as are states where the party is stronger and the turnout higher. Females, blacks, and young people also have been underrepresented, but since 1968 both parties have been trying to correct these imbalances, with the Democrats' efforts both more vigorous and more successful.

The first item of business is to seat delegates. Normally, a credential committee routinely certifies those who have been chosen by their states. Occasionally, however, a rival faction challenges a delegate or even an entire state delegation. The decision, ultimately made by those members of the convention who are already seated, may materially affect aspirants' chances.

Adoption of a platform is the second important item of business. A special committee that has long been in session presents its report, sometimes with strong dissenting views. Normally, convention leaders are able to march the document through without serious debate; but when challenges occur, they are apt to be bitter and to reveal cleavages within the party that can have a vast impact on the campaign strategies open to the eventual nominee.

It is easy enough to ridicule the average platform, for, as V. O. Key said, it "speaks with boldness and forthrightness on issues that are already well settled; it is likely to be ambiguous on contentious questions."[11] But evasive platforms often make it possible for parties to hold together long enough to elect a president who has the backing of 40 or 50 million voters—an achievement that should not be minimized. At the same time, the price is sometimes heavy in terms of muddling issues vital to the nation.

The convention's next step is to nominate a presidential candidate. A simple majority of votes is needed. If the party controls the White Houe and the president is eligible for re-election, the outcome is usually clear from the moment the president decides to run again. For the Republicans, two exceptions stand out: 1912, when Teddy Roosevelt tried to deny William Howard Taft's nomination; and 1976, when Ronald Reagan attacked Gerald Ford's claim to be leader of the party. In both cases, however, the challenge to the President failed. Also unsuccessful was the effort of Senator Edward Kennedy and his supporters to deny President Carter renomination in 1980, although Carter was forced into a bitter battle for the nomination which lasted through the convention and weakened his position in the general election.

A convention without a serious contest for the nomination also may occur if a candidate has won enough delegates in primaries to have or be close to a majority, as Carter had done in 1976 and Reagan in 1980. In most other situations, bargaining, maneuvering, and negotiation among candidates and delegates—often conducted before the convention meets—will be decisive. Only twice from 1932 through 1980 did the Democratic or Republican nominee not win on the first ballot.

The dynamics of the nominating process are much more complex. At the previous convention, some hopefuls were already befriending delegates and sized up potential rivals. In the intervening years, aspirants traveled around the country, meeting and negotiating with local leaders and generating publicity about their qualifications for the job. After these initial soundings come efforts to raise funds for primary campaigns and the staff needed to win votes and support. Holding public office is useful so that the candidate's name can stay in the news—which helps explain why governors and senators are so often among the presidential contenders taken most seriously.

The candidate's religion and region can also help or hurt in the quest for the nomination. With few exceptions, leading candidates for major party nominations have been Protestants (and all have been white males). Historically, candidates from large states have had an advantage, but the visibility provided by national television has dulled that edge considerably, witness the successful campaigns for the presidential nomination of Senators Barry Goldwater of Arizona in 1964 and George McGovern of South Dakota in 1972.

Selection of a vice-presidential nominee provides the convention's final work. Usually the presidential candidate announces his preference, and the convention quickly ratifies it, as was the case with George Bush and Walter Mondale in 1980. A central concern of the presidential nominee has been the ability of a running mate to "balance the ticket," to appeal to important segments of voters whom the presidential candidate cannot easily reach. The capacity of the vice-presidential candidate to succeed to the presidency in an emergency is often a marginal consideration, as Richard Nixon's cynical choice of Spiro Agnew in 1968 and 1972 attested.

☆ POLITICAL CAMPAIGNING

A campaign and election perform a number of functions. From the citizen's point of view, they provide an opportunity to obtain at low cost a great deal of information about politics and politicians, as well as an opportunity to participate in determining who will govern. In so doing, campaigns and elections also permit citizens to have a voice, although only a very small voice, in affecting the policies that will shape much of public and private life over the next few years.

From the point of view of the parties and their candidates, a campaign and election provide means of obtaining control of the government that are nonviolent and legitimate in the eyes of the governed. Further, by winning office, candidates and their colleagues can dispense patronage to keep their parties together and can create new public policies that they hope will increase votes at the next election and even do some good for the country.

From the point of view of the political system, a campaign and an election allow peaceful means of change, permitting shifts in personnel and policies while maintaining a high degree of stability. By involving masses of the people, a campaign and an election also reconfirm the basic legitimacy of the system itself and foster support for future governmental decisions, thus lowering the amount of force needed to preserve public order. The fact that presidents, senators, and representatives all have apparently been chosen by the people provides a powerful emotional argument for compliance with their decisions.

The difficulties of campaigning vary from office to office. We shall concentrate on the most dramatic, that for the presidency. Candidates for congressional, state, and local posts face some of the same problems, although the scale may be far smaller and the electorate more homogeneous in economic, social, and ethnic terms.

Patriotic backgrounds provide the setting for many campaign speeches. Ronald Reagan seeks votes in 1980 in San Antonio at the Alamo. (Herman Kokojan, Black Star)

Campaigns and Debates

An American presidential campaign involves expenditure of hundreds of millions of hours and only slightly fewer dollars. Candidates preempt prime television to deliver speeches, splatter radio and TV with spot announcements, and crisscross the country in jets specially equipped as flying dormitories for politicians and journalists. At the same time, thousands of volunteers ring doorbells, make telephone calls, distribute literature, and chauffeur hundreds of thousands of people to registration offices and later to voting booths.

But when the senses recover from torrents of booming oratory, waves of slick commercials, floods of junk mail, and scores of superficial analyses by television commentators, one cannot escape doubts that the campaign provided citizens with the quality of information they needed to make intelligent appraisals of issues or competitors. Candidates tend to talk past each other, not to the issues. More often, the candidates come out strongly for virtue and against sin—each assures the voters that he will make America strong, stimulate the economy, curb inflation, preserve free enterprise, and make government more efficient, while blaming the other side for most of the nation's problems.

Furthermore, campaigns typically emphasize the candidate's charm rather than sharply outlining the nation's problems, exploring alternatives, and justifying solutions in an intellectually respectable way. Differences in policy can sometimes be divined from both speeches and previous records. But a campaign seldom forms a stage on which presidential aspirants perform according to the script of democratic government, giving voters a choice between reasoned justifications for proposed policies. Even televised debates, interesting as they sometimes are, find the candidates talking around rather than to the questions or each other.

The causes of these performances are not hard to find. Two factors are basic. First, in peacetime, politics is usually not a fundamental concern of most Americans, and there is constant competition for the attention of voters more interested in family, job, recreation, hobbies, and popular entertainment. To compete successfully for voters' ears and eyes, most politicians believe, one cannot offer complicated discussions of policy issues. To rally supporters a candidate must first attract attention; and political folklore has it that an attractive family, an emotional

Mike Peters, © 1980 Dayton Daily News

charge of corruption in the opposition's ranks, suggestions that the other side cannot be trusted with America's security, and Madison Avenue gimmickry can be more effective than discussing specific policies that would reduce unemployment without aggravating inflation.

A second factor relates to the very broad spectrum of support that a successful candidate needs. To win, a large and diverse coalition must be pieced together that transcends regional, religious, class, and ethnic lines. Because of the inherent fragility of that coalition, a candidate usually finds it expedient to speak in vague terms that will offend no one of his targeted groups, while making promises that, if not actually incompatible, can be reconciled only with extreme difficulty.

Do Campaigns Make a Difference?

There is no simple answer to the question of how much difference all this frenzied activity makes on election day. Public opinion polls, summarized in Table 7-3, indicate that in presidential elections about one-half to three-quarters of those who actually vote have made up their minds by the time the national conventions have nominated candidates.[12] Thus, recent presidential campaigns have had, at most, a real chance of shaping choices of only half of the voters.

These figures also suggest what further research substantiates: A large share of the uncommitted are independents, who are generally

TABLE 7-3 **Time of Voting Decision in Presidential Elections**

Question: How long before the election did you decide that you were going to vote the way you did?

	Percentage of Voters								
	1948	1952	1956	1960	1964	1968	1972	1976	1980
Before the conventions	41	36	60	31	41	36	47	33	41
At the time of the conventions	31	32	19	31	25	24	18	21	18
After the conventions, during campaign	15	21	12	26	21	19	22	22	15
Last two weeks of campaign	10	9	7	9	9	14	8	17	17
On election day	3	2	2	3	4	7	5	7	9

SOURCE: Center for Political Studies, University of Michigan.

Gerald Ford campaigns with his wife, Betty, on the "Presidential Express" in Michigan. Once the main means of reaching voters, campaign trains today are one of the many devices used by candidates to attract the attention of television and newspaper reporters. (Wide World Photos)

less informed about and interested in politics than those who profess loyalty to a party. This fact, of course, reinforces campaign strategists' temptations to substitute drama for debate.

On the other hand, the figures in Table 7-3 conceal one of the purposes of a campaign; to bring the committed to the polls. Without a campaign, many who actually did vote might not have done so. A preference expressed at a cocktail party is welcome, but only when that preference is registered at the ballot box does it do a candidate much good. Gross statistics also obscure the fact that in many presidential elections—1948, 1960, 1968, and 1976, for example—a small switch in votes can be decisive. Harry Truman's hard-hitting whistle-stop tour in

1948 eroded just enough of Dewey's support to put Truman back in the White House. John F. Kennedy's effectiveness in the television debates of 1960 has been widely credited with providing his margin of victory. The effects of Gerald Ford's all-out effort during the final phase of the 1976 campaign can be seen in Table 7-3. As late as mid-October most pollsters agreed that Carter retained a commanding lead; but these same experts found on election eve that the gap had narrowed to the point where the contest would be too close to call. Carter's winning margin was 2 percent out of 81 million votes cast. And almost a quarter of the electorate made up their minds during the last two weeks before election day.

When victory or defeat hangs on such a relatively small number of votes, it is easy to understand why running an intelligently orchestrated campaign is so vital to professional politicians. Most candidates realistically see their efforts not as cracking huge blocs of voters already committed to opponents' causes, but rather as plucking out a few critical voters. In sum, campaigns are waged "to make marginal changes in political alignments."[13]

Campaign Strategy

The object is to win, but that is hardly a simple job in most precincts, much less in a country of 226 million people. The first problem a candidate faces is that of choosing a campaign manager and building a staff of close advisers on various campaign questions as well as policy issues. While the candidate may have to make many decisions, only a small fraction of the hundreds of problems that arise daily during a campaign can be handled personally.

In turn, lest the campaign manager be quickly swamped, he has to select a large staff of trusted assistants. These people will include a press secretary to oversee arrangements for newsmen, a finance director to coordinate myriad fund-raising activities, and personnel from one or more of the professional campaign consulting firms that have become increasingly prominent participants in electoral politics in the past decade. A major task of the campaign specialists is public relations and advertising, the shaping of the candidate's image and packaging of his message.

The campaign manager and the other chief advisers must map the candidate's strategy. The first problem is that of raising money, for American political campaigns are wonderfully expensive enterprises. The matter of money in politics is sufficiently important that we make it the subject of a full section of this chapter. Here we stress only that a presidential candidate must spend many millions of dollars to get—and keep—his name before the public. In the face of such costs, the question

Oliphant, © 1978 Universal Press Syndicate. Reprinted with permission. All rights reserved.

of how much money can be raised necessarily precedes that of how to reach voters most effectively. The question of raising money also affects other strategic choices, because a candidate cannot safely offend those who will be asked to pay the bills.

The next major decision involves how to form a coalition that offers maximal opportunities for winning and does so at minimal costs—in budget as well as programs that the candidate wants to carry out. Teachers, for instance, may promise to support a candidate in exchange for a commitment to create a federal department of education. A governor from the southwest may claim to be able to deliver several states if the candidate agrees to remove federal price controls from oil and natural gas. An appeal to one group, of course, may bring votes at the expense of lost votes in another sector. A pledge to support higher prices for agricultural products may win votes in the countryside but reduce support from consumers in the cities and suburbs.

The candidate's most rational approach is to set out clearly his objectives and what he is being asked to trade, and then begin to do his arithmetic. To bring his total up to 50.1 percent of the electoral vote, he has to be willing to pay a high price. After he passes that magic mark, additional increases in support become less and less valuable. Nevertheless, although a particular price—some particular tradeoff—may be too high, the worth is never zero, for a candidate can never be sure that his computations have been correct. Besides, "winning big" brings immense psychological and political advantages. In addition to demoralizing the opposition and attracting donors for his next campaign, a president who runs ahead of his ticket will have a much easier time leading Congress. If the president has demonstrated that he can attract votes, senators and representatives who are concerned about re-election will want his help; and nothing in politics is ever free, not even a campaign endorsement.

Modern survey research and data-processing techniques have been brought to bear on these campaign calculations. Computer models of voting patterns in key states were used with current survey data to help plan Reagan's electoral strategy in 1980. All such calculations are based on sketchy data at best. Past records do not necessarily predict the future accurately, and even evidence from current surveys of public opinion is often elusive. Both parties have certain historic strengths, however, on which they can build their coalitions—Democrats with blacks, Jews, Catholics, blue-collar workers, small farmers, and intellectuals; Republicans with white-collar workers, middle-class Protestants, large farmers, higher-income professionals, owners of businesses, and corporate executives. But none of these allegiances is permanent. In 1964, the Democrats wooed away many businessmen and white-collar workers from Barry Goldwater's ultraconservatism; and in 1972 the Republicans pried away a large portion of white ethnics (who were typically Catholic) by painting George McGovern as a man who would "run up the white flag" in international relations and at home take away the worker's hard-earned money to lavish it on blacks.

Strategists must also consider party allegiance in mapping their plans because these loyalties often exert strong emotional pulls. In order to win, the Democrats in recent decades have usually needed only to keep their adherents together and pick up a small portion of independents. This task is often difficult, since the Democratic party has drawn its strength from diverse groups such as conservative southerners, liberal white intellectuals, militant blacks, and white working-class ethnics. Moreover, party *identification* is not the same as party *loyalty*. The Electoral College adds another complicating dimension. The candidate must win not a majority of the popular vote but a majority of electoral votes.

As a party that is attractive to only a minority of Americans, the Republicans have an even more difficult task. They must keep their own followers in line, pick up a large share of independents, and also lure away a sizable number of Democrats. And, of course, Republicans have to be as concerned as Democrats about distribution of support in the Electoral College.

A third set of problems involves interlocking questions of focus, timing, and style. Most candidates concentrate their energy and re-

Franklin Delano Roosevelt campaigns in West Virginia in 1932, building the Democratic coalition that endured for the next half century. (United Press International)

sources in states where large electoral votes are at stake and the outcome is in doubt. It takes considerable political intelligence—usually gathered by analyses of past elections and of current public opinion polls—to select these states. If a choice has been unwise, the candidate may not only lose a state in which he has been working but others that his efforts might have brought into the fold. Timing is critical both in scheduling visits to specific areas and in setting the overall tempo of the campaign. Activity must start neither too early nor too late and must come to a crescendo at just the right moment—clearly identifiable only in retrospect—to sway the greatest number of voters.

The nature of a campaign is largely shaped by whether a candidate decides to attack his opponent relentlessly as Harry Truman did in 1948 and John F. Kennedy in 1960, or speak glowingly of his own record as did Lyndon Johnson in 1964 and Richard Nixon in 1972, or present a new and complicated program to revitalize society. In 1972, George McGovern offered proposals for alternative public policies on a broad range of domestic and international problems. As a result, the campaign of 1972 presented one of the clearest opportunities in recent decades for Americans to choose between candidates on the basis of their stands on public issues. Interestingly, survey research indicates that voters' choices were more influenced in 1972 by the candidates' stands on public issues than in other presidential elections for which comparable data exist.[14] Four years later, Jimmy Carter and Gerald Ford played down differences on public policies, following instead the more common strategy of each claiming he was the better man to solve problems. But in 1980 Ronald Reagan successfully emphasized his policy differences with Carter, particularly on economic policy, defense, welfare, civil rights, and the size and scope of the federal government.

The choice of whether to attack opponents, emphasize one's own purity of heart, or propose new public policies vitally affects the style in which a campaign can be effectively run. A thirty-second spot message on radio or television is ideal to pin a label on an opponent or an accolade on oneself. But commercials are inadequate to explain a new program or even a single proposal for a new public policy on a difficult issue. For that, one needs longer speeches rather than the catchwords that have come to dominate campaigns. And most of the speeches that candidates make as they crisscross the nation in their jets are strings of catchwords that are repeated endlessly as the campaign progresses.

When all these kinds of decisions have been made, attacks slashingly delivered, defenses righteously proclaimed, money collected and spent, votes counted, and results announced, both candidates are probably acutely aware of the huge role that chance played in the outcome. The "ifs" are numerous. If Richard Nixon's makeup man had been more skilled before the first television debate in 1960, if someone had probed more deeply into the Watergate break-in during the 1972 campaign, if Jimmy Carter had been able to secure the release of the hostages in Iran before election day in 1980 . . . if, on and on. Yet despite the capricious play of luck, a candidate who does not meticulously plan and carefully execute an intelligent strategy has no hope of being more than the leader of the loyal opposition for four years.

The Final Election of a President

By midnight of election day, it is usually obvious who will be the next president; in some recent elections, the television networks have proclaimed the winner before the polls have closed in the nation's largest state, California. But the outcome is not official until the new Congress assembles in January, counts the ballots of the members of the Electoral College, and proclaims the result. It is at this point that the House of Representatives would proceed to elect a president if no candidate had a clear majority of electoral votes.

Although the Electoral College has functioned reasonably well through the years, the system has three serious weaknesses. First, there is no provision in the Constitution or in federal law requiring an elector to vote for his party's candidates, and in 1948, 1960, 1968, and 1972 electors voted for an "outside" candidate. Only a few states expressly compel electors to fulfill their pledges to vote for particular candidates, although several others have laws that hint at such a requirement.

The second weakness is that the victor in the electoral vote might actually receive fewer popular votes than his opponent. This possibility results primarily from the fact that in each state the winning candidate receives the state's entire electoral vote, equivalent to the total of the state's two senators plus its representatives in Congress. Such an imbalance has occurred in two elections since the Civil War, 1876 and 1888. Moreover, the same result could have occurred in many other elections

Congress counts the electoral votes following the election of 1877. Samuel Tilden won the popular vote, but Rutherford B. Hayes captured a majority of the electoral votes, and the presidency. (The Bettmann Archive, Inc.)

had very small blocs of popular votes been cast the other way in certain states.

A third weakness is that the Electoral College could fail to give a majority to any candidate and throw the election into the House of Representatives. The House has had to make such a choice only once—1824—since the adoption of the Twelfth Amendment. But there have been other elections in which strong third-party candidates almost succeeded in deadlocking the Electoral College. In 1968 George Wallace won five states and received forty-six electoral votes. Had Hubert Humphrey rather than Nixon carried Alaska, Delaware, Missouri, Nevada, and Tennessee, states in which Nixon's combined margin of victory was less than 91,000, Nixon's electoral vote would have been 269 and Humphrey's 223, leaving no candidate with the majority of 270 votes needed in the Electoral College.

It takes only a moment's reflection to understand the problems caused by having the House choose a president. Voting in the House for president is by states and not by members, with states as different in population as Alaska and California each having one vote. It is also entirely possible for the minority party in the House to control a majority of state delegations and thereby to elect its candidate to the presidency even though he stood second in both popular and electoral votes. The constitutional requirement that the winning candidate receive the votes of a majority of states poses yet another problem. It is possible for party control of state delegations to be so scrambled that the House would have great difficulty in selecting a president, if it could do so at all.

If the House were unable to choose a president by inauguration day, the vice-president, elected by the Senate from the two candidates with the highest electoral votes for that office, would serve until the House could reach a majority decision or, if that did not happen, until the end of a regular four-year term. If the Senate were unable to elect a vice-president—fifty-one votes are needed, and enough senators might abstain to keep either candidate from winning—the speaker of the House of Representatives would serve as president, again until the House reached a decision or until the end of a four-year term.

The uncertainties of this complex system have stimulated periodic efforts to amend the Constitution to provide for direct popular election of the president. Each time—the last was in 1979—the champions of the Electoral College have prevailed, primarily by rallying those interests which benefit from the status quo. Small states want to retain a system which increases their weight in presidential elections. Blacks and other minorities concentrated in large metropolitan areas oppose change because the winner-take-all feature of the Electoral College increases the importance of blocs of voters in the big states. More generally, defenders argue that the current system of electing the president holds most voters inside our two federal parties, and the parties are thus held near the middle of the political road. To elect a President, even arrogant majorities must be solicitous of minorities; even alienated minorities must work with majorities. The system encourages moderation in radical times and protects against parochial passions. It discourages minor parties yet rewards their protest with major-party alternatives.[15]

★ CAMPAIGN FINANCING

Chapter 5 pointed out that money is an important source of political power; nowhere is it more important than in financing the extravaganzas called political campaigns. The costs of winning election to public office in the United States are staggering. In 1972, Richard Nixon and his supporters spent $68 million to ensure him a second term in the White House. Ten years later, $325 million was expended for campaigns for Congress. In recent elections, individual candidates for the Senate spent as much as $5 million, and a few candidates for the House spent more than a million.

To prevent a candidate's buying the White House, the Election Reform Act of 1974 offers substantial federal subsidies to those presidential candidates who comply with its provisions limiting expenditures. The act does not, however, subsidize campaigns for the House or Senate; and even presidential candidates still spend vast sums of money—over $150 million in the 1980 race.

How Money Is Spent

Campaign money is spent for a variety of purposes, of which the most important are the following:

1. *General overhead:* for headquarters at national, state, and local levels, including salaries, office rent, heat, light, telephones, and postage.

2. *Field activities:* candidate's speaking trips, often by leased aircraft, renting of halls, stadiums, and auditoriums, and other expenses involved in organizing mass meetings.

3. *Publicity:* telecasts and radio broadcasts, spot commercials, newspaper advertisements, campaign literature, special buttons and souvenirs; and the fees charged by the consulting firms that handle public relations, commercials, and related activity.

4. *Grants to subsidiary committees:* transfers of funds from national organizations to state and local organizations and to special committees and groups.

5. *Election day expenses:* transportation of voters to the polls and payments to watchers at the polls and to party workers who try to bring out the vote.

6. *Public opinion polling* to gauge the effects of various campaign strategies—in 1972, for example, the two parties spent almost $2 million for such surveys during the presidential primaries and the general election.

Where the Money Comes From

Apart from the huge amounts of money needed for campaigning, the most striking feature about party finances, at least before 1976, has been how much cash comes from so few donors. In 1972, for example, Nixon's five largest contributors kicked in $4.3 million, and five other well-heeled individuals gave more than a quarter of million dollars each. Most Americans, however, so generous in other respects, have been unwilling to make political contributions. The Gallup Poll reported in 1954 that only one family in eighteen had given in that year's campaign, and in 1968 the Survey Research Center of the University of Michigan found that the proportion had increased only to one family in thirteen. To spur small giving and thus protect parties and candidates from domination by a few rich donors—"fat cats," politicians call them—Congress now allows taxpayers to allocate one dollar of their income tax to a political party or to a fund to be divided among the parties.

In addition to fat cats, most of whom give in expectation of future favors or in payment for past help, politicians who are not themselves wealthy have had to rely heavily on three other sources of funds: labor unions, governmental employees, and the underworld. Since 1943 federal law has forbidden direct gifts by unions to candidates for national office. But unions have avidly spent money in conducting their own campaigns for labor's friends. Although it is always illegal to ask a federal civil service employee for money and usually illegal to ask a state civil service worker, many civil servants and appointive officials contribute as a form of job insurance. Many states and localities have unofficial (and illegal) sliding scales of contributions that party leaders expect from all government employees who owe their jobs to the party.

The underworld, from petty hoodlums to Mafioso dons, constitutes another source of funds. No matter how astute, no criminal can long conduct large-scale operations in loan sharking, narcotics, prostitution, gambling, milking labor unions, and shaking down legitimate businessmen without heavy governmental insulation. To survive, lucrative criminal enterprises need police officials who look the other way, district attorneys who do not prosecute, judges who let underworld figures off lightly, and elected officials who will pressure police, prosecutors, and judges to go easy on the mob. Returns from rackets are immense, totaling untold—and untaxed—billions each year; and campaign contributions to cooperative politicians and to the opponents of uncooperative officials are cheap forms of insurance.

Election Reform Act of 1974

Political parties or public officials who are beholden to a few large donors are a danger to honest government, but so are debt-ridden parties. The Democrats, for instance, entered the 1972 campaign with a debt of $9.3 million, a financial burden that imposed severe restrictions on their candidates' ability to campaign. Over the years, Congress enacted a series of ineffective laws designed to protect the integrity of the electoral process by regulating campaign contributions and expenditures. Finally, the scandals of Watergate and revelations that Nixon's aides had in 1972 routinely used promises of governmental aid or threats of governmental prosecution to collect millions of dollars led Congress to adopt the first regulatory scheme that has had any real chance of success, the Election Reform Act of 1974.

The nucleus of the statute is a system of heavy federal subsidies for presidential campaigns and restrictions on raising and spending money from other sources. (We shall limit analysis to provisions relating to presidential campaigns.) The act sets up three special funds, one for national nominating conventions, a second for presidential primaries, and a third for the general election.

Subsidies for national conventions. The national committee of each major party (one whose candidate for president received at least 25 percent of the votes at the last election) is eligible for $3 million to finance the national convention on the conditions that the national committee not spend any more money for the convention and that none of the funds be used to help any particular candidate or candidates. (Incidentally, the amounts of money specified in the statute automatically increase with inflation.) National committees of minor parties (those whose presidential candidates polled from 5 to 25 percent of the vote at the last election) can receive a smaller amount based on a formula that takes into account the number of votes received by any minor party and the number received by the major parties at the last election. New parties and those whose candidates received less than 5 percent of the votes at the last election are not eligible for federal assistance in holding a national convention.

Presidential primaries. In general, the act provides for matching federal funds to help defray costs of campaigning in primaries. To be eligible, a candidate must generate contributions of at least $5,000, with only the first $250 of any contribution counting, in each of twenty states. The candidate must also agree that total expenditures will not exceed a specified maximum—in 1980 it was almost $15 million. The candidate may not receive federal funds that exceed half of what is actually spent. In 1980, the federal government disbursed almost $31 million for the presidential primaries, which covered about one-third of the cost of the primaries.

Presidential elections. During the campaign, each candidate of a major party is entitled to another federal subsidy—in 1980 it was $29.4 million—on the condition that the candidate not accept any donations (including advertising material as well as money) in excess of the maximum federal grant. National, state, and local committees, however, can spend additional money to help their candidates. In 1980, each national committee was allowed to spend $4.6 million. Minor party candidates receive lesser federal aid based on the same sort of formulas for subsidies to their national conventions. Independent candidates and candidates of new parties or parties that received less than 5 percent of the vote at the last presidential election may also be eligible for federal aid. But because the formula used takes into account how many votes they received in proportion to other candidates, these independents and candidates of new parties receive federal support only after the campaign is over and the votes are counted. On the other hand, candidates from established parties receive their subsidies, in the form of a drawing account immediately after formal nomination by their parties.

The Election Reform Act also established a Federal Election Commission to enforce the statutes, requires detailed reporting by candidates and parties of fund raising and spending, and specifies heavy penalties for violations. In addition, the law sets limits on how much money an individual may contribute to political campaigns in any year: $1,000 to any one candidate; $5,000 to any political committee (except the national party committee—the limit there is $20,000); and $25,000 to all candidates and committees.

As one can imagine, this statute was highly controversial both as a matter of wise public policy and as conforming to constitutional provisions regarding equal treatment and freedom of political expression. Its constitutionality was immediately challenged in the courts by people as politically diverse as James Buckley, a conservative senator from New York, and the liberal American Civil Liberties Union.

The Supreme Court sustained most of the provisions of the act, but it did strike down, as violations of freedom of communication and association protected by the First Amendment, sections that set limits on the amount that a candidate could spend from his own private resources and on the sums that private citizens, acting without the consent of the candidate, could spend for that candidate. Somewhat surprisingly, the Court upheld the constitutionality of the quite different treatment accorded to the major parties and their candidates in comparison to minor and new parties and their candidates.[16]

Like all changes in complex systems, the Election Reform Act has had mixed effects. On the one hand, the law strengthened the two-party system by blatant favoritism toward Democrats and Republicans. On the other, public financing of presidential campaigns has weakened political parties by reducing their fund-raising role. The law's method of raising money—by allowing citizens to specify on their income tax returns that they wish a dollar of their taxes to go into a special fund for presidential campaigns—has worked very well. But the legislation also brought reams of red tape to presidential elections, as the Federal Election Commission has required detailed reports from candidates and compliance with complicated rules. One expert calls the Election Reform Act "the lawyers and accountants full-employment act."[17]

Political Action Committees

One of the most important unanticipated effects of public financing of presidential elections was the diversion of private campaign contributions—particularly large sums from organized interests—to candidates for Congress. Because the Election Reform Act imposed tighter limits on individual than group contributions to congressional campaigns—$1,000 per individual per campaign compared with $5,000 per campaign by a group—most contributions to congressional candidates have been funneled through political action committees, or PACs, a new breed of political animal that has multiplied rapidly. In the eight years following the enactment of the 1974 campaign reforms, political action committees created by corporations increased from under 90 to over 1,400, and in 1982 a total of more than 3,200 PACs of all kinds were active. Contributions from PACs to congressional candidates soared to $88 million in 1982, up from $12.5 million in 1974.

In addition to the political action committees established by corporations—such as the Nonpartisan Political Action Committee (General Electric) and the Civic Involvement Program (General Motors)—are those created by trade groups, labor, and other organizations. Examples are the Realtors Political Action Committee, the UAW Voluntary Community Action Program, and the NRA Political Victory Fund.

Jack Ohman. Reprinted by permission of Tribune Company Syndicate, Inc.

Some political action committees are not connected with a parent corporation, trade association, union, or organization. The political objectives of these PACs—such as the National Committee for an Effective Congress and the National Conservative Political Action Committee— are typically broader in scope than committees sponsored by business, labor, and other specialized interests. These independent committees are not bound by the spending limitations in the Election Reform Act as long as they are not directly involved with a particular candidate.

The vast majority of political action committees pursue narrow goals. Most of their contributions go to incumbents in Congress, and their objective is to influence recipients to support the interests of the particular corporation, industry, union, or group. To many, including some members of Congress, the process appears to be a sophisticated means of buying votes. Reinforcing this view are episodes such as the 1982 congressional veto of a proposed rule by the Federal Trade Commission that would have required dealers to inform potential buyers of defects in used cars, a vote that followed campaign contributions of more than $1 million by the Automobile and Truck Dealers Election Action Committee.

Growing concern over the rising costs of congressional elections and the influence of political action committees spurred an effort in the late 1970s to extend federal election subsidies to campaigns for the House and Senate. Opposed were most conservative members of Congress, particularly Republicans, who traditionally have been able to raise more money on their own than Democrats. Nor were the interests which finance political action committees eager to see their role in congressional campaigns diminished. These forces were able to defeat legislation for federal financing of congressional campaigns in 1977 and 1979.

⭐ SUMMARY

Elections and campaigns are among the most visible (and expensive) aspects of American politics. They also provide the most obvious expression of the democratic nature of the political system. But, as this chapter points out, the march to "one person, one vote" has been long and slow. We have also tried to emphasize that certain institutional arrangements, such as the electoral college and gerrymandering, the costs of running for public office, the character of campaign rhetoric, and widespread inattention to politics, leave the United States far short of achieving the democratic ideal.

NOTES

1. *Brown v. Board of Education*, 347 U.S. 483 (1954).
2. *Dunn v. Blumstein*, 405 U.S. 330 (1972), held thirty days to be sufficient; *Marston v. Lewis*, 410 U.S. 697 (1973), and *Burns v. Forston*, 410 U.S. 686 (1973), sustained requirements of fifty days.
3. 377 U.S. 186 (1964).
4. *Wesberry v. Sanders*, 376 U.S. 1 (1964).
5. 377 U.S. 533 (1964).
6. *Mann v. Howell*, 410 U.S. 315 (1973).
7. Edward R. Tufte, "The Relationship between Seats and Votes in Two Party Systems," *American Political Science Review*, LXVII (1973), 551.
8. *Gomillion v. Lightfoot*, 364 U.S. 339 (1961).
9. "Determinants of the Outcomes of Midterm Congressional Elections," *American Political Science Review*, LIX (1975), 812.
10. See Austin Ranney, *Participation in American Presidential Nominations, 1976* (Washington: American Enterprise Institute, 1977), pp. 20–22.
11. *Politics, Parties, and Pressure Groups*, 3rd ed. (New York: Thomas Y. Crowell, 1955), pp. 462–463.

12. See P. Lazarsfeld, B. Berelson, and H. Gaudet, *The People's Choice: How the Voter Makes Up His Mind in a Presidential Campaign* (New York: Duell, Sloan and Pearce, 1944); B. Berelson, P. Lazarsfeld, and W. McPhee, *Voting* (Chicago: University of Chicago Press, 1954); Angus Campbell, Phillip E. Converse, Warren E. Miller, and Donald E. Stokes, *The American Voter* (New York: John Wiley and Sons, 1960), especially Chapter 4; Warren Miller and Teresa E. Levitin, *Leadership and Change: Presidential Elections from 1952 to 1976* (Cambridge, Mass.: Winthrop Publishers, 1976): and the data released by the Survey Research Center of the University of Michigan after each presidential election.
13. Stanley Kelley, Jr., "The Presidential Campaign," in Paul T. David, ed., *The Presidential Election and Transition, 1960–1961* (Washington: Brookings Institution, 1961), p. 57.
14. See Miller and Levitin, *Leadership and Change*, especially Chapters 2, 5, and 6.
15. "A Vote for the Federal President," editorial, *New York Times*, July 9, 1979.
16. *Buckley v. Valeo*, 424 U.S. 1 (1976).
17. Herbert Alexander, Citizen's Research Foundation, quoted in "The Legacy of Watergate," *Newsweek*, June 14, 1982, p. 39.

SELECTED BIBLIOGRAPHY

Alexander, Herbert E. *Financing Politics: Money, Elections, and Political Reform*, 2d ed. (Washington: Congressional Quarterly Press, 1980). An introduction to the problems of money and political campaigns, written by the foremost American expert on the topic.

Barber, James David. *The Pulse of Politics: Electing Presidents in the Media Age* (New York: W. W. Norton, 1980). An attempt to explain presidential elections in terms of twelve-year cycles of conflict, conscience, and conciliation.

David, Paul T., Ralph M. Goldman, and Richard C. Bain. *The Politics of National Party Conventions*, paperback edition, K. Sproul, ed. (Washington: Brookings Institution, 1960). Brings together a wealth of information on the operations of national party nominating conventions.

Downs, Anthony. *An Economic Theory of Democracy* (New York: Harper & Row, 1957). A challenging investigation of the rational bases of political behavior.

Hess, Stephen. *The Presidential Campaign*, rev. ed. (Washington: Brookings Institution, 1978). An exploration of the implications of the way we elect the president.

Hinckley, Barbara. *Congressional Elections* (Washington: Congressional Quarterly Press, 1981). A thorough appraisal of the various elements in congressional campaigns.

Kayden, Xandra. *Campaign Organization* (Lexington, Mass.: D.C. Heath, 1978). A useful study of the sorts of organization it takes to win an election.

Keech, William R., and Donald R. Mathews. *The Party's Choice* (Washington: Brookings Institution, 1976). A thorough re-examination of the whole process of nominating presidential candidates.

Kelley, Stanley, Jr. *Political Campaigning: Problems in Creating an Informed Electorate* (Washington: Brookings Institution, 1969). The central concern here is how the distribution of policies and candidates in campaigns might make a greater contribution to electoral rationality.

Phillips, Kevin P. *The Emerging Republican Majority* (New Rochelle, N.Y.: Arlington House, 1969). A description of the so-called southern strategy that Richard Nixon followed in 1968 and to a lesser extent in 1972.

Polsby, Nelson W., and Aaron B. Wildavsky. *Presidential Elections: Strategies of American Electoral Politics*, 5th ed. (New York: Charles Scribner's Sons, 1976). An excellent introduction to the American electoral process and the implications of some proposals for reform.

Ranney, Austin. *Participation in American Presidential Nominations, 1976* (Washington: American Enterprise Institute, 1977). A brief but informative study of and the reasons for variations in turnout at presidential primaries in 1976.

Rosenbloom, David Lee. *The Election Men* (New York: Quadrangle Books, 1973). One of the better books on the management of political campaigns.

Sale, Kirkpatrick. *Power Shift: The Rise of the Southern Rim and Its Challenge to the Eastern Establishment* (New York: Random House, 1975). An examination of the political effects of the major shifts in population toward the sunbelt states.

8 Political Participation and Voting Behavior

The three preceding chapters have discussed some of the processes of politics. Chapter 5 looked at the distribution of political power in the United States; Chapter 6 examined the nature of the party system, one of the principal organizers and mobilizers of collective political power; and Chapter 7 analyzed campaigns and elections. In this chapter we shall look at the ways individual citizens participate in political processes and then narrow our focus onto patterns of voting behavior. From one point of view, this chapter forms an evaluation of the successes of parties in their appeals to particular groups. From a second point of view, these pages reanalyze some facets of the distribution of power: Who participates and how in politics? Who votes for whom? From yet another perspective, this chapter examines the problem of rationality in political behavior. Given their varied objectives, to what extent do private citizens maximize their opportunities to influence public policy?

# POLITICAL PARTICIPATION: THE DECISION TO VOTE

Voting represents perhaps the simplest form of political participation. It costs no money, takes only a small amount of time (although registering to vote can be more burdensome), and, according to democratic folklore, is a precious right. Yet not once in this century have as many as two-thirds of potential electors gone to the polls in a presidential election; and local contests often bring out only a small fraction of citizens. Indeed, about 10 percent of those who vote in presidential elections do not even bother to mark their ballots to choose among candidates for Congress. The turnout for off-year congressional elections (those when a president is not chosen) is anywhere from 20 to 50 percent less than for presidential elections. In short, the right to vote may be sacred, but many Americans seldom if ever avail themselves of its saving grace.

Who Is More or Less Likely to Vote?

More men than women voted in the past, but the gap had closed by 1982. The fading of differences in turnout reflects both the greater independence of women and their growing awareness of how they are discriminated against. Education directly affects the proportion of people casting ballots, the better-educated being more likely to vote. Similarly, people in upper-income brackets are more likely to vote than those in lower-income groups. Persons between thirty-five and fifty-five show greater interest in voting than do people either younger or older. A larger portion of urban dwellers turn out than do rural residents. Persons with strong attachments to a political party vote in relatively larger numbers than do political independents or those with weak party affiliations. Westerners have the highest rate of voting, and southerners the lowest. Protestants are less likely to vote than Catholics or Jews.

Although the legal and extralegal devices of southern communities have historically discouraged blacks from voting, so have, as the Civil Rights Commission has said, lethargy, lack of education, and simple despair.[1] Even in the north, blacks have in the past been less likely to vote than whites, but this statement is somewhat misleading. Blacks have been as likely to vote as whites of the same socioeconomic status, but blacks have tended to come from the lower-income and lower-educated strata of society, in which nonvoting runs high.[2]

Why People Stay at Home

Some people do not vote because they have only recently moved into a state or are ill, disabled, or away on vacation or business. Local party organizations try to minimize such problems by helping arrange for transportation and absentee ballots. Thus the number of people unable to vote for purely physical reasons is normally quite small, probably less than 6 percent of nonvoters.[3]

Some people, again a relatively small number, do not bother to vote because of their faith that whatever the rest of the people want will be right. Others—relatively fewer than we might expect—may feel that one side is so certain to win by a large majority that to cast their votes is to waste their time. Perhaps more important in keeping people at home are cross-pressures: for example, approval of Republican foreign policy but preference for Democratic approaches to domestic economic problems.

In addition, the issues and personalities featured in a campaign confuse some potential voters and bore others. Or they see no viable choice: Apparently millions of Americans in 1980 viewed Jimmy Carter and Ronald Reagan as equally unqualified to be president. More generally, nonvoting may indicate a lack of faith in one's own power, a feeling of political impotency, or a lack of faith in the political system and its processes, a belief that the system itself is too corrupt and inefficient to cope with important problems.

Nonvoting thus may result from a rational decision. Registration and voting consume time and energy; small amounts of each are involved, but still they bring what economists call "opportunity costs."

A traditional lion dance is used in New York City to attract attention to a voter registration drive for the 1976 election. Bilingual registration forms and information were available to Chinatown residents at tables like the one in the center of the photo. (Paul Hosefros/New York Times Pictures)

Similar and higher costs attend the process of obtaining information needed to choose intelligently between available alternatives. These costs also explain in part why many people find party labels handy guides to decision making. And, civic ideals to the contrary notwithstanding, the effect of any one vote must be discounted by the total number of other voters. That a single vote could ever swing an election above the precinct level is an infinitesimally small probability. Yet, what we know of typical nonvoters does not fit the model of shrewdly calculating people meticulously employing their resources. On the contrary, relatively uneducated people, indisposed to tolerate coldly rational analysis, are heavily overrepresented among nonvoters.

Several factors stand out in diagnoses of possible causes of nonvoting. The most obvious is the difficulty of registration. States that allow prospective voters only brief periods during the year to enroll have a much higher percentage of nonvoters than do states in which registration is relatively easy. And of those people who register, about three-quarters actually vote in presidential elections.[4] Of course, no one who is unregistered can legally vote in any election.

A second critical factor relates to civic mindedness and civic education. People who lack a sense of belonging to a political community or even a belief that one can profit from voting in a material way are not likely to go to the polls. According to two leading scholars, this disposition to participate in politics is heavily affected by a person's earlier education and training in the home:

> Through a variety of socialization mechanisms, parents and schools leave a legacy for later participation. . . . While it may be reflected in adult characteristics, this legacy is established long before adult characteristics have formed.[5]

Considerable light on the problem of nonvoting has been shed by a study conducted by the Bureau of the Census after the 1974 election.[6] In the largest political survey ever taken, the bureau interviewed people in 45,000 households across the country. The most common explanation

FIGURE **8-1**   **Percentage of Persons of Voting Age Who Actually Voted in Presidential Elections**

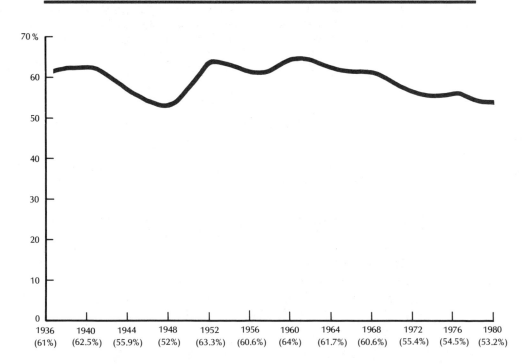

| 1936 | 1940 | 1944 | 1948 | 1952 | 1956 | 1960 | 1964 | 1968 | 1972 | 1976 | 1980 |
| (61%) | (62.5%) | (55.9%) | (52%) | (63.3%) | (60.6%) | (64%) | (61.7%) | (60.6%) | (55.4%) | (54.5%) | (53.2%) |

citizens offered for not even registering to vote was that they were not interested in doing so. A total of 41 percent of nonregistered citizens gave such reasons. Only 25 percent offered explanations relating to difficulties with registration, permanent illness, or inability to speak English. What we have said about the very tiny effect of any single vote is true, but apparently not important for most people: less than 2 percent of nonregistered citizens interviewed by the Bureau of the Census in 1976 expressed such a reason. On the other hand, many people feel a strong moral obligation to vote and experience a sense of power in doing so. Indeed, almost three-quarters of respondents in one study reported that voting gave them emotional gratification.[7]

Electoral competitiveness may be a third factor in a decision to vote, but the evidence is not clear-cut. Some studies have found that, when political contests appear tight, more people take the time to register and go to the polls. Other investigations have found a weak relationship between turnout and anticipated closeness.[8] At least, however, the probability of a close election can motivate political organizations to try to mobilize likely supporters and so perhaps increase the number of voters.

Much scholarly folklore holds that people who do not register and vote are more likely to be potential Democrats than Republicans. Several recent studies[9] indicate, however, that this description is too simple. People who would vote *solely* because of relaxed registration regulations are apt to favor Democratic over Republican candidates by only a small margin. Moreover, in congressional districts, more often than not it has been the minority party that has benefited from increased turnout among registered voters—perhaps because that increase has been caused by those who are unhappy with existing public policies. In any event, the relationship between turnout and partisan advantage is very complex.

★ OTHER FORMS OF POLITICAL PARTICIPATION

Voting, we said, is among the simplest, cheapest, and most obvious ways of participating in politics. There are dozens of other means by which a private citizen can influence the choice of public officials or public policies. (Some are listed in items 3 to 13 in Table 8-1.) Because more than one-third of people fail to vote even in presidential elections, it is reasonable to expect that far fewer attempt more expensive and difficult forms of participation. The data in Table 8-1 confirm that expectation. In fact, these figures are somewhat higher than those found by other researchers.

TABLE 8-1   **Percentage of People Engaging in Certain Kinds of Political Activity**

Type of political participation	Percentage
1. Vote regularly in presidential election	72
2. Always vote in local elections	47
3. Active in at least one organization involved in community problems	32
4. Have worked with others to try to solve some community problems	30
5. Have attempted to persuade others how to vote	28
6. Have ever actively worked for a party or candidates during a campaign	26
7. Have ever contacted a local government official about some issue	20
8. Attended at least one political meeting or rally within last 3 years	19
9. Have ever contacted a state or national government official about some issue	18
10. Have ever formed a group or an organization to attempt to solve some local community problem	14
11. Have ever given money to a party or a candidate during a compaign	13
12. Presently a member of a political club or organization	8

Number of people interviewed: 2,549

SOURCE: Copyright © 1972 by Sidney Verba and Norman Nie, *Participation in America* (New York; Harper & Row, 1972), p. 31.

Who Participates?

The most thorough study of political participation in American politics is that of Sidney Verba and Norman H. Nie.[10] Under their direction, the National Opinion Research Center interviewed a national sample* of 2,600 adults as well as officials in 64 of the communities from which the sample was drawn. The findings (partially reported in Table 8-1) distinguished six categories of citizens, one group that was politically inert,

---

* Pollsters cannot, of course, interview every person, even in a small town. Instead they interview only a portion (or sample) of the people in the particular town, city, county, state, or nation being studied. A *national sample* refers to a sample of people selected from every geographical region of the country. Although not free of problems, sampling has reached the status of a rather fine art. Most pollsters now use *random samples* of adults for voting studies, that is, samples in which every adult in the region being studied has an equal chance of being interviewed.

one that was fully active, and four that more or less specialized in certain kinds of participation:

1. *The Inactives.* These people seldom vote and rarely take part in other aspects of political life; indeed, they usually demonstrate neither knowledge of nor interest in matters political. This group constitutes a little more than one-fifth of the adult population, and it heavily over-represents blacks and those from lower socioeconomic levels, as well as young adults, very old people, and, during the time these samples were studied, women.

2. *The Voting Specialists.* These citizens typically vote but only occasionally perform other politically relevant activities, even though they often express strong identifications with a political party. These people are about as numerous as the Inactives, and they overrepresent older persons, those from lower socioeconomic strata, and inhabitants of big cities.

3. *Parochials.* This group is quite small, forming less than 5 percent of the sample. Its members vote less frequently than anyone except the Inactives. The Parochials' principal form of political participation comes through personal contacts—which they themselves initiate—with public officials, asking for assistance with problems peculiar to them or to a small segment of the population to which they belong. The Parochials overrepresent people of lower socioeconomic status, but not blacks. They are quite likely to be Catholics and to live in large urban centers.

4. *Communalists.* These people usually vote regularly, but seldom engage in other electoral activities such as campaigning. On the other hand, they, like the Parochials, make direct contact with public officials but do so about problems of wide significance within the community. The Communalists are also likely to form associations or join existing organizations to cope on a bipartisan or nonpartisan basis with social and political problems. They form about a fifth of the sample, underrepresenting blacks and Catholics and overrepresenting upper socioeconomic strata, Protestants, and people living in smaller towns and rural areas.

5. *Campaigners.* These are the citizens who are heavily involved in partisan political activities. They almost always vote, and they spend time urging others to do so—but in support of their own candidates. They often work energetically for candidates or parties, ring doorbells, distribute literature, attend rallies, and solicit and contribute money. The Campaigners have a number of political skills and are deeply partisan; but they tend to lack the sense of contribution to a community that the Communalists talk about. The Campaigners constitute about 15 percent of the population, overrepresenting persons of higher status, blacks, Catholics, and those who live in big cities.

6. *The Complete Activists.* These are the few (a little more than 10 percent of the sample) who fit the classic democratic model of the active,

informed citizen. They immerse themselves deeply in political life, voting, campaigning, contacting officials about personal and communal problems, and joining with others in both partisan and nonpartisan efforts to solve political and social problems. They heavily overrepresent the better-educated, the more affluent, and people of middle age. And, despite expectations, blacks make up a fully proportional share of this group.

Why People Participate in Politics[11]

If a sense of civic obligation and simple enjoyment of power are among the causes of political participation, very closely allied is the need that many people feel to understand the world around them and to exercise some control over what happens to their lives. Other motives vary from narrow self-interest—for instance, the Parochials—to selfless concern for the good of the whole community.

Desire for social activity—meeting with, talking to, and helping others—moves some people to political participation. Others, sometimes unconsciously, find in politics an outlet for emotional tensions, caused perhaps by personal problems, perhaps by broader concerns. Some white men who actively advocate busing to achieve integration may be assuaging the guilt they feel about past injustices done to blacks. Some public issues, especially those involving race or sex, can attract people with deep-seated neuroses. For some of them, participation acts as therapy. For others it may be a frenzied symptom of mental disturbance. There is no evidence, however, that those who participate in politics are more likely to be neurotic than less active citizens. In fact, nonparticipation is sometimes linked to emotional disorders that cause sufferers to withdraw from problems of the real world.

Participation is intuitively easier to understand than is nonparticipation. After all, politics makes a constant impact on the lives of most citizens. Yet the simple fact remains that relatively few people make the effort to become politically well informed or to take advantage of the range of opportunities open to them.

Results of Political Participation

The way an individual citizen votes is not likely to have much political impact—unless he or she acts in concert with others. And, of course, organizing individuals and massing their power is precisely what interest groups and, with a broader base, political parties try to do. It is necessary to read only an occasional newspaper to be aware of the effect that organized interest groups can have when they mobilize—or even seem to be able to mobilize—voters who share common concerns. If such organizations have money and some social prestige, their power further escalates.

The National Rifle Association, for example, has for decades been able to block effective federal gun-control laws despite the far more widely shared but unorganized concern about reducing the availability of weapons that contribute so hugely to violent crime and accidental deaths. Despite such daily demonstrations of the power of political organizations, only a very small percentage of Americans are members of such groups, as Table 8-1 shows. That figure would rise considerably, however, if it included such organizations as the American Legion, labor unions, chambers of commerce, or medical, educational, or bar associations, which, although ostensibly functioning for social, economic, or professional purposes, often work hard to block or secure passage of legislation to their own selfish advantage.

Even a lone citizen initiating contact with a public official can sometimes exercise real influence. Most elected officials pride themselves on their efficiency (usually their staff's efficiency) in hearing constituents'

Issues that private citizens perceive as important to them can bring people into the political arena. Here, jubilant voters celebrate their victory in having Proposition 13, limiting tax increases on property, approved by a statewide referendum in California. (Wide World Photos)

views and at least considering them in making decisions. In senators' and representatives' offices, much of the time is consumed in processing constituents' requests for help in dealing with various governmental agencies. And elected officials who have no strong personal views on some issues may find contacts initiated by individual citizens an excellent means of divining public opinion, especially when they want to build up records that will please voters.

In general, public officials do listen to and try to heed the suggestions, advice, requests, and even demands of politically active citizens. After interviewing officials in sixty-four of the communities from which their national sample was drawn, Verba and Nie wrote:

> If we accept as a measure of responsiveness the extent to which community leaders adopt the same agenda for community action as that of the citizenry, our data support the conclusion that where those citizens are participant, leaders are responsive.[12]

★ STUDYING ELECTORAL BEHAVIOR

So far we have been discussing individual citizens' decisions to participate in political affairs and the general patterns of their participation. Now, before moving to other aspects of political behavior, we shall explain how researchers have obtained data about voting and about most other forms of political participation.

Data for Study

The raw materials most readily available for the study of electoral behavior are the official voting returns, the records of the division of votes. These *aggregate data*, to use the technical term, are normally available down to the precinct level. They are useful for many purposes in analyzing either the results of a single election or changes over time in patterns of support. On the other hand, aggregate data have limited utility in explaining how different groups—Catholics or Jews, men or women, whites or blacks—voted. The means most frequently used to explore these differences is *survey research*, almost synonymous in the popular mind with the Gallup Poll.

To obtain information about how and why citizens vote (or participate in other ways), pollsters interview a sample of people—a small number randomly drawn so that all persons in the population have an equal chance of being selected—from an electoral district. For a presidential election, that "district" may be the entire nation; and in comparison with the entire population, "small" is indeed small. As few as 1,300 people, if truly randomly selected, meet statistical standards for a representative national sample; but one needs a much larger sample to analyze views of small groups, such as black women who vote Republican.

A variant of interviews with respondents at a single point in time is the so-called *panel*. Here pollsters interview each respondent on at least two occasions, perhaps once before and once after an election, or perhaps even a third and fourth time, before and after the next election. The advantages of a panel in discovering and accounting for changes over time are obvious. But the cost of any kind of survey research is high. And, because of the mobility of Americans, those costs spiral when a pollster tries to reinterview the same people after a lapse of several years.

Incidentally, there is no reason why students of voting behavior cannot combine analysis of aggregate voting data with survey research. And, in fact, most of the more competent analysts do use both sorts of information.

Limitations on Research and Analysis

Several cautions are in order before we look at the substantive findings about electoral behavior, cautions that also apply to what we said earlier about other kinds of political participation. First, none of the voting studies claims to explain the choices of all the voters. Each explanation is hedged by such words as "usually" and "typically." Second, most intensive studies of electoral behavior concern presidential or off-year congressional campaigns. We can generalize from national elections to all state and local contests, but only as hypotheses worth testing. Third, even at the national level, we have close investigations of only a handful of elections over a span of forty years. We should be careful not to assume that we are dealing with a static phenomenon. We may have discovered permanent patterns of behavior, but we should not reach such a conclusion without research extending over a much longer period.

This third qualification requires elaboration. Historically, presidential elections can be classified[13] as (1) *maintaining*, in which previously prevailing patterns of party loyalties persist; (2) *deviating*, in which basic partisan loyalties remain intact, but for some reason enough voters support the minority party candidate to swing this particular election to him; (3) *reinstating*, in which the majority party regains control following a deviating election; (4) *realigning*, in which old loyalties are disrupted to such an extent as to reshuffle majority and minority party statuses. The elections of 1940 (Roosevelt v. Willkie), 1944 (Roosevelt v. Dewey), and

1948 (Truman v. Dewey) were all *maintaining* elections. Thus similarities in findings during those years may mean only that in the same kind of electoral situation most people reacted in the same fashion.

The contests of 1952 and 1956 produced *deviating* elections. Dwight D. Eisenhower won handily in both, but a large number of those who voted for him continued to think of themselves as Democrats, and in 1954, 1956, and 1958 they elected a Democratic majority to both houses of Congress. The election of 1960 (Kennedy v. Nixon) was a *reinstating* election, and 1964 (Johnson v. Goldwater) provided another *maintaining* election. In 1968 (Humphrey v. Nixon) again was a *deviating* election. Richard M. Nixon captured the White House but with only 43 percent of the popular vote, and, at the same time, the Democrats retained control of both houses of Congress. In 1972 (McGovern v. Nixon), the Democrats were still bitterly divided among themselves, and their nominee clumsily pushed party loyalists into Nixon's camp. As in 1956, the result was a *deviating* election in which the Republicans won the presidency by a huge landslide but lost both houses of Congress. In 1976, enough Democratic loyalists came home, thus *reinstating* their party in power. Nineteen-eighty produced another *deviating* election. Jimmy Carter could not keep his party together, nor could Ronald Reagan generate enough enthusiasm to persuade large masses of voters to change their party allegiance.

Because there have been no *realigning* elections since survey research developed, we lack a study of the depth that would make a full comparison possible. Such contests, however, are relatively rare, those of 1896 and 1932 being the two that experts usually identify. The panic of 1893 apparently served as a catalyst to raise Republicans to the status of majority party. They retained this dominance, despite deviating elections in 1912 and 1916, until the Great Depression of 1929 started another cycle that brought the Democrats into power. Several prominent analysts have been predicting the coming of a new realignment, and many journalists leaped to proclaim 1980 as that epiphany. Close analysis of the data, however, shows that Reagan's supporters, outside the ranks of the Republican faithful, tended to be more fed up with Carter than committed to Reagan or his party.[14]

Some explanations of political behavior may change considerably when data of the same kind are available on each type of presidential election. Even without such data, there have already been some modifications of early theories. The first studies, which involved only *maintaining* electtions, agreed that a person's party preference was the best single determinant of his or her final vote. In the *deviating* elections of 1952 and 1956, however, large numbers of voters who continued to call themselves Democrats voted Republican, clearly attracted to General Eisenhower. Even in the *reinstating* election of 1960, a considerable number of Democrats again voted Republican. In 1964, vast numbers of Republicans supported the Democratic candidate; and in 1972, an equally vast number of Democrats voted for Nixon. But 1976 saw a strong resurgence of voting along party lines,[15] while 1980 brought another horde of line crossing and ticket splitting.

We should not, therefore, think of parties as holding together "like a sticky ball of popcorn." Rather, as V. O. Key put it, "no sooner has a popular majority been constructed than it begins to crumble."[16] Even a finding that the proportion of votes going to each party remains constant does not necessarily mean that the same people are always voting the same way. New voters come of age or participate in politics; old ones die or lose interest. Other voters become disenchanted with the administration and support the opposition; still others may be won over to administration policies and, for this election at least, vote for the incumbents.

★ PATTERNS OF PARTISANSHIP[17]

Political Knowledge

Despite different techniques of research and analysis and different interpretations of results, students of electoral behavior have produced findings that are in large measure consistent with each other. Those who hope to find an intelligent, informed electorate carefully weighing policy alternatives and candidates' records before voting can expect small comfort from available data. Such people exist, of course, but they are heavily outnumbered by citizens who know little about candidates and issues, even during a national campaign when the media are saturated with political information. Although the percentage of informed, carefully analyzing voters has grown as the educational level of Americans has increased, these people still form a distinct minority of the voting age population.

Furthermore, people's opinions and preferences about policies may be highly unstable over time. For example, when the University of Michigan's Survey Research Center asked a panel identical questions about certain public policies three times during a four-year period, a large segment of respondents gave answers that varied from strong support to strong opposition. And these questions concerned such apparently basic issues as the proper roles of the federal government in the fields of housing and public utilities.[18]

Socialization

Even when a voter believes that he or she has made a clear-cut choice based solely on considerations of public policy, a number of factors in that person's background may have helped form attitudes affecting and even distorting the images that the candidates have tried to project. Psychologists have often demonstrated the phenomenon of *selective perception*—what people see in a particular situation is greatly influenced by their own values. And early political education may affect both perceptions and preferences.

Cohesiveness of voting within families was a striking finding of an intensive study of Erie County, New York, in 1940,[19] a finding that has cropped up again and again in subsequent surveys. Because husbands and wives have tended to vote the same way, children have usually been reared in a one-sided political atmosphere. It is hardly surprising to find, then, that when they come of age children are inclined to vote in the same way as their parents. This pattern, however, is not immutable. Changes in social status or disagreements on important policy questions may weaken the "inherited" party allegiance. Lowering the voting age to eighteen, an age at which the young often take great pride in seeming to differ with their parents even when they really agree, may also widen cleavages between generations. Moreover, families' political coherence in the past normally resulted from wives following their husbands. What effect Women's Liberation has had on this coherence—and on children's inherited loyalties—remains to be seen.

Social Class

If we use occupation, income, and education as indexes of class (or what is sometimes called "socioeconomic status"), then we can say that, generally, the higher their education and income and the more professional the nature of their work, the more likely voters are to be Republican. Conversely, the lower their income and education the more closely their occupations are related to manual, unskilled labor, the more likely they are to be Democrats. There is, therefore, some evidence behind the old cliché that the rich are Republicans and the poor Democrats, but the full truth is far more complex. Republican strength is largely based on middle-class white-collar workers and semiprofessionals, and the Democrats often draw their leaders from the wealthy. There is also a striking exception to the rule of the better-educated being Republican. Intellectuals, particularly social scientists, are overwhelmingly Democratic. Moreover, many blue-collar workers supported Nixon in 1972, Ford in 1976, and Reagan in 1980, although without transferring any permanent allegiance to the Republican party.

Despite unions' claims to the contrary, there is probably more political cohesiveness among businessmen than among workers. If there were not and if general socioeconomic divisions were followed in every election, the Republicans would be hard put to win office except in wealthy suburbs, or they would be forced into becoming a more liberal party. One of the basic reasons for the absence of political solidarity among working-class people is that American culture has been predominantly white middle class. Geographical influences also cut across class lines. For example, in those small cities that are normally Republican communities, factory workers are less inclined to vote Democratic than are people who do the same sort of work in large urban centers.

Furthermore, the general relationship between class and party loyalty has declined since World War II. The Democratic party has made deep inroads into the middle class, especially its younger people, in part because of the upward mobility of traditionally Democratic families, and in part because of changing attitudes about the proper role of the federal government in social and economic affairs.[20]

Religion

Religion, too, is associated with partisan political loyalty, as Table 8-2 shows. White Protestants in northern states tend to vote Republican. Since the 1920s, the Jewish vote has been heavily Democratic by about a four-to-one margin. Historically, Catholics, even those in upper-income brackets, have been much more likely to vote Democratic, although this tendency has been more pronounced among Irish and Polish Americans than among Italian-Americans. Moreover, this historical attachment has weakened during the past few decades, as Catholics have become more assimilated into the mainstream of American life and issues other than economics and social welfare have increased in saliency. In 1956, Dwight Eisenhower's strong anti-communism helped him win almost half the Catholic vote. In 1972, George McGovern's support of abortion and Richard Nixon's opposition as well as his endorsement of public aid for parochial schools and his general effort to appeal to white urban, working-class ethnics, a group that is heavily Catholic, persuaded a majority of Catholics to vote Republican—but only for a presidential candidate and only in that election. In 1980, more Catholics voted for Reagan than for Carter, but the proportion was smaller than among the electorate as a whole.

Religion can be an explosive issue when it comes out openly in a campaign, and most politicians are careful to avoid the subject. In 1928, Al Smith's Catholicism was a major factor in his defeat. Again in 1960, it played a significant role, although its actual effect is more difficult to assess because the number of Catholic voters had greatly increased in the intervening thirty-two years. On balance, however, it seems that John Kennedy's religion cost him more votes than it gained him. "Prob-

TABLE **8-2**   **Voting Trends among Social Categories since 1952 (Presidential Vote, 1952–1976)**

Percent Democratic of two-party vote for President (three-party in 1968 and 1980)

	1952	1956	1960	1964	1968	1972	1976	1980
National	45	42	50	61	43	38	51	41
Men	47	45	52	60	41	37	53	38
Women	42	39	49	62	45	38	48	44
White	43	41	49	59	38	32	46	36
Nonwhite	79	61	68	94	85	87	85	86
College	34	31	39	52	37	37	42	35
High school	45	42	52	62	42	34	54	43
Grade school	52	50	55	66	52	49	58	54
Professional and Business	36	32	42	54	34	31	42	33
White collar	40	37	48	57	41	36	50	40
Manual	55	50	60	71	50	43	58	48
Under 30 years	51	43	54	64	47	48	53	47
30–49 years	47	45	54	63	44	33	48	38
50 years and older	39	39	46	59	41	36	52	41
Protestants	37	37	38	55	35	30	46	39
Catholics	56	51	78	76	59	48	57	46
Republicans	8	4	5	20	9	5	9	8
Democrats	77	85	84	87	74	67	82	69
Independents	35	30	43	56	31	31	38	29
Members of labor union families	61	57	65	73	56	46	63	50

SOURCE: The Gallup Poll, press release, December 14, 1972; the Gallup Opinion Index, December, 1976 (Report No. 137); the Gallup Poll, *Public Opinion 1980* (Wilmington, Del: Academic Resources Co., 1981), p. 243.

ably the best guess," V. O. Key wrote, "is that Kennedy won in spite of rather than because of the fact that he was a Catholic."[21] Anti-Catholicism may still be alive; but Catholics, though still a minority, have become the largest religious sect in the United States, and no sane national candidate can afford to antagonize such a large group.

Race

Minority racial status, like religion, correlates strongly with party allegiance. From Emancipation to the New Deal, blacks, at least those who voted, were strongly Republican; then Franklin D. Roosevelt won them away from the party of Lincoln. Although the Republicans have made a number of attempts to woo black support and black leaders frequently urge their followers to vote more selectively, blacks have remained since 1932 solidly Democratic. It was in part Republican despair at cracking the black vote in northern metropolitan areas that made it attractive for Nixon, Ford, and Reagan to make special appeals to whites.

Age

Age tends to stabilize party preferences. Typically, younger voters' party loyalties are not firm. In fact, younger citizens frequently call themselves independents, even when they vote for the same party their parents did. If a switch in allegiance occurs, it is likely to come during early adulthood, along with changes in income and social status. As voters grow older their attachment to a party is apt to harden, perhaps to a point where it becomes psychologically very difficult to vote for the traditional opposition.

Older voters are more apt to vote Republican than are younger voters, as Table 8-2 shows, the usual explanation being that age brings greater conservatism and, at least until retirement nears, larger income. But that table also shows considerable variations within each age group at any given election and indicates that voting behavior of any particular group varies from election to election. More specifically Table 8-2 demonstrates that it is wrong to think that most younger voters always vote Democratic.

Geography

Immigration from urban centers to the suburbs might benefit Republicans because this change normally involves moving from a lower to a higher income bracket and to an environment generally less hospitable to the Democratic party, or so some writers have speculated. While Republicans are somewhat more likely than Democrats to move out of the cities, there is little evidence of conversion among former city dwellers to Republicanism.

Farmers have perspectives that on many issues differ from those of people in urban areas; but it is possible to speak of a rural or an urban vote only in gross terms. Any remarks about voting behavior must be made with qualifications about income, race, religion, and a host of other factors. Northern farmers, for example, generally have a Republican tradition; southern farmers, at least until recently, a Democratic one. Outside the south, however, a considerable number of small farmers are quite likely to be Democratic; and even in the deep south, there have been rural Republican enclaves that trace their loyalty back to the Civil War.

Historically, farmers have been a prolific source of radical third parties that have received impressive rural support at one election, only to vanish within a few years. This tendency to support third parties may be dying out; but the two-party division among farmers outside the south still shows sharp fluctuations. Moreover, not only are farmers disinclined to be loyal to a party over time, but they are also less likely than city dwellers to vote a straight party ticket in any one election. And farmers' voting participation is erratic; they may turn out in mass for one election only to stay quietly at home for the next.

The Independents

Because membership in American political parties is loose and informal, it is not easy to determine what proportion of the electorate can accurately be labeled "independent." Many people who claim to be independents actually support one party with considerable regularity. The best

FIGURE **8-2**

Percentage of Population Calling Themselves Independents

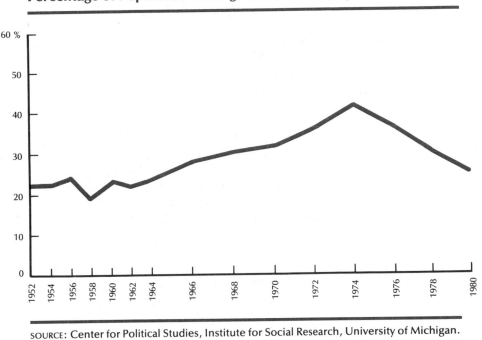

SOURCE: Center for Political Studies, Institute for Social Research, University of Michigan.

guesses place the proportion of real independents at somewhere between one-quarter and one-third of the electorate.

There is a venerable body of opinion that asserts the moral and intellectual superiority of independent voters. It is true that national surveys have found that a majority of the most knowledgeable respondents call themselves independents, but this group is small. The typical independent tends to have less political interest, awareness, concern, and information than the voter who asserts party allegiance.

Reactions against the war in Vietnam and the scandals of Watergate have reduced citizens' trust in government and these, along with the adoption of the Twenty-sixth Amendment in 1971 that lowered the voting age to eighteen, reduced willingness to identify with a political party. As Figure 8-2 shows, for many years about 75 to 80 percent of adults claimed to be Democrats or Republicans; but during the late 1960s the proportion of potential voters denying affiliation with either party began to rise steeply until 1974, when more than 40 percent of the electorate claimed to be independents. Then, with American forces out of Vietnam and Richard Nixon out of the White House, the share of people asserting party allegiance rose. By 1980, less than a quarter of voting age adults listed themselves as independents.

★ RATIONALITY AND POLITICAL CHOICE

The classical democratic model of a politically interested, informed, and active citizenry intelligently participating in the choice of public officials and public policies does not fit well with available data about political information and participation of a large majority of American adults—at least on first examination. Nor do these data support a model of highly informed "opinion leaders" guiding the political choices of the less sophisticated. The critical causes for the actual state of things, we have said, appear to lie in most citizens' failing to appreciate the importance of politics, not understanding how to influence public officials, and not enjoying participation—or at least lacking a feeling of civic duty to take part in politics. These shortcomings, as we shall discuss in a moment, are related to socioeconomic status. More immediately, we concentrate on the question of how rationally the mass of citizens behave. "Rationality" in this discussion is not a synonym for intelligence. Rather it concerns efficient allocation of available means (resources such as time, energy, and money) to achieve desired goals.

Rationality, Candidates, and Public Officials

First of all, whatever one can say about private citizens, it seems clear that, as a group, candidates for office behave rationally. The campaigning techniques described in Chapter 7 appear quite suited to the behavior of the American public, to whom "politics is a sideshow in the great circus of life."[22] Moreover, such traditional party appeals as those of the Democrats to the working class, blacks, Jews, and Catholics and those of the Republicans to whites, Protestants, professionals, semi-professionals, and other members of the middle class seem to hit a large share of their targets. More specifically, the fact that elected officials try to respond to the requests and suggestions of citizen-activists also indicates rational behavior by people who wish to be re-elected.

Rationality and Private Citizens

A closer look at private citizens shows, as we would expect, both far less political sophistication and much less rational behavior, in an objective sense, than among professionals. For, whether voters believe it or not, politics vitally affects the life of everyone in the country. Thus—and leaving aside voting for the moment—insofar as citizens do not take full advantage of their constitutional rights to contact government officials and join with others to engage in a whole range of activities that are politically relevant, those people are making very inefficient use of their resources.

That evaluation is correct, however, only to the extent that these people cannot act as "free riders" or actually do not want to destroy the system. It could make very good sense, of course, for a person opposing the system to refuse to use the means it offers to satisfy public needs. The problem of the free rider is much more complex. In brief, insofar as a group or another individual (such as Ralph Nader) will effectively further the interests of the inactive as well as the active, it is perfectly rational for a person to sit back and let others do the work. For example, a conservative, white male lawyer who knows that the powerful and highly politicized American Bar Association will fight vigorously to protect both his professional interests as a lawyer can quite rationally devote his time to making money.

Doing nothing, however, is not rational when such organizations or individuals either do not exist or lack money, skills, and other instruments of political power. And it is likely to be the poorer, less well-educated, aged, or sick—the very people who need governmental action most—who lack powerful organizations to fight for them. Thus it is objectively irrational for such people not to participate actively in politics. But these are also likely to be the people who lack the knowledge and verbal skills to participate effectively, and, in the case of the aged and the sick, the physical capacity to do so. As Chapter 5 pointed out, it is people of higher socioeconomic status who are best equipped to wield political instruments effectively.

Americans like to think that because the opportunity to participate politically is, as a matter of constitutional law, open to all, it is therefore *equally* open to all. As a matter of logic, the second proposition simply does not follow from the first. Nor is it empirically true. Of the ten countries that Verba and Nie have studied (Austria, Germany, Great Britain, Holland, India, Italy, Japan, Mexico, Nigeria, and the United States), only in India is political participation tied as closely to socioeconomic status as it is in the United States. The tight linkage in this country, they believe, is a paradoxical result of a relative absence of class consciousness and class-oriented political institutions. If most Americans were aware of the differences in political rewards received by different classes, and if there existed parties or interest groups that could awaken and exploit such an awareness, then, Verba and Nie believe, people of lower socioeconomic status would take fuller advantage of the political opportunities that are open to them. And there is some evidence to support this proposition. For instance, blacks who are able to articulate concern about racial problems tend to be more politically active than whites who have similar incomes, education, and social position.

Rationality and Voting

Assuming that it is rational to vote, the electoral behavior of almost two-thirds of American citizens demonstrates considerably more rationality than their generally low level of information might indicate. The small core of *Complete Activists*, of course, neatly fits the classic democratic model. Another, and probably larger, group of people from both the political left and right are also well informed and think with care about public issues. They tend, at least, to vote with great rationality. But before dismissing as irrational the way all the relatively inactive and uninformed members of the general public voters, we must carefully re-examine much of what we said earlier in this chapter.

First, there is a problem with our information, a methodological problem inherent in most of survey research. Having a stranger come into one's home and ask questions about politics creates emotional stress; and the questions require a degree of verbal facility that the respondent may simply not possess under the best of circumstances. The point is not that most voters are well informed, but rather that the way in which pollsters test their information tends to exaggerate their ignorance. Less structured and more informal interviews, involving talks with an interviewer who over a period of weeks becomes a friend, have produced a different picture.[23] It shows somewhat more coherence—though not necessarily more sophistication—among opinions that at first glance seem confused and even contradictory. This type of interview, however, may itself help produce coherence and consistency by forcing respondents to think hard about political problems, something they might never do unless prodded by a persistent interrogator.

Second, there is a distinction between acting on little information and acting irrationally. One cannot say that a gut reaction is irrational or even unintelligent. Rationality depends on the person's gut and the nature of the reaction. For example, it makes excellent sense in terms of economic self-interest for blacks and poor whites to vote for Democratic presidential candidates, just as it makes economic sense for upper-class white Protestants to vote Republican. By and large, Democratic presidents of this century have tried to use federal power to help the economically less fortunate. Republican presidents have been more concerned to protect upper-class whites.

Furthermore, those voters who want social change may reasonably prefer the more liberal party, just as those who look at the past for guidance may prefer the more conservative. Catholics and Jews, underdogs in a predominantly Protestant society and strongly motivated by religious teachings about government's positive obligations, act rationally in picking the candidate who preaches social justice through governmental action. Candidates and parties may give the public weak or even confusing clues to their stands on *specific* problems, but since

1932 the *general* policy orientations of presidential candidates has been clear. And the data in Table 8-2 are consistent with a rational response by most voters to those orientations.

Relationships between responses to policy questions and actual votes are weak, but, as we have said, this weakness may be due in part to difficulties in responding to interviewers' formal questions. This weakness may also be partly due to the fact that parties take stands on a great many issues, and the relative importance of these issues may vary widely among voters. It would hardly be surprising to see a white laborer, worried about his job and afraid of having blacks live next door, vote for a Democratic presidential candidate who is pressing for civil rights, *if* the white worker also associated the Democrats with prosperity and better jobs. Economic advancement might be more important to him than dislike of blacks. Besides, with more money he might be able to

"You're looking better in the polls . . . they show you with 51% as long as you don't have an opponents."

Grin and Bear It, by Lichty and Wagner, © 1978 Field Enterprises, Inc. Courtesy of Field Newspaper Syndicate

move to an all-white suburb. If this man used such social science jargon as "rank ordering of values" and "efficient allocation of resources," political scientists would be quick to proclaim the rationality of his decision, although they might deplore his goals. In short, we should be slow to equate lack of academic knowledge with irrational behavior.

There is a third, straightforward reason why one should be wary of dismissing as irrational voters' reactions in presidential elections. There is a close relationship between how voters perceive parties and candidates and how voters cast their ballots. To explain this linkage, Stanley Kelley and Thad Mirer have stated what they call the Voter's Decision Rule:

> The voter canvasses his likes and dislikes of the leading candidates and major parties involved in an election. Weighing each like and dislike equally, he votes for the candidate toward whom he has the greatest net number of favorable attitudes, if there is such a candidate. If no candidate has such an advantage, the voter votes consistently with his party affiliation, if he has such. If he does not identify with one of the major parties and if his attitudes do not incline him toward one candidate more than toward another, he will not vote.[24]

To test the validity of this rule, Kelley and Mirer analyzed the results of surveys of panels conducted just before five presidential elections. For each respondent they constructed a scale of attitudes toward parties and candidates based on his or her replies to questions asking what the person liked about the leading presidential candidates and major parties.* The farther the person was located on the negative (Republican) side of the scale, the more likely he or she was to vote Republican; the farther on the positive (Democratic) side of the scale, the more likely he or she was to vote Democratic. In fact, the scale accurately predicted the way an overwhelming percentage of voters would decide, as Table 8-3 shows. The scale's poorest performances came in 1968 and 1980, when there were three major candidates. But even in those years, the Voter's Decision Rule accurately predicted a larger porportion of votes than did any other explanation, including respondents' own statements, given in interviews shortly before the election, about how they planned to vote.

The results produced by the Voter's Decision Rule accord with Edward Tufte's analysis of off-year congressional elections, (reported in Chapter 7).[25] Tufte, it will be recalled, found that combining an index of

---

* For each respondent, Kelley and Mirer counted the number of favorable comments about Democrats and subtracted from that number all unfavorable comments the respondent made about Democrats. They performed the same simple arithmetic with each respondent's comments about Republicans. Then Kelley and Mirer subtracted each respondent's pro-Republican score from his or her pro-Democratic score. (The formula is more easily seen than said: [D+ − D −] − [R + − R −] = scale score.) The resulting scale gave pro-Democratic respondents positive scores and pro-Republicans negative scores. "The Simple Act of Voting," *American Political Science Review*, **LXVIII** (1974), 572.

TABLE **8-3**   **Percentage of Voters Whose Presidential Vote the Rule Accurately Predicted**

Year	Percentage	Number of respondents
1952	87	1,166
1956	85	1,251
1960	88	1,397
1964	90	1,109
1968	81	1,018
1972	84	827
1976	84	1,639
1980	75	949

SOURCES: Stanley Kelley, Jr., and Thad W. Mirer, "The Simple Act of Voting," *American Political Science Review*, LXVIII (1974), 572; and Stanley Kelley, Jr., *Interpreting Elections* (Princeton, N.J.: Princeton University Press, 1983), Appendix I.

economic well-being with presidential popularity accurately predicted the percentage of the national vote that the president's party would win. Thus it is reasonable to see off-year congressional elections as referendums on the president's performance in office.

There is additional evidence that many voters exercise rational choice. One piece of that evidence is indirect, but in the long run likely to be of great importance. The level of education in the United States, we noted earlier, has risen dramatically during the last generation. In 1948, almost half the electorate had not gone beyond grammar school. In 1980 a larger proportion of adults of voting age had college degrees than had only a grammar school education or less, and adults who had some education in college outnumbered by 3 to 1 those who had not gone beyond grammar school. Given the correlations among education, political interest, and political knowledge, we would expect that more voters are now giving thoughtful attention to politics than was the case forty years ago, when pollsters were first putting together an accurate picture of the American voter.[26]

The data that we have from surveys do not allow a definitive test of an increase in levels of political conceptualization (and thus, we would infer, rationality). But we can note several sorts of changes in answers to the questions that the Survey Research Center asks people regarding their likes and dislikes about presidential candidates.[27] First, the number of replies referring to candidates' personal characteristics remains steady over the years. Second, there has been a marked increase in responses referring to candidates' stands on particular issues of public policy. Before 1964 only about half the people interviewed mentioned issues; after 1964 about three out of every four respondents do so. Moreover, correlations between voting choice and these sorts of responses show a parallel course, steady for personal characteristics and a noticeable rise for stands on issues. Third, the number of people who mentioned candidates' parties as important elements in their choice declined from 1952 through 1972. As we have seen in 1976 there was a resurgence of party loyalty, but that resurgence does not necessarily imply—as 1980 showed—that voters once again were bewitched by the donkey or by the elephant. Rather, as two leading students of voting behavior put it:

> The analysis suggests that the increased role of party loyalty in voting reflects a complex process by which people connect their partisan predispositions to their policy preferences and to their evaluations of the policy and personal leadership qualities of the candidates.[28]

And the 1980 election showed a large number of Democrats voting for the Republican presidential candidate and an equal share of both Democrats and Republicans voting for John Anderson, an independent.

Neither individually nor collectively do these data *prove* that most people vote rationally. What the data do demonstrate, however, is that *in the aggregate* American electoral behavior meets at least minimal standards of rational choice—which is not to say, we repeat, that those choices are wise.

What complicates discussion—as well as practical politics—is that a sizable minority of voters, typically the least informed, least interested, and least committed to a political party, often supply the decisive margin of victory. And, as we saw in Chapter 7, campaign managers aim much of their propaganda at such people. With the uninformed, uninterested, and uncommitted a principal target, campaign strategists understandably prefer to rely on gimmickry rather than on hard evidence and cold logic, a decision that both dilutes the utility of the political knowledge that citizens already possess and discourages their acquiring new knowledge.

 SUMMARY

This chapter has described varying patterns of participation and nonparticipation in American politics and has offered a set of explanations about why some people do but most do not take anything like full advantage of available opportunities to influence politics. We also noted that the better-educated and more affluent citizens were more apt to participate than other people. More specifically, this chapter described the voting behavior of various groups and concluded that, despite low levels of information and the inability of a large portion of citizens to respond in a highly articulate fashion to pollsters' questions, the bulk of American voters make electoral choices that appear to be quite rational.

NOTES

1. *Report of the United States Commission on Civil Rights 1959* (Washington, D.C.: Government Printing Office, 1959), Book 1, p. 191.
2. See Richard D. Shingles, "Black Consciousness and Political Participation," *American Political Science Review*, LXXV (1981), 76.
3. Much information about recent causes of nonvoting is contained in U.S. Bureau of the Census, "Voter Participation in November 1974," *Current Population Reports*, Series P-20, No. 272 (January 1975).
4. See Stanley Kelley, Jr., Richard E. Ayres, and William G. Bowen, "Registration and Voting," *American Political Science Review*, LXI (1967), 359.
5. Paul Allen Beck and M. Kent Jennings, "Pathways to Participation," *American Political Science Review*, LXXVI (1982), 94.
6. See note 3, above.
7. Gabriel A. Almond and Sidney Verba, *The Civic Culture* (Princeton, N.J.: Princeton University Press, 1963), pp. 145–146.
8. For a discussion of the findings, see Jae-On Kim, J. R. Petrocik, and S. N. Enockson, "Voter Turnout among the Various States: Systemic and Individual Components," *American Political Science Review*, LXIX (1975), 107.
9. Steven J. Rosenstone and Raymond E. Wolfinger, "The Effect of Registration Laws on Voter Turnout," *American Political Science Review*, LXXII (1978), 22, and James De Nardo, "Turnout and the Vote: The Joke's on the Democrats," *American Political Science Review*, LXXIV (1980), 406. For a highly technical but still interesting analysis of nonvoting see Orley Ashenfelter and Stanley Kelley, Jr., "Determinants of Participation in Presidential Elections," *The Journal of Law and Economics*, XVIII (1975), 695.
10. *Participation in America: Political Democracy and Social Equality* (New York: Harper & Row, 1972). We draw especially heavily on Chapters 3–6.
11. See generally Robert E. Lane, *Political Life: Why People Get Involved in Politics* (New York: The Free Press, 1959).
12. P. 335.
13. This classification was developed by V. O. Key, Jr., "A Theory of Critical Elections," *Journal of Politics*, XVII (1955), 3; and elaborated by Angus Campbell, Philip E. Converse, Warren E. Miller, and Donald E. Stokes, *Elections and the Political Order* (New York: John Wiley and Sons, 1966), Chapters 2 and 3.
14. See, generally, Stanley Kelley, Jr., *Interpreting Elections* (Princeton, N.J.: Princeton University Press, 1983).
15. Warren E. Miller and Teresa Levitin, *Leadership and Change: Presidential Elections from 1952 to 1976* (Cambridge, Mass.: Winthrop Publishers, 1976), p. 230.
16. *The Responsible Electorate* (Cambridge, Mass.: Harvard University Press, 1966), p. 30.
17. Although we have used more recent works to bring data up to date, this section relies heavily on the classic study of electoral behavior: Angus Campbell, Warren E. Miller, and Donald E. Stokes, *The American Voter* (New York: John W. Wiley and Sons, 1960).
18. Philip E. Converse, "The Nature of Belief Systems in Mass Publics," in David E. Apter, ed., *Ideology and Discontent* (New York: The Free Press, 1964).
19. Paul F. Lazarsfeld, Bernard B. Berelson, and Hazel Gaudet, *The People's Choice: How the Voter Makes Up His Mind in a Presidential Campaign* (New York: Duell, Sloan & Pearce–Meredith Press, 1944).
20. Paul R. Abramson, "General Change in American Electoral Behavior," *American Political Science Review*, LXVIII (1974), 93.
21. "Interpreting the Election Results," in Paul T. David, ed., *The Presidential Election and Transition 1960–1961* (Washington: Brookings Institution, 1961), p. 175.

22. Robert A. Dahl, *Who Governs?* (New Haven, Conn.: Yale University Press, 1961), p. 305.
23. For examples, see Robert E. Lane's two books: *Political Ideology: Why the American Common Man Believes What He Does* (New York: The Free Press, 1962), and *Political Thinking and Consciousness: The Private Life of the Political Mind* (Chicago, Ill.: Markham Publishing Company, 1969).
24. "The Simple Act of Voting," *American Political Science Review*, LXVIII (1974), 574.
25. "Determinants of the Outcomes of Midterm Congressional Elections," *American Political Science Review*, XLIX (1975), 812.
26. See Philip E. Converse, "Change in the American Electorate," in Angus Campbell and Philip E. Converse, eds., *The Human Meaning of Social Change* (New York: Russell Sage Foundation, 1972).
27. Norman H. Nie, Sidney Verba, and John R. Petrocik, *The Changing American Voter* (Cambridge, Mass.: Harvard University Press, 1976), Chapter 10.
28. Miller and Levitin, *Leadership and Change*, p. 240.

SELECTED BIBLIOGRAPHY

Burnham, Walter Dean. *Critical Elections and the Mainsprings of American Politics* (New York: W. W. Norton, 1970). A study of American voting behavior that challenges many of the basic interpretations of the "Michigan School," exemplified by the work of Campbell, Converse, Miller, and Stokes listed below.

Campbell, Angus, Philip E. Converse, Warren E. Miller, and Donald E. Stokes. *The American Voter* (New York: John Wiley and Sons, 1960).

———. *Elections and the Political Order* (New York: John Wiley and Sons, 1966). Two thorough and insightful analyses of voting behavior in national elections, based on polls conducted by the University of Michigan's Survey Research Center.

Fuchs, Lawrence P., ed. *American Ethnic Politics* (New York: Harper & Row, 1968). A collection of essays dealing, as the title implies, with the political participation of white ethnic groups.

Kelley, Stanley, Jr. *Interpreting Elections* (Princeton, N.J.: Princeton University Press, 1983). A senior scholar's brilliant analysis of why elections come out as they do and what makes them "decisive" for the political system as a whole.

Key, V. O., Jr. *The Responsible Electorate: Rationality in Presidential Voting, 1936–1960* (Cambridge, Mass.: The Belknap Press of Harvard University Press, 1966). "The perverse and unorthodox argument of this little book," Key said shortly before his death, "is that voters are not fools."

Fiorina, Morris P. *Retrospective Voting in American National Elections* (New Haven: Conn.: Yale University Press, 1981). An effort to synthesize theories of voting behavior based on "rational choice" and "partisan predisposition" into a coherent intellectual framework.

Lane, Robert E. *Political Ideology: Why the American Common Man Believes What He Does* (New York: The Free Press, 1962). An effort to describe the sources and consequences of the ideology latent in the mind of "the urban common man," based on long and intensive interviews with fifteen lower-middle-class workers.

———. *Political Thinking and Consciousness: The Private Life of the Political Mind* (Chicago: Markham Publishing Co., 1969). A study, based on in-depth interviews with twenty-four young men, of how motivation shapes thinking about politics.

Lazarsfeld, Paul F., Bernard Berelson, and Hazel Gaudet. *The People's Choice: How the Voter Makes Up His Mind in a Presidential Campaign* (New York: Duell, Sloan and Pearce–Meredith Press, 1944). The first of the modern voting studies, interesting for its status as a piece of intellectual history.

Milbrath, Lester, and M. L. Goel. *Political Participation,* 2nd ed. (Chicago: Rand McNally, 1975). An insightful analysis of the modes of private citizens' involvements in politics.

Miller, Warren E., and Teresa E. Levitin. *Leadership and Change: Presidential Elections from 1952 to 1976* (Cambridge, Mass.: Winthrop Publishers, 1976). An imaginative use of survey research to discern and explain varying patterns of voting behavior; puts Carter's victory in historical perspective.

Nie, Norman H., Sidney Verba, and John R. Petrocik. *The Changing American Voter* (Cambridge, Mass.: Harvard University Press, 1976). A systematic effort to review, re-analyze, and rethink available evidence about voting behavior to discern patterns of change over the years.

Page, Benjamin I. *Choices and Echoes in Presidential Elections* (Chicago: University of Chicago Press, 1978). A sophisticated effort to test theories about elections.

Pomper, Gerald, et al. *The Election of 1980* (Chatham, N.J.: Chatham House Publishers, 1981). Commentaries on the 1980 elections by a group of experts.

Rogers, Lindsay. *The Pollsters* (New York: Alfred A. Knopf, 1949). An examination of the failure of the pollsters to predict the 1948 election that questions many of the fundamental assumptions and techniques of mass opinion surveys.

Scammon, Richard M., and Ben J. Wattenberg. *The Real Majority* (New York: Coward-McCann, 1970). An interesting and controversial analysis of the political attitudes and voting behavior of the "middle American."

Thompson, Dennis F. *The Democratic Citizen: Social Science and Democratic Theory in the Twentieth Century* (Cambridge University Press, 1970). An interesting effort to reconcile the empirical finding of voting studies with attempts of normative political philosophers to construct a democratic political theory.

Tufte, Edward R., ed. *Political Control of the Economy* (Princeton, N.J.: Princeton University Press, 1978). A study of the interactions among economic conditions, voting behavior, electoral results, and economic policies.

————. *The Quantitative Analysis of Social Problems* (Reading, Mass.: Addison-Wesley, 1970). A good collection of quantitative studies, several of which deal with voting behavior.

Verba, Sidney, and Norman H. Nie. *Participation in America: Political Democracy and Social Equality* (New York: Harper & Row, 1972). The most thorough and painstaking analysis of the varied patterns of political participation and what those patterns imply for the functioning of the political system.

PART IV

The
Congress

9 Congress and Its Members

The Congress of the United States was a product of the golden age of legislatures. In the eighteenth century the doctrine of legislative supremacy strongly influenced political thinking. Reflecting their commitment to representative government as well as the young nation's distrust of executive power, the founders created a strong national legislature to determine public policy, spend public funds, and command the executive.

Development of the modern state and its large bureaucracies, expansion of the stakes and instruments of diplomacy and warfare, and the ability of mass communications to dramatize and personalize chief executives have all contributed to the eclipse of the legislature by the executive branch of government. Congress has not been immune to these worldwide trends. Its relative importance has inevitably declined; but unlike most other national legislatures in the contemporary world, Congress has survived the growth of executive and bureaucratic power without losing a central role in the American system.

In recent years, however, the House of Representatives and the Senate have been severely tested. Presidential war making has largely bypassed the legislative process. Various presidents, particularly Richard Nixon, have asserted sweeping executive powers. In the wake of the Watergate scandals and Nixon's forced resignation, Congress sought with some success to regain its power over the purse and its checks on the executive branch. These efforts, however, seem unlikely to restore Congress to its constitutional role as the first branch of government, given the broad sweep of presidential power. Moreover, executive authority is concentrated in the Oval Office, while legislative power is dispersed among 535 representatives and senators. But the reassertion of congressional prerogatives in the 1970s demonstrates the underlying political strength of a national legislature unwilling to become a rubber stamp for the chief executive and his agents.

⭐ CONGRESS'S POLICY-MAKING FUNCTIONS

According to the traditional theory of representative democracy, the legislature has primary responsibility to determine public policy through its power to make laws. Article I of the Constitution provides that: "All legislative power herein granted shall be vested in a Congress. . . ." Laws such as the Social Security Act, the Wages and Hours Act, the Elementary and Secondary Education Act, and various civil rights, housing, and highway statutes passed by Congress are among the most important public policies developed over the past half century.

As Chapter 1 pointed out, however, a statute is only one of many forms of policy statements. Policy also emerges from customs, judicial decisions, executive orders, and administrative rulings. Often a rule of society begins as a custom that is observed more or less voluntarily. Later this custom may find expression in judicial decisions or administrative orders. Thus, when the time arrives for the legislature to enact a statute in a particular field, a good deal of relevant policy may already exist. Indeed, in most law-making situations the legislature does not create new policy. Instead, Congress reshapes proposals which have already taken shape.

Nor does the process of policy formation come to an end when Congress has acted. No matter what the character of a law, refinement and extension of policy are inevitable. The complex problems of modern society encourage legislatures to enact laws in general terms, indicating broad lines of policy and leaving details to other governmental agencies.

Constitutionally, Congress always retains power to erase or alter the actions of those agencies by passing new laws. But the national legislative process is exceedingly difficult and complex, and Congress does not legislate easily. Once a statute is passed, its moment is usually gone. Public attention is diverted elsewhere, old legislative coalitions dissolve, and new ones take their place. As a result, Congress has seldom been able to follow up initial policy decisions with periodic revisions. Nor can individual senators and representatives be familiar with the work of the hundreds of courts, commissions, and administrative agencies that interpret and enforce the law.

Policy Making without Statutes

Congress is not, of course, the only initiator of governmental policy. Policies can evolve without law making, particularly in foreign affairs. The Constitution gives so much power to the president in this field that he is capable of acting independently of Congress in many ways. The Monroe Doctrine is a famous example. So are the Korean and Vietnam wars, both of which began and ended without the formal involvement of Congress. Usually, the president takes influential members of Congress into his confidence in an effort to make the legislative branch a cooperative partner in his foreign policy. Occasionally, as in the case of the Gulf of Tonkin Resolution, which Congress passed in 1964 during the initial stages of American involvement in the Vietnamese conflict, the president seeks direct congressional approval of actions he has already taken in the international sphere.

To be sure, Congress always retains an important general check on presidential policy making through its control of the purse strings. But this power is of limited usefulness in checking the executive in most important areas of foreign affairs—especially once the president commits the armed forces. As congressional behavior during the Vietnam war illustrates, few members of Congress are willing to leave themselves open to the charge that they failed to support "our boys" who are risking their lives abroad. Only in 1973 after the withdrawal of American troops from Vietnam did both houses of Congress reject a presidential request for funds to pursue military operations in Southeast Asia.

The president also can make domestic policy without benefit of action by Congress. A good example is provided by the loyalty program for federal employees originally announced by means of an executive order in 1947. This controversial program subjected federal employees to intensive loyalty and security checks. Congress might well have made the first move by enacting a statute to establish for such a program, but it chose to permit the President to decide how the loyalty of federal employees should be judged.

Sharing the Legislative Function

The role of Congress, then, is limited by the fact that policy making in a complex government inevitably involves more than passing laws. It is further circumscribed by the fact that Congress shares legislative functions with the president. From the Constitution the chief executive derives power to veto legislation, call Congress into special session, report to the House and Senate on the State of the Union, and "recommend to their consideration such measures as he shall judge necessary and expedient."

Only in the twentieth century, however, have presidents regularly employed their constitutional powers so as to occupy a powerful role in the legislative process. Today, the president is the chief source of legislative initiative and leadership in the Congress. Because it prepares the budget, the White House proposes national priorities and, as a consequence, sets the legislative agenda. The president and his staff also organize support for his program in the Congress, using their own lobbyists and those of various departments and agencies. In addition, the president has means to reward and punish congressmen through federal programs that distribute benefits in every congressional constituency. Because of his instant access to television and the press, the president can influence public opinion far more effectively than can any congressional leader, particularly on matters involving foreign policy or national security.

Despite constant grumbling, frequent frustration, and an occasional revolt, Congress by and large accepts the president's legislative initiative, although not necessarily his specific policies. Given the size and complexity of its legislative task, Congress has no alternative. Congressional leaders rarely have the power to establish priorities or a legislative agenda. The president fills this gap with his legislative program and the leadership he provides for its enactment. In the process,

> Congress gains . . . a prestigeful "laundry-list," a starting order-of-priority to guide the work of each committee in both houses in every session. Since it comes from downtown [the White House], committee and house leaders—and all members—can respond to or react against it at their option. But coming from downtown it does for them what they, in their disunity, cannot do for themselves: it gives them an agenda to get on with, or depart from.[1]

Congress usually "gets on" with a fair amount of the president's program, but never with all of it. Congress inevitably views the president's program from a perspective different from that of the White House. No member of Congress shares the president's national constituency. Few congressmen, including party stalwarts, see their political

Budget Director David Stockman, Treasury Secretary Donald Regan, and Murray Wiedenbaum, chairman of the Council of Economic Advisers, on Capitol Hill, seeking support for President Reagan's economic program. (United Press International)

FIGURE **9-1**

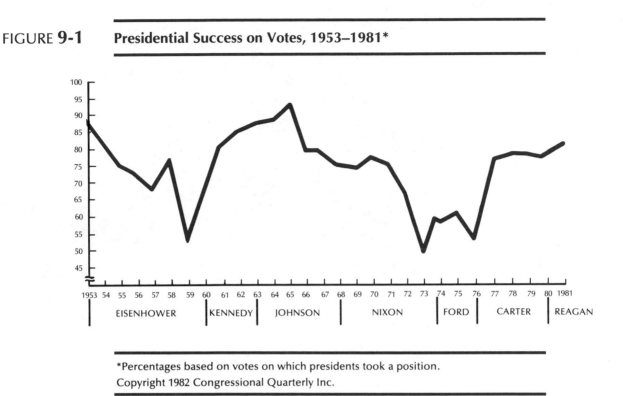

Presidential Success on Votes, 1953–1981*

*Percentages based on votes on which presidents took a position.
Copyright 1982 Congressional Quarterly Inc.

careers as closely tied to the fate of the president's program. In 1976, for example, only 22 of the 292 Democrats who won House seats received fewer votes in their districts than President Carter, and all but one of the Democrats elected to the Senate ran ahead of Carter in their states. "What can the President say to me when I know I'm more popular than he is in my district?" asked one Democrat. "What can he do for me? What can he do *to* me?"[2]

Influential members of Congress enjoy far longer tenure than the president. As President Kennedy pointed out in speaking of a powerful committee chairman: "Wilbur Mills knows that he was chairman of Ways and Means before I got here and that he'll still be chairman after I've gone—and he knows that I know it. I don't have any hold on him."[3] Indeed, Mills lasted as chairman until 1975, a dozen years after Kennedy's death.

Between 1964 and 1966, Lyndon Johnson dominated Congress as no president had since the early years of the New Deal. Yet the Eighty-ninth Congress rejected Johnson's proposal for home rule for the District of Columbia, blocked the administration's plan for merging the national guard and the reserves, refused to appropriate funds for the

"It's your move"

Don Hesse, St. Louis Globe-Democrat: Los Angeles Times Syndicate

newly enacted rent-supplement program, forced the White House to accept limitations on the secretary of defense's power to close military bases, and killed the attempt of the president and organized labor to repeal the provision of the Taft–Hartley Act that permits states to enact "right to work" laws.

In his first months in office, President Reagan rode the crest of his electoral victory in 1980 to a series of triumphs in Congress. Despite solid Democratic control of the House, Reagan persuaded Congress to accept tax cuts, the largest peacetime increase in military spending, substantial reductions in welfare and other domestic programs, consolidation of numerous federal programs into block grants, and sale of sophisticated reconnaissance aircraft to Saudi Arabia. But in his second year, Reagan was forced to abandon his budget and accept tax increases. Congress also rebuffed the President's recommendation that the Education and Energy Departments be abolished, and beat back Reagan's efforts to relax federal standards on air pollutants, pesticides, and use of wilderness areas.

More often than not, tax legislation has been written by the House Ways and Means Committee rather than the White House or the Treasury Department. This committee's leadership also played a central role in determining the fate of revenue sharing and welfare reform during the 1970s, helping to enact the first and to kill the second. Congressional influence has been substantial in legislation affecting agriculture, atomic energy, education, housing, labor-management relations, and social security.[4] In addition, much of the legislative initiative in air and water pollution, mass transportation, consumer protection, reform of the Electoral College, and women's rights has come from members of Congress.

⭐ OTHER FUNCTIONS OF CONGRESS

Law making usually is considered to be the paramount function of the legislature. But the work of Congress is not limited to enacting statutes. Congress also controls—formally, if not always actually—the budget, supervises administrative agencies, represents interests of constituents, and influences public opinion. In performing these functions, Congress often has more influence on policy making than it does through its power to legislate.

The Power of the Purse

Controlling the pursestrings is one of the oldest and most important functions of any legislative body; for example, it has much to do with the emergence of Parliament as an important part of the British government by the eighteenth century. The rallying cry of the American Revolution was "No taxation without representation," indicating how the idea of legislative control of tax policy had grown. The related notion that funds could be appropriated from the public treasury only by legislative action was a firmly established concept of Anglo-American political practice by 1787. Without hesitation the framers of the Constitution prescribed that "no money shall be drawn from the treasury, but in consequence of appropriations made by law." Writing in *The Federalist Papers*, James Madison argued that congressional control of the pursestrings was the chief safeguard against abuse of executive power:

> This power over the purse may, in fact, be regarded as the most complete and effectual weapon with which any constitution can arm the immediate representatives of the people obtaining a redress of every grievance and for carrying into effect every just and salutary measure.[5]

Over the years, Congress has delegated much of this power to appropriations committees, the House committee being more important than that of the Senate. Acting through subcommittees, the House Appropriations Committee each year reviews the president's budgetary requests. Hearings are held to permit agency officials to explain and justify proposed expenditures; there, legislators' questioning of administrators may be penetrating and even hostile. After the hearings, subcommittees make their recommendations to the full committee for action, which then submits its proposed appropriations bills to the House. The House measure is then transmitted to the Senate, which follows a similar procedure. When congressional action is completed, an appropriations bill goes to the president, who can veto it as a whole, but not specific items in it.

Part of Congress's problem in controlling the purse arises from the fact that its powers traditionally have been exercised "pluralistically, parochially, and episodically."[6] Authority over appropriations has been splintered among a dozen or more subcommittees in each house. These subcommittees were subject to only general oversight by the full appropriations committee and to even less control by the entire House or Senate. Many subcommittees were dominated by powerful chairmen with great personal influence over broad areas of federal activity. As a result, Congress gave piecemeal rather than comprehensive consideration to the budget as a whole. Until recently, the many segments of the appropriations process pursued their particular tasks in splendid isolation from each other. Moreover, the House and Senate considered each appropriations bill separately, with no formal reference to its impact on the budget as a whole.

Growing concern over the weaknesses of the decentralized appropriations process, combined with congressional desire to bolster its authority in dealing with the president, led Congress to enact sweeping reforms of its budgetary procedures in 1974. Under the new arrangements, Congress annually adopts an overall spending ceiling that must be honored in the appropriations process. If appropriations exceed the ceiling, both houses are obligated to impose new taxes or a higher national debt limit. To perform these functions, budget committees were created in the House and Senate. The Congressional Budget Office was established as the legislative counterpart to the executive branch's Office of Management and Budget.

The budgetary reforms of 1974 gave more cohesion to Congress's efforts to control the purse. Many members of Congress, however, were not happy about the necessity to make hard choices about spending priorities and tax levels, particularly as the budget process became increasingly contentious and time consuming in the face of growing federal budgets during the Carter and Reagan administrations. "In a rarefied atmosphere, taking politics out of the equation, the development of an overall spending plan is a good idea," noted one congressional critic. "But when you try to put it into practice in an atmosphere of partisan politics, it just won't work."[7] The new budget process also led to conflict between the budget committees and the appropriations committees and their subcommittees, which have lost some of their spending power but remain responsible for determining the funding of particular federal programs and agencies. Because of these internal difficulties and conflicts, the new budgetary procedures have not reduced significantly the pre-eminent role of the president in establishing the basic outlines of federal spending policy.

A more radical approach to reforming the power of the purse emerged in the 1970s in the form of demands that the Constitution be amended to require a balanced budget. Drawing on the dissatisfaction with increased public spending and higher taxes that fueled tax revolts in a number of states, supporters of a balanced-budget amendment by 1981 had won endorsement in thirty-one states of a constitutional convention to consider changing the Constitution to prohibit deficit spending. Congressional supporters of the amendment argued that "unless there is some constitutional discipline imposed, Congress will never by self-imposition follow a sound policy of fiscal prudence."[8] President Reagan embraced the amendment as an essential element in his effort to reduce government and taxes. Democrats found Reagan's endorsement in the election year of 1982 somewhat hypocritical, since his budget was unbalanced by more than $100 billion.

As noted in Chapter 3, a budget-balancing amendment was approved by the Senate in 1982, but died in the House. Under its terms, a balanced budget would be required unless the United States was formally at war, except that the requirement could be overridden by a three-fifths vote of the members of each house of Congress.

Administrative Oversight

Supervising administrative agencies is another major function of legislatures. The American Constitution does not spell out this legislative function in so many words. But the framers made congressional oversight inevitable when they assigned Congress control over appropriations, provided for senatorial confirmation of appointed executive officials, and permitted Congress to create and reorganize the administrative machinery of the national government. With the tremendous growth in the activities and personnel of the federal government in the twentieth century, administrative oversight has become an increasingly important congressional task, often overshadowing law making.

The Legislative Reorganization Act of 1946 charged congressional committees with maintaining "continuous watchfulness" over administration of the laws, a function most committees were already performing and have since continued with considerable zeal. The appropriations committees and their subcommittees monitor programs and personnel through control of the annual appropriations process. Other committees exercise influence because of requirements for annual review by Congress of such programs as foreign aid and space exploration. Committees also use hearings and investigations to expose mismanagement and corruption, to advocate projects and priorities they favor, and to compel policy changes in administering federal programs.

A number of committees and subcommittees have involved themselves directly in the administrative process. Appropriations subcommittees sometimes use detailed provisions in the appropriations statutes, subcommittee reports, and communications to executive agencies to instruct administrators on how to spend funds in order to avoid punitive action in the next round of the appropriations process. Some committees insist on a veto over such executive actions as closing military bases or require agencies to submit administrative determinations for committee clearance.

During the past decade, Congress has expanded substantially its general veto power over administrative and regulatory actions. Legislative vetoes have killed a variety of regulatory actions, including efforts by the Federal Trade Commission to ensure that funeral homes provide an itemized price list, and proposals by the same agency to require automobile dealers to disclose defects in used cars. In these two instances and many others, congressional vetoes have followed in the wake of heavy pressure from the regulated industry, often accompanied by substantial contributions from the regulated industry's political action committee. The power of Congress to veto administrative determinations has been challenged successfully in federal court, but the Supreme Court had yet to rule on the general question by the end of 1982.

Congress also influences the operations of the federal executive through the power of the Senate to confirm or reject the president's nominations. For example, senatorial criticism of the conservation and natural resources policies of Governor Walter J. Hickel of Alaska, President Nixon's nominee as Secretary of the Interior, stimulated Hickel's great concern with ecological issues after his confirmation.

Another major source of congressional involvement in administrative matters results from Congress's responsibilities for structuring and staffing the executive branch. Acts of Congress are necessary to create departments or agencies. Congress also can reject administrative reorganizations proposed by the White House and, in fact, it has vetoed one-third of the reorganization plans submitted by presidents over the past quarter of a century.

Congress also provides the legislation that establishes, regulates, and nourishes the civil service, the armed forces, and special groups of personnel as the Foreign Service, the Secret Service, and agents of the Federal Bureau of Investigation. In the process, Congress influences the managerial practices of federal executives and the pay, working conditions, and morale of federal workers. Through committees such as Armed Services, members of Congress become intimately involved with personnel issues and enormously influential with administrative officials and groups which promote the interests of federal employees.

A final, if rarely used, source of congressional control over the executive branch is the removal power. Responsibility for impeaching, or indicting, the president, vice-president, and other civil officers for "treason, bribery, or other high crimes and misdemeanors" rests with the House of Representatives. The Senate is responsible for trying those impeached by the House, and conviction by the Senate results in removal from office.

Despite the scope of these various powers, congressional oversight resembles Congress's attempts to control the nation's pursestrings. Oversight rarely has been systematic or comprehensive. Instead, various committees and subcommittees "look at programs . . . in a hop, skip and jump fashion."[9] Many programs and agencies have been largely immune from congressional oversight because of their political popularity, the influence of their administrators, the sensitivity of their tasks, or the sheer size and complexity of the federal establishment. The Senate also has failed to develop effective procedures to ensure careful scrutiny of the qualifications of presidential nominees. The result, as the Senate's majority leader confessed in 1978, is that "confirmations often have been rubber-stamped. There has been a feeling that this is a nominee the President wants, and he should have who he wants."[10]

Representing Constituents

Representation of the people is supposedly the principal reason for Congress's existence. More than any other political institution in Washington, it reflects the diversity of the American people and their interests. In practice, representing the people of a particular district or state usually means advancing and defending local interests in the nation's capital.

Most members of Congress spend a good deal of their own time— and most of their staffs'—servicing needs of constituents who want help on everything from information about voting to intercession in a federal criminal case. During a typical day, a representative or staff member may check with the Department of Agriculture on availability of agricultural agents to help suburban homeowners fight crabgrass, call the Defense Department to arrange an interview for a local businessman

A staff member works on some of the half million letters that Senator Daniel P. Moynihan (D., N.Y.) receives from constituents each year. (George Tames, New York Times Pictures)

seeking a federal contract, and contact the Civil Service Commission to inquire about how a constituent performed on a recent examination.

Representation of constituency interests also involves congressmen in a wide range of federal programs, as Chapter 4 pointed out. The importance of federal spending for state and local economies makes members of Congress active in promoting their localities as sites for federal facilities and in seeking federal contracts for industries within their districts. Of particular importance are federal outlays for defense, aerospace, and science, which can make the difference between prosperity and depression in a congressional district.

The larger the prize, the greater the legislative involvement, as indicated by the major roles of members of Congress from Texas and Washington in the battle between General Dynamics (Fort Worth) and Boeing Aircraft (Seattle) for the $6.5 billion TFX fighter plane contract. More recently, congressional supporters of Lockheed Corporation from Georgia have battled with Boeing defenders over a multibillion-dollar contract for a new military transport. Prospects of congressmen delivering on such campaign promises as Senator Edward M. Kennedy's pledge to "do more for Massachusetts" depend largely on increasing their constituencies" share of defense and space contracts. State delegations in Congress have organized to work closely with state and local officials and lobbyists of local industry in the quest for contracts and installations. One of the most active delegations in this respect is California's, whose goal is to maintain and expand the state's sizable share of military and space spending. Almost $17 billion in military contracts were awarded to firms in California in 1981, more than to any other state, and one-fifth of the national total.

Shaping Opinion

A democratic government has a particular obligation to acquaint the people with the nature of social problems and with possible courses of action. Moreover, it is to the legislature—the chief agency representing

Reprinted by permission of Tribune Company Syndicate, Inc.

the people and their interests—that a considerable part of this educational responsibility falls.

A speech on the floor of the House or the Senate by a well-known member of Congress may influence both public opinion and administrative action. In January 1945, Senator Arthur Vandenberg of Michigan publicly repudiated his earlier isolationist leanings and announced that he would henceforth support an American foreign policy looking toward closer international cooperation. That address influenced many Americans who had previously hoped that their country might "go it alone" but who trusted Senator Vandenberg's integrity and judgment. Similarly, the attacks of Senator William Fulbright of Arkansas on President Johnson's policies in Vietnam established an important rallying point for all groups who had doubts about the wisdom of American military participation in the Vietnam war.

Such influential speeches are not made in Congress every day or even in every session. But from time to time the stage is set for an address that will profoundly affect the thinking of important segments of the American public. Such remarks need not even be spoken on the floor of the House or Senate. So great is the attention paid by the press, television, and radio to certain members of Congress that a few words uttered at a press conference or over the air may drastically alter the course of public thinking or administrative policy. A notable instance occurred in 1950, when Senator Joseph McCarthy of Wisconsin announced that he held in his hands the names of 205 persons "that were made known to the Secretary of State as being members of the Communist party and who nonetheless are still working and shaping policy in the State Department." The speech marked the beginning of McCarthy's strong influence on American public opinion. That he never succeeded in documenting his charge—and kept changing the number of alleged Communists in the State Department—did not alter the effect of his speech. When a United States senator makes sensational charges, many people listen and are impressed.

Congressional Investigations

In performing its many functions, Congress often employs investigating committees. A congressional investigation differs from routine consideration of bills by standing committees. An investigation involves an inquiry into a subject or problem—like domestic spying by the CIA and the FBI, cost overruns in the Department of Defense, windfall profits for grain exporters, or the safety of food additives—rather than scrutiny of a particular legislative proposal. The most formal investigation occurs when Congress specifically authorizes an inquiry into a particular subject, designates a committee to make this study, votes an appropriation to cover costs of the inquiry, and grants the committee power to subpoena witnesses.

The motives that lead members of Congress to authorize an investigation are varied. First is the obvious need to obtain detailed and accurate information if Congress is to take intelligent action. A second purpose is to supervise or check administrative agencies. Each house has a committee on government operations, which frequently conducts such inquiries. A third purpose of investigations is to influence public opinion by giving wide circulation to certain facts or ideas, as Senator William Fulbright tried to do in the hearings his Committee on Foreign Relations held on the war in Vietnam.

These three purposes are often supplemented by others of a more personal and partisan character. More than one member of Congress has advanced his career because of a reputation as a hardheaded investigator. Accordingly, it is not surprising that hope of political profit should motivate congressional investigations. Similarly, Democrats or Republicans often undertake investigations to further their parties' interests or to embarrass the other side. When the Republicans won control of Congress in 1946, they facetiously announced that each day's session of the Eightieth Congress would "open with a prayer and close with a probe" of the Truman administration.

Congressional investigating committees sometimes encounter witnesses who refuse to appear before a committee or decline to answer its questions. Out of such episodes have come congressional statutes and Supreme Court decisions concerning the relative status and rights of investigating committees and witnesses. As early as 1857, Congress enacted a statute directing private persons to appear before investigating committees when subpoenaed and answer pertinent questions or risk a criminal prosecution in the courts and imprisonment up to one year. The constitutionality of this statute has repeatedly been upheld by the Supreme Court. But the Court has also ruled that a witness may properly refuse to cooperate with an investigating committee of Congress if the subject under examination lies outside the authority of the investigating committee, if a committee asks a witness questions that are not pertinent to the subject under investigation, or if a witness's answers would be self-incriminating.[11]

# THE MEMBERS OF CONGRESS

Whatever else it is, Congress is not an accurate cross section of the American people. In 1983, the "average" member of Congress was a white male approaching his fiftieth birthday. Only twenty-three women, twenty blacks, and six Hispanics were serving in Congress, and

King Of The Hill

© 1977 Engelhardt in the St. Louis Post-Dispatch, by permission

all except for Senators Paula Hawkins of Florida and Nancy Kassenbaum of Kansas were in the House. While younger Americans, women, and blacks continue to be significantly underrepresented in Congress, their ranks have grown in recent years. Only ten women were elected to the House of Representatives in 1964, compared with twenty-one in 1982. During the same period, black representation in Congress increased from six to twenty. And the influx of younger member of Congress has produced a steady decline over the last decade of the average age of representatives and senators.

Most members of Congress are professionals or businessmen with college educations who have been active in politics before coming to Washington. In 1982, 45 percent were lawyers, and 37 percent had been (or still were) active in business. In addition, sixty-nine members of the Ninety-seventh Congress were teachers, thirty-seven were farmers, twenty-eight were journalists, and seven were doctors. Over 80 percent of the membership of the two houses had previously been elected to public office or had otherwise been involved in governmental service before their arrival in Congress. Members of Congress are much wealthier than most Americans. In 1982, almost half of the hundred senators were millionaires.

Election to Congress provided a job in 1983 that paid senators $60,662 a year and representatives $69,800 annually, and as much as $1.2 million for senators to employ an office staff. Members also receive generous allowance for travel between Washington and home, substantial tax breaks for the costs of maintaining two households, free office space in Washington and in their states, postal privileges, access to television and radio studios in the Capitol, and substantial allowances for stationery, long-distance calls and telegraph messages, newsletters, and such special office equipment as automatic typewriters and signature machines. Another benefit is the opportunity to travel abroad on official business, to the tune of $2.8 million in 1981.

Staff assistance, mailing and telecommunications privileges, access to the media, and travel allowances offer substantial political advantages to the members of Congress seeking re-election. At government expense, the incumbent can stay in constant touch with residents of his district, as well as travel home for campaigning. Members of Congress

TABLE 9-1   **Incumbency and Congressional Elections, 1972–1982**

		*Number of Incumbents Running for Re-election**	*Percent Re-elected*
House	1972	390	94
	1974	391	88
	1976	384	96
	1978	382	94
	1980	398	91
	1982	393	90
Senate	1972	27	74
	1974	27	85
	1976	25	64
	1978	25	60
	1980	29	55
	1982	30	93

*Includes primary and general election.

also benefit from their status as senators or representatives, from the news their place in Washington allows them to generate, and from the favors incumbency permits them to distribute to constituents. The advantages are so great, contends a member of the House who served seventeen terms, that "no Congressman who gets elected and who minds his business should ever be beaten. Everything is there for him to use if he'll only keep his nose to the grindstone and use what is offered."[12]

As Table 9-1 shows, incumbents have fared very well indeed over the past decade, especially in the House of Representatives. On the average, over 92 percent of all House members running in general elections have been successful. With the exception of the presidential landslide of 1964 and the post-Watergate election of 1974, very few incumbents have been defeated in any recent election.

Increasing Tenure and Professionalization

In part because of the advantages provided in incumbency, congressional careers have tended to lengthen. During the nineteenth century, turnover in the House after elections ranged from 30 percent to 60 percent and the average representative had fewer than two terms of prior service. Not until 1900 was a Congress elected in which less than 30 percent of House members were newcomers and the average prior service more than two terms.[13] In the Ninety-fourth Congress, which experienced the largest turnover in a quarter of a century, only 21 percent of the representatives were first termers, 48 percent had won five terms or more, and the average member had served almost nine years. Longer tenure reflects the growth of safe seats throughout the nation. During the past two decades, close to three-fourths of the seats in the House have been safe. In recent years, however, the trend toward longer tenure has been moderated by the tendency of an increasing number of representatives and senators to leave Congress voluntarily. In the House, as indicated in Figure 9-2, the rise in early retirement has steadily reduced the ranks of those serving five or more terms.

With increased tenure have come profound changes in the nature of congressional service. Lengthening service has shifted "the balance in the careers and life styles of legislators from amateur to professional, from the status of temporary ambassador from home to that of member of the legislative group."[14] It has also bolstered the importance of seniority and made long tenure a requirement for leadership, especially in the House of Representatives. These developments, in turn, have increased the power of committees and subcommittees, encouraged specialization, and contributed to the general dispersion of power in Congress, all of which are discussed in the next chapter.

FIGURE **9-2**

Seniority and Turnover in the House of Representatives

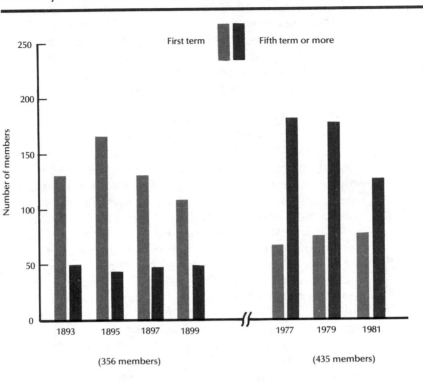

SOURCE: Adapted from H. Douglas Price, "The Congressional Career Then and Now," in Nelson W. Polsby, ed., *Congressional Behavior* (New York: Random House, 1971), p. 17. Data from various sources.

Rewards and Frustrations

The fact that most members seek re-election suggests a relatively high level of satisfaction with their jobs or at least a preference for staying in Congress rather than practicing law in Pocatello, Pascagoula, or Perry-opolis. Representatives and senators enjoy the prestige conferred by their offices and derive satisfaction from being in Washington at the center of national affairs. All acquire some influence, and a few are rewarded with great power. For most, being in Congress is itself a reward, either as the culmination of a political career begun in local government or as a way station on the road to higher office. For some, election to Congress is an opportunity for public service, a once-in-a-lifetime chance to advance a cause or change the nation's course. For others, a seat in the House or Senate becomes an easy job with a good salary, influential colleagues, and plentiful opportunities for personal gain and travel to the far corners of the earth at taxpayers' expense.

Most members of Congress work hard, spreading themselves too thin across the many tasks that compete for time and attention. For a member of the House, a typical day might begin with breakfast with a lobbyist, followed by two hours at his desk sampling the mail, consulting with staff on his weekly newsletter, meeting visitors, editing a speech to be given to a veterans' group, and helping constituents by making telephone calls to various administrative agencies. Next comes an hour at the executive session of a subcommittee, lunch with a group of colleagues to discuss tactics on a forthcoming bill, and an afternoon divided among the House floor, where amendments to a military appropriations measure are being considered, the corridors of Congress, where he talks briefly with colleagues and lobbyists on a variety of topics, and a meeting with Labor Department officials to discuss cutbacks in federal manpower-training funds to cities in his district. Before leaving for home, the congressman may spend another hour dictating and signing letters. After dinner, he works his way through a bulky briefcase containing the *Congressional Record* for the previous day's session, the morning newspapers, the rough draft of a committee report, and a thick file of housing data on his district supplied by the Department of Housing and Urban Development.

As Congress spends more and more of the year in session, such schedules become increasingly common. Because longer sessions shorten the time available to renew constituency ties and to campaign, weekends and recesses must be spent in the district. The pressures are particularly severe for House members, who must run for re-election every two years.

The growing volume of legislation, the mushrooming of federal programs, and the steady rise in communications from constituents also increase demands on congressmen. Because of these pressures, most have less time to master any subject. Even the more conscientious members find it necessary to vote on numerous issues that they only vaguely understand and on a vast amount of legislation that they have not read. The sheer volume of business increases reliance on their staffs, party leaders, committee associates, other congressmen, and lobbyists.

The hectic pace of life in Congress also strains family life and the personal resources of many members. Financial disclosure requirements and limitations on outside income have decreased the attractiveness of remaining in Congress, as have the rising costs of campaigns and the diminished prestige of Congress in recent years. Increasing the sense of frustration for many, particularly the more junior and activist members, is the slow pace of Congress, the concentration of power in the hands of committee and subcommittee chairmen, and the fact that "it takes so long to get anything done here."[15] For a growing number, as indicated above, these frustrations lead to early retirement. One of the fifty-six representatives and senators who retired in 1976 explained his decision in words increasingly heard in the halls of Congress: "My enthusiasm for public service has been waning under the weight of my frustrated hopes, others' unreasonable pressures and the job's persistent demands. Since I entered office, the duties have increased dramatically, exceeded only by public dissatisfaction with the Congress."[16]

Congressional Ethics

Public attention tends to focus on congressional ethics only when attracted by spectacular scandals involving personal use of campaign money, diversions of public funds for private pleasures, or exploitation of a congressman's name, office, and influence to further personal financial interests. In the most far-reaching of recent scandals, one senator and a number of House members accepted large amounts of cash from federal agents posing as Arab sheiks, in return for promises of help on various matters involving government. After their conviction, one of the representatives was expelled from the House, and the others resigned or were defeated.

More serious than these periodic scandals, however, is the widespread practice of senators and representatives engaging in private business while in public office. Congressmen frequently sit on committees considering new laws and overseeing administration of existing statutes that regulate the very businesses in which they themselves are involved. A member of the House Banking or Senate Finance Committee who maintains his position as a bank executive, a member of the Commerce Committee who owns an interest in a radio or television station, or the owner of a large farm who sits on the Agriculture Committee, each has an impossible job of serving the twin masters of the public good and personal financial interest. Even if he miraculously succeeds, it is not likely that he can appear to succeed. At the very least, he leaves not only himself but Congress open to a charge of corruption.

Despite the serious implications of widespread mixing of public and private responsibilities, Congress has been remarkably insensitive to conflicts of interest involving its own members. On the other hand, members of Congress have been quick to attack administrators and judges for possible violation of ethical standards. In 1962, Congress passed a far-reaching conflict-of-interest statute governing the behavior of almost all employees of the federal government, but carefully excluded themselves from the law. Congress took a timid first step toward putting its ethical house in order by adopting a code of conduct and requiring limited financial disclosure in 1968. Nine years later, in the wake of a series of scandals and pressures for change, the House and Senate accepted strict rules governing financial matters, including detailed disclosure of assets, limitations on outside income, and restrictions on gifts from lobbyists.

While approving these tougher financial rules, Congress remains reluctant to impose the same standards of conduct on its members as it does on others. Illustrative is the halfhearted congressional investigation in the late 1970s of highly suspect dealings between members of Congress and agents of the government of South Korea. Perhaps Congress only reflects society at large, since many voters seem willing to overlook wrongdoing on the part of congressmen. Two of the three representatives who were formally reprimanded by the House for their dealings with South Korea were re-elected in 1978.

★ STAFFING CONGRESS

Over the years, the rising volume of government business has led Congress to build up a bureaucracy that employs more personnel than many federal agencies. These professional staff members, who usually have more technical experience and greater expertise than the representatives and senators for whom they work, have come to play an increasingly important part in the legislative process. More generally, the growth of staff, the creation of a Congressional Budget Office and an Office of Technology Assessment, and the increasing use of computerized information systems have significantly bolstered Congress's ability to secure and assess information, thus reducing its dependence on materials provided by executive agencies.

Each member of Congress is given an allowance for the maintenance of a personal office staff. In the case of representatives, these funds provide for an administrative assistant, a legislative assistant, a professional secretary, two or three other aides, and several clerk-stenographers. A senator's allowance is more generous, and a senator from a populous state may have seventy or more persons working in his office. Administrative assistants and other aides answer a congressman's mail, deal with visitors, keep in touch with the executive agencies of the government, run errands to these agencies for constituents, and offer the congressman advice and assistance in studying bills, researching, writing speeches, and running for re-election.

Each of the standing committees also employs a sizable corps of professional and secretarial staff members, although, compared with the executive departments, congressional committees employ few economists, statisticians, demographers, operation analysts, and other specialists. Committee chiefs of staff are frequently extremely knowledge-

One of Senator Edward Kennedy's aides whispers advice during a public hearing.
(Julie Susman)

able and influential and often have years of experience. They organize committee hearings and investigations, draft legislation, and direct as many as seventy-five assistants. While many appointments to committee staffs are made on the basis of merit, party affiliation remains an important factor in filling these positions.

General staff services also are available to Congress. Chief among these are the Congressional Research Service, the Office of Legislative Counsel, the Congressional Budget Office, and the Office of Technology Assessment. The Congressional Research Service is a general research agency in the Library of Congress. It supplies various services and materials—pamphlets, digests of bills, data for use in speeches, abstracts of current literature, and studies of special legislative problems—requested by individual congressmen or by committees. The Office of Legislative Counsel's chief function is to draft bills at the request of congressmen or

Representative Bill Nelson (D., Fla.) with aide and computer used in preparing letters to constituents. (George Tames, New York Times Pictures)

committees, making certain that their legal language accomplishes the purposes that their sponsors have in mind.

Less closely tied to Congress is the General Accounting Office, the independent auditors of the federal government for Congress. GAO investigates all sorts of governmental activities to ensure that congressional appropriations are spent in the manner by law. Over the years, GAO's function has broadened to include a consideration of "whether the programs are really accomplishing their objectives or not."[17] As a result, GAO's investigators increasingly include engineers, statisticians, and medical experts as well as accountants.

Only recently has Congress begun to make use of modern methods available to assist organizations in coping with the vast flow of information characteristic of complex societies. Reformers, both inside and outside Congress, have argued persuasively that the House and Senate with their nineteenth-century procedures and techniques are unable to deal effectively with the executive branch and its banks of computers, program budget specialists, and the like. Reformers advocate widespread congressional use of computers and other electronic information storage and retrieval devices, as well as the employment by Congress of technicians trained in systems analysis, operations research, and related skills.

★ SUMMARY

Congress is the most representative of our national political institutions. Its 535 members reflect the diverse interests of a complex society. Members of Congress, however, are more homogeneous than the people they represent. Most are middle-aged college-educated white males with professional or business backgrounds. Senators and representatives and their growing staffs perform many functions: They make laws, control the purse, oversee the federal executive, and inform the public. Over the nation's history, Congress's *relative* influence in the American system of government has declined, largely as a result of the enormous increase in the power of the presidency. Among legislative bodies, however, Congress is perhaps the most influential representative assembly in the world. It initiates a good deal of important legislation, modifies much of what the executive branch proposes, and influences a wide range of other governmental activities.

NOTES

1. Richard E. Neustadt, "Politicians and Bureaucrats," in David B. Truman, ed., *The Congress and America's Future.* The American Assembly (Englewood Cliffs, N.J.: Prentice-Hall, 1965), p. 111.
2. See Steven V. Roberts, "Congress in No Mood to Help Out Carter," *New York Times,* March 27, 1979.
3. Quoted in Theodore C. Sorensen, *Kennedy* (New York: Harper & Row, 1965), p. 426.
4. See Ronald C. Moe and Steven C. Tell, "Congress as Policy-Maker," *Political Science Quarterly,* LXXXV (1970), 443–470.
5. *The Federalist* (New York: Random House, 1937), No. 58, p. 380.
6. Stephen K. Bailey, *Congress in the Seventies* (New York: St. Martin's Press, 1970), p. 89.
7. Representative Benjamin S. Rosenthal (D., N.Y.), quoted in Martin Tolchin, "Test for Budget Process in Congress," *New York Times,* May 4, 1982.
8. Senator Dennis DeConcini (D., Ariz.) quoted in Edward Cowan, "Congress Ponders Budget-Balancing Amendment," *New York Times,* April 2, 1982.
9. Walter Kravitz, staff director, Budget Committee, U.S. House of Representatives, quoted in "Congress May Step Up Oversight of Programs," *Congressional Quarterly Weekly Report* (March 22, 1975), p. 597.
10. Senator Robert C. Byrd, quoted in Barry M. Hager, "Confirmation Process: Weaknesses Abound," *Congressional Quarterly Weekly Report* (February 4, 1978), p. 297.

11. See *United States v. Rumely*, 345 U.S. 41 (1953); *Watkins v. United States*, 354 U.S. 178 (1957); *Quinn v. United States*, 349 U.S. 155 (1955); and *Emspak v. United States*, 349 U.S. 190 (1955).
12. Michael J. Kirwan, *How to Succeed in Politics* (New York: Macfadden Books, 1964), p. 20. Kirwan served for a number of years as chairman of the Democratic Congressional Campaign Committee.
13. See H. Douglas Price, "The Congressional Career Then and Now," in Nelson Polsby, ed., *Congressional Behavior* (New York: Random House, 1971), pp. 14–27.
14. Nelson W. Polsby, "Strengthening Congress in National Policymaking," *The Yale Review* (Summer 1970), p. 485.
15. Representative Edward G. Biester, quoted in James Goodman, "The House, It Is Slow A-Changing, They Say," *Evening Times* (Trenton, N.J.), July 14, 1971.
16. Representative William L. Hungate, quoted in Richard D. Lyons, "Patman Joins Growing List of Retiring Congressmen," *New York Times*, January 15, 1976.
17. Elmer B. Staats, Controller General of the United States, quoted in Jon Margolis, "The G.A.O. is Congress' Unpopular Watchdog," *New York Times*, May 18, 1975.

SELECTED BIBLIOGRAPHY

Arnold, R. Douglas. *Congress and the Bureaucracy* (New Haven, Conn.: Yale University Press, 1979). A theoretically rigorous examination of the fascinating ways in which Congress influences policy making in executive agencies.

Bolling, Richard W. *House Out of Order* (New York: Dutton, 1965). A critical analysis of the House of Representatives by an experienced member who proposes far-reaching reforms.

Clapp, Charles L. *The Congressman: His Work As He Sees It* (Washington: Brookings Institution, 1963). The House of Representatives from the perspective of the individual member of Congress.

Congress and the Public Trust (New York: Atheneum, 1970). Report on the Association of the Bar of the City of New York Special Committee on Congressional Ethics, James C. Kirby, Executive Director. A study of conflicting interests and ethical standards in Congress with recommendations designed to increase public confidence in the legislative process.

Davidson, Roger H., and Walter J. Oleszek. *Congress and Its Members* (Washington, D.C.: Congressional Quarterly Press, 1981). A comprehensive examination of the various elements that affect political life in Congress.

DeGrazia, Alfred, ed. *Congress, The First Branch of Government* (New York: Doubleday, Anchor Books, 1967). Twelve studies of congressional organization based on the premise that Congress itself must be strengthened, not made more dependent on party or the presidency.

Fenno, Richard E., Jr. *Home Style: House Members in Their Districts* (Boston: Little, Brown, 1978). A close examination of how congressmen behave when they are back home with their constitutents.

Kofmehl, Kenneth. *Professional Staffs of Congress* (West Lafayette, Ind.: Purdue University Studies, 1962). A useful analysis of the development of professional staffs for congressional committees.

Mann, Thomas, ed. *The New Congress* (Washington, D.C.: American Enterprise Institute, 1981). Essays on the changing nature of Congress.

Miller, Clem. *Member of the House* (New York: Charles Scribner's Sons, 1962), ed. by John Baker. A view of life in the House of Representatives as seen by a perceptive young congressman.

Orfield, Gary. *Congressional Power: Congress and Social Change* (New York: Harcourt Brace and Jovanovich, 1975). A defense of Congress, which argues that the national legislature is the prime source of public policy in a number of important issue areas.

Shick, Allen. *Congress and Money: Budget, Spending and Taxing* (Washington: Urban Institute Press, 1980). A thorough examination of the congressional role in the budgetary process.

Taylor, Telford. *Grand Inquest* (New York: Simon and Schuster, 1955). Probably the best general account of congressional investigating committees, treated historically and critically.

Wilson, Woodrow. *Congressional Government: A Study in American Politics* (Boston: Houghton Mifflin, 1885). A classic study analyzing the way in which nineteenth-century Congresses predominated over the presidency.

10 The Legislative System and Lawmaking

Visitors to the House or Senate galleries are often disillusioned. Having imagined an impressive parliamentary panorama with ceremonial pageantry, dignified debate, and dramatic clashes between famous personalities, they find instead that the usual scene is dull and inactive. Of the 435 representatives, perhaps 30 or 40 are present; of the 100 senators, maybe a dozen. A lone figure has the floor, and while he drones along in a unexciting monologue, a few inattentive colleagues read newspapers, work at their desks, or sit talking in back rows.

Such a glimpse of the House or Senate in session is hardly a reliable guide to the legislative process. "Like a vast picture thronged with figures of equal prominence and crowded with elaborate and obtrusive details," Woodrow Wilson wrote a century ago, "Congress is hard to see satisfactorily and appreciatively at a single view and from a single stand-point."[1] Congress goes about its work by means of a complex institutional system that has evolved slowly.

⭐ THE CONGRESSIONAL SETTING

Congressional behavior is influenced by many factors, not the least of which is the fact that no two of the 100 senators and 435 representatives have identical personal philosophies, perceptions of their roles, or habits of work. Some are conservatives, others liberals. Most, but not all, work hard, seek the respect of their colleagues, and conform to the customs of the House or Senate. Concerns about their constituencies preoccupy all members of Congress. But many of the more senior and influential representatives and senators have relatively safe seats and are less restricted by the periodic necessity of facing the voters. A majority are ready to follow the party line—if there is one—when they or their constituents have little concern with a measure. On the other hand, a significant minority are mavericks who pursue an independent course much of the time.

Despite these differences, every member of Congress is influenced by certain common factors. Almost all are Democrats or Republicans and have certain obligations to party. But, as Chapter 6 showed, national party organizations are typically weak. Also important in terms of pressure are each member's constituents. Because at the next election these people can end or continue a legislator's career, their wants—or the legislator's perception of their wants—typically form a powerful influence on a member's behavior. Complicating matters, every state and

A typical scene on the floor of the House of Representatives during the Seventy-ninth Congress. (United Press International)

a large number of districts contain a wide variety of economic, social, ethnic, and other groups whose interests compete if not conflict. In addition, members of Congress work in an institutional arena with specific structural characteristics such as two houses and a committee system, formal rules and procedures, and informal practices such as seniority and specialization.

The dominant characteristic of Congress in the twentieth century has been an increasing dispersion of power. More safe seats have lengthened tenure, increased the importance of seniority, lessened party leaders' influence, and bolstered the independence of individual members. In the House, party leadership is much weaker than it was during the half century following the Civil War. And in neither house do leaders have many resources to reward the faithful or punish the wayward.

Committees, and especially subcommittees, have steadily increased their power, contributing further to decentralization. More recently, reform that reduced the importance of seniority in selection of committee chairmen dispersed power more widely in both houses. So did changes that permitted new members to secure seats on major committees. Other reforms have improved access of the press, lobbyists, and the public to formerly closed committee sessions and party caucuses, thus increasing the number of knowledgeable participants and further reducing the influence of committee and party leaders. Underlying many of these changes was the arrival in Congress during the past decade of large numbers of aggressive younger members who insisted that authority be broadly distributed rather than concentrated.

As a result of these decentralizing forces, coalitions must be constructed on each major legislative issue; "inevitably the politics of such an institution is compounded of persuasion, bargaining and logrolling."[2]

⭐ THE ROLE OF POLITICAL PARTIES IN CONGRESS

Behavior in every legislative assembly is conditioned in part by the way its members are nominated and elected to office. In the case of Congress, these procedures are highly decentralized, reflecting the geographic fragmentation of influence in the American party system. For nomination, campaign assistance, and re-election, members of Congress rely primarily on party leaders and supporters within their constituency rather than on national parties. And on the national level, interest groups and their political action committees are more important sources of re-election support for most representatives and senators than the national parties or the Congressional campaign committees. The two parties' weak national organizations cannot even control the use of each party's label: Whoever wins the primary in a particular state or district can claim the tag. Except in rare landslides like those in 1936 and 1964, holding a safe seat insulates most congressmen from the ebb and flow of national party fortunes. And party mavericks are protected from purges by either the president or the party's leadership in Congress by the decentralized base of constituency support.

Party cohesion in Congress is also eroded by the broad spectrum of political perspectives encompassed by each party. Both Democrats and Republicans, as indicated in Chapter 6, come with a wide range of political viewpoints and represent constituencies in which the meaning of each party's label varies considerably. As a conservative Democratic member of Congress explains:

> We've always been a party of multiple philosophical beliefs on which there has rarely been unanimity on any issue. . . . This is a House of Representatives. We represent the people in our districts. We're voting the people we represent. We consider ourselves just as good Democrats as any other Democrats.[3]

Despite these weaknesses, the two political parties are the most comprehensive groupings in Congress. Every member of the Ninety-eighth Congress elected in 1982 was a Democrat or a Republican. Party is the primary identification both in Congress and on the ballot. Party affiliation determines which legislative leaders members will consult and follow; and whether they will be in the majority or minority in Congress, and thus whether an opportunity will exist to chair a committee or subcommittee. On election day the party label will provide a large share of the support, because "the candidate's party is the one piece of information every voter is guaranteed. For many it is the only information they ever get."[4]

Party also symbolizes the traditions and convictions a congressman shares with fellow party members in Congress. Shared identities, hazards, and rewards provided by party shape the general orientation of most senators and representatives toward policy and also provide the basis for most associations with congressional colleagues. Party also offers a source of support for efforts to enact a bill, investigate a bureaucracy, or secure a prize for a constituent. For the typical member,

> The life of an habitual maverick would be intolerable. Acting against the party involves a substantial amount of personal discomfort, which can even be expressed physically. The only Republican to vote against his party's recommittal motion on a major administration bill in 1963 answered the roll call while crouching behind the rail on the Democratic side of the House chamber. He explained: "It's 190 degrees over there [pointing to the Republican side]!"[5]

In short, party is something to be loyal to and expect loyalty from, albeit not all of the time, and certainly not when important constituency interests or compelling personal beliefs point the other way.

Party and Congressional Voting Behavior

Party, constituency, group pressures, and personal beliefs all affect the way a representative or senator votes in Congress. Of these factors, however, party has the most frequent influence on congressional voting behavior.

During the past half century, between two-thirds and three-quarters of the Democrats and Republicans in Congress have voted with a majority of their party colleagues on contested votes. Voting in the

House and Senate is more closely related to party affiliation than to constituency factors like urban-rural or sectional differences. Most Republicans tend to think and vote more like other Republicans than like Democrats—which is why they are Republicans. The parties tend to be most cohesive on votes involving partisan and ideological considerations, such as organization of the House and Senate, patronage, the size of the federal government, economic issues, taxation and fiscal policies, housing and welfare. Party is less important on foreign policy and on questions dealing with ethics, morals, and prejudice.

Nevertheless, except in periods like 1935–1938 and 1965–1966, when congressional majorities are exceptionally large, party cohesiveness is not sufficient in either house to guarantee victory to the majority party on most major issues. With the lengthening of congressional careers, the decentralization of power to committees and subcommittees, and the weakening of party discipline, parties have become less cohesive than they were earlier in the century. Among the Democrats, the majority party in Congress almost continuously since 1933, party cohesiveness has been further weakened by the insurgency of many southern Democrats on a substantial range of issues, including civil rights, labor, tariffs, foreign aid, and social welfare. For example, in 1977 a majority of southern Democrats opposed a majority of northern Democrats on one-third of the recorded votes in the Senate and 28 percent of those in the House. Support from conservative sunbelt Democrats enabled President Reagan to secure enactment of his tax and budget program in 1981 despite a solid Democratic majority in the House of Representatives.

Reflecting these differences among congressmen of the same party are informal and formal groupings, or factions, which strongly influence party voting patterns. These groups have been particularly important among Democrats in the House. Ties among southern Democrats traditionally were informal, with leadership provided by southern committee and subcommittee chairmen. Liberal Democrats, mostly from the north and west, are formally organized into the Democratic Study Group. In addition to marshaling voting strength on the House floor, the Democratic Study Group provides research and campaign assistance to its members. Middle-of-the-road Democrats in the House organized the Democratic Moderates of Congress as a counterweight to the liberal Democratic Study Group. And conservative Democrats in the House have formed the Conservative Democratic Forum.

Role of the Party Caucus

A *caucus* is a meeting of all members of a party in a legislative chamber. At the beginning of the twentieth century, caucuses determined party positions on controversial issues in Congress, particularly in the House of Representatives, and members were expected to cast their votes in accordance with decisions made in caucus. Over the past half century the role of the caucus in binding congressional votes has declined, primarily as a result of the weakening of party discipline and the decentralization of power in Congress.

Although party members often break ranks over legislation, both parties' caucuses stand firm in organizing the House and Senate. Caucuses select the party's candidates for speaker of the House and president pro tempore of the Senate, as well as party floor leaders, whips, and policy committees. In addition, caucuses have ultimate authority to determine committee assignments and chairmanships. Committee reforms of the 1970s greatly enhanced this authority, particularly among Democrats in the House. Now chairmen unable to retain support of a majority of the caucus face a very real threat of losing their positions, as did three chairmen of House committees when the Ninety-fourth Congress organized in January 1975.

★ CONGRESSMEN AND THEIR CONSTITUENCIES

Seats in the Senate and House depend on state and local constituencies, and national party leaders and organizations play a minor role in congressional campaigns. As a result, constituency influence is pervasive in Congress:

> An understanding of the risks of the electoral arena is important for an understanding of Congress, not because local pressures are always decisive on particular votes but because the local basis of election tends to promote a local orientation toward issues in general. Specific local pressures may only infrequently be decisive, but they constitute the pervasive milieu within which congressmen and Senators operate.[6]

Congressional opposition to the deployment of missile weapons systems provides a good example of this local orientation toward issues. Relatively few congressmen initially opposed the $58 billion Sentinel anti-ballistic missile system proposed by the Johnson administration as a means of protecting American cities from nuclear missile attack. Once Congress approved the program, the army began to acquire sites in a number of metropolitan areas. What happened next was graphically described by John W. Finney in the *New York Times:*

> In Boston, Chicago, Detroit, Seattle, San Francisco, Los Angeles and Honolulu, objections [were] raised by city councils, church groups, conservationists, union leaders, real estate developers, peace groups and scientists to the emplacement of nuclear-tipped missiles in their cities or suburbs. . . . What had been an abstract, highly technical issue suddenly

acquired a direct political interest for many Senators and Representatives. When opposition began mounting in Hawaii, for example, Senator Daniel K. Inouye, a Democratic member of the Senate Armed Services Committee, came out firmly against Sentinel deployment on the ground that it would be "a dangerous step backward" into a nuclear arms race. Senator Harry M. Jackson of Washington, who had championed the system on the Senate floor, found himself running into political flak back home when the Army proposed to put a Sentinel site at Fort Lawton in the heart of Seattle. At Senator Jackson's suggestion, the Army agreed to move the site to Bainbridge Island, across Puget Sound, but that only served to arouse Representative Thomas M. Pelly, who has a home on the island. . . . The Army also proposed to establish a Sentinel base at Cheli Air Force Base in the southeastern section of Los Angeles only half a mile from [Representative Chet] Holifield's home in Montebello. This . . . brought protests from the Los Angeles County Board of Supervisors, which [wanted] to use the World War II base for industrial and housing development and suggestions from Mr. Holifield that the Army should not build its Sentinel bases in populated areas.[7]

A decade later, the Defense Department's plan to deploy MX missiles among 4600 shelters scattered across thousands of square miles of

Benson, April 1982, The Arizona Republic: Washington Post Writers. Reprinted with permission.

Nevada and Utah stirred a similar hornet's nest of locally inspired opposition in Congress. Western senators and representatives, normally strong supporters of defense expenditures, responded to their constituents' concerns about the MX system's adverse impact on farming and grazing, on water and the environment, and on the quality of life in the sparsely populated area. And as with the Sentinel, the scatter-site MX system eventually was shelved, at least in part because of constituency-inspired opposition in Congress.

Promoting constituency interests also means "bringing home the bacon"—federal projects, programs, and public works—from the "pork barrel." The chief source of "pork" traditionally has been public works—dams, post offices, highways, and other federal construction projects for one's district or state that provide evidence to constituents of a member of Congress's efforts on behalf of the folks back home. Those most favored in this quest have been congressmen on the public works and appropriations committees and subcommittees, and the ability of the chairmen of these groups to secure or deny projects for other members has increased their power. While few members of Congress defend the pork barrel, most dip in, because projects for *their* district are always "essential." "Pork," explains one House member sarcastically, "is something that some other place gets."[8]

Constituency Interests and Voting in Congress

The importance of constituency concerns does not, however, make congressmen robots who automatically serve the interests of their districts. Indeed, such interests are not clear-cut on most issues. Districts typically encompass a variety of interests, which often cancel out one another, giving members of Congress considerable freedom of choice. On many questions, constituents express little or no concern, and most Americans never communicate with their senators or representatives. In the average House district, a majority of the people do not even know the name of their congressman.

Despite the general public's lack of knowledge and interest, most representatives and senators believe their voting records are of concern to their constituents. Usually, they vote in accord with their perceptions of their districts' interests. But these perceptions are significantly shaped by the kind of contacts a member has with constituents.

> The communications most Congressmen have with their districts inevitably put them in touch with organized groups and with individuals who are relatively well-informed about politics. The Representative knows his constituents mostly from dealing with people who do write letters, who will attend meetings, who *have* an interest in his legislative stands. As a result, his sample of contacts with a constituency . . . is heavily biased.[9]

Congress of the United States
House of Representatives
Washington, D.C. 20515

OFFICIAL BUSINESS

Charles E. Bennett
M. C.

CONGRESSMAN CHARLES E. BENNETT

PRINTED ON RECYCLED PAPER

February 5, 1982

Dear Friends

Two weeks ago, I wrote the President and the Secretaries of Defense and the Navy asking them to set up a federal Drug Interdiction Task Force to step up the government's pace in stopping the flood of illegal drugs into our country.

As you can see from this diagram pictured to the left, which I used to illustrate my remarks at a recent press conference, the flow of illegal drugs swirls around and through Florida, bringing with it crime and heartache. I was determined to do all I can to make 1982 the year that we achieve real progress in stopping the flow of illegal drugs into our country.

Last week the President advised me that he is forming an antidrug task force headed by Vice President Bush and senior administration officials. I hope this group, which was ordered to focus its attention on South Florida, will attack the drug problem on a national basis. Drug abuse caused by illegal drugs entering this country is the most pressing domestic problem facing this country.

* * * * * * * * *

Last week I was delighted to serve as a co-host for the Washington Military Conference of the Jacksonville Chamber of Commerce. The nearly 20 delegates from Jacksonville's business community met with members of the House Armed Services Committee and other members of Congress and federal officials. One of the high points of that Conference was a luncheon with the Secretary of the Navy, John Lehman. The Secretary emphasized the opportunity Jacksonville has in expanding its share of the Navy's ship repair contract business. With over 40 ships to be homeported in Mayport, Mr. Lehman and I both believe that there is great potential for Jacksonville's shipbuilding and repair companies. I am supporting legislation, requested by them, which would improve the Navy's ship repair contracting and bidding policies in a way helpful to the Navy and to private enterprise as well.

Concern with constituency interests is evident in a typical congressional newsletter. The first two items in Representative Bennett's "report" deal with the flow of illegal drugs into his state of Florida, and defense contracts for his district.

301   Congressmen and Their Constituencies

The average congressman's contacts among politically active constituents tends to be with members of his own party who already share his general outlook on national issues and district interests. As a result, "the Representative's perceptions and attitudes are more strongly associated with the attitude of his electoral *majority* than they are with the attitudes of his constituency as a whole."[10]

Because members of Congress are responsive to the views of their partisan electoral supporters, they tend to see party and constituency interests as similar on many issues. Contributing to this coincidence of interests is the fact that Democrats and Republicans typically represent states and districts that reflect the different socioeconomic bases of the two parties. Thus, congressmen often are able at the same time to vote for the interests of the party and of the dominant majority in their districts.

Party and constituency are most likely to conflict for members of Congress who represent districts that differ greatly from the party norm—urban Republicans and rural Democrats. Over the past three decades, Democrats in the House have divided along urban-rural lines nearly half of the time, while urban and rural Republicans have parted company on more than one-fifth of all important votes in Congress.[11]

As in the case of party, constituency interests stimulate formation of groupings within Congress. Representatives and senators from a state organize, regardless of party, to advance common interests. Larger constituency-based groupings include the Senate Western Coalition, the Congressional Sunbelt Council, the New England Congressional Caucus, and the Northeast-Midwest Congressional Coalition. Black members of Congress, almost all of whom represent inner-city districts, created the Congressional Black Caucus in 1970. More recently, caucuses have been organized by women, working-class, and Hispanic members of the House.

The Shifting Constituency Base

Congressional constituencies change over time. National demographic shifts have affected the composition of the electorate in every state and district—increasing the number of voters in the rapidly growing states of the south and west, reducing the number of farmers and younger people in midwestern states, replacing white voters with blacks in inner-city districts, and adding new residents to voting rolls in suburban districts.

These population movements require substantial reallocation of seats among the states each decade. Between 1948 and 1982, California gained twenty-two seats in the House and Florida thirteen, while New York was losing eleven and Pennsylvania ten. The 1980 census alone shifted seventeen House seats from the northeast and the midwest to

TABLE **10-1**   **Changes in Apportionment of Seats in the House Following the 1980 Census**

Florida	+4	New York	−5
Texas	+3	Illinois	−2
California	+2	Ohio	−2
Arizona	+1	Pennsylvania	−2
Colorado	+1	Indiana	−1
Nevada	+1	Massachusetts	−1
New Mexico	+1	Missouri	−1
Oregon	+1	New Jersey	−1
Tennessee	+1	South Dakota	−1
Utah	+1		
Washington	+1		

the south and west. Within states, metropolitan growth necessitates redistricting to provide more representation for spreading suburbs, and less for older cities with their declining populations.

Legal changes also alter constituencies and their electorates. In *Wesberry v. Sanders,* the Supreme Court ruled that congressional districts within a state must have equal populations, thus ordering an end to widespread malapportionment of House districts that had benefited rural areas and disadvantaged growing cities and suburbs.[12] The Civil Rights Act of 1965 enfranchised hundreds of thousands of southern blacks, while the Twenty-sixth Amendment gave an opportunity to 11.2 million young people between eighteen and twenty-one to join the electorate.

Changes in constituencies have steadily augmented the number of congressmen oriented to the interests of suburbs and newer cities, lowered the average age of members of Congress, and reduced the number of southern districts in which candidates can ignore black voters. Constituency changes have also affected the internal workings of Congress. Younger and newly elected congressmen played important roles in democratizing the selection of committee chairmen and in securing seats for less senior members on important committees.

Change has broadened the perspectives of newer members of Congress. Many are less localistic in their outlook than senior congressmen. Better educated and widely traveled, they are less likely than older members to have spent their entire lives in the district, and more likely to have worked for the federal government or some nationally based organization before coming to congress. "We represent that mobile generation of post-war America," noted one of the ninety-two freshmen representatives elected in 1974. "We don't have the local roots that some others have. Our group would style ourselves as national

Congressmen. . . . We're concerned about our districts, but we're even more concerned about national problems."[13]

No matter how concerned about national problems, however, members of Congress cannot afford to ignore their constituencies. In fact, constant changes within constituencies reinforce continual efforts of congressmen, young and old, to build solid political bases in their districts and states. Job security is the object of much legislative activity. The necessity for such activity is reinforced by the fact that control over House districts is decentralized in the American federal system. State legislatures, not Congress, determine boundaries of congressional districts, a task they often perform with considerable imagination. Partisan advantage is the name of the game when state legislatures redraw congressional lines. "We wanted a map that assures the reelection of all Democratic incumbents," explained the Democratic state legislator responsible for the serpentine New Jersey districts illustrated in Chapter 7, "and one that gives us a fighting chance with some other seats."[14]

★ THE STRUCTURE OF CONGRESS

Two Houses

The most obvious structural fact about the American Congress is its bicameral organization. At the Constitutional Convention, bicameralism was required to accommodate the interests of the larger and smaller states. It also was consistent with the principle of checks and balances, one of the strongest forces that motivated the work of the framers. The story is told that when Thomas Jefferson returned from France after the Philadelphia convention he objected to the bicameral feature and asked George Washington why the convention had taken such a step. The conversation occurred at breakfast, and Washington is said to have asked Jefferson, "Why did you pour that coffee into your saucer?" "To cool it," was Jefferson's reply. "Even so," answered Washington, "we pour legislation into the senatorial saucer to cool it."[15]

This original expectation has long since ceased to be realized. The Senate does not function primarily as a "check" on the House. Legislation, with very few exceptions, originates as readily in one house as in the other. Under the Constitution, the Senate has exclusive jurisdiction over the ratification of treaties, trials of impeachments, and the confirmation of presidential nominations. The constitutional responsibility for initiating measures to raise revenues rests with the House, but in fact the Senate has originated tax legislation. For example, in 1982 major tax legislation was written in the Senate, which then attached the measure to a minor bill that had been introduced in the House. Otherwise, the two houses are equal in power, and *all* legislation requires action by both the House and the Senate.

Bicameralism, however, influences the nature of the congressional setting in a number of ways. The difference in their constituency bases affects the behavior of members of the two houses. Representatives are chosen from districts with an average population of 520,000, whereas senators represent states that range in population from Alaska's 400,000 to California's 24 million. Regardless of their size, statewide constituencies tend to be more diverse than most House districts, and senators are subject to a greater variety of pressures than the typical House member. As a result, there are fewer safe seats and less immunity to national political trends in the Senate than in the House of Representatives.

Because the Senate is much smaller than the House, senators function in a less formal environment than do the 435 representatives. The pace in the Senate is more leisurely, the rules more flexible, and real debate and deliberation more frequent. The House is an impersonal institution, with rigid rules that limit consideration of legislation on the floor. Senators normally serve on twice as many committees as representatives; as a result, specialization is less intensive and opportunities for leadership come more quickly in the smaller Senate. All these differences provide individual senators with greater independence and visibility than their counterparts in the House.

Senators enjoy a six-year term, while representatives must face the ordeal of re-election every two years. In a competitive district, House members are almost perpetually campaigning. Because of the advantages of the Senate's size and term of office, as well as the greater prestige associated with being a Senator, many representatives aspire to seats in the Senate.

A New Congress Every Two Years

Congress operates on a two-year cycle. The Congress that convened in early January 1983 was the Ninety-eighth Congress, there having been 97 previous Congresses in the 194 years since the first Congress met. While not prescribed in the Constitution, this biennial cycle was the logical result of an electoral system whereby all the seats in the House of Representatives and one-third of the seats in the Senate become vacant every two years. Accordingly, the Congress that meets in January of an odd-numbered year is a new body, many of its members having just been elected two months before. The meeting in the odd-numbered year is called the *first session*. Assuming that no special session is called, the meeting in the following, even-numbered year is the *second*, and final, *session* of a Congress. Very early in the first session the two houses proceed to organize, and the resulting arrangements continue for the

Congressional Record

United States
of America

PROCEEDINGS AND DEBATES OF THE 97*th* CONGRESS, SECOND SESSION

Vol. 128   WASHINGTON, MONDAY, JUNE 28, 1982   *No. 84*

Senate

The Senate was not in session today. Its next meeting will be held on Tuesday, June 29, 1982, at 11:00 a.m.

House of Representatives

MONDAY, JUNE 28, 1982

The House met at 12 o'clock noon and was called to order by the Speaker pro tempore (Mr. WRIGHT).

DESIGNATION OF THE SPEAKER PRO TEMPORE

The SPEAKER pro tempore laid before the House the following communication from the Speaker:

WASHINGTON, D.C.,
June 25, 1982.

I hereby designate the Honorable JIM WRIGHT to act as Speaker pro tempore on Monday, June 28, 1982.

THOMAS P. O'NEILL, Jr.,
Speaker of the House of Representatives.

PRAYER

The Reverend Dr. Lee B. Sheaffer, Aldersgate United Methodist Church, Alexandria, Va., offered the following prayer:

Our Heavenly Father, who has so lavishly blessed this Nation. Make us humble and sensitive to Your will. Keep us ever aware that the good things we enjoy have come from You and that You loan them to us.

Impress upon our smugness the knowledge that we are not owners or rulers, but stewards and servants; remind us, lest we become filled with conceit, that one day an accountability will be required of us.

Sanctify our love of nation and our love of people, that our boasting may be turned into humility and our pride into a ministry to every person and to every need.

Guide our Congress and our national leaders as they enable today's people to live with freedom, happiness, re-

sponsibility, and with the opportunity for growth and development.

Help us to make this God's own nation by helping us to live like God's own people. Amen.

THE JOURNAL

The SPEAKER pro tempore. The Chair has examined the Journal of the last day's proceedings and announces to the House his approval thereof.

Pursuant to clause 1, rule I, the Journal stands approved.

MESSAGE FROM THE SENATE

A message from the Senate by Mr. Sparrow, one of its clerks, announced that the Senate had passed without amendment bills and a joint resolution of the House of the following titles.

H.R. 4569. An act to designate the U.S. Post Office Building in Hartford, Conn., as the "William R. Cotter Federal Building";

H.R. 4903 An act granting the consent of the Congress to an interstate compact between the States of Mississippi and Louisiana establishing a commission to study the feasibility of rapid rail transit service between the two States; and

H.J. Res. 518. Joint resolution to designate the week commencing with the fourth Monday in June 1982 as "National NCO/Petty Officer Week."

The message also announced that the Senate insists upon its amendments to the bill (H.R. 6133) entitled "An act to amend the Endangered Species Act of 1973," disagreed to by the House; agrees to the conference asked by the House on the disagreeing votes of the two Houses thereon, and appoints Mr. STAFFORD, Mr. CHAFEE,

Mr. GORTON, Mr. RANDOLPH, and Mr. MITCHELL to be the conferees on the part of the Senate.

The message also announced that the Senate had passed a joint resolution of the following title, in which the concurrence of the House is requested:

S.J. Res. 183. Joint resolution to authorize and request the President to issue a proclamation designating October 17 through October 23, 1982, as "Lupus Awareness Week."

COMMUNICATION FROM THE CLERK OF THE HOUSE

The SPEAKER pro tempore laid before the House the following communication from the Clerk of the House of Representatives:

WASHINGTON, D.C., *June 28, 1982.*
Hon. THOMAS P. O'NEILL, Jr.,
The Speaker, House of Representatives, Washington, D.C.

DEAR MR. SPEAKER: Pursuant to the permission granted in the Rules of the House of Representatives, the Clerk received at 6:05 p.m. on Thursday, June 24, 1982, the following message from the Secretary of the Senate: That the Senate passed without amendment H.R. 6682.

With kind regards, I am,
Sincerely,
EDMUND L. HENSHAW, Jr.,
Clerk, House of Representatives.

ANNOUNCEMENT BY THE SPEAKER PRO TEMPORE

The SPEAKER pro tempore. The Chair desires to announce that pursuant to clause 4 of rule I, the Speaker signed the following enrolled bill on Friday, June 25, 1982:

□ This symbol represents the time of day during the House proceedings, e.g., □ 1407 is 2:07 p.m.

● This "bullet" symbol identifies statements or insertions which are not spoken by the Member on the floor.

H 3971

The first page of an issue of the *Congressional Record.* Note the designation of the Congress and session. Much of what appears in the *Congressional Record* is not part of any "proceedings" or "debate," as is indicated by material marked with the "bullet" symbol, which is explained at the bottom of the page.

306   The Legislative System and Lawmaking

two-year period. Any bill introduced in the first session of a Congress may be taken up during the second session. But when the final session in the two-year cycle comes to an end, all unfinished business automatically dies.

The opening days of a new Congress, when the business of organization is done, are marked by activity and excitement. The presiding officers and other officials must be elected, members assigned to standing committees, a chairman selected for each committee, and in the House rules of procedure agreed upon. These organizational tasks give the House a good deal more concern than they do the Senate, because only one-third of the senators have been involved in the recent election. Unless party control of the Senate is changing in a new Congress, organizing is a relatively simple process.

★ THE LEADERSHIP

The primary centralizing force within Congress is the leadership, composed of the presiding officers and party leaders who manage the flow of business through the House and Senate. The leaders organize the parties in Congress, prepare the legislative schedule, promote attendance of party members for votes on important bills, collect and distribute information, try to persuade members to follow their lead, and maintain liaison with the White House.

As one would expect, the leaders are among the most influential and respected members of Congress. Because the average length of service has grown, most leaders are career congressmen with long tenure. The leaders, however, have modest formal powers with which to influence members. As we have seen, the White House rather than the leaders in the House and Senate sets much of the legislative agenda. Congressional leaders are further hampered by their lack of rewards and punishments. "How do you discipline a man? What goodies are there?" asks a House leader. "If a fellow says 'No' to us what can the Speaker and I do about it? What can we give them? There are no little goodies, no patronage."[16] Legislators with strong constituency bases usually can get re-elected, even if they have thumbed their noses at party leaders in Congress. Also limited is the authority of leaders over chairmen of committees and subcommittees. Thus, leaders with small powers attempt to steer a diverse legislative party whose members are largely independent of direct control. As the current House majority leader puts it: "You have a hunting license to persuade—that's about all you have."[17]

Presiding Officers

The most important formal officers of Congress are those who preside over the two houses: in the House, the *speaker,* chosen by the majority party caucus; in the Senate, the *vice-president,* who under the Constitution holds the post of presiding officer. In the Senate, the *president pro tempore* is chosen on a party basis to preside in the absence of the vice-president. (In fact the vice-president or the president pro tempore rarely presides; this dull duty is usually passed around among more junior senators.)

The presiding officers' authority and influence depend only in small part upon their formal powers. To a large extent, the leaders' importance is controlled by such intangible factors as their personalities, the respect they command from their colleagues, their skills in human relations, their party standing, the overall strength and cohesion of their party, and the state of relations between Congress and the president. The speaker of the House is almost always one of the most respected and influential members of the majority party. Unlike the vice-president, the speaker is a party leader, chosen by his colleagues. He is a regular member of the House who retains his right to vote and speak on any proposal. When the speaker does leave the chair to enter the debate, he is likely to exert great influence. The vice-president, on the other hand, has no regular right to participate in debate and may vote only to break a tie.

No member of the House or Senate may speak on the floor or offer any motion without first being recognized by the presiding officer. Occasionally, the course of the legislative process may be significantly affected by the recognition of a certain member at a particular moment, and the speaker and the vice-president sometimes deliberately weigh such considerations when they give the floor to members. But the power of recognition usually is exercised on an impartial basis.

The presiding officer also has authority to interpret and apply the rules when a procedural question arises. Usually, reference to precedent is enough to indicate the proper interpretation, but occasionally the presiding officer makes a creative and important decision. In 1890, for instance, Speaker Thomas B. Reed changed the interpretation of the quorum rule so as to include in the count members present but not voting on a bill. In so doing, Reed frustrated the attempts of the Democratic minority to prevent the transaction of business by not voting either way. Generally, however, opportunities to make new and significant interpretations of the rules are rare. Besides, any ruling of the presiding officer may be appealed to the floor and reversed by a majority of the members present.

In both houses, the presiding officers refer bills introduced by members to standing committees for consideration and action. Various legis-

Representative Sam Rayburn of Texas moves to the podium after re-election by the Democratic majority as Speaker of the House at the opening of the Eighty-seventh Congress in 1961. "Mr. Sam," as he was known to his colleagues, served eighteen years as speaker, a period which spanned the administrations of four presidents. (United Press International)

lative reform acts delineate the jurisdiction of committees in detail, but when a bill can be assigned to one of two or more committees, the presiding officer may have the option of choosing a friendly or an unfriendly committee.

In addition, the presiding officers of the House and Senate name members of special committees, among them conference committees (those organized to compromise the differences in the bills passed by the two houses) and special investigating committees. This function is usually so controlled by tradition, however, that it leaves very little freedom of choice. For example, members of conference committees normally are named in order of seniority from the standing committees that considered a bill.

Before 1910, the powers of the speaker of the House were far greater. As chairman of the Rules Committee, which determines what proposals reach the floor, the speaker controlled the flow of legislation in the House. He also appointed committee members and chairmen and had absolute discretion in recognizing representatives who wished to speak on the floor. All these powers were lost as a result of the revolt of 1910–1911 against the strong leadership of Speaker Joe Cannon. Since then, "the Speaker's formal authority has been modest, and his centralizing influence has been more informal and interstitial than formal and comprehensive."[18]

Most of the speaker's informal influence is derived from his role as the central party leader in the House. His views are usually influential in selecting the rest of the majority party leadership and in assigning members of his party to committees. He is at the center of a communications network that links committee chairmen, other powerful members of his party, and the minority leadership. He is also his party's chief persuader. As former Speaker Joseph Martin explained:

> The speaker himself is the grand strategist and guiding spirit. Each Speaker, of course, exercises his leadership according to his own character and the prevailing political situation. For my own part I was never dictatorial. I worked by persuasion and drew heavily on long-established personal friendships. I found that I could best keep my members with me by tact and discretion. Unless it was absolutely necessary, I never asked a man to side with me if his vote would hurt him in his district. Whenever I could spare a man this kind of embarrassment I did so and saved him for another time when I might need him more urgently.[19]

In these dealings, as adept speaker will make use of his formal powers, which include control over the House staff, allocation of offices, approval of foreign travel, as well as his influence on committee assignments and his ability to affect the fate of bills dear to the hearts of particular members.

Floor Leaders and Whips

Next to the speaker, the most important officers in Congress are the *majority* and *minority floor leaders* in each house. These leaders are chosen by the party caucuses. As their titles indicate, their main duty is to watch over and try to control business on the floor of the Senate and House in the interests of their parties. A floor leader keeps in touch with ordinary party members and key committee members, as well as leaders of state delegations and other groupings like the Democratic Study Group and the Black Caucus. He tries to persuade them to act in committee and vote on the floor in accordance with party policies and the wishes of party leaders. In addition, floor leaders supervise debate, direct the activity of party whips, and serve as their parties' legislative strategists. In consultation with the presiding officer and the minority leader, the majority leader in each house plans the order of business, a function shared in the House with the Rules Committee.

Each party in each house employs a *whip,* who is appointed by the floor leader. Aiding the whip are a number of assistant whips, all of whom are members of Congress. The basic function of the whip is to secure the support of party members when major issues reach the floor. In the process, whips find out how party members intend to vote, convey the wishes of the leadership to members, inform the party leaders of the views of the rank and file on pending bills, notify members when key votes are scheduled, and ensure that supporters are present to vote. In the House, particularly, the activities of whips often affect the outcome of votes on important legislation.[20]

Both parties also have created *policy committees* in each house of Congress. These committees are supposed to develop general legislative programs for their respective parties. None, however, has been able to formulate broad policies, largely because of the diversity of viewpoints within each of the parties and the decentralization of power within Congress.

★ THE COMMITTEE SYSTEM

Power is dispersed in Congress primarily because most of the work of the House and Senate is done in *standing committees* and their *subcommittees.* Furthermore, these committees exercise their considerable power independently of one another. In large measure, they also operate independently of the presiding officers, floor leaders, and other centralizing forces in Congress.

The committee system permits a division of labor in dealing with the numerous and complex proposals that come before Congress. It also encourages specialization by congressmen, most of whom develop detailed knowledge only in those areas of governmental activity that fall within the range of their committees. Respect and influence among colleagues, particularly in the House of Representatives, are won primarily by working hard in committee and developing expertise. In the words of one representative:

> The members who are most successful are those who pick a specialty or an area and become real experts in it. As a consequence, when they speak they are looked upon as authorities and are highly respected. Even though they may be an authority in only one field, their influence tends to spread into other areas.[21]

"You'll find 80% of the work is done in the committees my boy . . . and 90% of the goofing off."

Grin and Bear It, by George Lichty and Fred Wagner, courtesy of Field Newspaper Syndicate.

Grin and Bear It, by Lichty and Wagner, © 1975 Field Enterprises, Inc. Courtesy of Field Newspaper Syndicate

The congressman who relies on a colleague's judgment on some issue within this special sphere of competence expects that colleague's support on matters that come before his own committee. The relationship is reciprocal, and so committee influence increases.

Committees and Subcommittees

While the number of *standing* committees in the two houses differs slightly, twenty-two in the House and fifteen in the Senate, the division of responsibility among committees is similar. Both have committees on agriculture, appropriations, armed services, banking, budget, commerce, ethics, foreign affairs, government operations, labor, rules, taxation, and veterans (Table 10-2).

Over the years, responsibilities of various committees have expanded as new problems and issues have come before Congress. Movement of the banking committees into housing and urban policy provides a good example. Housing issues initially arose in the context of mortgage policies, which the banking committees handled. Once involved in housing politics, these committees began handling other urban issues such as planning, mass transportation, and open space. Eventually, the committee names were changed to reflect their new responsibilities.

Periodically, Congress has tried to reorganize its committee structure to reduce overlapping responsibilities, organize functions more logically, and provide better balance in the workload of committees. One such effort produced the Legislative Reorganization Act of 1946, which eliminated almost fifty standing committees. In 1974, another reform abolished the House's Internal Security Committee, as well as altering the responsibilities of a number of committees in the House. In 1977, the Senate reorganized its committee structure, eliminating the District of Columbia and Post Office Committees, and altering the responsibilities of many of the remaining standing committees.

Overhauling committee responsibilities intimately affects the fortunes of large numbers of legislators. Eliminating committees and subcommittees directly threatens the chairmen of the targeted bodies. Shifting a function such as mass transportation or health care from one committee to another means an irretrievable loss of influence for congressmen who have specialized in that activity because members of Congress cannot move with their area of specialization to a new committee. Thus, carefully nurtured relations with federal officials, state and local agencies, interest groups, and others with a concern in a particular policy area are bound to suffer. Because of the high stakes congressmen have in existing allocations of responsibilities, committee reform has been an extremely controversial issue, and opposition from potential losers has blocked many proposed reforms.

Each standing committee in Congress is organized on a bipartisan basis. Ratios of Democrats and Republicans on committees reflect the overall division between the two parties in the House and Senate. Each representative is assigned to one or two committees, and the typical senator to three. Committees in the House tend to be twice as large as those in the Senate, usually averaging forty members compared with around eighteen in the Senate.

Subcommittees have proliferated since the streamlining of the committee system in 1946. House and Senate standing committees now have more than 230 subcommittees, a growth that also reflects the increasing volume and complexity of legislation. Obviously, subcommittees permit greater specialization; and, even more important, subcommittees mean that more members of Congress occupy positions of leadership, a condition that further disperses power in Congress. In recent years, every member of the majority party in the Senate has chaired a subcommittee,

TABLE **10-2**   **Standing Committees and Their Subcommittees* in the 97th Congress**

House of Representatives	Senate
Agriculture (8)	Agriculture, Nutrition and Forestry (7)
Appropriations (13)	Appropriations (13)
Armed Services (7)	Armed Services (6)
Banking, Finance and Urban Affairs (8)	Banking, Housing and Urban Affairs (7)
Budget (9)**	Budget (0)
District of Columbia (3)	Commerce, Science and Transportation (7)
Education and Labor (8)	Energy and Natural Resources (6)
Energy and Commerce (6)	Environment and Public Works (6)
Foreign Affairs (8)	Finance (9)
Government Operations (7)	Foreign Relations (7)
House Administration (7)	Governmental Affairs (8)
Interior and Insular Affairs (6)	Judiciary (9)
Judiciary (7)	Labor and Human Resources (7)
Merchant Marine and Fisheries (5)	Rules and Administration (0)
Post Office and Civil Service (7)	Veterans' Affairs (0)
Public Works and Transportation (5)	Totals: 15 committees
Rules (2)	92 subcommittees
Science and Technology (7)	
Small Business (6)	
Standards of Official Conduct (0)	
Veterans' Affairs (5)	
Ways and Means (6)	
Totals: 22 committees	
140 subcommittees	

  *Number of subcommittees is shown in parentheses.
**The House Budget Committee calls its units "task forces" rather than subcommittees.

while almost half of the majority Democrats in the House have headed subcommittees.

Membership on Committees

Committee assignments largely determine the areas of public policy in which a representative will specialize, the administrative agencies on which they will have the greatest influence, and the subjects on which they will generate publicity. Both houses limit the number of committee assignments available to individual legislators. In the House, membership on the Appropriations, Rules, or Ways and Means committee usually precludes service on other standing committees.* All other House members are permitted to serve on two committees, but only one of these assignments can be on a major committee. The Senate restricts members to two major committees.

The party caucuses assign members of Congress to standing committees. In both the House and the Senate, the caucuses have delegated this task to party committees. Because standing committees are reasonably continuous bodies (most members carrying over from the previous Congress), the prime task of each party committee is to fill vacancies. Usually, there are more applications than openings on the important committees, as some senior congressmen try to obtain assignments that provide more influence and visibility. Pressures from younger members, however, have diluted the significance of seniority in committee assignments. The Democrats in the Senate try to give each newly elected Democratic senator an appointment to a major committee. In the House, the party committees consider a number of factors in addition to seniority, including the member's record as a legislator, his or her state or region, the nature of the district, the contribution of a particular committee assignment to chances for re-election, and the legislator's background before entering the House. Constituency considerations are especially important in assignments to such committees as Agriculture, Armed Services, Banking, Education and Labor, Interior, Merchant Marine and Fisheries, and Science and Technology.

Policy considerations can also play an important role in some assignments. Over the years, various factions have tried to bolster their influence by placing particular individuals on a committee. For example, in 1975, southern Democrats pressed for the assignment of Senator James B. Allen, a conservative from Alabama, to the Judiciary Committee. Allen was blocked in the Democratic Steering Committee by liberals strongly opposed to having another conservative on the committee that handles civil rights, criminal justice, and judicial nominations.

Normally, ratification by the party caucus of recommended committee assignments is a mere formality. Congressmen disgruntled with a committee assignment have no choice but to wait two years for another chance. Some freshmen, however, have successfully challenged their committee assignments in the Democratic caucus. In 1969, Shirley Chisholm—the first black woman elected to Congress—objected to her assignment to the Agriculture Committee as inappropriate to her inner-city district. Her appeal was accepted by the caucus, and she was as-

---

* The Appropriations Committee handles all spending bills, that is, those that *appropriate* public funds. The Rules Committee is the "traffic cop" of the House, because it determines what proposals reach the floor for debate and a vote. The Ways and Means Committee considers tax legislation and related matters, such as revenue sharing and social security.

signed to the urban-oriented Education and Labor Committee. Two years later, another New York City Democrat—Herman Badillo, the first congressman of Puerto Rican descent—also successfully challenged his assignment to the Agriculture Committee and won appointment to the Education and Labor Committee.

Role of Committee Chairmen

Because so much of Congress's work is done in committees and subcommittees, chairmen play a critical role in the legislative process. To a chairman belongs most of the power to arrange committee meetings and select staff to work with committee members. Chairmen play a major role in establishing subcommittees, appointing their members and chairmen, determining how specialized and independent they will be, deciding what matters will be referred to them, and assigning them staff and funds. The chairman also determines the order in which a committee considers bills, decides whether public hearings shall be held, arranges to have bills that the committee has approved brought to the floor, and manages floor debate on the committee's bills.

In both houses of Congress, committee chairmen are selected primarily on the basis of seniority on the committee. Rank within committees also is similarly determined, and subcommittee chairmen normally are selected from among the more senior committee members, particularly in the House. The Senate has used seniority since early in the nineteenth century, and the House since the revolt in 1910–1911 against Speaker Cannon. For much of the twentieth century, the only exception to the seniority rule has been the prohibition in both houses against a member's serving as the chairman of more than one standing committee.

Probably no aspect of the congressional system has been more controversial than the seniority rule. Critics argue that it rewards members from safe districts rather than those who work hard, are skillful, or demonstrate party loyalty. Seniority also sentences junior congressmen to lengthy periods of apprenticeship that frustrates newcomers and deters able and mature individuals from seeking election to Congress. New members, as one House freshman pointed out, do not want to "wait around five years to have a voice in making this a viable institution."[22] The seniority rule also comes under fire from those who want to strengthen the role of the parties in Congress. Under the system, committee chairmen can usually ignore the party leadership. As long as they have the support of a majority of voters in their states or districts, their seats in Congress are safe. So too are their chairmanships of committees, provided their party remains in the majority.

Seniority is defended on a number of grounds. It has brought or promises benefits to many members of Congress. Supporters also contend that seniority contributes to the stability of committee membership by rewarding experience, thus promoting specialization and expertise. Defenders further argue that no workable alternative exists. Abandoning seniority, they insist, would lead to endless factional and personal conflicts over distribution of chairmanships. The result would weaken Congress in its dealings with the president, federal agencies, and lobbyists.

Even with these reforms, seniority continues to play an extremely immen, pressures from junior members has produced significant modifications in the selection of committee chairmen. Since 1971, nominations for chairmen and ranking minority members of committees have been submitted to party caucuses for approval. In 1975, Democrats in the House dramatically broke with seniority. With the reformers' ranks bolstered by the addition of seventy-five freshmen, the Democratic caucus voted to deny reappointment to three venerable chairmen who had served a total of 118 years in Congress.

Despite these reforms, seniority continues to play an extremely important role in selecting committee chairmen. Nineteen of the twenty-two House chairmen chosen during the "revolt" of 1975 were the most senior members of their committees. In two of the three cases where chairmen were removed in 1975, the position went to the next senior Democrat on the committee. And since 1975, the Democratic caucus has always followed seniority in designating committee chairmen. As a result, most chairmen still are older members with long tenure who tend to represent districts or states in which competition between parties is relatively low.

Although modification of seniority has had relatively little impact on the *selection* of chairmen, the need to win caucus approval has significantly altered the *behavior* of chairmen. In the past, they could reward and punish individuals with little fear of retaliation. Now, in the words of one representative, chairmen "recognize they are not serving by divine right, but as elected representatives of the caucus."[23] Accountability to the party caucus has made chairmen more responsive to committee members, junior congressmen, and party leaders. As a result, there is more debate, conflict, and compromise within committees and subcommittees.

These developments have further dispersed power within Congress. Both floor leaders and committee chairmen must largely deal with subcommittee chairmen and, increasingly, with individual legislators, as equals. Paradoxically, greater democratization within Congress has made it more difficult to carry out any policy, even one that is popularly supported.

LOBBYING

Congress is a constant target of vigorous activity by groups that try to shape policy decisions. Lobbyists are involved in every stage of the legislative process, directly pressuring senators and representatives. They draft legislation, support or oppose proposals at hearings, urge committees to advance or block issues, and try to influence votes on bills that reach the floor of the House or Senate. Many groups also actively promote or oppose changes in the legislative process. For example, Common Cause, a national citizens' group, energetically supported the revolt of younger House members against the seniority system in 1975. Labor unions, on the other hand, successfully fought the proposed division of the House Education and Labor Committee into two committees. Groups also press to secure strategic committee assignments for members of Congress who are sympathetic to the particular interest.

An extraordinary range of groups seeks to influence Congress, and their numbers have grown rapidly in recent years as the public agenda has steadily broadened. Lobbyists for corporations and trade associations as well as a host of Washington law firms advance business interests. The AFL–CIO, individual unions, state labor federations, and large union locals all have agents in Washington to "inform" legislators. The diverse concerns of farmers are pressed by such national organizations as the American Farm Bureau Federation and the Farmers Union, as well as by commodity and cooperative groups. Veterans' groups, doctors, lawyers, conservationists, owners of firearms, religious organizations, welfare recipients, opponents of abortion, older citizens, and hundreds of other organized interests also lobby Congress.

Expansion of federal aid to states and localities has led to more and more lobbying by governors, state highway officials, county officials, mayors, school boards, local health officers, housing authorities, metropolitan transit agencies, and a multitude of other public bodies. Even representatives of foreign governments contact congressmen, seeking economic aid, military assistance, trade advantages, and similar benefits. On many issues before Congress, lobbyists for corporations, trade associations, and organizations form alliances such as the Clean Air Working Group or the National Coalition of Telephone Users and Providers.

The largest employer of lobbyists is the federal executive, whose corps of legislative representatives constantly tries to advance presidential and agency interests in Congress. At the top of the pyramid of federal lobbyists is the White House's congressional liaison staff, whose efforts to win support for the president's legislative program include a computerized information system containing basic information on every member of the House and Senate. Within the federal government, the biggest corps of lobbyists is employed by the Defense Department. Even the Supreme Court lobbies in Congress. The chief justice and one or two associate justices often are invited to testify on budgetary matters that concern the judicial system. Sometimes individual justices have pressed hard—albeit informally—for and against bills. Indeed, an occasional statute has been drafted by members of the Supreme Court.

Senators and representatives are more susceptible to pressures from lobbyists than would be the case if political parties were highly disciplined. The dispersion of influence among committees and subcommittees also provides lobbyists with a multitude of access points to decision-making processes. Perhaps the most successful groups are those that exploit the opportunities to forge an alliance of lobbyists, committees or subcommittees, and a federal bureau, which together control a particular area of policy. These "sub-governments," as they have been called, function in a variety of fields, including defense, oil, sugar, public works, and veterans' benefits.[24] In the case of public works, for example, the main allies are the National Rivers and Harbors Congress, the Public Works Committees, and the Army Corps of Engineers.

Techniques of Lobbying

Lobbying methods vary greatly. An approach that is effective with one member of Congress may put off another. The techniques that attract the most public attention—wining and dining, free plane trips and hotel rooms, gifts, sex, and money—are not necessarily the most effective, although these and other unsavory techniques undoubtedly secure results in some instances.

Lobbyists typically concentrate on legislators who are either already disposed to vote their way—the object is to reinforce loyalty and to secure active support—or on those who are uncommitted and thus open to persuasion. Seldom do lobbyists spend time, energy, and other scarce resources on those who are committed to the other side. Threats are rarely used, since members of Congress can easily retaliate against obnoxious lobbyists.

A lobbyist has four principal instruments of persuasion. First are *campaign contributions*, which are increasingly funneled through political action committees. With the costs of running for Congress soaring, even the most honest legislator is tempted to be more sympathetic to the pleas of special interests that make heavy campaign contributions. These contributions need not be monetary. They might include helping with registration drives, engaging in campaign debates, or getting out the vote on election day.

The second instrument is *friendship*. Many organizations hire former congressmen or staff members to represent them, because these people usually can gain access to their former colleagues. Obtaining access is

S. C. Rawls, Palm Beach Post: NEA

critical, but using it fruitfully is even more so. Operating in a selfish world of demands and counter demands, a legislator usually finds that he can trust only a small portion of those who come to him for help. As a result, he tends to listen more to those whose reliability and personal loyalty have been tested over time. The mark of a successful lobbyist is that officials on Capitol Hill look on him as a trusted friend and ally, not as an agent of a particular group.

Information is the lobbyist's third instrument. Congressmen need accurate information about the nature and extent of a problem, the feasibility of proposed solutions, and, not least, how constituents feel about the matter. Because of the thousands of demands on their time, legislators can be personally familiar with only a narrow range of problems. Even with the help of a large staff, many important matters cannot be given anything like the attention they deserve. One particularly persuasive kind of information concerns what a proposal will do for—or to—a legislator's constituents. Lobbyists increasingly try to generate grass-roots pressure by having members of their groups send letters and telegrams to their congressmen. Groups opposing the Panama Canal treaties solicited letters to Congress through appeals to three million people in 1977. As a variant to mass pressure, some lobbyists prefer to have friends or particularly influential constituents speak privately with the senator or representative about what a proposed bill is likely to do and how the people at home are viewing it.

Fourth is the ability of the lobbying organization to *deliver votes* in the constituencies of individual members of Congress. Obviously, "a congressman from a district with a high proportion of union members will not often risk alienating the labor lobby through his votes on the floor."[25] Other lobbies that can stimulate potentially large voting blocs are opponents of gun control, advocates of prayers in public schools, and supporters of strict controls on abortion and birth control. Of course, most lobbyists represent groups with more limited clienteles. Such groups pay less attention to mobilizing their supporters at the grass roots, or they focus their resources on a smaller number of congressmen. The latter strategy was followed in 1972 by environmental groups who sought to demonstrate their electoral strength to Congress by concentrating their efforts on the defeat of the "dirty dozen," twelve congressmen who had opposed environmental measures.

Interdependence of Legislator and Lobbyist

Lobbying is not a one-way street. Members of Congress frequently use lobbyists for their own purposes. A bargaining process is at work. The legislator can do things for the lobbyist—give his cause publicity, leak some inside information to him, talk to an uncommitted colleague for him, introduce him to a member of an important committee, invite him to social functions so he can enlarge his contacts, and, of course, speak and vote for his proposals. Negatively, the legislator can refuse to cooperate with the lobbyist or can launch a public attack on the selfish interests trying to pressure votes.

The lobbyist can help the legislator by doing research, writing speeches, running errands, lining up friendly witnesses for committee hearings, soliciting campaign contributions, supplying information, and using influence with other lobbyists and legislators to support proposals that the legislator wants enacted. In short, lobbyists and legislators need each other and use each other.

In addition, lobbyists' efforts to build up friendships with members of Congress are often based on mutual, if selfish, interests. Lobbyists and legislators frequently have the same aims. Planning and carrying out a coordinated campaign to secure or block passage of legislation comes easily to them in such circumstances. A senator from Kansas has little difficulty cooperating with lobbyists from farm organizations, a senator from Texas readily accepts the help of the petroleum industry in working out details of an oil bill, and a representative from Akron or Pittsburgh is likely to be predisposed to support organized labor's position on a full-employment bill.

Federal Regulation of Lobbying

In 1946, Congress for the first time undertook to control interest groups by the Regulation of Lobbying Act. Actually, the law is poorly named, because it provides for little actual *regulation*. Any person or organization soliciting or receiving money to be used "principally to aid," or any person or organization whose "principal purpose" is to aid passage or defeat of legislation before Congress is required to register with Congress. Each lobbyist is required to disclose the name and address of his employer and how much he is paid.

Lack of clarity in the law, as in vague phrases like "principal purpose," allows some politically active organizations to refuse to register on grounds that lobbying is only incidental to their objectives. Compounding difficulties, Congress did not establish any special agency to enforce the statute. Nor does publication of required data in the *Congressional Record* do much to improve the situation. The *Congressional Record* is hardly regular reading fare even for well-informed voters, and newspaper analysts have generally shown scant interest in the information available.

Federal regulation of lobbying also suffers from the difficulty of having to operate under tight constitutional restrictions. The First Amendment, which forbids Congress to make any law abridging the right of the people to assemble and to petition the government for a redress of grievances, protects the basic right of lobbying against any outright federal prohibition. In upholding the Regulation of Lobbying Act, the Supreme Court in 1954 gave the statute the narrowest possible interpretation. According to the Court, the act applies only to lobbyists who enter into direct communication with members of Congress with respect to pending or proposed federal legislation, and does not cover lobbyists who try to influence the legislative process indirectly by working through public opinion.

☆ THE MAKING OF A FEDERAL STATUTE

The cards are stacked against action by Congress. Bills can be pigeonholed as a result of committee or subcommittee inaction in either house, blocked by a negative vote in committee or subcommittee, or beaten by failure of the Rules Committee in the House to act. A negative vote by the Rules Committee or defeat of a proposed rule for the bill on the House floor, a successful motion in either house to send the bill back to committee, a negative vote on final passage by the House or Senate, failure of a conference committee to resolve differences between the houses, or rejection of the conference compromise on the floor of either house can each effectively kill a bill. Those who want action must win at every stage of the process in both houses. Opponents, on the other hand, can lose at five stages, win at the sixth, and carry the day.

Drafting and Introduction of Bills

With very few exceptions any member of either house may introduce a *bill* dealing with any subject over which Congress has authority. A bill carries the prefix "HR" in the House and "S" in the Senate, and a number that indicates the order of its introduction. Bills enacted into law are also numbered in sequence. The Voting Rights Act of 1965, for example, is Public Law (or P.L.) 89–110, the 110th public law adopted by the Eighty-ninth Congress. The title *public law* is used to differentiate statutes of general application from *private laws,* such as an act to admit a particular person to the United States as an exception to current immigration rules.

The wording of a major statute is usually determined by many persons. Few congressional committees report bills for action by the House or Senate in exactly the same language as that in which they were originally drafted. Bills may be initially written in congressional offices or committees, or by an executive agency or interest group. Almost no major legislation is written in Congress without outside help or advice.

Committee Action on Bills

Almost all bills are referred to standing committees for consideration. The committee stage is the most crucial in the life of a bill, since most proposals die there. Each bill is carefully scrutinized in committee, and often its final language is determined at this stage, by either the committee or subcommittee.

Committees usually hold public hearings on important bills, and these hearings may be impressive sessions at which members seek the advice and assistance of informed persons interested in the proposed legislation. On the other hand, they may be carefully staged productions in which a committee chairman seeks to confirm and give publicity to his own prejudices. Because the two houses accept so many committee recommendations without change, interest groups and lobbyists are very active at committee hearings.

After these public hearings, the committee or subcommittee meets to determine a bill's fate. Before passage of the Legislative Reorganization Act of 1970, most of these sessions were closed to the public. Today, both houses impose strict limits on secret or "executive" sessions. If a

97TH CONGRESS
2D SESSION

S. 2222

To revise and reform the Immigration and Nationality Act, and for other
purposes.

IN THE SENATE OF THE UNITED STATES

MARCH 17 (legislative day, FEBRUARY 22), 1982

Mr. SIMPSON (for himself, Mr. GRASSLEY, Mr. HUDDLESTON, Mr. MATTINGLY,
Mr. PROXMIRE, and Mr. SASSER) introduced the following bill; which was
read twice and referred to the Committee on the Judiciary

JUNE 9 (legislative day, JUNE 8), 1982

Reported by Mr. SIMPSON, with an amendment

[Strike out all after the enacting clause and insert the part printed in italic]

A BILL

To revise and reform the Immigration and Nationality Act, and
for other purposes.

1   *Be it enacted by the Senate and House of Representa-*

2 *tives of the United States of America in Congress assembled,*

3   ~~SHORT TITLE; REFERENCES IN ACT~~

4   ~~SECTION 1. (a) This Act may be cited as the "Immigra-~~

5 ~~tion Reform and Control Act of 1982".~~

**One of the thousands of bills introduced in each Congress. This particular bill was
the 2,222nd introduced in the Senate during the Ninety-seventh Congress. It was
introduced by Senator Simpson of Wyoming and cosponsored by five other
senators. The bill was referred to the Committee on the Judiciary.**

committee views a legislative proposal favorably, it usually proceeds to "mark up" (revise) the bill and to prepare a formal report on it. Often the committee is split and submits both majority and minority reports to the floor.

Floor Action on Bills

A bill that has been reported by a committee is listed on a calendar, although its position there has little to do with the order in which it is actually considered. Instead, both houses have developed varying procedures for determining the order of business.

Under Senate rules, any senator is entitled to move that the Senate take up a bill that has been reported by committee. If the motion is adopted by a majority vote, the Senate turns to the bill in question. In practice such motions are usually offered by the majority leader, who acts after consultation with committee chairmen who have bills awaiting consideration.

Because of the size of its membership, the House uses a more complex system to determine the order of business. Most bills cannot be called up by a simple motion from the floor. A few committees, such as Ways and Means, Appropriations, and rules, may move consideration of bills and are said to be "privileged" in this respect.

Important public bills are normally brought to the floor of the House by means of a *special rule* or order prepared by the Rules Committee and adopted by a majority vote of the House. It is standard procedure for the chairman of the committee reporting a bill to go to the Rules Committee to ask for such a rule. If granted, the special rule usually fixes the time that consideration by the House shall begin, limits the period of debate, and guarantees that the bill will be brought to a final vote. Most special rules are "open," but a few are "closed" or "gag" rules, which limit or forbid offering amendments to that particular bill from the floor.

A bill may also be brought to the floor of the House by *discharging a committee* from further consideration of it. Discharging a committee requires that a majority of all House members sign a petition and that the House then approve the motion to discharge by a majority vote of those present. If the Rules Committee refuses to report a special order for a bill, the same discharge petition method can be used to force a House vote on the special order. This procedure is rarely successful, in part because of the influence of senior members of committees, who are able to retaliate against those who sign a discharge petition.

Limitation on Congressional Debate

Under House rules, each member is entitled to speak for one hour on the subject under consideration, but this right means little in practice. First, it is usually in order for the member who has the floor to move to close debate. This motion must be voted on immediately. If it is supported by a majority, debate ends at once, and the bill or proposal is brought to a final vote. Furthermore, the House debates virtually all important measures while sitting as the *Committee of the Whole*. All 435 members serve on the Committee of the Whole. By sitting as the Committee of the Whole, the House is able to operate under rules that are designed to expedite business. Here, debate is divided into two sections; a period of general debate on a bill and a period when the bill is read section by section for amendment. The length of the period of general debate occurs under the so-called five-minute rule, by which five-minute speeches are in order for or against proposed amendments. General debate on important bills may consume two or three days. Further debate under the five-minute rule may on occasion lengthen House consideration of a bill to a period of a week or more.

Under Senate rules, senators may speak as long as they please on any matter under consideration. It is this privilege, plus that of a senator who has the floor to yield temporarily to a colleague whom he chooses, that allows a *filibuster*—a prolonged discussion by one or a few senators—to prevent the majority from passing a bill.

Opponents of unlimited debate argue that the filibuster enables a minority to frustrate the will of the majority. Defenders contend that unlimited debate protects a minority's right to present its views and so prevent hasty action. In fact, filibusters have defeated relatively few bills that would have been passed. Most casualties have been civil rights bills; and the most ardent defenders of the filibuster traditionally have been southern conservatives, with northern liberals the most outspoken critics. But liberal senators who had repeatedly gone on record as favoring a change in Senate rules to curb unlimited debate filibustered unsuccessfully against the Communication Satellite bill in 1962. In the 1970s, liberal filibusters killed federal aid for the development of supersonic transports and legislation opposing school busing for the purpose of desegregation.

As the pressure of legislative business has mounted over the years, the Senate has been forced to use certain means of limited debate:

Two-Speech Rule: No member may speak more than twice on a single subject on the same legislative day. By recessing, rather than adjourning, at the end of the day's session, the Senate can prolong a "legislative day" indefinitely and thereby limit the amount of speaking that can be done on a single item of business.

Cloture Rule: In 1917, prior to American entry into World War I, the Senate adopted a specific rule to close debate as the result of a particularly unpopular filibuster against a proposal by President Wilson for arming American merchant ships. Under the present version of the rule, a vote of sixty senators closes debate on a pending measure. After cloture has been voted, no senator can speak for more than one hour on the measure and its pending amendments. In practice, cloture has been extremely difficult to invoke. Senators attempt to use it only in the face of an extensive filibuster against a highly controversial bill.

Curtailment of Debate by Unanimous Consent Agreements: Debate on major bills is usually brought to a close in the senate by unanimous consent that a final vote will be taken at a set hour. Debate is closed by unanimous consent as a matter of convenience where there is no real opposition to letting a bill come to vote, particularly if the majority has allowed a reasonable time for debate.

Methods of Voting

Both houses employ several methods of voting. The simplest and most common is a *voice vote*, in which the members call out and yeas and then the nays and the presiding officer judges which side has prevailed. Any member who doubts the results can ask for a *rising*, or *division*, *vote*, in which the two groups rise alternately and are counted. In the House only, one-fifth of a quorum may request a *teller vote*, by which the two groups leave their seats, pass between tellers, and are counted. Finally, in both houses, one-fifth of the members present may demand a *record vote*, in which the clerk calls the roll and members vote yea or nay. The House now has an electronic system that allows such roll calls in a matter of seconds.

Conference Committee Action on Bills

Most important public bills pass each house in a different version. These differences must be compromised if the bill is to become law. Where differences are slight, time short, or the bill unimportant, one house often accepts the version approved by the other. But if each house stands fast on its own version, it is necessary to use a *conference committee* to effect a compromise. The members of conference committees are usually drawn in a bipartisan fashion from among the more senior members of the standing committee in each house that originally considered the bill.

A conference committee is supposed to produce a bill that falls somewhere between the House and Senate versions. Sometimes, however, conference committees find it expedient to introduce new provisions into bills, even though that practice is a violation of congressional rules. Members of conference committees are also expected to defend their house's version in the negotiations, but this does not always occur, especially when these conferees do not sympathize with the legislation passed by their house.

The end of the tortuous path for a major legislative proposal is an occasion for celebration. President Carter and congressional leaders congratulate each other after legislation revising the social security system was signed late in 1977. (United Press International)

To become a law, a conference committee's proposal must be accepted as it stands by both houses, and no amendments may be proposed on the floor of either house. Either house, however, may reject a conference report and send a bill back to conference a second time, making clear that a particular change is required before it will accept the bill.

Final Hurdles

Following final affirmative action by both House and Senate, a bill is signed by the speaker of the House and the president of the Senate, and then transmitted to the White House for the president's signature. The president may sign the bill, whereupon it becomes law. Or he may let it become law without his signature by doing nothing for ten days following congressional approval. But if Congress adjourns during that ten-day period (as often occurs because of the rush of legislation in the last ten days of a session), the bill is dead. Or the president may veto the bill. Congress in turn can override the president's veto by two-thirds majority in each house.

⭐ SUMMARY

Power is decentralized in Congress. Most of the work of the House and Senate is done in committees and subcommittees. Legislative leaders cannot enforce party discipline on most issues, although party affiliation has a strong influence on the behavior of congressmen. Decentralized constituencies reinforce the independence of most members of Congress. Because representatives and senators enjoy considerable freedom of action, they are more receptive to pressures of special interests than would be the case if the parties could effectively discipline their members. Recent reforms have further dispersed power by weakening committee chairmen. This decentralized environment makes positive action difficult. The existence of two houses, complex rules, highly independent committees, and crowded legislative agendas provide opponents with many opportunities to defeat proposals. Most bills—wise and foolish—never survive the run through the congressional gantlet.

NOTES

1. *Congressional Government* (Boston: Houghton Mifflin, 1885), p. 58.
2. Lewis A. Froman, Jr., and Randall B. Ripley, "Conditions for Party Leadership," *American Political Science Review*, LIX (1965), 52.
3. Representative Charles W. Stenholm (D., Texas), quoted in Martin Tolchin, "The Troubles of Tip O'Neill," *New York Times Magazine*, August 16, 1981.
4. Donald E. Stokes and Warren E. Miller, "Party Government and the Salience of Congress," *Public Opinion Quarterly*, XXVI (1962), 545.
5. Randall B. Ripley, *Party Leaders in the House of Representatives* (Washington: Brookings Institution, 1967), p. 159.
6. H. Douglas Price, "The Electoral Arena," in David B. Truman, ed., *The Congress and America's Future*, The American Assembly (Englewood Cliffs, N.J.: Prentice-Hall, 1965), p. 32.
7. "Halt of Sentinel Is Traced to a 10-Month Old Memo," *New York Times*, February 9, 1969.
8. Representative David Obey (D., Wis.), quoted in "How Congress Slices the Pork," *Newsweek*, August 2, 1982.
9. Warren E. Miller and Donald E. Stokes, "Constituency Influence in Congress," *American Political Science Review*, LVII (1963), 54–55.
10. Ibid., p. 52.
11. See Julius Turner, *Party and Constituency: Pressure on Congress.* Revised ed. by Edward V. Schneier, Jr. (Baltimore, Md.: Johns Hopkins University Press, 1970), p. 111.
12. 376 U.S. 1 (1964).

13. Representative Timothy E. Wirth (D., Colo.), quoted in Marjorie Hunter and David E. Rosenbaum, "Defeats Split Bitter House Democrats," *New York Times,* July 2, 1975. Wirth, thirty-five years old at the time of his election, had been employed by the Department of Health, Education and Welfare in Washington before running for Congress.
14. State Senator Matthew Feldman, quoted in William E. Geist, "The Art of Politics: Jersey District Map Is a Partisan Gem," *New York Times,* May 26, 1982.
15. Max Farrand, *The Framing of the Constitution* (New Haven, Conn.: Yale University Press, 1926), p. 74.
16. Representative Thomas P. O'Neill, Jr. (D., Mass.), quoted in Hunter and Rosenbaum, "Defeats Split Bitter House Democrats," *New York Times,* July 2, 1975. O'Neill was majority leader at the time.
17. Representative Jim Wright (D., Texas), quoted in Steven V. Roberts, "Eroding Loyalty Weakens House Leaders," *New York Times,* June 4, 1979.
18. Richard F. Fenno, Jr., "The Internal Distribution of Influence: The House," in David B. Truman, ed., *The Congress and America's Future,* The American Assembly (Englewood Cliffs, N.J.: Prentice-Hall, 1965), p. 63.
19. Joseph Martin *My First Fifty Years in Politics* (New York: McGraw-Hill, 1960), pp. 182–183.
20. See Randall B. Ripley, "The Party Whip Organizations in the United States House of Representatives," *American Political Science Review,* LVIII (1964), 561–576.
21. Quoted in Charles L. Clapp, *The Congressman: His Work as He Sees It* (Washington: Brookings Institution, 1963), p. 24.
22. Representative Edward Mezvinsky (D., Iowa), quoted in James M. Naughton, "Congress Getting Younger: Reform Period Is Foreseen," *New York Times,* October 3, 1974.
23. Representative Jonathan B. Bingham (D., N.Y.), quoted in James M. Naughton, "Upheaval in the House," *New York Times,* January 17, 1975.
24. See Douglas Cater, *Power in Washington* (New York: Random House, 1964).
25. Turner, *Party and Constituency,* p. 88.

SELECTED BIBLIOGRAPHY

The American Assembly. *The Congress and America's Future,* ed. David B. Truman (Englewood Cliffs, N.J.: Prentice-Hall, 1965). Perceptive essays by eight leading students of congressional behavior and national politics.

Bailey, Stephen K. *Congress Makes a Law* (New York: Columbia University Press, 1950). A lively study of the enactment of the Employment Act of 1946.

Fenno, Richard F., Jr. *The Power of the Purse* (Boston: Little, Brown, 1966). An exhaustive account of the political processes involved in congressional appropriations.

Gross, Bertram. *The Legislative Struggle: A Study in Social Combat* (New York: McGraw-Hill, 1953). A portrayal of the legislative process in terms of intergroup conflict.

Matthews, Donald R. *U.S. Senators and Their World* (Chapel Hill, N.C.: University of North Carolina Press, 1960). A detailed and well-written analysis of the formal and informal ways of the Senate.

Mayhew, David R. *Congress: The Electoral Connection* (New Haven, Conn.: Yale University Press, 1974). An incisive essay which argues that congressional behavior is best understood in terms of the congressman's constant quest for re-election.

Milbrath, Lester W. *The Washington Lobbyists* (Chicago: Rand McNally, 1963). An interesting analysis of the strategy and tactics of lobbyists, based on a series of interviews with both lobbyists and legislators.

Odegard, Peter H. *The Story of the Anti-Saloon League* (New York: Columbia University Press, 1928). A classic account of the effects on one group to control the legislative process.

Oleszek, Walter J. *Congressional Procedures and the Policy Process* (Washington: Congressional Quarterly Press, 1978). A detailed examination of the formal setting of politics in Congress, including rules, procedures, and organizational structure.

Polsby, Nelson, ed. *Congressional Behavior* (New York: Random House, 1971). A stimulating selection of readings on behavior in the Congress.

Redman, Eric. *The Dance of Legislation* (New York: Simon and Schuster, 1974). A fascinating account of Congress at work as seen by a bright young man just out of college, serving on a senator's staff.

Truman, David. *The Congressional Party* (New York: John Wiley & Sons, 1959). A case study of party leadership and cohesiveness in the Eighty-first Congress.

Turner, Julius. *Party and Constituency: Pressures on Congress.* Revised edition by Edward V. Schneier, Jr. (Baltimore, Md.: Johns Hopkins University Press, 1970). A thorough revision of a pioneering work which sought to measure the influence of party and constituency factors on the voting behavior of members of the House of Representatives.

11 Presidential Leadership

PRESIDENTIAL STYLES
Strong and Weak Presidents
Recent Presidents
Personal Style and Presidential Power

SOURCES OF PRESIDENTIAL POWER
Party Leader
Chief of State
Chief Legislator
Chief Administrator
Chief Diplomat
Commander in Chief

LIMITATIONS ON PRESIDENTIAL POWER
Public Opinion
Congress: Checks and Needs
Congress: Impeachment
Congress: Foreign and Military Affairs
The Bureaucracy
Judges and State Officials
Political Culture and Political Conscience

INSTRUMENTS OF PERSUASION
Molding Public Opinion
Influencing Congress: Formal Powers
Influencing Congress: Informal Means
Persuading the Bureaucracy
Persuading Judges and State and Local Officials

SUMMARY

PART V

The
Presidency

During much of the last half century the American presidency has grown enormously in power and prestige. Crisis after crisis in international and domestic affairs, the president's capacity to dramatize *his* solutions to those crises, and development of swift and awesome weapons demanding equally swift and awesome decisions have multiplied both the opportunities and the needs for presidents to exercise leadership. The president has come to symbolize the nation, to personify American government. The patrician reformism of Franklin D. Roosevelt and John F. Kennedy, the homey manner and dogged courage of Harry S Truman, the gentle patience of Dwight D. Eisenhower, the craftiness of Lyndon B. Johnson, the scheming vulgarity of Richard M. Nixon, the moralizing energy of Jimmy Carter, and the genial oversimplifications of Ronald Reagan all reflect various facets of the American character.

Despite errors in political judgment and moral failures, the presidency remains *the* great public office in the United States, a place not only of raw power and glittering glamour but also, as Teddy Roosevelt observed, a "bully pulpit" from which to exercise world leadership. In many respects, the American presidency has become an imperial office. The incumbent is the prime focus of the media that cover government, and he and his family are the first celebrities in a nation that never seems to tire of the personal lives of the famous. Every gadget of modern technology is at the president's disposal, from the automated pens that sign the chief executive's name to the tape recorders that spelled Richard Nixon's doom. He is guarded by a phalanx of security agents, whisked through cities in bullet-proof limousines, and shadowed by a military officer whose briefcase contains the codes that control America's nuclear arsenal. Surrounding the president is a swirling mass of courtiers—aides, advisers, speech writers, television experts, and confidants—who inevitably cut the president off from the people whose votes put him in the White House, and Camp David, and Air Force One.

If many persons and events have combined to expand presidential power, other factors continue to tug in a different direction. Fewer than half of the presidents—only sixteen of thirty-nine—have been able to win re-election. And the saga of recent chief executives reads like an epic tragedy. Of all the presidents who served from 1933 to 1980, only Eisenhower was able to leave office alive and undefeated; and even he had to participate in the inauguration of the other party's candidate. Roosevelt died before being able to complete his domestic reforms or to see the Allied victory in World War II. Truman withdrew from the 1952

TABLE **11-1**

Presidents of the United States

George Washington	1789–1793, 1793–1797
John Adams	1797–1801
Thomas Jefferson	1801–1805, 1805–1809
James Madison	1809–1813, 1813–1817
James Monroe	1817–1821, 1821–1825
John Quincy Adams	1825–1829
Andrew Jackson	1829–1833, 1833–1837
Martin Van Buren	1837–1841
William Henry Harrison	1841 (died in office)
John Tyler	1841–1845
James K. Polk	1845–1849
Zachary Taylor	1849–1850 (died in office)
Millard Fillmore	1850–1853
Franklin Pierce	1853–1857
James Buchanan	1857–1861
Abraham Lincoln	1861–1865, 1865 (assassinated)
Andrew Johnson	1865–1869
Ulysses S. Grant	1869–1873, 1873–1877
Rutherford B. Hayes	1877–1881
James A. Garfield	1881 (assassinated)
Chester A. Arthur	1881–1885
Grover Cleveland	1885–1889, 1893–1897
Benjamin Harrison	1889–1893
William McKinley	1897–1901, 1901 (assassinated)
Theodore Roosevelt	1901–1905, 1905–1909
William Howard Taft	1909–1913
Woodrow Wilson	1913–1917, 1917–1921
Warren G. Harding	1921–1923 (died in office)
Calvin Coolidge	1923–1925, 1925–1929
Herbert Hoover	1929–1933
Franklin D. Roosevelt	1933–1937, 1937–1941, 1941–1945, 1945 (died in office)
Harry S Truman	1945–1949, 1949–1953
Dwight D. Eisenhower	1953–1957, 1957–1961
John F. Kennedy	1961–1963 (assassinated)
Lyndon B. Johnson	1963–1965, 1965–1969
Richard M. Nixon	1969–1973, 1973–1974 (resigned)
Gerald Ford	1974–1977
James E. Carter	1977–1981
Ronald Reagan	1981–

campaign when it became evident that, even from the White House, he would have great difficulty in securing his party's nomination. Kennedy was murdered before Congress had approved any sizable portion of his legislative program. Lyndon Johnson's disastrous policies in Southeast Asia not only involved the country in a bloody and divisive war, they also undermined his grand dream to create a Great Society in which poverty had been eliminated. Nixon's crimes forced him to resign in disgrace, turning to dust the political advantages that resulted from his landslide re-election victory in 1972. Gerald Ford's efforts to reunite the country after Vietnam and Watergate earned him only defeat in 1976. Jimmy Carter was repudiated after four years in the White House by an electorate that blamed him for the humiliation of the hostages in Iran, raging inflation, and soaring federal deficits. Ronald Reagan came to Washington in 1981 promising to balance the budget and revive the economy, and, despite considerable success in pushing his programs through Congress, wound up after two years in office with the largest budget deficit in American history and a stagnant economy with the highest unemployment rates in four decades.

The picture with which we are left is not one Norman Rockwell would have painted. Rather, it is a surrealistic set of swirls of power and frustration, prestige and disdain, victories and defeats. This chapter will attempt to trace some of those swirls and to offer at least partial explanations for their shapes and colors.

Jack Ohman. Reprinted by permission of Tribune Company Syndicate, Inc.

PRESIDENTIAL STYLES

In the abstract, it might seem that one should talk first about sources of, limitations on, and instruments of presidential power and only afterward discuss ways in which various presidents have tried to maximize their advantages and minimize their disadvantages. But the presidency is such a personal office that one cannot speak intelligently about it without first fully understanding that the character, ambition, skill, and, not least, the vision of the incumbent are critical elements.

Strong and Weak Presidents

Presidents can be ranged along a spectrum of attitudes toward their office. At one extreme would be the "literalists."[1] Presidents like William Howard Taft, Warren Harding, and Calvin Coolidge viewed the office as a place of rest and repose. They saw carrying out congressional policies as the president's main function. Any positive presidential action had to be justified by a clear constitutional command. As Taft wrote:

> The true view of the Executive functions is . . . that the President can exercise no power which cannot be fairly and reasonably traced to some specific grant of power or justly implied and included within such express grant as proper and necessary to its exercise. Such specific grant must be either in the Federal Constitution or in an act of Congress passed in pursuance thereof. There is no undefined residuum of power which he can exercise because it seems to him to be in the national interest.[2]

At the other end of the spectrum have been "strong" presidents like Jackson, Lincoln, both Roosevelts, Woodrow Wilson, and Lyndon Johnson. They have thought of the presidency as the center of a tornado of activity, an ideal vantage point from which to lead the nation. Theodore Roosevelt summed up the outlook of these men:

> My view was that . . . every executive office in high position was a steward of the people bound actively and affirmatively to do all he could for the people. . . . I declined to adopt the view that what was imperatively necessary for the Nation could not be done by the President unless he could find some specific authorization to do it. My belief was that it was not only his right but his duty to do anything that the needs of the Nation demanded unless such action was forbidden by the Constitution or by the laws.[3]

Most presidents do not fall so neatly at one extreme or the other. Many sometimes behave more like literalists, sometimes more like strong presidents. But the kind of role outlined by Taft has become a less and less viable option. The problems of modern society and the demands as well as opportunities for leadership are likely to be too pressing for anyone who enters the White House with a modest conception of his functions to follow Taft's model. Moreover, the driving ambitions that propel most of those who seek the modern presidency are not apt to be satisfied with such a humble role.

Recent Presidents

Among recent presidents, only Dwight D. Eisenhower was not a professional politician. He achieved national support as a great war hero and grandfather figure. He sought national unity rather than personal power. He saw his main task as reconciling differences among Americans and among nations. He preferred to moderate change rather than initiate it. In an attempt to place the presidency "above partisan politics," Eisenhower emphasized tidy administrative arrangements and careful staff work for information, ideas, analyses, and insights. His assistants made the president's tasks more manageable. But, in the process, "he became typically the last man in his office to know tangible details and the last to come to grips with acts of choice."[4]

John F. Kennedy relished his job. He was a bubbling source of information, ideas, and energy. Impatient with staff efforts, he preferred to expose himself directly to free-flowing arguments and avidly sought details. Eisenhower functioned like a chairman of the board, but Kennedy tackled problems personally, by seeking his own information and defining the options himself. As a result, Kennedy's presidency was not very neat, and failures of coordination were sometimes embarrassing. But, like Franklin Roosevelt, Kennedy believed that it was *his* job to make decisions; and to do so intelligently he needed to know as many of the facts as he could absorb. Again like Franklin Roosevelt, he cut across normal administrative channels to obtain the information he wanted.

Lyndon Johnson served in the House and Senate for almost thirty years before coming to the White House and had acquired a reputation for political genius. Throughout his career, Johnson displayed cyclonic energy, great persuasiveness, and iron will. Flamboyant and emotional, Johnson was also acutely sensitive to "the art of the possible" in politics. But Johnson's experience was almost totally in domestic affairs, and he showed none of his usual cunning in foreign policy, and particularly in Vietnam, where he demonstrated much iron but little wisdom.

Personally, Johnson was hard-driving, purposeful, and often spiteful, able to beg a man one day to join his staff, the next day to dominate, and the third day to humiliate him with crude sarcasm. Yet for all his meanness, Johnson kept his attention on using power—and people—to achieve his policy goals. The many facets of the war against poverty and the Civil Rights Acts of 1964, 1965, and 1968 were all *his* measures, parts of *his* grand design for a "Great Society." And Johnson enormously enjoyed the whole business. As he summed up his years in the White House: "If the Presidency can be said to have been employed and to have been enjoyed, I have employed it to the utmost, and I had enjoyed it to the limit."[5]

Nixon's presidency mirrored his own character: self-serving, amoral, paranoid, and erratic. His record was more positive in foreign than in domestic affairs, reflecting Nixon's personal interests and the influence of Henry Kissinger, who guided foreign policy throughout Nixon's presidency. However slowly and bloodily, Nixon ended American participation in Vietnam, established relations with the People's Republic of China, and lessened tensions with the Soviet Union. In domestic affairs his primary concern was increasing his power. Nixon's style was heavily sanctimonious, interspersed with occasional slashing attacks on the integrity and patriotism of those who refused to accept his hyperbolic rhetoric as eternal truth. He tended to make policy in secret and to reveal decisions in surprise announcements that stressed their "historic" importance and his own originality.

Part of the explanation for Nixon's style lay in his need for power, a need shared by most modern presidents, but part can also be found in other facets of his personality.[6] Essentially an introvert, Nixon preferred quiet meditation to free-wheeling debates. To insulate himself, he gave his top aides license to act more as assistant presidents than as presidential assistants. Not only did they make many decisions, they also determined who could speak to the president. Much of the time, Nixon's lieutenants exercised precisely the kind of control over his sources of information—and so his choices—that the Roosevelts, Truman, Kennedy, and Johnson had carefully avoided.

Gerald Ford's simplicity etched a striking contrast to Johnson's guile and Nixon's duplicity. Honest and outgoing, Ford made no pretense of being an intellectual or a dynamic leader. Ideologically a conservative, he wanted to cool both anger against the presidency and demands for governmental action to solve domestic problems. Ford's apparent directness and simplicity concealed his skill as a manipulator of men. His long tenure in the House of Representatives had taught him how to deal effectively with people. His legislative background brought him to the White House determined to heal the wounds that Nixon had inflicted on Congress. But within a few months Ford had his own disagreements with a Congress controlled by the Democrats. His frequent use of the veto relit the inevitable coals of presidential-congressional tensions, although with nothing like the intensity with which they had burned during Nixon's administration.

Jimmy Carter arrived in Washington with trunks bulging with blueprints for reform. Trained as an engineer, he saw his task as seeking objective solutions to the nation's many problems. He announced plans to overhaul an antiquated system of welfare, simplify the jungle of tax regulations, and streamline an often inefficient civil service. He also brought ideas for a new agreement with the Russians on limiting arms, proposals for peace in the Middle East, an outline of a national program of health insurance, and hopes for a comprehensive policy toward creating, using, and conserving energy.

During the 1976 campaign, Carter had stressed that he was innocent of Washington and its dark doings. Once in office, he demonstrated the truth of his claims. He understood little about the limits of presidential power and less about dealing with Congress or the diverse Democratic coalition that had put him in the White House. Carter thought it sufficient merely to preach and was shocked to find that legislators and interest-group leaders did not desert their doctrines and special causes to embrace his gospel. Carter's staff was equally un-

President Carter with his homework, briefing books dealing with some of the issues that press for decisions in the Oval Office. (Wide World Photos)

sophisticated about Washington and only painfully adapted to the ways of the national capital.

Nor was Carter very effective at stirring the American people, although he made many attempts to rally them behind his policies. He was an uninspired speaker, who rarely moved his audiences emotionally. His relentless efforts to shed the trappings of the imperial presidency that Johnson and Nixon had loved—there was little ceremony at the Carter White House, and the President carried his own luggage and wore sweaters and blue jeans—deprived him of the majesty of the office. To most Americans, Carter seemed an ordinary fellow who was overwhelmed by his problems rather than *the president*, firmly in control.

The result was a presidency which failed more often than it succeeded, despite Carter's enormous energy and high intelligence. He immersed himself in the details of every important policy issue, and many that were not so important. Like Roosevelt and Kennedy, Carter refused to allow anyone to function as his executive officer. He encouraged debate while mulling over a decision, but insisted on absolute loyalty after making a determination. Yet he often embarrassed friends by backing down (without notice to his supporters) when they thought it time to dig in and fight, and, on other occasions, by stubbornly refusing to negotiate when a compromise was his only hope. These sorts of errors led critics to charge that Carter was alternatively a waffler and a mule.

President Reagan on television, explaining his tax relief program to the American people, two days before he won the key vote on the legislation in Congress. (Photo by Karl Schumacher, The White House)

Ronald Reagan offered striking contrasts to Carter—he was a master of public relations, with a relatively simple but sweeping program, who provided general rather than detailed direction of the executive branch. A former movie actor, television personality, and star performer on the conservative lecture circuit, Reagan was a persuasive speaker in formal settings. He used television skillfully as candidate and as President, and was widely perceived as sincere, dedicated to his programs, and reasonable in his efforts to secure their acceptance by Congress. His views on most issues were to the right of the mainstream of public opinion, but his humor, affability, and optimism disarmed many who disagreed with his conservative outlook on government's role, social programs, civil rights, military expansion, and relations with the Soviet Union.

When the chips were down, Reagan proved a highly effective political leader. He provided strong direction for his tax and budget program in 1981, overcoming formidable odds to rout the Democrats who controlled the House of Representatives and who consistently underestimated his political skills. In building support, Reagan was flexible and persuasive, winding up with the most striking set of legislative triumphs since the early days of Lyndon Johnson. The following year, Reagan demonstrated that he could be pragmatic when necessary, as he joined forces with the Democrats to secure passage of tax increases opposed by conservatives of both parties.

Reagan's personal style in the White House was closer to Eisenhower's or Coolidge's than to Kennedy's or Carter's. His preferred role was that of chairman of the board, with most of the details of the presidency left to staff members. His work day was short and his vacations long, particularly in comparison with those of his workaholic predecessor. Reagan's approach spared him involvement in many of the complex problems that enraveled Carter. But Reagan paid a price for his detachment—he often was out of touch, uninformed, or misinformed. And his leisurely, affluent lifestyle combined with his hard-nosed social policies and high unemployment to polarize the American people, at inevitable cost to Reagan's popularity and effectiveness.

Personal Style and Presidential Power

In a formal, constitutional sense, the authority of the presidency has remained almost constant from Washington to Carter. In another sense, the office has changed markedly from one incumbent to another. The presidency of Andrew Jackson was simply not the office he had taken over from John Quincy Adams, any more than Lincoln's was the same as Buchanan's, or Franklin Roosevelt's that of Herbert Hoover.

Thus the first source of presidential power is the president himself: his peculiar skills and the ideas he has about his own roles and those of his staff, of Congress, of the courts, and his notion of what is good for the country and his own position in history. The presidency at any given moment is in large part the creature of the political vision of its temporary possessor. The other sources of power lie in constitutional clauses or in less formal practices that have built up around the institution of the presidency. It is to these that we now turn.

⭐ SOURCES OF PRESIDENTIAL POWER

Most of the president's work, Harry Truman liked to say, consists of "trying to persuade people to do things that they ought to have sense to do without my persuading them."[7] A president's judgment about what others should do may not always be correct, but Truman was certainly right in stressing that the power of the president, in national as well as international politics, is based on persuasion rather than command. In domestic affairs, both state and national legislators, as well as governors, mayors, and a host of other officials, have independent sources of authority and their own electoral bases, while federal judges have virtual life tenure. Thus, there are few people outside the executive branch whom the president may command, and even there he may have problems with federal officials whose role, constituency, or support in Congress insulates them from presidential control. In dealing with foreign nations, the need to rely on persuasion is obvious. Threats of force, like

Kennedy's in dealing with Soviet missiles in Cuba, or uses of force, like Nixon's bombing North Vietnam, are typically designed to compel an opponent to negotiate.

The unique constitutional and political position of the president allows him to play many different roles, and in each he may exercise different kinds of persuasion. But two facts must be kept in mind when looking at these roles as sources of power and opportunities for leadership. First, the president "plays every 'role,' wears every 'hat' at once. Whatever he may do in one role is by definition done in all. . . . He is one man, not many."[8] Second, in no one role or combination of roles is the president sure of exercising effective persuasion. Even as canny a man as Lyndon Johnson may end in tragedy. Each facet of the presidency presents the incumbent with an opportunity—and, in another sense, a menace—but never a guarantee.

Party Leader

When a candidate receives the presidential nomination, he becomes head of his party. Whether the president becomes the party's leader as well as its head depends on his political skill. But without his party's support he cannot be elected or, after election, effectively perform his duties. Because American parties are loose coalitions of state and local factions, they cannot be easily directed by the president or anyone else. If the chief executive is a strong vote-getter, state and local leaders may feel indebted to him for helping them stay in power. As often as not, however, these leaders boast of *their* achievement in electing the president. To be at all successful, the president as party leader must use charm, patience, patronage, and federal funds to weld these factions into some reasonable facsimile of a political organization.

Chief of State

The president is the representative of the entire nation as well as his party. He symbolizes the government of the United States. Like the British monarch, he reigns; like the British prime minister, he governs. Thus, the president can try to rise above partisan politics and claim authority to lead in the name of the United States, gathering to himself all the emotions aroused by appeals to patriotism. It is very difficult for any American to ignore a president who says that the national interest requires a certain policy. A member of Congress or a private citizen may not necessarily be convinced by the president's logic, but most people will listen attentively and respectfully to his words.

The ritual of inauguration symbolizes the president's role as chief of state and representative of the entire nation. Except in the case of re-elected presidents, inauguration also marks the peaceful transfer of power from one administration to another, as when Franklin Roosevelt succeeded Herbert Hoover (at the far right in the first row), Roosevelt's bitter foe in the critical 1932 election. (Wide World Photos)

Chief Legislator

The Constitution makes the president part of the legislative process. Article II instructs him to "give the Congress information of the state of the Union" and to "recommend to their consideration such measures as he shall judge necessary and expedient." In addition, the president can call Congress into special session to act on his recommendations and adjourn a session if the two houses cannot agree on a date. Furthermore, he may veto bills that he does not like. Those formal grants of authority and the diffusion of power within Congress reinforce the chief executive's influence over legislation.

At least as important as these factors is the president's access to the mass media. The presidency is indeed a "bully pulpit" from which to preach to the nation and the world. As pointed out in Chapter 9, the president has the legislative initiative. He can frame the agenda of Congress because he can set the political agenda for the nation. If he has the skill and courage, he can, as Lyndon Johnson phrased it, put "Congress' feet to the fire" by stirring up public opinion.[9]

Chief Administrator

Article II of the Constitution charges the president "to take care that the laws be faithfully executed." The vague language of many statutes increases that burden, but it also enhances the president's discretion and so his power. As a means of compromise or as the only feasible way of coping with a complex problem, Congress often chooses general rather than specific phrasing, leaving final resolution of difficulties to administrators, judges, or future legislators.

Translating law—vague or specific—from statute books into rules of real life requires an enormous administrative apparatus. Later in this chapter and in the next, we discuss some of the president's difficulties in dealing with the vast federal bureaucracy. Here we note only that, despite a merit system in the career civil service, the president can appoint—usually subject to the approval of the Senate—several thousand people at the top ranks of executive agencies. Skillful use of this authority in selecting officials who will serve him loyally and ably can materially enhance his power to lead, just as can deft use of the discretion allowed by vague or general statutory language.

Chief Diplomat

The Constitution makes the president the principal officer in foreign affairs, although in some respects this authority is shared with Congress. The president alone receives ambassadors and thus "recognizes" foreign governments. With "the advice and consent of the Senate" he appoints American ambassadors and top-level officials in the State Department. Only the president or his agents can communicate with other governments in the name of the United States. Only the president or his agents can negotiate treaties or other international agreements, although to become binding a treaty must be approved by a two-thirds vote of the Senate. In addition, to become fully effective some treaties need to be supplemented by legislation, such as an appropriation, that must be passed by both houses of Congress.

Presidential authority has been enhanced by judicial interpretations of the Constitution that have decreed that the conduct of foreign affairs is a virtual federal monopoly. The authority of the federal government in international politics, the Supreme Court has ruled, is complete, limited neither to those powers specifically listed or implied in the Constitution nor by authority reserved to the states.[10] The national government derives these powers from "the fact that the American people are a sovereign entity at international law."[11]

The Supreme Court has also spoken expansively about the powers that the president derives from the national government's paramount

Personal diplomacy has become an increasingly important aspect of presidential power. President Carter joins President Anwar Sadat of Egypt and Prime Minister Menachem Begin of Israel in a triumphant handshake at the conclusion of the Camp David agreement in 1979. (Newsweek, Wally McNamee)

role in foreign affairs. In 1936, the Court spoke of "the very delicate, plenary and exclusive power of the president as the sole organ of the Federal government in the field of international relations—a power which does not require for its exercise an act of Congress."[12] On other occasions, the Court has held that the president's conduct of foreign policy is subject to congressional restraints.[13] But the president's ability to act swiftly and his access to secret information give him enormous advantages over Congress in this area of policy making.

Commander in Chief

Closely related to the president's diplomatic power is his designation by the Constitution as "commander in chief" of the armed forces of the United States. As part of their fracturing of power among the various branches of government, the framers gave Congress authority to declare war and assigned the president responsibility for the way a war is fought. Indeed, presidents from Washington to Reagan have interpreted their authority as permitting them to commit American forces to combat without any congressional declaration of war.

The way a president plays his role as commander in chief can have a significant impact on domestic politics. Increased military spending can generate inflation. New defense priorities can force cutbacks in a wide range of domestic activities, as occurred during the Reagan administration, when military expenditures were sharply accelerated. A decision to fight an undeclared war, as in Korea or Vietnam, can also drastically reduce a president's popularity at home and affect his ability to push measures through Congress or carry out existing programs. Lesser decisions, such as hiring and firing professional soldiers, can change a president's standing with Congress or the electorate, as Lincoln found out when he shuffled generals during the Civil War and Truman when he dismissed the legendary General Douglas MacArthur during the Korean conflict.

As commander in chief, the president may make another, very different kind of impact on domestic affairs. Section 4 of Article IV of the Constitution directs the national government to protect each state "on application of the legislature, or the executive (when the legislature cannot be convened), against domestic violence." Congress has authorized the president to use federal forces, including the national guard, in discharging this obligation. It was on this authority that Lyndon Johnson, at the request of the Governor, sent troops into Detroit to help put down race riots. Congress also has provided for use of troops when enforcement of federal laws by ordinary judicial proceedings is, in the president's judgment, impracticable. President Eisenhower used this authority in 1957 to dispatch troops to Little Rock, Arkansas, and President Kennedy in 1962 sent troops into Mississippi to enforce federal court decisions ordering school desegregation.

The president's responsibility to "take care that the laws be faithfully executed" also carries with it authority to use federal troops when federal property or activities are endangered. In its most drastic form, use of military power within the United States means establishment of martial law—replacement of civil law and civilian courts by military law enforced by military tribunals. Such a suspension of civil government must be authorized by Congress and is valid only, the Constitution stipulates, when the United States is invaded or a rebellion is in progress.

★ LIMITATIONS ON PRESIDENTIAL POWER

None of these formidable powers, however, is exercised in a vacuum. At every turn, the president faces substantial constraints on the effective use of executive authority. One of the most important limitations is the sheer number and complexity of problems that reach the Oval Office.

Americans expect the president to have answers to inflation, unemployment, poverty, pollution, the Arab–Israeli conflict, unrest in the Caribbean, Soviet aggressiveness, and scores of other problems, in part because the president indicated he had solutions during the last campaign.

Presidents are further constrained by the strong centripetal forces in American politics that have dispersed power in Congress, weakened the role of political parties, strengthened the influence of special interests of all kinds, and spread governmental authority around scores of federal agencies, fifty state governments, and thousands of local units. And the presidency has been on the defensive in recent years—the reaction against Johnson's adventure in Vietnam and Nixon's submergence in Watergate produced new laws restraining presidential authority, more intense scrutiny by a more skeptical press, and a public more fickle than ever in its attitude toward the current occupant of the White House.

Another limiting factor is the immediacy of modern communications, which provides the public with instant images and appraisals, while leaving presidents little breathing space on most issues. One wonders how earlier presidents would have fared in the era of instant replays. "What would we have thought of Lincoln during his presidency?" asks one political commentator. "Could the Civil War have survived the 7 p.m. news? Could General Washington hold his command after a TV special on Valley Forge? What would the *New York Times* and the Washington *Post* have said about Lincoln's suspension of habeas corpus?"[14]

Public Opinion

When a president wants to have his policies accepted and put into operation, he must persuade large segments of the voting public, a working majority of Congress, executive officials, influential segments of the press, and, often, many state and local officials. All can limit his effectiveness. He must consider judicial opinions, for in very different ways federal judges may also block attainment of presidential goals.

In dealing with other public officials, a president's reputation for having both the ability and the desire to make the most of his position is crucial. So too is the president's prestige—what other political leaders believe the general public thinks about the president. Although voters can defeat the president or his party only at election time, their opinions, at least what politicians perceive to be their opinions, can ignite or extinguish enthusiasm in Washington or in state capitals for a president's plans. Many legislators are as reluctant to support an unpopular president's programs as they are to oppose the proposals of a popular chief executive. Bureaucrats are also often sensitive to fluctuations in

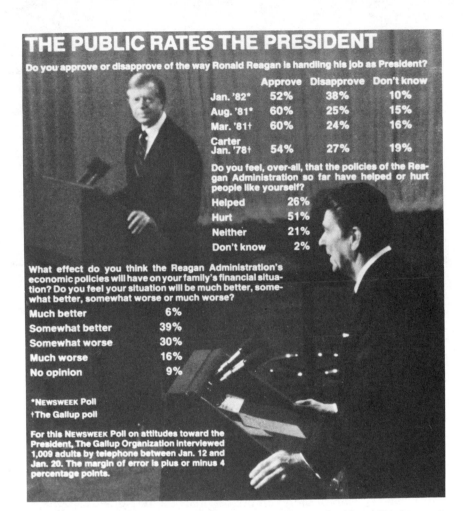

THE PUBLIC RATES THE PRESIDENT

Do you approve or disapprove of the way Ronald Reagan is handling his job as President?

	Approve	Disapprove	Don't know
Jan. '82*	52%	38%	10%
Aug. '81*	60%	25%	15%
Mar. '81†	60%	24%	16%
Carter Jan. '78†	54%	27%	19%

Do you feel, over-all, that the policies of the Reagan Administration so far have helped or hurt people like yourself?

Helped	26%
Hurt	51%
Neither	21%
Don't know	2%

What effect do you think the Reagan Administration's economic policies will have on your family's financial situation? Do you feel your situation will be much better, somewhat better, somewhat worse or much worse?

Much better	6%
Somewhat better	39%
Somewhat worse	30%
Much worse	16%
No opinion	9%

*NEWSWEEK Poll
†The Gallup poll

For this NEWSWEEK Poll on attitudes toward the President, The Gallup Organization interviewed 1,009 adults by telephone between Jan. 12 and Jan. 20. The margin of error is plus or minus 4 percentage points.

Fluctuations in presidential popularity are as closely watched by politicians and the press as are the vital signs of a patient in a hospital. (Newsweek)

both congressional and popular opinion. Thus public opinion, which can be a whip the president can crack against Congress, can snap back and coil around an unskilled user. And for most presidents, popularity is a perishable commodity. Over the past two decades, presidents have lost an average of five points a year in their standing in the public opinion polls.

Congress: Checks and Needs

Congress, like public opinion, poses major checks on presidential power. A president needs Congress to pass new legislation, to modify existing statutes, and to appropriate money to carry out his policies. To the extent that Congress refuses to perform these acts, it restricts presidential power. More positively, Congress can harass the president by adopting, perhaps over his veto, policies that he opposes. The reasons for friction between the president and Congress are varied.

First, conflict is built into a system of shared powers. The purpose of this constitutional arrangement, as Chapter 3 pointed out, is to check the power and ambition of one group of officials by the power and ambition of another group so that no one person, faction, or institution can obtain a monopoly of political authority. The system works well in that its overlapping grants of authority generate suspicion and antagonism among the three branches. Whether the president is a Democrat or a Republican, to all senators and representatives he is to some extent a dangerous rival.

Second, the president and members of Congress are elected by very different constituencies. Chosen in a national election with the support of 40 million or more voters, a president naturally tends to think in national terms. A senator or representative, on the other hand, is chosen by a single state or district and must necessarily be sensitive to more parochial demands. Indeed, a legislator is likely to be turned out of office if widespread local concerns are neglected.

Third, not only do constituencies differ, but so do responsibilities and perspectives. While a flood in central Pennsylvania will be catastrophic to the House member from that district, it probably will seem minor to a president trying to hammer out agreement on next year's budget or negotiate a treaty with the Soviet Union to limit nuclear weapons. Similarly, a president's requests for new federal programs for big cities may look to a senator from Wyoming or Idaho like just another give-away of taxpayers' dollars.

Complicating all presidential-congressional relations is the fact that Congress is not a single entity. As a former presidential adviser put it:

> A President does not face anything so simple as *the* Congress: such a cohesive assembly does not exist. Instead, he must confront a confounding array of Senate and House committees and subcommittees—each clutching its proud prerogatives and special responsibilities, all responding to chairmen as personally varied as the nation's Congressional districts in their presumptions and procedures.[15]

The growth of overall executive power in this century has displeased many legislators, and one might suspect that as a result Congress would easily and frequently stymie the president completely. Yet Congress frustrates the president less often than one might predict simply by looking at formal relations. In fact, the needs are mutual. Legislators often need what the president can give: his influence on other members of Congress; his signature on legislation that helps their constituents; his power to make useful appointments; or his support in campaigns for re-election. Thus, the relationship between congressmen and the president is hardly simple. Despite deep differences, they need each other, especially if they are members of the same party. If either is to accomplish any policy goal other than stagnation, there must be some cooperation.

In such situations, the most likely outcome is negotiation and compromise. At times, especially if the White House and Congress are controlled by different parties, relations may verge on all-out war, as happened in 1973–1974, when a Democratic majority in Congress, with the help of a sizable number of Republicans revolted against Nixon's leadership. At other times, a weak president like Warren Harding may enjoy quite chummy relations with Congress. At still other times, a strong president may dominate Congress, the extreme cases being Franklin Roosevelt in 1933–1934 and Lyndon Johnson in 1964–1966. Periods of total war, honeymoon, and domination have, however, usually been short. More often there is the give-and-take of bargaining, sometimes expressed, sometimes tacit. And as Lyndon Johnson once remarked, "I've never seen a Congress that didn't eventually take the measure of the President it was dealing with."[16] "Eventually," however, can be a long time; and Johnson's own legislative record demonstrates that a president can accomplish a great deal before being stalemated.

Congress: Impeachment

The Constitution creates an additional check on the president—and on federal judges as well—by allowing Congress to impeach and remove officials from office. This weapon is powerful but seldom used. Overall, from 1789 to the present, only twelve federal officials have been impeached (nine of them judges) and only four (all judges) convicted.*

With respect to the presidency itself, growth of political parties and the normal state of affairs in which the same party controlled both Congress and the White House have made impeachment highly unlikely. In fact, until Richard Nixon's troubles in 1974, Andrew Johnson had been the only president to be impeached, and he had been acquitted. Nixon, however, almost certainly would have been impeached and probably removed from office had he not resigned.

The Constitution speaks with deceptive simplicity about impeachment. Article II states that:

---

* These figures somewhat underestimate the effectiveness of impeachment. At least seventeen judges resigned during impeachment proceedings, and a large number of officials, including Richard Nixon, have left office because of real threats of such action. See Raoul Berger, *Impeachment: The Constitutional Problems* (Cambridge, Mass.: Harvard University Press, 1973), p. 166.

The President, Vice-President, and all civil officers of the United States, shall be removed from office on impeachment for, and conviction of, treason, bribery, or other high crimes and misdemeanors.

But nowhere does the Constitution define "high crimes and misdemeanors." Some have argued that impeachment need imply no more than that the group in control of Congress wants to take a public office from one person and give it to another. The House of Representatives, however, has taken the narrower view that an impeachable offense includes only crimes serious under ordinary law.

Article I of the Constitution gives the House sole power to impeach. Individual representatives introduce resolutions for impeachment as they do other proposals, and these resolutions go to the Committee on the Judiciary. If the committee thinks the charges have substance, it holds hearings, with the "accused" official given many of the rights of a defendant in court. At the conclusion of hearings and deliberations, the committee reports its recommendations to the House. If the committee's recommendation is to impeach, the House debates and votes on the question. A simple majority is sufficient to impeach—to accuse formally.

If the impeachment resolution passes, the Senate then sits as a court and proceeds much as any criminal court would. The impeached official is represented by counsel (as in the House proceedings), and one or more members of the House act as prosecutors. Both sides may make opening and closing statements; call, examine, and cross examine witnesses; and present documentary evidence. The Senate's rules provide that to pose a question an individual senator must submit it in writing to the presiding officer, who shall ask it. When the president or vice-president is on trial, the chief justice presides; otherwise the vice president, or the president pro tempore if there is no vice-president. A two-thirds vote is required to convict.

Punishment can extend no further than removal from office and a ban against ever again holding federal office. But the Constitution specifically states that conviction and punishment upon impeachment do not bar trial and additional penalties in regular criminal courts. The president's power to pardon—which reaches all other federal offenses, past, present, and possibly even future—does not extend to conviction upon impeachment, lest he pardon himself or his cronies. Whether there can be any judicial review of impeachment proceedings remains an unsettled and fascinating question.

Congress: Foreign and Military Affairs

Congress has a number of means of checking the president's power in foreign affairs. By refusing to consent to treaties and appointments of ambassadors and other officials, the Senate can frustrate the president's policies, as can both houses when determining appropriations and setting the size and composition of the armed forces. Historically, however, Congress has not restricted presidential power in foreign policy nearly as much or as consistently as in domestic affairs. The need for secrecy and speed in international relations although often exaggerated, is real; and Congress finds it difficult to act with dispatch and impossible to keep secrets. Moreover, constituents are apt to put far less pressure on legislators to intervene in foreign affairs than in domestic matters.

As did George Washington, some presidents have taken seriously the implicit constitutional command to share with Congress responsibility for foreign policy. Most recent presidents, however, have taken a sweeping view of their powers and have not merely controlled the day-to-day conduct of foreign relations but also dealt summarily with crises that threatened violence. In well over a hundred instances, presidents have ordered American forces into combat without an explicit congressional authorization, much less a declaration of war.

Almost always, a few senators or representatives have vigorously protested these "usurpations" of legislative authority, but the typical response of Congress as a whole has been sluggish inaction. Indeed, on occasion, as when it adopted the Gulf of Tonkin Resolution in 1964, approving "the determination of the President, as Commander in Chief, to take all necessary measures to repel any armed attack against the forces of the United States and to prevent further aggression," Congress has given the executive what amounts to a blank check.

On some occasions, however, one or both houses of Congress have attempted to reassert authority over foreign policy. In 1848, for instance, the House of Representatives adopted a resolution branding President Polk's military operations against Mexico as "unnecessarily and unconstitutionally begun." Several times during the 1950s both houses came close to proposing an amendment to the Constitution that would have restricted the scope of the treaty-making power and would also have subjected executive agreements to senatorial approval.* And during the late stages of the war in Vietnam, Congress rescinded the Gulf of Tonkin Resolution and prohibited use of American ground forces in Laos or Cambodia.

More generally, in the War Powers Act of 1973, the president was ordered to consult with Congress "in every possible instance" before sending troops into combat in an undeclared war. If the president does commit troops to combat without a declaration of war, the act requires

---

* An executive agreement is a covenant between heads of government. In international law, it is binding on the president who signs it but not on his successors. As domestic law, however, it has much the same effect as a treaty. See *United States v. Belmont*, 301 U.S. 324 (1937); and *United States v. Pink*, 315 U.S. 203 (1942).

him to submit a report to Congress within forty-eight hours. He must withdraw those forces, the statute says, when Congress so directs or within sixty days, unless during that period Congress (1) declares war; (2) extends the time limit; or (3) is unable to meet because of a physical attack upon the United States.

The extent to which such legislation is constitutional is an open question. Certainly a test in court would be difficult to arrange. Perhaps more critical is how Congress could enforce such a policy once the president actually sent troops into combat. As the most ardent doves discovered during the Vietnamese war, it is very difficult for congressmen to vote to cut off supplies for "brave American boys" who are under enemy fire, even if members of Congress disapprove of the war.

The Bureaucracy

Officials of administrative agencies present a third set of limitations on presidential power. One might think that, as chief executive, the president would be able to command his subordinates in much the same way a general commands an army. In practice, however, bureaucracy "more nearly resembles the arena of international politics than a group of disciplined subordinates responsible to the control of common superiors."[17] The next chapter talks in detail about the president's problems in leading *his* bureaucracy. Here we note only that the sheer magnitude of the president's work forces him to rely heavily on subordinates to carry out his policies. In turn, these officials must rely on their own subordinates to complete the tasks.

In effect, then, the same people who can contribute to the president's power by providing means to execute his policies may also be able to frustrate policies with which they disagree. The president may have been unwise in his appointments, choosing some people who were not especially competent or not staunchly loyal to him and his goals. The possibility of doubtful loyalty is increased by the frequent necessity for a presidential candidate, or even a president, to trade appointments for votes or support on some specific issue before Congress. Moreover, the tradition of senatorial courtesy gives senators from the president's party a large—sometimes decisive—share in choosing federal officials who will serve in their states, and a say in appointments of individuals from their states. Local U.S. attorneys, for example, are the federal equivalent of district attorneys. They are in charge of most prosecutions in federal courts; and because they are apt to owe their position to a senator or a local politico, they may be quite unsympathetic to the president's goals.

Less subject to presidential control are the permanent civil servants. At any particular time many of the men and women who run day-to-day governmental operations want policies that differ widely from those of the president and his immediate subordinates. Having seen presidents, agency heads, and their assistants come and go does little to make career officials ready to surrender their professional judgment, much less their agencies' interests. Even when they do not openly or consciously oppose the president, their lack of enthusiasm may hamper execution of a program.

Judges and State Officials

Once nominated and confirmed, federal judges are virtually immune to presidential control. And many executive policies face major tests before the courts. Judges may pass on the constitutionality of legislation or executive orders or interpret a statute to determine whether Congress in fact has authorized a particular course of action.

State officials may also check presidential policies. Given the decentralized nature of American politics, state and local officials are likely to influence the reactions of senators, legislators, and federal administrators to proposals from the chief executive. Moreover, the success of many national programs such as interstate highways, public housing, or employment compensation depends on cooperation by state and local officials who will be responsible for their implementation.

Political Culture and Political Conscience

Most presidents have been restrained by a sense of what is morally right and wrong in politics. As professional politicians, they have in most instances worked in public affairs for decades before coming to the White House, and to move ahead they have had to follow if not absorb at least a fair share of widely accepted norms about right and wrong, the so-called rules of the political game. Even when they do not personally believe in the prevailing standards of public morality, presidents have been deeply concerned about their place in history. The judgment of future generations thus usually acts as a powerful reinforcement to private conscience in restricting a president's choices. In an ironic way, it was a concern for history that hastened Nixon's downfall. His complicity in assorted felonies was proved beyond doubt by the record that he kept in the form of tapes of conversations in the White House.

⭐ INSTRUMENTS OF PERSUASION

Despite these interlocking checks, a president is in a position of immense influence—provided he has the desire, energy, and ability to exploit his opportunities for persuasion. He has at his command a number of instruments, not the least of which are availability of evidence to support his arguments and use of reason to convince other people. In addition, he has the prestige of his office, the hopes of his party, easy access to mass media, and certain specific constitutional grants such as power to nominate federal judges and executives. He may also have personal charm and skill in human relations. None of these instruments is likely to be effective alone; but if several of them are expertly combined, they may yield some measure of success.

To a certain extent, a chief executive may be hampered by the Twenty-second Amendment, which stipulates that a president may not be elected for more than two terms. In his second term, and especially in his last year, rival candidates for the nomination may attract considerable political support to themselves and away from the incumbent. But if a president uses his instruments of persuasion to control his party's choice of a candidate, he may still retain much of his power during this bowing-out period. Furthermore, he may, if he is extraordinarily gifted, even increase his power during this time by persuading others that, with his own career done, he is acting only for the good of the nation. Whether or not members of his own party are convinced, they may be willing to compromise with a president in such circumstances, because they, and not he, have to face the voters on *his* record.

Molding Public Opinion

With the mass media at his disposal, the president has an unequaled opportunity to convince the public that they should approve his policies, elect other officials who approve, and pressure incumbents to cooperate with him. For important speeches he may pre-empt prime television and radio time; newspapers carry his remarks on their front pages; and magazines publish feature articles on him and his family. By displaying confidence, knowledge, and intellectual agility, an adroit president can do much to build up a favorable image not only with the general public but also with legislators and administrators. Travel abroad can bolster presidential prestige, as television images are beamed home of solemn meetings with world leaders and triumphal parades through cheering throngs.

Press conferences, allowing exchanges with reporters, can be especially valuable not only in nabbing the next day's headlines but in per-

President Reagan in Westminster Palace, waiting to address the British Parliament. Pageantry has become an important part of presidential travel abroad, since ceremonies and parades are more interesting for television than working meetings with foreign leaders on complicated issues. (Wide World Photos)

suading journalists that the president knows what he is doing. Franklin Roosevelt was the first real master of this sort of exchange. John Kennedy took advantage of his quick wit by allowing television coverage of his press conferences. Any such triumphs, of course, are not merely the product of a president's intellect. Each conference is preceded by days of research by the White House staff to cope with, if not answer, questions that advisers think are most likely to be asked. Then come hard hours of briefing the president so that he may seem a font of spontaneous wisdom.

Inevitably, however, the president's desire to shape public opinion clashes with the interest of the press in reporting what goes on in the White House. The president and his aides seek to control information in order to portray their actions in the most favorable light. To do so, they "manage" the news, playing up accomplishments, attempting to bury adverse information, and leaking stories to favored reporters. Journalists, for their part, have become increasingly aggressive, particularly in the years since Vietnam and Watergate, in ferreting out stories about presidential fumbles and follies. And as the press has become more cynical and combative, presidents have grown more bitter about what they consider unfair treatment of their programs, performance, and personal behavior—of Jimmy Carter's energy proposals, or Ronald Reagan's bloopers in answering questions at press conferences, or Gerald Ford's occasional stumbles.

Underlying the acrimony between president and press is mutual need. The president relies on the television networks, news magazines, and daily press to reach the people and convey his perspective to a diverse and diffused society. The White House press corps, on the other hand, needs news. Since almost all executive decisions in Washington are made behind closed doors, reporters must depend heavily on sources in the White House and other executive agences. Under the circumstances, the press is bound to be used, and presidents are likely to feel abused. But a skillful president is likely to come out ahead in the exchange, since *he,* not the press, is the focus of public attention.

Influencing Congress: Formal Powers

Recommending legislation. To induce members of Congress to cooperate or at least compromise, a president has a number of instruments. First is his ability to recommend legislation and, in effect, to set the agenda of Congress. Article II of the Constitution instructs the president to "give the Congress information of the state of the Union" and to "recommend to their consideration such measures as he shall judge necessary and expedient." This power is important because it gives the president the initiative in the legislative process. In addition, he can call Congress into special session to act on his recommendations.

The veto. The President has another powerful weapon, the veto, that he can use both as a roadblock against unwanted legislation and as a prod to move Congress to pass bills that he wants in the form that he wants. Franklin Roosevelt and Jimmy Carter were very willing to use tacit threats of vetoes to influence legislators. Both ordered their staffs to search for bills they might veto, to remind recalcitrant congressmen of their need to cooperate with the White House.

The Constitution is specific in its provisions regarding the veto: Every bill, order, resolution, or vote to which the concurrence of the Senate and the House of Representatives may be necessary (except a question of adjournment) shall be presented to the president for his

President Reagan delivers his State of the Union message to a joint session of Congress in 1982. Vice-President George Bush is considerably more enthusiastic than the Democratic Speaker of the House of Representatives, Thomas O'Neill. (*Newsweek*, Larry Downing)

approval or disapproval.* The president has four choices when he receives a bill. The first is to sign it; then the bill becomes law. He may also veto the bill and return it to the house where it originated. If each house repasses the bill by a two-thirds majority, it becomes law without the president's approval; otherwise, the bill dies. Or he may let a bill remain on his desk for ten days without either signing it or returning it to Congress; then it becomes law without his signature. The fourth possibility is the *pocket veto*. If during the ten-day period during which a bill may sit on the president's desk Congress ends its session and adjourns, the bill automatically dies if the president does not sign it. Because Congress tends to pass many bills during the final days of a session, a chief executive has extensive opportunity to employ this weapon.

Early presidents rarely used the veto. Until after the Civil War, most vetoes were justified on the grounds of a bill's doubtful constitutionality. Since then, presidents have typically based their objections to a bill on its lack of wisdom.

Relatively few measures are ever repassed over a veto. Congress made no serious efforts to override any of Kennedy's or Johnson's vetoes, and the few attempts to override vetoes by Carter failed. In Reagan's first two years in office, Congress was able to override only two vetoes. Even heavily Democratic Congresses overrode only twelve of Ford's forty-five vetoes. The Constitution makes reconsideration mandatory, but this requirement is fulfilled by referring the bill to the standing committee that reported it to the house in which it originated.

Impoundment. The president cannot veto specific items in a bill (as can governors of some states). He must accept or reject a measure in its entirety. But some presidents have claimed authority not to spend—to impound—funds appropriated by Congress, thus giving themselves an *item veto* as far as appropriations are concerned. And programs without money are unlikely to survive.

The constitutional authority of the president to impound funds is unclear. Taft's conception of the presidency would sternly deny such authority. On the other hand, Teddy Roosevelt's stewardship theory would just as firmly justify presidential refusal to spend money if he thought such action was in the public interest. The only time that the Supreme Court considered a case involving impoundment, the justices restricted themselves to the narrow question whether in the Clean Waters Act of 1972 Congress had delegated to the president power to withhold funds. The Court unanimously agreed that Congress had made no

---

* Although the Constitution permits only this one exception, practice has added others. For instance, concurrent resolutions expressing "the sense of Congress" and constitutional amendments proposed to the states for ratification are not sent to the president. See the Supreme Court's decision in *Hollingsworth v. Virginia*, 3 Dallas 378 (1798).

President Lyndon Johnson signs the Civil Rights Act of 1964 into law. The other signatures are those of the Speaker of the House of Representatives and the President pro tempore of the Senate. (United Press International)

such delegation, but the justices offered no views on the larger constitutional question, whether the president could act on his own authority.[18]

Practical problems complicate the issue of impoundment. Most legislators would not want the president to spend money unnecessarily. Suppose, for example, Congress appropriated $10 billion for communications equipment for the armed services, and the Pentagon found that improved technology could provide even better equipment for $5 billion. A president who tried to force the manufacturer to accept $10 billion would surely incite screeches of congressional wrath. Because one can easily multiply such examples, members of Congress are loath to require the president to spend all funds they appropriate. The real dispute comes over priorities. A president may believe that government must reduce spending or bring on disastrous inflation or ruinous deficits. And he may impose cuts on programs of which he disapproves (such as welfare) but not on others (such as purchases of military hardware), which he likes. Faced with that same choice, a majority of Congress may well have different priorities.

Presidential spending power. Money is the lifeblood of governmental programs no less than of political campaigns, and according to Article II of the Constitution, "no money shall be drawn from the Treasury, but in consequence of appropriations made by law . . ." On its face, this clause gives Congress complete control over what can be spent from the public purse, subject only, of course, to the president's veto. Chief executives, however, have found some loopholes here.[19]

First of all, because of the complexities of governmental operations, Congress usually appropriates money in large lump sums to agencies or programs rather than specifying precise amounts to be spent for every purpose. The "understanding" among executive officials and appropriations subcommittees is that the money will in fact be spent for specific items spelled out in the president's budget and explained in testimony before Congress. Nevertheless, administrators sometimes take advantage of these broad grants to initiate programs that Congress specifically rejected.

Second, because of a need for secrecy in intelligence, foreign, and military operations, Congress normally gives the president certain blocks of money to be used at his discretion. And if he is imaginative, he can spend these funds in ways that help his programs. Because of the clandestine nature of the payments, monitoring by either Congress or its financial watchdog, the General Accounting Office, is very difficult.

Third, Congress also typically appropriates "contingency funds," especially for defense agencies, to meet emergencies or unforeseen major problems. The amounts involved can run into billions of dollars. Since there can be no exact definition of a "major" unforeseen problem or even of an emergency, the president and his subordinates have wide discretion. In 1973, for example, Nixon used $10 million of a contingency fund for disaster relief and national security to aid research on raising livestock in the Bahamas and less than $5 million to help victims of a catastrophic drought in Africa.

Additionally, a president may sometimes authorize an official to transfer funds given for one purpose to another. Presidents have also allowed agencies to use secret or contingency funds or unspent money from other accounts to begin projects and then explained to Congress the following year that unless the money to complete the project was forthcoming, the millions of dollars already spent would have been wasted.

Several of these techniques raise serious questions of breaches of faith with Congress, and a few are of dubious legality. But some executive discretion in using money is obviously necessary, especially in an era of rapidly changing technology. Thus the problems of presidential spending parallel those of impoundment. Congress simply cannot lay down, fifteen to eighteen months in advance, absolutely rigid rules specifying exactly how each dollar is to be spent. Historically, however, even when abuses have been flagrant, senators and representatives have done little more than whine. On the whole, Congress has been too lazy or too timid to challenge the president. In an effort to tighten congressional control over spending, Congress in 1974 passed the Budget and Impoundment Control Act. To date, there has been too little experience with the impoundment provisions of that law to know whether it will prevent shrewd presidents from continuing to pick Congress's purse.

Executive privilege. Congress needs information if it is to function intelligently, and often that information can be secured only from an executive agency. Thus, a president can sometimes stymie Congress by claiming "executive privilege," that is, the authority to refuse to supply, or allow other executive officials to supply, information.

Presidents have sometimes justified such refusals on claims of "national security," protecting the good names of innocent people, safeguarding informants or spies whose safety would otherwise be endangered, or preserving the chief executive's ability to obtain candid advice—advice that would not be forthcoming were assistants not guaranteed confidentiality. More broadly, presidents have made a constitutional argument: In separating institutions, the Constitution made the president independent of the legislature. Congress has no more "right" to learn about the president's information and his sources than he has a "right" to know what goes on in closed sessions of Congress or its committees or in conversations among individual legislators or between a legislator and his staff.

These arguments have convinced many presidents since George Washington, and members of Congress have often accepted them. On the other hand, most presidents have admitted, even while invoking the privilege, that Congress could override the claim. The Constitution itself makes no mention of executive privilege, and the scope of its legitimacy remains obscure. In ordering Richard Nixon to deliver to a special prosecutor tapes of certain conversations in the White House—and one should note that the conflict there was not specially between Congress and the President—the Supreme Court upheld a limited privilege:

> The President's need for complete candor and objectivity from advisers calls for great deference from the courts. However, when the privilege depends solely on the broad, undifferentiated claim of public interest in the confidentiality of such conversations, a confrontation with other values

arises. Absent a claim to protect military, diplomatic, or sensitive national security secrets, we find it difficult to accept the argument that even the very important interest in confidentiality of Presidential communications is significantly diminished by production of such material for in camera* inspection with all the protection that a district court will be obliged to provide.[20]

Like impoundment, presidential invocation of executive privilege is almost wholly negative in effect. That is, its use is not likely to persuade Congress to act in the way the president wishes. On occasion a president may give up a claim of executive privilege or "un-impound" funds in exchange for congressional action. But usually the most he can hope for is to make it impossible for Congress to act at all. Because of the fuzzy nature of the constitutional question and the vital legislative need for information, use of executive privilege may anger or even outrage many congressmen. Thus, a president can use it freely only when he wants nothing and fears nothing from Congress, a rare situation indeed.

Influencing Congress: Informal Means

To lead Congress, a president has to use informal as well as formal means of persuasion. Most obviously, he may invoke party loyalty. While that loyalty may be a sometime thing for most senior legislators, it can tug at their self-interest more insistently than at their emotions. Even if their own re-election is certain, congressmen's abilities to influence appointments may vanish if their party does not win the presidency again. If their party does not retain control of Congress, their positions of leadership and committee chairmanships will go to other people.

Still, a president cannot depend on the weak, decentralized party structure to bridge the gap between the executive and legislative branches. Far more often than not, only by means of bipartisan majorities is the president able to get measures through Congress. Piecing these majorities together is delicate work. Thus, in dealing with members of the opposition as well as of his own party, a president must learn to be a consummate manipulator of his fellow politicos, alternately friendly and stern, now shrewd and calculating, now seemingly open and frank, by turns acting as supplicant and commander, flatterer, and sharp critic. As Lyndon Johnson recalled about his own presidency, "I pleaded. I reasoned. I argued. I urged. I warned."[21] And he also threatened and badgered.

---

* The term *in camera* means in closed session. Thus the judge would examine the papers in the privacy of his office and there decide which could be used in the courtroom and seen by both sides, the jurors, and eventually the public.

To translate his legislative proposals into actual policy, a president has to weld congressmen into an effective team if he wants action—or play them off against each other if he wants inaction. His immediate goal is to persuade a working majority of senators and representatives that his program is good for the country, good for their constituents, and therefore good for themselves. For, as a former director of the Bureau of the Budget remarked, "Virtue is so much easier when duty and self-interest coincide."[22]

President Reagan seeks support for his tax cut legislation in 1981 from Democratic members of the House of Representatives at the presidential retreat at Camp David, in the Catoctin Mountains in Maryland. (Photo by Bill Fitz-patrick, The White House)

To ease the inevitable friction with senators and representatives, presidents try to find ways of making friendly overtures. Harry Truman now and then appeared suddenly at the Capitol and modestly asked to eat lunch with his old colleagues; John Kennedy often extended the hospitality of a formal White House dinner with vintage wine, French cuisine, and music from the Marine Band. Lyndon Johnson used the telephone to keep in touch with congressmen at all hours of the day—and night—and his entertaining was folksy. Carter tended to be stiff in his dealings with legislators, and he never was able to develop easy social relations with members of Congress. Reagan, on the other hand, wooed Congress with considerable success. He appeared on Capitol Hill before his inauguration, massaged congressional egos at gatherings at the White House and Camp David, and spent hours on the telephone seeking support personally for key elements of his legislative program.

It is doubtful that these efforts have often paid off directly in bills passed or not passed by Congress. But no president can afford to ignore friendly gestures. There are so many occasions when he must play the tough taskmaster that he must seize every opportunity to persuade legislators that he is a decent human being.

As we have seen, the president can sometimes swap with legislators. A promise of support for a congressman's pet bill, or a threat of presidential opposition to it, may produce support for the president's program. Frequently the president must bargain with members of Congress, and one of the chief purposes of regular consultations between the president and congressional leaders is to determine whether the lines can be held fast for a presidential proposal or whether compromise is in order, and if so, how much.

Perhaps the most notorious of the president's informal powers to influence Congress is patronage. Use of the appointing power to win over senators and representatives dates back to George Washington. Usually a president does not crudely offer to make a particular nomination if the congressman votes as the president wants. He is likely to use patronage more subtly as a means of cultivating friendly relations with legislators, thereby encouraging sympathetic consideration of his proposals. This kind of approach was illustrated in the special session of Congress in 1933, at which Roosevelt's New Deal measures were passed. The administration let it be understood that patronage would not be distributed until after the session. In this way, congressmen eager to control certain appointments were compelled to give favorable consideration to the president's legislative requests.

Patronage, however, is a two-edged sword. For one thing, an appointment that pleases one congressman may irritate other legislators as well as disappointed job seekers. Second, by trading patronage for congressional votes a president may be weakening his control over adminis-

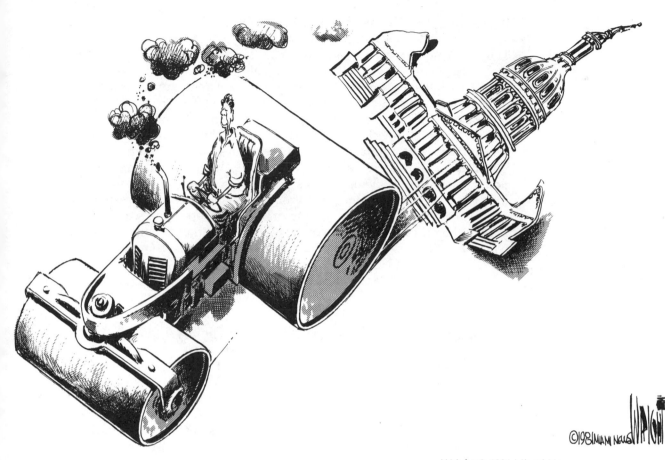

Wright © 1981 Miami News

tration, because appointees may feel a stronger loyalty to some members of Congress than to the chief executive.

A promise of presidential support at the next election can be an effective instrument of persuasion. In extreme circumstances, the president may hint at political reprisals against uncooperative congressmen. But he must be wary of actually carrying out this threat. He cannot dissolve Congress and call a new election, as can a prime minister. Even though a regular election may be near, if his quarrel is with members of his own party, the president cannot very well ask for election of members of the opposition. To purge his party of dissidents, he must go into state primaries and try to persuade party voters to replace them with new legislators who will be more loyal to him. Historically, this practice has not had great success.

369   Instruments of Persuasion

Persuading the Bureaucracy

The following chapter examines in detail the president's relations with the federal bureaucracy. We note here only that the president can increase his influence, first, by exercising great care in his appointments to cabinet and other top administrative posts. Neither personal loyalty, professional ability, nor political skill is sufficient in itself to make an administrator an especially useful subordinate. The president needs assistants who have a combination of these virtues. Second, the president can enhance his capacity to lead career officials by showing them that he understands the problems that his policies create and appreciates the difficulties of carrying them out. Third, congressmen, like the president, try to shape decisions of administrators, and the president's ability to protect the bureaucracy from congressional retaliation is critical to the way administrators will respond to competing demands from the White House and Capitol Hill.

Persuading Judges and State and Local Officials

In dealing with state and local officials a president can use almost the same instruments and tactics that he employs with Congress—reason, prestige, publicity, personal charm, promises of campaign support, patronage, and old-fashioned bargaining. In contrast, a president has as little chance of charming judges into agreement as he does of overawing them with his prestige or promises of patronage. Of course, since federal judges are not elected, campaign support is not of value to them, although a chance of promotion might be enticing to those on lower courts. Reasoned argument, usually presented by local U.S. attorneys or the staff of the Department of Justice, is the instrument most often used in dealing with judges. But a president's nominating power can also be important, in both choosing and promoting judges whose basic views tend to coincide with his own.

In addition, if courts hand down a decision or series of decisions that threaten his policy objectives, the president may deploy his instruments of persuasion in Congress to obtain some counteraction—perhaps a constitutional amendment, a more clearly worded statute, a change in the kind of cases federal courts can hear, or an increase in the number of judges. As a last resort, a president may refuse to enforce a court decision, as Lincoln did during the Civil War when Chief Justice Roger Taney ordered a southern sympathizer released from a military prison.[23]

In influencing public opinion in general, a president may also influence judges because he creates a climate of opinion in which all citizens must live. "The great tides and currents which engulf the rest of men," Justice Benjamin Cardozo once wrote, "do not turn aside in their course and pass the judges by."[24]

 SUMMARY

This chapter has stressed the political nature of the presidency. Emphasis on the necessity of manipulation and maneuvering does not in any way question the necessity of the president's having, or being receptive to, creative ideas that have substantive merit. Rather, the point is that many other governmental officials, officials who have power to check the president, also have firm policy views of whose worth they are sincerely convinced. Faced with these conditions and armed with only a limited authority to command, the president must persuade, negotiate, bargain, and compromise if he wants to achieve a positive program. As James David Barber remarks, the presidency represents a contradiction in power, for the president, "like most actors in the political system, is dependent on his dependents, subject to his subjects, forever in the position of supplicant for renewal of his license to rule."[25]

Knowing what policies to pursue requires the vision of a statesman; putting those policies into actual operation requires the talents of a masterful politician. A successful president needs not only strength of character and a thorough understanding of the long-run needs of the nation but also professional skills, personal charm, a feel for shifting winds of public opinion, a delicate sense of timing, and that quality which in enemies we call ruthlessness and in friends total dedication. For a president must be able to use, drain, and discard other people to achieve national goals. He must be able to distinguish among what is worth fighting for to the bitter end, what is worth compromising on, and what is worth only capitulation. He must know when to move and when to wait, when to argue and when to agree, when to stand firm and when to compromise, when to reason and when to bargain, when to cajole and when to command. Without doubt, such paragons of virtue and intelligence are rare. The amazing thing is that some have made their way through the labyrinthine paths of American politics to the White House.

NOTES

1. Louis Koenig, *The Chief Executive* (New York: Harcourt Brace Jovanovich, 1964), p. 13.
2. *Our Chief Magistrate and His Powers* (New York: Columbia University Press, 1916), p. 139.
3. *Theodore Roosevelt: An Autobiography* (New York: Macmillan, 1913), p. 389.
4. Richard E. Neustadt, *Presidential Power* (New York: John Wiley and Sons, 1960), pp. 164–167.
5. Lyndon Baines Johnson, *The Vantage Point: Perspectives of the Presidency, 1963–1969* (New York: Holt, Rinehart and Winston, 1971), p. 566.
6. See James David Barber, *The Presidential Character: Predicting Performance in the White House* (Englewood Cliffs, N.J.: Prentice-Hall, 1972), especially Part V; and Bruce Mazlish, *In Search of Nixon: A Psychohistorical Inquiry* (New York: Basic Books, 1972).
7. Quoted in Neustadt, *Presidential Power*, pp. 9–10.
8. Ibid., p. viii.
9. Johnson, *The Vantage Point*, p. 450.
10. *United States v. Curtiss-Wright Export Corp*, 299 U.S. 304 (1936), and *Missouri v. Holland*, 252 U.S. 416 (1920).
11. Edward S. Corwin, *The President: Office and Powers*, 4th ed. (New York: New York University Press, 1957), p. 172.
12. *United States v. Curtiss-Wright Export Corp.*
13. The earliest example is *Little v. Barreme*, 2 Cranch 170 (1804).
14. Hedley Donovan, "Fluctuations on the Presidential Exchange," *Time*, November 9, 1981, p. 122.
15. Emmet John Hughes, *The Living President* (Baltimore, Md.: Penguin Books, 1974), p. 205.
16. Quoted in Rowland Evans, Jr., and Robert D. Novak, *Lyndon B. Johnson: The Exercise of Power* (New York: New American Library, 1966), p. 490.
17. Robert A. Dahl and Charles E. Lindblom, *Politics, Economics and Welfare* (New York: Harper, 1953), p. 342.
18. *Train v. City of New York*, 420 U.S. 35 (1975); see also *Train v. Campaign Clean Water*, 420 U.S. 136 (1975).
19. Analysis in this section depends heavily on Louis Fisher, *Presidential Spending Power* (Princeton, N.J.: Princeton University Press, 1975).
20. *United States v. Nixon*, 418 U.S. 683 (1974).
21. Johnson, *The Vantage Point*, p. 30.
22. The remark was by Kermit Gordon; quoted in ibid., p. 440.
23. *Ex parte Merryman*, 17 Federal Cases 144 (No. 9487) (1861).
24. *The Nature of the Judicial Process* (New Haven, Conn: Yale University Press, 1921), p. 168.
25. Barber, *The Presidential Character*, pp. 17–18.

SELECTED BIBLIOGRAPHY

Barber, James David. *The Presidential Character: Predicting Performance in the White House* (Englewood Cliffs, N.J.: Prentice-Hall, 1972). An ambitious effort to develop tools of psychological analysis to explain, predict, and evaluate presidential performance.

Blum, John M. *The Republican Roosevelt* (Cambridge, Mass.: Harvard University Press, 1954). A sparkling study of Theodore Roosevelt as president.

Corwin, Edward S. *The President: Office and Powers*, 4th ed. (New York: New York University Press, 1957). The authoritative study of the presidency from a constitutional and legal perspective.

Cronin, Thomas E. *The State of the Presidency*, 2nd ed. (Boston: Little, Brown, 1980). An effort to answer two questions: How can the presidency become a more efficient executive institution and how can it be made more accountable to the people?

Fisher, Louis. *Presidential Spending Power* (Princeton, N.J.: Princeton University Press, 1975). A careful examination of the ways in which presidents have methodically picked Congress's purse.

Grossman, Michael Baruch, and Martha Joynt Kumar. *Portraying the President: The White House and the News Media* (Baltimore, Md.: Johns Hopkins University Press, 1981). An analysis of the various facets of the relationship between the press and the president.

Hughes, Emmet John. *The Living Presidency: The Resources and Dilemmas of the American Presidential Office* (Baltimore, Md.: Penguin Books, 1974). A beautifully written, sweeping examination of the character of the presidency from Washington to Nixon.

MacKenzie, Calvin. *The Politics of Presidential Appointments* (New York: Free Press, 1981). A thorough analysis of the process by which presidential appointments are made, including confirmation by the Senate.

Neustadt, Richard E. *Presidential Power: The Politics of Leadership* (New York: John Wiley and Sons, 1960). A perceptive study that deals with the president's problem of obtaining power for himself while holding office.

Pious, Richard M. *The American Presidency* (New York: Basic Books, 1978). A richly detailed study of all aspects of the presidency, which emphasizes the constitutional bases of presidential authority and the limits on the president's power.

Schlesinger, Arthur M., Jr. *The Age of Roosevelt*, a three-volume history of the years preceding and during FDR's administrations: Vol. 1: *The Crisis of Old Order*; Vol. 2: *The Coming of the New Deal*; Vol. 3: *The Politics of Upheaval* (Boston: Houghtom Mifflin 1957, 1959, 1960). A distinguished history, colorful and brilliant, illuminating an exciting era of ideas, events, and personalities.

12 The President and the Executive Branch

The preceding chapter looked at the presidency as an institution that offers a bundle of opportunities for political leadership, and discussed ways in which various presidents have exploited these opportunities. This chapter focuses on two aspects of presidential leadership: how the president obtains the information and advice needed to make intelligent decisions, and how he exercises control over the vast federal bureaucracy that is supposed to carry out policies that he and Congress formulate.

★ SECURING INFORMATION AND ADVICE

Before being able to recommend policies to Congress or to carry out policies under his own authority, a president needs a great deal of information as well as advice about what that information means in practical terms. No matter how intelligent and widely read, a president cannot be an expert on all the problems that confront the nation. Neither could any small group of people provide the knowledge to deal with such a variety of issues as how to gather and evaluate military intelligence about Soviet strategic planning, the implications of changes in personnel within the Chinese government, the causes of tensions in the Middle East, the extent to which Russians and Cubans are training guerrillas in Central America, how most effectively to equip and deploy American armed forces, or ways of dealing with the conflicting economic interests of the United States and its European allies.

Similarly in domestic affairs, a president needs a comparable range of expert advice in deciding how to dispose safely of nuclear wastes, regulate energy prices, manage federally owned land, reduce unemployment while curbing inflation, control federal spending, manage a huge and decentralized political party, carry on congenial relations with congressional leaders while pushing them to adopt his legislative program, find able executives for government, settle disputes between officials in different bureaucracies, and conduct press conferences and other public relations so as to convey to the electorate an image of informed, forceful leadership.

Obviously, a president has to surround himself not just with a few but with arrays of advisers, formal and informal. Formal advisers are those whom a statute or an executive order designates as presidential advisers; informal advisers are those whom the president selects without regard to such legalistic criteria.

The Cabinet

In most constitutional democracies the prime minister and his cabinet are chosen by and are immediately responsible to parliament. In those countries, the cabinet meeting is the formal institutional setting where the prime minister calls for discussion of almost all important questions of policy. At the end a vote is taken. By definition, an effective prime minister leads rather than follows his ministers, and he may on occasion go against the collective advice of his cabinet. But to do so is to run a grave risk of a rash of resignations by those ministers, collapse of his support in parliament, and the fall of his government.

In the United States, the situation is very different. The president is not responsible to Congress, nor, at least in a constitutional sense, are cabinet members—called *secretaries* (except for the attorney general, who heads the Department of Justice). Instead, cabinet members are supposed to be the president's men and women. To appoint them, he needs the consent of the Senate, but it is normal for nominees to the cabinet to win easy approval. As a matter of constitutional law, the president can dismiss any cabinet member whenever he wishes. But as a practical matter, a president is not always free to hire and fire cabinet officials. Thus the pressures on him to consult with his cabinet are exerted by prudence, not the Constitution.

How individual cabinet members run their particular departments is of vital concern to the president, for ultimately he bears responsibility for whatever goes on in the executive branch. Thus, a president may keep in close touch with individual secretaries. But most presidents have seldom sought the *collective* advice of the cabinet and have not been apt to follow it if given. It is true that any major policy decision inevitably has an impact on all other governmental action; at minimum it affects the amount of money available. But there is no reason to expect the attorney general, for example, to have an expert opinion about how to negotiate with the Chinese. Nor should anyone expect the secretary of state to be able to offer informed advice on how to cope with crime in the cities.

Perhaps even more important than lack of expertise is a presidential fear that the advice of a secretary may be biased toward the parochial concerns of his or her own department or the particular interests that department protects. That sort of special advocacy is easier to discern when the department's involvement in a problem is clear and direct. It is far more difficult to detect when a recommendation is supposedly objective. To be sure, a president may often ask an individual cabinet member for advice about problems that technically do not fall within his or her jurisdiction. But when that happens, the president is far more likely to consult in private with that secretary rather than seek help from the individual in a cabinet meeting.

Having all the members of the cabinet periodically sit down together with the president serves many useful functions. It allows the president to emphasize his priorities and to explain how each department will be affected; it gives the president an opportunity to convey his mood in a direct and personal manner and to stress the force with which he intends to carry out his job; and it provides the president with a forum to press the top administrators of the federal government to support vigorously the administration's programs. A cabinet meeting also permits secretaries an additional few moments to chat with each other and with the president—not easy tasks for busy people caught in the rush of hectic routines. But as a means of offering a president advice on general problems, the cabinet meeting has been a failure.

Despite this historical experience, the lesson is one that has not always been apparent to new presidents. For, as did Jimmy Carter in 1977 and Ronald Reagan in 1981, chief executives continue to come into office promising collegiality in running the federal government. Reagan, for example, indicated that his cabinet would be his "inner circle of advisers—almost like a board of directors."[1] Typically, however, chief executives soon find that, in governing under the American political system, collegiality in the executive branch means no leadership at all. Indeed, presidents may soon have reason for surprise, even anger, at the policies that emerge from particular departments.

President Reagan meets in the Cabinet Room with Ambassador Philip Habib, Secretary of State George Shultz, and Secretary of Defense Caspar Weinberger, to ponder U.S. policy in the Middle East. (Photo by Michael Evans, The White House)

The bases of conflicts over policy are not hard to find. Hardly ever has each member of the cabinet represented the president's own choice of people to head executive departments. American presidential hopefuls typically "run scared," and to gain votes in nominating conventions and to accrue electoral support during campaigns, they often bargain away some cabinet positions. Perhaps they will give a large union the prerogative of naming or at least vetoing anyone as the new secretary of labor; a group of corporate executives may secure a similar privilege regarding the secretary of commerce. The claims of different factions in the president's party, regional considerations, and the concern in recent years to represent women and blacks in the cabinet further constrain presidential options. Later, to move his legislative program through Congress, a president may have to bargain away other posts, or at least agree not to dismiss officials who are siding less often with him and more often with chairmen of important congressional committees or subcommittees. To win or keep the support of local politicos he may also have to place their people in important positions below that of secretary; and cabinet members typically want subcabinet political posts filled with individuals loyal to them rather than to the White House. As a result of these maneuverings, even high-level political appointees may feel no gratitude and little loyalty, personal or programmatic, toward the president.

Once in office, cabinet officers typically are more responsive to their department's constituencies, its employees, and its congressional supporters than they are to the president. The secretary of agriculture tends to be more concerned about farmers and their problems than about the president and his problems; and the secretary of state is likely to weigh more heavily the advice of foreign service officers than that of White House staff members or presidential cronies. Independence is reinforced by institutional realities—each cabinet member directs a huge department with scores of assistants and thousands of employees. In the colorful language of one former top presidential aide:

> A Cabinet officer is like a medieval duke out there in his dukedom, and all his vassals and all his apparatus very quickly convince him that he's the head of the whole operation. Yes, there's a President down there in the White House, but that's a remote problem. The duke is, by God, the head man of his dukedom, and all the perks and trappings—the huge offices, the gymnasiums, the private dining rooms, the limousines—reinforce all that. So it's very hard to find a Cabinet officer who has recently reminded himself that he is subservient to anybody.[2]

The Executive Office of the President

The White House, the Executive Office Building next door on Pennsylvania Avenue, and other buildings on Lafayette Square provide official

Questions on the Staff Evaluation Form

Office:_____
Name of Rater: _____

STAFF EVALUATION

Please answer each of the following questions about this person.

Name:_____
Salary: _____
Position:_____
Duties: _____

Work Habits

1. On the average when does this person:
   arrive at work _____
   leave work _____

2. Pace of Work:

1	2	3	4	5	6
slow					fast

3. Level of Effort:

1	2	3	4	5	6
below capacity					full capacity

4. Quality of Work:

1	2	3	4	5	6
poor					good

5. What is he/she best at? (rank 1-5)
   ____Conceptualizing
   ____Planning
   ____Implementing
   ____Attending to detail
   ____Controlling quality

6. Does this person have the skills to do the job he/she was hired to do?
   yes ___
   no ___
   ? ___

7. Would the slot filled by this person be better filled by someone else?
   yes ___
   no ___
   ? ___

Personal Characteristics:

8. How confident is this person? (circle one)

x	x	x	x	x	x
self-doubting		confident			cocky

9. How confident are you of this person's judgment:

1	2	3	4	5	6
not confident					very confident

10. How mature is this person?

1	2	3	4	5	6
immature					mature

11. How flexible is this person?

1	2	3	4	5	6
rigid					flexible

12. How stable is this person?

1	2	3	4	5	6
erratic					steady

13. How frequently does this person come up with new ideas?

1	2	3	4	5	6
seldom					often

14. How open is this person to new ideas?

1	2	3	4	5	6
closed					open

15. How bright is this person?

1	2	3	4	5	6
average					very bright

16. What are this person's special talents?
    1 _____
    2 _____
    3 _____

17. What is this person's range of information?

1	2	3	4	5	6
narrow					broad

Interpersonal Relations:

18. How would you characterize this person's impact on other people? (for example, hostile, smooth, aggressive, charming, etc.)
    1 _____
    2 _____
    3 _____

19. How well does this person get along with

Superiors	1	2	3	4	5	6
Peers	1	2	3	4	5	6
Subordinates	1	2	3	4	5	6
Outsiders	1	2	3	4	5	6
	not well				very well	

20. In a public setting, how comfortable would you be having this person represent:

	1	2	3	4	5	6
you or your office	1	2	3	4	5	6
The President	1	2	3	4	5	6
	uncomfortable			comfortable		

21. Rate this person's political skills.

1	2	3	4	5	6
naïve					savvy

Supervision and Direction

22. To what extent is this person focused on accomplishing the
    Administration's goals ___%
    personal goals ___%
    _____
    100%

23. How capable is this person at working toward implementing a decision with which he/she may not agree?

1	2	3	4	5	6
reluctant					eager

24. How well does this person take direction?

1	2	3	4	5	6
resists					readily

25. How much supervision does this person need?

1	2	3	4	5	6
a lot					little

26. How readily does this person offer to help out by doing that which is not a part of his/her "job"?

1	2	3	4	5	6
seldom					often

Summary:

27. Can this person assume more responsibility?
    yes ___
    no ___
    ? ___

28. List this person's 3 major strengths and 3 major weaknesses.
    Strengths: 1 _____
    2 _____
    3 _____
    Weaknesses: 1 _____
    2 _____
    3 _____

29. List this person's 3 major accomplishment.
    1 _____
    2 _____
    3 _____

30. List 3 things about this person that have disappointed you.
    1 _____
    2 _____
    3 _____

In an effort to improve the effectiveness and loyalty of political appointees, President Carter asked agency heads to complete this form on their subordinates. The effort had little noticeable impact on Carter's ability to secure support from "his" people in the departments and agencies. (© 1979 by The New York Times Company. Reprinted by permission.)

homes for as many as 4,000 people whose jobs are lumped together under an institution called the Executive Office of the President. Most of the president's formal advisers are lodged in the Executive Office.

The number of presidential advisers has been constantly increasing. Abraham Lincoln handled the business of the presidency with the aid of two or three clerks and even allotted time almost weekly for appointments with private citizens who had come to Washington to ask for favors. Even in the twentieth century, William Howard Taft was embarrassed by a need for twenty-five clerks and stenographers. Shortly after Franklin Roosevelt took office, he had thirty-seven assistants in the White House and several hundred officially carried on the rosters of various agencies around Washington. In 1939, Congress created the Executive Office of the President to bring presidential advisers together under one institutional roof. Growth continues, with each of Roosevelt's successors surrounding himself with more and more people performing an increasingly diverse set of tasks.

The White House Staff. Usually the most influential formal advisers are the men and women the president appoints to his personal staff in the White House. At barest minimum, he needs a press secretary, a liaison officer to be in charge of dealing with Congress, a speechwriter, and a personal secretary. But recent presidents have added national security and domestic policy aides, pollsters, and communication specialists. Each of these people needs assistants, and sometimes assistants need assistants. All, of course, need secretaries and other office staff to generate, sort, and file a flood of paper.

Just how many aides a president will have and how duties and authority will be divided among them depend on the president and how he views the job. "The White House," one close student of the presidency has written, "is peculiarly idosyncratic. It must and will reflect the habits of its occupant."[3]

As we saw in Chapter 11, presidents have followed many models of organizing their staffs: Dwight Eisenhower and Franklin D. Roosevelt fall at the polar extremes. Eisenhower, relying on his experience as a general, preferred to arrange his staff in a structure much like that of a military command, with a chief of staff channeling an orderly stream of information and recommendations to the president and directing neat rivers of decisions from the White House to various departments and agencies. Roosevelt, on the other hand, demanded a free-flowing system—or nonsystem—in which aides had vague and overlapping missions and information and recommendations tumbled around the president like clothes spinning in a gigantic dryer. FDR would not tolerate a "chief of staff" to run *his* White House. Rather he "intended his administrative assistants to be eyes and ears and manpower for *him*, with no fixed contacts, clients, or involvement of their own to interfere

President Eisenhower with his chief of staff, Sherman Adams. Eisenhower organized the White House along military staff lines, with responsibility centered in Adams at the top. (Courtesy Dwight D. Eisenhower Library)

when he needed to redeploy them."[4] Truman, Kennedy, and Johnson were more like FDR, although none had his tolerance for turmoil and disorder. Nixon was quite close to Eisenhower; and Ford, while tending toward Eisenhower, did not rely on his assistants as much as Nixon had, except perhaps in foreign policy.

Carter followed Roosevelt much more than Eisenhower. Legislators, lobbyists, bureaucrats, and newsmen complained that it was often difficult to know who was in charge of what, or, indeed, if anyone was. In the absence of a chief of staff, officials in Carter's White House contradicted each other, and at times failures in coordination were blatant. "Things run wild and fly crazily," a disgruntled staff member told *Newsweek*. But, like FDR, Carter believed Clausewitz's dictum that it is a fortunate commander whose subordinate disagree, for then he can make the important decisions himself.

Like Eisenhower and Nixon, Reagan delegated much of the day-to-day operations of the presidency to his staff, but his organizational pattern was more complex than that employed by his Republican predecessors. Directing the efforts of the 500 or so White House staffers under Reagan was an inner circle of three top aides: one was in charge of policy development, the cabinet, and the White House staffs for national security and domestic policy; a second directed legislative and political activities as well as the operations of the White House; while a third was the president's alter ego, serving as confidant, personal aide, and shield against the outside world.

Recent presidents have come to rely more heavily on their immediate staffs as their term advances. They come to office talking in terms of collective or collegial government. But the White House staff has qualities that presidents quickly find lacking in the cabinet and other officials—loyalty, familiarity, and dedication to the chief executive's policies and programs. Key aides usually have known the president for years, often having worked in his campaigns, and frequently are from his home state—Johnson's Texans, Carter's Georgians, and the Californians who predominated in the Nixon and Reagan White House. While the president undoubtedly benefits from having a devoted inner circle whom he can trust, he usually pays a price, because his staff tends to

President Reagan celebrates the passage of the 1981 tax cut legislation with Vice-President Bush (fourth from right), Treasury Secretary Regan (fourth from left), and members of the White House staff. (Photo by Michael Evans, The White House)

insulate and isolate him, too often shielding him from criticism, and equating dissent by cabinet members and other "outsiders" with disloyalty.

As presidential reliance on the White House staff has increased, the number of assistants has proliferated. Today, the staff is so large that few members have much contact with the president. Tasks are divided and subdivided, with specialists on a variety of topics. In the process of advising the president and coordinating the various departments and agencies, the White House staff replicates and frequently supersedes the functions of the entire executive branch. Presidential assistants bargain with Congress, talk with leaders of interest groups, develop policies, and negotiate with foreign governments. In effect, the staff has become a government within the government and in the process has been transformed from a personal instrument of the president into an increasingly formal institution whose functions carry over from administration to administration.

Office of Management and Budget (OMB). Next to the White House staff, the Office of Management and Budget is the most important of the agencies whose primary mission is to help the president control and direct the executive branch. It acquired its present significance in 1939, when its predecessor, the Bureau of the Budget, was transferred from the Treasury Department to the Executive Office of the President. It is headed by a director, who is nominated by the president and confirmed by the Senate. The director of OMB's primary activities are formulation and execution of the federal budget that the president sends to Congress each year.

By law, all executive agencies must submit their budgetary estimates to the president. The chief executive, however, rarely gets involved in the details of budgetary decision making. Rather, he makes the grand decisions that express general policies and priorities, leaving main responsibility for making detailed judgments to OMB. Because the budget is of necessity one of the most important instruments of executive direction and influence, it is difficult to overestimate the impact of these judgments. As President Johnson's budget director wrote:

> The budget [is] seen from the White House as the central focus of efforts to achieve the Presidential vision of national purpose. What appears from lower vantage points to be a catalogue of discrete decisions is viewed from the highest perspective as a series of *choices* among alternatives, many of them perplexing and some of them agonizing.[5]

Another major task of OMB is to improve management of the executive branch. It provides technical assistance in preparing plans for reorganizing executive agencies. OMB also offers advice to executive departments and agencies about how to improve their internal organization and operating procedures.

A third activity involves acting as a clearing house for legislative matters. OMB participates in developing legislative programs by gathering and coordinating departmental advice on proposed legislation and by recommending presidential action on legislative enactments. It also reviews legislative proposals submitted by various agencies, examines them for conformity with the president's general program, and seeks views of other agencies that have an interest in the legislation. The OMB's staff is thus often able to discover conflicts in proposals from different agencies and perhaps prevent incompatible plans from being submitted to Congress as administration bills. Armed with information from OMB, the president is able to tell legislative leaders whether he is supporting, indifferent to, or opposing a particular bill. OMB also reviews proposals for new regulations by executive agencies, to see if they are necessary, cost effective, and consistent with an administration's overall regulatory policies.

For bills that have been passed by Congress and on which the president must act, OMB surveys interested departments and agencies to find out how they would be affected. If the consensus is against a bill, OMB drafts a veto message. The president, of course, consults legislative leaders as well as executive officials; but he should find it easier to make up his own mind because of the information assembled by the Office of Management and Budget.

The National Security Council (NSC). The National Security Act of 1947 placed the three military departments—army, navy, and air force—under one cabinet-level office, the Department of Defense, and established a National Security Council to help advise the president on international relations and military affairs. The council's functions are to "assess and appraise the objectives, commitments, and risks of the United States in relation to our actual and potential military power" and to coordinate the various political, technological, and military factors necessary to plan for national security.

By statute, the NSC's members are the secretaries of state and defense, the president, and the vice-president; but the president normally invites a scattering of other people to participate. Frequently these include—but are by no means limited to—the chairman of the joint chiefs of staff, the director of the Central Intelligence Agency, and the secretary of the treasury. To assist deliberations, the NSC has its own professional staff, mostly experts on loan from the Department of Defense, the military, and various intelligence agencies.

While more effective than cabinet meetings in formulating policy, the National Security Council has been less than an ideal institution. Each president has used it in his own fashion, and in varying degrees each has felt that it does not include precisely the people whose advice he needs—which explains why "outsiders" so often participate in its deliberations. More important than the National Security Council in

Jack Ohman. Reprinted by permission of Tribune Company Syndicate, Inc.

many policy matters are the president's national security adviser and his staff (which also constitutes the staff for the NSC), McGeorge Bundy under Kennedy and Johnson, Henry Kissinger with Nixon, and Zbigniew Brzezinski for Carter made the national security adviser the keystone of the national security structure.[6]

The Council of Economic Advisers. The Employment Act of 1946 requires the president to send an annual economic report to Congress. It also created the Council of Economic Advisers to help the president prepare that report, which usually describes trends in employment and production and appraises federal programs that are affecting the economy. The council has three members, usually highly respected academic economists who are sympathetic to the president's general political goals. He appoints all three with the advice of the Senate. Their function, in addition to preparing the annual economic report, is to recommend actions to maximize employment, production, and purchasing power.

Educating the president and other public officials is an inescapable part of advising in any technical field. As Walter Heller, a former chairman of the council, put it, "The explanatory and analytical models of the economist must be implanted—at least intuitively—in the minds of Presidents, congressmen, and public leaders if economic advice is to be accepted and translated into action."[7]

Because the president knows that the council's advice is not diluted by interests of particular government agencies or pressure groups, its members tend to be listened to by the White House. But influence on presidential decisions is by no means automatic. According to Heller:

> Unless the White House took a hand in directing economic traffic through the Council, the policy train often flashed past before we could get out the flag to stop it. One of our major tasks was to establish constructive relationships with the men around the President to help insure that the Council's voice would be heard before final decisions were made, even if it had not been drawn into the early stages of the policy-making process.[8]

Moreover, economics is neither an exact science nor a discipline in which consensus exists on either analysis or policy prescription. Disagreement among economists inevitably weakens the authority of the council. Nor are presidents bound to accept the council's advice if arguments from other quarters seem more compelling, as is sometimes the case on matters as politically sensitive as inflation, taxes, unemployment, and interest rates.

Bob Englehart, The Hartford Courant: Los Angeles Times Syndicate

Special Boards, Task Forces, and Commissions

Depending on his personal style or the image that he wishes to transmit, a president may also appoint a bevy of special boards and commissions of distinguished private citizens to gather data and offer recommendations on pressing policy issues. In addition, a chief executive may utilize special task forces composed of officials from a variety of agencies to study and advise on problems that cut across normal lines of responsibility within the executive branch.

Since Herbert Hoover, presidents have frequently used presidential commissions.[9] Typically made up of prominent private citizens and perhaps a few senior officials, these commissions are asked to investigate and report on problems ranging from reorganization of the executive branch to civil rights to criminal justice. The period of time such an outside commission—aided by a professional staff of its own choosing—needs to study a problem and prepare a report generally prevents hasty action and allows the president an opportunity to plan his own approach. Perhaps even more important, precisely because most of these people are outsiders, they can approach a problem free from commitment to any particular policy or to the interests of any bureau and its clientele. They can take a fresh look and, if they think it feasible, offer a solution that cuts across established jurisdictional lines of existing agencies. Furthermore, since commission members are distinguished citizens, their report can win congressional and administrative attention and also generate reactions from reporters and analysts from the news media.

The principal disadvantage of advisory commissions is inherent in their chief advantage. Because the members tend to be outsiders without roots in the federal bureaucracy, they will not remain in office to carry through on the long, hard process of translating ideas into viable, operational policy decisions. A second disadvantage lies in their vulnerability to abuse. It is not uncommon for presidents (or governors or mayors or university officials) to establish commissions as means of burying rather than confronting problems. Indeed, a commission report that is not in accord with the policy that a president may have already chosen is shelved in a very dark corner.

Informal Advisers

Whatever the differences of presidential style and the effectiveness of formal sources of advice, most presidents have drawn heavily on advice from people outside the official chain of command or even outside of government. Indeed, during the last 70 years, informal advisers have often exerted decisive influence on critical presidential choices. Nor is that practice new. Andrew Jackson had his "kitchen cabinet" of old friends—the two most prominent were journalists—and Woodrow Wilson's relationship with Colonel Edward M. House is legendary.[10] Wilson's reliance on Louis D. Brandeis, while less famous, was also significant. Brandeis was, according to Wilson's biographer, the "chief architect" of the President's economic program of "the New Freedom."[11]

As one would suspect, it was Franklin Roosevelt who most thoroughly exploited unofficial advisers. His friendship with Harry Hopkins was, if anything, more productive of policy recommendations than Wilson's with Colonel House.[12] And in the early days of the New Deal, Brandeis, though a Supreme Court Justice, was in spirit if not in body at the center of debates in the White House. In those days, FDR referred to him as "Old Isaiah" and continually sought his views on economic policy. But Roosevelt also gathered opinions from dozens of other people, prominent government officials, young men fresh out of Harvard Law School, journalists, professors, and even, his opponents claimed, his dog Fala. He sent his wife around the country as an ambassador to discover what formal advisers could never have learned or would have feared to report. Visitors who came to talk about one problem might find their whole appointment consumed by the president's inquiries about totally unrelated matters. Newsmen who tried to question Roosevelt often found themselves being used as sources of information.

One could recite whole litanies of presidential reliance on unofficial sources of information and advice. Truman, Eisenhower, Kennedy, Johnson, Nixon, Ford, and Carter kept old friends busy pondering the president's problems, a practice Reagan has continued. Many of these people were private citizens; some of them, like Clark Clifford and Abe Fortas under Lyndon Johnson and Bert Lance under Carter, were later given official positions; others, like James Reston, were journalists. Some held governmental offices but not positions that would normally include offering advice to the president. Truman's reliance on Fred Vinson and Johnson's on Abe Fortas, for example, continued after the two had gone to the Supreme Court.

The essential elements in these informal relationships have been intellectual respect, loyalty, and friendship, usually old friendship. Needing advice they can rely on, and suspicious of most of those who offer suggestions, presidents understandably tend to turn to those whose personal loyalty has been proved by time.

Information, Advice, and Decision Making

All these advisers, councils, staff members, and friends are critical in formulating policy. A decision maker—whether a president, a governor, a business executive, or a dean—can act only on the information that he or she has. Thus, by screening information, by keeping out some kinds of data and stressing other kinds, officials in supposedly subordinate positions can severely narrow the choices that a decision maker sees as open. Furthermore, to the extent that the information contains technical material outside the decision maker's expertise, the people who evaluate the data can further influence his opinions.

No effort at sabotage or selfishness need be involved. Each of us sees the world only through his or her own eyes. And even the most conscientious assistant can overlook or underestimate a fact. Problems here are magnified by the possibility of less innocent distortions. Insofar as each governmental agency has its own character and peculiar goals, its officials are likely to have their own institutional clientele, and perhaps even personal objectives to pursue. Indeed, to promote their particular goals is the reason why special-interest groups such as farmers or businessmen or union leaders have fought to have cabinet-level departments. Frequently, if not invariably, both agency heads and career bureaucrats have come to associate the interests of their "clients" with those of their departments or agencies. Even those departments without obvious clients, such as State, have their own institutional commitments, whether to certain policies, such as containment of communism, or to allocations of authority to certain kinds of personnel, such as professional foreign service officers.

Thus, the president who relies solely on a single source for information or advice becomes to some extent a captive of that source. As FDR explained to Wendell Willkie, whom he defeated in the 1940 election:

> Someday you may well be sitting here where I am now as President of the United States. And when you are, you'll be looking at that door over there and knowing that practically everybody who walks through it wants something out of you. You'll learn what a lonely job this is, and you'll discover the need for somebody like Harry Hopkins, who asks for nothing except to serve you.[13]

But if even the most loyal person can have blind spots and pet theories that color his or her outlook, so, too, friends can build up certain interests apart from those of the president, if only a desire to be known as a person with influence. The president's need, therefore, is for advice that is unpolluted by institutional or personal bias, something that mere humans are not likely to be able to give on a regular basis. The improbability of achieving semidivine assistance leaves the president with three basic alternatives: (1) to consult with several agencies and individuals who have different—and if possible competing—perspectives; (2) to rely principally on his own staff and friends, for at least he is apt to know their biases and to be able to discount them with greater accuracy; or (3) to combine the first two and at the same time read as widely as possible, while cultivating or maintaining friendships with academics and journalists. The more successful presidents have tended to follow the third alternative. When presidents have narrowed their circles of communication to keep out dissenting views, as Johnson did regarding Vietnam and Nixon after Watergate, they have courted—and sometimes won—disaster. The basic point is that if a president is to choose intelligently, he must have alternatives from which to select and know more about each alternative than any single person can tell him.

 **EXECUTING PUBLIC POLICY**

On occasion, every president must have looked out the window of the Oval Office and imagined that he saw not a garden but a creeping jungle that was about to engulf him. The Constitution says that he is the head of the executive branch of government. But a weary president must sometimes have grave doubts about his power to control the almost three million civilians who fill federal posts. To ensure that it is truly "his" policy the bureaucracy is carrying out, a president also needs advice and information. But, to some extent, the very civil servants he is trying to control form an important source of his information. At least some of them may see little advantage in telling him all they know or even all that he wants to know.

The Independent Regulatory Commissions

Some agencies operate outside of the president's authority. The Federal Power Commission, the Federal Reserve Board, and the Interstate Commerce Commission are examples of so-called independent regulatory commissions. They are partly legislative, partly judicial, and partly administrative bodies that are supposed to formulate, within broad guidelines established by Congress, specific rules to control aspects of economic and social life—how much, for example, producers can charge for natural gas, how much the "prime rate of interest" will be, or how truckers or railroads can price their services. These commissions also apply their rules to particular situations and, subject to appeal to federal courts, can impose monetary penalties.

With the advice and consent of the Senate, the president appoints the members of each board. In that respect, he has some control. But Congress has stipulated that there must be representation from both political parties and that members serve for set terms. A president may not fire them except for neglect of duty or criminal actions. The Supreme

Court has ruled that disagreement with the president, no matter how deep, on matters of policy is not grounds for removal.[14] Because these commissions can have immense impacts on national policy—affecting, for instance, the amount of energy available, the volume of money in circulation, or priorities in transportation among truckers, airlines, and railroads—their actions can either reinforce or sap the strength of presidential decisions.

The Chain of Command and the Career Bureaucracy

Most federal agencies fall under the president's control; at least legally they do. The Constitution and various statutes establish a chain of command from the White House to the janitor in a social security office in Topeka. Each member of the cabinet is formally responsible to the president for the operations of his department. (In 1982, there were thirteen cabinet-level departments: Agriculture, Commerce, Defense, Education, Energy, Health and Human Services, Housing and Urban Development, Interior, Justice, Labor, State, Transportation, and Treasury.) So are the chiefs of other federal agencies headed by officials who are not members of the cabinet, such as the Veterans Administration, the Environmental Protection Agency, and the Central Intelligence Agency. In turn, each secretary has various deputy secretaries, under secretaries, assistant secretaries, directors of programs, and heads of bureaus, agencies, and offices who are responsible for specific functions and satellite institutions. Each of these officials has his or her own line of subordinates. On paper, the system is clear, although complicated by great masses of people. One can see the chain of command run through organizational charts like a bright—and thick—red line. But yanking on that chain often gives the president only a strained back.

Among the factors restricting the president's power are the interests and perspectives of the bureaucrats themselves. All but the very top few layers of federal officials are apt to be career civil servants, people who have already spent years in government service and usually plan to spend many more. And of the two or three thousand officials at the top, some have been career civil servants who have accepted "political" appointments to become agency chiefs or similar heads of offices. Like most bureaucrats, they were selected and promoted by a "merit system" operated free from partisan influence. The criteria for selection are administrative, professional, or technical skills, sometimes reflected in scores on competitive examinations, sometimes by achievement in a profession such as law, engineering, or medicine. Advancement is supposed to be based on demonstrated excellence in performance, with retention throughout a career protected against removal by changes in party government and directions in public policy.

Despite this insulation from partisan influence, both the actual operations of civil servants and public perceptions of those activities can affect a president's popularity with voters. After all, it is not unreasonable for citizens to judge a chief executive by the efficiency and courtesy of those federal officials with whom they deal on a face-to-face basis. Furthermore, civil servants can vitally affect the way in which presidential policies operate. Middle- and upper-level bureaucrats are usually the officials who make such specific decisions as whether a university is complying with guidelines regarding equal employment, whether a particular project is entitled to federal aid, or whether the government should prosecute a corporation for violation of the antitrust laws. These civil servants may apply presidential policies with force and imagination, or they may be content to wait for people to complain before taking action. When they do act, it may be with a maximum of speed and energy or with a maximum of red tape and delay.

To the extent that protection against civil servants' being discharged for partisan political reasons protects them against discharge for inefficiency, to the extent that bureaucrats, like the rest of humanity, tend to prefer old ways of operating even when confronting new problems, whole public programs can sink in a paper sea. Administrative efficiency is obviously important to a president in other ways, not the least of which are the costs that it imposes on public programs—and, ultimately, upon taxpayers.

The situation is complicated by at least four factors: bureaucrats' interests in their own professional careers and thus typically in their agencies' continuation and even expansion; their perception of the public interest; the influence of members of Congress in the administrative processes; and similar influence, often exerted through congressmen, of leaders of interest groups.

Bureaucrats' Career Interests. It is hardly realistic to expect many civil servants to be absolutely unselfish, ready to sacrifice their careers to carry out the president's policies. On the whole they may be willing to work hard to further the president's goals, but few would risk professional suicide. As a group, civil servants share a common interest as bureaucrats, just as officials of particular agencies share common interests as members of the Internal Revenue Service, the Veterans Administration, or the Federal Bureau of Investigation. As the cartoon on page 000 shows, President Carter found out just how fiercely bureaucrats can defend their shared interests when, in 1977, he proposed to reform the Civil Service to make it easier to hire, fire, and transfer personnel and to substitute bonuses based on tangible achievements for automatic increases in salary. Carter's plan came under heavy fire from a bevy of federal employees' unions worried by potential threats to job security and by congressmen and interest-group leaders concerned that their

'This could be trouble — get those desks into a circle!'

own programs might suffer if presidential control of the bureaucracy were enhanced.

Congress finally approved civil service reform late in 1978, after making extensive changes. Under the new law, the Civil Service Commission was replaced by two agencies, an Office of Personnel Management to oversee the operation of the civil service system, and a Merit Systems Protection Board to hear employees' grievances. In addition, federal officials were allowed a bit more freedom in firing incompetent employees, merit pay was authorized for the upper ranks of the federal bureaucracy, a new Senior Executive Service of 8,000 top federal officials was established with less job protection but higher compensation than regular civil servants, and federal employees were given the right to organize and bargain collectively (which previously had been granted by executive order rather than by statute). Notably missing from the bill signed by President Carter was his proposal to curtail the preference received by veterans in federal hiring and promotion, which had been vehemently opposed by veterans' organizations, federal employees who were veterans, and their numerous supporters in Congress.

Bureaucrats' Perception of the Public Good. Normally, senior civil servants have worked for the government for a decade or more. They are, as a group, intelligent men and women who consider themselves, usually with good reason, to be experts in their fields. Moreover, they have seen presidents and cabinet members come and go, and expect to see

Government workers protest the Reagan administration's plans to cut pay and workers at the U.S. Government Printing Office, part of the widespread reductions in federal programs undertaken during the early 1980s. (Chick Harrity, *U.S. News and World Report*)

others enter and exit from the White House. With their expertise and experience, these bureaucrats often develop their own ideas about proper public policies. To some extent, of course, those ideas are influenced by their career interests, but they may also be largely products of years of study and hard work. From a careerist's perspective, the president may simply appear to have chosen the wrong policy or the wrong agency to execute his policy. As a former bureaucrat has noted:

> It would be unreasonable to expect this official to see his program in the Presidential perspective. The President wants him to be a zealot about his mission, to pursue the goals of his program with skill, enthusiasm, and dedication. To ask him at the same time to be Olympian about his role and his claim or resources—to see in a detached way that he is part of a hive in which many other bees have missions of equal or greater urgency—is to ask him to embrace a combination of incompatible attitudes.[15]

Few bureaucrats deliberately sabotage presidential policies; most try to execute the president's program, though not always with the same zeal they would have in pushing their own ideas. When sabotage does occur, however, a president beset by several dozen problems each day may be among the last to know. When, for instance, Richard Nixon ordered destruction of American stores of deadly nerve gas, some CIA officials, believing the president to be mistaken in his judgment, neglected to carry out the order. A decade earlier, during negotiations over the Cuban missile crisis, President Kennedy was surprised to hear the Russians ask the United States to withdraw its medium-range missiles from Turkey. In fact, Kennedy had issued that order some months earlier, but the Air Force had failed to obey. In each of these instances, the president simply did not realize that his policy had been ignored.

Temptations to sabotage a president's program may afflict even members of the cabinet. These officials, Vice-President Charles Dawes used to assert, "are the President's natural enemies."[16] Dawes was exaggerating, but there is a hard kernel of truth in his claim. Some secretaries may covet the presidency for themselves and remember that Jefferson, Madison, Monroe, John Quincy Adams, William Howard Taft, and Herbert Hoover were cabinet members. More often—and more realistically—cabinet members may earnestly wish to pursue policies that differ markedly from those of the president. During the heyday of Franklin Roosevelt's New Deal, William O. Douglas, who then was chairman of the Securities and Exchange Commission, and Jesse Jones, a rock-ribbed conservative whom Roosevelt kept as Secretary of Commerce to placate conservatives in Congress, were summoned to the Oval Office and ordered to coordinate their activities to develop regional electric systems. "Now, Jesse," Roosevelt ended, "you get together with Bill and work this out." As they left the White House, Douglas asked, "Jesse, when shall we get together? How about now?" "Not now, not tomorrow, never," Jones replied. Then, taking off his hat and pointing to his gray thatch, he added, "When your hair gets the color of mine, you'll be wise. You will know by then that the President is a very busy man. He's so busy that he'll never remember this talk we've had."[17]

Congressional Influence. As we have seen earlier, few members of Congress want to see federal bureaucrats become a disciplined army prepared to carry out the president's orders. Rather, most legislators want the bureaucracy to be sympathetic toward the needs of constituents in the legislators' states and districts and so to help strengthen the law makers' electoral support.

Senators and representatives, especially chairmen of committees and subcommittees, can influence executive agencies not only through general legislation but also through annual appropriations that, in effect, mean for an agency a larger or smaller staff as well as projects added or deleted. Complicating such situations is the fact that the bureau chief often is more sympathetic to the legislator's views than to those of the president, for reasons of either policy or personal loyalty. For occasionally, the person who heads an agency, office, or bureau may hold that position because of the support of one or more members of Congress.

The Influence of Interest Groups. We have several times noted that governmental agencies have often been created to serve rather than regulate particular aspects of economic or social life. Farmers and their organizations look to the Department of Agriculture more for help than for rules, as do businessmen to the Department of Commerce and unions to the Department of Labor. Over the years, high-ranking civil servants will have worked with leaders of interest groups, seeking advice and information about how their agencies can better fulfill their functions or how to deal with particular senators and representatives.

Here is the third leg of the famous triangle of power that sometimes confronts a president: a bureau or agency whose senior administrators are dedicated to a specific set of missions that may or may not be dear to a president's heart; a set of congressional committees and subcommittees friendly to the agency's self-determined goals; and active groups that are prepared to pressure or assist both of the other two elements in order to advance the interests of their members.

"Then it's agreed. The problem's not *our* fault, because the country's run by *low*-level bureaucrats."

Dana Fradon, © 1981 The New Yorker Magazine, Inc.

Tensions within the Executive Branch

One should be careful not to perceive the federal bureaucracy as an anarchistic band of saboteurs, anxious to destroy a president's policies. That picture would be a gross caricature. On the other hand, one must realize that the American political system generates tensions between the president and the bureaucracy. Intensifying these tensions over the past third of a century has been the continual struggle over the bureaucracy size and role. Republican presidents from Eisenhower to Ford promised to reduce the role of the national government and its bureaucrats. Jimmy Carter echoed similar themes in 1976, reflecting growing public concern over the expansion of federal influence over more and more aspects of American life. With the election of Ronald Reagan, conflict over the scope of the federal government moved to center stage, as most federal bureaucracies were battered by budget cuts.

★ MEANS OF CONTROL

In attempting to exercise control over the federal bureaucracy, presidents have available substantial instruments of persuasion and command. The chief executive can seek professional skill and personal loyalty in the administrative posts that are filled with political appointees. While these goals are difficult to achieve for all the political appointments that are made, because of the variety of claimants, commitments, and constituencies that must be satisfied through the patronage process, the president can insist on high standards of skill and loyalty for those top positions that he fills himself.

Of considerable importance is the president's ability to capitalize on the commitment of most bureaucrats to public service. In planning his programs and in explaining them, he can take into account administrators' justifiable concerns about how to carry out the policies involved and those policies' likely effects on their agencies and their own careers. By doing his homework, a president can demonstrate to these professionals that he understands the complexities and difficulties of administering vast federal projects and that his choices of particular means and reliance on certain agencies are based on careful analysis rather than whim. By speaking and acting tactfully, he can demonstrate his appreciation of jobs loyally and efficiently done. In sum, the president can apply to the bureaucracy the same sorts of reasoned persuasion mixed with personal charm, firm determination, and skillful use of political resources that he must use to move Congress.

Close control over the budget provides another instrument of command. A president can insist that agencies give to the Office of Management and Budget detailed explanations of how they intend to use requested funds and, later, progress reports on how they are spending that money. Cross-checking of sources of information can also be important. Obviously, to control his subordinates, a president must first know what they are doing. If he depends solely on the bureaucrats themselves for information, he again becomes their prisoner. That is why Franklin Roosevelt instructed an old friend: "Go and see what's happening. See the end product of what we're doing. Talk to people. Get the wind in your nose."[18]

In monitoring what federal agencies are doing, a president has the same sorts of alternatives available as in gathering information and advice about formulating policy. Some, like talking to journalists and reading newspapers, may be especially valuable in tipping off a chief executive about his subordinates' actions. But no single means is likely to be sufficient, and successful presidents are likely to use combinations of techniques, as they do in gathering advice. Franklin Roosevelt added a twist of his own: He would sometimes deliberately assign two departments or agencies the same or overlapping missions in the hope that competition would spur each to do a better job or at least give each an incentive to tattle on the other.

The Vice-President

With respect to overseeing the variegated operations of the executive branch, it might appear that the vice-president would make an ideal chief of staff. To date, however, no vice-president has played that role. Even Carter, who honored his promise to treat Vice-President Walter Mondale as a "senior adviser," did not go that far. Vice-President George Bush was named chairman of the Reagan administration's "crisis management" committee and its task force on regulatory reform, but neither body was very important; and Bush's role has been far less significant than that of Reagan's inner circle of White House aides.

In part, the explanation may lie in the sort of people who have been vice-president. Even as humorless an individual as Richard Nixon would have laughed at the suggestion that a petty grafter like Spiro Agnew could have helped run the federal government. And Dwight Eisenhower retained deep suspicions about Nixon's character. But such considerations are only part of an explanation, since many able and honest men have held the office. Nelson Rockefeller was certainly a competent political leader, with substantial executive experience as Governor of New York, but his expansive views on the role of government were not shared by Gerald Ford or most other Republican leaders. Besides, like Lyndon Johnson's talented Vice-President, Hubert H. Humphrey, Rockefeller had a history of chronic "presidentitis" that made him a strong rival for power. "The history of the Vice Presidency," Walter Mondale astutely observed to a reporter for the *New York Times*, "has been so unrelievedly grim that I came to the conclusion that . . . there was something inherent in the relationship that made it unworkable."

For some presidents much of the explanation may lie in a subconscious reaction against close relations with the person who will gain the White House if the president dies in office. Furthermore, many presidents have refused to include the vice-president on their "team" because of a deliberate choice regarding power. To the extent that a president delegates power, he loses a measure of control. Much delegation is necessary, of course; but the vice-president is the only high-ranking member of the executive branch whom the president cannot legally dismiss.

Bureaucratic Independence and Limited Government

The independence of bureaucratic structures can impose high costs on the coherence of presidential programs. As conceived in the White House, an attack on a particular problem may involve closely coordinated sets of action by several federal agencies. If one agency drags its heels, another proceeds in a ploddingly begrudging fashion, while a third and fourth leap enthusiastically into the battle. The final program will be a mishmash, and the president is likely to seem a blunderer.

Such a price in programmatic coherence may be steep; nevertheless, it is inherent in the Madisonian system. It is easy to bemoan the cost and think of ways to "reform" the system. But reformers have to ask themselves precisely how far they wish to go in making bureaucracy responsive to the White House. An answer to that question must consider several points.

First, because of the complexity of serious political problems, Congress tends to legislate in general terms, setting broad objectives rather than specifying details. For all the reasons already discussed, no president or small group of advisers can possibly know enough to fill in every major gap in legislation, much less complete every detail. And, even if they had the technical knowledge, they would lack the time.

As a result, if most policies are to be effective, administrators, from cabinet secretaries to bureau chiefs to heads of field offices around the country, have to make intelligent, imaginative decisions. The kinds of people who can make such choices are not apt to come to or remain in jobs that limit them to shuffling papers and filling out forms. If the federal government is to recruit and retain effective executives, it must provide reasonably regular opportunities for creative leadership. Choices made by such executives will not always coincide with those the president would have made. But the president has no choice but to rely on hundreds and hundreds of others to carry out his policies.

Here is a dilemma that is common to popes and prime ministers, to dictators and corporate executives, as well as to presidents. To cope with complex problems, a leader needs subordinates who are loyal, diligent, and creative. Otherwise the leader will be overwhelmed with decisions. On the other hand, to the extent that creative people, even though loyal and diligent, exercise *their* judgment, they will shape policy in ways that are likely to diverge from what the leader had in mind. In so doing, these subordinates subtract from their leader's power. The chiefs of most governments of constitutional democracies are sufficiently realistic—and tolerant of disagreement—to be satisfied with keeping bureaucratic independence within bounds rather than trying to stomp it out.

There are other potential benefits to bureaucratic independence in a *constitutional* democracy founded on the desirability of *limited* government. A president who cannot command absolute, unquestioning obedience is restricted from doing evil as well as good. In this regard, it should be remembered that many of the sordid details of Watergate became public in 1973–1974 partly because of officials and former officials of the White House who became disgusted with the immorality of Nixon and his henchmen. The famous "Deep Throat," who fed or confirmed reports to the newsmen who did the most to break the full story of Watergate, may have been a mythical composite of several informants, but his—or their—resistance to the president was an important factor in Nixon's fall.

American government has been and remains presidential government, but presidential government is not the same as presidential dictatorship. Checking the president is not a trivial matter in a constitutional system. Indeed, what is at work here is another manifestation of the now familiar Madisonian strategy of preserving liberty by fracturing and fragmenting power. The costs in coherent public policy as well as in governmental responsiveness to public needs can be high, however. As Stephen Hess remarks, "Autonomous agencies are certainly preferable to presidential corruption but are no substitute for enlightened presidential leadership."[19]

 **SUMMARY**

This chapter has had two major objectives. First, it has tried to explain the president's need for information and advice in order to make decisions, and to describe the formal and informal systems of advice that are available to him. Second, and closely related, this chapter has attempted to show how a president's reliance on others to carry out his decisions inevitably reduces his power—but need not, if the president is astute, drain his ability to see that his program is carried out. Nor do these checks on presidential power constitute mere flaws in the political structure. They can serve positive functions in preserving limited, constitutional government.

NOTES

1. See "Cabinet Government Fades Away Once More," *U.S. News and World Report*, March 29, 1982, p. 28.
2. John Ehrlichman, quoted in "The Presidency: Can Anyone Do the Job?" *Newsweek*, January 26, 1981, p. 42.
3. Stephen Hess, *Organizing the Presidency* (Washington: Brookings Institution, 1976), p. 156.
4. Richard E. Neustadt, "Approaches to Staffing the Presidency," *American Political Science Review*, LVII (1963), 857.
5. Kermit Gordon, "Reflections on Spending," in J. D. Montgomery and A. Smithies, eds., *Public Policy* (Cambridge, Mass: Harvard University Press, 1966), Vol. 15, 12–13.
6. For assessments of the National Security Council, see the articles collected in Keith C. Clark and Laurence J. Legere, eds., *The President and the Management of National Security* (New York: Frederick A. Praeger, 1969), as well as the introduction by the editors. See also Morton H. Halperin with Priscilla Clapp and Arnold Kanter, *Bureaucratic Politics and Foreign Policy* (Washington: Brookings Institution, 1974).
7. *New Dimensions of Political Economy* (Cambridge, Mass.: Harvard University Press, 1966), p. 17.
8. Ibid., p. 54.
9. See Norman C. Thomas, "Presidential Advice and Information: Policy and Program Formulation," *Law and Contemporary Problems*, 35 (1970), p. 540.
10. For a close analysis of Wilson and House, see Alexander L. George and Juliette L. George, *Woodrow Wilson and Colonel House: A Personality Study* (New York: John Day, 1956). For a general view of such "inside advisers," see Louis W. Koenig, *The Invisible Presidency* (New York: Holt, Rinehart & Winston, 1960).
11. Arthur Link, *Woodrow Wilson and the Progressive Era 1900–1917* (New York: Harper & Row, 1954), p. 28.
12. For a brilliant account of the relationship between FDR and Harry Hopkins, see Robert E. Sherwood, *Roosevelt and Hopkins* (New York: Harper & Brothers, 1948).
13. Quoted in ibid., p. 3.
14. *Humphrey's Executor v. United States*, 295 U.S. 602 (1935).
15. Gordon, "Reflections on Spending," op. cit., p. 14.

16. Quoted in Richard E. Neustadt, *Presidential Power* (New York: John Wiley & Sons, 1961), p. 39.
17. William O. Douglas, *Go East Young Man: The Early Years* (New York: Random House, 1974), p. 305.
18. Quoted in Hughes, *The Living Presidency*, p. 141
19. Hess, *Organizing the Presidency*, p. 150.

SELECTED BIBLIOGRAPHY

Appleby, Paul. *Big Democracy* (New York: Alfred A. Knopf, 1945). Stimulating lectures on administrative problems of the federal government; just as fresh today as they were when originally published.

Balzano, Michael P. *Reorganizing the Federal Bureaucracy: The Rhetoric and the Reality* (Washington: American Enterprise Institute, 1977). A former official's brief case study of efforts to reorganize his agency and the general lessons that experience reveals about bureaucratic reform.

Fenno, Richard F., Jr. *The President's Cabinet* (Cambridge, Mass.: Harvard University Press, 1959). The best account of the cabinet as a political institution, pointing up its weaknesses as a policy-making body.

Goldstein, Joel K. *The Modern American Vice Presidency* (Princeton, N.J.: Princeton University Press, 1982). A new look at the vice-president, which concludes that the office has become much more important in recent years.

Halperin, Morton H., with the assistance of Priscilla Clapp and Arnold Kanter. *Bureaucratic Politics and Foreign Policy* (Washington: Brookings Institution, 1974). An effort by a former national security adviser to explain the process by which decisions are made regarding international relations and military affairs.

Heclo, Hugh. *A Government of Strangers: Executive Politics in Washington* (Washington: Brookings Institution, 1977). A thoughtful appraisal of national policy development and administration.

Hess, Stephen. *Organizing the Presidency* (Washington: Brookings Institution, 1977). The case for more presidential reliance on cabinet members as the principal sources of advice and accountability.

Johnson, Richard Tanner. *Managing the White House: An Intimate Study of the Presidency* (New York: Harper & Row, 1974). A former White House Fellow's analysis of the president's problems in organizing and running his office.

Kaufman, Herbert. *The Administrative Behavior of Federal Bureau Chiefs* (Washington: Brookings Institution, 1981). An intensive examination of the activities of the chiefs of six major federal bureaus.

Rourke, Francis E. *Bureaucracy, Politics, and Public Policy* (Boston: Little, Brown, 1969). A thoughtful treatment of bureaucratic contributions to the formulation of public policy.

Seidman, Harold. *Politics, Position, and Power: The Dynamics of Federal Organization*, 2d ed. (New York: Oxford University Press, 1975). A penetrating analysis of the ways in which the federal bureaucracy operates—both its internal politicking and its ultimate external effects on national policies.

Sindler, Allan P. *Unchosen Presidents: The Vice-President and Other Frustrations of Presidential Succession* (Berkley: University of California Press, 1976). Although mainly concerned about presidential succession, this brief study provides valuable insight into the vice-presidency.

Stanley, David T., Dean E. Mann, and Jameson W. Doig. *Men Who Govern* (Washington: Brookings Institution, 1967). An analysis of those who serve in political executive positions in the departments, agencies, and regulatory commissions of the federal government.

Wildavsky, Aaron. *The Politics of the Budgetary Process*, 2d. ed. (Boston: Little, Brown, 1974). A thorough study of the role of the OMB and other participants in the formulation of the president's budget.

PART VI

The Judiciary

13 The Judicial Process

Chapters 11 and 12 examined Congress and the presidency. This chapter and the one that follows look closely at the third branch of government, the judiciary. Here we analyze the roles thtat judges play in the political system. This chapter investigates the origins, discretion, jurisdiction, organization, and personnel of the entire system of federal courts. The next chapter focuses on the Supreme Court of the United States.

★ JUDGES AND THE DEVELOPMENT OF ANGLO-AMERICAN LAW

Divisions among legislative, executive, and judicial functions are clear neither in the abstract nor in the tangled webs of real government. We have just seen that legislators become involved in administration and that it is frequently difficult to tell whether an executive official is creating, interpreting, or applying rules. Similarly, while the role of judges is supposedly to interpret the law, they often create the very legal rules that they are supposed to interpret. Indeed, in England and the United States, judges made far more law than did legislators until well into the second half of the nineteenth century.

The Common Law

There are solid historical reasons for this fusion of these functions. The roots of American law run far back into medieval Britain, where judges—if one can even use that term—were executive officials and Parliament's basic function was to levy taxes. Some of the time, early English "judges" conferred with the king at Westminster and at other times traveled around the country to settle disputes on the basis of "common" custom, rather than the particular usages of any single region. Undoubtedly, however, judges' own biases were important elements in deciding what was "common" and what was local practice. To minimize arbitrariness and maximize consistency, judges soon adopted a practice called *stare decisis*—to follow their previous decisions when encountering similar cases. It was not until.centuries later, when reports of judicial decisions were regularly published, that stare decisis could become a firm rule. But even its loose application of common custom created a system of judge-made law.

Equity

As the common law developed, it hardened into rigid forms that covered only certain problems. The English social system, on the other hand, was still evolving, and old rules could not solve all the new problems. Therefore, aggrieved persons came to the king for justice, and his staff referred them to the royal chancellor. Gradually the chancellor's office, the chancery, also developed into a court, separate from the courts of the common law, and it applied a different and more informal set of rules, which came to be known as *equity*.

The most important difference between equity and common law lies in their objectives. Common law mainly provides *compensatory* justice; its chief remedy is money to pay for damages. Equity, on the other hand, offers *preventive* justice. It can order a defendant not to act, to stop acting, or to undo the effects of a previous action.

Federal seizure of the steel mills in 1952 supplies a clear illustration of these differences. When President Truman ordered the secretary of commerce to take over the mills to prevent a national strike, the mills' owners could, under the common law, have sued the United States, the secretary, or both for damages. Equity offered a different remedy, an *injunction* (a court order) directing the Secretary to return control of the mills to their managers. Naturally, management sought an injunction.[1] In other situations, one might seek an injunction to forbid an official or a private citizen to take a particular action; for example, a Chicano might ask for an injunction prohibiting a registrar from enforcing an English literacy test for voting.

Although in England courts of law and courts of equity were separate institutions, Congress in 1789 authorized federal judges to hear cases arising under either common law or equity, a practice accepted today in most of the states and even in Britain.

Toward an Independent Judiciary

The personnel who staffed the British tribunals of common law and equity gradually split off from the king's court and developed a professional identity as judges. By the early seventeenth century, they claimed a monopoly of interpreting the law. True independence from the king, however, came even more slowly. It was not until 1701 that judges served for good behavior during the reign of the king who appointed them, with removal during the king's life subject to parliamentary approval. And it was not until 1760 that judges did not have to leave office when the king died.

Eventually, the notion of an independent judiciary took firm hold in British and American culture. Royal abuse of this principle was one of

During the nation's early years, justice was brought to remote settlements by judges who rode the "circuit," moving from town to town to hear cases that fell within their jurisdiction. (The Bettmann Archive, Inc.)

the grievances listed in the Declaration of Independence. Today, even though two-thirds of American states provide for popular election of judges, the political system grants them a great degree of independence.

★ POLITICAL EFFECTS OF JUDICIAL DECISIONS

The rules that judges apply can have important impacts on the political system. In deciding cases that appear to concern only two private citizens, a court may apply an old rule, modify that rule, or create a new one. That rule—old, new, or modified—can affect the rights of many other citizens, because of either lawsuits or out-of-court advice given by lawyers. More broadly, the interests involved in a case may be widely shared in society and perhaps even represented by organized groups. For instance, a case may revolve around the duties of manufacturers to their customers. A decision holding a car maker liable for injuries suffered because of inadequate safety features can immediately affect the lives and property of millions of people.

On another level, a lawsuit, or perhaps a criminal prosecution, might raise issues fundamental to relationships between citizens and government. Another kind of case may concern relations among governmental officials. In what circumstances, for instance, can the president invoke executive privilege to withhold documents from Congress or the courts?

Like governmental officials, leaders of interest groups are keenly aware of the effects of judicial decisions and frequently try to shape the content of judicial rulings. Lobbying, in the sense the term is used in the legislative process, has no legitimate place in the judicial process. Private contacts with judges or jurors about a matter before a court are always unethical and usually illegal.

"Morning, sweetheart."

Stevenson, © 1978, The New Yorker Magazine, Inc.

Yet, in a broader sense, interest groups can legitimately lobby in the judicial process. First, they can use their influence to help select judges whose general political philosophy is favorable to the group's objectives. For instance, the American Bar Association, a conservative group that does not represent all or even a majority of lawyers and long barred Jews and blacks from membership, has succeeded in obtaining an institutional voice in the choice of federal judges.

Second, interest groups can file lawsuits or help others do so. This sort of aid may be critical. Lawyers are expensive, and there are usually court fees and perhaps large bills for research. A technical procedure known as a *class action* eases group access to courts. Here, a single person or a few people sue not only for themselves but for all other members of a clearly defined group who share a legal right, and the resulting decision affects the entire "class." For example, a black might file a class action for an order forbidding voting registrars to discriminate not only against her but also against *all* qualified black voters.

A group can also legitimately lobby by entering a legal dispute already in progress as an *amicus curiae*, a friend of the court, and offer its views about the proper way to resolve the dispute. The U.S. Supreme Court has held that the First Amendment's protection of freedom of speech, association, and petition gives organizations as well as individuals a constitutional right to use the courts to further their goals.[2]

A decision, even by the Supreme Court, does not necessarily end conflict over policy. The political process provides avenues of attack on judicial decisions just as it provides ways to contest legislative or administrative action. Thus, a decision by the Supreme Court that is unfavorable to the objectives of a particular interest group may trigger a fresh campaign in the legislative or administrative process. Groups hurt by a decision seek new legislation, constitutional amendments, or new judges; groups who benefit from the ruling talk about the sanctity of law and fight to prevent counteraction.

⭐ JUDICIAL DISCRETION

The effects of their decisions make judges important political actors; and in making decisions, they do not function as dispassionate computers, searching memory banks of prefabricated rules and then applying relevant rules to particular facts. Judges frequently exercise choice among competing values and competing policies, and they are forced to do so by the nature of their office.

If the streams of the law—customs, previous judicial decisions, statutes, and constitutional clauses—were crystal clear and all ran in the same direction, and if the needs of society were static, judges might be able to exercise only technical skills. But none of these conditions obtains. Most basically, the problems and the needs of society are constantly changing. "The law," Dean Roscoe Pound once observed, "must be stable, yet it cannot stand still." This dilemma of providing a known set of rules while adapting those rules to cope with changing conditions makes judging a creative process. Furthermore, the sources of the law rarely settle difficult cases. Custom is of little help when a new problem arises; indeed custom—the custom of dumping industrial wastes in the nearest stream, for instance—may be the cause of the problem. Previous judicial decisions may not cover the situation or, what is more likely, may offer conflicting guidelines. American courts have been functioning for such a long time that it takes an incompetent attorney not to be able to unearth a half dozen precedents to support either side of almost any kind of claim.

Statutory and constitutional clauses may be more helpful, but they do not necessarily settle the problem. The Constitution contains a wide variety of provisions. The Fourth Amendment does not forbid *all* searches and seizures but only those that are "unreasonable." The Fifth and Fourteenth Amendments forbid not the taking of "life, liberty, and property," but only their taking "without due process of law," and that phrase defies precise definition.

Important statutes also tend to be general—in part because vagueness of language is one way of compromising among competing interests, in part because there are problems inherent in using words, and in part because members of Congress have at times wanted to encourage judges to become creative partners in the legislative process. The Sherman Antitrust Act, for example, declares it illegal to "monopolize, or attempt to monopolize" trade in interstate commerce. But the statute offers no definition of "monopolize," and Senator Sherman conceded:

> I admit that it is difficult to define in legal language the precise line between lawful and unlawful combinations. This must be left for the courts to determine in each particular case. All that we, as lawmakers, can do is to declare general principles, and we can be assured that the courts will apply them so as to carry out the meaning of the law.[3]

When judges exercise discretion, they are apt to be influenced by their own values. They are also influenced by their perceptions of the nature of a problem. To a judge like William O. Douglas, who as a poor young man riding a freight train from Yakima, Washington, to law school in New York was almost killed by a railroad detective, police brutality seems a more real danger than it does to a judge from a socially prominent family.

Perception and values reinforce each other to the point that judges, like the rest of us, may see much that they want to see in particular controversies. A number of analyses of the voting behavior of justices of the Supreme Court have found a strong relationship between those votes and the values the justices endorse.[4] When he was still a judge on the Court of Appeals of New York, Benjamin Cardozo summed up the matter:

> My analysis of the judicial process comes then to this, and little more: logic, and history, and custom, and utility, and the accepted standards of right conduct, are the forces which singly or in combination shape the progress of the law. Which of these forces shall dominate in any case must depend largely upon the comparative importance of value of the social interest that will thereby be promoted or impaired. . . .
>
> If you ask how [the judge] is to know when one interest outweighs another, I can only answer that he must get his knowledge just as the legislator gets it; from experience and study and reflection; in brief from life itself.[5]

Discretion, however, is not equivalent to license. Judges do not fit the model of completely impartial arbiters; they have prejudices and predilections. But these are usually not biases for or against particular persons but for or against certain principles and policies. If the ideal judge is one who is impartial between litigants, then most federal judges come reasonably close to this model. But they are not likely to be impartial between competing ideas. Before lamenting this fact, one should consider whether a judge who did not treasure certain values, such as respect for human dignity, would be a proper official in a civilized society. The troublesome aspects about judicial discretion are how much of it a judge exercises and for what purposes he or she uses it.

⭐ THE FEDERAL SYSTEM OF COURTS

Federal Jurisdiction

One of the peculiar features of American law is a dual court structure, one for the federal government and a different set of tribunals run by each state government. Federalism itself does not require this double system. In Australia, Canada, and India, state courts handle most judicial business, with a national role confined to a federal supreme court that hears appeals. Although the U.S. Constitution permits a similar arrangement, the First Congress opted in 1789 for a complete set of federal courts. But Congress has given federal courts exclusive *jurisdiction*—authority to hear and decide a case—only in certain kinds of controversies—patents, for instance—listed in Article III of the Constitution as being under national control. (We repeat that listing on pp. 000–000).

Because of overlapping state and federal jurisdiction, a potential litigant often has a choice of using either set of courts. Moreover, in matters of criminal law, a defendant may be prosecuted in *both* state and federal courts, because by one act—robbing a national bank, for exam-

UNITED STATES DISTRICT COURT

FOR THE DISTRICT OF COLUMBIA

RICHARD NIXON, individually)
   and as the former President)
   of the United States,   )
)
       Plaintiff   )
)   Civil Action No. 74-1852
         v.   )
)
ADMINISTRATOR OF GENERAL SERVICES)
)
        and   )
)
THE UNITED STATES OF AMERICA,   )
)
       Defendants   )

AFFIDAVIT OF RICHARD NIXON

County of San Diego
State of California   ss:

Richard Nixon, being duly sworn under oath, deposes and says as follows:

1.   I am a citizen of the United States and a resident of the State of California, my residence being at San Clemente, California.

2.   From January 3, 1947 to November 30, 1950 I served as a Member of the House of Representatives. From December 1, 1950 to January 1, 1953 I served as a United States Senator from the State of California. Thereafter, from January 20, 1953 until January 19, 1961 I served as Vice President of the United States. I was elected President of the United States and served in that office from January 20, 1969 until my resignation on August 9, 1974.

3.   During the time I served in each of these four Constitutional offices it was my practice to retain and preserve nearly all of the materials produced or received by myself or my staff. Following the practice of all other Congressmen, Senators and Vice Presidents, when I

Contests in the courts involve a variety of legal documents, such as the affidavit or sworn statement. After Richard Nixon's resignation from the presidency in 1974, Congress passed a law ordering that the papers and tapes amassed during his years in the White House remain under governmental control. Nixon then sued to have them returned to his custody, alleging that the statute was unconstitutional. This is the first page of the affidavit justifying his claims. He lost the case.

ple—he may violate the law of both governments. The Supreme Court has ruled such a possibility constitutes "double amenability," or "double accountabilities," not "double jeopardy."[6]

Article III further limits federal jurisdiction to *cases* and *controversies*. These are technical terms and refer to situations in which opposing litigants have real interests that are in conflict and that conflict either has injured or threatens imminent injury to a right that the law protects. The gist of this restriction is that federal courts are not supposed to give *advisory opinions*.* To these "case" requirements, judges have added rules regarding "standing to sue." Basically, these require that a person who invokes federal juridiction show that: (1) the question raised is one that courts can answer and not one whose solution the Constitution leaves to Congress or the president; and (2) this particular clash of interests involves a personal right of the litigants, not a right of the public in general or of some other person. The Supreme Court has sometimes relaxed the latter requirement when it would be difficult for the individual whose rights were threatened to bring suit.[7] (A class action does not violate the rules regarding standing because the one who sues must demonstrate that a real personal interest of his or her own is involved.)

Further, Article III restricts the kinds of cases federal courts may decide. Federal jurisdiction depends either on the nature of controversy itself or on the status of one of the parties to the suit.

A. Nature of the controversy
   If the case involves:
   1. a question of the interpretation of the federal Constitution or any federal statute or treaty; or
   2. a question of admiralty or maritime law.

B. Status of the parties
   Where one of the parties is:
   1. the United States government or one of its officers or agencies;
   2. an ambassador, consul, or other representative of a foreign government;
   3. a state government suing:
      a. another state;
      b. a citizen of another state;
      c. a foreign government or its subjects;
   4. a citizen of one state suing a citizen of another state;
   5. an American citizen suing a foreign government or citizens of a foreign nation;
   6. a citizen of one state suing a citizen of his or her own state where both claim land under grants of different states.

---

* An *advisory opinion* is a statement of a court's views about a legal question where no real case, in the technical sense of that term, is before the court. A few state courts and many courts in foreign countries are required to offer such advice to executive or legislative officials.

State Jurisdiction

Because of the limited scope of federal jurisdiction, most lawsuits begin and end in state tribunals. Indeed, courts of a large state like California may handle more cases in a year than does the entire federal system. The organization of state courts varies widely, but normally, in addition to such specialized tribunals as juvenile courts, there are two sets of trial courts, one for minor criminal and civil matters, the other for more serious litigation. There is also at least one appellate court, and in some states there are two such layers, headed, as in the federal system, by a supreme court.

☆ FEDERAL JUDICIAL ORGANIZATION

District Courts

Congress has created three tiers of federal courts plus several special tribunals. At the first, or trial, level are district courts. In 1982 there were 91 of these, at least one in every state. At the next level are twelve U.S. courts of appeals, which review decisions of district courts, and at the top is the U.S. Supreme Court, which reviews decisions of federal courts of appeals and also decisions of state supreme courts on federal questions.

The bulk of federal judicial work is done in the *district courts.* Except for some local matters in the District of Columbia and the territories, all federal criminal cases and most civil cases start here, as do all federal suits in equity. Several hundred thousand cases a year are filed in district courts, but a large share of these are informally settled by the parties themselves. Except for infrequent civil suits requiring a special panel of three judges, a single judge presides over a trial, although the court itself may have as many as 27 judges attached to it.

District judges are influential public officials. In pretrial conferences they act as mediators and try to persuade litigants to settle their differences without further judicial proceedings. These solutions are seldom appealed because the parties themselves have agreed to them. Even when a formal trial is held, only a bit more than half of the decisions in civil cases will be appealed and less than a quarter of the decisions in criminal cases (although the latter figure represents about two-thirds of convictions obtained after full trial). Thus the district court's decision is not only the first, but, more often than not, the final, judicial ruling in a case.

Other factors widen district judges' power. First, legal rules are no more clear when a district judge has to interpret them than when the Supreme Court does. Indeed, they may be far less so, because, if the case presents a new problem, the Supreme Court has the advantage of the district judge's insights. In addition, even where the Supreme Court has apparently spoken, the justices may not have spoken clearly. Besides normal problems of communication, judges, like framers of constitutions and statutes, often have difficulty reaching clearcut agreement. One way of compromising differences is to use vague phraseology and leave some issues for future resolution. Supreme Court justices may also take this course when they are unsure of the best solution, hoping to gain wisdom from the experience of lower court judges as they transform broad pronouncements into specific rules. The generality of the Supreme Court's directives in the School Segregation Cases[8] and early Reapportionment Cases[9] was in part an attempt to learn from the efforts of district judges.

When a district judge faces a muddy pronouncement by the Supreme Court or senses that the justices are about to change an old rule, he or she must exercise choice—not completely unfettered choice, but choice nonetheless. And selection can shape public policy as well as public law. Even if that decision is appealed, argument at the next level will be shaped by the district judge's work.

Fact Finding. Cases seldom present only questions about legal rules. Probably most lawsuits center on disputes of fact. Witnesses to the same event—especially when the event happened months or years earlier—vividly recall quite different actions; experts often offer conflicting diagnoses of a defendant's mental health or financial condition.

Appellate judges are reluctant to disturb a district judge's or a jury's weighing of conflicting testimony. A witness's demeanor may strengthen or weaken his or her credibility, and appellate judges never see or hear witnesses. They must depend on a cold record of the trial.

Trial by Jury. The judge's tasks narrow when a jury is used. In federal courts, a litigant may ask for a jury trial in any lawsuit (but not in a suit in equity) where the amount in dispute exceeds $20. In a federal criminal prosecution, a defendant must be tried by jury unless both sides waive that right. The jury takes over the task of fact finding; the judge is supposed only to ensure that the trial follows regular procedures and to instruct the jury on the law to be applied to the facts. Yet a sharp distinction between facts and law is frequently impossible to maintain. In deciding what evidence the jury can hear, a judge participates in fact finding; moreover, a judge can often comment to the jury on the weight that should be given to certain kinds of evidence. In turn, juries in their deliberations probably often interpret or even create legal rules.

Although still numerous, jury trials are becoming less common. There is considerable debate whether that decrease bodes ill or good for the legal system. Only two facts are clear: (1) jury trials take much longer

"The jury will disregard the witness's last remarks."

and so contribute to the growing burdens of administering justice; and (2) juries are much freer than judges in arriving at a judgment because they do not have to explain or justify their decision.[10] An appellate court can never be sure what mixture of law and fact a jury used to decide a case. And judges are supposed to overturn a jury's verdict only on a finding that the judgment could not have been based on evidence presented at the trial—a most difficult conclusion to justify, though sometimes easy to suspect.

Courts of Appeals

Trial judges may make mistakes. More often, losing litigants think trial judges have made mistakes. Even when judges have committed no technical error, other judges may have offered different solutions to the same sort of problem. Thus, for greater certainty and uniformity, most judicial systems have established a way to review trial judgments.

Generally speaking, an American *court of appeals* does not retry the facts of a case, but the distinction between facts and law is as blurred at the appellate as at the trial level. Appellate judges frequently must decide for themselves whether congressional districts are as equal in population as they can be, or whether a business is mostly in local or interstate commerce. The Supreme Court has said that its duty to review is "not limited to the elaboration of constitutional principles; we must also in proper cases review the evidence to make certain that those principles have been constitutionally applied."[11]

The federal judicial system has two appellate layers, courts of appeals and the Supreme Court. Congress has divided the country into twelve circuits, each presided over by a court of appeals, all of which are collegial courts, that is, courts on which several judges hear cases together. Circuit judges normally sit in panels of three, but in rare instances all those in a circuit may sit together—*en banc*—to decide a controversy. In 1982, 132 judges staffed these tribunals.

As its name implies, a court of appeals hears only cases initially decided elsewhere. A few decisions can be taken directly from a district court to the Supreme Court, but most losing litigants in district courts must, if they wish to appeal, first go to a court of appeals. In addition, a U.S. court of appeals may review orders of certain federal administrative agencies, such as the Interstate Commerce Commission and the Federal Trade Commission.

The Supreme Court

The Constitution refers to a Supreme Court but leaves it to Congress to determine the Court's size and organization and to establish its appellate jurisdiction. From time to time, Congress has set the number of justices at from five to ten. Changes in the Court's size—or attempts to change its size, as in 1937—have usually been at least partially efforts to change the Court's decisions. The number nine has no inherent magic, but because this has been the number of justices since 1869, it has taken on sanctity over the years.

The Supreme Court is almost exclusively an appellate tribunal. Article III does provide that the Court shall have original jurisdiction in a few instances; but the justices exercise that jurisdiction almost solely in suits between states—which come up once or twice a year—and the even less frequent suits between a state and the federal government.

The procedure by which controversies reach the Supreme Court under its appellate jurisdiction is complex. Generally speaking, cases come up in one of three ways: *certification, appeal,* or *certiorari.* A U.S. court of appeals may *certify* to the Supreme Court a question of federal law that the judges feel is of such significance that it should be resolved immediately by the highest tribunal in the country. This procedure is uncommon.

Appeal is more often used. Under existing statutes a losing party may take his or her case to the Supreme Court when: (1) a federal court has declared a state or federal law unconstitutional; (2) the highest court

of a state has declared a federal statute, executive order, or treaty unconstitutional; or (3) the highest court of a state has sustained the validity of
a state law that has been challenged as violating the U.S. Constitution.
Cases under the last heading are numerous, and, while jurisdictional
statutes appear to oblige the Supreme Court to hear nearly all of them,
the justices dismiss the overwhelming majority on grounds that the
constitutional challenges are insubstantial.

Most cases are brought to the Court by a *writ of certiorari* (from the
Latin, "to be made more certain"). The losing party in a U.S. court of
appeals or in the highest court of a state, if the claim involves a question
of federal law, may petition the Supreme Court for review. Granting
certiorari, that is, agreeing to hear the case, is strictly a matter of discretion. The justices vote on whether or not to take each of these cases, four
votes, one less than a majority, being necessary to accept the dispute.

Special Federal Courts

There are also several federal courts of special jurisdiction, among them
the Customs Court, the Court of Customs and Patent Appeals, the
Court of Claims, and the Court of Military Appeals. Decisions of these
tribunals are reviewable by the Supreme Court under much the same
procedures as cases from courts of appeals.

⭐ JUDICIAL RECRUITMENT

Judicial office poses problems for democratic theory. On the one hand,
judges are supposed to personify justice. On the other hand, they are
powerful political officials. Periodically, cries are raised to take judicial
recruitment "out of politics" and leave selection to lawyers acting
through their bar associations. In practice, this suggestion means removing choice from one kind of politics, where voters indirectly exercise
some control, and putting it into another, the politics of bar associations,
where voters have no control at all.[12]

Historically, the British king appointed judges. Early practice in the
United States tended toward election by state legislatures or nomination
by the governor subject to legislative consent. In the nineteenth century
the tides of Jacksonian democracy swept over the courts. Every state
admitted to the Union since 1846 provides for popular election of all or
most judges, as do many older states. Federal judgeships, however,
have remained appointive offices.

The status of judges in common law countries differs from that in
European nations whose legal systems draw on Roman (or civil) law. On

the Continent, judges form a distinct profession that one enters immediately after graduating from law training and having passed a special set of examinations and undergone apprenticeship. Promotion comes much as for career civil servants. In contrast, American judges come from the ranks of practicing lawyers, public officials, and law professors. These people seldom have any special training other than having once studied law; indeed, minor state judges may have had no legal education at all.

Formal Steps in Appointing Federal Judges

The formal steps in appointing federal judges are simple. The president nominates a candidate whom the Senate confirms or rejects. If confirmed, the judge takes an oath of office and serves during good behavior at a salary that cannot be lowered.

The informal processes are far more complex. A campaign for appointment usually begins long before a vacancy occurs. Judgeships are marvelously rich pieces of patronage—"grand political plums," Senator Everett Dirksen once called them. The attraction is not financial. Indeed, because federal judges are not well paid* when compared to successful practicing attorneys, many lawyers who would make excellent justices cannot afford to give up their private practices. The critical factors attracting people to the bench are the power and prestige a federal judge commands. Many ambitious lawyers covet these rewards and begin early in their careers to try to achieve them by working hard and faithfully for political organizations or by running for elective office themselves.

Before disparaging this ambition, one should examine its effects. It does make judges appear less like high priests and more like other public officials, but such an image is not necessarily bad for democratic government. Second, this ambition helps keep able, highly trained people in politics. Third, it provides a large pool of professionally qualified and practically experienced candidates from which both parties can draw.

A judge's basic political philosophy is also an important element in selection. A president would be a fool willingly to put on the bench a judge who would declare the administration's most cherished policies unconstitutional or interpret statutes so as to block the administration's goals. Richard M. Nixon candidly stated the primary criterion that most presidents have applied in selecting judges: "First and foremost, they

---

* Federal judges' salaries are now adjusted annually to reflect increases in the cost of living. In 1982, district judges received $70,300, circuit judges $74,300, associate justices of the Supreme Court $93,000, and the chief justice $96,800.

had to be men who shared my legal philosophy. . . ." It may turn out, of course, that the president misjudges a person or has to choose the lesser evil; but when he has free choice, a president will opt for a judge whose constitutional philosophy accords with his own. It is no accident that more than nine out of ten federal judges have come from the same political party as the presidents who nominated them and that presidents tend to pick people whose views have been tested. As Lincoln said:

> We cannot ask a man what he will do [if appointed], and if we should, and he should answer us, we should despise him for it. Therefore we must take a man whose opinions are known.[13]

Still, the wide spectrum of views encompassed by both political parties means that a president is not limited to his own party for "right thinking" people. He can nominate members of the other party to enhance an image of nonpartisanship while hoping to secure a judge favorably disposed toward his general policies. A president may also reward senators or congressmen from the other party by naming some of their supporters to the bench. Although a chief executive or his staff rarely bargains along straight lines of "You support my bill and I'll nominate your candidate," presidents cannot consistently ignore the wishes of those legislators on whom they depend. And a president often has to rely on members of the opposing party to supply critical votes for his programs.

Nomination

Once a vacancy occurs, a dramatic game begins. Unlike most contests, its object is to get off the field and onto the bench. Candidates quickly mass the support they have been building over the years and prod bar associations, friendly interest groups, local politicos, senators, and congressmen. Interest groups rally around their own candidates or endorse or oppose candidates already active. Public officials join in, sometimes to ensure that one of their people is selected, sometimes to win posts for themselves. Even incumbent judges may be drawn into the whole process of selection; indeed, they may inject themselves into the activities with gusto. During William Howard Taft's justiceship (1921–1930), the scent of a vacancy on the federal bench triggered a series of letters, telephone calls, and visits from "the Big Chief" to the Department of Justice and the White House.

Presidents usually delegate authority in the nominating process to the attorney general, who passes this task to the deputy attorney general, who, in turn, usually works through a small staff. The leeway executive agents have depends on the judgeship. Since George Washington, senators have played a crucial—at times a dominant—role in naming district judges. If one of the senators from the state in which the vacancy occurs is from the president's party, senatorial courtesy gives that legislator a great advantage. A senator cannot capriciously invoke this tradition to blackball any nominee, but he or she can come close to doing so. If both senators are from the president's party, his agents may play one off against the other. But even when the two senators are both in the opposition party, the deputy attorney general's staff is well advised to listen to their views, although probably—and usually quite acceptably—local leaders in the president's party will carry more weight.

At the level of the courts of appeals, a president is less constrained by senatorial influence. Every circuit includes at least three states—except the District of Columbia circuit, but the District has no senators—and while considerations of geographical representation do come into play, a senator cannot assert the same proprietary interest as for district judgeships because all districts fall totally within a single state.

When filling vacancies on the Supreme Court, the president is even less restricted than he is at the circuit level. But the Senate's refusals in recent years to confirm Abe Fortas to be chief justice and Homer Thornberry, Clement Haynsworth, and G. Harrold Carswell as associate justices show the president does not have completely free choice.

When a vacancy occurs at any level of the federal bench, the deputy attorney general's staff compiles a list of promising candidates. At the same time, senators, congressmen, local leaders, interest-group representatives, officials of other executive agencies, members of local and state bars, and perhaps members of the White House staff will be sorting out their own preferences.

When the deputy attorney general's staff has completed its list—and in the case of district judges that list invariably overlaps with those of the state's senators—he asks the Federal Bureau of Investigation to investigate the moral characters and professional reputations of at least the front runners. At the same time, the staff usually asks the American Bar Association's Standing Committee on Federal Judiciary to report on candidates' professional qualifications. It rates these people on a three-point scale: "Meets the highest standards"; "Not opposed"; and "Not qualified."

These investigations may screen out some candidates, but they rarely determine the winner. For district judgeships and to a lesser extent circuit judgeships, the remaining names on the list are subjects of continuing negotiation among the staff and the senator or senators. Even for a district judgeship, a senator cannot dictate final choice, unless the president has given that prerogative in exchange for other considerations. But a senator can block almost any nominee from being confirmed. Faced with a potential stalemate, both sides typically negotiate.

Confirmation

The president announces the nomination by sending the candidate's name to the Senate, where the matter is referred to the Committee on the Judiciary. The committee's staff has usually been in contact with the deputy attorney general and has completed some preliminary investigations of its own. A member of the Department of Justice goes over the FBI report with the chairman, but no other senator is supposed to see it. The American Bar Association's committee formally submits its evaluation to the committee. Meanwhile, the committee's staff solicits views of senators from the nominee's state, then schedules hearings. Because of the work that has preceded nomination, hearings on district or circuit judgeships are generally dull recitations of virtue more appropriate to funeral eulogies.

In contrast, hearings on Supreme Court appointments are frequently dramatic performances. Legal experts may offer searing critiques of the nominee's judicial philosophy while others present stirring endorsements. A crackpot may provide comic relief by explaining how the candidate's refusal to condemn the United Nations spells corruption of American youth. Committee members and other senators may praise or damn the nominee's political opinions, questioning the potential justice with the zeal of an ambitious district attorney cross examining a notorious kidnapper. The hearings may expand into debates among the committee members on such topics as the nature of the Union or the relationships between Congress and the courts.

The hearings in 1968 on the nomination of Justice Abe Fortas to be chief justice provide a vivid illustration of what can happen, as Senator J. Strom Thurmond of South Carolina thundered at the nominee:

> Mallory—I want that word to ring in your ears—Mallory. . . . Mallory, a man who raped a woman, admitted his guilt, and the Supreme Court turned him loose on a technicality. . . . Can you as a Justice of the Supreme Court condone such a decision as that? I ask you to answer that question.[14]

His ears, and those of most people within a hundred yards, ringing from the senator's shouting, Fortas did refuse to comment and exposed himself to hours of additional berating.

After the hearings, the committee deliberates and recommends that the Senate confirm or reject the nominee. Both majority and minority members may file reports. The question is then discussed on the Senate floor. Again, the matter has usually been long settled for district and circuit judgeships. It is not unusual, however, for debates over confirmation of Supreme Court nominees to be both angry and informed.

At this stage, lobbying is normally at a minimum; opponents usually know they are beaten and content themselves with formal speeches. When the opposition has a chance, however, lobbying may become intense, with agents of the AFL–CIO, the National Association of Manufacturers, the NAACP, the American Bar Association, officials of the Department of Justice, members of the president's personal staff, and senators crossing one another's trails with promises, blandishments, and fresh evidence about the nominee.

Federal Judges

The products of this process have generally been honest, competent, and politically knowledgeable public officials. The sanction of punishment at the polls reinforces the moral imperatives that a president, his assistants, and senators bring to bear on such problems. To speak of judgeships as a form of patronage by no means implies that they are auctioned off. As one official said, "We feel that we owe certain people jobs but we do not feel that we owe them *specific* jobs."[15] Judgeships are very special kinds of jobs, requiring very special qualifications.

In addition to being competent and honest, the typical federal judge has been a white, male, upper-middle-class, highly educated Protestant, who is in middle to later life. Ethnic pressures affect this area of politics, too, and there are many members of white ethnic groups on the bench, although blacks and Hispanics are grossly underrepresented, as are women.

Perhaps more important than ethnic or socioeconomic backgrounds of judges is that they have almost all been successful lawyers whose commitment to the system has been tested in the crucible of practical politics. Some, as William O. Douglas and Louis Brandeis were, may be devoted to political, legal, and social reform; but federal judges come almost exclusively from people clustered just to the right and left of the political center. This collective biographical fact may help account for the conservatism of the bench. Judges may work for social change, but for change that improves the existing system rather than creating a new system.

Retirement of Federal Judges

Judges on state courts usually serve for specified terms, and many countries have set ages for compulsory retirement from the bench. Article III of the Constitution, however, specifies that federal judges "shall serve during good behavior." Still, this clause does not protect judges from problems of ill health and old age, and they may stay on the bench after they can function effectively. In 1895, for example, Justice Stephen J. Field cast the decisive vote to invalidate the income tax when he was senile. He, like Robert Grier earlier and Oliver Wendell Holmes later, was asked by his colleagues to resign.

Because impeachment is a harsh remedy for bad health or old age, policy makers have sought other solutions. Many people have suggested a constitutional amendment setting a compulsory retirement age. More positively, Congress has enacted generous retirement provisions. A federal judge who reaches seventy and has had ten years of service—or sixty-five after fifteen years' service—may retire at full salary. If he or she is in ill health, both requirements of age and service may be waived. Nevertheless, most judges do not retire at seventy. "It is extraordinary," Chief Justice Charles Evans Hughes once remarked, "how reluctant judges are to retire."[16] Yet he himself stayed on the bench until he was seventy-nine, even though he had earlier suggested that seventy-five was an appropriate time for retirement.

 SUMMARY

This chapter has described the development of judicial institutions, begun a discussion of the capacity of federal judges to shape public policy, explained the jurisdiction and organization of federal courts, outlined the procedures by which those judges are chosen as well as some of the problems raised by tenure "during good behavior," and sketched a composite silhouette of the jurists who staff the federal bench. We have not, however, sufficiently emphasized that courts perform an important emotional function for the political system by providing a forum in which disputants may angrily, but peacefully, attack each other. In the courtroom, advocates gently examine friendly witnesses and mercilessly cross examine hostile witnesses; and opposing counsel make eloquent pleas to the judge, to the jury, and to the Deity for justice, mercy, or revenge. On the whole, courts perform this function so well that in common speech "a day in court" is synonymous with a fair chance.

NOTES

1. *Youngstown Sheet and Tube Co. v. Sawyer*, 343 U.S. 579 (1952).
2. *NAACP v. Button*, 371 U.S. 415 (1963).
3. *Congressional Record*, XXI, 2460.
4. See especially the two books by C. Herman Pritchett, *The Roosevelt Court* (New York: Macmillan, 1948) and *Civil Liberties and the Vinson Court* (Chicago: University of Chicago Press, 1954); and Glendon A. Schubert, *The Judicial Mind* (Evanston, Ill.: Northwestern University Press, 1965).
5. Benjamin N. Cardozo, *The Nature of the Judicial Process* (New Haven, Conn.: Yale University Press, 1921), pp. 112–113.
6. See *United States v. Lanza*, 260 U.S. 377 (1922); *Abbate v. United States*, 359 U.S. 187 (1959); and *Bartkus v. Illinois*, 359 U.S. 121 (1959).
7. See, for example, *Pierce v. Society of Sisters*, 268 U.S. 510 (1925); and *Barrows v. Jackson*, 346 U.S. 249 (1953).
8. *Brown v. Board of Education*, 349 U.S. 294 (1955); there were four cases here, one each from Delaware, Kansas, South Carolina, and Virginia.
9. *Baker v. Carr*, 369 U.S. 186 (1962); *Wesberry v. Sanders*, 376 U.S. 1 (1964); and *Reynolds v. Sims*, 377 U.S. 533 (1964).
10. But Harry Kalven and Hans Zeisel, *The American Jury* (Boston: Little, Brown, 1966), have shown that judges typically come to the same conclusions as jurors.
11. *New York Times v. Sullivan*, 376 U.S. 254, 285 (1964).
12. See Richard A. Watson and Rondal G. Downing, *The Politics of Bench and Bar: Judicial Selection under the Missouri Nonpartisan Court Plan* (New York: John Wiley and Sons, 1969).
13. Quoted in David M. Silver, *Lincoln's Supreme Court* (Urbana: University of Illinois Press, 1956), p. 208.
14. U.S. Senate, Committee on the Judiciary, *Hearings on the Nomination of Abe Fortas to be Chief Justice of the United States*, 90th Cong., 2d Sess. (Washington: Government Printing Office, 1968), p. 191.
15. Quoted in Harold W. Chase, "Federal Judges: The Appointing Process," *Minnesota Law Review*, LI (1966), 204.
16. *The Supreme Court of the United States* (New York: Columbia University Press, 1928), p. 75.

SELECTED BIBLIOGRAPHY

Abraham, Henry J., *The Judicial Process: An Introductory Analysis of the Courts of the United States, England, and France*, 4th ed. (New York: Oxford University Press, 1980). A first-rate introduction to the business of judges and their inevitable involvement in making public policy.

Auerbach, Jerold S. *Unequal Justice: Lawyers and Social Change in Modern America* (New York: Oxford University Press, 1976). A blasting criticism of the American legal profession for its failure to achieve justice.

Cardozo, Benjamin N. *The Nature of the Judicial Process* (New Haven, Conn.: Yale University Press, 1921). An eloquent and insightful description of the problems of judicial decision making.

Chase, Harold W. *Federal Judges: The Appointing Process* (Minneapolis: University of Minnesota Press, 1972). The most thorough study yet produced of the appointing process.

Danelski, David J. *A Supreme Court Justice Is Appointed* (New York: Random House, 1964). A fascinating analysis of the events that led to the appointment of Pierce Butler to the Supreme Court.

Frank, Jerome. *Law and the Modern Mind* (New York: Brentano's, 1930). A brilliant and provocative analysis of the role of law in modern society.

Friedman, Lawrence M. *A History of American Law* (New York: Simon and Schuster, 1973). A one-volume history of the development of American legal institutions and doctrines.

Grossman, Joel B. *Lawyers and Judges: The ABA and the Politics of Judicial Selection* (New York: John Wiley and Sons, 1965). A case study of the efforts of a pressure group to influence federal judicial appointments.

Horowitz, Donald L. *The Courts and Social Policy* (Washington: Brookings Institution, 1977). A sharply critical analysis of the ways in which judges have been shaping public policy.

Jacob, Herbert. *Justice in America: Courts, Lawyers, and the Judicial Process*, 3d ed. (Boston: Little, Brown, 1977). A brief but useful "political analysis of how justice is administered in American courts."

Kalven, Harry, and Hans Zeisel. *The American Jury* (Boston: Little, Brown, 1966). A fascinating empirical study of the work of juries and how their decisions differ from those of judges.

Murphy, Walter F., and C. Herman Pritchett. *Courts, Judges, and Politics*, 3d ed. (New York: Random House, 1979). An introduction to the judicial process in the United States.

Murphy, Walter F., and Joseph Tanenhaus. *The Study of Public Law* (New York: Random House, 1972). An explanation of why and how political scientists study courts and judges.

Peltason, Jack W. *Federal Courts in the Political Process* (New York: Random House, 1955). A stimulating analysis of judges' involvement in American government.

Ulmer, S. Sidney, ed. *Courts, Law, and Judicial Processes* (New York: The Free Press, 1981). An excellent collection of articles on the nature of law and the functions of courts.

Watson, Richard A., and Rondal G. Downing. *The Politics of Bench and Bar* (New York: John Wiley and Sons, 1969). A close examination of the political maneuverings of lawyers and judges to influence judicial selection under a supposedly nonpartisan method of choice.

White, G. Edward. *The American Judicial Tradition* (New York: Oxford University Press, 1976). An ambitious effort to construct an intellectual history of American law through penetrating sketches of leading judges, both state and federal.

14 The Supreme Court

Chapter 13 provided an overview of the judiciary. This chapter examines in greater depth the United States Supreme Court—its procedures, the sources of its power, the instruments it may use to affect public policy, restraints on the Court's power, and some general consequences the justices' decisions have for the political system.

⭐ DECISION-MAKING PROCEDURES

The Supreme Court's building provides a fitting home for the magic and majesty that surround the law. The huge marble palace radiates the solidity and serenity of a temple of justice. From the first Monday in October until sometime in July, the justices attend to the mass of cases that roll in. The issues directly involved are always legal, but their ramifications affect political power.

A long summer vacation and the justices' practice of recessing every several weeks to read, write, and reflect make the Court's pace seem leisurely. In fact, the work load is staggering, and as much in self-pity as in jest the justices have referred to themselves as "a chain gang" as they confront each year's docket of 5,000 cases.

Just before ten o'clock Mondays through Wednesdays, during the weeks when the Court is in session, the justices meet in the chamber behind the red-veloured courtroom, shake hands, and don their black robes. Precisely at ten, the curtains part and the justices take their places behind the great mahogany bench that dominates the small room. As they enter, the crier slams down his gavel and chants:

> The Honorable, the Chief Justice and Associate Justices of the Supreme Court of the United States!
>
> Oyez, oyez! All persons having business before the Honorable, the Supreme Court of the United States are admonished to draw near and give their attention, for the Court is now sitting. God save the United States and this Honorable Court.

Administrative matters may consume a few minutes; then the Chief Justice calls the first case. Each side's contentions have already been carefully explained in written arguments called briefs and reply briefs. Now counsel have a chance at oral argument. Usually, the Court allots only thirty minutes to each side, but in extraordinarily important disputes it may allow more time. In front of the justices in their high-backed leather chairs, counsel stands at a lectern and begins, "Chief Justice, may it please the Court. . . ." A white light on the lectern flashes

At the apex of the federal court system is the United States Supreme Court, whose majestic building proclaims the lofty goal of "equal justice under law." (United Press International)

when five minutes are left; when a red light goes on, the lawyer stops instantly. Chief Justice Charles Evans Hughes once cut off a prominent attorney in the middle of the word "if."

The justices prefer a Socratic dialogue to a lecture, and lucid explanation to rhetoric. Questions, sometimes three and four at once, fly at counsel as the justices probe for clearer explanation of the dispute and for informed speculation on probable consequences of alternative solutions. The justices can be ruthless in pursuit of the truth—or of the lawyer, if he or she annoys them.

If the justices find a presentation tedious, they do not hesitate to show their feelings. They may stare glumly at the ceiling, whisper and send notes to each other, or dispatch messengers to fetch law books. Oliver Wendell Holmes used to sketch an outline of an attorney's probable argument and, if counsel followed a predictable course, catch a short nap.

At noon, the Court recesses for an hour, then goes back into session until three. On Wednesday after argument and all day Friday, the justices meet in conference to discuss and vote on the cases they have just heard argued and to decide what other cases to accept. These conferences are secret. Only the justices may enter the room, but some have scribbled notes to guide themselves in writing opinions and perhaps to enlighten history. These notes reveal informed, lively, and often heated discussions. As at oral argument, the justices are concerned about more than technical legal rules; they explore—and debate—possible impacts of decisions on public policy. The Chief Justice speaks first, then the others in order of seniority. Each is supposed to talk without interruption, but ideas—and sometimes tempers—flash. When the Chief feels that further discussion would serve no useful purpose, he calls for a vote. Until recently, voting was in reverse order of seniority, with the Chief last. Earl Warren, however, surrendered his prerogative of casting the final vote. The justices now vote in the same order in which they spoke.

If the Chief Justice votes with the majority—and before Warren some Chiefs used the advantage of voting last to join the majority—he assigns responsibility for writing the opinion of the Court either to himself or to another majority justice. If the Chief Justice is in the minority, the senior associate justice in the majority appoints the opinion writer. That justice circulates drafts to the entire Court, so that those in the majority may make suggestions for change and the minority may have an opportunity to reply. The justices typically propose many, and sometimes basic, changes—Oliver Wendell Holmes complained that "the boys generally cut one of the genitals" from his opinions. In an important case, an opinion is likely to go through at least a half dozen revisions.

Each justice may write his or her own opinion, dissenting or concurring, although custom requires circulation to all the Court. Occasionally a concurring or dissenting opinion persuades other justices to change their minds and so becomes the opinion of the Court. A justice is free to switch his or her vote up to the moment the decision is announced, and even after that if the loser petitions for a rehearing.

SUPREME COURT OF THE UNITED STATES

No. 80–251

Bernard Rostker, Director of Selective Service, Appellant, v. Robert L. Goldberg et al.	On Appeal from the United States District Court for the Eastern District of Pennsylvania.

[June 25, 1981]

JUSTICE REHNQUIST delivered the opinion of the Court.

The question presented is whether the Military Selective Service Act, 50 U. S. C. App. § 451 *et seq.*, violates the Fifth Amendment to the United States Constitution in authorizing the President to require the registration of males and not females.

I

Congress is given the power under the Constitution "To raise and support Armies," "To provide and maintain a Navy," and "To make Rules for the Government and Regulation of the land and naval Forces." Art. I, § 8, cls. 12–14. Pursuant to this grant of authority Congress has enacted the Military Selective Service Act, 50 U. S. C. App. § 451 *et seq.* ("the MSSA" or "the Act"). Section 3 of the Act, 50 U. S. C. App. § 453, empowers the President, by proclamation, to require the registration of "every male citizen" and male resident aliens between the ages of 18 and 26. The purpose of this registration is to facilitate any eventual conscription: pursuant to § 4 (a) of the Act, 50 U. S. C. App. § 454 (a), those persons required to register under § 3 are liable for training and service in the Armed Forces. The MSSA registration provision serves no other purpose beyond providing a pool for subsequent induction.

Decisions are the final products of those cases heard by the Supreme Court. This is the opening page of the ruling in 1981 sustaining the constitutionality of drafting only males.

JUDICIAL POWER

In 1788, one opponent of the Constitution complained of "the stupendous magnitude" of power[1] conferred on the Supreme Court. American constitutional history makes the gentleman appear guilty of understatement. The justices function as members of a coordinate branch of government, and they have sometimes fully exploited their potential to influence immediate public policy as well as long-range development of the political and social systems. John Marshall's nationalism, Stephen Field's classic economic liberalism, and Earl Warren's civil libertarianism have been dynamic forces shaping American society. Yet the justices are not all-powerful. Although they operate from a strong political base and can wield sharp weapons, they are also subject to many restrictions. Understanding the sources and instruments of, and limitations on, judicial power is necessary to comprehending the roles that the Supreme Court—indeed all courts—play in American government.

SOURCES OF JUDICIAL POWER

Legal Sources

As Chapter 13 showed, the multiplicity of legal rules and the generality of language of many important statutes force judges to act as policy makers, and the Constitution reinforces this push. By its own terms, the Constitution is law—"the supreme law of the land"—and, so the justices have successfully claimed, as subject to judicial interpretation as other kinds of law.

In practice, constitutional interpretation means judicial review, the authority to declare invalid actions of other public officials. Although the Constitution makes no mention of any such authority, in several early cases the justices assumed they could declare statutes unconstitutional.[2] The first clear use of judicial review came in *Marbury v. Madison* (1803).[3] The specific point involved was a narrow, technical one of jurisdiction; but, as frequently happens, important political issues crackled below the surface.

Before going out of office, President John Adams had persuaded the lame-duck Federalist Congress to create a number of new judgeships, which Adams filled up with deserving Federalists. Some of these appointments were made so late that John Marshall, who saw no ethical problem in serving as Adams's Secretary of State while he was also Chief Justice, did not have time to deliver them before Adams left office. President Jefferson refused to send out the remaining commissions, and

William Marbury, a disappointed justice of the peace in the District of Columbia, went to law to gain his judgeship.

He filed suit in the Supreme Court for an order directing James Madison, the new Secretary of State, to deliver the commission. Marbury claimed that the Judiciary Act of 1789 gave the Court original jurisdiction, that is, as a trial court, to issue a mandamus—an order to a public official to do his duty—in such a case. Chief Justice Marshall, like many conservatives, was fearful of the havoc a radical like Jefferson might wreak on the country and was determined to establish once and for all the character of judicial power. He put aside the easy course, which was to declare that the act of 1789 did not give the Court original jurisdiction in this kind of case—a fair reading of the statute.

First, Marshall wrote a biting criticism of Jefferson's refusal to deliver the commission, concluding that Marbury indeed had been wronged. The next question, Marshall said, was whether Marbury had sought the correct remedy. At that point the Chief Justice took up the constitutional issue and found a conflict between Article III's description of the Court's original jurisdiction and what was supposedly added by the act of 1789. He then deduced the principle of judicial review by means of a syllogism. *Major premise:* The Constitution is the supreme law. *Minor premise:* It is the function of judges to interpret the law, and they take an oath to support the Constitution. *Conclusion:* Courts must declare invalid any inferior law—for example, an act of Congress—in conflict with the higher law, that is, the Constitution.

Marshall's tactics were clever: He had declared a statute unconstitutional in a case whose political context made it impossible for the President to defy the decision. Jefferson, after all, did not want to give Marbury his commission, and Marshall ruled that the Court could not order him to do so because Marbury had sued under an unconstitutional statute. Nevertheless, the Chief's logic was not invulnerable. The Constitution, critics noted, was different from ordinary law; it was a political document. As for the judicial oath, every office holder took a similar pledge to support the Constitution. Perhaps the most telling point was made by Senator Breckinridge of Virginia: "Is it not extraordinary," he asked, "that if this high power [of judicial review] was intended, it should nowhere appear [in the Constitution]?"[4]

Marshall's decision enraged the Jeffersonians, though more because of his searing attack on the administration than for his assertion of judicial review. In retaliation, they impeached Justice Samuel Chase and came within a few votes of convicting him. Had they succeeded, Marshall might have been next; but they failed, and the principle of judicial review—next used by Marshall to declare invalid an executive order issued by President Adams,[5] a decision with which the Jeffersonians found it difficult to quarrel—became part of the American political tradition.

Although few people today seriously question the legitimacy of judicial review itself, just how far a Supreme Court decision obligates coordinate branches of the federal government is still unsettled. Few responsible critics would deny judges' supremacy over the kinds of courtroom procedures covered by Article III of the Constitution. For instance, were Congress to provide for a conviction for treason on testimony of one witness rather than two as Article III commands, no one would claim that the Court should enforce the statute. Probably also a broader policy that uniformly denied other officials use of judicial machinery to enforce laws that the justices thought unconstitutional would find little opposition.

Some writers, however, have implied a much wider claim: A Supreme Court decision binds not only the parties to a case; it also binds the president and Congress in their own policy-making roles. Without a doubt, the possibility of an adverse Supreme Court decision has inhibited administrative and legislative behavior, but the extent of legal and moral obligations involved poses a different sort of question. Strong presidents like Thomas Jefferson, Andrew Jackson, Abraham Lincoln, and Franklin Roosevelt have asserted that in performing their duties they must follow their own interpretations of the Constitution. Jackson vetoed the bank bill of 1832[6] because he thought a national bank unconstitutional, even though the Supreme Court had held in *McCulloch v. Maryland* (1819)[7] that Congress could establish such an institution. In his veto message the President said:

> If the opinion of the Supreme Court covered the whole ground of this act, it ought not to control the coordinate authorities of this Government. The Congress, the Executive, and the Court must each for itself be guided by its own opinion of the Constitution. Each public officer who takes an oath to support the Constitution swears that he will support it as he understands it, and not as it is understood by others.

Lincoln put it more generally. He conceded that a Supreme Court decision was binding on the parties to a case and that public officials must treat with great respect the principles announced by the Court, but added:

> At the same time the candid citizen must confess that if the policy of the government, upon vital questions, affecting the whole people, is to be irrevocably fixed by decisions of the Supreme Court, the instant they are made, in ordinary litigation between parties, in personal actions, the people will have ceased to be their own rulers, having to that extent, practically resigned their government, into the hands of that eminent tribunal.[8]

Jackson's and Lincoln's arguments, incidentally, would not support state officials who claimed authority to nullify a Supreme Court decision, because they are not officers of a coordinate branch of government.

Judicial review is not a power unique to the U.S. Supreme Court. It is shared by every federal court and by all state courts of general jurisdiction, although usually the Supreme Court can, if asked, review decisions of these other courts. Other countries—including Australia, Canada, West Germany, India, Ireland, Italy, and Japan—have also adopted judicial review, to some extent modeling their processes on those of the United States.

Prestige

Prestige can be a vital source of power. Because they lack physical force, judges ultimately have to depend on the feeling that one ought to obey a court's decision and that if one of the parties does not, then other public officials ought to use their power to compel obedience.

From time to time, scholars, newspapermen, lawyers, elected politicians, and judges themselves point to the high or low prestige in which the Supreme Court is currently held. Unfortunately, we have little hard data to gauge the popularity of the Court in different periods. Some decisions irritate some groups, ethnic, regional, or ideological, and at the same time those decisions please yet other groups. But the correlation between general public opinion and noisy praise or condemnation is doubtful. What does seem clear, however, is that if one looks at what critics have been saying since 1788, the justices began with no prestige whatever and have fallen steadily in public esteem. "The Supreme Court," C. Herman Pritchett once remarked, "is not what it used to be, and what's more it never was."[9]

Mass polling promises some clarification, but its use on a scientific basis goes no further back than the 1930s; and even since then there has been scant sampling of public attitudes on judicial issues. one systematic study[10] reveals some awareness of specific Court decisions. About 45 percent of national samples of voting-age adults in 1964, 1966, and 1975 could recall a recent Supreme Court action—names of cases were not, of course, asked. When a respondent could recollect a decision, it was likely that he or she disapproved of what the Court had done. Yet more than two out of three of the people who had an opinion—including 40 percent of those who had expressed only critical views of particular decisions—thought that the Court was doing its basic job very well. This difference between criticism of individual decisions and approval of the Court as an institution indicates that the justices have a reservoir of public support on which they can draw in emergencies. Other surveys of practicing attorneys and professional politicians, as well as views expressed by better-educated people in national samples, indicate that this institutional support is deeply and widely shared among those who could be termed political activists and opinion leaders.

Yet three pieces of evidence imply that the justices' reservoir of public support is not unlimited. First, and perhaps most critical, replies showed emotion ranging from respect, admiration, pleasure, and approval on the one hand, to disapproval, anger, and contempt on the other. But there was no evidence of adulation that would remotely imply automatic acceptance of any judicial decision.

Second, variations in evaluations of the Court were closely associated with respondents' overall political views, usually lumped under liberalism and conservatism. This connection indicates a complex relationship. In part, public approval of certain policies may be due to Supreme Court decisions. This connection may also mean that certain kinds of decisions can severely drain the Court's reservoir of support and that as general political attitudes change, so may those toward the Court—if the Court's rulings do not change in much the same way as public opinion.

Third, a large portion of the public either is unaware of the Court's work or so slightly aware as to be unable to answer simple questions. Thus we do not know how deeply, if at all, the support of this silent mass runs. Moreover, ignorance or apathy may occur among those most helped by judicial decisions and whose political support the Court would most need in time of crisis. In the mid-1960s, for example, one would have expected blacks to be among the most ardent defenders of the Court, and so knowledgeable blacks were. But proportionately far fewer blacks than whites had much knowledge of the Court in particular or politics in general.

The Need for an Umpire

A third source of judicial power is a practical one: A federal system that divides power among state and national units of government, denies some power to each, and then further fragments power among units of the national government needs some kind of umpire. The framers planned this division to cause friction, and in that sense it works very well. But just as individuals living together in society need an arbiter to settle disputes, so do governmental officials who share power.

In a related fashion, governmental officials may need the Court to help legitimize controversial decisions.[11] In a pluralistic society, any important public policy is likely to hurt the interests of many individuals and groups. Opposition will be based in part on the *wisdom* of a policy; but, especially when a vaguely worded constitutional clause is involved, doubts about the policy's *validity* will occur.

To survive, every governmental structure must provide some means of quieting basic constitutional doubts of this kind. In American politics the campaign speech, the ballot box, and the constitutional amendment may perform this legitimizing function, but so may a Supreme Court decision. Indeed, the justices are far more likely to declare a contested congressional statute constitutional than unconstitutional. From 1789 to 1982 the Supreme Court invalidated national laws in less than a hundred instances.

⭐ INSTRUMENTS OF JUDICIAL POWER

The most basic instrument of judicial power is *jurisdiction*, the authority to hear and decide cases as well as to issue orders to the parties involved. The effectiveness of this instrument increases if, as American judges can, courts can issue orders to governmental officials. Reinforcing this authority is the practice of writing opinions. These may be merely turgid explications of technical rules. In the hands of a master, however, they can become means of influencing not only current but also future public opinion. The eloquent rhetoric of the opinions of John Marshall, Louis Brandeis, Oliver Wendell Holmes, and Harlan Fiske Stone all took on lives of their own in helping to mold the thinking of later generations.

Just as *prestige* is an important source of judicial power, so it can also become a weapon of judicial power—precisely what an opinion writer wants it to be. Prestige can be strongly reinforced by *professional reputation*, the respect that other governmental officials have for the skill and determination with which the justices use their power. When the justices can combine a popular feeling that their decisions ought to be obeyed with a belief that the justices can create a political backfire to burn those officials who do not aid compliance, they have forged an instrument to bludgeon the very people who possess the physical force to defy them.

The justices also control certain passive instruments. Without giving any reason whatever, they can refuse to hear almost any case. Moreover, even when they take a case, they may use a variety of technical devices to delay a decision on the merits until a time they consider more favorable for the objectives they wish to achieve.

⭐ LIMITATIONS ON JUDICIAL POWER

Technical Checks

A series of interlocking restrictions limit judicial power. As judges, the justices must follow certain formal procedures. These are flexible, but not infinitely so. Unlike administrators, judges cannot initiate action.

Someone must bring a case to them, and in a form that meets jurisdictional and standing requirements. The justices can, for instance, sustain the conviction of a brutal sheriff under a civil rights law, but they cannot start such a prosecution themselves.

A second restriction limits the effect of a decision. A court order legally obligates only the parties to that particular case, those who cooperate with them, and those who succeed to their office or status. A decision that the legislature of Tennessee is gerrymandered does not, of itself, *legally* oblige the government of another state using exactly the same representational formula. A separate suit must be brought, although, of course, existence of the first judgment might well move officials of the second state to act on their own. Earlier, we mentioned the class action, a procedure that allows one litigant or a small group of litigants to sue for themselves and all others similarly situated. These kinds of options widen access to the courts, but the resulting order still binds only the specific defendants named in the court's final order.

Judges are also restricted in the kinds of orders they can issue. In general, they can far more easily forbid action than they can command positive action, especially where public officials are involved. The justices can hold a civil rights statute or social security law constitutional, but they cannot compel Congress to pass such a statute. They can, of course, loosely interpret existing statutes and surprise congressmen by discovering more policy than legislators thought they had set. In 1956, for example, Representative Howard Smith, author of the Smith Act, which punishes advocacy of violent overthrow of the U.S. government, expressed stunned disbelief at the Court's decision[12] that this statute forbids states to adopt similar laws to protect the United States. But, despite occasional opportunities to reap a bigger harvest than Congress has thought it has sown, limitations on the kinds of orders a court can issue are very real.

Public Opinion

If the Court draws much of its power from public esteem, popular attitudes can also check judicial power—unless, of course, the public considers the Court incapable of error, and, as we have seen, there is no evidence of such adulation. Like the Lord, the public taketh away as well as giveth, and it may act considerably more capriciously than the Deity.

Internal Restrictions

The justices are also limited by their own ideas of how they, as judges, ought to act. Because they come to the bench after a long period of legal training and usually a far longer period of apprenticeship in public service, they probably have absorbed many prevailing norms about judicial action. These norms may be vague, yet they do broadly distinguish between behavior perfectly proper for legislators and administrators but improper for judges. For instance, a legislator who informally consults with experts might be looked on as energetic. On the other hand, a judge who discusses a pending case with a person not a member of the court, unless attorneys for both sides are present, is slipping into unethical conduct.

In addition, the justices cannot help being aware that they are appointed officials serving what amounts to life terms in a government that is in many respects democratic. The apparent oddity of this situation has caused justices to hesitate to substitute their own judgment for

"My DISSENTING OPINION WILL BE BRIEF: 'YOU'RE ALL FULL OF CRAP!'"

that of popularly elected officials. (Candid judicial acknowledgment that the United States is a *constitutional* democracy, as explained in Chapter 3, would ease but not remove this difficulty.)

Institutional Limitations

The simple fact that the Supreme Court is staffed by nine justices constitutes a further check. To hear a case requires a vote of four members and to decide it requires five votes. Since nine is an uneven number, one might expect clear-cut decisions in all cases where every justice sat; but complex litigation often presents more than two options. Furthermore, an opinion, to be labeled that of the Court, must win the assent of a majority of the justices. It is no easy matter to persuade five or more individualistic, strong-willed lawyers to agree on a closely reasoned document based on controversial assumptions of political philosophy that may have immediate as well as long-run effects on public policy.

A justice who is determined to write exactly as he or she wishes is apt to write for her- or himself alone. Not since the days of John Marshall has a single justice been able to dominate the Court. Decisions and opinions are products of what Justice Felix Frankfurter described as orchestral rather than solo performances.[13] When the justice assigned the task of writing for the Court circulates each draft, suggestions for change may pertain to literary style or to the heart of the substance of a case. Securing agreement, if the case is at all important, typically involves negotiation, compromise, and even bargaining. This sort of operation is complex, for a change demanded by one member of the majority may anger another. The opinion writer thus sometimes writes vaguely so as to alienate as few collegues as possible. The final product, as Justice Holmes once observed, may be a mass of dough. But if no single judge or small coterie can dominate the Court, the alternatives to bargaining are each judge's writing a separate opinion, as is done in England and Australia, or publishing no opinions at all.

The justices have incentives and sanctions for their bargaining. The main incentive is to enshrine as those of the Court the principles he or she thinks best cover this and similar situations. The major sanction available to the opinion writer is to ignore a colleague's wishes—if he or she can still muster five votes. Those who disagree may write separate opinions and persuade other justices to join them. Clearly, the effectiveness of either sanction depends on the closeness of the vote and the intellectual powers of individual justices. A 5–4 division puts the opinion writer at a considerable disadvantage, just as an 8–1 judgment gives great latitude. So too a threat to circulate a separate opinion means much more from a Holmes or a Brandeis than from a less skillful writer. Helping to keep negotiations within bounds is the knowledge among the

The justices of the Supreme Court, 1982. *Front, left to right:* **Thurgood Marshall, William J. Brennan, Chief Justice Warren E. Burger, Byron R. White, Harry A. Blackmun.** *Rear, left to right:* **John P. Stevens, Lewis F. Powell, William H. Rehnquist, Sandra Day O'Connor.** (Courtesy the Supreme Court Historical Society)

justices that they will work together for many years, and during that time each is likely to have to write hundreds of opinions of the Court.

That the Supreme Court rarely makes either the first or the final decision in a case imposes another set of institutional checks. As the preceding chapter showed, the Court's jurisdiction is almost totally appellate. It reviews a lower court decision, reverses or affirms it, writes an opinion explaining the principles behind choices, and usually sends *(remands)* the case back to the court where the litigation began for final disposition. Thus, like the president, the justices operate through a bureaucracy; and they have even less control over their bureaucracy than does the president over his. The justices can exercise little influence in appointing, retaining, or promoting lower federal judges and probably no control whatever in state judicial affairs. The sheer volume of business, the frequency with which new issues arise, and the vagueness of many legal rules mean that the justices are at most leaders of their branch of government, not its masters. The analogy of bureaucracy—judicial or administrative—to international politics, where independent and semi-independent leaders negotiate, is apt.[14] The military model of disciplined subordinates saluting and unquestioningly carrying out orders is one that presidents and justices may sorely envy but never see.

Political Restraints

The Supreme Court can interpret statutes and executive orders; it can even declare them unconstitutional. These are great powers, but Congress and the president have weapons they can turn against the justices. Congress can impeach and remove judges, increase the number of justices, withdraw at least some of the Court's appellate jurisdiction, cut off money for the Court's administrative staff or deny funds to execute decisions, enact new statutes to "correct" judicial interpretations of old law, and propose constitutional amendments to counter the effects of a judicial decision, as the Fourteenth and Sixteenth Amendments did, or even to strike at judicial power itself, as the Eleventh Amendment did. During Jefferson's administration, Congress, although its action was unconstitutional, abolished a whole tier of federal courts and turned the judges out without salaries; and after the Civil War, several Radical Republican legislators threatened to abolish the Supreme Court itself.

The president may refuse to enforce judicial decisions, and he can pardon anyone convicted of criminal contempt of court for disobeying judicial orders. In choosing judicial nominees, the president can try to influence future decisions, as can senators in approving or disapproving a nominee. The president can also try to persuade Congress to use any of its powers against the Court; and, as can senators and congressmen, he can draw on his own prestige to attack the justices.

Although the national supremacy clause of Article VI of the Constitution puts state officials on a lower level than federal officers, state officials can still challenge the Court. They too can pass new statutes or issue fresh orders and so force apparent winners back to court for additional battles. Like national officials, state officers may try to undermine the justices' prestige. And because the decentralized structure of both political parties makes senators, representatives, and even federal administrators dependent on local politicos, state officials may pressure federal officials to oppose Supreme Court decisions. Efforts to impede implementation of the Court's rulings regarding segregation and school prayers demonstrate how effectively states may retard judicial action.

☆ POWER AND PRUDENCE

So many restraints coming from so many sources raise the question of why the Supreme Court has been so powerful. In part, the answer lies in the fact that these checks are limitations, not barriers. Having had practical political experience, judges are typically aware of these restrictions and know how to work within them. Moreover, judicial decisions that offend some groups usually delight others. And defenders of the Court as well as its attackers can use channels of political influence. Critical in these struggles is the fact that it is always easier to prevent Congress from acting than to persuade it to act.

A president, too, is likely to be cross-pressured. Much of the power he can wield against the Court requires congressional cooperation. Furthermore, refusal to enforce decisions can expose him to political dangers, not only from public opinion but from the fact that recalcitrants are usually state officials whose challenge to the Court may also threaten national supremacy, on which the president's own power rests.

Another part of the answer lies in the internal restraints to which all governmental officials are subject. Presidents, members of Congress, and most state officials take their oaths of office as seriously as do judges and are as devoted to preserving the political system. And an independent judiciary exercising judicial review is an integral part of that system. Closely related is the fact that public officials often feel they *ought* to obey Supreme Court decisions even when they disagree with them. There are, of course, limits on how far officials will go in following a judicial decision—limits determined partly by officials' guesses about how far their constituents will push them or let them go.

In short, Supreme Court justices and other public officials are commonly products of the same general culture—the white upper-middle class—and of the same political subculture—professional politicians. They share beliefs in the "rules of the game" and existing governmental processes. Presidents, senators, congressmen, and justices are also held together by the bond of all being officers of the *federal* government.

Furthermore, because of the frequency with which vacancies occur on the Court (about once every twenty-seven months), it is usual for at least a sizable minority, if not a majority, of the justices to be quite sympathetic with the goals of an administration. Bitter disagreements may arise, as in the early 1800s or the mid-1930s, when a majority of the justices are from a different political generation from that of the president and a majority of the Congress. More likely to occur are difficulties with state officials whose local orientation may put them out of the mainstream of national politics.

Other prudential concerns may deter Congress and the president from using their weapons against the Court. The president and Congress are inevitably rivals for power, and each may need the Court to check the other. Because of the president's easy access to mass media, legislators may believe that by crushing judicial power they would give the chief executive the upper hand in that rivalry. Even when they agree with him on substantive issues, they may feel that a strong judicial check on the White House protects legislative power. In 1937, for instance, many liberal Democrats who had been foes of the Supreme Court attacked Roosevelt's plan to add six new justices. These people sensed what one of FDR's advisers put into words: "If the President wins the court fight, everything will fall into his basket."[15]

Moreover, either branch may need the justices, as John F. Kennedy and Lyndon Johnson did in the civil rights field, to help push the other into taking certain courses of action. The president and Congress may also need the Court to legitimize certain controversial policy decisions or to take the blame for failures to act.

As a result of all these factors, there has been intermittent guerrilla warfare between Congress and the Court and between the Court and the president, but not since Jefferson was in the White House have Congress and the president joined to launch a major attack against the justices, and even that alliance was short-lived. The three branches of government coexist, occasionally in harmony, more often in armed truce, even more frequently in competition, and sometimes in open conflict; but the conflict has typically been for limited objectives.

⭐ SUMMARY

This chapter has described a set of roles that Supreme Court justices and to some extent all federal judges play in the American political system. The Supreme Court is a legal tribunal operating within a flexible but still recognizable set of procedural rules; it is also a dispenser of justice as well as an interpreter of law; at the same time the Court is a coordinate branch of government responsible for helping shape public policy.

Like the president, Supreme Court justices simultaneously play many roles. *First*, they arbitrate disputes between individual citizens and thus often between conflicting social interests. *Second*, where public officials are involved in a case, the Supreme Court frequently defines boundaries of authority between various governmental agencies and between government and individual citizens. *Third*, in defining boundaries of public authority, the Supreme Court may not only check governmental power but also help legitimize controversial policies. *Fourth*, the justices supervise the federal judicial system, and even state judicial systems insofar as federal law is concerned. *Fifth*, in deciding cases, the Court often modifies existing rules or fashions new rules for new problems. Thus, the justices play a legislative role.

Sixth, like bureaucrats, Supreme Court justices may play a representational role in the sense of being "chosen from" rather than "acting for." Customs surrounding appointments require that the justices come from all sections of the country and that there usually be at least one Catholic and one Jew on the Court. The appointment of Thurgood Marshall probably began a tradition of having at least one black justice, just as Sandra Day O'Connor's appointment in 1981 shows that women have won token representation.

The Court may perform an additional representational function by providing a forum for those who have no real access to other governmental processes. The justices may also play an ancillary representational role by protecting the integrity of the electoral processes, by safeguarding, as in the white primary cases,[16] the rights of racial minorities to vote, or, as in the reappointment decisions,[17] the right of every person to have his or her vote counted equally with those of every other citizen.

Seventh, by the opinions they write, the justices may help educate the public at large and governmental officials in particular. These opinions may be read only by a cluster of lawyers, public officials, newsmen, scholars, and students experiencing the joys of political science courses. Yet, because these people also write and talk, a general idea of what courts do percolates through some of the community. And knowledge that the justices have declared that the Constitution permits or forbids certain kinds of policies may well affect public attitudes. Like the presidency, the Supreme Court can be a "great pulpit" in American politics. Here, incidentally, may be the most important legacy of the Court under Chief Justice Earl Warren (1954–1969): It reminded Americans of the basic concepts like democracy, constitutionalism, and equality that underlie their political system.

The justices may play these roles well or badly. The Dred Scott Case[18] held in 1857 that Congress could not prohibit slavery in the territories; and what the justices thought would stabilize the Union by ending the divisive debate on slavery helped bring on the Civil War. The School Segregation Cases,[19] on the other hand, supplied a much-needed sermon that free government cannot rest on a caste society.

Three points are fundamental: First, the justices play these roles whether they want to or not. As Justice Robert H. Jackson once said, "We act in these matters not by authority of our competence but by force of our commissions."[20] A decision that school segregation was constitutional would have had different but no less important political effects from those of the actual decision.

Second, the direction that Supreme Court decisions take and the persuasiveness and persistence with which the Court pushes its jurisprudence are highly dependent on the values, talents, and courage of the justices themselves. Neither precedents nor procedural rules predetermine the course the Court will follow, and rarely do statutes or the precise words of the constitutional document. All of these usually permit choice.

Third, a judicial decision is not necessarily final. New statutes, new constitutional amendments, even new judges are practical possibilities. The American political system forces judges to participate in policy making and requires them to share power not only with each other but also with a large number of other public officials.

NOTES

1. Quoted in Alpheus T. Mason, *The Supreme Court: Palladium of Freedom* (Ann Arbor: University of Michigan Press, 1962), p. 72.
2. These early cases are discussed in Charles Warren, *The Supreme Court in United States History* (Boston: Little, Brown, 1922), Chapter 1. The most important decisions were: *United States v. Yale Todd*, decided in 1794 but not officially reported until 1852, 13 Howard 52; *Hylton v. United States*, 3 Dallas 171 (1796); and *Calder v. Bull*, 3 Dallas 386 (1798).
3. 1 Cranch 137 (1803).
4. *Annals of Congress*, 7th Cong., 1st Sess., p. 179.
5. *Little v. Barreme*, 2 Cranch 170 (1804).
6. James D. Richardson, ed., *A Compilation of the Messages and Papers of the Presidents* (Washington: Bureau of National Literature and Art, 1908), II, 582.
7. 4 Wheaton 316 (1819).
8. Richardson, *A Compilation of the Messages and Papers of the Presidents*, VI, 9.
9. U.S. Senate, Subcommittee on Separation of Powers, *Hearings: The Supreme Court*, 90th Cong., 2d Sess. (1968), p. 130.
10. Walter F. Murphy and Joseph Tanenhaus, "Public Opinion and the United States Supreme Court," in Joel Grossman and Joseph Tanenhaus, eds., *Frontiers of Judicial Research* (New York: John Wiley and Sons, 1969), p. 273; Murphy, Tanenhaus, and Daniel L. Kastner, *Public Evaluations of Constitutional Courts* (Beverly Hills, Cal.: Sage Publications, 1973).
11. Robert A. Dahl, "Decision-Making in a Democracy: The Supreme Court as a National Policy-Maker," *Journal of Public Law*, VI (1957), 279; and Charles L. Black, Jr., *The People and the Court* (New York: Macmillan, 1960), Chapter 3.
12. *Pennsylvania v. Nelson*, 350 U.S. 497 (1956). See also *Brotherhood of Railroad Trainmen v. Howard*, 343 U.S. 768 (1952), and *Sullivan v. Little Hunting Park*, 396 U.S. 229 (1969).
13. For a discussion of the group phase of decision making on the Supreme Court, see Walter F. Murphy, *Elements of Judicial Strategy* (Chicago: University of Chicago Press, 1964), Chapters 3 and 7.
14. Robert A. Dahl and Charles E. Lindblom, *Politics, Economics, and Welfare* (New York: Harper, 1953), p. 342.

15. The statement was by Thomas Corcoran, quoted in Louis Koenig, *The Invisible Presidency* (New York: Holt, Rinehart and Winston, 1960), p. 286.
16. *Smith v. Allwright*, 321 U.S. 649 (1944); and *Terry v. Adams*, 345 U.S. 461 (1953).
17. See Chapter 15 for a listing and discussion of these cases.
18. *Dred Scott v. Sandford*, 19 Howard 393 (1857).
19. *Brown v. Board of Education*, 347 U.S. 483 (1954).
20. *West Virginia v. Barnette*, 319 U.S. 624, 640 (1943).

SELECTED BIBLIOGRAPHY

Beveridge, Albert J. *The Life of John Marshall* (Boston: Houghton Mifflin, 1916), 4 vols. The first major biography of a Supreme Court justice: a classic of its kind.

Bickel, Alexander M. *The Supreme Court and the Idea of Progress* (New York: Harper & Row, 1970). A well-written evaluation of the work of the Warren Court by a former law clerk of Justice Felix Frankfurter.

Ely, John Hart, *Democracy and Distrust* (Cambridge, Mass.: Harvard University Press, 1980). An elegant but controversial effort to carve out a limited set of functions for the Supreme Court in the political system.

Friedman, Leon, and Fred L. Israel, eds. *The Justices of the United States Supreme Court 1789–1969: Their Lives and Major Opinions* (New York: Chelsea House, 1969). A 4-volume work containing a lengthy biographical article on each justice who sat from 1789 until 1969, with a reprinting of one or two of his most important opinions.

Freund, Paul A., ed. *History of the Supreme Court of the United States* (New York: Macmillan, 1971—). A projected 11-volume history of the Court, financed through a bequest of Justice Oliver Wendell Holmes. As of 1982, 4 volumes had been published, written by Charles Fairman; Julius Goebel, Jr.; Carl B. Swisher; and George L. Haskins and Herbert A. Johnson.

Harmon, M. Judd, ed. *Essays on the Constitution of the United States* (Port Washington, N.Y.: Kennikat Press, 1978). A collection of lectures by leading scholars on the work of the Supreme Court in interpreting the Constitution.

Jackson, Robert H. *The Supreme Court in the American System of Government* (Cambridge, Mass.: Harvard University Press, 1955). A justice's short, trenchant essays on his Court.

Kluger, Richard. *Simple Justice: The History of Brown v. Board of Education and Black America's Struggle for Equality* (New York: Alfred A. Knopf, 1976). By focusing on the School Segregation Cases, Kluger shows the way the Court functions in the political system.

Mason, Alpheus T. *Harlan Fiske Stone: Pillar of the Law* (New York: Viking, 1956; and *William Howard Taft: Chief Justice* (New York: Simon and Schuster, 1965). Two richly detailed political studies of chief justices by a masterly biographer.

McCloskey, Robert G. *The American Supreme Court* (Chicago: University of Chicago Press, 1960). A superb historical introduction to the work of the Court.

Murphy, Walter F. *Congress and the Court* (Chicago: University of Chicago Press, 1962). A case study of efforts in the 1950s to curb the Supreme Court.

———. *Elements of Judicial Strategy* (Chicago: University of Chicago Press, 1962). An analysis of the political power of the Supreme Court, based on the private papers of several justices.

Pritchett, C. Herman. *The Roosevelt Court: A Study in Judicial Politics and Values, 1937–1947* (New York: Macmillan, 1948). A path-breaking study of decision making in the Supreme Court.

Vose, Clement E. *Caucasians Only: The Supreme Court, the NAACP, and the Restrictive Covenant Cases* (Berkeley: University of California Press, 1959). An interesting account of how a pressure group utilized judicial power to achieve one of its goals.

Woodward, Bob, and Scott Armstrong. *The Brethren* (New York: Simon and Schuster, 1979). A best-selling effort to present an "inside" account of the Court from 1969 to 1976, heavily based on gossip among and leaks from law clerks, some of which is accurate.

PART VII

Civil Liberties

15 Civil Liberties

Chapters 6–14 centered on various political processes and particular governmental institutions. In discussing topics like campaigning, electoral behavior, and lobbying, we occasionally alluded to such issues of civil liberties as the right to vote and petition government. Chapters 15 and 16 focus directly on constitutional rights. This chapter examines some of the freedoms that judicial decisions have singled out as "fundamental"—for instance, rights to speak out on public issues, to worship (or not worship) as one deems appropriate, and to enjoy privacy. Chapter 16 analyzes the rights of persons accused of crime.

★ THE HISTORIC AMERICAN CONCEPT OF RIGHTS

Every American schoolchild can repeat from memory the second paragraph of the Declaration of Independence:

> We hold these truths to be self-evident, that all men are created equal, that they are endowed by their Creator with certain unalienable rights, that among these are life, liberty, and the pursuit of happiness. That to secure these rights, governments were instituted among men, deriving their just powers from the consent of the governed, that whenever any form of government becomes destructive of those ends, it is the right of the people to alter or abolish it. . . .

In these two sentences, Jefferson succinctly outlined the essential elements of a political philosophy around which the new nation should be organized: (1) by their human nature, not by the gift of society or government, *all* men have certain fundamental, *"natural" rights*; (2) men created government to protect those rights; and (3) thus, respect for and protection of natural rights form a standard by which to judge the legitimacy of governmental action, and habitual governmental abuse of those rights gives citizens the right, if not the duty, to overthrow that government.

The proximate sources of the idea of natural rights included Sir Edward Coke (1552–1634) and Sir William Blackstone (1723–1780), authors of treatises on English law that were required reading—often the *only* required reading—for fledgling lawyers in colonial America. Coke and, less consistently, Blackstone argued that no act of government could validly abridge natural law or natural rights. British political philosophers, most prominently John Locke (1632–1704), more systematically linked natural rights with limited government. Widely read in the colonies, they acted as spiritual godfathers to the Revolution.

For Americans of the eighteenth century no less than of the twentieth, civil liberties were to be enjoyed for their own sake or as means to achieve other ends. Without rights to enjoy privacy, to write, talk, and associate with others, to worship or not worship, to own and use property, and to be secure from arbitrary arrest and imprisonment, the good life, however defined, would be impossible. Actually, writers of the seventeenth and eighteenth centuries were apt to place heaviest emphasis on the right to property. For them, however, "property" usually had a broader scope than it does in current usage, closer in meaning to what chemists call "the properties" of a particular element. Property included not only tangible things like land and buildings but intangibles as well. Thus, Chief Justice John Marshall could speak of freedom of the press as a "property" of newspapers.

The doctrine of natural rights also formed an important theoretical cornerstone to the concepts of constitutionalism and of limited government that we discussed in Chapter 3. Any successfully asserted claim to individual rights limits governmental authority. Freedom to speak and to write, for instance, permits self-expression, essential to individual autonomy.

Moreover, this right, along with freedom of assembly, provides a legitimate means of organizing opposition to challenge and perhaps unseat incumbents. In this sense, freedom of communication and association is also essential to democracy. If opposition is illegal, if alternative policies cannot be formulated, defended, and tested in the electoral process, then democracy cannot exist. The right to discuss public affairs, Justice Oliver Wendell Holmes once said, "is more than self-expression; it is the essence of self-government"[1] In a similar fashion, other protections, such as a fair, public trial by jury in a criminal case, function not merely to defend the rights of a particular person but also to protect society as a whole from overzealous or corrupt officials.

But civil liberty also depends on governmental power. Without a government sufficiently strong to keep the peace and protect people from fellow citizens who feel little moral restraint in taking what they want, real freedom is impossible. On the other hand, possession of physical force can tempt governmental officials to use their power for personal benefit. The history of Nazis and Fascists in Germany, Italy, and Spain provides ample evidence of the dangers from unchecked "defenders of the people," evidence as brutal as the record of Stalinism in the Soviet Union.

Protecting civil liberties thus poses a delicate problem of blending freedom with governmental power. "It is a melancholy reflection," James Madison wrote to Jefferson in 1788, "that liberty should be equally exposed to danger whether the Government have too much or too little power, and that the line which divides these extremes should be so inaccurately defined by experience."[2]

The Bill of Rights

The original Constitution did not contain a bill of rights, although it did provide some explicit protections for individuals. Article I forbids states to pass bills of attainder, ex post facto laws (defined in Chapter 3), or laws "impairing the obligation of contracts." Article IV provides that citizens of each state are entitled to "all privileges and immunities of citizens in the several states"—a vague clause that might have been shorthand for the contemporary doctrine of natural rights.

Article I also forbids Congress to enact bills of attainder or ex post facto laws, or to suspend the writ of habeas corpus*—the common law's basic protection against arbitrary arrest and imprisonment—unless "when in cases of rebellion or invasion the public safety may require it." Article III guarantees trial by jury in federal criminal cases, narrowly defines treason, and outlaws the British practice of punishing a traitor's family.

These protections were hardly trivial, but they did not guard the sweep of what contemporaries thought were natural rights or even historic legal rights. The framers' primary justification for the omissions was that the Constitution gave the federal government no authority to violate these rights. They also argued that to try to list such rights would be dangerous, because if one were accidentally omitted, officials might later deny its existence. Moreover, Madison and some of his colleagues believed that the Constitution's complex system of pitting power against power and ambition against ambition better protected civil liberties than would the "parchment barriers" of a bill of rights.

But, bowing to pressure from those who objected strenuously to the absence of a bill of rights, the First Congress proposed twelve amendments to the Constitution. The states ratified ten of these, and collectively they have become known as the Bill of Rights. (Inclusion of the Ninth Amendment—"enumeration . . . of certain rights, shall not be construed to deny or disparage others retained by the people"—was an attempt to meet the problems of possible omissions.)

Madison continued to believe that the Constitution's complex institutional structure of shared powers would provide as effective armor for civil liberties; but he argued for the amendments because they would serve to educate (modern social scientists would say "socialize") citizens about the sacredness of their fundamental rights. In addition, like Jefferson, Madison stressed that a written bill of rights would encourage judges to protect civil liberties.

---

* A *writ of habeas corpus* (literally, "if you have the body") is an order from a court directing a jailer or other official who is holding a prisoner to bring that person before the court and justify his detention.

And, indeed, American judges have come to "consider themselves in a peculiar manner the guardians of those rights," though they have not always functioned as an "impenetrable bulwark" against popular frenzy or governmental arrogance. To understand civil liberties in the United States, one must begin by learning what judges—especially justices of the U.S. Supreme Court—have said about them. As we have already seen, decisions and opinions of the Supreme Court can exert a powerful influence on the policies governmental officials pursue and, by helping to shape the general political culture, can affect the ways in which individual citizens think and behave. But a Supreme Court ruling seldom immediately settles a policy problem. Before a problem is solved—or outlived—Congress, executive officials, state and local officers, and many private citizens usually become involved.

States and the Bill of Rights

Most provisions of the Bill of Rights are general enough to prohibit state as well as federal action. But there was a widespread assumption that they would restrict only the *federal* government. In 1833, speaking for a unanimous Court in *Barron v. Baltimore*, Chief Justice John Marshall wrote that assumption into constitutional law.[3] As we shall see, however, in this century the justices have used the Fourteenth Amendment to revise Marshall's holding.

It did not follow, however, even from *Barron*, that individuals—at least white individuals—were at the mercy of state officials. First of all, most states had their own bills of rights. Second, many judges reiterated the notion of natural rights as a positive limit on government—although in keeping with the Constitution's compromise they usually exempted slavery from its reach.

After the doctrine of natural rights had begun to wane, the Fourteenth Amendment—ratified in 1868—became a part of the Constitution, and it specifically restricted state power. Its second sentence reads:

> No State shall make or enforce any law which shall abridge the privileges and immunities of citizens of the United States; nor shall any State deprive any person of life, liberty, or property, without due process of law; nor deny to any person within its jurisdiction the equal protection of the laws.

Gradually that sentence, especially its second clause, became a protection against state and local efforts to regulate business and property, with "property" taking on the rather narrow modern usage. (It should be kept in mind in this discussion that, in terms of constitutional law, there are only two levels of government, state and federal. All city, county, or other local officials are *state* officers.)

Nevertheless, for many decades the Supreme Court continued to follow Marshall's ruling that the Bill of Rights limited only the federal government. It did, however, provide broad protection against state action for rights relating to tangible property or freedom to contract to buy, sell, or lease one's goods or labor. These rights, the Court said, fell within the specific terms of the Fourteenth Amendment's clause forbidding states to deny any person rights to "life, liberty, or property without due process of law."

Then in 1925, without warning, the Court held that the "liberty" guaranteed by the "due process" clause of the Fourteenth Amendment included freedom of speech.[4] In the 1930s, the Court included freedom of religion and, although only under limited conditions, a right to free legal counsel. In 1937, speaking through Justice Benjamin Cardozo, the Court offered a justification for its process of "selective incorporation." Some rights are

> of the very essence of a scheme of ordered liberty. . . . If the Fourteenth Amendment has absorbed them, the process of absorption has had its source in the belief that neither liberty nor justice would exist if they were sacrificed. . . . This is true, for illustration, of freedom of thought and speech. Of that freedom one may say that it is the matrix, the indispensable condition of nearly every other form of freedom.[5]

Shortly thereafter, Justice Hugo Black claimed that the Fourteenth Amendment incorporated *all* of the Bill of Rights. Much of his reasoning was based on what he thought was the intent of the framers of the Fourteenth Amendment, but he also argued that "selective incorporation" gave too much power to judges. The Bill of Rights itself listed those rights essential and unessential to "ordered liberty." The Supreme Court has never accepted Black's reasoning, but it has gone beyond the substantive results he urged. "Selective incorporation" now encompasses all of the first nine amendments except the requirements of indictment by grand jury and trial by jury in civil cases where the amount in controversy exceeds $20. Moreover, the Court has included in "due process" some rights not specifically listed in the Constitution, such as privacy, bodily integrity, a presumption of innocence, and freedom to travel within the country.

★ FUNDAMENTAL SUBSTANTIVE RIGHTS

Civil liberties are at once values in themselves and limitations on government. Some rights partake more of one character than the other, although it is not always easy to tell which function they may be performing at any given moment. This section looks at several fundamental rights that are more values in themselves—the intangible goods of individual liberty which constitutionalism seeks to protect. The next sections analyze rights that operate more to restrict government.

The Right to Be Free

Slavery blatantly contradicted constitutionalism and natural rights. In fact, Jefferson's early drafts of the Declaration of Independence had indicted the slave trade as "execrable commerce" that "waged cruel war against human nature itself, violating it's [sic] most sacred rights of life and liberty." But, fearful of alienating southerners, he removed those sentences. Adoption of the Thirteenth Amendment in 1865 ended slavery as a legal institution, although twelve decades later the country still suffers from its wounds.

The Thirteenth Amendment is the only provision of the Constitution that operates against private citizens as well as against governmental officials. In practice, relatively few controversies have arisen under this amendment; those that have come up have centered on "involuntary servitude" rather than slavery. In 1867, Congress passed an act making it a federal crime to hold persons in peonage—" a status or condition of compulsory service, based upon the indebtedness of the peon to the master." Thus, attempts to force anyone to work off a debt are illegal.

Compulsory military service contains an element of involuntary servitude; but in 1917 a unanimous Supreme Court held that "contributing to the defense of the rights and honor of the nation" is a citizen's "supreme and noble duty."[6] While this decision is still ruling law, the Supreme Court in 1968 struck down as "blatantly lawless" a local draft board's revocation of an exemption because the man had turned in his registration card in protest against the war in Vietnam.[7]

Integral parts of the basic right to freedom itself are protection against arbitrary arrest and presumption of innocence. Habeas corpus, explicitly guaranteed by Article I of the Constitution, guards against capricious arrest, but no constitutional clause mentions the presumption of innocence. The Supreme Court, however, has held the latter to be so fundamental a right as to be included within the concept of due process.[8]

The Right to Citizenship

In a world of nation-states, citizenship is "the right to have rights."[9] To be deprived of citizenship can mean being condemned to the status of a perpetual nomad. "Stateless persons" can be deported at official whim. Because they have no passports, they often find themselves unable to travel—legally—to other countries. If they do manage to emigrate, they usually are not entitled to work or even remain in the host country for more than a few months.

The Fourteenth Amendment—aimed at the infamous *Dred Scott*[10] ruling that a black could not be an American citizen—opens with a straightforward sentence: "All persons born or naturalized in the United States, and subject to the jurisdiction thereof, are citizens of the United States and of the State wherein they reside." After some backing and filling, the Supreme Court has held that Congress may not remove a person's citizenship for any reason. An individual may voluntarily renounce it, but only by a clear, specific repudiation. Neither desertion from the armed forces in wartime, draft evasion, nor voting in a foreign election constitutes a clear repudiation.[11]

The Right to Travel

American citizenship, the Court has said, carries with it a right to travel within the United States, free from legal restrictions, and a similar right to travel abroad, subject only to carefully drawn provisions that involve the federal government's authority to regulate foreign commerce, control immigration, or conduct foreign relations.[12] The justices sustained, for example, revocation of a former CIA officer's passport after the agent announced he was going to travel around the world and expose American intelligence agents.[13]

The right to move freely within the United States means not only that a state may neither forbid nor regulate immigration from other states, but also that a state may not impose unreasonable disabilities on new arrivals. The Supreme Court has held unconstitutional state requirements for long periods of residence before a new member of the community can vote, receive welfare benefits, or have free hospital care.[14]

The Right to Equal Justice

The Constitution explicitly forbids only states, but not the federal government, to deny any person "the equal protection of the laws." Yet the right to equal treatment seems so basic that the Supreme Court has ruled that it is included in the concept of "due process" embodied in the Fifth Amendment and so limits federal no less than state power.[15]

Racial Equality. Blacks have been the most obvious, though by no means the only, victims of discriminatory governmental treatment. In 1896, the Supreme Court in *Plessy v. Ferguson* held that state laws requiring "separate but equal"[16] accommodations for the races satisfied the Fourteenth Amendment. Many decades elapsed before judges—and a longer time before other officials—took the second half of the formula seriously. By the late 1930s, however, the Supreme Court had begun undermining "separate but equal"; and when the fatal blow came in the School Segregation Cases of 1954,[17] the justices pointed to sixteen years

An employee of the Dallas Transit Company removes a sign requiring racially segregated seating from a bus following a 1956 ruling of the U.S. Supreme Court banning racial segregation on public transportation vehicles operating within a state. This decision (*Gale* v. *Browder*, 352 U.S. 903) was one of a number of court rulings which applied the basic doctrine of the school segregation cases of 1954 to other aspects of life. (United Press International)

of rulings that had chipped away the legal foundations of racial segregation. Despite judicial rulings and a bevy of important civil rights laws enacted by Congress, much racial discrimination still exists in private business and governmental policies, most obviously in continued segregation in public schools.

Its historic defense of equality notwithstanding, the Supreme Court has refused in several important ways to move against educational discrimination. First, a majority of the justices have held that states are not required to tackle problems of school desegregation on a metropolitan or regional basis unless all school districts in that area have discriminated. Thus the Court reversed a district judge's order the Michigan carry out desegregation by reassigning pupils not merely within the city of Detroit but also in surrounding suburbs.[18] Because Detroit itself is largely black, the Court's restriction of remedies to the city has made full school integration there impossible.

Second, *San Antonio v. Rodriguez* (1973) ruled that states need provide only a portion of the costs of education and can leave it to local communities to supplement these funds as best they can through property taxes.[19] This decision means that children in poorer areas run a substantial risk of receiving educations inferior to those of children in richer areas. In effect, the dissenters argued, *Rodriguez* changes the constitutional guarantee of "equal protection" to "minimal protection."

Unequal Justice and Disparities in Wealth. Other kinds of inequalities abound in the legal system. That system is slow, cumbersome, and costly. People with more skillful—and typically more expensive—attorneys have a decided advantage. The Supreme Court has tried to compensate by ruling that government must waive for the poor certain fees charged for use of the judicial system[20] and has held that in all serious criminal cases government must provide, free of charge, a lawyer if the defendant is too poor to afford his or her own.[21] But these attorneys, usually from legal aid bureaus, are often heavily overburdened. Moreover, although help from legal aid organizations is sometimes available to the poor, neither a state nor the federal government has a constitutional obligation to provide free counsel in civil cases.

Statutory Classifications and Equality of the Sexes. Perhaps the surest way to treat people unequally is to apply exactly the same rules to everyone in all situations. Laws that did not exempt paraplegics from the draft or that taxed poor orphans the same amount as millionaires would impose unequal as well as unfair burdens.

Judges have tried to formulate rules to sort out permissible from impermissible distinctions. In the late 1960s, the Supreme Court constructed a two-tiered test. One tier requires "strict scrutiny" by judges to make certain there is an essential connection between a "compelling public interest" and the classification. The other tier demands only a showing of a reasonable relation between the classification and a valid governmental purpose. The Court invokes "strict scrutiny" under either of two circumstances: (1) where a "fundamental" right such as freedom of speech is involved, or (2) where government uses a "suspect classification" such as race.

Coping with discrimination by sex has led the Court to create an intermediate tier of tests. Sex is not sufficiently suspect a classification to trigger "strict scrutiny," the justices have held; but neither is it so benign a distinction as to allow government to show only that its regulations are reasonable. Instead, the justices insist, such distinctions must serve "important governmental objectives" and also be "substantially related" to their achievement.[22] Defeat of the proposed constitutional amendment to outlaw discrimination because of sex is likely to impose an even heavier burden on the Court to formulate rules to distinguish between permissible and impermissible legal distinctions between men and women.

Affirmative Action. Racial classification can be used for "benign" as well as for harmful purposes. The effects of centuries of discrimination against certain minorities, especially blacks, Hispanics, and Indians, still persist, often making it difficult for many of these people to compete on equal terms with members of the white middle and upper classes. To help undo the effects of legally sanctioned segregation, the Supreme Court has on occasion ordered states to take race into account in assigning teachers and pupils to schools. Furthermore, Congress requires institutions receiving money from federal agencies to institute plans of *affirmative action;* that is, to go beyond mere passive policies that do not discriminate, and actively recruit members of minorities. Some states have enacted similar requirements for their own agencies and private organizations, and many private institutions and businesses have, on their own, begun such programs.

The most famous legal test of affirmative action came in *California v. Bakke* (1978).[23] There, the medical school of the University of California at Davis set aside sixteen of the one hundred places in each entering class for members of certain minority groups. To fill these places, the school imposed far less rigorous standards than it applied to whites. For example, it demanded that whites score in the upper 5 percent of the country on standardized tests of verbal and scientific aptitude but admitted blacks and Hispanics whose scores placed them in the lower half (and sometimes lower third).

Allan Bakke, a white male who was twice rejected at Davis even though he scored in the upper 4 percent on the aptitude tests and had college grades far above those of most members of minority groups Davis accepted, sued in a state court for admission. Eventually, California's supreme court ordered him admitted, holding that Davis's plan violated both the Fourteenth Amendment and the provision of the U.S. Civil Rights Act of 1964 forbidding institutions receiving federal money to discriminate because of race.

The university appealed to the U.S. Supreme Court. The justices divided in a bizarre 4–4–1 fashion. Four refused to reach the constitutional question; they thought that the Civil Rights Act of 1964 clearly outlawed the school's plan. Thus they voted to order Bakke admitted. Four others thought the Civil Rights Act encouraged rather than forbade such programs. Furthermore, they thought that Bakke lost on constitutional grounds as well. They reasoned that, in light of the extensive history of denials of equal opportunity in education, a state

> may adopt race-conscious programs if the purpose of such programs is to remove the disparate racial impact its actions might otherwise have and if there is reason to believe that the disparate impact is itself the product of past discrimination, whether its own or that of society at large.

This 4–4 division made the views of the ninth justice, Lewis F. Powell, critical. On the one hand, he agreed with the four justices who thought that the Civil Rights Act of 1964 did not outlaw Davis's plan. On the other hand, he agreed with the four who thought Davis had violated the Fourteenth Amendment. By allowing members of certain minorities to compete for a hundred places and Bakke for only eighty-four, Davis had denied him an equal chance solely because of his race. "The guarantee of equal protection," Powell wrote, "cannot mean one thing when applied to one individual and something else when applied to a person of another color."

But even the issue of affirmative action was not settled. Powell carefully added that he did not think that affirmative action was of itself necessarily unconstitutional. The fatal flaw in Davis's plan was that race *automatically* blocked applicants from being considered for certain places. Later cases have not done much to clarify the situation,[24] though they have sustained other, less sweeping plans for affirmative action.

The Right to Freedom of Religion

When Madison proposed a bill of rights in 1789, he especially wanted to protect "liberty of conscience." In final form, however, what became the First Amendment read: "Congress shall make no law respecting an establishment of religion, or prohibiting the free exercise thereof. . . ."

There are two separate provisions here, one relating to "establishment of religion," the other to "free exercise." In many disputes the two are closely linked and sometimes demand opposite policies. For example, a draftee may need a chaplain in order to practice his religion. On the other hand, making chaplains military officers entangles government with religion. Similarly, either or both clauses may conflict with other constitutional guarantees. A statute that provides free bus transportation for all schoolchildren except those attending religious schools may deny those children "equal protection."

Anti-Establishment. For a time, the Supreme Court's practice was to speak dogmatically about "a wall of separation between church and state," but to act pragmatically. More recently, the justices have conceded that the Constitution does "not call for total separation between church and state; total separation is not possible in an absolute sense. Some relationship between government and religious organizations is inevitable."[25]

The Court has come to favor a flexible, three-pronged test to determine the constitutionality of governmental aid to religion: (1) the purpose of the aid must be secular, not religious; (2) the primary effect of the aid must not be to advance one religion or all religions; and (3) aid must not constitute "excessive entanglement" of the state in religious affairs. The Court has allowed government to supply free bus transportation[26] and textbooks[27] to parochial schoolchildren and to make funds available to church-affiliated colleges and universities.[28] On the other hand, the justices have found "excessive entanglement" in a state's paying a portion of the salaries of parochial schoolteachers to teach such subjects as mathematics or science.[29]

Efforts to integrate religious training into curricula of public schools have had a mixed judicial reception. In 1948, the Court invalidated a "released time" program for religious instruction[30] under which unpaid volunteers from local churches taught on school property children whose parents wanted them to have such training. Four years later, however, the Court upheld a plan similar in almost all respects except that instructions were given off school property.[31]

The justices have also struck down requirements for prayers and/or Bible reading in public schools, even programs that excused students whose parents so requested.[32] The Court's general approach has been that government "should stay out of the business of writing or sanctioning official prayers and leave that purely religious function to the people themselves and to those the people choose to look to for religious guidance."[33]

Free Exercise. The earliest case in which the Supreme Court considered free exercise of religion involved an act of Congress outlawing polygamy in the territories. The statute was directed against Mormons, but in 1879 the Court sustained its validity, distinguishing between the right to *believe*, which was absolute, and the right to *act*, which was subject to normal criminal law.[34] Sixty-seven years later, the Court held that a federal anti-prostitution statute could legitimately be applied to Mormons practicing polygamy.[35]

Sunday-closing laws have also raised questions relating both to establishment—sanctioning the Christian day of rest—and of free exercise in that they force Jewish merchants to recognize the Christian sabbath and put them at a competitive disadvantage if they observe their own as well. The Court rejected both arguments,[36] but a few years later held that a state could not deny unemployment compensation to a Seventh Day Adventist who refused to accept a job that required work on Saturdays.[37]

Small religious sects have sometimes suffered from governmental regulations impinging on their rituals and taboos. The Jehovah's Witnesses have been especially active in bringing offending public officials into court, and their litigation in the 1940s helped develop much of the law of the First Amendment. The most notable victory of the Witnesses was over compulsory flag salutes. Because they take literally the biblical Commandment not to worship "graven images," the Witnesses refused to allow their children to participate in saluting the flag. In 1943 the

Supreme Court reversed an earlier ruling and held that such laws were unconstitutional interferences with religious freedom.[38]

Almost thirty years later, the Court sustained the right of the "old Order Amish" to take their children out of all schools after the eighth grade.[39] The justices reasoned that the state's interest in keeping children in school until they were sixteen was not sufficient to override the religious importance to the Amish of having their children immersed in the life of their own community, free from the "worldly" influences of modern society.

Conscientious objection presents more dramatic problems. Congress has allowed exemptions from military service to those who object to *all* war on religious grounds, and the Court has interpreted "religious" to encompass "philosophical" views and so to include atheists who object to all war.[40] Both Congress and the Court, however, have refused to exempt "selective conscientious objectors," that is, people whose religious tenets—such as those of Roman Catholics—allow them to participate only in "just wars."[41]

The Right to Privacy

Justice Louis D. Brandeis once spoke of "the right to be let alone" as "the most comprehensive of rights and the right most valued by civilized men."[42] But Brandeis spoke in dissent. Despite the Fourth Amendment's protection against "unreasonable searches and seizures," the Supreme Court did not recognize a general right to privacy until 1965. Then, in *Griswold v. Connecticut*,[43] a majority held that specific provisions of the Constitution had "penumbras"—shadowy regions next to specific things, here constitutional clauses. The right to privacy, Justice William O. Douglas said for the Court, grew not only out of the Fourth Amendment but also from the First Amendment's protection of freedom of religion and association, the Third's prohibition against quartering troops in civilian homes in time of peace, the Fifth's ban against self-incrimination, and the Ninth's sweeping maxim that the rights listed in the first eight amendments were not exhaustive of basic civil liberties.

The specific issue in *Griswold* was whether a state could punish a physician who advised married couples on contraception. The Court's answer was, of course, no. A few years later the justices struck down a Massachusetts statute that forbade distribution of contraceptives to unmarried people.[44] "If the right of privacy means anything," the majority held, "it is the right of the *individual,* married or single, to be free from unwarranted governmental intrusion into matters so fundamentally affecting a person as the decision whether to bear or beget a child."

The Court has also invoked the right of privacy to invalidate state laws that forbid abortions unless the health of the mother is seriously

DID YOU KNOW

This is how big you were when you were only 11 weeks old. From then on you breathed (fluid), swallowed, digested, urinated, and had bowel movements, slept, dreamed, and awakened, tasted, felt pain from touch and heat, reacted to light and noise, and were able to learn things.

After 11 weeks no new organs began functioning; you just grew more mature.

Reprinted with permission from *Did You Know?* (Hayes Publishing Co., Willke, Cincinnati, Ohio)

endangered: "The right of privacy is broad enough to encompass a woman's decision whether or not to terminate her pregnancy," at least during the first three months of that pregnancy. After that time, as the fetus becomes more and more capable of sustaining life on its own, the mother's right to privacy recedes and the state's interest in protecting life increases. "We therefore conclude," the majority said, "that the right of personal privacy includes the abortion decision, but that this right is not unqualified and must be considered against important state interests in regulation."[45]

The Court has also held that a married woman does not need her husband's consent to obtain an abortion nor a minor child her parents' consent,[46] though a state may require a doctor to inform the parents of a minor that she has asked for an abortion.[47] On the other hand, a majority of the justices have ruled that a state is not obliged, even under a general health plan for the poor, to provide free abortions for women who cannot afford the costs.[48]

The Right to Bodily Integrity

The justices have indicated that a right to bodily integrity exists; but, however fundamental, it is not absolute. The Court has sustained compulsory vaccinations even against a challenge by a man who had a history of allergic reactions to such measures,[49] upheld state authority to sterilize a feeble-minded young woman,[50] and validated obligatory blood tests for people accused of drunken driving.[51] On the other hand,

the Court has struck down a law imposing sterilization as a punishment for crime[52] and invalidated use by police of a stomach pump to obtain evidence from an accused.[53] There may be an intelligent way of reconciling these decisions, but no justice has yet had the imagination to do so.

★ BASIC RIGHTS: COMMUNICATION AND ASSOCIATION

We now turn to rights that are associated with democratic values in that they function to make government more responsive to its citizenry. We focus here on freedom of expression.

Because freedom of speech, press, assembly, association, and petition are vital to democratic political processes as well as being fundamental to self-expression, some justices have said that these rights deserve a "preferred position" in the Constitution's hierarchy of values. But no formula can solve all the problems that freedom of communication presents in a modern society. Even if rights to voice political opinions and join with others who share those opinions are absolutely necessary in a democracy, one still must confront questions about limits on such rights. Do those rights include a right to: urge violent destruction of the constitutional system? publish documents that contain military secrets? call a neighbor dirty names or print false stories about her life? screen movies or stage live shows involving performances of sexual intercourse?

All these questions basically ask at what point government may regulate rights of communication so as to protect other values. As would be expected from the diversity of American life, we have not one answer but many. In the cases after World War I, Justice Oliver Wendell Holmes proposed sustaining regulations of communication if what was spoken or written posed a "clear and present danger" to some important interest that government could protect.[54] In this test's first applications, the Court used it to justify sending people to jail for arguing that the draft was unconstitutional and that the United States should not intervene in the Russian civil war. Later, Holmes and Brandeis tried to refine "clear and present danger" to protect rather than threaten free speech. As Brandeis explained in 1927:

> Those who won our independence by revolution were not cowards. They did not fear political change. They did not exalt order at the cost of liberty. . . . [N]o danger flowing from speech can be deemed clear and present, unless the incidence of evil apprehended is so imminent that it may befall before there is opportunity for full discussion. If there be time to expose through discussion the falsehood and fallacies . . . the remedy to be applied is more speech, not enforced silence. Only an emergency can justify repression. . . .
>
> Moreover, even imminent danger cannot justify resort to prohibition of these functions essential to effective democracy, unless the evil apprehended is relatively serious. . . . The fact that speech is likely to result in some violence or in destruction of property is not enough to justify its suppression. There must be the probability of serious injury to the State.[55]

"The Constitution only covers freedom of speech, Senator....It doesn't guarantee anyone will listen."

Grin and Bear It, by Lichty and Wagner, © 1978 Field Enterprises, Inc. Courtesy of Field Newspaper Syndicate

In the 1930s and 1940s, the Court did occasionally use the test as Holmes and Brandeis wished; but by the early 1950s both those who were terrified by the specter of domestic communism and those who dismissed communist agitators as "miserable merchants of unwanted ideas" agreed that "clear and present danger" was not a useful rule to interpret the First Amendment. The former thought it was too restrictive of governmental power, the latter found it too restrictive of freedom of speech.

Since then judges and scholars have debated five general approaches to interpretation of the First Amendment. We shall briefly summarize each.

Preferred Position

In the 1930s,[56] Chief Justice Harlan Fiske Stone reasoned that, because freedom of expression is vital to the democratic process, it deserves special judicial protection—hence the term "preferred position." Where such rights are involved, Stone said, courts should relax the usual presumption of constitutionality accorded statutes and require government to justify any restrictions. (The similarity to the rule of "strict scrutiny" in equal protection is no accident; that rule, too, originates in Stone's work.)

Two very different kinds of objections have been lodged against this approach. First, the Constitution does not authorize judges to make distinctions in the importance of its various clauses. What rights a judge sees as "vital" or "fundamental" may be no more than personal value judgments. Second, the notion of a preferred position for First Amendment freedoms does not go far enough. That amendment does not say that Congress shall bear the burden of proof when it regulates freedom of speech or press; rather it says simply, "Congress shall make no law," none at all, regulating speech, press, petition, or religion.

Balancing

As the term implies, "balancing" calls for judges to weigh against one another the interests that compete in a case and determine which prevails, or perhaps how much of each can coexist. Specifically, such an approach requires judges to "balance" rights claimed under the First Amendment with other rights or with governmental authority— perhaps to maintain national security or preserve public peace.

There are immediate problems with this approach. The most serious is that no one has been able to explain and justify the weights that should be put on various interests, First Amendment or other. Nor has anyone explained how a judge's scale of values should be calibrated. Without such explanations and justifications, balancing may do no more than cloak judges' reading their own values into the Constitution.

Reasonableness

Another approach, often associated with Justice Felix Frankfurter, who served on the Court from 1939 until 1962, rejects the notion of judges' "preferring" or balancing rights in First Amendment cases. He agreed that often a balance must be struck. But in a democracy, he argued, the legislature must strike that balance, not the judiciary.

Courts are not representative bodies. They are not designed to be a good reflex of a democratic society. . . . Primary responsibility for adjusting the interests that compete . . . of necessity belongs to the Congress.[57]

Judges, he maintained, should only ensure that the "balance" that the legislature set is reasonable, not whether it is "correct" or the "best" of possible alternatives.

Critics have retorted that this approach turns courts into lunacy commissions, for judges could intervene only where they thought a legislature had acted irrationally. Others have pointed out that Frankfurter's approach would change the First Amendment to read:

Neither Congress nor the states shall make any law abridging the freedom of speech or press unless a majority of the appropriate legislature and the Supreme Court think such abridgment is reasonable.

Literalness

The simplest solution has been that of Hugo L. Black, who was an associate justice from 1937 to 1971:

My view is, without deviation, without exception, without any ifs, buts, or whereases, that freedom of speech means that government shall not do anything to people . . . either for the views they have or the views they express or the words they speak or write. . . . I simply believe that "Congress shall make no law" means that Congress shall make no law.[58]

Thus Black voted against governmental power to punish those who spoke in favor of violent overthrow of the constitutional order or who showed movies that many people thought obscene. He also voted against the right of individuals, private citizens as well as public officials, to sue anyone who wrote falsehoods about their character. "Our First Amendment," he summed up, "was a bold effort . . . to establish a country with no legal restrictions of any kind upon the subjects people could investigate, discuss and deny."[59]

But, critics point out, Black excluded action as well as "symbolic speech" from the First Amendment's protection. He thought that such "symbolic" acts of communication as picketing,[60] wearing armbands,[61] or burning a draft card[62] or an American flag[63] were not protected by the First Amendment. Black also voted to convict demonstrators for parading in an orderly fashion outside a courtroom.[64] "Justice cannot be rightly administered," he explained, "nor are the lives and safety of prisoners secure, when throngs of people clamor against the processes of justice outside the courthouse or jailhouse door."

These distinctions may be reasonable, but they imply that communication of ideas is not an absolute that should always take precedence over other values. Any distinction between words and deeds is very thin. Not only is the usual purpose of words to cause deeds—words are also "the triggers of action," Judge Learned Hand once wrote—but verbal persuasion is typically interlaced with symbols. The flag, the log cabin, the full dinner pail, Watergate, the donkey, the elephant, parades, and demonstrations express politically laden values.

Public versus Private Issues

Another approach, put forth by Professor Alexander Meiklejohn, combines literalness and reasonableness.[65] Insofar as *public issues* are involved, he asserted, officials must follow the words of the First Amendment and "make *no* law." Because freedom of communication is essential to self-government, it cannot legitimately be limited by governmental action. Only when political debate is completely unlimited can the people see all the alternatives and intelligently choose among them.

On the other hand, Meiklejohn argued, where no issues of public policy are involved but only issues of, say, obscenity or pornography, the true test of constitutionality is whether the means are reasonably related to a valid governmental purpose.

The obvious difficulty with this approach lies in drawing a line between public and private issues. What books people may read or movies they may see are inherently public issues. More specifically, sexual rules may be closely related both to a nation's general political culture and more specifically to how authoritarian or permissive it will be. Restrictions on discussions of sex limit debate on issues that are politically relevant and thus cut into self-government.

Judicial Practice

None of these approaches fully solves the problems of freedom of expression; indeed, each creates serious problems of its own. As one would thus expect, the Supreme Court has not followed a consistent doctrinal path, and most cases have provoked bitter dissents. As with controversies involving religion, the justices have acted more pragmatically than they have spoken. Still, outlines of different patterns dimly emerge for various subissues.

National Security. When national security has been involved, the justices have tended to balance—although still without telling us anything about the scale or the weights assigned to competing interests—government's authority to protect the political processes from violence against an individual's right to speak out.[66] Predictably, by stating the problem in this way, the Court has tended to decide in favor of restricting freedom.

Reputation and Free Press. When rights to freedom of the press (and less often freedom of speech) have conflicted with another person's right to privacy or a decent reputation, the justices have also been pragmatic. If the injured party has been a public official or a "public figure"—such as a labor-management negotiator or a noted football coach—the Court has allowed a suit for damages only on a showing that not only was the information false but the writer knew it was false or wrote it with reckless disregard for its truth or falsity. Political debate in a democracy, the Court has reasoned, must be "robust," and that debate would become tame and tepid with a constant threat of a lawsuit hanging over participants' heads.[67]

On the other hand, when the injured party has been a private citizen, the justices have said that the normal rules for slander (for damaging oral attacks) or libel (written slurs) should apply, providing that the writer or speaker can be shown to have been at fault.[68]

Obscenity and Pornography. Cases involving sex make fascinating reading but hard law. On the one hand, most judges accept the notion that freezing sexual morality exempts politically important matters from public choice. On the other hand, judges also know that many advocates of sexual freedom are hypocritically mouthing slogans to profit from pandering to lust. Thus judges have searched for "redeeming social value" in literature and movies that have been attacked as obscene or pornographic.

To say that the justices have been less than consistent in this area is a gross understatement. There is, however, some coherence. *Roth v. United States* (1957) forms a landmark because there the justices faced up to problems of definitions and tests.[69] They did not reject the old rule that obscenity is not constitutionally protected but emphasized that "sex and obscenity are not synonymous." They defined the latter term as "material which deals with sex in a manner appealing to prurient interest." Expressly denying that a book might be judged obscene because of isolated passages, the Court established a new test: "whether to the average person, applying contemporary community standards, the dominant theme of the material taken as a whole appeals to prurient interest."

For effort and courage *Roth* rates high marks, but not for clarity. "Prurient" as defined in contemporary dictionaries means "a restless craving" or "itching," and is hardly more clear than "obscene." Under Chief Justice Earl Warren (1953–1969) the Court wrestled with the problem of definition on several later occasions, but without much more success. The justices did say, however, that the way in which material was advertised might indicate whether its basic appeal was to prurient interest.[70]

The general approach of the Warren Court was to allow as little restriction as possible. In contrast, the Court under Chief Justice Warren

Burger has been less fearful of censorship and more concerned about stopping the spread of "immoral" ideas. *California v. LaRue* (1972) upheld state regulations banning "bottomless dancers" or acts of sexual intercourse in floor shows of establishments that sold liquor. The majority admitted that these regulations outlawed "some forms of visual presentation which would not be found obscene under *Roth* and subsequent decisions of the Court." Nevertheless, the justices found the state's interest in controlling alcoholic beverages—and the state's authority under the Twenty-first Amendment—sufficient to legitimize standards that could not be constitutionally applied in other situations.[71]

"THAT'S TO TAKE CARE OF OBSCENITY CASES"

From Herblock *On All Fronts* (New American Library, 1980)

What *LaRue* treated as an exceptional circumstance *Miller v. California* (1973) turned into a general rule to allow governmental officials to forbid commercial exploitation of sex or nudity or "patently offensive representations or descriptions of ultimate sexual acts, normal or perverted, actual or simulated."[72] Speaking for six justices, Burger reiterated that obscenity was not protected by the First Amendment and that whether a work was obscene was a question of fact:

> The basic guidelines for the trier of fact must be: (a) whether "the average person, applying contemporary community standards" would find that the work, taken as a whole, appeals to the prurient interest . . . (b) whether the work depicts or describes, in a patently offensive way, sexual conduct specifically defined by the applicable state law, and (c) whether the work, taken as a whole, lacks serious literary, artistic, political, or scientific value. . . .

"Contemporary community standards," the Chief added, are local, not national, and probably vary from area to area.[73]

Censorship. On one point, at least, there has historically been wide agreement: Freedom of speech and press protect against prior restraint, that is, against censorship. In some circumstances, most judges have said, a person may be held responsible for the effects of his or her words, but no one should have to submit the content of his or her communication to a censor for clearance. Yet enough cases—frequently decided by divided votes—crop up to indicate that censorship is more prevalent in the United States than fiercely libertarian judicial pronouncements would lead one to expect.

In 1931, *Near v. Minnesota* centered on a state law that branded as a public nuisance any periodical that regularly published obscene, lewd, or scandalous material. A district attorney obtained an injunction against future publication of *The Saturday Press*, a newspaper that mixed anti-Semitism with charges of corruption in Minneapolis politics. "This," a majority of the Supreme Court said about the injunction, "is the essence of censorship"; but four justices dissented.[74]

Problems of censorship have often arisen where towns require licenses for parades or public meetings. The Court has sustained such ordinances only where they contain non-discretionary regulations pertaining to the time, place, and manner of the demonstration. If the official has discretion to issue a permit to one group and deny it to another, the justices have struck down the ordinance.[75] It was these rulings that lower courts followed when in 1978 they invalidated efforts by officials in Chicago and Skokie, Illinois, to ban parades by neo-Nazis preaching racial and religious hatred.

The most famous of American disputes over censorship occurred in 1971, during the Vietnamese war, when several newspapers began publishing classified documents popularly known as "the Pentagon

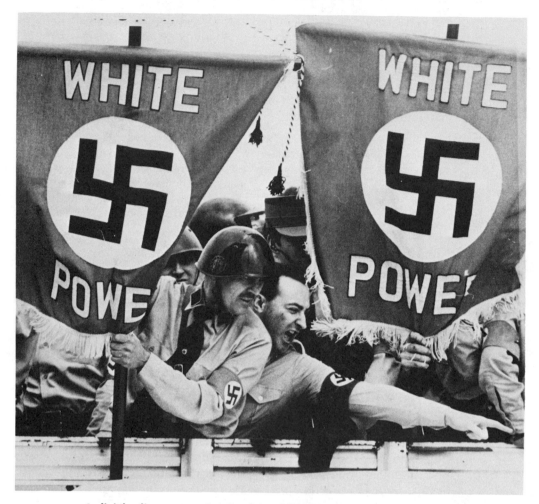

Judicial rulings protecting the right of potentially or actually oppressed groups to parade and demonstrate also protect those people who would deny others their civil rights. Here a group of Nazis proclaim their racial and religious bigotry in St. Louis in 1978. (United Press International)

Papers." Claiming that publication would endanger national security, the Department of Justice sought injunctions forbidding the newspapers to print the papers. The cases raced through the entire judicial process in eight days. Over protests from three justices against that feverish haste, the Court held there was a presumption that any previous restraint of expression was unconstitutional and that, in this instance, the government had not met the heavy burden of overcoming that presumption.[76]

Free Press and Fair Trial. The potential impact on jurors of newspaper stories or radio or television broadcasts poses a serious problem for justice. Here a defendant's right under the Sixth Amendment to a fair trial by an "impartial jury" may conflict with newspeople's rights under the First Amendment to publish information. On occasion the Supreme Court has reversed convictions when the justices have thought it probable that news media had so prejudiced a community that a panel of impartial jurors could not be chosen.[77]

The basic solution to excessive pretrial publicity lies in preventing police and prosecutors from giving information to reporters. Until that Eden arrives, a trial judge has several remedies, including delaying trial until passions have eased; allowing, if the defendant requests, the trial to be held in another community; and questioning potential jurors more closely than normal about possible prejudice. If the publicity continues during a trial at a pace that might affect jurors already chosen, the judge may order them isolated from the rest of the world, including their families, until they have reached a verdict.

In cases that are likely to provoke great notoriety, some judges have taken the further step of barring newsmen from hearings that precede the actual trial as well as from the trial itself, at times even forbidding reporters to write about the evidence. In 1976 the Supreme Court struck down such "gag" orders as prior restraints. Pointing out the range of lesser means available to protect jurors against prejudicial information, the Court held that only truly extraordinary circumstances could justify such censorship.[78] In 1980 the Court took the further step of declaring that public attendance at a criminal trial was a constitutionally protected right.[79]

Disclosure of Sources. Are reporters obliged to disclose their informants' names and testify about criminal activity of which they have knowledge? Many journalists have invoked the First Amendment as grounds for refusing to divulge such information, claiming that if they testify, future informants will be unwilling to provide the evidence from which convincing stories can be written and through which effective pressure can be brought to bear on government.

The issue is a delicate one. Without doubt, full disclosure can dry up many sources of news, especially where, as in the Watergate scandals, those sources are public officials who prudently fear reprisal by more powerful public officials. On the other hand, reporters have the same obligation as other citizens to cooperate with law enforcement agencies; and people do not become incorruptible when they become professional writers. The Supreme Court, by a 5–4 vote, has come down on the side of requiring journalists to reveal their sources.[80]

In 1978, the Supreme Court imposed an even more drastic restriction on the media. Believing that photographers for *The Stanford Daily*

"We find the defendant guilty as charged by the media."

had taken pictures that might identify people participating in a riot, police obtained a search warrant and went through the newspaper's files. The *Daily* argued that because no member of its staff was accused of aiding criminals, the proper procedure was for the police to obtain a subpoena ordering the editors to produce in court any pictures of the riots contained in their files. The danger, the paper pointed out, of having police go through the files was that they might learn the identities of informants for other stories not related to crimes and curb reporters' ability to get at the truth about official conduct and thus limit the public's right to know.

A narrow five-judge majority brushed aside this argument and held that "valid warrants to search property may be issued when it is satisfactorily demonstrated to a magistrate that fruits, instrumentalities, or evidence of crime is located on the premises."[81] That the premises were those of a newspaper was irrelevant.

☆ THE DARKER SIDE OF CIVIL LIBERTIES

Americans have taken great pride in their freedom to vote; to criticize governmental officials; to form, join, and leave associations and political parties; to speak out on religion or politics or anything else that interests them. Americans have also felt secure from the prying eyes of government's spies. They have believed that their government would let them alone unless they committed some act that was defined by law as criminal. The notion of constitutional liberty—"a government of laws and not of men"—has been a long-standing national ideal.

In some measure, this pride has been justified. Americans enjoy a far greater range and depth of civil liberties than do citizens of communist countries or rightist dictatorships. But some of that pride, the scandals of Watergate (1972–1974) showed, was inflated. Even more ominously, some of Watergate's uglier violations of constitutional rights were common practices, and many are perhaps still corroding ideals of freedom.

At least since the 1930s, several federal agencies have been systematically spying on American citizens, opening their mail, tapping their telephones, "bugging" their homes, hotel rooms, and offices, and in several instances kidnapping and threatening them with bodily injury. The information so obtained has been carefully retained in computers' memories. During the mid-1970s the Federal Bureau of Investigation alone was keeping files on more than a half-million Americans.

The people subjected to these sorts of crimes have generally not been spies, terrorists, or even Mafiosi, but law-abiding citizens whose political views and activities did not conform to what officials of the FBI, the Central Intelligence Agency, the National Security Agency, or the Internal Revenue Service thought "proper." For instance, FBI operatives infiltrated the Women's Liberation Movement and manfully recorded names of people who were so brazen as to attend meetings.

In carrying out such policies, the FBI frequently resorted to burglary, or, as the bureau called it, "black bagging." Between 1960 and 1966, for example, agents robbed offices of the Socialist Workers Party more than ninety times. And President Reagan, despite pronouncements about restoring respect for law and order, pardoned the FBI agents convicted of these crimes.

In another instance, FBI agents carried on a concerted campaign to destroy the reputation of the Reverend Martin Luther King, Jr., the great black civil rights leader. Recognizing King's magnetic attraction to blacks and white liberals, J. Edgar Hoover, then Director of the FBI, reasoned that if King abandoned his advocacy of nonviolence and brotherly love he could lead a revolution. Therefore, Hoover concluded, the smart tactic would be to discredit King so that he could never pose a threat.

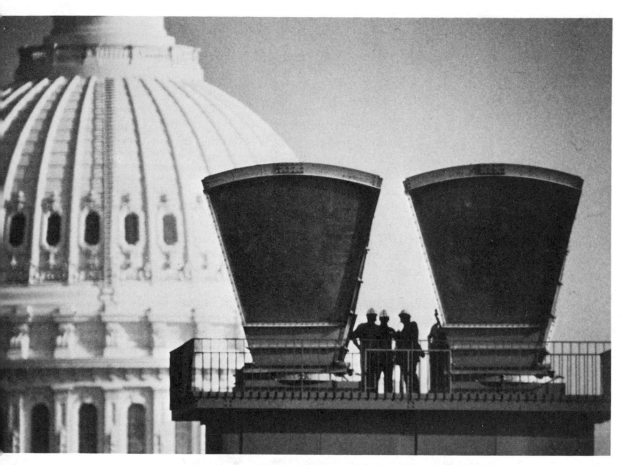

In the shadow of the Capitol, federal officials guard microwave towers used in the interception of private communications. (AT&T)

"No holds were barred," the investigator in charge of the operation stated. FBI men followed King, tapped his telephone, and bugged his hotel rooms. They even threatened to make public an allegedly damaging tape recording unless he committed suicide.[82]

The Internal Revenue Service ran its own criminal operations. Ignoring the law that requires tax returns of citizens to be kept confidential, the IRS speedily opened its records to almost any federal official—and many state officers—who asked for them. The IRS also conducted special audits of individuals of whose political views the service disapproved—in addition to cooperating with the White House to harass Richard Nixon's political opponents and with the FBI to keep its critics busy arguing with accountants.

Some of these officials have been overzealous. They have rightly feared organizations, like the Weathermen and Black Panthers, that advocated and practiced violence. But as Justice Louis Brandeis warned a half century ago, "Men feared witches and burnt women."[83] These particular men began by fearing spies and terrorists and ended by violating the rights of those who dared to think political thoughts different from those of leaders of the FBI, the CIA, or the IRS.

Other officials have merely been corrupt. They have leaped at an opportunity to advance their careers by obtaining information that might please their superiors. Their oaths to uphold the law faded before the chance for advancement. Testifying before a Senate committee, William Sullivan, Assistant Director of the FBI, conceded that the Bureau's

---

TABLE 15-1 **Uncle Sam Has His Eye on You**

	Files on People	
In thousands of computers and elsewhere, the federal government keeps track of Americans. Within these systems, at last count, were 3,529,743,665 files related to everything from payrolls to Social Security data to criminal charges to loans and grants—most available at the touch of a button.	Departments of Education and Health and Human Services	1,033,999,891
	Department of Treasury	780,196,929
	Department of Commerce	431,427,589
	Department of Defense	333,951,949
	Department of Justice	201,474,342
	Department of State	110,809,198
	Department of Agriculture	33,727,730
	Copyright Office	28,408,366
	Department of Transportation	24,023,142
	Federal Communications Commission	20,870,078
	Department of Housing and Urban Development	20,340,642
	Department of Labor	16,785,015
	Department of the Interior	16,708,016
	Office of Personnel Management	16,016,779
	Department of Energy	8,929,999
	Executive Office of the President	30,655
	All other federal agencies	452,043,345
	Grand total	3,529,743,665
		Or 15 files on average for each American

SOURCE: Reprinted from *U.S. News & World Report.* Copyright 1982 *U.S. News & World Report.* Basic data: Office of Management and Budget.

---

effort to "get" Martin Luther King "is not an isolated phenomenon . . . this was a practice of the Bureau down through the years. I might say it often became a real character assassination." Sullivan added:

> . . . never once did I hear anybody, including myself, raise the question, is this course of action which we have agreed upon lawful, is it legal, is it ethical or moral? We never gave any thought to this realm of reasoning. . . .[84]

One result of governmentally sponsored crime could be cynicism about honesty in politics and, far worse, perhaps even disdain for honesty and decency themselves. As Justice Brandeis noted:

> Our Government is the potent, the omnipresent teacher. For good or for ill, it teaches the whole people by its example. Crime is contagious. If the government becomes a lawbreaker, it breeds contempt for law; it invites every man to become a law unto himself; it invites anarchy.[85]

Most important, these criminal activities could impose a "chilling effect" on political freedom—a fear that to join unpopular organizations or to voice unorthodox ideas will bring harassment by tax investigators, invasions of privacy by FBI agents, and perhaps even blackmail. To the extent that people do not exercise their constitutional rights because of fear of governmental repression, both the First Amendment and the cherished ideals of the American political tradition will shrink.

 ## SUMMARY

This chapter has presented a double, even schizophrenic view of American civil liberties. The United States has a venerable tradition of individual freedom. Where formal constitutional clauses, statutes, executive orders, and judicial decisions have been involved, the record is generally in favor of liberty. That record has had glaring faults, such as slavery and racial discrimination, but, over the long haul, it has improved. Reasonable people can reasonably differ about whether existing statutes are too broad or judicial decisions too narrow; but, over the years, arguments have more and more tended to converge within a context of respect for human dignity and liberty under law.

Yet there is also a darker side. Spurts of repression occasionally occur in American history. The Alien and Sedition Act of 1798, prosecutions for sedition during World War I, the "Great Red Scare" of the 1920s, imprisonment during World War II of a hundred thousand American citizens of Japanese ancestry, the Cold War fright of the late 1940s and early 1950s, the FBI and the IRS during the 1960s and 1970s—

Over 100,000 American citizens of Japanese descent were denied their rights by the federal government during the Second War War. Aliens and citizens were indiscriminately evacuated from their homes, as with this group shown leaving San Francisco, and placed in detention camps in remote areas. (United Press International)

all show hysterical officials violating their oaths of office in fierce determination to advance their careers and to protect the American people from imaginary seducers.

That the system has failed in the past and yet recovered does not guarantee that it will continue to survive crises. Governmental bureaucracies now have much more dangerous instruments than they did even a few decades ago. Sophisticated electronic devices can listen to conversations in the bedroom or telephone booth. Computers can store hundreds of millions of bits of information and, within a split second, regurgitate them in any pattern the operator desires. After recording a few innocent sentences of a telephone conversation, a skilled technician can now reconstruct a tape that has the speaker confessing to rape and murder or planning to bomb the White House. Most ominous is the evidence that hundreds, perhaps thousands, of officials in powerful agencies like the FBI, CIA, IRS, and the White House itself have had little commitment to, or understanding of, the American Constitution.

NOTES

1. *Abrams v. United States*, 250 U.S. 616, dissenting opinion (1919).
2. Letter of October 17, 1788, in Gaillard Hunt, ed., *The Writings of James Madison* (New York: G. P. Putnam's Sons, 1904), V, 274.
3. 7 Peters 243 (1833).
4. *Gitlow v. New York*, 268 U.S. 652 (1925).
5. *Palko v. Connecticut*, 302 U.S. 319 (1937).
6. Selective Draft Act Cases, 245 U.S. 366 (1917).
7. *Osterreich v. Board No. 11*, 393 U.S. 233 (1968).
8. *In re Winship*, 397 U.S. 358 (1970); *Jackson v. Virginia*, 443 U.S. 307 (1979).
9. Chief Justice Earl Warren in *Trop v. Dulles*, 356 U.S. 86 (1958).
10. *Dred Scott v. Sandford*, 19 Howard 393 (1857).
11. See especially *Afroyim v. Rusk*, 387 U.S. 253 (1967).
12. For foreign travel, see: *Kent v. Dulles*, 357 U.S. 116 (1958), and *Aptheker v. Rusk*, 378 U.S. 500 (1964); for domestic travel, see: *Shapiro v. Thompson*, 394 U.S. 618 (1969), *Dunn v. Blumstein*, 405 U.S. 330 (1972), and *Memorial Hospital v. Maricopa County*, 415 U.S. 250 (1974).
13. *Haig v. Agee*, 453 U.S. 280 (1981).
14. For welfare benefits, see *Shapiro*, cited in note 12; for voting, *Dunn*, cited in note 12; and for free hospital care, see *Memorial Hospital*, also cited in note 12.
15. *Bolling v. Sharpe*, 347 U.S. 497 (1954).
16. 163 U.S. 537 (1896).
17. 347 U.S. 483 (1954).
18. *Milliken v. Bradley*, 418 U.S. 717 (1974).
19. 411 U.S. 1 (1973).
20. For example, waiver of fees: charged to prepare a transcript for an appeal—*Griffin v. Illinois*, 351 U.S. 12 (1956); to begin a divorce suit—*Boddie v. Connecticut*, 401 U.S. 371 (1971); but, curiously, the Court has held that government is not required to waive the fee to file for bankruptcy—*United States v. Kras*, 409 U.S. 434 (1973).
21. *Gideon v. Wainwright*, 372 U.S. 335 (1963); *Argensinger v. Hamlin*, 407 U.S. 25 (1973).
22. *Craig v. Boren*, 429 U.S. 190 (1976), is the basic case.
23. 438 U.S. 265 (1978).
24. *United Steelworkers v. Weber*, 443 U.S. 193 (1979); *Fullilove v. Klutznick*, 448 U.S. 448 (1980). For an excellent summary of recent developments, see Jesse H. Choper, "The Constitutionality of Affirmative Action," *Kentucky Law Journal*, LXX (1981), 1.
25. *Lemon v. Kurtzman*, 403 U.S. 602 (1971).
26. *Everson v. Ewing Township*, 330 U.S. 1 (1947).
27. *Cochran v. Louisiana*, 281 U.S. 370 (1930); *Board of Regents v. Allen*, 392 U.S. 236 (1968); *Meek v. Pittinger*, 421 U.S. 349 (1975).
28. *Tilton v. Richardson*, 403 U.S. 672 (1971); and *Roemer v. Maryland*, 426 U.S. 736 (1976).
29. *Lemon*, cited above in note 25.
30. *McCollum v. Board*, 333 U.S. 203 (1948).
31. *Zorach v. Clauson*, 343 U.S. 606 (1952).
32. *Engel v. Vitale*, 370 U.S. 421 (1962); *Abington School Dist. v. Schempp*, 374 U.S. 203 (1963); *Chamberlin v. Dade County*, 377 U.S. 402 (1964).

33. *Engel,* cited in note 32.
34. *Reynolds v. United States,* 98 U.S. 145 (1879); *Davis v. Beason,* 133 U.S. 333 (1890).
35. *Cleveland v. United States,* 319 U.S. 14 (1946).
36. *McGowan v. Maryland,* 366 U.S. 420 (1961); *Gallagher v. Crown Kosher Super Market,* 366 U.S. 617 (1961); *Two Guys v. McGinley,* 366 U.S. 582 (1961); *Braunfeld v. Brown,* 366 U.S. 599 (1961).
37. *Sherbert v. Verner,* 374 U.S. 398 (1963).
38. *West Virginia v. Barnette,* 319 U.S. 624 (1943).
39. *Wisconsin v. Yoder,* 406 U.S. 205 (1972).
40. *United States v. Seegar,* 380 U.S. 1 (1965); *Welsh v. United States,* 398 U.S. 333 (1970).
41. *Gillette v. United States,* 401 U.S. 437 (1971).
42. *Olmstead v. United States,* 277 U.S. 438, dissenting opinion (1928).
43. 381 U.S. 479 (1965).
44. *Eisenstadt v. Baird,* 405 U.S. 438 (1972).
45. *Roe v. Wade,* 410 U.S. 113 (1973).
46. *Planned Parenthood v. Danforth,* 428 U.S. 52 (1976); *Bellotti v. Baird,* 428 U.S. 132 (1976).
47. *H. L. v. Matheson,* 450 U.S. 398 (1981).
48. *Maher v. Roe,* 432 U.S. 464 (1977); *Harris v. McCrae,* 448 U.S. 297 (1980).
49. *Jacobson v. Massachusetts,* 197 U.S. 11 (1905).
50. *Buck v. Bell,* 274 U.S. 200 (1927).
51. *Breithaupt v. Abram,* 352 U.S. 432 (1957).
52. *Skinner v. Oklahoma,* 316 U.S. 535 (1942).
53. *Rochin v. California,* 342 U.S. 165 (1952).
54. *Schenck v. United States,* 249 U.S. 47 (1919).
55. *Whitney v. California,* 274 U.S. 357, concurring opinion (1927).
56. Especially *United States v. Carolene Products,* 304 U.S. 144 (1938).
57. *Dennis v. United States,* 341 U.S. 494, concurring opinion (1951).
58. *A Constitutional Faith* (New York: Alfred A. Knopf, 1969), p. 45.
59. "The Bill of Rights," *New York University Law Review,* XXXV (1960), 865.
60. *Milk Wagon Drivers Union v. Meadowmoor Dairies,* 312 U.S. 287, dissenting opinion (1941); *Giboney v. Empire Storage,* 336 U.S. 490 (1949).
61. *Tinker v. Des Moines,* 393 U.S. 503, dissenting opinion (1969).
62. *United States v. O'Brien,* 391 U.S. 367 (1968).
63. *Street v. New York,* 394 U.S. 576, dissenting opinion (1969).
64. *Cox v. Louisiana,* 379 U.S. 559, dissenting opinion (1965).
65. *Free Speech and Its Relation to Self-Government* (New York: Harper, 1948), and *Political Freedom* (New York: Oxford University Press, 1965).
66. *Dennis v. United States,* cited above in note 57; *Yates v. United States,* 354 U.S. 298 (1957); *Barenblatt v. United States,* 360 U.S. 109 (1959).
67. The basic case here is *New York Times v. Sullivan,* 376 U.S. 254 (1964).
68. The basic case here is *Gertz v. Welsh,* 418 U.S. 323 (1974).
69. 354 U.S. 476 (1957).
70. *Ginzburg v. United States,* 383 U.S. 463 (1966).
71. 409 U.S. 109 (1974).
72. 413 U.S. 15 (1973).
73. See also *Smith v. United States,* 431 U.S. 291 (1977), reaffirming *Miller* on this point; but *Pinkus v. United States,* 436 U.S. 293 (1978), held that children could not be included as members of the community whose views were being considered. *Ginsburg v. New York,* 390 U.S. 629 (1968), sustained state regulations forbidding sales of "girlie magazines" to minors.
74. 283 U.S. 697 (1931).
75. For instance: *Lovell v. Griffin,* 303 U.S. 444 (1938); *Cox v. New Hampshire,* 312 U.S. 569 (1941); *Nietmotko v. Maryland,* 340 U.S. 268 (1951).
76. *New York Times v. United States,* 403 U.S. 713 (1971).
77. See, for instance, *Sheppard v. Maxwell,* 384 U.S. 333 (1966).
78. *Nebraska Press Association v. Stuart,* 427 U.S. 539 (1976).
79. *Richmond Newspapers v. Virginia,* 448 U.S. 555 (1980).
80. *Branzburg v. Hayes,* 408 U.S. 665 (1972).
81. *Zurcher v. Stanford Daily,* 436 U.S. 547 (1978).

82. Most of the evidence in this section comes from the hearings and report of the Church Committee: U.S. Senate, Select Committee to Study Governmental Operations with Respect to Intelligence Activities, *Hearings*, 7 vols; and *Final Report*, 6 books, plus supplemental material, 94th Congress, 2d Session (1975–1976); Book III of the committee's *Final Report* contains a 106-page summary of the FBI's efforts to discredit the Rev. Mr. King.
83. *Whitney v. California*, cited in note 55.
84. Quoted in Church Committee, *Final Report*, Book III, p. 135.
85. *Olmstead v. United States*, cited in note 42.

SELECTED BIBLIOGRAPHY

Abraham, Henry J. *Freedom and the Court: Civil Rights and Liberties in the United States*, 4th ed. (New York: Oxford University Press, 1982). An excellent general survey of the constitutional law of civil rights.

Ackerman, Bruce A. *Private Property and the Constitution* (New Haven, Conn.: Yale University Press, 1977). A very sophisticated analysis of the meaning of the modern right to property.

Anastalpo, George. *The Constitutionalist: Notes on the First Amendment* (Dallas, Texas: Southern Methodist University Press, 1971). A sometimes strange but always wonderful book, filled with unique insights into the meaning of the First Amendment for a functioning constitutional democracy.

Becker, Carl. *Freedom and Responsibility in the American Way of Life* (New York: Alfred A. Knopf, 1945). A beautifully written analysis of the compatibility of political authority and individual liberty.

Berns, Walter. *Freedom, Virtue and the First Amendment* (Baton Rouge: Louisiana State University Press, 1957). A vigorous attack on the American tradition of freedom of expression. Berns continues his analysis, though in a more positive vein, in *The First Amendment and the Future of American Democracy* (New York: Basic Books, 1976).

Boggan, E. Carrington, Marilyn G. Haft, Charles Lister, and John P. Rupp. *The Rights of Gay People* (New York: Avon Books, 1975). One of a series of handbooks, sponsored by the American Civil Liberties Union, on the rights of particular groups.

Chafee, Zechariah. *Free Speech in the United States* (Cambridge, Mass.: Harvard University Press, 1941). A classic in civil rights literature, by a noted legal scholar and defender of human liberty.

Clor, Harry M. *Obscenity and Public Morality: Censorship in a Liberal Society* (Chicago: University of Chicago Press, 1969). A sophisticated attempt to develop a justification for censorship against obscenity in a free society.

Dworkin, Ronald. *Taking Rights Seriously* (Cambridge, Mass.: Harvard University Press, 1977). A constitutionalist's defense of rights against utilitarian theories.

Emerson, Thomas I. *Toward a General Theory of the First Amendment* (New York: Random House, 1963). An effort to construct a formal legal doctrine to guide judges in deciding First Amendment cases.

Friendly, Fred W. *The Good Guys, the Bad Guys and the First Amendment: Free Speech vs. Fairness in Broadcasting* (New York: Random House, 1975). A provocative discussion of problems of open debate and governmental regulation of television and radio.

Goldman, Alan H. *Justice and Reverse Discrimination* (Princeton, N.J.: Princeton University Press, 1979). A closely reasoned argument that only limited programs of affirmative action are just.

Lasswell, Harold D. *National Security and Individual Freedom* (New York: McGraw-Hill, 1950). An analysis of the dangers of a garrison state, even a supposedly democratic garrison state.

Levy, Leonard W. *Legacy of Suppression: Freedom of Speech and Press in Early American History* (Cambridge, Mass.: Harvard University Press, 1960). A myth-puncturing account of the rather low legal protection accorded freedom of expression in the good old days.

Meiklejohn, Alexander. *Free Speech and Its Relation to Self-Government* (New York: Harper, 1948). A provocative and influential thesis that freedom of political expression ought to be an absolute right.

Mill, John Stuart. *On Liberty* (New York: Appleton-Century-Crofts, 1947). Originally published in 1851, a famous attempt to define the proper limits of freedom and authority.

Report of the Commission on Obscenity and Pornography (Washington: Government Printing Office, 1970). A thoughtful, heavily documented, and much discussed report of a presidential commission.

Schlissel, Lillian, ed. *Conscience in America: A Documentary History of Conscientious Objection in America, 1757–1967* (New York: E.P. Dutton & Co., 1968). The subtitle accurately describes this useful collection of documents.

Sorauf, Frank J. *The Wall of Separation: The Constitutional Politics of Church and State* (Princeton, N.J.: Princeton University Press, 1976). A scholarly analysis of a set of problems ranging from prayers in public schools to public aid to parochial schools.

Twentieth Century Fund, *Rights in Conflict: Report of the Twentieth Century Fund Task Force on Justice, Publicity, and the First Amendment* (New York: McGraw-Hill, 1976). A penetrating analysis of the potential conflict between freedom of the press and an individual's right to a fair trial.

Thoreau, Henry D. *On the Duty of Civil Disobedience* (New Haven, Conn.: Yale University Press, 1928). Originally published in 1849; an impassioned disquisition on the moral obligation of the individual to resist unjust governmental authority.

Wills, Garry. *Inventing America* (New York: Doubleday, 1978). A controversial reinterpretation of the intellectual roots of the Declaration of Independence.

16 Criminal Justice

Criminal justice poses once again the basic dilemma that Madison put to the framers of the Constitution: how to make government strong enough to protect society without allowing government to be so strong as to oppress society. How a nation treats people accused of breaking its laws reflects its values and also shapes much of its politics. That process not only involves serious questions of civil liberties, it also involves the quality of life that a society can enjoy free from restraint by either criminals or public officials.

This chapter looks at the scope of crime in the United States, examines the formal procedures designed to protect the constitutional rights of those accused of crime, and analyzes practices that allow police, prosecutors, and judges to evade those protections. We then discuss some of the implications that prison conditions pose for the future of American society.

THE SCOPE OF CRIME

The streak of violence that Chapter 2 described as running through American history still leaves an ugly stain on the nation's face. "Organized crime" is a huge industry that stands at the throat of big cities, controlling some judges, prosecutors, police, and legitimate businesses as effectively as it does loan sharking, gambling, prostitution, and narcotics. On a smaller scale, street gangs sometimes terrorize entire neighborhoods. Disorganized crime, in the form of muggers who assault and rob at random, threatens to turn urban streets into jungles. In that sort of environment, no person enjoys real civil rights.

Accurate figures regarding the incidence of crime are difficult to obtain. Many, possibly most, crimes are not reported to the police, and police departments often find it politically expedient to inflate or deflate the figures that they have. The Federal Bureau of Investigation estimated that 12 million crimes against property and another 1.3 million against persons were committed in the United States during 1981.[1] Polling data suggest that these estimates are low.

Costs

Crime does not equally affect all segments of the population. On the contrary, the victims are disproportionately the poor. A study of thirteen large American cities in 1974 showed that residents with annual

TABLE 16-1

1. SPREADING FEAR, CHANGING LIVES

Is there any area within a mile of your home where you would be afraid to walk alone at night?

Yes	53%
No	46%
Don't know	1%

Which of the following have happened to you in the past twelve months?

Property vandalized	20%
Money or property stolen	21%
House broken into or attempt made	14%
Assaulted or mugged	3%
Car stolen	3%

Which of these precautions against crime have you taken?

Try not to go out alone at night	64%
Never carry very much cash	79%
Avoid certain areas even during the day	60%
Avoid wearing expensive jewelry	64%
Keep a gun or other weapon	31%
Keep a dog for protection	44%

Is there more crime in your area than there was a year ago?

More	58%	The same	24%
Less	14%	Don't know	4%

Do you think criminals today are more violent than they were five years ago?

Yes 75%	No 21%	Don't know 4%

What is most responsible for the increasing rate of crime?

Unemployment	37%
Courts too lenient	20%
Breakdown of family, society, values	19%
Punishment not severe enough	13%
Drugs	13%
TV violence, movies	3%

2. DISTRUST

How much confidence do you have in the police to protect you from violent crime?

A great deal	15%
Quite a bit	34%
Not very much	42%
None at all	8%
Don't know	1%

How much confidence do you have in the courts to sentence and convict criminals?

A great deal	5%
Quite a bit	23%
Not very much	59%
None at all	11%
Don't know	2%

What effect, if any, will Ronald Reagan's election have upon reducing the crime rate?

Great effect	9%
Some	32%
Hardly any	27%
None	19%
Don't know	13%

incomes under $3,000 were twice as likely as those with incomes over $25,000 to be the victim of crimes involving violence, more than three times as likely to be robbed and injured, and four times as likely to be raped—ratios that were similar to those obtained a decade earlier by the President's Commission on Law Enforcement and in 1979 by the Department of Justice.[2]

Furthermore, crime's injury to the poor is likely to be far more painful than to the well-to-do. A theft of $100 from a business executive is an inconvenience; that loss might cause a poor family to go hungry. When the target of a robbery is a store in a ghetto area, the cost, even the added cost of insurance, is passed on to the neighborhood in the form of higher prices.

To prevent robberies, private industry spends billions of dollars each year for guards, special equipment, and insurance. These costs are passed on to consumers. The public bill for law enforcement—directly

3. WHAT'S TO BE DONE?

Leaving aside those cases in which there is a murder, how do you feel a criminal who carries a gun when committing a crime should be sentenced?

Life in prison	15%
5 to 10 years added to sentence	51%
Sentence should be the same as with no gun	20%
Depends on circumstances	8%
Don't know	6%

Are you in favor of or opposed to the death penalty for persons convicted of murder?

Favor	65%
Opposed	24%
Don't know	11%

Do you approve or disapprove of these alternatives for dealing with crime?

	Approve	Disapprove	Don't know
Allowing the police to stop and search anybody on suspicion	48%	50%	2%
Allowing the police to wiretap the telephone of anyone they suspect	30%	67%	3%
Allowing the police to search a home without a warrant	13%	86%	1%
Encouraging citizens to carry defensive weapons such as Mace	65%	32%	3%

For this NEWSWEEK Poll, The Gallup Organization conducted 1,030 telephone interviews across the nation between Jan. 16 and 23. The margin of error is plus or minus 3 percentage points. Percentages may not add up to 100 because of rounding or multiple responses. (The NEWSWEEK Pool, © 1981 NEWSWEEK, Inc.)

paid for by taxpayers and indirectly by those who need other governmental services—is staggering, now exceeding $30 billion each year. Maintaining prisons, courts, police stations, specially equipped vehicles, radios, and arsenals of weapons is extraordinarily expensive, as are feeding and clothing 400,000 people in penitentiaries and thousands more in smaller jails, and paying the salaries of more than 1,275,000 prosecutors, police officers, prison guards, and probation officials.

The high rate of violent crime also lowers the quality of life for potential as well as actual victims, as Table 16.1 shows. It keeps people from enjoying theaters, libraries, parks, and other facilities for leisure, education, and cultural enrichment. For a man—much less a woman—to go out at night in many urban centers is risky; and only a thief, a police decoy, or a fool walks alone after dark in lonely places like public parks. American tourists are surprised to see people strolling around Paris, Madrid, or Rome at midnight. In the United States most city residents double-lock themselves in at dusk, and more than half have guns in their homes to protect against burglars.[3]

Perhaps the most significant cost of crime is erosion of community. Awareness among whites that blacks and Hispanics commit a high percentage of crimes of violence intensifies ethnic prejudices. For their part, blacks and Hispanics, as the most frequent victims of violent crime, blame the police in particular for their problems and Anglos in general both for restricting their legitimate economic opportunities and for denying them adequate protection

Risk Taking and Profit Making

The profits from crime are both enormous and tax-free. The cost of goods stolen, embezzled, or destroyed by criminals now approaches $100 billion a year. The risks are low. Few crimes—perhaps only one in five—result in arrests; only a small percentage of those arrested are convicted; and a bare majority of those convicted go to prison.

⭐ PROTECTING SOCIETY

Law and Order

Unhappily for those who like simple solutions, "law and order" are two concepts, not a single idea. Law is frequently in tension with order, for one of the essential functions of law is to restrain officials who keep order. If order were the primary value in a society, the standard for police conduct would be efficiency in arresting criminals. But even then one could not be sure of achieving order; once freed from outside restraints, police might opt to further their own aims at the expense of society. It is hardly disrespectful to suggest that as human beings police are vulnerable to the temptations that beset the rest of humanity.

The real question is how to preserve order *with* law and liberty, and there are no easy answers. Neither the Constitution nor statutes systematically state the objectives of American criminal law. And those aims that can be deduced from those sources are not necessarily consistent with each other. Historically, the criminal law was a substitute for private revenge, and it still retains much of that character. In part, the purpose of criminal law has also been to serve as a secular equivalent of Purgatory, cleansing the criminal of moral guilt by forcing him "to pay his debt to society." Another purpose has been to protect society either by deterring lawbreaking or by isolating criminals. Criminal law may also operate as a means of rehabilitating and reforming the offender. What it seldom if ever does is to help the victim beyond occasionally offering public revenge.

Confusion about the purposes of criminal justice is compounded by the multiplicity of causes of crime. A few people are born psychopaths who, by definition, cannot obey laws regarding decent conduct. Others have been so twisted by their home environments or the flaws of society that they are no longer capable of existing without running afoul of legal rules. Some of these people might be helped, but identifying them and providing treatment that would be truly effective are both difficult and expensive. Others simply make mistakes of moral and practical judgment and commit crimes that seem at the moment rational in terms of self-interest. Others commit crimes out of sheer passion, mindlessly venting rage or jealousy.

Measures that might prevent crimes caused by one factor are likely to be ineffective in dealing with others. Furthermore, crime may have many causes, with several of these factors combining rather than acting singly. Yet, except perhaps for psychopaths, these causes do not invariably produce criminal action. Sometime in some important way society will wound most of its members; all humans are likely, at more than one moment in their lives, to become enraged; most people sometime face situations in which breaking the law promises tangible rewards at small risk. Yet most men and women do not commit serious crimes.

We face the philosophical problem of free will. Legal systems in the Western world presume free will, and thus individual moral responsibility—which is one reason why pleas of insanity cause the system such great difficulty. But many psychiatrists, social scientists, and public officials believe that environment limits that will and so dilutes individual responsibility. These authorities argue that it is almost always impossible to discern accurately the degree to which an individual is responsible for his or her actions and the degree to which society shares the blame. To the extent that these experts are correct, even the most sophisticated programs to deal with individual behavior will fail unless coordinated with equally sophisticated programs of social reform.

Constitutional Provisions

Differences among the aims of criminal law, disagreements among political leaders as to the relative importance of these aims, and fundamental philosophical disputes about individual responsibility multiply problems of administering justice. Less confused, but by no means clear, are the boundaries of the substantive rights that the constitutional system tries to protect from abuse by those charged with applying criminal sanctions. By *substantive rights* we mean the essence of what is protected, in contrast to *procedural rights*, the obligations of public officials to follow certain specified steps before imposing punishment. The Constitution originally mentioned no substantive rights, although we can deduce from the various procedural guarantees there and in the Bill of Rights that the basic rights in the field of criminal justice are those to dignity and privacy, to physical freedom, to a fair trial if accused of crime, and to protection, if convicted, against certain kinds of punishment.

As written in 1787, the Constitution directly referred to only three of these. The framers safeguarded the right to a fair trial by forbidding both state and national governments to pass bills of attainder or ex post facto legislation. (We defined these terms in Chapter 3.) Article III also carefully defines treason and limits the punishment that can be imposed for such a crime:

> Treason against the United States shall consist only in levying war against them, or in adhering to their enemies, giving them aid and comfort. No person shall be convicted of treason unless on the testimony of two witnesses to the same overt act, or on confession in open court.
>
> The Congress shall have power to declare the punishment of treason, but no attainder of treason shall work corruption of blood or forfeiture except during the life of the person attainted.*

More generally, the framers protected the basic right to freedom itself by providing in Article I that: "The privilege of the writ of habeas corpus shall not be suspended, unless when in cases of rebellion or invasion the public safety may require it." Sometimes called "the great writ of liberty," habeas corpus was designed to prevent arbitrary arrest or unlawful imprisonment. Where this right is available, any prisoner—

---

* "Corruption of blood or forfeiture" refers to English practices of punishing the family of a convicted traitor.

or the lawyer or a friend of the prisoner—may ask the nearest court to order the police (state or federal) to show legal cause for detention. If the police do not show such cause, the court will order the prisoner released.

⭐ "FORMAL" STAGES OF CRIMINAL JUSTICE

To understand the system of criminal justice, it is necessary to have a clear view of the rights that accused persons have from the time they become suspects until they go to prison. At the same time, one must recognize that actual practices may differ from these formal rules. This section describes the stages outlined by law, and the next turns to common practices.

Arrest

To arrest a suspect, police are supposed to have "probable cause" to believe that the person has committed or is about to commit a crime. The difference between mere suspicion and probable cause is imprecise. The Supreme Court has defined "probable cause" as "reasonable ground of suspicion supported by circumstances sufficiently strong in themselves to warrant a cautious man in the belief that the party is guilty of the offense with which he is charged."[4] Generally speaking, a policeman should have some tangible evidence implicating a suspect—perhaps the officer sees a person commit a crime or a witness identifies the suspect as the guilty party.

Wherever possible, an arresting officer should have a *warrant*—an order from a judicial official, to whom the officer's evidence of probable cause has been submitted—to take a person into custody. (We use the term "judicial official" because in federal district courts a magistrate, an assistant to a judge, rather than the judge, normally issues arrest and search warrants, hears charges against an accused, informs him or her of constitutional rights, and sets bail. In state systems a magistrate is usually a minor judge who performs similar rather routine duties.) Obviously, there are many situations in which police do not have time to go to court, and judges have ruled, somewhat vaguely, that a warrant is not an absolute requirement for a valid arrest.

Search

Once officers have made an arrest, they may search the prisoner, but judges have been divided over just how extensive that search can be unless police have obtained a *search warrant* that follows the Fourth Amendment's requirements that the thing sought and the person or area to be examined be specified. Indeed, the Supreme Court has crossed its own trail so often that the justices have become wary of laying down broad principles, claiming that this problem "can only be solved in the concrete factual context of the individual case."[5]

In general, the Supreme Court has restricted the area to be searched without a warrant to the person of the suspect and the immediate area under his or her control. The only lawful purposes of such a search are protecting the safety of the arresting officer and preventing destruction of evidence.[6] But these are elastic terms.

If police wish to look into a suspect's home or place of work for evidence, they must, under normal circumstances, obtain a search warrant. The crucial word here is "normal." As in arrest, there may be many circumstances, such as "hot pursuit" of a criminal, in which courts allow police to proceed without a warrant. The most troublesome exceptions to requirement of a warrant involve searches of automobiles. After tripping over itself several times, the Court ruled in 1982 that, if police have probable cause to believe an automobile is carrying evidence of a crime, they may stop the vehicle and search it thoroughly.[7]

Interrogation

The Fifth Amendment provides that no person "shall be compelled in a criminal case to be a witness against himself." The Supreme Court, since its controversial decision in *Miranda v. Arizona* (1966),[8] has required police to warn a suspect of his or her rights to say nothing and to have a lawyer present—at the government's expense if the suspect cannot afford to hire one.

Although today American police probably seldom use violence to obtain a confession, only an exceptional person detained in a police station and surrounded by detectives would not experience considerable fear. To ensure that emotion does not subtly coerce, federal law requires U.S. officials to bring prisoners "without unnecessary delay" before a judicial officer, who examines the charge and the evidence to make sure suspects are being lawfully detained and informs them once again of the charges as well as their constitutional rights to silence and to free counsel. The judicial officer also sets the bail that prisoners must post to be released, if the offense allows bail. In some jurisdictions, the magistrate can release an accused on his or her assurance of returning for trial.

Law Enforcement Code of Ethics

As a Law Enforcement Officer, *my fundamental duty is to serve mankind; to safeguard lives and property; to protect the innocent against deception, the weak against oppression or intimidation, and the peaceful against violence or disorder; and to respect the Constitutional rights of all men to liberty, equality and justice.*

I will *keep my private life unsullied as an example to all; maintain courageous calm in the face of danger, scorn, or ridicule; develop self-restraint; and be constantly mindful of the welfare of others. Honest in thought and deed in both my personal and official life, I will be exemplary in obeying the laws of the land and the regulations of my department. Whatever I see or hear of a confidential nature or that is confided to me in my official capacity will be kept ever secret unless revelation is necessary in the performance of my duty.*

I will *never act officiously or permit personal feelings, prejudices, animosities or friendships to influence my decisions. With no compromise for crime and with relentless prosecution of criminals, I will enforce the law courteously and appropriately without fear or favor, malice or ill will, never employing unnecessary force or violence and never accepting gratuities.*

I recognize *the badge of my office as a symbol of public faith, and I accept it as a public trust to be held so long as I am true to the ethics of the police service. I will constantly strive to achieve these objectives and ideals, dedicating myself before God to my chosen profession . . . law enforcement.*

There is no bright line distinguishing necessary from unnecessary delay. The Court has said that federal police may wait to bring a prisoner before a magistrate until they have completed routine arrest procedures, checked out any alibi, and talked to the principal witnesses immediately available.[9] But federal officers may not begin close interrogations of suspects before they have been brought before a magistrate. The obvious purpose of this rule is to make certain that defendants know their rights, not to promote police efficiency.

The Supreme Court has not imposed on state officials quite the same requirement of rapid appearance before a magistrate, but *Miranda* obliges *all* enforcement officers to inform accused of their rights. Furthermore, a suspect's lawyer may be present at all times the prisoner is under interrogation. If at any stage the prisoner changes his or her mind after first waiving a right to counsel, the interrogation is supposed to stop until an attorney can be present. The burden of proof that a defendant has freely and intelligently waived these rights is on the prosecution, if it attempts to introduce at a trial evidence obtained from questioning the accused.

Formal Charge

The Fifth Amendment requires that, for all major federal crimes, the accusations be made by an *indictment* lodged by a *grand jury*. That group is convened by the prosecutor and hears evidence presented by the prosecutor; only on rare occasions does it gather evidence on its own. If a majority of the jurors feel there is sufficient reason to bring a suspect to trial, they present a *true bill* and indict—that is, accuse—the person.

The grand jury is a cumbersome instrument, and its use is one of the few provisions of the Bill of Rights that the Supreme Court has not made obligatory on the states. Although some states still use this process to initiate judicial proceedings, most allow prosecutors to accuse a defendant by filing with a court what is called an *information*.

Once a prisoner has been charged, the magistrate may review any earlier decision regarding bail. The Eighth Amendment provides only that "excessive bail shall not be required,"* a stipulation that does not prevent a judge's denying bail in grave cases. The judicial officer, if he or she decides to allow bail, sets a sum of money which the defendant will have to deposit (post) with the court. The amount is that which in the judicial officer's judgment is sufficient to ensure the defendant's appearance at the trial. Because most defendants are not prosperous, bail bondsmen do a brisk business. For a fee, usually about 10 percent of the bail, they will post a bond guaranteeing the defendant's presence at the trial. In most jurisdictions, these bondsmen can arrest and return defendants who try to flee.

When bail is denied or set very high, a suspect may have to stay in prison for many months. Not only will his or her earning power be at least temporarily destroyed, the person's ability to gather evidence and prepare a defense will be curtailed. It is ironic that, although suspects may be jailed without being found guilty, if convicted they may be promptly freed, because suspended sentences are common for first offenders.

After several studies showed that suspects released without bail appeared for trial about as often as those who had to put up money,

---

* As of October 1982 the Supreme Court had never explicitly held that states are bound by this clause, but that states are so bound logically follows from many decisions.

Congress passed the Bail Reform Act of 1966. This statute, affecting only federal criminal procedure, requires magistrates to release on their own recognizance people accused of noncapital offenses* who are unable to raise bail, unless the judicial official has strong reason to believe that the accused will not appear for trial. The statute also authorizes, but does not require, magistrates to apply the same procedure to capital offenses. In addition, Congress provided for swift appellate court review of decisions refusing bail and ordered the attorney general to give credit toward any prison sentence for the time a defendant spent in custody awaiting trial.

The problem of bail also involves society's interests in protecting its other members. Some criminals released on bail commit fresh crimes soon after regaining freedom; others intimidate potential witnesses or jurors. On the other hand, the law's presumption of innocence bars imprisonment without trial. Traditionally, however, bail practices have resulted in a degree of *preventive detention*. Where judges believe that accused are dangerous to society, they often set very high bail or deny bail altogether.

Trial

The Sixth Amendment says that an accused person has a right to a "speedy" trial, but delays between arrest and trial are often long. In 1974 Congress authorized criminal defendants in federal cases not brought to trial within a hundred days of arrest to petition a district judge to dismiss the charges. The statute, the Speedy Trial Act, excludes from the hundred days certain periods, such as those during which a defendant was not available for trial or was undergoing tests to determine fitness to stand trial. But if none of the specifically listed circumstances is present, the judge must dismiss the charges. The Speedy Trial Act does not, of course, affect state courts, but several states are applying similar rules.

Federal and state trials for all important crimes must be by jury, unless the defendant and, in some jurisdictions, the prosecution waive that right. At least in state courts, the vote to convict need not be unanimous, and, for lesser offenses (still undefined), the jury may consist of fewer than twelve persons.[10] Neither the trial nor the grand jury has to be a statistically neat cross section of the community, but the government may not systematically exclude people from jury service because of race, ethnic origin, or sex.[11]

The Sixth Amendment sets procedural minimums for all trials "the accused shall enjoy the right . . . to be informed of the nature and cause

---

* A "noncapital offense" is one for which the punishment is less than execution or life imprisonment.

"We agree with the defense that the defendant is of strong moral fiber, and feel that our prison system could use a man of his caliber."

Grin and Bear It, by Lichty and Wagner, © 1979 Field Enterprises, Inc. Courtesy of Field Newspaper Syndicate

of the accusations; to be confronted with witnesses against him; to have compulsory process for obtaining witnesses in his favor, and to have assistance of counsel for his defense." As at interrogation, the state or federal government must provide a lawyer for the accused if he or she cannot afford to hire one, and the attorney must have ample time to prepare the case.

The defendant cannot be required to take the witness stand, nor can the prosecutor or judge comment adversely to the jury about the defendant's not testifying. "The constitutional foundation underlying the privilege [against self-incrimination]," the Supreme Court has said, "is the respect a government—state or federal—must accord to the dignity and integrity of its citizens."[12]

The trial as a whole must be fair in substance as well as procedure. It cannot, for example, be conducted in an atmosphere of mob rule; the presiding judge must be unbiased; the prosecutor may not introduce perjured testimony; and a reasonable group of people must have been able to conclude from the evidence presented that the accused was guilty beyond a reasonable doubt.

The Fourth Amendment may come into play again at the trial, as may the Fifth, when the question of admissibility of evidence is involved. Since 1914 the Supreme Court has not allowed federal courts to hear evidence that was illegally obtained;[13] and since 1961 state courts have been obliged by this limitation as well.[14] This so-called "exclusionary rule" has a double purpose. First, it is virtually the only practical means, though certainly not a completely effective one, of making police respect defendants' rights to privacy and to silence. Second, the exclusionary rule protects the integrity of the judicial process, preventing courts from becoming a "party to lawless invasions of the constitutional rights of citizens. . . ."[15]

Since the early 1970s a majority of the Supreme Court has taken a less favorable view of this rule, looking on it as a crude instrument to police the police.[16] The most important decision was *Stone v. Powell* (1976),[17] which held that a person convicted in a state court could not use a federal court to challenge his conviction if he or she had had a fair opportunity to raise the exclusionary rule before a state tribunal.

Electronic surveillance generally and wiretapping in particular add another dimension to already complex problems. The first wiretapping case, *Olmstead v. United States* (1928), held 5–4 that intercepting telephone conversations was not a search and seizure forbidden by the Fourth Amendment.[18] Gradually, however, the Supreme Court came to view *Olmstead* as wrong and saw wiretapping and similar forms of bugging as searches and seizures within the scope of the Fourth Amendment's prohibitions.[19] Evidence so obtained is admissible in court only if the requirements of the Fourth Amendment are met.

In the Omnibus Crime Control Act of 1968 Congress made it a crime under most circumstances for private citizens or governmental officials to intercept messages without a warrant. Officials must petition a court for permission and show the same probable cause as in applying for a search warrant. In emergency situations involving national security or organized crime, the attorney general may authorize bugging for as long as forty-eight hours, if the government uses that time to apply for a court order.

Some troublesome legal problems remain. First, an order for wiretapping is far more inclusive than the traditional search warrant, which allows only one examination. Second, the privacy of people other than the person named in the judicial authorization may be invaded, since the suspect may talk to—and about—a large number of people. Third, notice of the authorization will normally be given the suspect only after the surveillance is completed, not, as with a search warrant, when the order is executed.[20]

A fourth problem concerns the president's authority to order wiretapping under his constitutional duty "to take care that the laws be faithfully executed." In 1972 *United States v. U.S. District Court* ruled that, in investigations of "domestic security," wiretaps without judicial authorization violated the Fourth Amendment.[21] The Department of Justice had based its case on the inherent power of the chief executive as well as on a provision of the Omnibus Crime Control Act that nothing in the statute shall "limit the constitutional power of the President to take such measures as he deems necessary to protect the United States against the overthrow of the Government by force or other unlawful means, or against any other clear and present danger to the structure or existence of the Government."

The justices, however, found that this language "merely provides that the Act shall not be interpreted to limit or disturb such power as the President may have under the Constitution. In short, Congress simply left presidential powers where it found them." Stressing that a different situation might exist if the executive were tracking foreign agents, the Court held that where domestic organizations were concerned, the president and his subordinates could conduct a "reasonable" search of telephone conversations only by submitting the case to a magistrate and obtaining a warrant. "Security surveillances," the justices lectured Richard Nixon,

> are especially sensitive because of the inherent vagueness of the domestic security concept, the necessarily broad and continuing nature of intelligence gathering, and the temptation to utilize such surveillances to oversee political dissent. . . . [T]he President's domestic security role . . . must be exercised in a manner compatible with the Fourth Amendment.

Appeal

The Bill of Rights does not mention a right to appeal a conviction, but the federal government and all the states allow at least one appeal as a matter of statutory right. State procedures are usually more restrictive than federal; but state prisoners who can show that their trials were unfair and that the state judicial system does not allow a full review can ask a federal district judge for a writ of habeas corpus.[22] Whatever appellate procedure a state provides cannot discriminate on the basis of ability to pay. A state must, for example, furnish impoverished convicts with free transcripts of the trial and legal counsel for at least one appeal.

Punishment

The Eighth Amendment forbids imposition of "cruel and unusual punishments." That prohibition is vague, and some justices have candidly conceded that they interpret it in light of the "evolving standards of decency that mark the progress of a maturing society."[23] In 1910 the

Court invalidated a statute that authorized twelve years at hard labor in chains for embezzlement[24] and in 1962 a California law that made drug addiction a crime.[25]

The death penalty poses the most awesome constitutional problem. In 1972 *Furman v. Georgia* held by a 5–4 vote that death was a cruel and unusual punishment.[26] Each justice wrote his own opinion; two thought that it was basically offensive to human dignity, and three others believed that it was being imposed capriciously.

Isadore Hodges, one of the thirteen inmates of "death row" at the Tennessee State Prison, was spared execution by the electric chair by the U.S. Supreme Court's ruling in 1972 that the death penalty as then applied was unconstitutional. (United Press International)

Four years later, after Congress and thirty-five states had enacted new statutes to meet some of the objections of *Furman*, the justices ruled (7–2) that death was not of itself constitutionally forbidden, at least for murder.[27] At the same time the Court placed strict procedural restrictions on sentences of death, striking down in the process statutes that made death an automatic punishment for certain crimes. The justices were again badly divided in their reasoning and wrote six opinions, none of which commanded more than three votes.

These and later decisions seem to require that, to impose the death sentence, government must divide the trial into two sections. The first determines the guilt or innocence of the accused. In the second part, assuming a verdict of guilty, the defendant *must*[28] be allowed to present evidence showing mitigating circumstances and the prosecutor evidence of aggravating circumstances. The latter include such factors as the defendant's having been earlier convicted of another murder or having committed this murder while in the act of another felony. The court must then consider these circumstances and can impose a death sentence only on a finding that the aggravating circumstances outweigh the mitigating circumstances. A further necessary check is automatic and full review by the state's highest court, which goes beyond the usual kinds of appellate review and ensures that the penalty is consistent with that imposed in similar cases within the state.

Double Jeopardy

The clear message of the Fifth Amendment—"nor shall any person be subject for the same offense to be twice put in jeopardy of life or limb"— is that, if acquitted, a defendant can never be retried for that offense. Although this clause now applies to state as well as federal cases, it is subject to certain exceptions. If a particular crime violates *both* state and federal law, a person could be prosecuted by both governments. Even where a person has violated only a federal or a state law, that single deed may be criminal under several statutes. In such circumstances the accused may be tried for each separate offense. Again, freedom from double jeopardy does not prevent the prosecution from bringing a person to trial a second time when a higher court has set aside the original finding of guilt because of procedural errors.

⭐ ACTUAL PRACTICES OF CRIMINAL JUSTICE

It is easy to understand why police would prefer wider discretion than the Constitution, statutes, and judges permit. As trained experts, most of them take professional pride in their work—the business of apprehending criminals and protecting society.

It is also easy to understand—although not to justify—why police officers sometimes break the law to catch criminals. To dedicated officers crime is not simply a mass of unpleasant statistics. They work every day amid the suffering it causes and see the blood, gore, wasted lives, and crippled minds of adults and, worse, of youngsters who will never have a chance at a decent life. Police are likely to come to despise lawbreakers and to be deeply motivated to protect society from their activities. They are also likely to be angry at the restraints that the legal system often imposes on them. For instance, when police make an arrest, they do not presume the accused innocent. If honest officers were not convinced of the suspect's guilt, they would not make the arrest. They have conducted an investigation, examined the evidence, and drawn what to them are logical conclusions.

At the same time, the desire of police to curb crime is functional for their careers. Promotion depends in large part on success in making arrests that lead to convictions. And there can be little doubt that operating *within* the law often makes catching criminals more difficult.

Investigatory Procedures

Especially when working on a serious felony like murder or large-scale sale of narcotics, police almost always scrupulously follow the letter of the law. They know the case is likely to produce a lengthy trial, during which a judge will carefully examine not only the nature of the evidence but also the way in which it was obtained. Police are apt to be equally scrupulous in dealing with affluent citizens or successful criminals, because both types of people know their legal rights, retain their own attorneys, and perhaps also have easy access to reporters or public officials. In many instances, when the police think that the crime does not cause a disturbance and the offender is basically a decent citizen, they accord far more lenient treatment than the law specifies.

In the usual case, however, law enforcement officers are tougher in their actions, knowing that seldom will there be an examination in open court of the way in which evidence was obtained.[29] As a practical matter, police are familiar with the habits of many small-time criminals. They can detain most of these people and search them for incriminating evidence without probable cause. Both the suspect and the officer may know that the law forbids such action, but both also know that if the petty criminal, or even the innocent poor man or woman, insists on constitutional rights, the police can make life miserable. For the same reasons, after being taken into custody, accused often do not insist on their right to silence—although they may lie outrageously—or to an attorney, at least at the interrogation stage.

Studies of the impact of *Miranda* have shown that a large percentage of prisoners who are advised of their rights quickly waive them.[30] In part they do so because they wish to appear cooperative; in part because they do not understand what is being told them; and in part because they do not trust lawyers to take their side against the police. The *Miranda* rules, of course, make no difference to professional criminals, who know precisely what their rights are.

A standard police technique is to allow petty crooks to go free, letting them know that they can be leaned on any time, and then to use both gratitude and fear to persuade them to act as informers. In exchange for occasional tips, police may give these people a few dollars and not check closely into how they earn their living otherwise. The efficiency of a police force in arresting major criminals is a function of its intelligence system, which in turn is based largely on underworld informants. The society of criminals has its own networks of communications, and tapping these can provide steady payoffs that police believe are worth the cost of letting a few lesser offenders roam the streets.

The Trial Substitute

One of the most important facts about American criminal justice is that most cases never go to full trial. An overwhelming majority and, in some jurisdictions, as many as nine out of ten nontraffic convictions are obtained through guilty pleas that result from *plea bargaining*, negotiating between the accused and the prosecution. Suspects may tacitly begin bargaining by cooperating with the police by not insisting on their rights. It is with prosecutors, however, that the hard bargaining typically takes place. In some state jurisdictions—but not in the federal system—trial judges may participate in the negotiations; in a few states, both sides must stipulate that no bargaining has occurred, although everyone, including the judge, knows that it has.

In essence, the defendant offers to plead guilty if the prosecutor will ask the judge for leniency or will reduce the charge—for example, from assault with a deadly weapon to simple assault. Both sides are pushed toward bargaining. The defendant often has a criminal record and knows that the evidence is weighty, possibly damning. And, of course, he or she can usually plead guilty to a lesser crime. Even if innocent and able to put up a good defense, a defendant who cannot raise bail may have to stay in jail longer awaiting trial than if convicted and sentenced. Moreover, although the statistical evidence is shaky, there is a widespread belief that judges impose stiffer punishment on persons convicted after a full trial than they do if the accused pleads guilty.[31]

For their part, prosecutors usually have small, overworked staffs facing huge backlogs of cases. If busy prosecutors can get rid of less important business without riling the police or making a mockery of the law, they are generally happy to do so. To maximize their bargaining positions, prosecutors often charge defendants with a more serious

"I find you not guilty because the criminal justice system just isn't working."

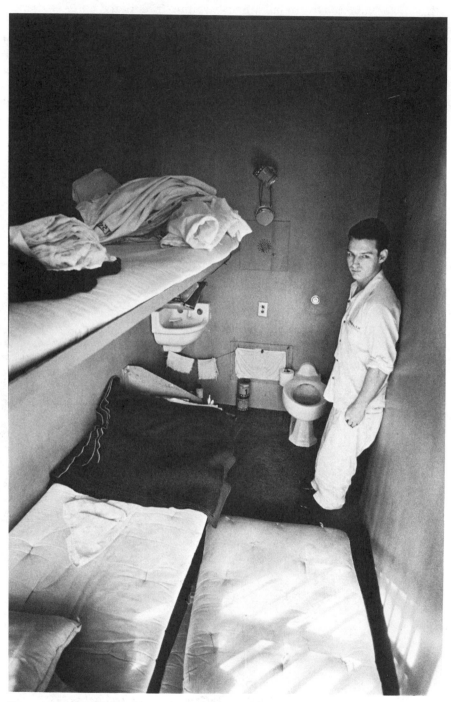

Overcrowded prisons: Three men live in this cell in a Texas penitentiary. (Tomas Pantin/*Texas Monthly*)

crime than the one on which they think they can get convictions if the cases actually go to trial.

Judges usually know what is going on, even where plea bargaining is illegal. They also realize that they preside over courts originally designed to serve a small, uncomplicated rural society; their tribunals, as currently staffed, could not possibly function in an urban environment if they had to accord a full and fair trial to every defendant. Dockets are stacked with cases. A typical judge on an urban court that handles lesser criminal cases may have to dispose of more than a thousand nontraffic cases every month, and perhaps as many traffic offenses. Courts of higher jurisdiction have fewer but more complicated cases, and they too are usually far behind in their dockets.

Justices of the Supreme Court have sustained plea bargaining, provided that the trial judge makes sure that the negotiations have been "intelligent and voluntary." Indeed, the Court said in 1971 that plea bargaining "is an essential component of the administration of justice. Properly administered, it is to be encouraged."[32] On the other hand, the National Advisory Commission on Criminal Justice Standards and Goals, a group of distinguished police, lawyers, judges, professors, and penologists, reviewed the evidence for and against the practice and condemned it. The only concession that the commission was willing to make "is that total elimination of the practice will take appreciable time."[33]

In 1982, California became the first large state to abolish plea bargaining. It remains to be seen whether its criminal courts will be swamped, as have been those of some smaller communities that have done away with bargaining.

⭐ PRISONS, REHABILITATION, AND SOCIAL REFORM

A Society of Captives

Confusion over the purposes of criminal law is reflected in what happens to that small percentage of criminals who are imprisoned. At best, most prisons are custodial institutions that do little to rehabilitate offenders. At worst—and the worst seems normal—prisons are merely schools that have very strict rules about attendance, maim the minds and bodies of amateurs, and train them to become professional criminals.

If a prisoner goes to a newer, minimum-security institution, the process is likely to be boring rather than oppressive. Confinement in a penitentiary, however, entails severe, even savage punishment. The

Efforts to provide prison inmates with opportunities to learn something besides the criminal trades vary greatly from prison to prison. At the Federal Correction Institution at Fort Worth, Texas, some prisoners are trained in the construction trades in preparation for admission into union apprenticeship programs upon release. (Leo M. Dehnal, U.S. Bureau of Prisons)

facilities are usually dilapidated and badly overcrowded. Florida, for example, recently packed into single cells measuring twelve by fifteen feet as many as ten inmates. In Alabama, prisoners sometimes had to sleep between urinals in crowded men's rooms infested with roaches and other vermin. In 1982, twenty-eight states were under court orders to reduce overcrowding or release their prisoners.

Even worse than the physical conditions is the atmosphere of terror that pervades a penitentiary. Sociologists have coined the word "prisonalization" to describe the social and psychological processes by which an inmate is assimilated into the life of a prison.[34] The new prisoner joins a society of criminals who live a life of more sordid violence inside the walls than they knew outside. Inmates quickly learn that, while guards keep them from freedom, the real determinants of how they live are fellow convicts. When the doors shut, the *prisoners'* rules operate, and penitentiaries abound in extortion; assaults that often result in serious injuries, sometimes in blindings or cripplings, and occasionally in death; as well as homosexual activities that include prostitution and brutal gang rapes. These conditions do little to help a person prepare for a useful, productive life outside.

Generally speaking, the larger society takes little interest in what happens to human beings inside penitentiaries. "It must be ironic to a prisoner," Chief Justice Burger has remarked, "to recall that society spared no expense to provide him with three, four, or five trials and appeals, at enormous costs, but then proceeds to forget his plight" once he has been imprisoned.

In some respects, the situation in most maximum-security penal institutions is likely to get worse even if more money is spent to improve physical facilities. Legislators, judges, prosecutors, and prison officials try to keep young offenders, first offenders, and those guilty of nonviolent crimes out of penitentiaries by giving suspended sentences, providing alternative facilities where some contact with normal life can be maintained, and allowing early parole when there seems a chance for rehabilitation. These may all be needed reforms; but, insofar as each is effective, it screens out for penitentiaries the more vicious criminals, the professionals as well as the psychopaths.

"Repeaters" form the core of hardened men and women who populate penitentiaries. Few persons go to maximum-security prisons unless previously *convicted* of a felony. Because the odds of arrest and conviction are low, it is probable that most of these people had *committed* many felonies. According to the FBI's data, about two out of every three prisoners who serve time or receive pardons are rearrested, though not necessarily reconvicted, within three years, on serious charges. The corresponding figure for those paroled—and thus supposedly supervised by law enforcement officers—is almost the same, reflecting in part the fact that the heavy work load of parole officers seldom allows them to offer more than token supervision or assistance.

 SUMMARY

This chapter underlined the gnawing problem of crime and stressed the difficulties of controlling such "deviant conduct" while maintaining government under law, a wide measure of individual freedom, and respect for human dignity. A free society needs protection both from criminals and from public officials, including police.

Police who are both efficient and law abiding, judicial procedures that are scrupulously fair, and prisons that reform rather than brutalize are all important elements in coping with the myriad problems of crime. But no matter how honest, fair, dedicated, and efficient they are, neither police, prosecutors, judges, nor prison officials can get at the roots of crime. Whatever the exact mix of individual and societal responsibility, no program can be successful over the long run unless linked to broader social reform. Frustrations of life in overcrowded urban slums, of discrimination, and of humiliations of unemployment and of living off welfare in a land of plenty may not cause crime, but they often make crime appear an attractive alternative—a means, perhaps the only visible means, of escape from the nightmares of the ghetto or barrio.

Moreover, many "habitual criminals" have made breaking the law a life's work and, having become skilled at their trade, see no point in joining the "straight" world. Others may not be capable of living peacefully in a community. Whether because of moral weakness, genetic defects, mental disease, scars from earlier abuses by parents or society, these warped humans again and again commit crimes of violence. Prison terms can interrupt but not end their careers. Some or all of these people may be re-educated to live useful lives, but only through intricate and costly programs.

NOTES

1. Federal Bureau of Investigation, *Uniform Crime Reports for the United States—1981* (Washington: Government Printing Office, 1982), p. 36.
2. Law Enforcement Assistance Administration, *Criminal Victimization Surveys in 13 American Cities* (Washington: Government Printing Office, 1975); T. J. Flanagan, D. J. van Alstyne, and M. R. Gottfredson, *Sourcebook of Criminal Justice Statistics—1981* (Washington: Government Printing Office, 1982), Section 3.
3. Law Enforcement Assistance Administration, National Criminal Justice Information and Statistics Service, SD-EE No. 7, and Bureau of the Census, *State and Local Government Special Studies, No. 77* (Washington: Government Printing Office, 1976).
4. *Stacey v. Emory*, 97 U.S. 642 (1877).
5. *Sibron v. New York*, 392 U.S. 59 (1968).
6. *Chimel v. California*, 395 U.S. 752 (1969).
7. *United States v. Ross*, 72 L. Ed 2d 572 (1982).
8. 384 U.S. 436 (1966).
9. *Mallory v. United States*, 354 U.S. 449 (1957).
10. *Johnson v. Louisiana*, 406 U.S. 356 (1972); *Apodoca v. Oregon*, 406 U.S. 404 (1972).

11. Race: *Norris v. Alabama,* 294 U.S. 587 (1935); ethnic group: *Hernandez v. Texas,* 347 U.S. 475 (1954); sex: *Taylor v. Louisiana,* 419 U.S. 522 (1975).
12. *Miranda,* cited above, note 8.
13. *Weeks v. United States,* 232 U.S. 383 (1914).
14. *Mapp v. Ohio,* 367 U.S. 643 (1961).
15. *Terry v. Ohio,* 392 U.S. 1 (1968).
16. For example, see Chief Justice Burger's dissent in *Bivens v. Six Unknown Federal Narcotics Agents,* 403 U.S. 388 (1971).
17. 428 U.S. 465 (1976).
18. 277 U.S. 438 (1928).
19. *Berger v. New York,* 388 U.S. 31 (1967); *Katz v. United States,* 389 U.S. 347 (1967).
20. *Scott v. United States,* 436 U.S. 128 (1978), recognized the danger of police eavesdropping on innocent and private conversations but held that peril to be constitutionally permissible as long as police had obtained a valid warrant for the wiretap.
21. 407 U.S. 297 (1972).
22. *Francis v. Henderson,* 425 U.S. 536 (1976); see also *Stone v. Powell,* 428 U.S. 465 (1976). These decisions actually restricted use of habeas corpus by state prisoners. The earlier rule had been that a state prisoner could seek habeas corpus as a means of challenging the constitutionality of state action against him unless it could be shown that he was deliberately avoiding state procedures that were open to him.
23. Chief Justice Earl Warren in *Trop v. Dulles,* 356 U.S. 86 (1958).
24. *Weems v. United States,* 217 U.S. 349 (1910).
25. *Robinson v. California,* 370 U.S. 660 (1962). In *Powell v. Texas,* 392 U.S. 514 (1968), however, the Court ruled that the factual record was not adequate to determine if drunkenness was a disease and so sustained the constitutionality of a statute punishing public intoxication.
26. 408 U.S. 238 (1972).
27. The leading cases are *Gregg v. Georgia,* 428 U.S. 153 (1976); *Roberts v. Louisiana,* 428 U.S. 325 (1976); *Woodson v. North Carolina,* 428 U.S. 280 (1976); and *Green v. Oklahoma,* 428 U.S. 907 (1976). The following year, *Coker v. Georgia,* 433 U.S. 584 (1977), held that a state could not execute a man convicted of rape if he had not killed his victim.
28. *Lockett v. Ohio,* 438 U.S. 586 (1978); *Eddings v. Oklahoma,* 71 L. Ed 2d 1 (1982).
29. Jerome H. Skolnick, *Justice Without Trial: Law Enforcement in Democratic Society* 2d ed. (New York: John Wiley and Sons, 1975), and Arthur Rosett and Donald R. Cressey, *Justice by Consent: Plea Bargains in the American Courthouse* (Philadelphia: J. P. Lippincott Co., 1976), provide two useful, well-written accounts of how the system actually works.
30. Many of these studies are discussed in U.S. Senate, Committee on the Judiciary, *Hearings: Controlling Crime through More Effective Law Enforcement,* 90th Cong., 1st Sess. (1967). See also, Note, "Interrogations in New Haven: The Impact of *Miranda,*" *Yale Law Journal,* LXXVI (1967), 1519; and Richard H. Seeburger and R. Stanton Wettick, Jr., "Miranda in Pittsburgh—A Statistical Study," *University of Pittsburgh Law Review,* XXIX (1967), 1; and Walter F. Murphy and C. Herman Pritchett, eds., *Courts, Judges, and Politics,* 3d ed. (New York: Random House, 1979), Chapter 10.
31. Compare the evidence and analysis in Note, "The Influence of the Defendant's Plea of Judicial Determination of Sentence," *Yale Law Journal,* LXVI (1956), 204, with the more recent and sophisticated analysis by James Eisenstein and Herbert Jacob, *Felony Justice: An Organizational Analysis of Criminal Justice* (Boston: Little, Brown, 1977), pp. 269–271.
32. *Santobello v. New York,* 404 U.S. 257 (1971).
33. National Advisory Commission on Criminal Justice Standards and Goals, *National Conference on Criminal Justice* (Washington: Government Printing Office, 1973).
34. See the literature excerpted in Leon Radzinowicz and Marvin Wolfgang, eds., *Crime and Justice,* vol. 3, *The Criminal in Confinement* (New York: Basic Books, 1971), Part I.

SELECTED BIBLIOGRAPHY

American Enterprise Institute. *Reform of Federal Criminal Law* (Washington: American Enterprise Institute, 1978). A brief but useful analysis of efforts to rewrite the entire federal criminal code.

Brown, Michael K. *Working the Street: Police Discretion and the Dilemmas of Reform* (New York: The Russell Sage Foundation, 1981). A scholarly study of police behavior and the effects of bureaucratization on officers' individual discretion.

Campbell, James S., J. R. Sahnid, and D. P. Stang. *Law and Order Reconsidered: A Staff Report to the National Commission on the Causes and Prevention of Violence* (Washington: Government Printing Office, 1969). A very useful re-evaluation of earlier work done by the President's Commission on Law Enforcement and Administration of Justice, cited below.

Caspar, Jonathan D. *American Criminal Justice: The Defendant's Perspective* (Englewood Cliffs, N.J.: Prentice-Hall, 1972). A description of the way the police, prosecutors, and courts operate, based on interviews with people charged with criminal activity.

Chevigny, Paul. *Police Power: Police Abuses in New York City* (New York: Pantheon Books, 1969). A sharply critical account of the behavior of a relatively good police force; argues that abuses are the results of social pressures on the police.

Doig, Jameson W., ed. *Criminal Corrections: Ideals and Realities* (Lexington, Mass.: Lexington Books, 1982). A group of distinguished experts writes on problems of street crime, including the roles of criminal and juvenile courts and prison conditions in fighting and/or fostering crime.

Ermann, M. David, and Richard J. Lundman, eds. *Corporate and Governmental Deviance* (New York: Oxford University Press, 1978). A revealing set of essays dealing with "white-collar" crime by corporate and governmental officials.

Gaylin, Willard. *Partial Justice: A Study of Bias in Sentencing* (New York: Alfred A. Knopf, 1974). Examining in depth several case studies, a practicing psychiatrist who is also a professor of law argues that it is not overt biases but subconscious values that make sentencing behavior so varied.

Goldfarb, Ronald L. *Jails: The Ultimate Ghetto of the Criminal Justice System* (New York: Doubleday, Anchor Books, 1975). A study of jails as pretrial detention centers.

Hawkins, Gordon. *The Prison: Policy and Practice* (Chicago: University of Chicago Press, 1976). A short but penetrating study of penal institutions.

Heumann, Milton. *Plea Bargaining: The Experiences of Prosecutors, Judges, and Defense Attorneys* (Chicago: University of Chicago Press, 1978). A comprehensive study of plea bargaining.

Levin, Martin A. *Urban Politics and the Criminal Courts* (Chicago: University of Chicago Press, 1977). Using aggregate statistical data as well as interviews with judges, prosecutors, and defense attorneys, the author presents several models of judicial systems and probes their effects on recidivism and deterrence.

Mitford, Jessica. *Kind and Usual Punishment: The Prison Business* (New York: Vintage Books, 1974). A popular but useful (and readable) account of life in prison.

National Advisory Commission on Criminal Justice Standards and Goals. *National Conference on Criminal Justice* (Washington: Government Printing Office, 1973). An effort by a distinguished group of public officials and private citizens to formulate a program to reform the entire system of criminal justice.

Packer, Herbert L. *The Limits of the Criminal Sanction* (Stanford, Cal.: Stanford University Press, 1968). An exciting inquiry into the relations between society and criminal law, and a challenge to the social utility of much of that law.

President's Commission on Law Enforcement and Administration of Justice. *The Challenge of Crime in a Free Society* (Washington: Government Printing Office, 1967). A monumental study surveying the entire field of criminal justice and making more than 200 specific recommendations for reform.

Radzinowicz, Leon, and Marvin E. Wolfgang, eds. *Crime and Justice* (New York: Basic Books, 1971). 3 vols. A massive collection, available in an inexpensive paperback edition, of leading articles by lawyers, philosophers, and social scientists.

Rosett, Arthur, and Donald R. Cressey. *Justice by Consent: Plea Bargains in the American Courthouse* (Philadelphia: J. P. Lippincott Co., 1976). A nontechnical analysis of plea bargaining by a lawyer and a sociologist, both of whom had earlier worked for the President's Commission on Law Enforcement and the Administration of Justice.

Skolnick, Jerome H. *Justice without Trial: Law Enforcement in Democratic Society*, 2d ed. (New York: John Wiley and Sons, 1975). A skillfully done work combining the rich detail of an original case study with broad generalizations from existing knowledge.

Sykes, Gresham M. *The Society of Captives: A Study of A Maximum Security Prison* (Princeton, N.J.: Princeton University Press, 1958). A short but fascinating account of life in a state prison.

Ungar, Sanford J. *FBI* (Boston: Little, Brown, 1975). A journalist's detailed and critical study of the FBI. Although completed before the scandals that racked the FBI in 1976 produced much new valuable information about the bureau's operations, this volume is still the best account.

Van den Haag, Ernest. *Punishing Criminals* (New York: Basic Books, 1975). A controversial argument by a psychiatrist that society has not only the right but the duty to make punishment fit the crime rather than the criminal, as much of modern criminology holds.

Whittemore, L. H. *Cop: A Closeup of Violence and Tragedy* (New York: Holt, Rinehart & Winston, 1969). Three vignettes of the working lives of policemen; provides a series of informative insights into the human problems of law enforcement.

Wilson, James Q. *The Investigators: Managing FBI and Narcotics Agents* (New York: Basic Books, 1978). The central thesis of this short, well-written book is that bureaucratic behavior, whether in government or private business, is largely shaped by the organization's central tasks; thus control and reform are far more difficult than most people imagine.

PART VIII

Conclusion

17 Politics and Policy in Perspective

A COMPLEX POLITICAL SYSTEM

THE ILLUSTRATIVE CASE OF THE SST

PROSPECTS

We have tried to further understanding of the American system of government by first placing it in its historical, cultural, and institutional setting and then analyzing how its formal and informal processes operate—the choice of leaders, the practical and legal restrictions on their power, and the character of citizens' rights. We have also described the way the system produces and carries out policy decisions and some of the ways these policy choices shape American life.

⭐ A COMPLEX POLITICAL SYSTEM

To this point our analyses have of necessity been organized around the various separate components of the American system, not the process as a whole. In reality, of course, Congress, the courts, the president and federal executives, political parties, the Constitution, federalism, and other elements of American politics constantly interact with each other. Rarely does one component operate in isolation. Instead, many elements of the political process are involved in developing and implementing almost all public policies.

An act of Congress, for example, may first take shape in an executive agency, or in a congressional subcommittee, or in an interest group. The problem addressed by this law may have been an issue in a presidential or congressional campaign. Or what happened in the campaign may have delayed consideration of a new policy. For example, despite widespread dissatisfaction with the welfare "mess," neither a Democratic Congress nor a Republican president was willing to give the other potential credit at the polls by cooperating to produce more rational and effective legislation before the election of 1976. No serious efforts at reform were undertaken by Congress or President Ford, at least in part because of the impending national election.

In some instances, widespread constituency pressures may greatly increase the importance to elected officials of such issues as abortion, prayers in public schools, or gun control. Public attitudes, reflected in polls, election results, and letters to newspapers and elected officials, can play a significant role in framing legislative agendas and in determining the content of policies.

More generally, particular policy proposals inevitably are influenced by widespread public attitudes about government, its responsibilities, and its effectiveness. Shifts in public concerns, priorities, and confidence in government constantly shift through to elected officials and so affect the nature and content of public policy. So does the nation's pattern of economic and social development. Both domestic and foreign policy making are shaped at every stage by the social, economic, demographic, and technological realities of a highly urbanized and industrialized society.

As any important legislative proposal moves through the maze of government, its content is affected by a variety of officials—federal bureaucrats, the president and his aides, representatives and senators on the appropriate committees and subcommittees, other members of Congress, and congressional staff. If the proposal deals with domestic affairs, state and local governments will try to ensure that their particular constituencies are treated fairly in the distribution of federal funds and responsibilities. The shape of the legislation is also influenced by past and anticipated rulings of federal courts, as well as by the general powers of and limitations on government set forth in the Constitution.

Once passed, a law continues to involve many elements of the political system. Enacting legislation is only one step in the policy process. Carrying out laws means action by federal administrative or regulatory agencies, the White House, and congressional committees and subcommittees. Rules and regulations must be developed within the executive branch or federal regulatory agencies. To implement the law, new administrative structures may have to be created, or old ones reorganized. Staffs usually have to be acquired, professional expertise developed, and equipment purchased.

All these activities depend heavily on the availability of funds to carry out the particular policy. To secure funds, administrative agencies submit budget requests to the Office of Management and Budget in accordance with general guidelines developed by the president and his advisers. OMB officials review these requests in light of overall resources and priorities. Their recommendations for particular programs and agencies become a key element in the development of the president's budget. Next comes detailed review in Congress, by the budget committees and the appropriations committees and their subcommittees in each house.

After securing legal authority and appropriations, agencies move on to make thousands of determinations necessary to carry out almost any public policy. Is a particular businessman or individual eligible for assistance under the statutory provisions and administrative regulations? Does an exporter qualify for an exemption from a particular trade restriction? Do the laser guns ordered by the Department of Defense meet federal contract specifications? Are the matching arrangements proposed by a city consistent with the rules governing a federal sewer program? Which of two hundred applicants should receive the fifteen federal grants available in the field of energy conservation?

"Hey! After we spend the Russians into the ground, if there's any money left let's give a little party!"

Dana Fradon, © 1982, The New Yorker Magazine, Inc.

For most domestic programs, implementation also depends heavily on the activity of state and local governments. Lack of matching funds or different local priorities may preclude participation in some federal programs. Differences in funding and administrative capabilities produce very different results among states and localities in "national" programs for welfare, health, job training, and education. Implementation may be slowed by political pressures, as in the case of major changes in federal transportation policy enacted by Congress in the early 1970s, which permitted use of highway taxes for mass transit. In many states, road builders, highway users, and other automotive interests strongly resisted diversion of "their" funds to public transportation. Another factor in implementation is lack of information among many local officials about new federal policies, a factor that reduced use of highway funds for public transportation.

At every step in the process of implementation, other elements of the political system become involved. Administrative agencies constantly compete for funds and responsibilities. Agencies lobby with budget officials, the White House, and congressional committees and subcommittees. So do interest groups of all kinds. Particular administrative decisions are closely watched by some members of Congress, as well as by corporations, unions, state and local governments, foreign nations, and other interests affected by the powers and actions of the agency in question. Judicial rulings may expand or restrict an agency's power, discretion, or procedures. Public opinion can affect the carrying out of policy, as can disclosures of official cupidity or stupidity by enterprising journalists or disgruntled public employees. From time to time, election results alter implementation, as well as policy. Newly elected leaders at the national, state, and local levels usually shift priorities, change policies, and replace some top officials.

Laws, of course, are only one type of policy. Other kinds of determinations of policy also involve a variety of the components of the political system. Decisions by federal courts ordering desegregation of public schools have resulted largely from lawsuits filed by civil rights groups challenging policies of local school officials. In the wake of actions by federal judges, opponents of integration have rioted, local school boards have wrestled with complex plans designed to implement or evade court orders, and mayors and other elected officials have tried to satisfy the courts without losing their local base of support. In Washington, presidents have unhappily resorted to military force to quell disturbances resulting from efforts to desegregate schools. Intense constituency pressures have led Congress to attempt to eliminate busing from the remedies available to federal judges in dealing with school desegregation. And officials of the Departments of Justice and Education have been consistently criticized, both for applying too much and too little pressure on local school districts that failed to desegregate.

Because of the complexity of the political process, issues rarely can

A message from the United Steelworkers of America poses the tradeoff between jobs and free trade in stark terms.

65,000 Jobs Endangered by Imported Specialty Steel

IS YOUR JOB NEXT?   PHONE: 344-4533

be neatly compartmentalized. Even such broad categories as foreign policy and domestic policy are seldom watertight. Defense spending and assistance to other nations reduce resources available for domestic needs. Development of new weapons is justified on the grounds of threats from abroad, but support for and opposition to particular military programs often depend on which sections of the country will obtain defense contracts and bases. Policy on the Middle East affects petroleum prices, and thus the cost of oil, and so the entire domestic economy. Encouraging favorable trade relationships with friendly nations may threaten domestic industries that cannot meet the competition of cotton goods produced in Taiwan or shoes made in Brazil. The question of how far the United States extends its jurisdiction over coastal waters is hardly an abstract issue of international law for commercial fishermen in Maine and California who compete with the formidable fishing fleets of Japan and the Soviet Union.

★ THE ILLUSTRATIVE CASE OF THE SST

Development of public policy on commercial supersonic aircraft provides an excellent example of the interplay of foreign and domestic policy and the involvement of most political components of the American system in a single issue. During the late 1950s, advances in aviation technology stirred interest in supersonic airliners. Builders of aircraft and federal aviation officials saw great promise in supersonic airplanes, as did the commercial airlines. Supersonic transports—or SSTs—soaring at over twice the speed of sound would drastically reduce travel time between major cities of the world. Development of the SST by American firms would permit the United States to retain its pre-eminent role in the production of commercial aircraft. But the estimated costs of designing and testing a supersonic airliner were beyond the resources that the aviation industry was willing to invest. As a result, the Federal Aviation Agency concluded that public funds would be required to assist development of the new airplane, and in 1961 Congress responded with an initial appropriation of $11 million.

The following year, the French and British governments announced a joint effort to develop their own SST, the Concorde, and similar work was also under way in the Soviet Union. The prospect of foreign competition created a sense of urgency in the United States. In 1963, President Kennedy decided to commit the federal government wholeheartedly to underwriting the development of an American SST by private industry. Under Kennedy's plan, which was announced one day after Pan American World Airways ordered six Concordes, 75 percent of the estimated development costs of the SST would be financed by taxpayers' dollars.

Over the next decade, Congress appropriated almost $1 billion for the SST. Supporters of the program, led by the two senators from Washington, the home of Boeing Aircraft, rested their case on national prestige and the necessity of ensuring continued American superiority in civil aviation. Failure to develop the SST, they argued, would adversely affect the nation's balance of payments by as much as $16 billion by 1980, because dollars to purchase new aircraft would flow out of, rather than into, the United States. Strong support for the SST came from business, labor, and political leaders, including Boeing's chairman, the president of the AFL–CIO, and the Governor of Washington. Groups like the National Committee for SST and Industry and Labor for SST were formed to bolster congressional backers of the SST and the then Federal Aviation Agency, which was the principal supporter of the project within the executive branch.

On the other hand, opposition to federal subsidies for the SST also grew steadily during the 1960s. The planes promised to be extremely noisy, generating sonic booms that could disturb millions of people, thus adding significantly to already severe noise problems around major airports. In addition, the new aircraft would pollute the upper atmosphere, perhaps adversely affecting the ozone layer that protects the earth from the sun's radiation. Because of the high cost of the aircraft itself and its prodigious consumption of fuel, travel on SSTs would be expensive. Why, asked critics, should the federal government subsidize an aircraft that would serve only a small proportion of the population, mostly affluent businessmen and wealthy "jet-setters"? More generally, increasing numbers of Americans were no longer convinced that expensive technological advancements like the SST automatically meant "progress." And environmental concerns were rising to the forefront of national political consciousness. Among the foes of the SST were such groups as the Friends of the Earth, Environmental Action, the Sierra Club, and Zero Population Growth.

By 1971, the opponents of the SST in Congress were sufficiently numerous to reverse the policy of three presidents who had supported federal subsidies. Bolstering opposition were persistent doubts within the executive branch over the economic feasibility and scientific desirability of SSTs. After weeks of intense lobbying by both sides, the SST was killed on close votes in the House and Senate. With President Nixon strongly in favor of the SST, party lines were relatively important in the congressional voting, particularly in the House, where most Republicans backed it. A key factor in the House vote was the Legislative Reorganization Act of 1970, which provided for recording teller votes. With environmental concerns rising, many congressmen who had previously supported the SST on unrecorded votes were unwilling to antagonize environmentalists on a recorded vote.

With federal support ended, Boeing and General Electric, the prime contractors, abandoned the project. The issue of supersonic aircraft,

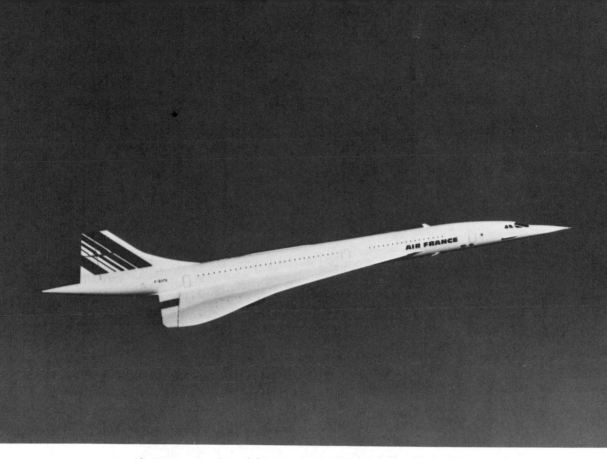

Air France's version of the Concorde SST, which was finally allowed to land in New York in 1977. (Courtesy Air France)

however, was not yet resolved. During the same year that Congress was rejecting additional funds for the SST, both the Anglo-French Concorde and the Russian TU-144 were undergoing test flights. By 1975, Concorde was ready for regular passenger service. Now the question became whether the United States would permit SSTs to operate within its territorial limits. Requests from Air France and British Airways for permission to fly Concorde into New York and Washington were favorably received by the Federal Aviation Administration. In recommending that the secretary of transportation approve SST service, FAA concluded that the aircraft was neither excessively noisy nor a significant threat to the atmosphere.

Residents of areas surrounding jet airports vigorously protested. Noise levels, they argued, would be intolerable. To support their case, they pointed to FAA's own statement on the environmental impact of Concordes, which conceded that the SST would be four times noisier during takeoff than the newest subsonic jets. Support for these objections came from the U.S. Environmental Protection Agency, which found Concorde's noise levels unacceptable for operations in densely settled areas such as those surrounding Kennedy International Airport in New York. Environmental groups also protested that the SST wasted fuel and that not enough was known about the hazards posed to health by Concorde's impact on the atmosphere. Responding to these concerns, members of Congress sought to amend federal airport legislation to ban Concorde.

Proponents of Concorde contended that local worries should not be permitted to endanger relations with Britain and France. The secretary of state urged fair treatment for two of the nation's oldest allies. British and French officials argued that agreements with the United States protected their airliners against discriminatory treatment. London and Paris also spoke ominously about retaliating against American airlines and commercial aircraft produced in the United States. To press their case, Britain and France and their airlines dispatched top officials, hired lobbyists, and engaged politically influential Washington law firms.

Early in 1976, the secretary of transportation decided to approve a limited number of daily flights into New York and Washington for a trial period of sixteen months. The American system of government, however, provides multiple means of access to power, and the way was not yet cleared for Concorde to fly to the two cities. Opponents continued to seek support in Congress for legislation to ban SSTs, arguing that the limited number of flights would grow, once Concorde had its sleek nose in the door. Anti-SST groups went to court as well in an effort to overturn the decision.

Although these efforts to block Concorde at the national level failed, supporters of Concorde had additional hurdles to overcome elsewhere in a decentralized political system. In New York, permission was required from the Port Authority of New York and New Jersey, the bistate agency that controls the metropolitan area's airports. Any action by the Port Authority, in turn, could be vetoed by the governor of New York or the governor of New Jersey. By now, the Concorde was an emotional issue in New York, and Governor Hugh Carey had come out strongly against Concorde flights into Kennedy International Airport. Other local officials, as well as such groups as the Metro Suburban Aircraft Noise Association, the National Organization to Insure a Sound-Controlled Environment (NOISE), and the Emergency Coalition to Stop the SST, immediately began to press the Port Authority to deny permission to Air France and British Airways.

Responding to these pressures, the New York legislature quickly passed a bill establishing noise standards that effectively barred supersonic aircraft from Port Authority airports. For the New York law to have any effect, however, New Jersey had to pass similar legislation. To prevent enactment, London and Paris dispatched officials to Trenton to lobby for the SST. Although New Jersey took no action, the Port Authority, in deference to the opposition of Governor Carey, rejected the requests of Air France and British Airways for permission to inaugurate

Concorde service at Kennedy International Airport. Only after evaluating Concorde operations at other airports, especially the impact of the SST's noise levels, would the Port Authority reconsider its policy. Britain and France refused to accept the Port Authority's prohibition and went into federal court to test the constitutional authority of a state agency to interfere with interstate and foreign commerce.

A complex legal battle ensued, as is often the case in American politics. The first round was won by Concorde, with a federal district court ruling that the Federal Aviation Act of 1958 provided clear authority for SSTs to land at Kennedy, and thus superseded the action of the Port Authority under the supremacy clause of the Constitution. This decision, however, was reversed by the U.S. Court of Appeals for the Second Circuit, which upheld the right of the Port Authority to ban the Concorde as long as the prohibition was fair, reasonable, and nondiscriminatory. The issue was referred back to district court for a hearing on the fairness of the Port Authority's action, where the judge once again overturned the SST ban, this time on the grounds that the Port Authority's behavior was arbitrary, unreasonable, and discriminatory. This finding was upheld by the appeals court, which ordered the Port Authority to permit immediate use of Kennedy by the Concorde. A last-ditch attempt to secure a delay from the U.S. Supreme Court failed. So did a final round of demonstrations by opponents, which tied up traffic

French and British lobbyists press the case for the Concorde SST with a legislator on the floor of the New Jersey Assembly in Trenton, the state capital. (Wide World Photos)

"A few more delays, gentlemen, and it'll be obsolete anyway!"

By courtesy of Paul Rigby, New York Post

around Kennedy, but did not prevent arrival of the Concordes in October 1977.

What is abundantly clear from the SST's travails is the complexity of American political processes. Political conflict over the SST involved basic constitutional questions, international relations, questions of national purpose and priorities, shifting public attitudes on technology and environmental protection, and different views of the costs and benefits of public actions. Experts differed over scientific, economic, and technological questions raised by development and use of supersonic aircraft. International, national, and varying local perspectives produced clashing views and interests. And almost every component of the political system became involved over the years—Congress and its committees and voting methods, the president and a variety of executive officials and agencies, political parties, federal courts, state and local governments, and a host of interest groups ranging from foreign governments and their agents to neighborhood civic associations.

 PROSPECTS

In the course of examining the varied components of the American political system, what may have escaped notice—but should not have— is the fragility of constitutional democracy. The ideals and trusts that together form a democratic system are brittle. They can be shaped into anarchy or demagoguery. Like most aspects of modern industrial societies, constitutional democracy depends on adherence to norms of peaceful behavior and free exchange of ideas. Acceptance of these norms rather than physical force makes what the framers called free government possible. Public officials can be murdered; speakers can easily be shouted down; universities closed; constitutional rights trampled by police or mobs of neighbors or strangers; and the electoral process corrupted by the apathy of voters or by the grandiose ambitions of candidates.

Despite this inherent fragility, essentially the same governmental structure has survived in the United States for almost two hundred years—a monument to the wisdom of the framers of the Constitution but also to the skill of succeeding generations of politicians. That this governmental structure has survived *and* produced a great measure of individual freedom and a general level of prosperity unequaled in most of the world is even more significant. Yet for contemporary Americans there are dismaying items on the debit side of the ledger: the United States continues to face serious crises in both foreign and domestic affairs.

The current international situation raises many issues of the debate over America's role as a world power that has gone on intermittently since 1898. One could almost say that the issues are similar to those George Washington discussed with his advisers after the outbreak of the French Revolution or those that Thomas Jefferson considered before sending the navy and marines to retaliate against the Barbary pirates. There is one all-important difference, however: The present problems occur against a backdrop of nuclear and biological weapons that can obliterate life on this planet.

The conflict with the Soviet Union has framed American foreign policy for a third of a century, resulting in enormous expenditures for ever more sophisticated weapons on both sides. Despite occasional "thaws" in relations with the USSR, competition with the Soviets affects American policies in every corner of the globe. The end of the war in Southeast Asia, which preoccupied U.S. foreign policy and domestic politics for almost a decade, settled few questions. Relations with Vietnam, Thailand, China, Korea, and other Asian nations still pose a variety of problems and opportunities. Equally troublesome are questions of American policy toward Israel and the Arab world, black Africa, and Latin America. Relations with close allies in western Europe are not straightforward and simple. Nor is it clear how the United States can help developing nations maintain their independence, attain some degree of internal freedom, and achieve a measure of prosperity or, in the case of some, feed their growing and hungry populations. If imperialism has become repugnant to most Americans, isolationism can only be a fatuous dream in a shrunken world.

The problem in foreign affairs is to find wisdom. In domestic politics, the problem is to find both wisdom and the power to carry out that wisdom. Previous chapters have stressed the ways in which the American system divides political power and makes it difficult to transform energy from a potential to a kinetic state. The results of that difficulty are plain.

More than a hundred years after Emancipation, racial injustice is still eroding ideals of human dignity as well as a constitutional command of equality; urban blight is spreading; private industries continue to scar the landscape, pollute the water, and foul the air at murderous rates. The welfare system can be most charitably described as inadequate, if indeed it is a system at all. In the midst of abundance and monumental agricultural surpluses, Americans permit millions of children to go hungry. Black and Hispanic ghettos are crowded with well-fed rats and ill-nourished people, people as rejected as the white poor of Appalachia or the Indian poor on the reservations. Unemployment has reached epidemic proportions in much of the older industrial belt of the northeast and midwest. Well-off Americans apparently continue to hope that the patience of these people is as boundless as their poverty.

Crime threatens to turn cities into jungles, and epidemics of narcotics addiction menace entire generations. The judicial system—state and federal—are in dire trouble. That they function at all is largely due to the fact that only a small percentage of crimes ever result in actual trials. Deep divisions have developed between those who would rehabilitate criminals and those who prefer simply to punish them. Only a handful of dedicated officials show concern enough to reject simplistic solutions and continue to search for ways to serve society and treat convicted felons with fairness and some humanity.

It is difficult to explain how the richest nation in the world, one that can wage massive wars, rebuild the economy of western Europe, design and deploy intercontinental ballistic missiles, and put men on the moon and rockets on Mars, cannot muster the physical resources and the will to conquer poverty, crime, and racial injustice at home. The cause may lie in what Duane Lockard has called "perverted priorities," putting second things first.[1] Or it may result from what Theodore H. Lowi terms "interest group liberalism," a belief that government not only *does* work through a bargaining process among powerful interest groups, but that it is the way government *ought* to function.[2]

In either case, the Madisonian system of fragmented power must bear much of the blame. As we have seen, the legal structure of federalism itself poses no real obstacle to the exercise of national power. The difficulties lie in the fragmentation that permeates American government. The parties, Congress, the bureaucracy, and even the national

"You heard the President. We're in this together."

courts are to some extent infused with a kind of fractionalism that shatters and obscures authority and responsibility. To be adopted, a national policy must usually be cut and sewn into a bizarre, almost psychedelic patchwork so that almost every influential constituency interest gets a piece of the action. To be carried out, a policy must be further tailored to fit the ideas and ambitions of federal, state, and local bureaucrats and the interests they represent. Rationality, in terms of programmatic efforts to attack a serious problem, rarely plays a central role in this bargaining process.

As long as the demands on government were small, as long as those making the demands could be satisfied with immediate symbolic gains and gradual material gains, the Madisonian system performed well. It still performs well for groups who have become politically entrenched and who want only to make minor adjustments in the status quo. But it is hard on newcomers. And there are now large groups of blacks, Indians, Hispanic Americans, and poor whites who are relatively new actors in politics and who do not seem likely soon to be absorbed into the mainstream of American life.

The Madisonian system also makes difficult the development of coherent policies on complex problems. With so many claimants seeking to protect their interests, and so many agreements needed to proceed, policies are never easily formulated for energy, trade, inflation, unemployment, and scores of other issues that press their way on to the public agenda.

For all the debits, there is also a credit side to the political ledger. The values protected by a system of fragmented power are numerous. Such arrangements safeguard the rights of many minorities by providing them with vantage points from which they can oppose and even block hostile governmental action. It promotes stability and peaceful change by encouraging negotiation, bargaining, and compromise. It produces public policy by a process approaching consensus, albeit consensus among a restricted clientele.

The system not only checks power against power and ambition against ambition—and so provides a strong incentive for one set of officials to counter efforts by the president to set himself above the Constitution. It also checks intelligence against intelligence and virtue against virtue. Built in is the assumption that no single individual or small group is all-wise or all-virtuous or is likely to have a monopoly of what wisdom and goodness humans do possess. The system, when it works, thus forces competition among ideas as well as among individuals, and so allows voters a choice. These are not trivial accomplishments. Limited government and even popular government must inevitably rest on the legitimacy of opposition to those currently in power and in favor.

The crux of the dilemma facing the United States is how to preserve the obvious benefits the Madisonian system bestows while lowering the costs of operating that system to the point where government, especially the federal government, can cope effectively and democratically with the unholy trinity of crime, poverty, and racial injustice. By "effectively" we imply no utopian vision of governmental officials wiping out social problems as if erasing a blackboard; we mean only that government must formulate and administer programs that will bring remedies substantial enough to provide real help in the present and realistic hope for the future. By "democratically" we mean securing the approval of a majority of the people in the country, not for the details of any plan but for the general ends and means of a coherent program.

To win approval for what must be done requires leadership that is skilled both in persuasion and, in the best sense of the word, in manipulation. In the past, the United States has sometimes found that kind of leadership, usually in war, but occasionally in peace. Most recently, Lyndon B. Johnson was able to build on the legacy of John F. Kennedy to begin a war against poverty and a campaign for civil rights that went far beyond tokenism. His tragedy was in dissipating his financial resources and his moral as well as political capital in Vietnam just when his management of Congress was creating and exploiting opportunities for far-reaching social reform.

If an open political system is to survive in the United States, it will do so because of positive political leadership that faces up to existing problems and convinces both private citizens and public officials that these problems are serious and interrelated; that they must be attacked, attacked immediately, and attacked together by coordinated and expensive programs.

In spite of Watergate, effective American government remains presidential government. Because of the moral or political ineptitude of a particular president, Congress may frustrate or even dominate the White House. In fact, if they are doing their work properly, members of Congress should be able to restrain presidential power and even, on occasion, to neutralize that power, for the president is neither infallible nor impeccable. But over the long run, as we have said in this book, if there is to be positive, effective leadership in American politics, it can come only from the White House. Even then, the Madisonian system may produce stalemate, as it did on most problems throughout the 1970s. But without presidential leadership, there can be no hope that the system can move with any speed or in a controlled direction. This was demonstrated anew in 1981 when President Reagan proposed major reductions in the role and scope of federal responsibilities and was able to secure approval from Congress and compliance from an often reluctant bureaucracy.

The great challenge to a president is to bring a whole people together. No recent president has met this challenge. Confronting problems of foreign or domestic politics, his first legitimate task is to persuade by evidence and reason—not by violence, repression, or deception—other public officials and a large majority of private citizens to face up to existing problems, for they cannot be wished away or hidden behind glib phrases coined by hucksters from Madison Avenue. His second and more difficult task is to motivate those people to act. His function is, quite simply, to *lead*.

NOTES

1. Duane Lockard, *The Perverted Priorities of American Politics* (New York: Macmillan, 1970).
2. Theodore J. Lowi, *The End of Liberalism: Ideology, Policy, and the Crisis of Public Authority* (New York: W. W. Norton and Company, 1969).

Glossary

Accountability   The concept that elected officials in a democratic political system are responsible to the people for their actions.

Administrative rules and regulations   Policy determinations made by administrative agencies in order to implement constitutional provisions, laws, treaties, and executive orders.

Advise and consent   The power of the U.S. Senate to ratify treaties and confirm presidential appointments. Ratification of treaties requires a two-thirds vote; appointments are confirmed by majority vote.

Advisory opinion   An opinion issued by a court, answering in the absence of an actual case or controversy a particular question of law. Federal courts may not issue such opinions; some state courts must do so if asked by an appropriate public official. Advisory opinions are fairly common in some countries, for example, Canada. See **Case.**

Affirmative action   Policy under which a governmental agency or private institution not only ceases to discriminate against particular racial, ethnic, religious or sexual groups but also tries to undo damage caused by past discrimination by actively seeking out and assisting members of the groups previously discriminated against.

Aggregate voting data   The actual results in voting subdivisions, such as precincts, wards, cities, states, or the country as a whole. Available from official records; thus, while accurate do not offer any way of telling how specific classes of individuals within the particular subdivision voted.

Amendment   An addition, alteration, or deletion by a legislative body of an existing statute or legislation under consideration. Most laws enacted by Congress are amendments to existing laws. See **Constitutional amendment.**

Amicus curiae   Literally "friend of the court." A private citizen, representative of an interest group, or public official not immediately involved in a lawsuit but who asks, or is asked by the court, to offer his or her views to enlighten the judicial mind.

Annexation The addition of new territory by a unit of government, permitting its physical expansion.

Appeal Generally a request from a losing litigant to a higher court to review the case in which he or she lost. More specifically, appeal refers to the process that losing litigants may follow in the limited circumstances that give them a right to a hearing before the U.S. Supreme Court.

Appellate jurisdiction Authority of a court to review decisions made by courts lower in the judicial hierarchy. See **Jurisdiction; Original jurisdiction.**

Apportionment The distribution of seats in a legislative body among electoral districts within a governmental unit. See **Gerrymandering.**

Appropriation A statute enacted by a legislative body authorizing the expenditure of public funds for the purposes set forth in the statute.

Arrest warrant An order from a judicial official, issued only upon probable cause, authorizing a public officer to take a named person into custody. See **Warrant; Search warrant; Probable cause.**

At large Election of members of a legislative body by the voters of the entire governmental unit rather than from districts within the governmental unit. U.S. senators are elected at large in each of the fifty states.

Bail An amount of money or property an accused or convicted person pledges as security that, if released from custody, he or she will appear in court at the proper time.

Balancing An approach to civil liberties issues which calls for judges to weigh against one another the interests that compete in a case and determine which prevails, or much of each can co-exist.

Bicameral legislature A legislature with two houses; in the case of the Congress, the House of Representatives and the Senate.

Bill of Attainder A legislative act that, without judicial trial, convicts a specific person of a crime and orders him or her punished.

Bipartisanship Cooperation between the two major political parties in the development of a policy or program, most commonly in the field of foreign affairs. Bipartisanship usually involves close consultation between leaders of the two parties in Congress, and between these leaders and the President.

Block grant Grants-in-aid made to units of government for broad general purposes such as community development or public health.

Case A technical term in law referring to a real clash of legally protected interests in which one interest is suffering or is about to suffer serious injury. Federal courts have jurisdiction only to hear "cases and controversies," not to issue advice or to settle academic questions, however interesting. See **Advisory opinion.**

Categorical grants Grants-in-aid made to units of government for specific purposes, such as the construction of highways or the education of handicapped students, usually involving requirements and conditions from the government that makes the grant.

Caucus In general, a meeting of a select group of people. In nominations for elections, caucus refers to a process by which party leaders meet together and choose candidates; in legislatures, it refers to meetings held solely among members of one party to decide on party policy. In Congress, the party caucuses select the party's legislative leaders and determine committee assignments and chairmanships.

Central city A city with 50,000 or more residents which forms the core of a Standard Metropolitan Statistical Area.

Certification The procedure used by a U.S. court of appeals to send certain questions before it to the Supreme Court for answers before the court of appeals proceeds to decide the actual case. The court of appeals, when it certifies questions to the Supreme Court, says the queries are of such difficulty or sweeping importance as to need settlement by the highest federal court. The procedure is seldom used.

Certiorari A writ (order) from the Supreme Court to a lower court (usually a court of appeals or a state supreme court) to send a case to the Supreme Court for review. The litigant who lost in the lower court may petition the Supreme Court for certiorari; granting the writ is completely within the discretion of the Justices. The Supreme Court's rules require a vote of four of the nine Justices to grant the writ. The Court annually rejects, without a hearing or explanation, more than 90 percent of such petitions.

Checks and balances Method of limiting the power of the components of the government by providing in the Constitution for shared responsibilities, so that one element may check the actions of another.

Civil rights Governmental actions usually in the form of statutes such as the Civil Rights Act of 1964 designed to protect individuals against arbitrary or discriminatory treatment.

Class action A law suit begun by a single person or small groups of persons suing not only on behalf of himself or herself but also for all other members of an easily identifiable group (or class) who share a common legal interest. The resulting decision affects not only the specific litigant(s) but all other members of that class.

Clientele interests Groups that benefit from a particular governmental activity, and thus usually provide the most important source of political support for the activity.

Closed primary A primary election in which only people who have declared their allegiance to a particular party may vote to select that party's nominees for the general election. Use of the closed primary prevents the "cross-over" of supporters of one party into the primary of another party. See **Primary election; Open primary.**

Cloture Motion to close debate and thus bring a matter to a vote. Cloture is particularly important in the Senate, where a vote of sixty senators is needed to restrict a senator to no more than one hour on a bill and its amendments.

Committee of the Whole Committee composed of all 435 members of the House of Representatives. By sitting as the Committee of the Whole, the House can operate under rules that expedite debate and consideration of issues.

Common law The body of law developed through decisions of English judges and carried on and adapted to changing conditions by American judges. Common law is usually concerned with providing damages for injuries inflicted by one private citizen on another. See *Stare decisis:* **Equity.**

Confederation A system of government in which local units (states in the United States prior to adoption of the Constitution of 1787) retain most of the important governmental powers and the nation can exercise only limited authority over the local units and can regulate conduct of individual citizens only through local units.

Conference committee A committee appointed by the House of Representatives and Senate to effect a compromise when, as usually happens, the House and Senate versions of a bill are not identical. Members of conference committees are usually drawn from the more senior members of the committee that considered the bill.

Confirmation Legislative approval of nominations for executive and judicial positions. Under the Constitution, presidential nominations are confirmed by a majority vote of the Senate.

Consensus Agreement among most of those concerned with a matter. In more general terms, consensus refers to widespread acceptance of a society's basic goals and fundamental political arrangements.

Conservatism Preference for maintenance of the status quo; thus the desire to conserve existing economic, political, and social institutions. Conservatives in the United States generally oppose governmental regulation of the economy, increased governmental expenditures, and the expansion of the national government into areas that traditionally have been the responsibility of the states, localities, or individual citizens. See **Liberalism.**

Constitution A fundamental set of rules to which all governmental actions are expected to conform. A constitution, whether written or unwritten, expresses a set of general political principles about society's ideals, objectives, and legitimate processes.

Constitutional A change or addition to a constitution. Amendments to the U.S. Constitution are proposed by a two-thirds vote of both houses of Congress or by a convention called by Congress at the request of two-thirds of the states. To date, only the first of these methods has been used. Proposed amendments must be ratified by three-fourths of the states. Only the Twenty-first Amendment, which repealed Prohibition, was ratified by state conventions.

Constitutionalism A belief that governmental power, whether of all the people, a majority of the people, or some smaller segment of society, must respect certain rights and liberties of individual citizens. See **Natural rights.**

Contingency funds Money appropriated by Congress for use by an executive agency to meet problems unforeseen when Congress approved the budget.

Controversy A legal term having the same meaning as *case.* See **Case.**

Delegated powers Powers granted by the Constitution to the national government.

Democracy A belief that government derives its legitimacy from popular consent. It may be *direct,* as in a New England town meeting in which all citizens were entitled to participate, or *representative,* as in U.S. state and national governments in which all citizens are entitled to vote to select major public officials who will. A democratic system may or may not include limitations on the power of the people or their representatives to enact certain kinds of public policy. See **Constitutionalism; Free government.**

Deviating election   An election in which a minority party captures the presidency and/or Congress but without disturbing previously existing patterns of party loyalty. See **Maintaining election; Reinstating election; Realigning election.**

Discharge petition   A petition signed by a majority of the members of the House of Representatives which, if approved by the House, forces a committee to bring a bill to the floor for consideration.

Double amenability   Being subject to two different governmental bodies (for example, the federal and state governments) and thus answerable to both for the same act; that is, for the same criminal act of robbing a national bank one might be separately tried and punished by both the federal and state governments. (Note that for the purposes of this concept as for much of American law, all municipal, town, city, county, and other local courts are *state* courts.) See **Double jeopardy.**

Double jeopardy   A highly technical term referring to a government's trying an accused for the same criminal offense for which a court earlier acquitted him. Note the difference between double jeopardy and double amenability.

Due process of law   A legal concept that for centuries referred to the procedures to which an accused person or a litigant was entitled in a court of law. It has now taken on certain substantive aspects. That is, it now also refers to what can be done by government, not merely how (the procedures it follows) government must act. For instance, not only must a state government provide a fair trial for persons accused of crime (procedures again) but also a state cannot make certain things legally punishable, for instance, religious beliefs.

Economic message   Annual report on general economic trends, employment, production, and prices submitted by the President to Congress in January, as required by the Employment Act of 1946.

Electoral College   A misnomer because it never meets together; the collective name given to the people for whom we actually vote in presidential elections; the winners, typically pledged to one of the major or minor parties, meet in their state capitols in December after presidential elections and cast their ballots for one of the candidates for President and one for Vice President. Each state has a number of electors equal to the sum of its senators and representatives; the District of Columbia has three. The ballots are sent to Congress, where they are counted in joint session the following January.

Equity   A legal procedure that began in medieval England as an alternative to common law, equity tends to prevent a wrong that a litigant will suffer in the future, whereas the common law typically offers monetary damages for wrongs already suffered. See **Common law.**

Executive agreement   An exchange of promises between two or more heads of government. Unlike a treaty, which binds the nations signing the pact, an executive agreement obligates only the incumbent heads of government. Its legal, but not necessarily its practical, force ceases when one of the signers leaves office.

Executive order   A policy determination made by the president, the governor of a state, or a mayor, on the basis of authority derived from constitutional or statutory law.

Executive privilege Controversial authority claimed by many presidents to withhold information from the legislative or judicial branches of government.

Ex post facto law A law that makes an act, innocent when committed, a crime, or that retroactively lowers the amount of proof needed to convict for a particular crime or that retroactively increases the punishment for a specific crime.

Extradition The process by which one government transfers a person within its jurisdiction to another government that wishes to try the person for a crime committed within its own jurisdiction.

Favorite son A state political leader nominated for the presidency at a national convention by members of the state's delegation, either as a means of gaining national publicity for the individual or in order to hold back the state's votes so as to improve the state's bargaining position at the convention.

Federal question The legal issues Article III of the Constitution says federal courts may decide.

Federalism A system of government in which authority is divided between local units (states in the United States) and the nation, with both sets of government having authority to act directly on individual citizens.

Federalist Papers, The A series of essays written in 1787 by Alexander Hamilton, John Jay, and James Madison in support of the proposed Constitution. The articles were published in New York newspapers and were designed to persuade New Yorkers to support the adoption of the new Constitution. The *Federalist Papers* provide an excellent insight into the aims and political philosophy of the framers of the Constitution.

Fiscal year The yearly accounting period used by a government for budgeting, appropriating funds, collecting taxes, and other financial purposes. The fiscal year for the national government now runs from October 1 to September 30, so that FY1979 began on October 1, 1978, and ends on September 30, 1979. Before 1977, the fiscal year for the national government was July 1 to June 30.

Filibuster A prolonged discussion by one or more senators designed to prevent the passage of a bill.

Floor leaders Members of Congress chosen by their party caucus to direct business on the floor of the House of Representatives and the Senate in the interest of their party.

Franchise The right to vote. See **Suffrage.**

Free government A name that many of the framers of the Constitution applied to the form of government they created, that is, a mixture of constitutionalism and democracy. See **Constitutionalism; Democracy.**

Full faith and credit A provision of the Constitution that requires states to honor each other's official acts.

Gerrymandering An apportionment of legislative seats so as to give an advantage to a particular political party or set of political interests. See **Apportionment.**

Grandfather clause A state statute that exempted a potential voter from having to comply with certain laws restricting the right to vote providing his grandfather had voted; a blatant way of allowing voting officials to block blacks whose grandfathers had been slaves and thus unable to vote from political participation; declared unconstitutional by the Supreme Court. See also **Literacy test; Understanding clause; White primary.**

Grand jury A body convened to hear evidence presented by the prosecuting attorney against persons accused of serious crimes. If a majority of the members of the grand jury feel there is sufficient reason to try the accused, the jury indicts the person who then must stand trial. See **Indictment.**

Grant-in-aid A sum of money derived from a tax levied by a higher level of government for expenditure and administration by a lower level of government in accordance with certain standards or requirements.

Grantsmanship The art of securing federal categorical grants for state and local governments, requiring skill in mastering complex regulations and winning political support from granting agencies.

Habeas corpus A writ order from a court, usually issued at the request of a friend or an attorney of a prisoner, directing a jailer or other official who is holding the prisoner to bring that person before the court and justify his or her detention. Literally, "if you have the body."

Head tax See **Poll tax.**

Impeachment One method the Constitution provides for removing appointive federal officials from office. The House of Representatives impeaches (formally accuses) an official of serious crimes, and the Senate then tries the accused. The House can impeach by a simple majority vote, but a two-thirds majority is needed in the Senate to convict.

Implementation The carrying out of policy determinations made by government.

Implied powers Powers of the national government derived from the authority explicitly specified in the Constitution.

Impoundment A refusal by an executive official, usually acting under direct presidential order, to spend money appropriated by Congress for certain specified purposes. The money is retained in the U.S. Treasury.

Indictment A formal accusation by a grand jury that a named person or persons is/are guilty of a particular crime. See **Information.**

Information A formal accusation by a prosecutor that a named person is guilty of a particular crime. See **Indictment.**

Injunction A court order directing a private citizen or a public official not to perform a particular action or to undo the effects of a particular action.

Interest group An organization whose principal objective is to secure support for policies favored by leaders of the group.

Interstate compact An agreement between two or more states.

Judicial review The authority of a court to declare unconstitutional an act or actions of the legislative and/or executive branch(es) of government.

Jurisdiction The authority of a court to hear and decide certain kinds of controversies.

Kitchen cabinet An informal group of advisers to the President, governor, or mayor, which can have more influence on the chief executive than cabinet members and other formal advisers.

Lame duck An elected official who has either been defeated for reelection or has chosen not to run for reelection but whose actual term of office has not yet expired.

Legislation Public policy formally enacted by legislative bodies such as Congress and state legislatures; it has the force of law, and violation of its terms could bring criminal penalties on the violator.

Liberalism Desire to change the status quo in order to advance the interests of individuals. Liberals in the United States generally favor the expansion of government to increase economic security and protect civil rights. See **Conservatism.**

Limited government A political system in which a constitution or other fundamental rules impose severe constraints on those who rule. See **Constitutional democracy; Free government.**

Literacy test A device, often used to keep blacks from voting, requiring a prospective voter to demonstrate to the satisfaction of a state official that he or she could read and write English; now forbidden by amendments to the Voting Rights Act of 1965. See also **Grandfather clause; Understanding clause; White primary.**

Litigant One who sues or is sued in a court. A party to a lawsuit.

Lobbying Efforts to persuade public officials to support the policies favored by a particular group.

Logrolling An agreement among two or more legislators to support legislation favored by the other; usually refers to the trading of votes for measures that benefit the logrollers home district.

Magistrate A minor judicial official authorized by law to try certain petty offenses and to issue some orders, such as subpoenas and warrants. See **Warrant.**

Maintaining election An election in which previously prevailing patterns of party loyalty persist. See **Deviating election; Reinstating election; Realigning election.**

Majority rule An underlying principle of democracy whereby the majority of citizens in any political unit are empowered to elect officials and through them determine public policies.

Mandamus An order from a court to a public official commanding him to perform a specific act about which the order allows him no discretion. In effect, a mandamus says to a public official, "Do your duty."

Martial law Replacement of regular legal and judicial processes by military orders enforced by troops and tribunals staffed by officers of the armed forces. At the federal level, the President may declare martial law only as authorized by Congress, and Congress may authorize martial law only where rebellion or invasion close the regular, civilian courts.

Matching funds Money or other public goods provided by state and local government as their share of categorical grants from the national government.

Metropolitan area An urbanized area composed of a large city or cities and surrounding suburban communities. See **Central city.**

Metropolitan government A single local governmental unit which encompasses all or most of a metropolitan area.

Midterm elections Congressional elections held in the middle of a President's four-year term; also called *off-year elections*.

Multimember district A legislative constituency that elects two or more representatives to a legislative body.

Multiparty system A political system with three or more political parties which regularly elect their candidates. Multiparty systems are rare in the United States, although minor parties are common.

National committee Party unit composed of members from each state, the District of Columbia, and territory whose primary function is to determine the date and place of the national convention.

National convention The formal assembly of the Democratic and Republican parties composed of delegates from each of the states and territories which nominates candidates for President and Vice President and ratifies the party platform.

National sample A relatively small number of people whom pollsters select from various parts of the entire country. Pollsters usually choose this sample on a random basis so that if of adequate size, one may generalize from the views of those in the sample to those of the population at large. See **Sample; Random sample; Panel.**

National supremacy A doctrine set forth in Article VI of the Constitution which established the Constitution, federal laws, and treaties as the supreme law of the land which may not be infringed upon by any state.

Natural law A belief that there exist certain rules of moral conduct among human beings, rules that all normal adults may perceive and understand through their ability to reason.

Natural rights A belief that every human being has certain unalienable rights which all people, groups, and government are morally obliged to respect. See **Constitutionalism.**

Nomination The official designation of an individual as a candidate for public office; also, the initial step in the appointment of an individual to an executive or judicial position. See **National convention; Primary election.**

Off-year elections See **Midterm elections.**

Open primary A primary in which people may decide at the time of the primary itself in which party's choice of nominees they wish to participate. See **Primary election; Closed primary.**

Original jurisdiction Authority of a court to hear a case by holding a trial. See **Jurisdiction; Appellate jurisdiction.**

Panel A sample of respondents whom pollsters interview two or more times in order to measure change in views. See **Sample; Random sample; National sample.**

Party identification A psychological relationship. Most Americans are not members of a political party in the sense of paying dues to the party or regularly and actively participating in party affairs. Most Americans do, however, think of themselves as being identified more with one party than another or with none at all.

Party platform   A document containing the position of a political party on some of the issues of the day.

Patronage   The public jobs an officeholder may dispense without regard to the formal rules of the Civil Service.

Plea bargaining   A process by which an accused person and a prosecutor negotiate. In exchange for the accused's providing evidence against others or for pleading guilty, a prosecutor offers to dismiss or reduce the charges or perhaps to recommend that the judge impose a light sentence.

Pluralism   In its most general sense, the term refers to the existence within a specific community of people of different social classes, occupations, religions, ethnic groups, or races. More particularly, in political analysis it refers to the dispersal of political influence among a wide range of individuals and groups.

Pocket veto   A means by which a President may kill a bill passed by both houses of Congress. If, within ten days of a bill's reaching the President, Congress ends its session and adjourns, the President may refuse to sign the bill. If he does refuse, the bill automatically dies. See **Veto.**

Policy committees   Groups created by each political party in the House of Representatives and the Senate which are supposed to develop general legislative programs for their parties, but have been unable to do so because of the decentralization of power in Congress.

Political culture   Ideas and social practices that are relevant to the development of a political system.

Political fragmentation   The division of a metropolitan area among a variety of local governmental units.

Political machine   A party organization headed by a single individual or a small group of leaders who exercise strong discipline over their followers. Political machines secured and maintained power by their control over nominations to public office, patronage, and favors. Machines have been most common at the city or county level. Their influence has declined with the spread of civil service and the growth of governmental social service programs.

Political party   An organization whose principal aim is to win control of the governmental machinery.

Political power   The ability to make others feel, think, or act as one wants with respect to governmental or other authoritative decision making.

Political socialization   The means by which a political system indoctrinates a new generation, as well as a means by which members of the new generation learn to become mature political participants following an old or a new set of values.

Politics   The authoritative processes that determine the goals of a society, mobilize its resources to achieve these goals, and distribute rights, duties, costs, benefits, rewards, and punishments among members of that society.

Poll   A survey of public opinion to obtain information about voting behavior and candidates, particular issues, and other political attitudes. See **Sample.**

Poll tax   Also known as a "head tax" or a "capitation tax." A tax of a fixed amount levied on all persons regardless of income or property; usually collected only when a person attempts to vote.

Polls   The official place where one votes in an election.

Populist revolt Effort during the early 1890s of the reformers known as Populists to mount a powerful third party to advance the cause of small and middle-level farmers. See **Populists.**

Populists Agrarian reformers who, especially in the last decade of the nineteenth century, tried to organize in the south and midwest to form a third party, though many were content to work within the Democratic party. They were opposed to what they saw as an eastern establishment as well as local rich who benefited from the gold standard, owned much land, and controlled the railroads, warehouses, and storage facilities. Among other reforms, the Populists advocated direct election of senators, federal loans for farmers, a graduated income tax, a secret Australian ballot, and the initiative and referendum. Populists pretty much disintegrated as a party after 1896.

Power elite A group that effectively monopolizes political influence, usually through its control over wealth and credit.

Power of the purse Control of the finances of government by the legislature. The Constitution lodges the power of the purse for the national government in Congress, providing that "no money shall be drawn from the treasury, but in consequence of appropriations made by law."

President pro tempore The presiding officer of the U.S. Senate in the absence of the Vice President, nominated by the caucus of the majority party and elected by the Senate.

Pressure group See **Interest group.**

Primary election An election, held under state law, in which those who declare themselves adherents of a particular party choose the nominees of that party to run in the next election. See **Closed primary; Open primary; White primary.**

Probable cause "Reasonable ground of suspicion supported by circumstances sufficiently strong in themselves to warrant a cautious man in the belief that the party is guilty of the offense with which he is accused."

Procedural rights The obligations of public officials to move only in certain specified ways when taking action against a private citizen or person.

Public authority Specialized units of government created to construct and operate toll roads, public housing, airports, and other public facilities.

Public law A statute or law of general application.

Public policy The actions or inaction of government with respect to a particular problem.

Quasi-judicial body A regulatory agency whose policy decisions have similar legal impact as court orders.

Radical Republicans The group of Republicans who controlled Congress during Reconstruction. See **Reconstruction.**

Random sample A relatively small number of people whom pollsters select from a larger population of a city, state, the nation, or from particular economic, ethnic, or other groups, by a method giving each person in the larger sample an equal chance of being chosen. See **Sample; National sample; Panel.**

Rationality In political analysis, concerns efficient allocation of available resources such as time, energy, or money to achieve the goals one desires.

Realigning election An election marking disruption of old party loyalties to the extent that the majority and minority parties switch places on a comparatively long-term basis. See **Maintaining election; Deviating election; Reinstating election.**

Reconstruction The period in American history after the Civil War, usually dated from 1865–1877, when the federal government directly ruled, frequently by means of the army, the former states of Confederacy, imposing a sort of period of atonement and reform before allowing those states to reassume their position as equals of the "loyal" states.

Registration A system used in most states to prevent fraud in the electoral process; to be eligible to vote a citizen must go to a designated state office and show proof of age, citizenship, and residence in the area. The citizen may then have his or her name placed on electoral rolls and is eligible to vote at the next election. Some states now allow registration at the time of election itself.

Reinstating election An election in which the majority party regains control following a deviating election. See **Deviating election; Maintaining election; Realigning election.**

Representative A member of the House of Representatives in the U.S. Congress, or of the lower house of a state legislature. There are 435 representatives in Congress, who serve two-year terms.

Revenue sharing Distribution of federal funds to states and localities for general use.

Rule of law The concept that all governmental actions must be based on previously announced general rules.

Sample A relatively small number of people whom pollsters interview and from their responses generalize about opinions held by larger segments of the population. See **Random sample; National sample; Panel.**

Search warrant An authorization issued only upon probable cause, from a judicial official to a public officer, allowing him to search specified persons or premises for particular objects described in the order itself. See **Warrant; Arrest warrant; Probable cause.**

Selective perception A psychological phenomenon which causes people to see events in terms of their personal values.

Senator A member of the U.S. Senate, or of the upper house of a state legislature. There are two senators for each of the fifty states, and they serve six-year terms.

Seniority Period of continuous service of a member of Congress, which determines rank within committees and is a major factor in the selection of committee and subcommittee chairmen.

Separation of power The term often used to describe the allocation of powers among the major components of the national government. Rather than separating power, the Constitution created a governmental system in which separate institutions share power. See **Checks and balances.**

Session The period during which a legislature meets. The U.S. Congress has a regular session each year. Since each Congress operates on a two-year cycle, there are two sessions per Congress. In addition, the President may call special sessions of Congress.

Single-member district A legislative constituency that elects one representative to a legislative body.

Special rule An order prepared by the Rules Committee and adopted by majority vote of the House of Representatives that sets the ground rules for consideration of a major bill on the floor of the House.

Standard Metropolitan Statistical Area (SMSA) A county or two or more counties with substantial urban population that contain at least one central city of 50,000 persons or a city of 25,000 which together with settled contiguous areas form a community of 50,000.

Standing committees The regular committees of the House of Representatives and the Senate, which are responsible for broad areas of public policy, such as foreign affairs, commerce, or appropriations.

Standing to sue A technical legal term referring to the requirements a litigant must meet, in addition to showing that the court has jurisdiction before being allowed to sue in a federal court. The essential requirements are that the questions raised can be handled by judges and are not ones whose solutions the Constitution delegates to Congress and/or the Executive; and that the legal interest that the litigant asserts involves a personal right and not a general right such as to "good government" shared by all citizens.

Stare decisis Literally, "let the decision stand." The rule adopted by English common law judges and followed by American judges generally to use the reasoning behind previous decisions as the basis for deciding current controversies.

Statutes Public policy formally enacted by legislative bodies such as Congress and state legislatures.

Straight party voting Voting for all the candidates nominated by one party.

Subcommittee A specialized component of a standing committee of the House of Representatives or the Senate that is responsible for much of the detailed work of the committee.

Substantive rights The essence of what is protected, such as privacy or free speech. See **Procedural rights.**

Suburbs The portion of a Standard Metropolitan Statistical Area that lies outside the central city.

Suffrage The right to vote. See **Franchise.**

Survey research A method of obtaining information about general public opinion or behavior by interviewing a sample of people from a particular population. See **Sample.**

Swing ratio The advantage a political party receives when it obtains a higher percentage of legislative seats than it received of the popular vote.

Ticket-splitting Voting for candidates of different parties for different public offices; for example, voting for a Democrat for President but a Republican or Independent for Congress. See **Straight party voting.**

Treaty A solemn agreement between two or more nations; it obliges them to perform or not perform certain kinds of actions and remains in force for the number of years specified in the agreement itself. Treaties are signed by the President and ratified by the Senate.

Understanding clause A state regulation, designed to keep blacks from voting, requiring a prospective voter to explain to the satisfaction of a public official, always white, the meaning of any clause in the state or federal constitution. See also **Grandfather clause; Literacy test; White primary.**

Unitary government A political system in which subnational units are created by and under the direct control of the central government.

Veto The President's refusal to consent to a bill's becoming law. He returns the bill to Congress, with his objections. Congress can "override" the veto, that is, enact the bill into law over the President's objections only by a two-thirds majority in both houses.

Voter's Decision Rule A theory of voting that explains the citizen's choice as consisting of weighing what is liked and disliked about one candidate against what is liked and disliked about the other. The candidate who gets the larger positive rating will be the one for whom the citizen votes.

Warrant An order from a judicial official authorizing a public officer to proceed in a manner specified by the terms of the order. See **Search warrant; Arrest warrant.**

Whips Members of Congress appointed by the floor leaders to secure support of party members when major issues come before the House of Representatives and the Senate for consideration.

White Citizens' Council A group founded in Winona, Mississippi, shortly after the Supreme Court's School Segregation Cases (1954), to prevent, by economic pressure on blacks and political pressure on public officials, implementation of those rulings.

White primary A primary election in which participation is limited to white people; declared unconstitutional in various forms by the Supreme Court. See **Primary election; Grandfather Clause; Literacy test; Understanding clause.**

Writ A formal written order from a court.

The Constitution
of the United States

and

Amendments
to the Constitution

The Constitution of the United States

We the People of the United States, in Order to form a more perfect Union, establish Justice, insure domestic Tranquility, provide for the common defence, promote the general Welfare, and secure the Blessings of Liberty to ourselves and our Posterity, do ordain and establish this Constitution for the United States of America.

Article I

SECTION I
[Legislative Powers]

All legislative Powers herein granted shall be vested in a Congress of the United States, which shall consist of a Senate and House of Representatives.

SECTION 2
[House of Representatives, How Constituted, Power of Impeachment]

The House of Representatives shall be composed of Members chosen every second Year by the People of the several States, and the Electors in each State shall have the Qualifications requisite for Electors of the most numerous Branch of the State Legislature.

No Person shall be a Representative who shall not have attained to the Age of twenty-five Years, and been seven Years a Citizen of the United States, and who shall not, when elected, be an inhabitant of that State in which he shall be chosen.

Representatives and *Direct Taxes** shall be apportioned among the several states which may be included within this Union, according to

---

* Modified by Sixteenth Amendment.

their respective Numbers, *which shall be determined by adding to the whole Number of free Persons, including those bound to Service for a Term of Years,* and excluding Indians not taxed, *three fifths of all other Persons.** The actual Enumeration shall be made within three Years after the first Meeting of the Congress of the United States, and within every subsequent Term of ten Years, in such manner as they shall by Law direct. The Number of Representatives shall not exceed one for every thirty Thousand, but each State shall have at Least one Representative; *and until such enumeration shall be made, the State of New Hampshire shall be entitled to chuse three, Massachusetts eight, Rhode-Island and Providence Plantations one, Connecticut five, New-York six, New Jersey four, Pennsylvania eight, Delaware one, Maryland six, Virginia ten, North Carolina five, South Carolina five, and Georgia three.*†

When vacancies happen in the Representation from any State, the Executive Authority thereof shall issue Writs of Election to fill such Vacancies.

The House of Representatives shall chuse their Speaker and other Officers; and shall have the sole Power of Impeachment.

SECTION 3
[The Senate, How Constituted, Impeachment Trials]

The Senate of the United States shall be composed of two Senators from each State, *chosen by the Legislative thereof,*‡ for Six Years; and each Senator shall have one Vote.

Immediately after they shall be assembled in Consequence of the first Election, they shall be divided as equally as may be into three Classes. The Seats of the Senators of the first Class shall be vacated at the Expiration of the second Year, of the second Class at the Expiration of the fourth Year, and of the third Class at the Expiration of the sixth Year, so that one third may be chosen every second Year: *and if vacancies happen by Resignation, or otherwise, during the Recess of the Legislature of any State, the Executive thereof may make temporary Appointments until the next Meeting of the Legislature, which shall then fill such Vacancies.*#

No person shall be a Senator who shall not have attained to the Age of thirty Years, and been nine Years a Citizen of the United States, and who shall not, when elected, be an Inhabitant of that State for which he shall be chosen.

The Vice President of the United States shall be President of the Senate, but shall have no Vote, unless they be equally divided.

---

* Modified by Fourteenth Amendment.

† Temporary provision.

‡ Modified by Seventeenth Amendment.

Ibid.

The Senate shall chuse their other Officers, and also a President pro tempore in the Absence of the Vice President, or when he shall exercise the Office of President of the United States.

The Senate shall have the sole Power to try all Impeachments. When sitting for that Purpose, they shall be on Oath of Affirmation. When the President of the United States is tried, the Chief Justice shall preside: And no Person shall be convicted without the Concurrence of two thirds of the Members present.

Judgment in Cases of Impeachment shall not extend further than to removal from Office, and disqualification to hold and enjoy any Office of honor, Trust or Profit under the United States: but the Party convicted shall nevertheless be liable and subject to Indictment, Trial, Judgment and Punishment, according to Law.

SECTION 4
[Election of Senators and Representatives]

The Times, Places and Manner of holding Elections for Senators and Representatives, shall be prescribed in each State by the Legislature thereof; but the Congress may at any time by Law make or alter such Regulations, except as to the Places of chusing Senators.

*The Congress shall assemble at least once in every Year, and such Meeting shall be on the first Monday in December, unless they shall by Law appoint a different Day.**

SECTION 5
[Quorum, Journals, Meetings, Adjournments]

Each House shall be the Judge of the Elections, Returns and Qualifications of its own Members, and a Majority of each shall constitute a Quorum to do Business; but a smaller Number may adjourn from day to day, and may be authorized to compel the Attendance of absent Members, in such Manner, and under the Penalties as each House may provide.

Each House may determine the Rules of its Proceedings, punish its Members for disorderly Behavior, and, with the Concurrence of two thirds, expel a Member.

Each House shall keep a Journal of its Proceedings, and from time to time publish the same, excepting such Parts as may in their Judgment require Secrecy; and the Yeas and Nays of the Members of either House on any question shall, at the Desire of one fifth of the present, be entered on the Journal.

Neither House, during the Session Congress, shall, without the

---

* Modified by Twentieth Amendment.

Consent of the other, adjourn for more than three days, nor to any other Place than that in which the two Houses shall be sitting.

SECTION 6
[Compensation, Privileges, Disabilities]

The Senators and Representatives shall receive a Compensation for their Services, to be ascertained by Law, and paid out of the Treasury of the United States. They shall in Cases, except Treason, Felony and Breach of the Peace, be privileged from Arrest during their Attendance at the Session of their respective Houses and in going to and returning from the same; and for any Speech or Debate in either House, they shall not be questioned in any other Place.

No Senator or Representative shall, during the time for which he was elected, be appointed to any civil Office under the authority of the United States, which shall have been created, or the Emoluments whereof shall have been encreased during such time; and no Person holding any Office under the United States shall be a Member of either House during his Continuance in Office.

SECTION 7
[Procedure in Passing Bills of Resolutions]

All Bills for raising Revenue shall originate in the House of Representatives; but the Senate may propose or concur with Amendments as on other Bills.

Every Bill which shall have passed the House of Representatives and the Senate, shall, before it becomes a Law, be presented to the President of the United States; if he approve he shall sign it, but if not he shall return it, with his Objections to that House in which it shall have originated, who shall enter the Objections at large on their Journal, and proceed to reconsider it. If after such Reconsideration two thirds of that House shall agree to pass the Bill, it shall be sent, together with the Objections, to the other House, by which it shall likewise be reconsidered, and if approved by two thirds of that House, it shall become a Law. But in all such Cases the Votes of both Houses shall be determined by Yeas and Nays, and the Names of the Persons voting for and against the Bill shall be entered on the Journal of each House respectively. If any Bill shall not be returned to the President within ten Days (Sundays excepted) after it shall have been presented to him, the Same shall be a Law, in like Manner as if he had signed it, unless the Congress by their Adjournment prevent its Return, in which Case it shall not be a Law.

Every Order, Resolution, or Vote to which the Concurrence of the Senate and House of Representatives may be necessary (except on a question of Adjournment) shall be presented to the President of the United States; and before the Same shall take Effect, shall be approved by him, or being disapproved by him, shall be repassed by two thirds of the Senate and House of Representatives, according to the Rules and Limitations prescribed in the case of a Bill.

SECTION 8
[Power of Congress]

The Congress shall have Power

To lay and collect Taxes, Duties, Imposts and Excises, to pay the Debts and provide for the common Defense and general Welfare of the United States; but all Duties, Imposts and excises shall be uniform throughout the United States;

To borrow Money on the Credit of the United States;

To regulate Commerce with foreign Nations, and among the several States, and with the Indian Tribes;

To establish an uniform Rule of Naturalization, and uniform Laws on the subject of Bankruptcies throughout the United States;

To coin Money, regulate the Value thereof, and of foreign Coin, and fix the Standard of Weights and Measures;

To provide for the Punishment of counterfeiting the Securities and current Coin of the United States;

To establish Post Offices and post Roads;

To promote the Progress of Science and useful Arts, by securing for limited Times to Authors and Inventors the exclusive Rights to their respective Writings and Discoveries;

To constitute Tribunals inferior to the supreme Court;

To define and Punish Piracies and Felonies committed on the high Seas, and Offences against the Law of Nations;

To declare War, grant Letters of Marque and Reprisal, and make Rules concerning Captures on Land and Water;

To raise and support Armies, but no Appropriation of Money to that Use shall be for a longer Term than two Years;

To provide and maintain a Navy;

To make Rules for the Government and Regulation of the land and naval forces;

To provide for calling for the Militia to execute the Laws of the Union, suppress Insurrections and repel Invasions;

To provide for organizing, arming, and disciplining, the Militia, and for governing such Part of them as may be employed in the Service of the United States, reserving to the States respectively, the Appointment of the Officers, and the Authority of training the Militia according to the discipline prescribed by Congress;

To exercise exclusive Legislation in all Cases whatsoever, over such District (not exceeding ten Miles square) as may, by Cession of particular States, and the Acceptance of Congress, become the Seat of the Government of the United States, and to exercise like Authority over all Places purchased by the Consent of the Legislature of the State in which the Same shall be, for the Erection of Forts, Magazines, Arsenals, dock-Yards, and other needful Buildings;—And

To make all Laws which shall be necessary and proper for carrying into Execution the foregoing Powers, and all other Powers vested by this Constitution in the Government of the United States, or in any Department or Officer thereof.

SECTION 9

The Migration or Importation of such Persons as any of the States now existing shall think proper to admit, shall not be prohibited by the Congress prior to the Year one thousand eight hundred and eight, but a Tax or Duty may be imposed on such Importation, not exceeding ten dollars for each Person.*

The privilege of the Writ of Habeas Corpus shall not be suspended, unless when in Cases of Rebellion or Invasion the public Safety may require it.

No Bill of Attainder or ex post facto Law shall be passed.

No Capitation, or other direct, Tax shall be laid, unless in Proportion to the Census or Enumeration herein before directed to be taken.†

No Tax or Duty shall be laid on Articles exported from any State.

No Preference shall be given by any Regulation of Commerce or Revenue to the Ports of one State over those of another; nor shall vessels bound to, or from, one State, be obliged to enter, clear, or pay Duties in another.

No Money shall be drawn from the Treasury, but in Consequence of Appropriations made by Law; and a regular Statement and Account of the Receipts and Expenditures of all public Money shall be published from time to time.

No Title of Nobility shall be granted by the United States: And no Person holding any Office or Profit or Trust under them, shall, without the Consent of the Congress, accept of any present, Emolument, Office, or Title, of any kind whatever, from any King, Prince, or foreign State.

SECTION 10
[Restrictions upon Powers of States]

No State shall enter into any Treaty, Alliance, or Confederation; grant Letters of Marque and Reprisal; coin Money; emit Bills of Credit; make any Thing but gold and silver Coin a Tender in Payment of Debts; pass any Bill of Attainder, ex post facto Law, or Law impairing the Obligation of Contracts, or grant any Title of Nobility.

---

* Temporary provision.

† Modified by Sixteenth Amendment.

No State shall, without the Consent of the Congress, lay any Imposts or Duties on Imports or Exports, except what may be absolutely necessary for executing its inspection Laws: and the net Produce of all Duties and Imposts, laid by any State on Imports or Exports, shall be for the use of the Treasury of the United States; and all such Laws shall be subject to the Revision and Control of the Congress.

No State shall, without the Consent of Congress, lay any Duty of Tonnage, keep Troops, or Ships of War in time of Peace, enter into any Agreement or Compact with another State, or with a foreign Power, or engage in War, unless actually invaded, or in such imminent Danger as will not admit of Delay.

ARTICLE II

SECTION 1
[Executive Power, Election, Qualifications of the President]

The executive Power shall be vested in a President of the United States of America. *He shall hold his Office during the Term of four years and, together with the Vice President, chosen for the same Term, be elected as follows.**

Each State shall appoint, in such Manner as the Legislature thereof may direct, a Number of Electors, equal to the whole Number of Senators and Representatives to which the State may be entitled in the Congress; but no Senator or Representative, or Person holding an Office of Trust or Profit under the United States, shall be appointed an Elector.

The electors shall meet in their respective States, and vote by ballot for two Persons, of whom one at least shall not be an Inhabitant of the same State with themselves. And they shall make a List of the Persons voted for, and of the Number of Votes for each; which List they shall sign and certify, and transmit sealed to the Seat of the Government of the United States, directed to the President of the Senate. The President of the Senate shall, in the Presence of the Senate and House of Representatives, open all the Certificates, and the Votes shall then be counted. The Person having the greatest Number of Votes shall be the President, if such Number be a Majority of the whole Number of Electors appointed; and if there be more than one who have such Majority and have an equal Number of Votes, then the House of Representatives shall immediately chuse by Ballot one of them for President; and if no person have a Majority, then from the five highest on the list the said House shall in like Manner chuse the President. But in chusing the President, the Votes shall be taken by States, the Representation from each State having one Vote; A quorum for this Purpose shall consist of a Member or Members from two-thirds of the States, and a Majority of all the

---

* Number of terms limited to two by Twenty-second Amendment.

States shall be necessary to a Choice. In every Case, after the Choice of the President, the person having the greatest Number of Votes of the Electors shall be the Vice President. But if there should remain two or more who have equal vote, the Senate shall chuse from them by Ballot the Vice President.*

The Congress may determine the Time of chusing the Electors, and the Day on which they shall give their Votes; which Day shall be the same throughout the United States.

No Person except a natural born Citizen, or a Citizen of the United States, at the time of the Adoption of this Constitution, shall be eligible to the Office of President, neither shall any Person be eligible to that Office who shall not have attained to the Age of thirty-five Years, and been fourteen Years a Resident within the United States.

In Case of the Removal of the President from Office, or his Death, Resignation, or Inability to discharge the Power and Duties of the said Office, the same shall devolve on the Vice President, and the Congress may be Law provide for the Case of Removal, Death, Resignation, or Inability, both of the President and Vice President, declaring what Officer shall then act as President, and such Officer shall act accordingly, until the Disability be removed, or a President shall be elected.

The President shall, at stated Times, receive for his Services, a Compensation, which shall neither be encreased nor diminished during the Period of which he shall have been elected, and he shall not receive within that Period any other Emolument from the United States, or any of them.

Before he enter on the Execution of his Office, he shall take the following oath or Affirmation: "I do solemnly swear (or affirm) that I will faithfully execute the Office of President of the United States, and will to the best of my Ability, preserve, protect and defend the Constitution of the United States."

SECTION 2
[Powers of the President]

The President shall be Commander in Chief of the Army and Navy of the United States, and of the Militia of the several States, when called into the actual Service of the United States; he may require the Opinion, in writing, of the principal Officer in each of the executive Departments, upon any Subject relating to the Duties of their respective Offices, and he shall have Power to grant Reprieves and Pardons for Offences against the United States, except in Cases of Impeachment.

He shall have Power, by and with the Advice and Consent of the Senate to make Treaties, provided two thirds of the Senators present

---

* Modified by Twelfth and Twentieth Amendments.

concur; and he shall nominate, and by and with the Advice and Consent of the Senate, shall appoint Ambassadors, other public Ministers and Consuls, Judges of the Supreme Court, and all other Officers of the United States, whose Appointments are not herein otherwise provided for, and which shall be established by Law: but the Congress may by Law vest the Appointment of such inferior Officers, as they think proper, in the President alone, in the Courts of Law, or in the Heads of Departments.

The President shall have Power to fill up all Vacancies that may happen during the Recess of the Senate, by granting Commissions which shall expire at the End of their next Session.

SECTION 3
[Powers and Duties of the President]

He shall from time to time give to the Congress Information of the State of the Union, and recommend to their Consideration such Measures as he shall judge necessary and expedient; he may, on extraordinary Occasions, convene both Houses, or either of them, and in Case of Disagreement between them, with Respect to the Time of Adjournment, he may adjourn them to such Time as he shall think proper; he shall receive Ambassadors and other public Ministers; he shall take Care that the Laws be faithfully executed, and shall Commission all the Officers of the United States.

SECTION 4
[Impeachment]

The President, Vice President and all civil Officers of the United States shall be removed from Office on Impeachment for, and Conviction of, Treason, Bribery, or other high Crimes and Misdemeanors.

Article III

SECTION 1
[Judicial Power, Tenure of Office]

The judicial Power of the United States, shall be vested in one supreme Court, and in such inferior Courts as the Congress may from time to time ordain and establish. The Judges, both of the supreme and inferior Courts, shall hold their Offices during good Behavior, and shall, at stated Times, receive for their Services, a Compensation, which shall not be diminished during their Continuance in Office.

SECTION 2
[Jurisdiction]

The judicial Power shall extend to all Cases, in Law and Equity, arising under this Constitution, the Laws of the United States, and Treaties made, of which shall be made, under their Authority;—to all Cases affecting Ambassadors, other public Ministers and Consuls;—to all Cases of admiralty and maritime Jurisdiction;—to Controversies to which the United States shall be a party—to Controversies between two or more States;—*between a State and Citizens of another State;*—between Citizens of different States;—between Citizens of the same State claiming Lands under Grants of different States, *and between a State,* or the Citizens thereof, *and foreign States, Citizens or Subjects.**

In all Cases affecting Ambassadors, other public Ministers and Consults, and those in which a State shall be Party, the supreme Court shall have original Jurisdiction. In all the other Cases before mentioned, the supreme Court shall have appelate Jurisdiction, both as to Law and Fact, with such Exceptions, and under such Regulations as Congress shall make.

The Trial of all Crimes, except in Cases of Impeachment, shall be by Jury; and such Trial shall be held in the State where the said Crimes shall have been committed; but when not committed within any State, the Trial shall be at such Place or Places as the Congress may by Law have directed.

SECTION 3
[Treason, Proof and Punishment]

Treason against the United States, shall consist only in levying War against them, or in adhering to their Enemies, giving them Aid and Comfort. No Person shall be convicted of Treason unless on the Testimoney of two Witnesses to the same overt Act, or on Confession in open Court.

The Congress shall have Power to declare the Punishment of Treason, but no Attainder of Treason shall work Corruption of Blood, or Forfeiture except during the Life of the Person attained.

Article IV

SECTION 1
[Faith and Credit among States]

Full Faith and Credit shall be given in each State to the public Acts, Records, and judicial Proceedings of every other State. And the Con-

---

* Modified by Eleventh Amendment.

gress may by general Laws prescribe the Manner in which such Acts, Records and Proceedings shall be proved, and the Effect thereof.

SECTION 2
[Privileges and Immunities, Fugitives]

The Citizens of each State shall be entitled to all Privileges and Immunities of Citizens in the several States.

A person charged in any State with Treason, Felony or other Crime, who shall flee from Justice, and be found in another State, shall on Demand of the executive Authority of the State from which he fled, be delivered up to be removed to the State having Jurisdiction of the Crime.

*No person held to Service or Labour in one State, under the Laws thereof, escaping into another, shall in Consequence of any Law or Regulation therein, be discharged from such Service or Labour, but shall be delivered up on Claim of the Party to whom such Service or Labour may be due.** *

SECTION 3
[Admission of New States]

New States may be admitted by the Congress into this Union; but no new State shall be formed or erected within the Jurisdiction of any other State; nor any State be formed by the Junction of two or more States, or Parts of States, without the Consent of the Legislatures of the States concerned as well of the Congress.

SECTION 4
[Guarantee of Republican Government]

The United States shall guarantee to every State in this Union a Republican Form of Government, and shall protect each of them against Invasion; and on Application of Legislature, or of the Executive (when the Legislature cannot be convened) against domestic Violence.

Article V

[AMENDMENT OF THE CONSTITUTION]

The Congress, whenever two thirds of both Houses shall deem it necessary, shall propose Amendments to this Constitution, or, on the Application of the Legislatures of two thirds of the several States, shall call a Convention for proposing Amendments, which, in either Case, shall be valid to all Intents and Purposes, as Part of this Constitution, when

---

* Repealed by the Thirteenth Amendment.

ratified by the Legislatures of three fourths of the several States, or by Conventions in three fourths thereof, as the one or the other Mode of Ratification may be proposed by the Congress; *Provided that no Amendment which may be made prior to the Year One thousand eight hundred and eight shall in any Manner affect the first and fourth Clauses in the Ninth Section of the first Article,** and that no State, without its Consent, shall be deprived of its equal Suffrage in the Senate.

Article VI

[Debts, Supremacy, Oath]

All Debts contracted and Engagements entered into, before the Adoption of this Constitution, shall be as valid against the United States under this Constitution, as under the Confederation.

This Constitution, and the Laws of the United States which shall be made in Pursuance thereof; and all Treaties made, or which shall be made, under the Authority of the United States, shall be the supreme Law of the Land; and the Judges in every State shall be bound thereby, any thing in the Constitution or Laws of any State to the Contrary notwithstanding.

The Senators and Representatives before mentioned, and the Members of the several State Legislatures, and all executive and judicial Officers, both of the United States and of the several States, shall be bound by Oath or Affirmation, to support this Constitution; but no religious Test shall be required as a Qualification to any Office or public Trust under the United States.

Article VII

[RATIFICATION & ESTABLISHMENT]

The Ratification of the Conventions of nine States, shall be sufficient for the Establishment of this Constitution between the States so ratifying the Same.†

---

* Temporary provision.

† The Constitution was submitted on September 17, 1787, by the Constitutional Conventions, was ratified by the conventions of several states at various dates up to May 29, 1790, and became effective on March 4, 1789.

done in Convention by the Unanimous Consent of the States present the Seventeenth Day of September in the Year of our Lord one thousand seven hundred and Eighty seven and of the Independence of the United States of America the Twelth. *In Witness* whereof We have hereunto subscribed our Names.

G:⁰WASHINGTON—
Presidt, and Deputy from Virginia

New Hampshire	John Langdon Nicholas Gilman		Geo Read Gunning Bedfor Jun
Massachusets	Nathaniel Gorham Rufus King	*Delaware*	John Dickinson Richard Bassett Jaco: Broom
Connecticut	Wm Saml Johnson Roger Sherman	*Maryland*	James McHenry Dan of St Thos. Jenifer
New York	Alexander Hamilton		Danl Carroll
New Jersey	Wil: Livingston David Brearley Wm Paterson Jona: Dayton	*Virginia*	John Blair James Madison Jr.
	B Franklin Thomas Mifflin Robt Morris Geo. Clymer	*North Carolina*	Wm Blount Richd Dobbs Spaight Hu Williamson
Pennsylvania	Thos. FitzSimons Jared Ingersoll James Wilson Gouv Morris	*South Carolina*	J. Rutledge Charles Cotesworth Pinckney Charles Pickney Pierce Butler
		Georgia	William Few Abr Baldwin

Amendments
to the Constitution

The first ten amendments were proposed by Congress on September 25, 1789; ratified and adoption certified on December 15, 1791.

Amendment I

[Freedom of Religion, of Speech, and of the Press]

> Congress shall make no law respecting an establishment of religion, or prohibiting the free exercise thereof; or abridging the freedom of speech, or of the press; or the right of the people peaceably to assemble, and to petition the Government for a redress of grievances.

Amendment II

[Right to Keep and Bear Arms]

> A well regulated Milita, being necessary to the security of a free State, the right of the people to keep and bear Arms, shall not be infringed.

Amendment III

[Quartering of Soldiers]

> No Soldier shall, in time of peace be quartered in any house, without the consent of the Owner, nor in time of war, but in a manner to be prescribed by law.

Amendment IV

[Security from Unwarrantable Search and Seizure]

> The right of the people to be secure in their persons, houses, papers, and effects, against unreasonable searches and seizures, shall not be

violated, and no Warrants shall issue, but upon probable cause, supported by Oath or affirmation, and particularly describing the place to be searched, and the persons or things to be seized.

Amendment V

[Rights of Accused Persons in Criminal Proceedings]

No person shall be held to answer for a capital, or otherwise infamous crime, unless on a presentment or indictment of a Grand Jury, except in cases arising in the land or naval forces, or in the Militia, when in actual service in time of War or in public danger; nor shall any person be subject for the same offence to be twice put in jeopardy of life or limb; nor shall be compelled in any criminal case to be a witness against himself, nor be deprived of life, liberty, or property, without due process of law; nor shall private property be taken for public use, without just compensation.

Amendment VI

[Right to Speedy Trial, Witnesses, Etc.]

In all criminal prosecutions, the accused shall enjoy the right to a speedy and public trial, by an impartial jury of the State and district wherein the crime shall have been committed, which district shall have been previously ascertained by law, and to be informed of the nature and cause of accusation; to be confronted with the witnesses against him; to have compulsory process for obtaining Witnesses in his favor, and to have the Assistance of Counsel for his defence.

Amendment VII

[Trial by Jury in Civil Cases]

In suits at common law, where the value in controversy shall exceed twenty dollars, the right of trial by jury shall be preserved, and no fact tried by a jury shall be otherwise re-examined in any Court of the United States, than according to the rules of the common law.

Amendment VIII

[Bails, Fines, Punishments]

Excessive bail shall not be required, nor excessive fines imposed, nor cruel and unusual punishments inflicted.

Amendment IX

[Reservation of Rights of People]

> The enumeration in the Constitution, of certain rights, shall not be construed to deny or disparage others retained by the people.

Amendment X

[Powers Reserved to States or People]

> The powers not delegated to the United States by the Constitution, nor prohibited by it to the States, are reserved to the States respectively, or to the people.

Amendment XI

[Proposed by Congress on March 4, 1794; declared ratified on January 8, 1798.]

[Restriction of Judicial Power]

> The Judicial power of the United States shall not be construed to extend to any suit in law or equity, commenced or prosecuted against one of the United States by Citizens of another State, or by Citizens or Subjects of any Foreign State.

Amendment XII

[Proposed by Congress on December 8, 1803; declared ratified on September 25, 1804.]

[Election of President and Vice-President]

> The Electors shall meet in their respective state, and vote by ballot for President and Vice-President, one of whom, at least, shall not be an inhabitant of the same state with themselves; they shall name in their ballots the person voted for as President, and in distinct ballots the person voted for as Vice-President, and they shall make distinct lists of all persons voted for as President, and all persons voted for as Vice-President, and of the number of votes for each, which lists they shall sign and certify, and transmit sealed to the seat of the government of the United States, directed to the President of the Senate;—The President of the Senate shall, in presence of the Senate and House of Representatives, open all the certificates and the votes shall then be counted;—The person having the greatest number of votes for President, shall be the President, if such number be a majority of the whole number of Electors appointed; and if no person have such majority, then from the persons

having the highest numbers not exceeding three on the list of those voted for as President, the House of Representatives shall choose immediately, by ballot, the President. But in choosing the President, the votes shall be taken by states, the representation from each state having one vote; a quorum for this purpose shall consist of a member or members from two-thirds of the states, and a majority of all states shall be necessary to a choice. And if the House of Representatives shall not choose a President whenever the right of choice shall devolve upon them, before the fourth day of March next following, then the Vice-President, shall act as President, as in the case of the death or other constitutional disability of the President. The person having the greatest number of votes as Vice-President, shall be the Vice-President, if such a number be a majority of the whole numbers of Electors appointed, and if no person have a majority, then from the two highest numbers on the list, the Senate shall choose the Vice-President; a quorum for the purpose shall consist of two-thirds of the whole number of Senators, and a majority of the whole number shall be necessary to a choice. But no person constitutionally ineligible to the office of President shall be eligible to that of Vice-President of the United States.

Amendment XIII

[*Proposed by Congress on January 31, 1865; declared ratified on December 18, 1865.*]

SECTION 1
[Abolition of Slavery]

Neither slavery nor involuntary servitude, except as a punishment for crime whereof the party shall have been duly convicted, shall exist within the United States, or any place subject to their jurisdiction.

SECTION 2
[Power to Enforce This Article]

Congress shall have power to enforce this article by appropriate legislation.

Amendment XIV

[*Proposed by Congress on June 13, 1866; declared ratified on July 28, 1868.*]

SECTION 1
[Citizenship Rights Not to Be Abridged by States]

All persons born or naturalized in the United States, and subject to the jurisdiction thereof, are citizens of the United States and of the State wherein they reside. No State shall make or enforce any law which shall abridge the privileges or immunities of citizens of the United States; nor shall any State deprive any person of life, liberty, or property, without due process of law; nor deny to any person within its jurisdiction the equal protection of the laws.

SECTION 2
[Apportionment of Representatives in Congress]

Representatives shall be apportioned among the several States according to their respective numbers, counting the whole number of persons in each State, excluding Indians not taxed. But when the right to vote at any election for the choice of electors for President and Vice-President of the United States, Representatives in Congress, the Executive and Judicial officers of a State, or the members of the Legislature thereof, is denied to any of the male inhabitants of such State, being twenty-one years of age, and citizens of the United States, or in any way abridged, except for participation in rebellion, or other crime, the basis of representation therein shall be reduced in the proportion which the number of such male citizens shall bear to the whole number of male citizens twenty-one years of age in such State.

SECTION 3
[Persons Disqualified from Holding Office]

No person shall be a Senator or Representative in Congress, or elector of President and Vice-President, or hold any office, civil or military, under the United States, or under any State, who, having previously taken an oath, as a member of Congress, or as an officer of the United States, or as a member of any State legislature, or as an executive or judicial officer of any State, to support the Constitution of the United States, shall have engaged in insurrection or rebellion against the same, or given aid or comfort to the enemies thereof. But Congress may by a vote of two-thirds of each House, remove such disability.

SECTION 4
[What Public Debts Are Valid]

The validity of the public debt of the United States, authorized by law, including debts incurred for payment of pensions and bounties for services in suppressing insurrection or rebellion, shall not be questioned. But neither the United States nor any State shall assume or pay any debt or obligation incurred in aid of insurrection or rebellion against the United States, or any claim for the loss of emancipation of any slave; but all such debts, obligations and claims shall be held illegal and void.

SECTION 5
[Power to Enforce This Article]

> The Congress shall have power to enforce, by appropriate legislation, the provisions of this article.

Amendment XV

[Proposed by Congress on February 26, 1869; declared ratified on March 30, 1870.]

SECTION 1
[Negro Suffrage]

> The right of citizens of the United States to vote shall not be denied or abridged by the United States or by any State on account of race, color, or previous condition of servitude.

SECTION 2
[Power to Enforce This Article]

> The Congress shall have power to enforce this article by appropriate legislation.

Amendment XVI

[Proposed by Congress on July 12, 1909; declared ratified on February 25, 1913.]

[Authorizing Income Taxes]

> The Congress shall have power to lay and collect taxes on incomes, from whatever source derived, without apportionment among the several States, and without regard to any census or enumeration.

Amendment XVII

[Proposed by Congress on May 13, 1912; declared ratified on May 31, 1913.]

[Popular Election of Senators]

The Senate of the United States shall be composed of two Senators from each State, elected by the people thereof, for six years, and each Senator shall have one vote. The electors in each State shall have the qualifications requisite for electors of the most numerous branch of the State Legislature.

When vacancies happen in the representation of any State in the Senate, the executive authority of such State shall issue writs of election to fill such vacancies: Provided, That the Legislature of any State may empower the executive thereof to make temporary appointment until the people fill the vacancies by election as the Legislature may direct.

This amendment shall not be so construed as to affect the election or term of any Senator chosen before it becomes valid as part of the Constitution.

Amendment XVIII

[Proposed by Congress December 18, 1917; declared ratified on January 29, 1919.]

SECTION 1
[National Liquor Prohibition]

> *After one year from ratification of this article the manufacture, sale or transportation of intoxicating liquors within, the importation thereof into, or the exportation thereof from the United States and all territory subject to the jurisdiction thereof for beverage purposes is hereby prohibited.*

SECTION 2
[Power to Enforce This Article]

> The Congress and the several states shall have concurrent power to enforce this article by appropriate legislation.

SECTION 3
[Ratification within Seven Years]

> This article shall be inoperative unless it shall have been ratified as an amendment to the Constitution by the legislatures of the several states, as provided in the Constitution, within seven years from the date of the submission hereof to the states by the Congress.

Amendment XIX

[Proposed by Congress on June 4, 1919; declared ratified on August 26, 1920.]

[Women Suffrage]

> The right of the citizens of the United States to vote shall not be denied or abridged by the United States or by any state on account of sex.
>
> Congress shall have power, by appropriate legislation, to enforce the provision of this article.

Amendment XX

[Proposed by Congress on March 2, 1932; declared ratified on February 6, 1933.]

SECTION 1
[Terms of Office]

The terms of the President and Vice-President shall end at noon on the 20th day of January, and the terms of the Senators and Representatives at noon on the 3rd day of January, of the years in which such terms would have ended if this article had not been ratified; and the terms of their successors shall then begin.

SECTION 2
[Time of Convening Congress]

The Congress shall assemble at least once in every year, and such meeting shall begin at noon on the 3rd day of January, unless they shall by law appoint a different day.

SECTION 3
[Death of President-Elect]

If, at the time fixed for the beginning of the term of the President, the President-elect shall have died, the Vice-President-elect shall become President. If a President shall not have been chosen before the time fixed for the beginning of his term, or if the President-elect shall have failed to qualify, then the Vice-President-elect shall act as President until a President shall have qualified; and the Congress may by law provide for the case wherein neither a President-elect nor a Vice-President-elect shall have qualified, declaring who shall then act as President, or the manner in which one who is to act shall be selected, and such person shall act accordingly until a President or Vice-President shall have qualified.

SECTION 4
[Election of the President]

The Congress may by law provide for the case of the death of any of the persons from whom the House of Representatives may choose a President whenever the right of choice shall have devolved upon them, and for the case of the death of any of the persons from whom the Senate may choose a Vice-President whenever the right of choice shall have devolved upon them.

SECTION 5

Sections 1 and 2 shall effect on the 15th day of October following ratification of this article.

SECTION 6

This article shall be inoperative unless it shall have been ratified as an amendment to the Constitution by the legislatures of three-fourths of the several States within seven years from the date of its submission.

Amendment XXI

[Proposed by Congress on February 20, 1933; declared ratified on December 5, 1933.]

SECTION 1
[National Liquor Prohibition Repealed]

The eighteenth article of amendment to the Constitution of the United States is hereby repealed.

SECTION 2
[Transportation of Liquor into "Dry" States]

The transportation or importation into any State, Territory, or Possession of the United States for delivery or use therein of intoxicating liquors, in violation of the laws thereof, is hereby prohibited.

SECTION 3

This article shall be inoperative unless it shall have been ratified as an amendment to the Constitution by conventions in the several States, as provided in the Constitution, within seven years from the date of the submission hereof to the States by the Congress.

Amendment XXII

[Proposed by Congress on March 21, 1947; declared ratified on February 26, 1951.]

SECTION 1
[Tenure of President Limited]

No person shall be elected to the office of President more than twice, and no person who has held the office of President, or acted as President, for more than two years of a term to which some other person was elected President shall be elected to the Office of the President more than once. But this Article shall not apply to any person holding the Office of President when this Article was proposed by the Congress, and shall not prevent any person who may be holding the office of President, during the term within which this Article becomes operative from holding the office of President or acting as President during the remainder of such term.

SECTION 2

This Article shall be inoperative unless it shall have been ratified as an amendment to the Constitution by the legislatures of three-fourths of the several states within seven years from the date of its submission to the States by the Congress.

Amendment XXIII

[Proposed by Congress on June 21, 1960; declared ratified on March 29, 1961.]

SECTION 1
[Electoral College Votes for the District of Columbia]

The District constituting the seat of Government of the United States shall appoint in such manner as the Congress may direct:

A number of electors of President and Vice President equal to the whole number of Senators and Representatives in Congress to which the District would be entitled if it were a State, but in no event more than the least populous States; they shall be in addition to those appointed by the States, but they shall be considered, for the purposes of the election of President and Vice President, to be electors appointed by a State; and they shall meet in the District and perform such duties as provided by the twelfth article of amendment.

SECTION 2

The Congress shall have power to enforce this article by appropriate legislation.

Amendment XXIV

[Proposed by Congress on August 27, 1963; declared ratified on January 23, 1964.]

SECTION 1
[Anti-Poll Tax]

The right of citizens of the United States to vote in any primary or other election for President or Vice President, for electors for President or Vice President, or for Senator or Representative of Congress, shall not be denied or abridged by the United States or any State by reasons of failure to pay any poll tax or other tax.

SECTION 2

The Congress shall have power to enforce this article by appropriate legislation.

Amendment XXV

[Proposed by Congress on July 7, 1965; declared ratified on February 10, 1967.]

SECTION 1
[Vice-President to Become President]

In case of the removal of the President from office or his death or resignation, the Vice-President shall become President.

SECTION 2
[Choice of a New Vice-President]

Whenever there is a vacancy in the office of the Vice President, the President shall nominate a Vice-President who shall take the office upon confirmation by a majority vote of both houses of Congress.

SECTION 3
[President May Declare Own Disability]

Whenever the President transmits to the President pro tempore of the Senate and the Speaker of the House of Representatives has written declaration that he is unable to discharge the powers and duties of his office, and until he transmits to them a written declaration to the contrary, such powers and duties shall be discharged by the Vice-President as Acting President.

SECTION 4
[Alternative Procedures to Declare and to End Presidential Disability]

Whenever the Vice-President and a majority of either the principal officers of the executive departments, or of such other body as Congress may by law provide, transmit to the President pro tempore of the Senate and the Speaker of the House of Representatives their written declaration that the President is unable to discharge the powers and duties of his office, the Vice-President shall immediately assume the powers and duties of the office as Acting President.

Thereafter, when the President transmits to the President pro tempore of the Senate and the Speaker of the House of Representatives his written declaration that no inability exists, he shall resume the powers and duties of his office unless the Vice-President and a majority of either the principal officers of the executive department, or of such other body as Congress may by law provide, transmit within four days to the President pro tempore of the Senate and the Speaker of the House of Representatives their written declaration that the President is unable to discharge the powers and duties of his office. Thereupon Congress shall decide the issue, assembling within 48 hours for that purpose if not in session. If the Congress, within 21 days after receipt of the latter written declaration, or, if Congress is not in session, within 21 days after Congress is required to assemble, determines by two-thirds vote of both houses that the President is unable to discharge the powers and duties of his office, the Vice-President shall continue to discharge the same as Acting President; otherwise, the President shall resume the powers and duties of his office.

Amendment XXVI

[Proposed by Congress on March 23, 1971; declared ratified on June 30, 1971.]

SECTION 1

The right of citizens of the United States, who are eighteen years of age or older, to vote shall not be denied or abridged by the United States or by any State on account of age.

SECTION 2

The Congress shall have the power to enforce this article by appropriate legislation.

Index

Campaigns, *see* Campaign finances; Elections; Presidential elections
Cannon, Joseph G., 310, 316
Cardozo, Benjamin N., cited 84, 371, 413, 459
Carey, Hugh, 528
Carswell, G. Harold, 423
Carter, James Earl ("Jimmy"), 208, 216, 220, 269, 335, 337, 340–42
  civil service reform under, 392–93
  executive office under, 381
  style of, 340–42, 343
Categorical grants, 107–9
CBS News, 19
Censorship, 477–78
Central Intelligence Agency (CIA), 17, 391, 481
Centralized (unitary) government, 95, 552
Certification, judicial, 419
Certiorari, writ of, 419, 420, 541
Chase, Samuel, 436
Chavez, Cesar, 147
Chicanos, 45, 52
Chisholm, Shirley, 315–16
Cities, 31–33
Citizenship, 460–461
  deprivation of, 461
  education for, 61
Civil Aeronautics Board (CAB), 126
Civil liberties
  basic, substantive, 459–80
  government agency violations of, 481–84
  hierarchy of, 458–59
  historic sources of, 455–56
  statutory classifications and, 463–64
  see also Bill of Rights; Equality; Rights; *and specific types by name*
Civil Rights Act (1964), 197–98, 339, 464
Civil Rights Act (1965), 303, 339
Civil Rights Act (1968), 339
Civil Rights Commission, 197, 234
Civil service, employees, 224, 391–95
  presidential policies and, 356–57, 390–95
  reform of, 393
Civil Service Commission, replacement of, 393
Class action, 411
Class consciousness, 165–66, 170–71
Clay, Henry, 163
Clean Waters Act (1972), 362
"Clear and present danger" test, 470–71
Cleveland, Grover, 98
Clifford, Clark, 388
Cloture rule, 326, 541

Coercion, by government, 5, 139–40
Coke, Edward, 455
Collective action, 131–34
Committee for Economic Development, 143
Common Cause, 143, 318
Common law, 407, 541
Communication, freedom of, 456, 470–80
Communist Party, 170
Concorde, Anglo-French, 525–30
Confederation, defined, 542
Conflict, political, *see* Political conflicts
Congress, U.S., 264–329
  administrative oversight by, 85, 273–75
  admission of states by, 98–99
  under Articles of Confederation, 75–76
  bicameral organization of, 304–5
  budgetary role of, 271–73
  bureaucracy and, 395
  committee organization and operations, 295, 310–17, 323–25
  conference action by, 327–28
  constituency representation in, 200–2, 275–77, 300–4
  decentralization and, 117, 295
  election to, 165, 203–5, 295, 305
  fiscal role of, 267, 271–73, 362–65
  foreign policy role of, 267, 354–56
  impeachment functions of, 85, 275, 353–54
  investigational functions, 278–79
  judicial roles of, 84–85, 275, 354, 413
  leadership of, 307–11
  legislative functions, 266–71, 307–17, 322–29
  lobbying in, *see* Lobbying
  membership in, 279–82, 302–4; *see also* Congressmen
  opinion shaping by, 277–78
  party affiliations in, 295–98, 311, 314–16
  policy making by, 265–71
  powers delegated to, 82, 90, 97
  presidential limitations by, 83–85, 88–90, 267–71, 273–75, 351–56
  public opinion and, 300–2
  seniority system, 294, 309, 315–17
  staff support services, 287–88
  Supreme Court and, 419, 441, 445–46
  terms and sessions of, 305–7
  veto overrides by, 362
  warmaking role of, 266–67, 355
  see also House of Representatives; Senate

Congressional Budget Office, 272, 286, 287
Congressional Record, 322
Congressional Research Service, 287
Congressmen
  committee assignments of, 311–17
  constituency representation by, 200–2, 275–77, 298–304
  duties of, 283–85
  ex-, as lobbyists, 319–20
  financial disclosure by, 285–86
  lobbyists and, 319–21
  perquisites of, 281–2, 286
  political behavior of, 293–5, 305, 352
  reform of, 288–89
  tenure of, 282, 294
  voting by, 296–97
  see also Congress
Congress of Racial Equality (CORE), 150
Connally, John, 174
Constitution, U.S., 68–90
  attitude toward, 42
  amendment of, 71
  amendments to, *see specific ones, as* First Amendment, etc.
  bill of rights, *see* Bill of Rights
  on courts, *see* Court system
  on distribution of powers, 82, 101–5; *see also* Federal government
  and federalism, 95–101
  framing of, 74–82; *see also* Constitutional Convention
  judicial review of, 84, 435–36, *see also* Federal courts; Supreme Court
  language of, 84
  on national supremacy, 96
  natural rights under, 455, 547; *see also* Civil liberties; Rights
  potentialities of, 88–89
  public policies in, 22
  on religion, *see* Religion
  restraints on power by, 82–85
  on states, *see* States
  on substantive rights, 496; *see also* Bill of Rights; Constitutional Convention; Constitutionalism; *and specific concepts and issues by name*
Constitutional Convention (1787), 72, 74–82
  controversies at, 78–82; *see also specific issues by name*
  delegates to, 76–78
  federalism issue at, *see* Federalism
  principles and goals, 74, 78–82
Constitutionalism, 70–71, 89–90
  definitive role of, 69–74; *see also*

Federalism
  flaws in, 89–90
Consumer Product Safety Commission, cited, 16
Coolidge, Calvin, 173, 338
"Corruption of blood and forfeiture," 496n
Council of Economic Advisers, 385–86
Counties, 101
Court system, *see* Appellate court; Federal courts; State courts; Supreme Court
Crime,
  fiscal cost of, 491–94
  national deterrence of, 532
  organized, 491
  poor as victims of, 491–93
  presidential campaign contributions, and, 224–25
  punishment for, *see* Punishment
Criminal justice system, 497–513
Criminal law
  authority for, 496
  basic rights under, 496
  courts of, 416
Criminals, treatment of, 507–13

Dahl, Robert A. cited, 131
Dawes, Charles, cited, 395
Death sentence, 505–6
Debates, and presidential campaigns, 212–14
Decentralization, 103–19
Declaration of Independence, 49, 409, 455–56
Defendant's rights, 498–500
Defense Department, 318
Democracy, 5–8, 542
  belief in, 39–40
  citizen participation in, 252–58
  civil liberties and, 456
  constitutional, 6, 79, 400, 531
  Constitution's framers on, 79
  decentralization and, 103–5
  development of, U.S., 195–202
  electoral process and, 193–95
  permissiveness and, 38
Democratic Party, 172–73, 225, 297
  campaign strategies, 218–20
  convention technicalities, 207, 208–9
  development of, 163
  electoral coalition, 167–69
Democratic Study Group, 297, 310
Dewey, Thomas E., 216
Dickinson, John, cited, 78
Dirksen, Everett, cited, 421
Discrimination
  economic, 49, 52

racial, 49–51, 461–65; *see also* Race relations
  sex, 54, 463–64
  voting rights and, 195–96
District courts, 416–18
Dixiecrat Party, 170
Double amenability, 415
Double jeopardy, 506
Douglas, William O., 395, 412, 425
  on Constitution, cited, 90
  on inherent rights, cited, 70
  on privacy, cited, 467
Draft, 460
Dred Scott decision (1857), 448, 460–61
Du Bois, W. E. B., cited, 46
Due process clause, 84, 461

Economy, U.S., 36
Education, political, 58–61
Eighth Amendment, 500, 504
Eisenhower, Dwight D., 173, 244, 247, 335, 339, 349, 397, 398
  staff organization under, 380
Elderly persons, 14, 144–45
Election(s), 43, 82–83, 184, 193, 204–6
  candidate spending for, 223–24
  federal subsidies for, 225–27
  lobbyists and 319–20; *see also* Special interest groups
  political issues in, 521
  see also Congress, election to; Presidential elections; Voter participation
Election districts, 165–67, 200–2
Election Reform Act (1974), 225–27
Elective office(s), 128–31, 193–4
  blacks holding, 199
  decentralization of, 114–16
Electoral College, 163, 206
  defects of, 221–23
  as majority restraint, 87
  selection of, 195
Electoral process, 193–225
  reform of (1974), 225–27
Electorate, *see* Political participation; Voter behavior
Elitism, 8, 127–31, 145–47
Ellsworth, Oliver, 78, 81
Employment Act (1946), 385
Environmental activism, 321, 526
Environmental Protection Agency, 391, 527
Equality, 6–8, 29–30, 461–65
  blacks in struggle for, 41, 51, 149; *see also* Blacks
  in education, 461–65
  racial, *see* Race relations
  statutory classifications and, 463–64
  see also Democracy; Rights
Equity, in law, 408, 417–18

Equal Rights Amendment, 54
Ethnic identity, and politics, 247
Evidence, admissibility of, 503–4
Executive agreements, 23, 355
Executive branch, 83–85, 374–400
  cabinet level departments, 391
  congressional oversight, 85, 273–75
  legislative activities, 83–84, 267–68, 319
  presidential control, 397–400
  reorganization of, 274
Executive Office, 378–86
Executive orders, 23
Executive privilege, 365–66, 410
Ex post facto laws, 83, 457, 496
Extradition, 119

Fact finding, 417
Fair trial, 457, 479, 496
Farmers, political activism of, 249–50, 318
Farmer-Labor Party, 169
Farmers' Union, 318
Federal agencies, 15–16, 356–57, 391–95; *see also specific agencies by name*
Federal aid, 105–14
Federal Aviation Agency, 525, 526, 527
Federal Bureau of Investigation (FBI), 17, 392, 423, 481–84, 491
Federal courts, 413–26
  appellate, 418–19, 529
  circuit, 419
  Constitution on, 413
  criminal cases in, 414, 416, 497–506
  district courts, 416–18
  judicial appointments to, 420–26
  judicial review by, 84, 437–38
  organization of, 416
  see also Judges, Judicial procedures; State courts; Supreme Court
Federal Election Commission, 227
Federal employees, *see* Bureaucracy
Federal government, 12–19, 89–90, 95–101
  decentralization of, 116–19
  implied powers, 97
  local governments and, *see* Local governments
  political growth of, 101–3
  services of, 15–18
  state relations with, 80–82, 97–100, 114–19; *see also* State(s)
  see also Federalism; Government; Public policy
Federalism, 119
  and Constitution, 95–101
  decentralization and, 103–5
  of judiciary, 413, 415, 439

and democracy, 193–95
  discrimination and, 195–96
  of ex-slaves, 196–97
  poll taxes and, 196
  property and, 78
  state determination of, 195
  of women, 54, 196
Voting Rights Act (1965), 198, 199
  amendment of 1970, 199

Wallace, George, 163, 170, 208, 222
Wallace, Henry, 163, 170
"War on Poverty," 90, 339
Ward organization, 181–83
War Powers Act (1973), 355–56
Warrant
  for arrest, 497
  for search, 498
Warren, Earl, cited, 38, 200, 433, 448
Washington, George, 38, 78, 304
  on party affiliation, 161
WASPs, 51
Watergate episode, 18, 220, 225, 251,
    350, 400, 481
Water pollution control, 271
Wealth, political role of, 125–28, 134–
    36, 463
Weathermen, 493
Webster, Daniel, 163
Welfare
  civil liberties and, 464
  federal support for, 271
  public opinion on, 19
  reform of, 521
Westberry v. Saunders, 303
Whig Party, 163
White ethnics, 51–52
White House staff, 339, 341–42, 359–
    60, 378–86
Willkie, Wendell, 389
Wilson, James, 78
Wiretapping, 503–4
Women
  in Congress, 279–80
  discrimination against, 54
  liberation of, 54
  political behavior of, 54–55, 233
  voting rights of, 195–96, 233
Work ethic, 36

Zero-sum game, 104–5